THE COMPLETE
Do-It-Yourself
Human Resources
Department

Third Edition

MARY F. COOK

PRENTICE HALL

Library of Congress Cataloging-in-Publication Data

Cook, Mary F.

    The Complete do-it-yourself human resources department / Mary F. Cook—3rd ed.

      p. cm.

    Includes index.

    ISBN 0-13-092219-6

    1. Human Resources management   2. Human Resources management—Forms.   I. Title.

HR5549.C7239   2001   01-6352

658.3—dc21   CIP

Printed in the United States of America

10 9 8 7 6 5 4 3 2 1

This publication is designed to provide accurate and authoritative information in regard to the subject matter covered. It is sold with the understanding that the publisher is not engaged in rendering legal, accounting, or other professional service. If legal advice or other expert assistance is required, the services of a competent professional person should be sought.
—*From the Declaration of Principles jointly adopted by a Committee of the American Bar Association and a Committee of Publishers and Associations*

ISBN 0-13-092219-6

ATTENTION: CORPORATIONS AND SCHOOLS

Prentice Hall books are available at quantity discounts with bulk purchase for educational, business, or sales promotional use. For information, please write to: Prentice Hall Special Sales, 240 Frisch Court, Paramus, New Jersey 07652. Please supply: title of book, ISBN number, quantity, how the book will be used, date needed.

PRENTICE HALL

Paramus, NJ 07652

On the World Wide Web at http://www.phdirect.com

ABOUT THE AUTHOR

MARY F. COOK is the President of Mary Cook & Associates, a Scottsdale, Az. based human resources and management consulting firm. Ms. Cook has many years experience as both a corporate human resources generalist and as a human resources consultant. She has written articles for business magazines, newspapers and trade journals. She is an award-winning author of more than a dozen books. Ms. Cook's HR trends forecasts have been quoted in *Success Magazine, Management Review, Franchise Update,* and *Federal Credit Union* magazine.

Ms. Cook is a recipient of the top national research award from the Society for Human Resources Management and awards from the Colorado Society for Human Resources Management. She is a member and past president of the Colorado Author's League and the Denver Women's Press Club. Ms. Cook can be reached at MaryCookBooks.com.

Current Books by the Author

The Complete Do-It-Yourself Human Resources Department, 3ʳᵈ Edition, Prentice Hall

The AMA Handbook on Recruitment and Retention, AMACOM Books

Consulting on the Side, John Wiley & Sons

Outsourcing Human Resources Functions, (English, Spanish, and Chinese Editions), AMACOM Books—1-800-262-9699

Ms. Cook's books published by Prentice-Hall may be ordered by calling 1-800-288-4745. When ordering *The Complete Do-It-Yourself Human Resources Department,* ask for ISBN 0-13-092219-6.

CONTENTS

About the Author   iii
Preface   xiii
What This Book Will Do for You   xv

CHAPTER 1
RECRUITING, INTERVIEWING, AND SELECTION:
PROCEDURES AND FORMS—1

Recruiting Has Gone Hi-Tech 3
Recruiting Ads 4
Where to List Your Jobs 5
Using a Recruitment Advertising Agency 10
Identifying and Recruiting the Best Workers 10
Recruiting and Employment Routine 12
Checklist of Recruiting and Employment Forms 14
Ad Checklist 18
Sample Forms and Letters 19
The Application Forms (English & Spanish) 20
Checking References 34
Twelve Tips for Giving References 34
Background Checks 37
Making a Job Offer 39
Sample Forms & Letters 40
Seven Steps to Successful Selection 53
Pros and Cons of Employment Testing Including Drug Testing 54
Sample Interviewing and Selection Handbook 57
Other New Hire Forms You'll Need and Why You Need Them 57
An Internal Job-Posting System 82
Recruiting Persons with Disabilities—An Important and Underutilized Resource . . . 84
How to Save Money by Using Temporary Help 88
Illegal Employment Practices 89
New Employee Orientation 90
Handling Relocation 91

CHAPTER 2
PERSONNEL RECORDKEEPING—93

New Hire Reporting Mandatory 96
Employee Information and Recordkeeping Requirements. 96
Information to Include in the Personnel File 96
Payroll Procedures and Relevant Statutes 98
Pay Terminology and Definitions 103
Record Retention Requirements. 105
Maintaining Control of Staffing Levels. 120
Monthly Payroll Trend 120
How to Figure Recruiting and Selection Costs. 124
Frequently Used Personnel Calculations, Formulas, and Tables 126
Sample Human Resources Calculations and Reports 126
Auditing the HR Function 132

CHAPTER 3
REGULATORY COMPLIANCE—135

Key Federal Statutes Affecting Employment, Termination, EEO,
    Compensation, and Benefits 137
Fair Labor Standards Act (FLSA). 143
Federal Guidelines on Affirmative Action 149
Affirmative Action Plans 150
Drug-Free Workplace Act of 1988. 153
Making the Decision About Having a Drug and Alcohol Testing Policy 155
Drug and Alcohol Testing 155
Employee Polygraph Protection Act. 157
What to Do When a Wage-Hour Investigator Calls to Announce a Visit 159
Do You Use Independent Contractors? The IRS May Not Think So. 160
What You Need to Know About the Consolidated Omnibus Budget
    Reconciliation Act (COBRA). 162
Employers Who Have Medical Plans Must Provide Notice of
    COBRA Amendments. 164
Posters Required by Federal Statute. 179
Termination Day Requirements by State 179
State by State Analysis of EEO Laws. 189
Complying with the Immigration Reform and Control Act of 1986 196
The Objective of Workers' Compensation 205
What to Do About Workers' Comp Costs 209
Worker's Comp Checklist 212

Unemployment Compensation 217
Personal Privacy and Employee Rights. 217
ADA Compliance Checklist and Sample Accommodation Letter 221
Family and Medical Leave Act and Certification Form. 223
What You Should Know About an Employee Returning to Work Under
  the Family Medical Leave Act. 226

CHAPTER 4
EMPLOYEE COMMUNICATIONS—231

Making the Personal Connection Is Important to Your Company's Success 233
25 Management/Employee Communications Channels You Can Implement
  in Your Company 233
Communicating Through Corporate Intranets. 235
How to Start an Employee Newsletter 236
Sample Employee Handbook 237
Employee Handbook Acknowledgment Form. 259

CHAPTER 5
PERSONNEL POLICIES—261

Keys to Successful Implementation of Personnel Policies 263
Checklist for Personnel Policy Manual 264
Fifteen Ways to Communicate Your Policies 266
Personnel Policy Manual Key Instructions 267
Sample Personnel Policy Manual. 268
E-Mail, Internet & Other Electronic Information Resources 284

CHAPTER 6
COMPENSATION AND BENEFITS—325

How Compensation Programs Are Changing. 327
Designing and Evaluating Your Compensation Program 328
Compensation Program Evaluation Checklist 328
Job Descriptions and Job Evaluations: How to Choose the Best System
  for Your Company 332
The DOs and DON'Ts of Writing Job Descriptions 334
Understanding "Essential Job" Functions Under the Americans with
  Disabilities Act (ADA) 336
Sample Statements That Can Be Used in Job Descriptions to Describe
  Physical and Mental Demands 336

Sample Job Description 339
The Three Most Common Methods of Job Evaluation 342
Making Job Evaluation Simple but Effective 342
Model of Wage Grades and Rates for a Small Company 345
Sample Job Descriptions 347
Sample Salary Program 359
Pay for Performance and Performance Management 366
Employee Benefits 376
Glossary of Benefits Terms 377
Work and Family Benefits 388
Examples of Employee Benefits 389

CHAPTER 7
HANDLING DISCIPLINE AND DISCHARGE—391

Performance Improvement 393
Determining Discipline and Discharge Policy 397
Sample Discipline Policy 397
Discipline and Discharge Forms 399
Sample Letters on Discipline 409
Preventing Discrimination Complaints 412
Policy Against Harassment 415
Investigating Claims of Sexual Harassment 415

CHAPTER 8
SAFETY, ACCIDENT REPORTING, AND OSHA REGULATIONS—417

Occupational Safety and Health Administration's Leading Violations 419
Employer Obligations for Reporting Occupational Injuries and Illness
    Under OSHA 420
Sample Guide to Accident and Injury Reporting 421
Guide to Compliance with the Federal OSHA Hazard Communication Standard . . 422
Accident Reporting Forms 425
Glossary of Occupational Safety and Health Terminology 438

CHAPTER 9
LABOR RELATIONS—443

Key Issues in Labor Relations 445
Questions and Answers on Retaining Union-Free Status 446

What You Should Know About Plant Closings and Layoffs/Sample
    Labor Relations Letters. 450
Arbitration of Employment Disputes 456
Outsourcing HR Functions 456

CHAPTER 10
PERSONNEL LETTERS AND MEMOS—463

Letter to Applicant Confirming Employment Offer 465
Replies to Applicants. 466
Applicant Rejection Letter 469
Sample ADA Accommodation Letter 470
Letter Requesting Employment Verification 471
New Employee Welcome. 472
New Employee Orientation Schedule. 473
Orientation Schedule 474
Employee Secrecy Agreement. 478
Confidentiality Agreement 479
Letter to New Employee Regarding Conflict of Interest. 480
Letter Regarding Rehire and Reinstatement of Benefits 481
Job Sharing Proposal 482
Confirmation of Transfer Decision 483
To Employee Regarding Request for a Leave of Absence 484
Letter to Branch Manager on Use of Independent Contractors. 485
To Employees Informing of an Impending Layoff. 486
Notification of Layoff. 487
Letter to Employees Regarding Notice of Plant Closing. 488
To All Employees Regarding Company Relocation 489
Letter Informing Employee of Being Placed on 30-Day Performance
    Improvement Plan 490
Unacceptable Work Performance—Must Improve 491
Letter Informing Employee of Disciplinary Action 492
Letter to Employee Regarding Suspension Without Pay 493
Written Warning for Excessive Absenteeism. 494
Letter to Employee on Termination for Excessive Absenteeism 495
Termination for Theft of Company Property 496
To Employee with a Substance Abuse Problem. 497
Letter to Employee on Termination for Intoxication on the Job 498
Warning on Internet Use 499
Memorandum to All Employees Regarding Drug Testing 500

Department Managers on Turnover Analysis. 501

Request for Additional Salary Budget 502

Reviewing Company Policy on Salary Increases When Employee Is on
    Leave of Absence. 503

To Employee Regarding Company Privacy Policy 504

To Human Resources Manager Regarding Employee Privacy 506

Letter to Personnel Manager Regarding Corporate Procedures for Employees
    Wishing to File a Complaint 507

Memorandum to Division Manager Regarding Sexual Harassment. 509

To Manager Regarding Sexual Harassment Complaint 510

To Employee Regarding Her Sexual Harassment Complaint 511

To EEOC Regarding Allegation of Age Discrimination Charge 512

To Employees Covering Annual Report of Employee Benefit Plans. 513

Letter Questioning Claims Processing Time. 514

Letter to Employee Requesting 401(k) Hardship Withdrawal 515

Memorandum to Employees Announcing a New Company Benefit 516

Confirming Company Participation in Support of Employee Bowling League 517

To Employees Regarding United Way Drive 518

Sample COBRA Letter to Employees: Summary of Rights and Obligations
    Regarding Continuation of Group Health Plan Coverage 519

Sample COBRA Letter to Terminating Employee or Dependent 523

Sample Alternative COBRA Letter to Employees 524

Condolences on Death of Employee's Spouse 526

CHAPTER 11
PERSONNEL CHECKLISTS—527

50 Ways to Save Money in the Human Resources Area 529

Employee Planning Checklist 532

Checklist of Eight Uses for Temporary Help to Lower Payroll Costs 533

Checklist to Use When Writing Recruiting Ads. 534

Applicant Interview Checklist 534

Checklist of Questions You May Not Ask in an Interview 536

Checklist for Use in Evaluating Interview or Appraisal Data. 537

New Employee Orientation Checklist. 540

Affirmative Action Planning Checklist. 542

Checklist for Investigating Sexual Harassment Complaints 543

Yearly Salary Program Checklist. 544

Training and Development Checklist 545

Checklist for Meeting Your Training Needs While Saving Money 546

Checklist for Developing New Communications Programs. 547

Checklist and Guidelines for Using an Outside Consultant 548
Human Resource Management (HRM) Merger Checklist 549
Checklist and Manager's Guidelines for Handling Drug or Alcohol
    Problems on the Job. 550
Checklist for Avoiding Litigation When Terminating an Employee. 551
Checklist for Use in Preparing for a Layoff 552
Checklist of Security Activities 553
Checklist for Maintaining a Safe Workplace. 554
Checklist for Establishing a Complaint or Grievance Procedure 555
An ADA Checklist for Employers 555

CHAPTER 12
SAMPLE PERSONNEL FORMS—559

Personnel Requisition 562
Applications for Employment (English & Spanish). 563
Applicant Appraisal Form 572
Telephone Reference Check 573
Employee Agreement (E-Mail, Internet) 574
Approval of Estimated Relocation Expenses and Allowances 576
Personnel Action Notice 577
Payroll Time Report. 578
Overtime Hours Worked Report. 579
Employee Attendance Record 581
Sample Employee Benefit Program—Plan Highlights. 582
Job Description Outline. 583
New Employee Orientation. 585
Employee Agreement (Employment). 588
Education Verification Reference 589
Employee Transfer Request. 590
Vacation Request Form 591
Employee Absence Report Form 592
Leave Request/Return from Leave Form. 593
Application for Funeral Leave 594
Mileage Reimbursement Report. 595
Travel and Expense Reimbursement Request 596
Performance Appraisal Worksheet 597
Employee Counseling Activity Sheet 599
Supervisor's Checklist and Report for Effective Discipline. 600
Disciplinary Warning Notice 602
Employee Warning Notice. 603

Exit Interview Form 604
Accident/Injury Report 605
Supervisor's Report of Accident Investigation. 606
Attending Physician's Return to Work Recommendations Record 607
First Aid Report Log 608
Quarterly Safety Performance Record 609

GLOSSARY OF HUMAN RESOURCES TERMS—611

INDEX—643

PREFACE

The response from users of the first and second editions of *The Complete Do-It-Yourself Human Resources Department* has been most gratifying. Since those editions were published, there have been changes in regulations relating to the Human Resources (HR) function. In addition changes in the economy and the workplace have affected personnel policies, procedures, and employee relations issues in organizations of all sizes.

There are constant changes in the environment in which the HR function is managed. The need for information on the part of practicing HR managers, CEO's, and those people who are charged with the responsibility for establishing and managing an HR function has grown dramatically in the last five years.

This Third Edition of *The Complete Do-It-Yourself Human Resources Department* provides in-depth updates on the various issues that fall under the umbrella of the HR function. It provides hundreds of checklists, reproducible forms, sample policies, and quick-reference procedures. It is also a comprehensive guide for dealing with the many difficult personnel issues managers face daily such as employee performance, discipline, and termination. There are sample letters to use in many tough management situations, and step-by-step guidance for managing scores of specific issues like recruiting, training, safety and health, recordkeeping, and so on.

The many forms and checklists make your life easier when you face a difficult situation such as a layoff or plant or office closure. The book covers federal regulations you should be familiar with and it provides updated information and easily understood guidelines for resolving everyday HR problems. The CD provides readily available forms which you can revise, adding your company's information. You also have the ability to customize the forms to suit your individual needs.

This is such a handy, comprehensive, and easy-to-use resource you will wonder what you ever did without it! You may want to recommend it to your business associates. It can be ordered by calling 1-800-288-4745 and citing ISBN 0-13-092219-6.

WHAT THIS BOOK WILL DO FOR YOU

The Third Edition of *The Complete Do-It-Yourself Human Resources Department* provides the up-to-date information you will need to establish or manage a complete HR function in your organization. If you are an HR Manager, an accounting professional charged with the responsibility for HR in your organization, the CEO of a small or mid-sized company, an administrator for a professional organization, or an HR consultant, you will find the policies, procedures, handbooks, systems, guidelines, forms, and checklists that you will need to do the HR job in a professional and effective manner. This book will save you hours of valuable time. Here is just a sampling of what you will find:

- The latest in Internet Recruiting Sites
- E-Mail, Internet Usage Policy
- Sample Letters/Memo
- Sample Job Descriptions
- Interview Checklists
- Application Forms (English & Spanish)
- Performance Evaluation Form
- Matrix of Federal Regulations
- Layoff Checklist and Sample Notice
- Discipline Procedures and Forms
- Termination Checklist and Form
- Overview of the Fair Labor Standards Act
- Guidelines on Using Independent Contractors

- Tested Personnel Letters
- Sample Employee Handbook
- Sample Personnel Manual
- Family Med. Leave Policy
- Salary Program Format
- Workers' Comp Guides
- 50 Ways to Save Money
- Investigating Sex Harass.
- New OSHA Standards
- Sample COBRA Letter
- Policy on Drug Testing
- Outsourcing Guidelines
- Lists on HR Terminology

The book also includes tips, glossaries, and most-used tables and formulas for quick reference.

HOW TO USE THIS BOOK

Each chapter of the book provides short, practical, easy-to-use policies, procedures, and tools in a key area of the HR function. If you need a sample employment advertisement, or some interview questions quickly before a last minute interview, turn to Chapter 1. This chapter also includes an *Interviewing and Selection Handbook* that will get you up-to-speed quickly on the latest information about this topic. If you want to be sure that you are keeping appropriate personnel records, turn to Chapter 2 on Personnel Recordkeeping and you will find exactly what you should and should not be keeping in an employee personnel file. This chapter also includes the federal record retention requirements that will tell you how long you need to keep personnel records.

Large corporations and small businesses alike find it difficult to keep up with federal regulations that relate to organizations and know which ones actually apply to them. Chapter 3 provides an easy-to-read matrix of key federal regulations. This matrix also provides information on what posters a business must display and where anyone can quickly order the state or federal posters they need. This chapter also provides a list of termination pay requirements by state. There is also an American with Disabilities (ADA) compliance checklist and a sample letter to change and use to fit your needs in case you are asked to provide an accommodation under the ADA.

Chapter 4 provides a sample employee handbook which you can tailor to your own needs and have your attorney review, saving hours of costly time. Chapter 4 also includes valuable information on starting an employee newsletter and offers other ideas for effective employee communications.

Chapter 5 includes a checklist for writing a personnel policy manual and lists the key issues in the successful implementation of personnel policies. There is also a sample personnel policy manual that you can adapt to fit your company's needs. Chapter 6 provides easy-to-implement ideas for designing a salary program including model wage grades and salary rates and ranges adaptable to any company. This chapter also includes information on employee benefits and examples of what other companies offer in the way of benefits. The difficult subjects of discipline and discharge are covered at length in Chapter 7. There is a sample disciplinary policy, and sample forms and letters to assist in this hard-to-manage area.

Chapter 8 addresses concerns about safety, accident reporting, and OSHA issues. It includes a list of the top OSHA violations. You will also find a sample Guide to Accident and Injury Reporting which you can adopt to your needs. There is also a glossary of Occupational Safety and Health Terminology. Chapter 9 discusses key issues in labor relations and what you need to know about plant closings and layoffs.

Any CEO manager, or HR consultant can save hours of effort by using the many sample HR letters that are included in Chapter 10. This chapter is a real time-saver for anyone who has to write a letter or memorandum about a personnel issue.

Chapter 11 contains checklists that will quickly assist in any personnel area when you are rushed and need to know the key issues you face in managing the elements of the HR function. Then to make your life even easier, Chapter 12 provides sample forms that you can copy and adapt to fit your specific needs. Again, this chapter will save you hours of invaluable time hunting for a form when you are in a hurry and need to get a specific personnel issue covered quickly.

Take a few minutes to read the Table of Contents and leaf through the book to get an understanding of what is included in each area of the HR function. Then you'll have a good idea of how and when the book can save you valuable time.

1

RECRUITING, INTERVIEWING, AND SELECTION

Procedures and Forms

- Recruiting Has Gone Hi-Tech
- Recruiting Ads
- Where to List Your Jobs
- Using a Recruitment Advertising Agency
- Identifying and Recruiting the Best Workers
- Recruiting and Employment Routine
- Checklist of Recruiting and Employment Forms
- Ad Checklist
- The Application Forms (English & Spanish)
- Checking References
- Twelve Tips for Giving References
- Background Checks
- Making a Job Offer
- Sample Forms & Letters
- Seven Steps to Successful Selection
- Pros and Cons of Employment Testing Including Drug Testing
- Sample Interviewing and Selection Handbook
- Other New Hire Forms You'll Need and Why You Need Them
- An Internal Job-Posting System
- Recruiting Persons with Disabilities—an Important and Underutilized Resource
- How to Save Money by Using Temporary Help
- Illegal Employment Practices
- New Employee Orientation
- Handling Relocation

Recruiting, Interviewing, and Selection
Procedures and Forms

Attracting and hiring the best employees are two of the most important elements for success in any business. If you don't have the right people in your jobs when you need them, your bottom line will be adversely affected. Your management and supervisory people have a tremendous responsibility to recruit and hire the people who will be effective and who will stay with your organization in order to achieve a positive return on your investment in recruiting and training. We need to continuously look for new and better ways to recruit competent workers.

The old methods of recruiting and employment won't attract the people we want to attract today. What can you do to turn your recruiting activity into a "with it," savvy business operation that hits the right market?

RECRUITING HAS GONE HI-TECH

Employers are finding that it's necessary to list their jobs on national web sites in order to reach the numbers of job applicants they need to fill all of their open positions. Increasingly, corporations are finding this high-tech resource a positive employment tool.

The sites listed here are the most commonly used national web sites. There are other sites in each state and many local high-tech resources for companies who need an ongoing source of job applicants. Local sources are usually accessed by the name of the city, state, or county government.

Example

In Phoenix an excellent resource is www.maricopa.edu/recruiter. Maricopa is the largest county in Arizona. Big employers, and local governments list their jobs and job search register and list their skills and competency levels. When at least 50 percent of the employer's skill requirements are met, both parties are notified via e-mail.

Online Job Interviews

A new trend in retail hiring is the computer-conducted interview. Big-name retailers including Target, Hollywood Video, Macy's, and Longs Drug Stores are replacing paper applications and in-person interviews with computer kiosks in the initial screening of applicants.

The computer programs query prospective employees on job history and work habits. They then typically delve into psychological tests that the companies say can help match job skills and personalities with openings. Employers say the automation gives them an edge in the tight labor market, enabling them to sift through applications quickly, weed out applicants who don't fit their jobs, identify talent and attract candidates who might not otherwise have taken the time to apply.

The next step in automated recruiting is to have job seekers apply for jobs from their home via the Internet. As technology advances, companies foresee putting prospective employees into virtual video environments to see how they might react to a variety of work situations.

The entire recruiting and employment process is changing and becoming more automated and more global.

RECRUITING ADS

Design recruiting ads that attract today's worker. People today are concerned with the quality of work life and self-fulfillment. The style of ads and other recruiting literature is a barometer of a company's philosophy and commitment to employee concerns.

ADVERTISING Only certain jobs today are filled through help-wanted ads. They are basically technical, service and clerical, white- and blue-collar jobs. Exceptions to this are professional jobs advertised in your local paper or the *Wall Street Journal,* or high-level positions that warrant an expensive box ad on the financial page of your local paper. These ads are usually "blind" ads that list a box number for replies and don't show the company name. Remember, however, that some people will not reply to blind ads.

TELEVISION ADVERTISING TV ads are popular. They are often used by large companies as demand for skilled employees has increased. The main consideration here, naturally, is the cost. Local commercial spots can cost as little as $100, depending on the market, while national 60-second spots can cost hundreds of thousands of dollars. The key here is to identify accurately the audience you wish to reach before you spend the money.

RECRUITING SOURCES Keep track of sources when you hire people in order to identify the best recruiting sources for each job. Eliminate those activities that are not providing the best candidates and gear up the ones that are. Trim the recruiting efforts that are not paying off and spend the money where it brings the best return. Use association contacts, networking sources, and your current employees as recruiters.

How to Implement These Ideas

One of the quickest ways to get up-to-speed on current advertising techniques is to read the classified ads in the newspapers in which you wish to run your ads. Find the style and wording that appeals to you and fits your jobs. Read through the ads a second time as

WHERE TO LIST YOUR JOBS

SITE	THE MONSTER BOARD www.monster.com	AMERICA'S JOB BANK www.ajb.dni.us	CAREERPATH.COM www.careerpath.com	HOTJOBS.COM www.hotjobs.com	ONLINE CAREER CENTER www.occ.com
DESCRIPTION	Resume City, the site's job bank, posts more than 25,000 openings and more than 300,000 resumes.	A government site. State agencies post an average of 5,000 new openings per day. Companies contribute another 3,000.	Classifieds from more than 65 newspapers, including the *New York Times*, the *Los Angeles Times*, and the *Boston Globe*.	A member-based site that charges companies a fee to post openings or to search through resumes.	A pioneer in online recruiting. OCC started in 1992 and moved to the Web in 1993.

SITE	NATIONJCB NETWORK www.nationjob.com	CAREERMOSAIC www.careermosaic.com	4WORK www.4work.com	AMERICA'S EMPLOYERS www.americasemployers.com	E.SPAN www.espan.com
DESCRIPTION	More than 15,000 jobs listed nationwide, with an emphasis on those in the Midwest.	More than 70,000 jobs, updated daily.	Specify the state and your job, and 4Work emails you.	Maintained by consultants. It offers several thousand updated job listings.	A pioneer in online employment services. The site is easy to navigate.

SITE	THE CAREER-BUILDER NETWORK www.careerbuilder.com	COMPUTERJOBS.COM www.computerjobs.com	DIVERSITY FORUM www.diversityforum.com	WETFEET www.wetfeet.com	JOBDIRECT www.jobdirect.com
DESCRIPTION	This site focuses on the needs of companies and includes database of 20,000 openings.	A variety of career-oriented content, including lists of IT jobs organized by region and skill set.	Provides a recruiting source for companies seeking a diverse workforce.	Provides more room on site to tell candidates why they should take your job.	Networks you directly on line to thousands of pre-qualified pre-screened candidates.

SITE	CAREERENGINE www.careerengine.com	JOBOPTIONS www.joboptions.com	RECRUIT USA www.recruitusa.com	CAREERJOURNAL www.careerjournal.com	RESUMIX www.resumix.com
DESCRIPTION	Provides category-specific job sites in 20 fields, pre-screens.	Provides search technology so candidates can find the right job quickly.	Submit jobs once. Their technology reformats and delivers to destinations you select.	The Wall Street Journal recruits executive and managerial candidates. Lists jobs directly from your database.	Accessible to all members of your hiring team at home or on the road. Pay only a monthly fee.

though you were an applicant looking for that job. What attracts you? What turns you off? Do the ads reflect an open, interested attitude on the part of the employer? Do you get a feel for their management style? Is it participatory or autocratic? Will people of all ages and ethnic backgrounds respond? Will both men and women apply and feel welcome? Will disabled applicants feel you want them to respond? The ad form provided in this chapter will assist you in writing and placing your ads.

Placing an Ad

Call the classified ad department of the newspaper of your choice. If you haven't received a classified ad packet and know exactly what size type and the size of the ad you need ask the ad taker to help you. Tell the person how you want it to look and provide an idea citing an ad in one of their recent papers as an example. They can look it up and quickly see what you want.

If you are placing TV ads it's best to go to the TV station the first time or ask an account executive to come to your office and help you design your spot. You can get a better idea of what it will cost you. Following are a few sample ads:

Sample Help-Wanted Ad

CHIEF EXECUTIVE OFFICER

We're an exciting new company that could become one of the great international growth stories of the century. We design, manufacture, and market an advanced new communication system based on a major electronic breakthrough. This exciting new technology enables us to produce a system that is smaller, more effective, and less expensive than any other product of its kind on the market today.

We are looking for a dynamic, effective leader who can guide this new company to a successful future in the world marketplace. We have already secured our financing and now seek an extraordinary manager/CEO with impeccable credentials, an entrepreneurial spirit, and a hands-on approach to the top position in the company.

We need a person with consumer-oriented product experience. The ideal candidate will have no illusions about the prodigious amount of talent, effort, and commitment required to reap the substantial rewards that are possible. This CEO will assume full authority for the worldwide operations of this company. An exceptional compensation package including a significant equity position will be negotiated. This is a once-in-a-lifetime opportunity for the right person.

Send your resume in strictest confidence.

Box CO222, New York, NY l0110

Note

This ad is designed to appeal to a top-level executive with impeccable credentials. It communicates that this is a fantastic opportunity with the best package of compensation and benefits available today, that only the most highly qualified persons should bother to apply. It conveys the idea that it's a wonderful opportunity for the right person and there will be pressure to succeed. The successful applicant must be prepared to expend whatever effort and personal time is necessary to get the job done.

Sample Help Wanted Ad

NATIONAL SALES MANAGER

At XXX Company our people have taken us farther, faster than any company in history. What makes us so different? We've created a unique corporate environment—an environment that fosters creativity and personal satisfaction. We give our employees the opportunity to stretch and explore their talents.

Our distinctive approach to business translates into much more than producing a great product. It means personal achievement and satisfaction in a job well done.

As the Regional Sales Manager for our company you'll provide leadership in the New York office. Our sales staff will look to you for guidance in setting and achieving mutually agreed upon goals and objectives.

To qualify you should have sales experience in our field, be technically qualified, and be a dynamic, goal-oriented professional. You'll need a BS degree or equivalent experience. You must have leadership qualities as evidenced by previous experience. You'll need excellent presentation skills, and you must be willing to travel.

We offer you excellent compensation and benefits in an unequaled work environment. If you're interested in this position, please submit your resume to XXX Company, Dept. SM322, P.O. Box 43271, New York, NY 10110.

We are an Affirmative Action employer M/F/V/D

Note

The ad appeals to today's worker. It tells prospective applicants the company has a forward-thinking, creative, and participatory management environment that gives employees an opportunity for personal satisfaction in their work. The ad makes the reader feel that this company is truly interested in its employees.

Sample Help Wanted Ad

NURSING PROFESSIONALS

DIVERSIFICATION   **CHALLENGE**

Whatever your area of expertise, we have a great place for you to work. Our healthcare facility offers the opportunity to work in several areas ranging from acute care to community health. We serve a multicultural patient population. If diversification and challenge are not currently part of your current job description, come and check out the opportunities available at ABC Health Care Systems.

We are proud of our current staff and are pleased to announce the recipient of our third quarter Excellence in Nursing Award. She's Jane Brown, RN, BSN, MSN. Jane is coordinator of the children's program and another fine example of our high standards of nursing excellence. Jane says, "Our healthcare system offers a unique advantage in the industry, the opportunity to diversify and use all of your skills. We are large enough that we can provide many unusual opportunities."

PICTURE

We offer excellent pay and benefits and the opportunity for personal and professional growth. To find out more about the positions available now, send your resume to:

ABC Healthcare Systems
Equal Opportunity Employer M/F/V/D

Note

This ad immediately addresses two of the biggest complaints nurses have about their jobs: the inability to do the type of nursing they like to do and the lack of opportunity for diversification. Because nurses reading the ad might not believe it, the picture and statement of a currently-employed and highly qualified nurse is included.

Sample Help-Wanted Ad

RETAIL SALES PROFESSIONALS

$80,000 per year
COMMISSION . . .

THAT'S WHAT HAPPENS
WHEN YOU SELL QUALITY

XYZ Company-you've heard our name and you know our quality. We want your class and your entrepreneurial spirit.

If you have a warm demeanor, a great deal of confidence, and a track record of selling top quality merchandise to elegant customers in an opulent environment, you're someone we'd like to talk to.

$80,000 is an average annual figure for a full-time sales professional in our store. It can be much greater if you are a capable energetic salesperson.

We offer excellent benefits and a 30% store discount. Please apply in person.
Equal Opportunity Employer M/F/V/D

Note

This ad appeals to an experienced person who has a track record of selling expensive merchandise in a classy store. It says: "We want a go-getter who can sell, and we will pay the right person well." It appeals to a narrow group of people who are probably doing the same job now in another store. This ad gets the job done. It will probably attract qualified people from a more down-scale store wanting to move up in the retail industry.

Sample Help-Wanted Ad

SECRETARY/ADMINISTRATIVE ASSISTANT

Our company, one of the leading computer organizations in this area, has an exciting opportunity for a Secretary/Administrative Assistant to one of our executives.

The person in this job will have a lot of variety in an entrepreneurial setting with a great deal of autonomy and opportunity for creative problem solving. There is occasional travel to plan and set up group meetings around the country.

We are looking for a person who is flexible and has good interpersonal skills. You will need Microsoft Word and a good working knowledge of business systems. You must be organized and a self-starter.

We offer an exciting participatory business environment, excellent compensation and benefits including tuition refund, and other personal growth opportunities.

Send resume and salary requirements to:

Equal Opportunity Employer M/F/V/D

Note

The ad conveys the sense that this company is forward-thinking and uses a participatory management approach to its people. Many companies are trying to attract young professionals, and this company is trying to do it by offering a tuition refund program. It also says that this company is interested in "growing" its people and promoting from within.

Manager's Tip

Notice that the organizations running these ads are appealing to applicants by stating that they want the best people and in order to get them they are providing a good place to work, a place to be proud of. Not only that, they are providing competitive benefits and pay and an atmosphere of excellence with growth opportunities. Read other ads in the paper and compare. Many of them only tell the applicant what the company wants and expects. They are one-dimensional. They convey an attitude of autocratic management and show little interest in what the applicant is looking for.

Many classified ads in newspapers and magazines include a picture of the company's current employees to show their apparent satisfaction with the organization.

EFFECTIVE METHODS OF FILLING OPEN POSITIONS

Most Effective Ways to Fill Jobs	Executives	Managers	Professionals	Technical, Including Data processing	Administrative, Accounting, etc.	Clerical	Laborers and Service Workers
Internet job postings	x	x	x	x	x		
Ads in local newspapers	x	x	x	x	x	x	x
Ads on TV and radio		x	x	x	x	x	x
Employment agencies		x	x	x	x	x	
Executive search firms	x						
College campus recruiting			x	x	x		
Employee referrals	x	x	x	x	x	x	x
State Job Service						x	x
Walk-in applicants, unsolicited resumes						x	x

Note: There are times when one of the above methods of filling a job would work better than another, but over a long period the ones checked should prove most effective.

Manager's Tip

When recruiting hard-to-fill jobs: Flexibility is the answer. Be open-minded regarding working hours, job-sharing, working at home, temporary help and other alternative working situations. Gear company procedures to workers needs.

USING A RECRUITMENT ADVERTISING AGENCY

Recruit advertising agencies provide a valuable service to companies when it comes to notifying the public of employment opportunities available in their company. A specialized recruitment agency deals with recruitment communications and nothing else. It is expert at handling the whole business of recruitment advertising and employee communications, from in-column ad placement to technologies like the Internet and the World Wide Web.

Specifically, a recruitment advertising agency develops, prepares, and places advertising to help a company communicate its recruitment message. This message may appear in print media (newspapers, trade publications, directories, direct mail), in broadcast media (radio, television), and other media (billboards, transit signs, point-of-purchase displays). It may also appear in brochures or on specialty items, display booths, and the Internet.

In choosing the right recruitment advertising agency, you should consider an agency that is familiar with your company's employment marketplace, has experience handling a similar budget, has a history of success using a variety of media, and has a proactive approach to total quality.

The basic service areas of a recruitment advertising agency include:

- Account Management—Account executives, and account coordinators can provide ad placement, ad tracking, strategic media planning, creative services coordination, Internet services, project management, and proof of publication. Other specialty services include a confidential reply service and answering, prescreening, and interviewing services.

- Creative copy, design, and production—Copywriters provide headlines, body copy, and conceptual art suggestions. Art directors can provide original design, illustration, and photography. Also, production artists can work with your staff using an integrated computer network to generate fast, error-free camera ready art.

- Research—Advanced research systems offer recruiters round-the-clock access to extensive databases. They also compile facts, figures, and recommendations for a variety of business needs.

- Accounting—Provide custom invoicing and tear sheets of your ads.

One company that provides these services is Nationwide Advertising Services at (800) 627-4723.

IDENTIFYING AND RECRUITING THE BEST WORKERS

If you are going to have all the workers you need to fill your jobs you must be flexible in the way you deal with a more diverse workforce. Today's worker may:

- work shorter hours and a shorter work week
- work at home

- work part time
- share a job with another person
- ask to work early evenings to share child care with a working spouse
- request help with child care because he or she is a single parent and works the night shift
- get an extension of company benefits for a domestic partner
- be retired from one job and seeking a second career
- be over fifty
- be a person with a disability
- meet his/her future spouse on the job or participate in at least one work romance
- work together with a spouse in the same company and possibly in the same department
- bring a child to work if the job can be done effectively with a child present—or bring the child to an on-site day-care center
- have to change careers and be retrained at least twice in a lifetime
- lose at least one job either through merger, or to a computer or robot
- be healthier because of health and fitness programs offered on the job
- use a personal computer on the job
- own company stock through a profit-sharing program
- own a share in the company through a leveraged buyout
- be more outspoken on personal rights issues like privacy and termination-at-will
- want more say in the way his/her job is done
- refuse to take lie-detector or other controversial types of tests
- be more likely to have tried or used drugs in the past
- be bilingual—probably Spanish speaking
- have legally or illegally immigrated to the United States
- be a member of a minority group—Asian, Hispanic, or African-American
- be a two-income family member or be a single-parent head of household
- want comparable pay for work of comparable worth, an issue that won't go away as more women enter the workforce. An estimated 75 percent of all women over the age of sixteen will be in the workforce in the 1990s.
- insist on flexible benefits so that, in a two-income household, the benefits won't overlap
- hold several jobs off and on through a lifetime in order to attain a desired life style

Get your management group together over gourmet snacks some early evening and brainstorm ways to identify and recruit the types of employees you need to fill your open positions. Tap the brainpower you have on staff to help in the recruiting function.

RECRUITING AND EMPLOYMENT ROUTINE

Two of the key personnel functions are recruiting and employment. Certain forms should be completed and procedures followed in order to comply with government regulations.

1. When a job opens that you cannot fill from within the company, have the manager complete an employment requisition form. This form describes the job and assists the person who has to place the ad, to understand the job. In case of a civil rights suit it also helps you to remember what jobs have been open and who filled them. Maintain requisitions in a looseleaf binder. The requisition also helps you keep track of the number of open jobs you have. Review job descriptions before you place ads and interview to ensure you know the job.

2. If you are going to place an ad, type it up ahead of time and make a copy. Keep that copy with the employment requisition or in a separate file. Insist that all ads be placed through the personnel administrator and that they carry the EEO/AAP designation.

3. Have all applicants fill out the employment application. Even if they have a resume, they must complete and sign the application. The application is the legal document. Be sure the application conforms to state and federal regulations and gives you permission to investigate a prospective employee.

4. Set up files on applicants. You can file them by job category and then alphabetically. You must maintain applicant files for one year. Don't accept applications unless you have jobs available, because you will build a tremendous backlog of applications.

5. You may wish to keep a computerized applicant log. It saves a great deal of time when applicants call in to see if their resume or application is still on file. The log can be maintained by year and month. The log is a great help if you are a federal contractor and have a desk audit by the Office of Federal Contract Compliance and need to furnish applicant data.

6. Screening applicants is an important step in the hiring process. You will save hours of your time and the managers' time in interviewing if you learn to screen applicants using your application form. Train your receptionist or personnel clerk to look for:
   - Breaks in employment
   - Omissions on the application
   - Overall professionalism in completing the application

7. Interviewing process and skills are important; The interview should be planned. You should know the job to be filled and plan the questions to be asked. Avoid overlap by using a list of questions to be asked in personnel and a separate list of more technical questions to be asked by the department manager. There are some questions you may not ask. Get together after the interview and compare notes. Post-interview forms can be used to record interview information.

8. Reference checking is an important element of the hiring process. No one should be hired without a reference check. There has been a tremendous rise in negligent hiring lawsuits in the past few years. Use reference check forms and guidelines.

9. After the person has been hired to fill the open position, you can pull the employment requisition out of the pending looseleaf binder and file it in a "filled requisition file," noting the name of the person who filled the job and the hire date.

10. Federal contractors should use a "filled position summary sheet." It greatly simplifies your job in case of a desk audit.

11. When a person is hired, send a "new employee confirmation letter." This letter confirms the details under which the person was hired so there is no misunderstanding later. Always quote salary as a monthly figure. Courts have ruled that when a yearly salary was quoted in an employment letter it implied the person was guaranteed the job for a year.

12. Be sure the new employee receives an employee handbook and signs the acknowledgment form and that the employee is given an orientation to the company and a review of company benefits.

13. Set up an employee personnel file. The type of file you use is up to you. Some people like to clip down every piece of paper in a heavy file. Others like to put everything into an envelope-type file. If you use a regular file, put clips on both sides. File everything to do with status changes on the right hand side and everything to do with hiring, promotion, and termination on the left. Set up a separate file for benefits.

   Maintain a personnel data sheet on the top of the right side of the file folder, and log all personnel changes on the sheet as you file them. Then, when you have to pull out a file and look to see when the employee's last raise or last promotion occurred, you have information quickly available. Also, maintain emergency contact and phone numbers on this sheet for quick reference. Retain these files for five years after termination.

14. Send the payroll information sheet with all the employee information on it to the payroll department to be processed.

15. Use a PC to purchase a software package that will maintain your entire employee base on the computer. When you get calls about employees all you have to do is call up the data on the screen. You don't have to pull the individual personnel files.

16. Have all necessary employment forms completed as soon as the employee is hired.

Manager's Tips

- Always have classified ads run by your personnel person to control costs and content.
- Review the requisitions form and be sure you know the job before you run an ad and conduct interviews. This saves a lot of time and effort.
- If you take applications all the time—even when you don't have jobs open—you must file the applications and you then have a obligation to call those old applicants when a new job opens. You can build a tremendous backlog of paper in your files. You could also be building statistics that could have an adverse impact on your affirmative action program. It's a good idea to accept applications only when you have a job to fill.

CHECKLIST OF RECRUITING AND EMPLOYMENT FORMS

❏ Job Description

❏ Employment Requisition

❏ Ad Checklist

❏ Classified ad form

❏ Application

❏ Telephone Reference Check Guide

❏ Education Reference Verification

❏ Employment Confirmation Letter

❏ Applicant Rejection Letter

❏ Post-Employment Form

❏ Immigration Form I-9, Employment Eligibility Verification

❏ Filled Position Summary

❏ Employee Agreement and Handbook Acknowledgment Form

❏ Confidentiality Agreement (if applicable)

❏ Personnel Data Sheet

❏ New Employee Orientation Checklist

❏ Personnel Action or Status Form

JOB DESCRIPTION OUTLINE

JOB TITLE:	STATUS
JOB CODE:	DATE:
DIVISION:	REVISION NO.:
REPORTS TO:	REVISION DATE:

POSITION SUMMARY:

Please provide a brief summary of the position. This information will be used for position announcements and advertisements.

PRINCIPAL ACCOUNTABILITIES:

Please make a list of job tasks stating what is done and how it is done. Begin each sentence with a verb using present tense singular. For example: <u>Analyze</u> financial data using spreadsheet software. <u>Prepare</u> reports using Wordperfect 5.1 software.

THIS JOB DESCRIPTION DOES NOT CONSTITUTE A CONTRACT FOR EMPLOYMENT

JOB TITLE:
DATE:
PAGE____ OF____

JOB REQUIREMENTS:

EDUCATION:

List minimum acceptable educational requirements to do this job.

EXPERIENCE:

List number of years of experience in the job and specific knowledge requirements.

SKILLS:

List analytical, organizational, interpersonal, technical, managerial skills, and so on.

SUPERVISORY RESPONSIBILITIES:

Please list the number of people supervised and their job titles. If you do not supervise, put "none."

EQUIPMENT TO BE USED:

Please list computers, fax machines, telephones, calculators, floor waxers, power tools, fork lifts, and so on.

TYPICAL PHYSICAL DEMANDS:

Please list job requirements such as lifting standing, sitting, and so on. Try to be specific. Example: "Must be able to lift 50 pounds," "must sit 7 hours a day," "must be able to drive a car."

TYPICAL MENTAL DEMANDS:

List the mental requirements of the job. Example: "must be able to do simple math calculations" or "must be able to analyze complex information."

WORKING CONDITIONS:

Please list examples such as "must work evenings and/or weekends," "job requires driving ____% of the time," "works in a typical office setting," "works outside 90% of the time," and so on.

THIS JOB DESCRIPTION DOES NOT CONSTITUTE A CONTRACT FOR EMPLOYMENT

PERSONNEL REQUISITION FORM (Please type)

Job Title	Salary Range	Hourly Rate	Requisition Number	
			Department/Location	Current Date

☐ Replacement   ☐ *New Position   Approved _____ Yes _____ No

☐ Exempt   ☐ Non-exempt   Date Needed

Name of Vacating Employee

Regular Full-time _____   Regular Part-time _____

Temporary _____ (3 mo. max) Agency _____

Reason for Vacancy or New Position

Skills Required

Education or Equivalent Experience

Essential Job Functions

1. _____
2. _____
3. _____
4. _____

5. _____
6. _____
7. _____
8. _____

Additional Job Information Including Physical/Mental Demands

*Board Approval/Signature (if $40,000 annual salary)

Schedule Interviews Through (Name/Extension)

Supervisor

Manager's Signature

Director or Vice President's Signature

President's Signature

HUMAN RESOURCE DEPARTMENT USE ONLY

Position Filled By	Start Date	Starting Salary	HR Approval

Ad Checklist

A high percentage of jobs will be filled by help-wanted ads and recruiting literature, but many ads are sterile and boring. There is no way to know exactly how effective advertising is, even if you keep records of applicants who respond to your ads. Here are some ideas to keep in mind when running ads:

❏ People are attracted by class. If you can afford it, use display ads. Be sure the ads reflect the company personality.

❏ Use a clean-cut type style and graphics.

❏ The first few words need pizzazz to hook the reader and appeal to the people you want to attract. They should be printed in large type.

❏ Make sure your ad is placed under the appropriate job classification.

❏ Use your company logo.

What you're looking for:

❏ List specific skills.

❏ List work experience required.

❏ State whether relocation is necessary.

❏ State educational requirements.

❏ Indicate whether the job requires regular travel.

❏ State whether you will train.

❏ Use the EEO/AAP designation.

Benefits:

❏ Provide a good review of your overall benefit program and any other items (such as "mountain location" or "mild year-round climate") that you consider a benefit.

What *not* to include:

❏ References to age or sex or any other discriminatory language.

HELP WANTED ADVERTISING FORM

Position _____ Reg. # _____

Department/Division _____

Charge To _____Cost Center

Person Requesting Ad _____

     Phone Ext. _____

Ads must be sent to the Human Resources Department by:

     Monday 5:00 P.M. for Wednesday placement

     Thursday 5:00 P.M. for Sunday placement

_____

Newspaper _____

Run Ad _____Day(s) _____Date(s)

Under Heading(s) _____

Please insert the following ad for the above position:

EOE/M/F/D/V

_____

FOR HUMAN RESOURCES DEPARTMENT USE ONLY

Ad Ordered_____(Date) _____(Newspaper)

Price $ _____

Re-run: Run Ad _____Day(s) _____Date(s)

Re-run Ordered _____(Date) _____(Newspaper)

Re-run Price $ _____

THE APPLICATION FORMS

The application form is important, it is the legal document that provides the information you need on an applicant in order to make an effective hiring decision. It is also the form that provides concrete information on an applicant's qualifications. Insist that your application form be fully completed.

The Fair Credit Reporting Act also requires that an applicant read an accompanying statement and sign it. This gives you the ability to run credit and background checks on the applicant with their permission. Some states like the state of California have additional requirements. Be sure to check the regulations in your state.

With the growing diversity in today's workforce many companies find they need the employment application also done in the Spanish language, therefore, I have included both an English and Spanish Employment Application form. You can adjust them to fit your specific needs.

Note

You may wish to have your attorney review the form that you decide to use to ensure your application conforms to the regulations in your state and fits your specific purposes.

APPLICATION FOR EMPLOYMENT
An Equal Opportunity Employer

We do not discriminate on the bases of race, color, religion, national origin, sex, sexual orientation, age, or disability. It is our intention that all qualified applicants be given equal opportunity and that selection decisions be based on job-related factors.

Each question should be answered fully and accurately. No action can be taken on this application until all questions have been answered. Use blank paper if you do not have enough room on this application. **PLEASE PRINT**, except for signature on back of application. In reading and answering the following questions, be aware that none of the questions are intended to imply illegal preferences or discrimination based upon non-job-related information.

Job Applied For _____ Today's Date _____

Are you seeking: Full-time ___   Part-time ___   Temporary ___   When could you start work? _____

Last Name	First Name	Middle Name	Telephone Number

Present Street Address _____ City _____ State _____ Zip Code

Are you 18 years of age or older?   Yes ___ No ___   (If you are hired you may be required to submit proof of age.)

Social Security Number _____ If hired, can you furnish proof you are eligible to work in the U.S.?   Yes ___ No ___

Have you ever applied here before?   Yes ___ No ___   If yes, when? _____

Were you ever employed here?   Yes ___ No ___   If yes, when? _____

Have you ever been convicted of or pleaded guilty to any law violation (except speeding or parking violations)? Yes___ No___

   If yes, give details _____
   (A "Yes" answer does not automatically disqualify you from employment, because the nature of the offense, date, and the job for which you are applying will also be considered.)

Are you now or do you expect to be engaged in any other business or employment?   Yes ___ No ___

   If yes, please explain _____

For Driving Jobs Only: Do you have a valid driver's license?   Yes ___ No ___

   Driver's License Number _____ Class of License _____

   Have you had your driver's license suspended or revoked in the last 3 years?   Yes ___ No ___

   If yes, give details: _____

List professional, trade, business or civic activities and offices held. (Exclude labor organizations and memberships which reveal race, color, religion, national origin, sex, age, disability or other protected status.) _____

_____

LIST NAME AND ADDRESS OF SCHOOLS	Number of Years Completed	Diploma/ Degree/ Certificate	Subjects Studied
High School or GED:			
College or University:			
Vocational or Technical:			

What skills or additional training do you have that are related to the job for which you are applying? _____

_____

What machines or equipment can you operate that are related to the job for which you are applying? _____

_____

List names of employers in consecutive order with present or last employer listed first. Account for all periods of time including military service and any periods of unemployment. If self-employed, give firm name and supply business references. **PLEASE GIVE MONTH AND YEAR.**

NAME OF EMPLOYER

ADDRESS

CITY, STATE, ZIP CODE

SUPERVISOR   TELEPHONE

JOB TITLES AND DUTIES

DATE OF EMPLOYMENT: FROM _____ TO _____

PAY: START $_____ FINAL $_____

REASON FOR LEAVING

NAME OF EMPLOYER

ADDRESS

CITY, STATE, ZIP CODE

SUPERVISOR   TELEPHONE

JOB TITLES AND DUTIES

DATE OF EMPLOYMENT: FROM _____ TO _____

PAY: START $_____ FINAL $_____

REASON FOR LEAVING

NAME OF EMPLOYER

ADDRESS

CITY, STATE, ZIP CODE

SUPERVISOR   TELEPHONE

JOB TITLES AND DUTIES

DATE OF EMPLOYMENT: FROM _____ TO _____

PAY: START $_____ FINAL $_____

REASON FOR LEAVING

NAME OF EMPLOYER

ADDRESS

CITY, STATE, ZIP CODE

SUPERVISOR   TELEPHONE

JOB TITLES AND DUTIES

DATE OF EMPLOYMENT: FROM _____ TO _____

PAY: START $_____ FINAL $_____

REASON FOR LEAVING

Have you worked under any other name? Yes ___ No ___
    If yes, give names: _____

Are you presently employed? Yes ___ No ___ If yes, may we contact your present employer? Yes ___ No ___

Have you ever been fired from a job or asked to resign? Yes ___ No ___
    If yes, please explain: _____

Give three references, not relatives or former employers.
Name   **Address**   **Phone**

PLEASE READ EACH STATEMENT CAREFULLY BEFORE SIGNING

I certify that all information provided in this employment application is true and complete. I understand that any false information or omission may disqualify me from further consideration for employment and may result in my dismissal if discovered at a later date.

I authorize and agree to cooperate in a thorough investigation of all statements made herein and other matters relating to my background and qualifications. I understand that any investigation conducted may include a request for employment and educational history, credit reports, consumer reports, investigative consumer reports, driving record, and criminal history. I authorize any person, school, current and former employer, consumer reporting agency, and any other organization or agency to provide information relevant to such investigation and I hereby release all persons and corporations requesting or supplying information pursuant to such investigation from all liability or responsibility to me for doing so. I understand that I have the right to make a written request within a reasonable period of time for complete disclosure of the nature and scope of any investigation. I further authorize any physician or hospital to release any information which may be necessary to determine my ability to perform the job for which I am being considered or any future job in the event that I am hired.

I understand that compliance with the Company's Corporate Code of Conduct is a condition of my employment.

I understand I may be required to successfully pass a drug-screening examination. I hereby consent to a pre-and/or post-employment drug screen as a condition of being hired or of my continued employment, if required.

I UNDERSTAND THAT THIS APPLICATION OR SUBSEQUENT EMPLOYMENT DOES NOT CREATE A CONTRACT OF EMPLOYMENT NOR GUARANTEE EMPLOYMENT FOR ANY DEFINITE PERIOD OF TIME. IF EMPLOYED, I UNDERSTAND THAT I HAVE BEEN HIRED AT THE WILL OF THE EMPLOYER AND MY EMPLOYMENT MAY BE TERMINATED AT ANY TIME, WITH OR WITHOUT CAUSE AND WITH OR WITHOUT NOTICE.

I have read, understand, and by my signature consent to these statements.

Signature _____   Date: _____

This application for employment will remain active for a limited time. Ask the organization representative for details.

FAIR CREDIT REPORTING ACT

DISCLOSURE

The Company, when evaluating your application for employment, when deciding whether to offer you employment, when deciding whether to promote you, reassign you, or to continue your employment (if you are hired), and when making other employment-related decisions directly affecting you, may wish to obtain and use a "consumer report" about you, from a "consumer reporting agency." These terms are defined in the Fair Credit Reporting Act, 15 U.S.C.S. 1681 et seq. ("FCRA") which applies to you. As an applicant for employment or employee of our company, you are a "consumer" with rights under the FCRA.

"Consumer reporting agency" means a person or business which, for monetary fees, dues, or on a cooperative nonprofit basis, regularly assembles or evaluates consumer credit information or other information on consumers for the purpose of furnishing "consumer reports" to others.

"Consumer report" means any written, oral or other communication of any information by a consumer reporting agency bearing on a consumer's credit worthiness, credit standing, credit capacity, character, general reputation, personal characteristics, or mode of living which is used or expected to be used or collected for the purpose of serving as a factor in establishing the consumer's eligibility for, among other things, employment purposes.

If we obtain a consumer report about you, and if we intend to make an employment-related decision that adversely affects you based in whole or in part on the consumer report, you will be provided with a copy of the consumer report before the decision is made final by our Company. Any decision regarding your employment will be made by us and not by the consumer reporting agency. You are also free to contact the Federal Trade Commission about your rights under the FCRA, as a "consumer," with regard to consumer reports and consumer reporting agencies.

AUTHORIZATION FOR ___(Company Name)___
TO OBTAIN CONSUMER REPORT FOR EMPLOYMENT PURPOSES

By signing below, I hereby certify that I have read and understand *completely* the Fair Credit Reporting Act Disclosure (the "Disclosure") that has been provided to me by _____ , and I hereby authorize _____ to obtain for employment purposes a consumer report and/or a motor vehicle report about me and to consider such reports when making decisions regarding my employment. I understand that I have rights under the Fair Credit Reporting Act, including the rights discussed in the above Disclosure provided to me by _____ .

_____   _____
Applicant/Employee Name   Date   Witness's Name   Date

_____   _____
Signature   Signature

Un empleador que brinda igualdad de
opportunidades
SOLICITUD DE EMPLEO

Nombre: _____
                Apellido   Primer Nombre   Segundo Nombre

No. de Telèfono: _____ No. de Seguridad Social: _____

Dirección Actual: _____
                        No.   Calle   Ciudad Estado   Código Postal

---

Puesto al que se postula: _____

¿Empleo a tiempo completo?   **?** Sí   **?** No
¿Empleo a tiempo parcial?   **?** Sí   **?** No

¿En qué días y horas puede usted trabajar? _____
_____

En caso de ser contratado/a, ¿cuándo puede comenzar a trabajar? _____
¿Alguna vez presentó una solicitud de empleo en nuestra compañía en el pasado?_____
_____
? Sí **?** No   En caso afirmativo, ¿cuándo?_____ ¿Dónde?_____
¿Usted ha trabajado con nosotros en el pasado? **?** Sí **?** No En caso affirmativo, _____
¿Cuándo?_____ ¿Dónde?_____
¿Cómo llegó a nosotros? Publicidad **?**   Agencia de Colocaciones **?**

Empleado actual **?** Especifique el nombre: _____
Otros **?** Especificar: _____

INFORMACIÓN PERSONAL

¿Tiene usted 18 años de edad o es mayor de 18 años?   **?** Sí   **?** No

(**Nota:** La contratación podrá estar sujeta a la verificación de que usted posee la edad mínima requerida
por ley.)

¿Usted cumple con los requisitos legales para trabajar en los Estados Unidos? **?** Sí **?** No

(**Nota:** La contratación está sujeta a la verificación de que es ciudadano/a estadounidense o que posee
status de inmigrante autorizado de acuerdo con la Ley de Control y Reformas de Inmigración de 1986.)

¿Alguna vez fue condenado/a por cualquier delito, exceptuando violaciones de transito de poca
gravedad?   **?** Sí   **?** No

En caso afirmativo, especifique la naturaleza del/los delito/s, cuándo y dónde fue declarado/a culpable y
la resolución del caso: _____
_____
_____

(**Nota:** No se negará *automáticamente* la contractación a los postulantes que hayan sido acusados de un
delito. La naturaleza del delito, la fecha del delito, las circunstancias que lo rodearon, y la importancia
del delito con respecto al/los puestos al/los que la persona se postula podrán ser tenidos en cuenta, no

**ENUMERE A CONTINUACIÓN TODOS LOS EMPLEOS
ACTUALES Y PASADOS, COMENZANDO POR EL MÀS RECIENTE**

Nombre de la Compañía	Dirección/Número de Telèfono	Empleado		Salario	
		Desde	Hasta	Inicial	Final

Describa sus tareas: Motivo por el cual dejó de trabajar:

Supervisor:

Nombre de la Compañía	Dirección/Número de Telèfono	Empleado		Salario	
		Desde	Hasta	Inicial	Final

Describa sus tareas: Motivo por el cual dejó de trabajar:

Supervisor:

Nombre de la Compañía	Dirección/Número de Telèfono	Empleado		Salario	
		Desde	Hasta	Inicial	Final

Describa sus tareas: Motivo por el cual dejó de trabajar:

Supervisor:

Nombre de la Compañía	Dirección/Número de Telèfono	Empleado		Salario	
		Desde	Hasta	Inicial	Final

Describa sus tareas: Motivo por el cual dejó de trabajar:

Supervisor:

¿Podemos ponernos en contacto con los empleadores enumerados anteriormente?_____
En caso negativo, favor indicar con cuál/es usted no desea que nos pongamos en contacto: _____

ESTUDIOS, CAPACITACIÓN Y EXPERIENCIA

Colegio	Nombre y Dirección	No. de Añós que asistió	¿Se Graduo?	Titulo obtenido o Curso que realizó
Enseñanza Primaria			Sí ☐ No ☐	
Enseñanza Secundaria			Sí ☐ No ☐	
Instituto/ Universidad			Sí ☐ No ☐	
Oficio Actividad			Sí ☐ No ☐	
Otros (Especificar)			Sí ☐ No ☐	

Responda las siguientes preguntas en caso de postularse para un *cargo administrativo:*

¿Escribe a máquina? Sí ☐ No ☐   En caso affirmativo, ¿cuántas palabras por minuto? _____

¿Tiene experiencia en el uso de computadoras? Sí ☐ No ☐ En caso affirmativo, favor explicar: ___
_____

Enumere cualquier otro aparato de oficina que usted sepa manejar: _____

¿Posee usted experiencia, capacitación o habilidades adicionales que sienta que lo/la capacitan especialmente para el/los cargo/s al/los que se postula? En caso afirmativo, favor explicar: _____
_____
_____

REFERENCIAS   **(Escriba a continuación el nombre de tres personas, que *no* sean parientes syuos y que *no* sean antiguos empleadores suyos, y a quienes conozca desde hace al menos un año.)**

Nombre: _____
Dirección: _____
          No.   Calle   Ciudad Estado   Código Postal

                                        Número de años
No. De teléfono: _____ Que se conocen: _____
Nombre: _____
Dirección: _____
          No.   Calle   Ciudad Estado   Código postal

                                        Número de años
No. De teléfono: _____ Que se conocen: _____
Nombre: _____
Dirección: _____
          No.   Calle   Ciudad Estado   Código postal

                                        Número de años
No. De teléfono: _____ Que se conocen:_____
Nombre: _____
Dirección: _____
          No.   Calle   Ciudad Estado   Código postal

FAVOR LEER Y FIRMAR ABAJO

Por la presente certifico que no retuve a sabiendas ningún tipo de información que pudiera afectar en forma adversa mis posibilidades de contratación, y que mis respuestas son verdaderas y correctas, y que no poseo reserva mental alguna. Comprendo que cualquier omisión o declaración en falso de un hecho material contenido en esta solicitud, en cualquier documento utilizado para asegurar la contratación, o durante la entrevista previa a la contratación constituirá causal para que se rechace esta aplicación o para que se me despida inmediatamente en caso de que resulte contratado/a, independientemente del tiempo que haya transcurrido antes de que se descubra tal hecho.

Por la presente autorizo a   a investigar exhaustivamente mis referencias, antecedentes laborales, educación y cualquier otro asunto relacionado a mi idoneidad para el cargo y, asimismo autorizo a mis antiguos empleadores a revelar a todos y cualesquiera de mis antecedentes laborales, incluyendo informes disciplinarios y cartas de reprimenda, sin mediar notificación a mi persona de tal divulgación. Asimismo, por la presente eximo a o a mis antiguos empleadores, sus respectivos directores, funcionarios, empleados y agentes y a todas las demás personas, de todo reclamo, demanda y responsabilidad derivados o relacionados en cualquier forma con tal investigación o divulgación.

Comprendo y acepto que, en caso de ser contratado/a, mi contratación y compensación no se aplican a un período definido o determinado, sino que pueden cesar en cualquier momento, con o sin mediar causa, y con o sin mediar aviso, ya sea por decisión mía o de   Además comprendo y ningún representante de   posee autoridad alguna para celebrar ningún acuerdo de empleo por ningún plazo específico ni para realizar ninguna representación vinculante o acuerdos, ya sea en forma oral o escrita, contraviniendo lo anteriormente mencionado o aduciendo la finalidad de garantizar cualesquiera beneficios, plazos o condiciones de contratación en particular.

NOTA

Esta solicitud permanecerá vigente por noventa (90) días. Si usted no tuvo noticias de luego de noventa (90) días y aún desea ser tenido en cuenta para un empleo, deberá llenar y presentar una nueva solicitud de empleo.

_____   _____
                Fecha   Firma del Postulante

COMENTARIOS ADICIONALES: _____

_____

_____

_____

_____

_____

_____

_____

_____

_____

_____

AVISO A LOS POSTULANTED RESPECTO DE LOS INFORMES DE ANTECEDENTES/CONSUMO

Antes de cualquier oferta de empleo se podrá obtener un informe de consumo y/o un informe de antecedentes que incluya información respecto de su personalidad, antecedentes laborales, reputación general, antecedentes judiciales, antecedentes sobre la conducción de un vehículo motorizado, modo de vida y/o actividad crediticia y endeudamiento. Mediante una solicitud por escrito, presentada oportunamente por el Departamento de Personal de la Compañía, y dentro de un plazo de 5 (cinco) días de presentada la solicitud, se le informará a usted el nombre, la dirección y el número de teléfono del organismo informante, así como la naturaleza y el alcance del informe.

Antes de que se tome ninguna medida adversa en todo o en parte como consecuencia de la información contenida en el informe de antecedentes/consumo, se le proporcionará una copia del informe, el nombre, la dirección y el número de teléfono del organismo informante, un resumen de los derechos que usted posee según la Ley Justa para la Divulgación de Información Crediticia, así como la información adicional sobre sus derechos legales.

CONSENTIMIENTO PARA OBTENER INFORMES DE ANTECEDENTES/CONSUMO

Leí la información arriba mencionada y por el presente autorizo a la Compañía a obtener un informe de antecedentes/consumo, tal como se describió anteriormente. Comprendo que poseo el derecho de realizar una solicitud por escrito dentro de un plazo razonable para recibir información adicional y detallada sobre la naturaleza y el alcance del informe, incluyendo el nombre, la dirección y el número de teléfono del organismo informante.

_____

Firma

_____

Nombre en letra de imprenta

_____

Fecha

CONSENTIMIENTO PARA DIVULGAR INFORMACIÓN

Por favor llene la siguiente información a los efectos de identificar sus antecedentes:

Nombre (tal como figura en su licencia de conducir o documento de identidad):

En letra de imprenta: _____
                    Nombre   Appelido   Segundo Apellido

Indique cualesquiera otros nombres que usted haya utilizado, que no figuren en la solicitud o el curriculum vitae que presentó (Apellido de soltera, otros apellidos de casada, sobrenombres, etc.).

En letra de imprenta: _____

Enumere todas las direcciones en las que haya vivido <u>en los últimos cinco años</u> (incluya el número de calle, nombre de la calle, ciudad, estado y código postal):

Actual: _____

_____

Direcciones Anteriores   Fechas aproximadas

1. _____

2. _____

3. _____

4. _____

Número de licencia: _____ Fecha de emisión:_____
Número de seguridad social: _____ Fecha de nacimiento: _____

De conformidad con la Ley de Privacidad (5 C.E.U.A.), la Ley para la Libertad de Información y la Ley para la Justa Divulgación de Información Crediticia, expresamente autorizo a cualquier persona vinculada a cualquier institución educativa, empleador actual o pasado (incluyendo gobiernos federales/estatales/locales), cualesquiera organizaciones militares (federales o estatales), cualquier organismo para el cumplimiento de la ley (federal/estatal/local), cualquier organismo de información crediticia, cualquier institución u oficina de asistencia médica pública/privada, o cualquier persona que posea un conocimiento personal acerca de mi personalidad, antecedentes laborales, antecedentes médicos (incluyendo resultados de análisis de drogas y/o antecedentes de rehabilitación correspondientes) y modo general de vida a DIVULGAR tal información al organismo informante de mis antecedentes a los efectos de ser considerado para la contratación en un emploe. Por el presente acepto EXIMIR a   empleados, agentes y cualesquiera otras personas u otras entidades de todas y cualesquiera responsabilidad por daños de cualquier especie y naturaleza, conocidos o desconocidos, que pueden en cualquier momento recaer sobre mi persona debido a 1) que tales personas o entidades confien en la información presentada en mi solicitud de emploe, 2) que tales personas o entidades confíen en la información obtenida en virtud de esta autorización, 3) el cumplimiento o cualquier intento de cumplir con esta autorización y 4) el cese de mi contratación basado en información obtenida en virtud de esta autorización. Por el presente autorizo a que una copia de esta DIVULGACIÓN sea considerada tan válida como el original.

Firma:_____ Fecha:_____

APPLICANT EEO OR AFFIRMATIVE ACTION INFORMATION

It is the policy of this organization to provide equal employment opportunity to all qualified applicants for employment without regard to race, color, religion, national origin, sex, age, veteran status or disability. Various agencies of the government require employers to invite applicants to identify themselves as indicated below.

COMPLETION OF THIS FORM IS VOLUNTARY AND IN NO WAY AFFECTS THE DECISION REGARDING YOUR APPLICATION FOR EMPLOYMENT. THIS FORM IS CONFIDENTIAL AND WILL BE MAINTAINED SEPARATELY FROM YOUR APPLICATION FORM.

PLEASE PRINT

Name: _____ Date: _____
        Last   First   Middle

Position Applied for: (list only one) _____

What is your race/ethnic origin?   **What is your sex?**
 ❑ White   ❑ Male
 ❑ Hispanic   ❑ Female
 ❑ American Indian/Alaskan Native
 ❑ Black
 ❑ Asian/Pacific Islander

Are you a Vietnam Era Veteran? . . . . ❑ Yes   ❑ No

A person who served on active duty for a period of more than 180 days any part of which occurred between 8/5/64 and 5/7/75, and was discharged or released therefrom with other than a dishonorable discharge or for a service connected disability.

Are you a disabled veteran? . . . . ❑ Yes   ❑ No

A person entitled to disability compensation under laws administered by the Veterans Administration for disability rated at 30% or more, or a person whose discharge or release from active duty was for a disability incurred or aggravated in the line of duty.

Do you have a mental or physical disability? . . . . ❑ Yes   ❑ No

A person who has a mental or physical impairment that substantially limits one or more major life activities, who has a record of such impairment, or who is regarded as having such an impairment.

APPLICANT APPRAISAL FORM

Name of Applicant _____ Position _____

Department/Company _____ Interview Date_____

This rating form will become a part of the applicant's personnel record which may be made available to governmental compliance agencies upon request.

	Outstanding	Above Average	Average	Below Average
DO NOT FILL OUT IN THE PRESENCE OF APPLICANT Review the current job description and your interview notes and rate the candidate in all categories below. Comment in each section.				
ESSENTIAL JOB FUNCTIONS—Comment on ability to perform the essential functions of this job.				
EXPERIENCE—How does previous experience relate to current job opening?				
MENTAL/PHYSICAL CAPABILITIES—Verbal ability, judgment, analytical skills, logic, decisiveness, and so on. Can the applicant perform the physical requirements of the job?				
EDUCATION/SKILLS—Degree(s), professional licenses, registration, certifications, languages, equipment, computer skills, and so on.				
ADDITIONAL COMMENTS:				

Reason applicant was/was not hired (use applicant disposition codes and comments as needed—see other side for codes).

_____

_____

For additional comments use back of form.

Overall Appraisal:

    Outstanding _____ Above Average _____ Average _____ Below Average _____

Recommend employment for current opening: Yes _____ No _____ Applicant Disposition Code _____

Future consideration: Yes _____ No _____ If yes, for _____ position

Recommendation based upon: Application Review _____ Interview _____ References _____

Signature of Interviewer: _____ Date Completed: _____

APPLICANT APPRAISAL FORM

Name of Applicant _____ Date _____

Position _____

Interviewer _____ Division _____

Please comment on the following items	**Rate from 1 to 6**

Knowledge and Experience—How does previous knowledge and experience relate to current open position?

_____   _____
_____
_____
_____
_____
_____

Mental and Physical Capabilities as They Relate to This Job—Verbal ability, judgment, analytical, logical, decisive, resourceful, imaginative, can/cannot meet specific physical requirements of this job. Explain.

_____   _____
_____
_____
_____
_____
_____

Interpersonal Skills—Does applicant communicate with credibility and confidence?

_____   _____
_____
_____
_____
_____

Goals. Maturity, Adaptability, Self Confidence—Does applicant show initiative, persistence, drive, defined goals, a mature outlook, seem adaptable, flexible and confidant in abilities? Explain.

_____   _____
_____
_____
_____
_____
_____

Applicant Appraisal Form
Page 2

| Rate from
| 1 to 6

Supervision and management experience Discuss in depth management training and experience, including managing a diverse workforce.

_____ _____

_____

_____

_____

_____

_____

_____

_____

Knowledge of budgeting, financial analysis, business and human services planning.

_____ _____

_____

_____

_____

_____

_____

_____

_____

Rate applicant on other factors relevant to this job.

_____ _____

_____

_____

_____

_____

_____

_____

_____

Total Points _____

References checked: Yes _____   No _____

Background checked: Yes _____   No _____

CHECKING REFERENCES

Reference checking is one of the least favorite things HR Managers have to do, but it is an important activity. You should have a clear waiver of liability of former and prospective employers for information given in a reference check.

In order to speed the process ask applicants to specifically list periods of unemployment on their application. Request that all names ever used by the applicant be listed on the application. Then in the interview, ask the applicant to give you four job-related references. If there are people who should not be contacted ask them for those names and ask why they should not be contacted.

If you are in an industry where you know your competitors and are on a friendly basis with them, and feel comfortable providing reference information, you are more likely to get good reference information in return.

TWELVE TIPS FOR GIVING REFERENCES

Many companies today forbid managers from giving references. People have sued former employers for defamation of character for bad employment references and some have won settlements. However when you don't give references it's hard to get references when you need them. Two reasons for giving references are that they can be an asset in outplacement activities, and they reward strong performers. Because of this some firms have started giving references but have established hard and fast rules for their managers to follow. Here are 12 tips for giving references:

1. Develop a formal policy on handling reference requests that include who may actually provide a reference, what type of information they can give, and the format in which references will be given, i.e., that the request be in writing on the company's letterhead with the requester's signature.

2. It is important to communicate your policy to all of your managers and employees.

3. Ask separating employees to sign a form permitting your company to give references to prospective employers. Don't provide references on former employees unless you have a signed release and waiver. Tell terminating employees that this is your policy.

4. Never provide "to whom it may concern" reference letters to terminating employees.

5. To maintain consistency, centralize responsibility and authority to provide references to one or two responsible individuals.

6. It's best not to give references by telephone, but if you decide to do that be sure you know who you are talking to and that your conversation is not being recorded. Ask the person for their name, position and phone number and call them back. Ask if the party is alone and that the conversation not be recorded.

7. Provide only truthful, job-related information. Ask if the person has the former employee's permission to call you.

8. Ensure factual information given in a reference is based on documentation.

9. Don't volunteer information that is not requested. Keep the conversation focused and based on facts.

10. Provide the same type of information about former employees at all levels.

11. Document the specifics pertaining to the references you give.

12. If the former employee exhibited dangerous tendencies or was fired for dangerous acts, consult your attorney about requests for references. There are liabilities here when you do and when you don't give a reference on this type of ex-employee.

TELEPHONE REFERENCE CHECK

Applicant's Name _____

Company Contacted _____ Phone No. _____

   1. When did the applicant work for your company? From_____ To_____

   2. What was the applicant's position/title? _____

   3. What information can you give concerning:

       Quality of work?

       _____

       _____

       _____

       Quantity of work?

       _____

       _____

       _____

       Attendance?

       _____

       _____

   4. Did this person get along well with others?   Yes_____   No_____

   5. Why did he/she leave your company?

       _____

       _____

       _____

   6. Is he/she eligible for rehire with your company?   Yes_____   No_____

       If not, why? _____

       _____

       _____

Additional Comments: _____

_____

_____

Information From _____ Title _____

Reference Check Made By _____ Date _____

BACKGROUND CHECKS

Most organizations use background checks as prescreening tools. Even though many companies are finding it difficult to recruit good employees, a majority of organizations across all business sectors believe background checks are a vital prescreening tool. In fact, 76 percent of the 316 responding organizations in a recent poll conducted by *Human Resource Executive* magazine use background checks as a prescreening tool. The reason they do is because of the legal liability a firm has to find out about a prospective employee's background.

You may have read about the lady who was raped by a Domino Pizza delivery man in Oklahoma City. She was awarded $600,000 because Domino's had not done a background check on their employee. This instance brought the subject of background checks to the attention of the whole country. You should not assume that your insurance carrier will insure you for this type of crime. Insurance carriers take the position that it's the legal responsibility of the employer to perform the check.

In addition, an overwhelming majority of organizations conduct background checks on a job applicant's previous employment as well as a check for a criminal conviction record.

The most common type of background checks are on: the employment record, criminal conviction, professional references, education, driving record, credit and financial, social security, residency and salary.

Many organizations do their own background checks, but it is increasingly common to find that companies outsource this function. Two firms that do background checks are Profiles International on the web at www.ProfilesArizona.com and U.S. Search at www.ussearch.com.

EDUCATION VERIFICATION REFERENCE

Employer's Request for Information

The EMPLOYER will fill in the appropriate areas and send this form to the college, together with a stamped, self-addressed return envelope.

Date_____

NAME AND ADDRESS OF SCHOOL	TO BE RETURNED BY THE SCHOOL TO
	EMPLOYER _____
	EMPLOYER REPRESENTATIVE _____
	ADDRESS _____
ATTN: OFFICE OF THE DEAN	_____

REQUEST TO SCHOOL: The individual named below is being considered for employment as_____
(Type of position)

Applicant indicates attendance at above school. Your cooperation in furnishing the following information will expedite consideration of the applicant.

APPLICANT'S NAME AND ADDRESS			ON REGISTER OF THIS SCHOOL			
		Class	MONTH	YEAR	MONTH	YEAR
LAST *(fill in)*	FIRST *(fill in)*	Number (1)	FROM		TO	
APPLICANT INDICATES ATTENDANCE AT THIS COLLEGE			DATE OF BIRTH AS GIVEN BY APPLICANT (FOR SCHOOL RECORD IDENTIFICATION AND VERIFICATION)			
FROM	TO		MONTH	DAY		YEAR
GRADUATION DATE	TYPE OF DIPLOMA		GRADE POINT AVERAGE			
HAS APPLICATION BEEN MADE FOR ADMISSION TO GRADUATE SCHOOL OR OTHER SPECIAL SCHOOL? NO ❏ YES ❏						

This information supplied below will be treated as confidential by the employer.

REMARKS· (AWARDS, HONORS, CLASS OFFICES HELD, ACTIVITIES)

_____

_____

_____

_____

_____

SIGNED _____   TITLE _____   DATE _____

MAKING A JOB OFFER

There are pros and cons on the subject of whether or not you should confirm an employment agreement in writing. Some attorneys prefer their clients not put employment statements in a letter to a prospective employee, fearing a court might later say the letter is an employment contract. The problem with not putting your employment offer in writing, however, is that an employee might later say you offered more at the time you hired the person than you actually did. For example: You offer an applicant a salary of $6,000 per month plus an incentive bonus which is discretionary. Later, when the bonus is awarded, it is $10,000 and the employee feels it is not enough and says that you promised an incentive bonus of $25,000. You state again that the bonus is discretionary, and he says in your initial hiring discussions, you told him the bonus would be at least $25,000. Setting out the specifics of a compensation package eliminates the possibility of a misunderstanding. If you do make a compensation offer in writing, be sure to state clearly more than once that you are an "At-Will" employer, and that the letter should not be construed in any way as an employment contract. Put a line at the bottom of the letter and the words "Accepted and Agreed" and ask the applicant to sign and return the letter for the personnel file.

Be sure to state the salary as a monthly rather than an annual amount. Courts have ruled that because the salary stated in an offer letter was stated as an annual amount the employee who was terminated before the end of the year, should have received the full annual amount of compensation.

SAMPLE EMPLOYMENT CONFIRMATION LETTER

Date _____

Name
Address

Dear _____:

We want to welcome you to the _____ Company as _____(job title)___ of the _____ Division located in _____. This position is an important one to our organization and we look forward to having you join our company and contribute your excellent experience and technical expertise.

Your first day of employment is _____, and your monthly salary will be $_____. In addition, after completing our 90-day evaluation period you will be eligible to participate in the medical, dental and life insurance benefits. Long term disability and family medical coverage under our medical plan is also available at your cost.

We want to start out on a positive note, but it is also important for both of us to understand our employment arrangements. Our company is an "At Will" employer and we think it is important to understand that either of us can terminate our employment arrangement at any time.

We are very pleased to be working with you and look forward to your participation on our management team. Best wishes for success in your new position. If you accept these employment terms, please sign below and return one copy of this letter to me.

Sincerely,

Vice President
Human Resources

Accepted:

_____   _____
Name   Date

LETTER REQUESTING EMPLOYMENT VERIFICATION

Mr. John Smith
Personnel Director
Financial Services Corporation
815 16th Street NW
Washington, D.C. 20006

Ref: Employment Verification
Carol L. Mills

Dear Mr. Smith:

The person identified above is being considered for employment and has signed our employment application form authorizing this inquiry. We would appreciate a statement of your experiences with this person when she was employed by your company. Please provide the information requested on the bottom of this letter and return the letter to us in the enclosed self-addressed stamped envelope at your earliest convenience. Your reply will be held in strict confidence. We sincerely appreciate your cooperation and will reciprocate with employment information on your applicants should the need arise.

Sincerely,

John Watson
Velcare Corporation

CONFIDENTIAL

Applicant Name _____
and Address: _____

Name and Location of _____
Former Company: _____

Dates Employed:_____
General Work Record: _____

APPLICANT REJECTION LETTER

Date _____

Dear _____:

Thank you for your response to our recent advertisement for the position of _____
_____.

We appreciated the opportunity to review your credentials and were pleased that you are interested in employment with the _____ Company.

We have narrowed our search to those few applicants who have the specific qualifications and experience we need for this position. Although your credentials do not specifically meet our current needs, we will retain your resume for six months in the event that an appropriate career opportunity becomes available.

Thanks again for your interest. We wish you the best of luck in your job search.

Sincerely,

Vice President
Human Resources

POST EMPLOYMENT FORM

This questionnaire can be completed after a person is hired. Please complete the following:

EMPLOYEE'S NAME: _____

    Date of Birth: _____

    Social Security Number: _____

    Marital Status: _____ Date of Marriage: _____

    Maiden Name: _____

    Previous Married Name: _____

    Dates of Military Service: _____ to _____

EMERGENCY INFORMATION:

Name of Person to Notify' in Emergency: _____

Telephone: (Home) _____ *(Business)* _____

Any medical condition the agency should be aware of: _____

_____

NAME OF EMPLOYEE'S SPOUSE: _____

    Date of Birth: _____

    Social Security Number: _____

    Maiden Name: _____

    Address if different: _____

    Employed by: _____

    Phone: (Home)_____ (Business) _____

    Occupation: _____

DEPENDENTS CLAIMED/RELATIONSHIP:

_____

_____

_____

_____

Our Affirmative Action Program and Governmental Reporting Requirements require the following information:

Sex: Male   Female

Ethnic Group: _____Caucasian _____Black _____Asian _____Hispanic _____American Indian

Handicapped Status: _____Yes _____No   If yes, what is handicap?_____

Disabled Veteran: _____Yes _____No   If yes, do you receive disability pay? _____Yes _____No

Vietnam Veteran? _____Yes _____No   U.S. Citizen? _____Yes _____No

Manager's Tip

This information can be requested after the person is hired, and is needed for company records and EEO reporting.

U.S. Department of Justice
Immigration and Naturalization Service

OMB No. 1115-0136
Employment Eligibility Verification

Please read instructions carefully before completing this form. The instructions must be available during completion of this form. **ANTI-DISCRIMINATION NOTICE.** It is illegal to discriminate against work eligible individuals. Employers **CANNOT** specify which document(s) they will accept from an employee. The refusal to hire an individual because of a future expiration date may also constitute illegal discrimination.

Section 1. Employee Information and Verification. To be completed and signed by employee at the time employment begins

Print Name: Last	First	Middle Initial	Maiden Name

Address (Street Name and Number)	Apt. #	Date of Birth (month/day/year)

City	State	Zip Code	Social Security #

I am aware that federal law provides for imprisonment and/or fines for false statements or use of false documents in connection with the completion of this form.

I attest, under penalty of perjury, that I am (check one of the following):
☐ A citizen or national of the United States
☐ A Lawful Permanent Resident (Alien # A_____)
☐ An alien authorized to work until ____/____/____
  (Alien # or Admission #_____)

Employee's Signature	Date (month/day/year)

Preparer and/or Translator Certification. (To be completed and signed if Section 1 is prepared by a person other than the employee.) I attest, under penalty of perjury, that I have assisted in the completion of this form and that to the best of my knowledge the information is true and correct.

Preparer's/Translator's Signature	Print Name

Address (Street Name and Number, City, State, Zip Code)	Date (month/day/year)

Section 2. Employer Review and Verification. To be completed and signed by employer. Examine one document from List A OR examine one document from List B and one from List C as listed on the reverse of this form and record the title, number and expiration date, if any, of the document(s)

List A	OR	List B	AND	List C
Document title: _____		_____		_____
Issuing authority: _____		_____		_____
Document #: _____		_____		_____
Expiration Date (if any): ___/___/___		___/___/___		___/___/___
Document #: _____				
Expiration Date (if any): ___/___/___				

CERTIFICATION - I attest, under penalty of perjury, that I have examined the document(s) presented by the above-named employee, that the above-listed document(s) appear to be genuine and to relate to the employee named, that the employee began employment on (month/day/year) ____/____/____ **and that to the best of my knowledge the employee is eligible to work in the United States. (State employment agencies may omit the date the employee began employment).**

Signature of Employer or Authorized Representative	Print Name	Title

Business or Organization Name	Address (Street Name and Number, City, State, Zip Code)	Date (month/day/year)

Section 3. Updating and Reverification. To be completed and signed by employer

A. New Name (if applicable)	B. Date of rehire (month/day/year) (if applicable)

C. If employee's previous grant of work authorization has expired, provide the information below for the document that establishes current employment eligibility.

Document Title: _____ Document #: _____ Expiration Date (if any): ___/___/___

I attest, under penalty of perjury, that to the best of my knowledge, this employee is eligible to work in the United States, and if the employee presented document(s), the document(s) I have examined appear to be genuine and to relate to the individual.

Signature of Employer or Authorized Representative	Date (month/day/year)

Form I-9 (Rev. 11-21-91) N

LISTS OF ACCEPTABLE DOCUMENTS

LIST A		LIST B		LIST C
Documents that Establish Both Identity and Employment Eligibility	**OR**	**Documents that Establish Identity**	**AND**	**Documents that Establish Employment Eligibility**

LIST A — Documents that Establish Both Identity and Employment Eligibility

1. U.S. Passport (unexpired or expired)

2. Certificate of U.S. Citizenship (INS Form N-560 or N-561)

3. Certificate of Naturalization (INS Form N-550 or N-570)

4. Unexpired foreign passport, with I-551 stamp or attached INS Form I-94 indicating unexpired employment authorization

5. Alien Registration Receipt Card with photograph (INS Form I-151 or I-551)

6. Unexpired Temporary Resident Card (INS Form I-688)

7. Unexpired Employment Authorization Card (INS Form I-688A)

8. Unexpired Reentry Permit (INS Form I-327)

9. Unexpired Refugee Travel Document (INS Form I-571)

10. Unexpired Employment Authorization Document issued by the INS which contains a photograph (INS Form I-688B)

LIST B — Documents that Establish Identity

1. Driver's license or ID card issued by a state or outlying possession of the United States provided it contains a photograph or information such as name, date of birth, sex, height, eye color, and address

2. ID card issued by federal, state, or local government agencies or entities provided it contains a photograph or information such as name, date of birth, sex, height, eye color, and address

3. School ID card with a photograph

4. Voter's registration card

5. U.S. Military card or draft record

6. Military dependent's ID card

7. U.S. Coast Guard Merchant Mariner Card

8. Native American tribal document

9. Driver's license issued by a Canadian government authority

For persons under age 18 who are unable to present a document listed above:

10. School record or report card

11. Clinic, doctor, or hospital record

12. Day-care or nursery school record

LIST C — Documents that Establish Employment Eligibility

1. U.S. social security card issued by the Social Security Administration (other than a card stating it is not valid for employment)

2. Certification of Birth Abroad issued by the Department of State (Form FS-545 or Form DS-1350)

3. Original or certified copy of a birth certificate issued by a state, county, municipal authority or outlying possession of the United States bearing an official seal

4. Native American tribal document

5. U.S. Citizen ID Card (INS Form I-197)

6. ID Card for use of Resident Citizen in the United States (INS Form I-179)

7. Unexpired employment authorization document issued by the INS (other than those listed under List A)

Illustrations of many of these documents appear in Part 8 of the Handbook for Employers (M-274)

EMPLOYEE AGREEMENT AND HANDBOOK ACKNOWLEDGMENT FORM

This employee handbook describes the highlights of the company policies, procedures, and benefits. In all instances the official benefit plan tests, trust agreements, and master contracts as appropriate are the governing documents. Your employee handbook is not to be interpreted as a legal document or an employment contract. Employment with the Company is at the sole discretion of the Company and may be terminated with or without notice at any time for any reason. Nothing in this handbook constitutes an express or implied contract or assurance of continued employment or implies that just cause is required for termination.

Understood and agreed:

_____

(Employee's signature)

_____

Date

Manager's Tip

It is important that every employee sign such an employee agreement and that it be retained in the personnel file. This will help protect the Company if there is legal action by the employee charging that he or she did not know the company policies and procedures. A thorough employee orientation and review of the handbook followed by receipt of this signed acknowledgment form could help the company.

Confidentiality Agreement

The nature of services provided by the (organization's name here) requires that information be handled in a private, confidential manner.

Information about our business or our employees or clients will not be released to people or agencies outside the company without our written consent; the only exceptions to this policy will be to follow legal or regulatory guidelines. All memoranda, notes, reports, or other documents will remain part of the company's confidential records.

Personal or identifying information about our employees (such as names, addresses, phone numbers or salaries) will not be released to people not authorized by the nature of their duties to receive such information, without the consent of management and the employee.

I agree to abide by this Confidentiality Agreement.

_____

Name

_____

Witness

_____

Date

Manager's Tip

This form can be used for organizations that have goods or services of a proprietary nature, but it doesn't fit all situations. Adjust accordingly, or have it reviewed by legal counsel.

PERSONAL DATA SHEET

Name _____   Change of Address _____

Address _____   _____

_____   _____

Hire Date _____   Emergency Contact and Phone:

Telephone No. _____   _____

SS Number _____   _____

Marital Status _____   Spouse Name _____

Spouse Work Phone _____

Type of Personnel Change	Date	Pay Increase	Merit/Promotion/Other

Note _____

Place this form in the front of the personnel file and update as each personnel change occurs. This saves you a great deal of time when you need to check the employee's current status and past history. You may prefer to maintain this information in the computer.

NEW EMPLOYEE ORIENTATION

NOTE: All employees must attend an orientation session.

Employee's Name: _____   SSN: _____

Job Title: _____   Dept. _____   Date: _____

HUMAN RESOURCES DEPARTMENT: The information checked below has been given or explained to the employee.

Compensation and Benefits

- Time sheet/card ( )
- Payroll procedures ( )
- Insurance Program Booklet ( )
- Voice Booklet ( )
- Educational Assistance ( )
- Credit Union ( )
- Stock Purchase Plan ( )
- Savings Bond Plan ( )
- Sick Benefits—A&S—Limitations, and so on ( )

Leaves, Promotions, and Transfers

- Performance Evaluations ( )
- Promotions ( )
- Transfers ( )
- Vacations ( )
- Holidays ( )
- Absences—Tardiness ( )
- Jury Duty ( )
- Leaves of Absence—
- Maternity—Medical & Family, and so on ( )

General

- Code of Conduct ( )
- Employee Handbook ( )
- Complaints and Grievance Procedures ( )
- I.D. or Entrance Card ( )
- Introduction to the Department ( )
- Parking Facilities ( )
- Safety Guidelines ( )
- First Aid and Requirements for Reporting Injury ( )
- Bulletin Boards/Company Events ( )
- Voluntary Resignation Notice ( )
- Termination Procedures ( )

SUPERVISOR: The following is a checklist of information necessary to orient the new employee to the job in your department. Please check off each point as you discuss it with the employee and return to the Human Resources Department to be placed in the employee's personnel file.

Welcome the New Employee

- Review copy of employee's application. Be familiar with employee's   ( )
  experience, training, and education.
- Review job description with employee, including the duties, responsibilities, ( )
  and working relationships.
- Discuss with the employee the unit organization and the department division ( )
  organization. Explain the function of your department/division as related to
  the total organization and how the employee fits in.
- Confirm that employee has a copy of employee handbook, and has read and ( )
  understands it.

Introduce Employee to Co-Workers

- Indicate to each co-worker the new employee's position.   ( )
- Explain the functions of each person as you introduce the new employee.   ( )

Show New Employee Around the Facility

- Tour the department, plant, or company.   ( )
- Explain where lavatories, coffee areas, and parking facilities are located. ( )
- Explain the various departments within the organization.   ( )

Introduce the New Employee to Job

- Insure that new employee's working area, equipment, tools and supplies are ( )
  prepared and available.
- Explain the levels of supervision within the department.   ( )
- Provide new employee with necessary or required training.   ( )
- Explain use of: Telephone (personal/company calls)   ( )
                    Copy machines   ( )
                    Company vehicles   ( )
                    Mail procedures   ( )
                    Supply procedures   ( )
                    Personal expense reimbursement   ( )

- Explain hours of work/overtime/call-in procedures.   (   )
- Give new employee department telephone number.   (   )
- Review location of department's first aid equipment.   (   )
- Explain housekeeping responsibilities.   (   )

Future Follow-Up

- Set date and time within one week to cover any questions or concerns   (   )
  of the new Employee.

_____

Supervisor's Signature

Employee's Signature

_____

Supervisor's Title

Date

_____

Department

_____

Date

Note: Return this form to the Human Resources Department.

PERSONNEL STATUS FORM

Name			Effective Date	

Address			Social Security Number	

Department	Salary Grade	☐ Full Time ☐ Exempt
		☐ Part Time ☐ Nonexempt
Job Title	Salary	☐ Temporary ☐ Other _____
		Hours per week _____
		Schedule _____

Employment

☐ New Hire ☐ Reinstatement

☐ Rehire ☐ Other

_____

Termination

☐ Resignation ☐ Layoff

☐ Quit Without Notice ☐ Other

☐ Discharged _____

Status Change	**From**	**To**
☐ Exempt/Nonexempt	_____	_____
☐ Schedule	_____	_____
☐ Department	_____	_____
☐ Salary Grade	_____	_____
☐ Salary	_____	_____
☐ Title	_____	_____
☐ Leave of Absence	_____	_____
☐ Other	_____	_____

Comments _____

_____

_____

_____

Requested by _____ Date _____

Approved by _____ Date _____

Approved by _____ Date _____

SEVEN STEPS TO SUCCESSFUL SELECTION

The recruiting and selection process takes a great deal of time. Most of us spend too much time interviewing applicants who are not qualified. We need to work smart to attract the right people. Consider adding the following seven steps to your selection process:

1. Much time is spent interviewing applicants for jobs when the position's specifications and requirements are not clear. Many times even hiring managers haven't defined the job clearly in their own minds. Job responsibilities are frequently blown out of proportion, resulting in too high an expectation of the job on the part of the person hired. To avoid a lengthy, costly recruiting process and a poor selection decision, it is important to know the precise job specifications, including daily interfaces, ability to commit to the company, interpersonal skills, and levels of sophistication and experience.

2. A brief discussion with the hiring manager could save hours of interviewing time later. It's important to understand what the manager wants in the person to be hired. What are the person's obvious objectives and "hidden agendas"?

3. Identify the best recruiting source for the open position. The interviewing process will be successful only if you are able to attract the most qualified candidates for the job. You frequently have to try several sources until you're successful at attracting the best candidates for a job.

4. Use an assessment approach to reviewing applicants and choosing the top candidates. Assess the following qualities:
   - Technical skills
   - Academic credentials
   - Credentials for the position
   - Experience in the field
   - Past successes
   - "Can do" qualities
   - "Will do" qualities
   - Past promotions
   - Attitudes
   - Interpersonal skills
   - Knowledge of your business

5. Check the applicant's credentials, employment references, academic history, and so on.

6. Conduct a thorough selection interview. Cover such items as education, work experience, the "can do" qualities of the applicant; watch for good listening, speaking, and interpersonal skills. Determine the applicant's technical expertise by asking open-ended questions about job assignments. Encourage open discussion by putting the applicant at ease at the beginning of the interview.

7. After you have put together a complete file of information on your top three candidates, the hiring manager must make a decision based on the data collected. Use a form to evaluate the top candidates initially. A form tends to make you more objective about the data gathered. Ask yourself which candidate best fits the job specifications and the internal environment of the department and the company.

An effective employee selection program should be tailored to the needs of the organization and should be simple to carry out on a day-to-day basis. Eliminate unnecessary and redundant paperwork.

PROS AND CONS OF EMPLOYMENT TESTING INCLUDING DRUG TESTING

Employers can hardly be blamed for wanting to test applicants and employees for drug use and for honesty. According to experts, drug and alcohol abuse account for business losses of over $33 billion annually. Some estimates have gone as high as $60 billion. Another $40 billion is attributed annually to employee theft. On the other hand, applicants, employees, and civil libertarians feel that all testing is frustrating, nerve-wracking, and an invasion of privacy. What direction will the issue of testing take in the next few years?

Testing is now more prevalent than ever in the United States. The use of tests to measure the qualifications of employees and job applicants has been recognized as a valid employment practice under Title VII of the Civil Rights Act. Any professionally developed ability test that is not designed, intended or used to discriminate against persons in one of the protected groups, that is, women, minorities, older workers, and the handicapped, is specifically authorized for use. The professionally developed test must also be professionally validated as a true predictor of job performance.

The Equal Employment Opportunity Commission and the Office of Federal Contract Compliance still look at adverse impact when they review an employer. Adverse impact in testing is considered to be demonstrated where there is a three-point score spread on a hundred-point scale between the average score of whites on an employment test and the average score of minority group persons. The disparity is regarded as statistically significant.

When an organization is concerned about honesty—for example, a bank employee who handles a great deal of money—the bank may use some type of honesty test on the employee. During the past few years the most popular honesty test has been the polygraph. Hundreds of thousands of businesses across the country began using polygraph exams in the 1980s, until more and more evidence surfaced showing the polygraph was not always 100 percent accurate as a predictor of honesty. The Polygraph Protection Act passed by Congress in 1988 prohibits private employers from giving lie-detector tests to current or prospective employees.

Today organizations have turned to a paper and pencil honesty test. John E. Reid & Associates of Chicago pioneered the paper and pencil honesty test. The Stanton Corporation based in Charlotte, N.C. is probably the largest publisher of honesty tests in the U.S. Stanton sells millions of tests each year to hotels, restaurants, retailers, convenience stores, manufacturers, and so on. A sample question on the Stanton tests states: "The amount I stole from my employer was (a) 0, (b) $5, (c) $25, (d) $100, or (3) $500."

There is a space for an explanation. Many job applicants actually circle one of the last four items and provide an explanation. You wouldn't think you could identify a thief by simply asking, but sometimes you can. Over 2 million people have taken the Stanton test. Some states are moving to outlaw the paper- and-pencil honesty test. Massachusetts is one state that has passed a law that refers to them as the paper and pencil polygraph.

Another controversial area is drug testing. Drug testing for new hires is becoming more common. The number of companies testing current employees and applicants has risen from 5 percent in 1982, to over 60 percent today. A positive drug test will almost always result in being rejected for a job or perhaps being fired from a current job. Many companies have turned to employee assistance programs (EAPs) for help in getting current employees off drugs or alcohol. Some legal questions remain unanswered about who can test whom for what, but more employers are administering drug tests, especially for new hires.

The Drug-Free Workplace Act requires federal contractors and federal grantees to maintain drug-free workplaces through anti-drug policies and drug-awareness programs for employees. A number of federal agencies, including the Department of Transportation and the Department of Defense, have issued regulations requiring employers to have drug-free workplace policies that include drug testing of employees under certain circumstances and specific sanctions against violators. Mandatory drug testing policies under these and other provisions have come under legal scrutiny. Employers currently administering a drug and alcohol testing policy or considering the adoption of such a policy should thoroughly review federal and state laws and agency regulations to ensure that they are in compliance and, where deficient, take the necessary corrective steps prior to implementation.

Here are some additional facts:

- False positives are rare, despite widespread reports to the contrary. The American Association for Clinical Chemistry, conducted a test of 47 labs. It showed a 99.2 percent accuracy rate. Most false positives result from mishandling at the lab, although a false positive can result if a person has taken ibuprofen, a common nonprescription drug found in some pain relievers. Pre-test questioning can avoid most false positives.

- Tests are harder to beat than people realize. Diluting a urine sample with water or substituting a drug-free sample isn't as easy as it sounds. Water taps are not available in rooms where tests are taken, and most "clean" samples purchased through the mail require that water be added.

New, more sophisticated tests are being examined. Testing human hair may be a far more reliable way to test for drugs and is already being used by the Navy in California.

Personality tests, once very popular, seemed to take a nose-dive in the late 1970s but they have come back strong in some mid-size and large organizations today. The tests run the gamut from the standard psychological test such as the 46-year-old Minnesota Multiphase Personality Inventory (MMPI) to the Myers Briggs Type Indictor and the personality assessment test sold by Praendix, Inc. of Wellesley Hills, Massachusetts. The MMPI consists of up to 566 statements and requires a true, false or "cannot say" answer to questions such as "I avoid getting together with people," or "I have a great deal of self-confidence." The Praendix test produces a personality assessment that consists of a list of phrases and adjectives including "life of the party," "sympathetic," and "aggressive," and two questions: "Which of these adjectives describes how you think you are expected to act by others?" and "which of these adjectives describes who you *really are*?". In this test, if you select the word *patient*, for example, as an apt description of yourself, it might mean you are good at detail and work best when reporting to others of higher authority. Those who select *impatient* might be good managers, focusing on the big picture. These kinds of tests are frequently challenged in court when hiring decisions are made based on the results of the tests.

The Equal Employment Opportunity Commission has issued Guidelines on Employment Testing Procedures. These guidelines lay down the ground rules for employers to use in the administration and use of employment tests. Prior to this time, there were no rules concerning the use of tests by employers other than the somewhat educationally oriented *Standards for Educational and Psychological Tests and Manuals* published by the American Psychological Association.

The Equal Employment Opportunity Commission Guidelines were largely ignored by most employers until court decisions began to give great deference to the Equal Employment Opportunity Commission Guidelines and upheld them as proper administrative rules. The use of tests continued unabated until court decisions such as *Griggs v. Duke Power Company* and *United States v. Georgia Power Company* startled employers who then began to limit their use of tests.

In the *Agreement Between United States Steel Corporation and the United Steelworkers of America* (September 1, 1965) the parties agreed to conduct a survey of written tests, to examine the relationship of the test to qualifications required for work and to study the administrative procedures used in conjunction with testing programs. In the next labor agreement in the steel industry, the parties agreed that any test used in determining the qualifications of an employee must be a job-related test. This is the first occurrence of the term *job-related* as applied to testing and which later appeared in a court decision. The agreement further required that:

- Tests shall be fair in their makeup and in their administration.
- Tests shall be free of cultural, racial, or ethnic bias.
- Testing procedures shall include procedures for notifying an employee of his/her deficiencies and offering counseling as to how they may be overcome.

The Equal Employment Opportunity Commission has revised its guidelines which were issued in 1966. The 1966 Guidelines had been called "Guidelines on Employment Testing Procedures." The revision of these guidelines was called "Guidelines on Employee Selection Procedures." The Office of Federal Contract Compliance has also issued guidelines on testing.

The key issue in all the regulations and guidelines is that tests used for employment or promotions must be job-related, fair, and uniformly administered.

The following is a testing "Bill of Rights." Employees should have the:

- Right to know the title, nature, and use of a test
- Right to a second chance (retesting)
- Right to minimal age-sex-race-culture bias
- Right to knowledge of score with interpretation
- Right to counseling or feedback on performance and means of improvement

- Right to fair and accurate administration and scoring
- Right to use of a valid test
- Right to examination or evaluation of test by a neutral third party
- Right to know method of scoring
- Right to appeal or challenge the procedure

SAMPLE INTERVIEWING AND SELECTION HANDBOOK

Key Instructions

The following interviewing and selection handbook is provided here to give you step-by-step guidelines for interviewing applicants and selecting new employees. These guidelines include sample questions, questions you may not ask until after the applicant is hired, ways to interview, preparing for the interview, and how to interview difficult applicants. It also provides information on how to select the best employees and specific guidelines for rating applicants.

This interview and selection handbook can be invaluable not only to you but to all of your supervisors and managers who have hiring responsibility. Copy it and furnish it to your outlying offices and field personnel. It can also be the basis for a supervisor's workshop on the topic of interviewing and selection.

OTHER NEW HIRE FORMS YOU'LL NEED AND WHY YOU NEED THEM

Application for Employment—California Addendum

This form is a requirement in the State of California and must be included in the employment application. It is a Credit Report Processing Authorization Form.

Employee Benefits Verification Form

This form protects the employer when employees sign the form saying that they have been provided the opportunity to enroll in company benefits plans, and that if they do not sign the form and enroll within a specific period of time the company will assume they have declined coverage. They then must wait until the next formal benefit enrollment period before they can enroll.

Worker's Compensation Employee Verification Form

Your company should establish a working relationship with a local medical group so that you can send your employees to this one group when there is an illness or accident covered by Worker's Compensation. Then you provide this form to employees to sign stating that they will use this facility for medical attention for work-related injuries and illnesses. If they do not use your facility, you will not be financially responsible for that care. This policy will help you control work-related medical costs.

APPLICATION FOR EMPLOYMENT
CALIFORNIA ADDENDUM

CREDIT REPORT PROCESSING AUTHORIZATION

In processing this employment application, the company may request that a consumer credit report be prepared. In the event that a credit report is ordered, please indicate whether you wish to receive a copy of the credit report at no cost to you by checking the appropriate space No_____ Yes_____, The company agrees that if you are not offered employment and the reason was based either wholly or partly because of information contained in the credit report, you will be advised of this fact and supplied with the name and address of the consumer credit reporting agency.

I have read, understand, and by my signature consent to the above authorization.

Signature: _____ Date: _____

EMPLOYEE BENEFITS VERIFICATION FORM

I have been notified by my employer of my rights for medical, dental and long-term disability benefits subject to the eligibility requirements applicable to each of the insurance plans.

My employer has informed me of my options to enroll in the DPP or PPO medical plans and Pre-Paid or Indemnity Dental Plans.

I understand that I must complete and deliver the benefit plan enrollment forms to the Human Resources Department within 30 days of the effective date of my benefit qualification, or earlier, in order to evidence my selection of coverage under the plans. If I do not deliver the election form within such time, the company will assume that I have declined coverage and I will have to wait until the next open enrollment period to elect coverage under the plans.

_____

Name of Employee (Please Print)

_____   _____

Signature of Employee   Date

_____

Social Security Number

WORKER'S COMPENSATION
EMPLOYEE VERIFICATION FORM

I have been notified by my employer of the procedure to follow in the event I incur a work-related injury or illness. I understand that my employer has designated _____ _____ as the primary provider for all work-related injuries and illnesses. I understand that if I do not receive my medical care for work-related injuries and illnesses from the facility listed above, I may be financially responsible for that care. See attached directions for healthcare locations.

I have been informed that authorization is required from my employer before I access medical care for non-emergency, work-related injuries and illnesses.

_____   _____
Name of Employee (Please Print)   Location

_____   _____
Employee Signature   Date

_____   _____
Human Resources Manager Signature   Date

Interviewing and Selection Handbook

CONTENTS

- Introduction
- Basic Concepts
- Applicants
- Applicant Forms
- Application
- Interviews
- Questioning Techniques
- Unstructured Questions
- Sample Questions
- Inappropriate Questions
- Common Interviewing Errors
- Checklist for Evaluating Interview Data
- Decision and Implementation
- When Not to Accept Applications

INTRODUCTION

This handbook will assist managers with interviewing skills, provide appropriate systematic selection tools, and reduce overlap between personnel and departmental interviews. The information is based on sound personnel selection techniques.

Regardless of its size or type of organization, the key to successful operation of any business depends on the recruiting, selection, and placement of individual employees in timely fashion.

There are no shortcuts to the selection process. Proper systematic selection consists of matching the individual to the job. The best way to achieve effective selection is with a structured interview program in which the interviewer maintains control-ensuring that the applicant's education and experience are reviewed from the broadest standpoint, keeping questions from overlapping, cutting the amount of time spent on the interview, helping to objectively evaluate the applicant, and evaluating the applicant immediately after the interview.

Interviewing and selection don't have to be difficult. Make it simple by organizing yourself. Get the necessary information and tools you need to do the job and then set aside the time you need to do it well.

Turnover is expensive. A business can save a great deal of money by having effective screening, interviewing, and selection processes.

Basic Concepts

This is a how-to manual. The basic principles are stated in the following concepts:

1. The effectiveness of any organization depends largely on its human resources. While many factors are important in developing a good team, selection is critical because the basic capacity of an individual places a ceiling on his or her ultimate performance.

2. Selection is based upon the concept that no applicant is good or bad *per se*, but qualified/qualifiable or unqualified for a given job. In the final analysis, selection is an individual prediction of whether *this* person fits the requirements of *this* job.

3. The evaluation of job applicants assumes that the reasons which cause a person to succeed or fail on the job can be predicted in advance. While the prediction of human behavior is not an exact science, giant strides have been made which can greatly improve your "batting average" in selecting good employees.

4. Proper selection is as much in the interests of the applicant as the employer. A poor choice of jobs can retard an individual's career progress, impairing self-confidence and even placing the person in the position of failing. Appropriate selection, on the other hand, helps an individual grow and develop at a healthy pace in a career which provides personal fulfillment as well as job satisfaction and financial rewards.

5. The selection process is an expensive one. The *direct* costs of recruiting, screening, testing, and interviewing applicants are high enough, to say nothing of the expense involved in training and supervising new employees. But the *indirect* costs of poor selection are much higher. Lost productivity, poor service, high turnover, and low morale all result from poor selection decisions.

6. The best predictor of future behavior is past behavior. Long-standing habits, attitudes, and needs seldom change; they are formed early and remain relatively constant throughout life. Of course, significant changes in human behavior do occur. Just as good athletes tend to repeat their successes year after year, problem employees likewise tend to remain problems year after year. A sound selection system examines past performance through the interview (in addition to review of current skills) to predict future behavior.

7. Efficient and economic selection must be a systematic process, following a logical, step-by-step procedure. Each step in the selection process should be designed to help you make good choices. Initial techniques, such as the review of a resume or application form, are gross screening devices intended to eliminate the obviously unqualified. The more expensive and time-consuming procedures, like the comprehensive interview, are reserved for qualified applicants who warrant a full evaluation.

8. While the system helps you gather data in an orderly fashion, the final interpretation requires judgment. After the job has been analyzed and the person evaluated, someone must match the job as a whole to the individual as a whole. A systematic selection program can help provide as much information as possible and thereby minimize the chances of a poor decision.

9. Many factors are required for success on the job, but the lack of any one characteristic may cause a person to fail. It is relatively easy to identify the limitations of an applicant. What is more difficult—and far more important—is identifying the attributes of success. Successful selection does not occur until the "right" person has been placed in the "right" job.

10. Supportive interviewing is a relatively new factor in the interviewing process. The purpose of a supportive interview is to screen applicants "in" instead of screening them "out." Basically, this means not taking the information received in an interview at face value. Whether it is negative or positive, probing allows you to look at the applicant more objectively.

APPLICANTS

While the basic principles of efficient selection remain the same for all kinds of people, procedures necessarily vary depending upon the professional level of the applicant. There is a distinction between technical, clerical, and professional or managerial applicants. The interviews are handled in a slightly different manner.

To elicit the necessary responses, good questioning techniques must be established. This is accomplished by various methods: (1) the unstructured question and structured question; (2) the use of silence; (3) reflecting feelings; (4) active listening; (5) assertions of understanding and the like. All of the above methods will provide the required information to make an objective selection.

The technical or clerical applicant interview is inclined to deal more with the applicable skills. The questioning technique applies directly to previous education and on-the-job experience—that is, primarily job-related questions.

On the other hand, the clinical/professional/managerial interview takes longer to conduct, and the questioning techniques include verbal communication abilities, management philosophies, as well as job-related questions dealing with education and previous on-the-job experience.

It is important in all interview situations to initially establish a climate of rapport, mutual interest, and respect.

Screening the Applicant

Your human resources person will screen applications to determine whether they meet the minimum requirements for the job. If they do, the applications should be forwarded to the department manager.

Interviewing Applicants

After the decision is made that the applicant is qualified for the position, a thorough interview should be conducted.

Accepting the Applicant

When an applicant is interviewed and hired, references should be checked.

Rejecting the Applicant

Applicants who do not get a job should receive a letter thanking them for applying for the position.

APPLICANT FORMS

A position requisition form should be completed to assist managers in communicating their needs. The requisition form should be retained, it provides information needed to complete annual EEO reports. This form should be completed in full, specifying information on education, skills, and duties to be performed. To accomplish this, refer to the job description which will provide a basic understanding of the job and state the job requirements.

Once the essential and desired requirements have been established, each manager should state needs clearly and simply on the requisition form. If, for example, the individual must be able to function with virtually no supervision, this should be listed; if a college degree or equivalent experience is desired, this should be entered. The job accountabilities should be stated as simply as possible.

List as much information as possible including job duties, starting salary, travel requirements, and necessary skills.

APPLICATION

Preliminary Screening

Initial information on an applicant may be obtained by screening applications and resumes. This information is used to screen out applicants who fail to meet the basic specifications for the job. If, for example, a college degree is required, but one of the applicants did not complete high school, he or she can be screened out on the basis of that information alone, thereby saving time to evaluate more completely those candidates who meet the initial requirements. *Note:* There must be a bona fide, job-related need to insist on a college degree or a high school diploma. In most jobs you must consider applicants who have equivalent job experience.

Resumes

While resumes do provide some data, their value is limited because it is the applicant who decides which facts to include and which to omit. Obviously, the individual is more interested in marketing himself/herself than providing information needed for effective screening. You can't always rely on the information contained in resumes.

Application Form

Your application form should be designed to obtain maximum data without imposing on the applicant, either by asking the individual to complete a unnecessarily lengthy form or by requesting information of a private nature. The form must comply with civil rights and affirmative action program guidelines. By analyzing the data on the application form, the employer can determine whether the applicant meets the minimum requirements for the position, especially in terms of such evident characteristics as experience and skills. The application form also provides the information necessary for conducting reference checks after the interview. Finally, by examining the application form carefully, the employer can be alerted to special areas which require a thorough investigation in the interview. It is necessary that every candidate complete the application form as one of the basic steps in the selection system. The application form is the formal document.

EEO and affirmative action guidelines indicate certain questions are inappropriate to ask applicants. It is appropriate to ask these questions after the person has been hired, however, and a post-hiring form may be completed.

INTERVIEWS

A *comprehensive* interview follows a definite plan, and the interviewer may pursue important points in detail. A sample form has been included in this manual for use as a guide for comprehensive interviews.

Interview Checklist

As interviewers gain experience, they develop their own style. The following items may prove useful in the development stage:

Preparing for the Interview   The interviewer should study the application form and any other information about the applicant *before* beginning the interview. In this way, the interviewer can plan to explore those areas which require special attention and skip over questions already answered.

Setting the Stage   It is essential that the interview be conducted in quiet surroundings with a minimum of distractions. If at all possible, a private office should be used and interruptions avoided.

Establishing Rapport   The interviewer must ease the tension and make the applicant feel welcome and comfortable. Techniques such as offering coffee and getting on a first-name basis are still valid. But a word of caution is in order. Some interviewers go beyond the bounds of rapport and become friendly to the point that their objectivity is biased by personal consideration. While it is all very well to discuss skiing with the applicant, for example, this can be disastrous if it prejudices one's thinking about the individual's job qualifications.

Conducting the Interview   A good interview progresses from nonthreatening, job related questions to more personal and potentially sensitive areas. It begins with a discussion of work history, career interests, and education—all matters which the applicant expects.

Encouraging the Candidate to Talk   In the fact-finding stages of the interview, it is the applicant who has the facts and the interviewer who wants the information. Hence, the candidate should be encouraged to talk and the interviewer to listen (try for at least 75 percent of the time). On occasion, an interviewer may have to use "silence" to stimulate an otherwise reluctant applicant, but most candidates will be happy to talk given the chance. The danger is that the interviewer will seize on the applicant, propounding personal ideas and opinions to this "captive audience," and generally dominate the conversation.

Taking Adequate Time   It takes time to conduct a thorough interview. As much as one to two hours may be needed to review the background of a mature, professional or managerial prospect. An inexperienced clerical applicant, truck driver, or geologist, on the other hand, might be interviewed in twenty minutes. The cardinal rule in all cases is to take whatever time is needed to get all the facts required for making a good decision.

Using the Conversational Approach   While the interview should follow a plan, specific questions should be phrased in a natural, conversational way. Sometimes, there are good reasons for varying the sequence of the interview. The interviewer should remain in control at all times. It is dangerous to let an applicant "run away with the interview and as in the resume, present his or her story as he or she sees fit. Direct questions may be needed to pinpoint the specific reasons underlying such common generalities as "no opportunity for advancement," which is often given as the reason for leaving a previous place of employment.

Avoid Leading Questions   A leading question is one which gives the respondent a cue to what the audience expects to hear. Questions should be asked in such a way that the applicant must provide a narrative answer—not just a "yes" or "no." Ask open-ended or unstructured questions.

Emphasizing the Important   The employment interview should focus on work history in particular (and what the applicant has done in general) in order to predict successfully what the applicant is likely to do in the future. Past behavior is the best predictor of future performance. Most of the interview time should be devoted to experience and education.

Avoiding Moral Judgments   You should suppress personal feelings about the behavior, morals, and standards of an applicant. Nor should you assume that you are a counselor whose role in life is "helping" applicants or criticizing their pattern of life. Instead, it is your purpose to find out what the applicant has done—and then, later, to decide whether the applicant meets the requirements of the position under consideration.

Taking Notes   It may be necessary to take notes of the information collected in the interview. It helps the interviewer to analyze the data after the applicant has gone. It also helps the individual be thorough and systematic in covering all important aspects of the applicant's background. Few candidates will be disturbed by the note taking process. This note taking, however, should be limited, with the interviewer maintaining as much eye contact with the applicant as possible while writing.

Obtaining Precise information   It is human nature for candidates to fill out the application in such a way as to make themselves look "good." Likewise, the applicant will not call attention to periods of unemployment, involuntary terminations and so forth. For this reason, it is important that the interviewer find out what the applicant has done by accounting for all time in his or her life since the individual has left school. Reasons for leaving jobs must be probed carefully. Then, if contradictions between the application form and the interview are obtained, it is necessary to examine the reason for the inconsistency. It is unfortunate, but true, that a significant number of applicants will provide false information—much of which can be uncovered in a careful interview.

Listening with the Third Ear The skillful interviewer listens to what is really being communicated, not just what is being said. It is estimated that a person can think seven times as fast as normal speech; an alert interviewer will use that time to analyze in depth what the interviewee is saying. Good listening is an active, not a passive, process. One can become very perceptive in the interview by listening hard to the undertones of the conversation.

Selling the Job The interview is a two-way street. After the interviewer has the necessary information from the applicant, it is only fair to discuss the job and the organization. It is best to hold this discussion at the end of the employment interview, to avoid the applicant's slanting answers to meet the qualifications of the job. There is another reason as well: if the interviewer is convinced that an applicant is highly desirable, the interviewer should make every effort to interest the individual in joining the organization. If, on the other hand, the interviewer believes the applicant is not qualified or qualifiable for employment, then he or she should not try to "sell" the candidate. Never "oversell" applicants. After they get into the job they might be disappointed and leave.

Concluding the Interview After sufficient information has been exchanged between the interviewer and the applicant, and both are satisfied they have the information needed, the interviewer should then discuss the next step in the selection process. This step may well be a meeting between the applicant and the prospective supervisor to ascertain the personal chemistry between them and to discuss the technical requirements of the job. If the applicant is not to receive further consideration for employment, he or she should be notified graciously and tactfully-so that time may be spent more profitably in seeking work elsewhere.

QUESTIONING TECHNIQUES

To obtain the necessary answers from an applicant, use good questioning techniques. These include the following:

Unstructured Question   Cannot be answered by a "yes" or "no"—will enable the applicant to speak openly. This helps the interviewer to better ascertain and understand the applicant's views. Questions beginning with *who, what, when, where, why,* and *how* will elicit unstructured answers.

Structured Question   Places the applicant in a position to answer either "yes" or "no." The answer need not be elaborated on. For example:

Q.   Did you like your last job?
A.   Yes.

Unstructured Question Combined with Structured Question   A structured question may be followed by an unstructured question to help clarify the applicant's feelings, pinpoint a fact, or obtain additional information. For example:

Q.   Did you like your last job?
A.   Yes.
Q.   What in particular did you like?
A.   Well, . . .

Use of Silence   A brief pause between questions allows the applicant time to elaborate on an answer if he or she desires.

Reflective Feelings   The interviewer paraphrases the applicant's statement as to content and feelings. Phrases beginning with: "it seems that . . ." or "it sounds like . . ." reflect feelings.

Active Listening   The interviewer repeats or restates what the applicant has said, usually in the form of a question. Applicant is then aware of the interviewer's interest. For example:

Q.   What did you think of your previous supervisor?
A.   He was all right, but a bit overbearing.
Q.   Overbearing? Would you explain?
A.   Well, he . . .

Assertions of Understanding   Neutral phrases that will place the applicant in a position so as to elaborate on his or her answer. These phrases include: "I understand," "Uh-huh," "Yes, I see," and the like.

UNSTRUCTURED QUESTIONS

Open-Ended Questions

- Tell me about . . .
- Would you tell me about . . .
- I'd be interested in knowing . . .
- How did you feel about . . .
- Would you explain . . .
- I'm not certain I understand . . .
- Would you explain in more detail?
- What do you mean by that?
- Tell me more about . . .
- Perhaps you could clarify . . .
- What was there about . . . that appealed to you?
- Has there been any opportunity to . . .

SAMPLE QUESTIONS

- One of the things we want to talk about today is your experience. Would you tell me about your present job?
- What do you feel were your major responsibilities in your last job?
- In your last job, what duties did you spend most of your time on?
- What were some of the things about your job that you found difficult to do? Why do you feel this way about them?
- How do you feel about the progress you have made with your present company?
- In what ways do you feel your latest job has developed you to take on even greater responsibilities?
- What are some of the reasons you had for leaving your last job?
- What were some of the things you particularly liked about your last job?
- Most jobs have "pluses" and "minuses." What were some of the "minuses" in your last job?
- Do you consider your progress on the job representative of your ability? Why?
- What do you feel is a satisfactory attendance record?
- In what areas do you feel your supervisor in your past job could have done a better job?
- What are some of the things your boss did that you particularly liked or disliked?
- How do you feel your supervisor rated your job performance?
- What did your supervisor feel you did particularly well? What were major criticisms of your work? How do you feel about these criticisms?
- What kind of people do you like working with? What kind of people do you find most difficult to work with? How have you successfully worked with this type of person?
- What are some of the things in a job that are important to you? Why?
- What are some of the things you would like to avoid in a job? Why?
- How do you feel your last company treated its employees?

QUESTIONS TO ASK CANDIDATES
FOR MANAGEMENT POSITIONS

- Please describe a time when you were working with a problem employee to turn them around. What steps did you take? How did you follow-through? What were the final results?
- Describe a difficult decision you've had to make. How did you communicate that decision and how did you get people to work with you to implement your decision?
- Have you ever found yourself faced with an ethical or value conflict in your job? How did you react? What was the result?
- Describe a time when you made a mistake in judgement that effected your peers or subordinates. What was the decision? What did you do when you realized your mistake? What was the outcome?
- Describe your most effective subordinate. Your least effective subordinate.

INAPPROPRIATE QUESTIONS

Questions That Are Inappropriate to Ask Candidates for Employment

Questions seeking the following information may not be asked of an applicant before he or she is hired:

- Date of birth
- Maiden name
- Previous married name
- Marital status
- Name of spouse
- Spouse's occupation and length of time on the job
- Spouse's place of employment
- Number of children and their ages
- Arrest record
- Convictions may be asked about, but you may not refuse employment before conviction unless it is a bona fide job qualification
- Whether child care has been arranged for the children
- Reasons which would prevent an applicant from maintaining employment
- Ancestry
- National origin/race
- Age
- Sex
- Religion
- Whether or not the person has a disability
- Affiliations with a union
- Garnishment of wages

Keep in mind that much of the above is the type of information necessary for personnel records and employee benefit programs once the individual is employed. However, the point that must be understood is that the information is obtained after employment and, therefore, can have no bearing on the employment decisions.

Questions That Are Inappropriate to Ask Candidates for Promotion

Again, the same type of information listed above is illegal to seek from any candidate being considered for promotion or transfer within the company. Since the employee has a work history with the company, discussions with the current supervisor and review of the personnel records as to work performance and potential are far more valuable in evaluating an employee's qualifications than any of the above information. The interviewer should concentrate on the employee's qualifications, past performance, and potential ability to meet the job needs. It is not appropriate to ask an applicant or an employee being considered for promotion about disabilities.

COMMON INTERVIEWING ERRORS

- Asking leading questions
- Making decisions too early in the interview
- Following a set pattern of investigation, not recognizing individual differences
- Lacking knowledge of precise job requirements
- Letting pressure of duties shorten interview time
- Doing more talking than the candidate
- Failing to direct the interview, thereby wasting time
- Becoming overly enthusiastic about a person during the initial interview
- Not knowing what to look for
- Tending to be overly influenced by individual factors, rather than considering the applicant as a whole
- Lacking skill in asking questions, in motivating the applicant, in probing, and in recording interview data

Other criticisms made of interviews and the mistakes that are frequently made in an interview include:

- Allowing one undesirable factor to influence judgment
- Lack of preparation for the interview
- Under the pressure to fill a job, making a decision before the facts are in, and then setting up the interview so that the candidate is selected
- Tending to become too routine, instead of adapting each interview to the individual
- Being interviewed by the candidate instead of doing the interviewing

CHECKLIST FOR EVALUATING INTERVIEW DATA

Items preceded by a minus sign represent examples of unfavorable findings with respect to a given trait; those preceded by a plus sign represent examples of favorable or positive findings:

Maturity

- − Tends to rationalize failures
- + Has learned to accept limitations
- • Displays chronic dissatisfaction with jobs, working conditions, peers, and superiors
- + Has career goals and is optimistic about them
- + Has mature outlook on life and work in general

Emotional Adjustment

- + Has shown an ability to maintain composure in face of adversity or frustration
- + Has been able to maintain emotional balance in face of trying personal circumstances
- − Has had problems with bosses or teachers on more than one occasion
- − Is unable to deal with others' shortcomings
- − Evidence that person allows emotions to rule business decisions

Team Player

- + Seems to have operated successfully as a member of a team
- − Is strongly motivated to be the "star"
- + Seems to place the accomplishments of the group ahead of personal ego
- + Has a degree of empathy and social sensitivity
- − Displays poor interpersonal skills and shows tendency toward intolerance

Tact

- + The manner in which person phrased remarks during interview reflects tact and consideration
- − In discussing relationships with subordinates, the person seems to reflect a lack of consideration and sensitivity
- + The person is a good listener

Adaptability

- + Has shown an ability to handle a number of job assignments simultaneously
- − Applicant's approach reflects a tendency to be structured . . . maybe a perfectionist

+ Seems to like jobs involving contact with many types of people and diverse job situations

Tough-Mindedness

+ Seems willing to take a stand for what is right
− Might not be sufficiently demanding of subordinates when the situation calls for it
− Seems overly concerned with the feeling of others
− Ability to delegate might be questionable based on what seems to be an unreasonable attention to detail
+ Has a positive assertive nature

Initiative

+ Has demonstrated ability to operate successfully without close supervision
+ Seems to have reached out for increasing responsibility
+ Evidence indicates the person is a self-starter
− Seems to dislike unstructured situations

Follow-Through

− Changes jobs too often
+ Once the person starts a job, seems to hang in there
− Seems to start more things than can be completed
+ Has achieved one or more career goals

Self-Confidence

+ Reflects a realistic appraisal of abilities
+ General manner and style reflect poise
− Does not have sufficient confidence to discuss shortcomings
− Appears over-confident and boastful
− Lacks a sense of self-confidence in the interview process

Personality

+ Personality has considerable impact
− Tends to be introverted
+ Has an outgoing, personable style
− Is ego-oriented
+ Displays empathy and sensitivity

Honesty and Sincerity

+ Is willing to give credit when credit is due.

− Tends to exaggerate own accomplishments

− Stories seem to be inconsistent in terms of other statements or findings

− Bragged about "pulling a fast one"

+ Willing to discuss unfavorable aspects of work experience in interview

These items are just a few elements that can be used effectively to assist in evaluating an applicant. Not all of them pertain to every applicant, but they will trigger ideas that will get you thinking about specific qualities you need for a particular job. You will come up with other questions and be able to make evaluations as you become more proficient at the interviewing process.

Remember: Half of interviewing is *listening.* When you listen to an applicant, you glean far more information than when you are talking to an applicant

It is helpful to write a summary of assets and shortcomings immediately after the interview has taken place. Concern yourself with the most important findings in terms of the applicant's overall qualifications. Summarize your findings.

Interviewing is an art. As you progress and get better at it, you can relax and enjoy the interaction and the personal give and take that makes the effort worthwhile. It is worthwhile when you find yourself hiring the best people for your jobs, and when your "batting average" improves over time.

Decision and Implementation

The final decision must match the "whole person with the "whole job." This requires a thorough analysis of both the person and the job; only then can an intelligent decision be made as to how well they will "fit" together. To evaluate the person, it is necessary to analyze all the data collected on the individual: resume, application form, reference checks, interview materials. To understand the job, it is necessary not only to review the formal job description, but also to identify some feeling for the supervisor and work group to which the prospective employee will be assigned.

Then you must weigh all the facts intelligently and come to a sound conclusion. *This element of judgment is of critical importance.* Up to this point the selection system will have helped gather data together in a systematic fashion—but how this data is evaluated depends upon the judgment of the evaluator. A summary form has been provided to help you make a decision on the critical strengths and limitations of the applicant. The ultimate decision—whether to hire the person—depends not only upon the individual and the organization, but also upon the labor market and other factors. Other factors include such items as government regulations, your affirmative action program, and company needs, and should be taken into account when making employment decisions.

Final decisions are generally made with two factors in mind: the applicant's qualifications for a given job opening and potential for future promotion. These two should be kept separate. The best decisions are generally those which match an applicant to a specific position. Looking into the future and trying to determine what a person's potential may be five or ten years from now is difficult. Nevertheless, this may have an important bearing on the employment decision and must be taken into account.

"Can Do" vs. "Will Do" Characteristics

Can do qualities denote a person's intelligence, education, training, experience, skills, aptitudes, and so forth. But, it is the *will do* characteristics—drive, determination, stability, and maturity—that determine whether the person will put these basic abilities to good use.

The unskilled evaluator will often pay more attention to *can do* factors than *will do* qualities—the former are easier to evaluate. But it is equally true that more failures may be attributed to a lack of the necessary *will do* characteristics.

In essence, *an employer is interested in hiring an achiever,* a person who performs on the job and gets the work done, or gets work done through others. What the person will do in the future is best determined by what has been done in the past. Hence, the emphasis in this manual has been placed on work history in particular and achievement in general.

This emphasis on *will do* characteristics is based upon several well-established principles:

- Actual behavior is largely determined by a person's habits or character traits, such as initiative and perseverance.

- These traits develop early in life and seldom change.

- These habits can be determined from a detailed analysis of past behavior.
- Future behavior can be accurately predicted by looking at past behavior.

The interview and reference checks provide the basic data on *will do* characteristics. The interview largely measures the *can do* qualities. Taken together, they provide a good picture of the whole person.

WHEN NOT TO ACCEPT APPLICATIONS

If you do not have an open position, don't keep accepting applications. You are required to retain applications for five years and to call those people *before* you interview current applicants. Also, by taking applications when you do not have a job open, you are *building* your applicant statistics. You could open yourself to a charge of "adverse impact," that is, not hiring a significant number of women and minorities based on their representations in your applicant base.

You don't have to accept applications if you don't have a job opening. Applicants constantly walking in your office can disrupt your business. Have a sign made to put in your reception area that says:

"We are not accepting applications today, but thanks for coming in."

When you do have openings and are accepting applications, you can save a great deal of your manager's time by establishing interview hours. Have a sign made such as:

"We are accepting applications from 9:00 to 11 :00 and 2:00 to 4:00."

AN INTERNAL JOB-POSTING SYSTEM

Before you go outside the company to recruit new employees it's a good idea to consider people you already have on the payroll. A frequent complaint of employees is that their company goes outside to fill open positions rather than give promotional opportunities to current employees who might be qualified for the job.

A few years ago, it was unthinkable to post open positions in a nonunion salaried environment. But over the past few years, with Equal Employment Opportunity, the need for companies to maximize their human resources and increasing concern for individual career progression, job posting has become common.

How One Company's Job-Posting System Works

ELIGIBILITY

- All regular employees who have completed their evaluation period and are not under a performance improvement or disciplinary warning plan are eligible to use the open position listing policy in order to request consideration for a position that would constitute a growth opportunity.
- Employees who have been promoted or transferred, or who have changed jobs for any reason, must wait six months before applying for a different position.

POLICY

- A list of open positions will be communicated to all employees in all facilities. Notices will include information on job title, salary grade, department, supervisor's name and title, location, brief description of the job content, qualifications, and instructions concerning whether candidates will be expected to demonstrate their skills during the interview process.
- Basic job qualifications and experience needed to fill the job will be listed on the sheet. Employees should consult with the human resource department if there are questions concerning the promotional opportunities associated with the job.
- Open position lists will remain on bulletin boards for five working days.
- Forms for use in requesting consideration for an open position may be obtained from the human resource department.
- The human resource department will review requests to substantiate the employee's qualifications for the position.
- The hiring manager will review requests for employees inside the company before going outside the company to fill the position.
- It is the responsibility of the employees to notify their managers of their intent to interview for an open position.
- The hiring manager makes the final decision when filling the position; however, the guidelines for filling any open position are based on the employees' ability, qualifications, experience, background, and the skills they possess that will allow them to carry out the job successfully. It is the responsibility of the hiring manager to notify the previous manager of the intent to hire the employee.

- Employees who are aware of a pending opening, and who will be on vacation when the opening occurs, may leave a request with the human resource department for consideration.

- It is the manager's responsibility to ensure that the human resource department has notified all internal applicants that they did or did not get the job before general announcement by the manager of the person who did get the job.

- "Blanket" applications will not be accepted. Employees should apply each time a position they are interested in becomes available.

- Since preselection often occurs, employees should be planning for their career growth by scheduling time with potential managers before posting, to become acquainted with them, and to secure developmental information to be used in acquiring appropriate skills for future consideration.

- There are occasions when jobs will not be listed. Two such examples might be (1) when a job can be filled best by natural progression or is a logical career path for an employee, and (2) when a job is created to provide a development opportunity for a current high-performance employee.

- In keeping with this policy, managers are encouraged to work with employees in career development in order to assist them in pursuing upward movement in a particular career path or job ladder.

What the Human Resource Department Does

- Reviews applications for open positions, and checks to see if applicants meet minimum time-on-the-job requirements.
- Reviews background material of applicants with hiring manager. Hiring manager selects the employees qualified for interviews.
- Notifies all applicants who will not be interviewed, and gives them the reasons why.
- Provides counseling to applicants who will not be interviewed.
- Answers questions from interviewed candidates concerning selection, if the interviewing extends beyond the normal three-week period.

What the Manager Does

- Selects employees to be interviewed for the position.
- Screens interviewed applicants (may contact previous manager for reference).
- Decides who is the best-qualified candidate.
- Informs the human resource department of the selection and provides reasons for rejecting unsuccessful applicants.
- Notifies the successful applicant and his or her current manager. Arranges release dates with the current manager (normally two weeks).
- Completes application forms in full, at the bottom of the form, and answers all appropriate question blocks as necessary.

- Notifies the unsuccessful candidates, advising them of reasons for rejection.
- Makes sure that the interview process does not extend more than three weeks beyond the date the notice comes off the bulletin board.

Some Pros and Cons of Posting Open Positions

PROS

- Fewer employees look for new jobs or transfers because they find suitable jobs through the posting system.
- The program makes upward mobility easier.
- It creates better morale by making employees aware of open positions.
- Employees have more control over career progression.
- It assists with affirmative action programs.
- It affords better use of the human resources.

CONS

- The program lengthens the process of filling jobs.
- It creates a chain reaction, and more jobs have to be filled. Employees who don't get jobs require counseling and may become disgruntled.

RECRUITING PERSONS WITH DISABILITIES—AN IMPORTANT AND UNDERUTILIZED RESOURCE

The Americans with Disabilities Act (ADA) was signed into law by President Bush on July 26, 1990. Unlike most other federal legislation prohibiting discrimination against persons with disabilities, it broadly covers private industry and does not require that entities covered receive federal funding or be a government contractor. The definition of disability means with respect to an individual:

1. A physical or mental impairment that substantially limits one or more major life activities of such individual,
2. a record of such impairment; or
3. being regarded as having such impairment.

   Who needs to comply:

- All employers with 25 or more employees must comply effective July 26, 1992.
- All employers with 15–24 employees must comply effective July 26, 1994.

JOB BID FORM

Name _____ Date _____

Current Department _____

Current Supervisor_____

Job Applying for _____ Dept._____

Your qualifications for the job: _____

_____

_____

_____

_____

_____

_____

Other qualifications such as degrees, licenses: _____

_____

_____

_____

_____

_____

_____

_____

_____

_____
Employee Signature

- -

TO BE COMPLETED BY THE HUMAN RESOURCES DEPARTMENT

Date employee was interviewed _____

Did this employee get the job? _____yes _____no

Why didn't employee get the job? _____

_____

_____

Has employee's supervisor been notified? _____

Has employee been notified? _____

_____
Human Resource Representative

Employment criteria:

- Employers may not discriminate against an individual with a disability in hiring or promotion if the person is otherwise qualified for the job.
- Employers can ask about one's ability to perform a job, but cannot inquire if someone has a disability or subject a person to tests that tend to screen out people with disabilities.
- Employers will need to provide "reasonable accommodation" to individuals with disabilities. This includes steps such as job restructuring and modification of equipment.
- Employers do not need to provide accommodations that impose an "undue hardship" on business operations.

In addition to complying with the Americans with Disabilities Act, any employer with a federal contract must include an affirmative action clause in all contracts or subcontracts. The clause must include the following:

- The contractor agrees not to discriminate against any handicapped person who is qualified to perform the job and also agrees to take affirmative action to hire, advance, and treat handicapped people without discrimination.
- The contractor agrees to abide by all Department of Labor rules and regulations.
- In the event of noncompliance, the contractor will be declared in default.
- The contractor agrees to post notices of affirmative action in conspicuous places around the plant.
- The contractor agrees to notify all union or worker representatives that they are covered by the affirmative action law.
- The contractor includes the affirmative action clause in all subcontracts or purchase orders of more than $2,500.

Each contractor holding a contract or subcontract of $50,000 or more and having at least fifty employees is required to develop and maintain an affirmative action program that sets forth policies and practices regarding handicapped employees. A sample program is provided in this kit.

This program may be kept separate from other affirmative action programs, or it may be integrated into the other programs; if this is done, it must be identifiable and retrievable.

The program must be reviewed and updated each year. Explanations of major changes must be readily available to employees and to applicants for jobs. There have been proposals to increase the dollar amounts and the number of employees covered.

Handicapped job applicants and employees who want to be covered by affirmative action may be asked to identify themselves. They are told that:

- The information is to be given voluntarily and will be kept confidential.
- Refusal to give it will not subject the person to any kind of adverse treatment.

We've talked about the letter of the law, but how do you go about creating an environment where persons with disabilities are welcomed into the organization? Here are some ideas and some actions to be taken:

- Build acceptance of persons with disabilities by managers, supervisors, and all employees through internal communications.
- Use personnel audits to ensure that affirmative action programs are followed.
- Use all recruiting sources, such as state employment services, vocational rehabilitation, sheltered workshops, college placement officers, state education agencies, labor organizations, and organizations of and for handicapped people.
- Recruit candidates at schools for handicapped students—blind, deaf, mentally handicapped, physically handicapped.
- Get advice on placement, recruitment, training, and accommodations from vocational rehabilitation, voluntary health organizations, handicapped groups, and others.
- Review employment records of persons with disabilities to find out whether their full abilities are being used.
- Try to attract qualified persons with disabilities from outside the labor force, through organizations to which they belong.

SPREADING THE WORD To gain full support of affirmative action within the company, it should be publicized in the policy manual; in company publications; by special meetings for executives, managers, and supervisors; in employee orientation programs; in meetings with unions; in nondiscrimination clauses in union contracts; and on company bulletin boards.

EXECUTIVE RESPONSIBILITY An executive of the company should be appointed director of affirmative action activities and should have top-management support. The director's duties should include developing policy statements, affirmative action programs, and communications activities; identifying problem areas and developing solutions; arranging for audit and reporting systems; serving as liaison between the contractor and enforcement agencies and organizations of and for handicapped people; keeping management informed of developments in affirmative action; and arranging for career counseling of handicapped employees.

CARRYING OUT THE PROGRAM To make certain that the greatest possible number of people benefit from affirmative action, the contractor should do things such as:

1. Look over the employee selection process to be sure handicapped people aren't being considered only for certain stereotyped kinds of jobs.
2. Hold briefing sessions for recruiting sources, letting them know about company policies, future job openings, and the like.
3. Carefully select personnel people to ensure that they will implement affirmative action.

4. Include handicapped people in the personnel department.

5. Take part in career days, work-study programs, and other efforts that reach out into the community, as well as other activities that include handicapped people.

HOW TO SAVE MONEY BY USING TEMPORARY HELP

One of the fastest growing industries in the country today is the temporary help industry. Industry figures show that more than 90 percent of American businesses and practically all of the Fortune 500 companies currently use temporary help on a regular basis. An estimated 5 percent of the entire work force works on a temporary basis, and that number is expected to triple.

Temporary help fills two key needs:

- The need of most organizations for a readily available work force for short periods.
- The need of many experienced skilled people to work, but not on a permanent, full-time basis.

Organizations all over the country have been merging, downsizing and eliminating entire levels of management. Where they once were quick to hire full-time personnel, they now are more likely to fill jobs on a temporary basis. By keeping permanent staff lean and supplementing with temporary help, companies are eliminating significant payroll costs.

Eight Creative Uses for Temporary Help That Can Lower Payroll Costs

1. Placing employees on the payroll of a temporary help service during their evaluation period can minimize a company's unemployment compensation rates.

2. Temporary help teams are a new service offered by some agencies. Teams of word processors, data processors, sales people, and so on, can staff a whole department until permanent staffing is arranged.

3. Retirements cause an organization to lose valuable employees at a time when a particular project is crucial to the business plan. A temporary help service can assist by transferring the person to their payroll, thus easing the pressures on both the company and the employee.

4. Before a company recruits a regular, full-time employee for a new position, a temporary worker can be used to determine if a valid position really exists.

5. Use temporary help for one-time demands involving special projects such as product sampling, assembling an annual report, taking or doing the extensions on inventory, and a data processing conversion program. A temp can go in for a short term and complete the project.

6. Smoother transitions can be delivered when temporary workers are used during office or plant relocation as job vacancies occur.

7. Temporaries can fill crucial spots until a hiring freeze is lifted.

8. Sometimes exactly the right applicant comes along, but it takes a week or more to process the paperwork for authorization to hire the person. During this delay, the prospect may consider another attractive offer. If a manager can place the applicant on the job, but on a temporary service firm's payroll immediately, the problem of losing the applicant may be averted.

If you are in the process of choosing a temporary help service, here are six questions you should ask in order to make a good decision:

1. How long has the temporary help service been in business? (It takes a fair amount of time to develop a backlog of well-trained, experienced personnel.)

2. What recruiting methods and screening procedures are used in hiring temporary employees?

3. What kinds of training programs are there for temporaries, particularly in the more specialized areas such as word processing? (Dig for detailed information.)

4. What sort of insurance or bonding coverage is carried for the protection of the company in case of loss?

5. What are the billing rates for various job classifications?

6. What is the policy on transferring a temporary employee to the client company's payroll?

Some advance planning before the temporary arrives will save time and get the work flowing as quickly as possible. Here's a checklist of seven items to help you get organized before the temporary arrives:

1. A list of the basic duties and responsibilities of the position, including a list of work priorities.

2. A summary of company procedures, work hours, lunch periods, parking areas, and so on.

3. A calendar of important events that will affect the temporary person.

4. A current list or file of frequently used names, titles, telephone numbers, and addresses.

5. Directions on how mail is to be handled and how additional supplies may be secured.

6. An index to office files, indicating any that are to be locked at the close of the day.

7. A set of samples of regularly prepared reports and forms that will be used.

ILLEGAL EMPLOYMENT PRACTICES

Under current legislation it is unlawful to:

1. Refuse to consider for employment, or otherwise discriminate against any person because of race, color, national origin, sex, religion, physical disability, or age.

2. Show a bias in help-wanted advertising for or against applicants based on race, color, national origin, sex, religion, or age unless you can prove your requirements are bona fide occupational qualifications.

3. Use any screening techniques for employment or promotion, such as paper and pencil tests or questionnaires that cannot be proved to be directly job related.

4. Categorize job candidates on the basis of race, color, national origin, sex, religion, or age.

5. Condone or permit sexual harassment of employees.

6. Segregate employees by race, religion, or national origin with respect to working areas, toilets, lockers, and recreational facilities.

7. Cause or attempt to cause an employer to discriminate against any person because of race, age, religion, national origin, sex, or veteran status through actions initiated by a union.

8. Refuse to hire a woman because separate facilities would have to be provided. Nor can an employer refuse to hire a woman because he/she would have to pay her special benefits such as premium overtime or rest periods required by state law. (Note: An employer would have to give men the same benefits as women.)

9. Perpetuate past discriminatory practices that have led to statistical imbalances in the workforce.

10. Discharge, lay off, or otherwise terminate an employee on the basis of race, religion, sex, national origin, or age.

Manager's Tip

These practices reflect the thrust of current legislation and the dangers inherent in careless personnel practices and techniques. Most of you are aware of these issues, but you may want to provide your staff with this extra emphasis on employment practices.

NEW EMPLOYEE ORIENTATION

It is important to get the new employee up to speed quickly. It saves you money in lost work time and helps maintain the quality of your work product.

Design a new employee orientation that covers all the company policies and procedures, the employee's compensation and benefits package, the departmental procedures, and any other items of general interest. Be sure the employee is introduced to everyone in the department. Also, the employee should know everyone in the company with whom he or she will be working or interacting in any way.

Use the New Employee Orientation Form furnished in this chapter and revise it to fit your specific needs.

Handling Relocation

Relocation can be expensive. Most mid-size and small companies try not to hire someone they have to relocate. If you do decide to relocate an applicant, however, use a relocation form like the one that follows and ensure costs are approved in advance.

APPROVAL OF ESTIMATED RELOCATION EXPENSES AND ALLOWANCES

Name _____   Social Security Number _____

Account to be Charged _____   Position Title _____

Old Location _____   New Location _____

Effective Date of Hire _____   Present Residence: Own_____   Rent ____

Married_____   Single_____   Head of Household_____   Number of Dependents _____

	Estimated Cost	*Actual Cost*
Cost of moving household goods	_____	_____
Employee travel and lodging to new location	_____	_____
Family travel and lodging to new location	_____	_____
Househunting travel and lodging for employee and/or spouse	_____	_____
Federal income tax allowance	_____	_____
Any other special items to be allowed	_____	_____

Employee's signature _____   Date _____

APPROVALS:

Department Manager _____   Date _____

Vice President _____   Date _____

Chief Financial Officer _____   Date _____

President _____   Date _____

Board (if required) _____   Date _____

2

PERSONNEL RECORDKEEPING

- New Hire Reporting Mandatory

- Employee Information and Recordkeeping Requirements

- Information to Include in the Personnel File

- Payroll Procedures and Relevant Statutes

- Pay Terminology and Definitions

- Record Retention Requirements

- Maintaining Control of Staffing Levels

- Monthly Payroll Trend

- How to Figure Recruiting and Selection Costs

- Frequently Used Personnel Calculations, Formulas, and Tables

- Sample HR Calculations and Reports

- Auditing the HR Function

Personnel Recordkeeping

Recordkeeping is important, and employee personnel records should be maintained in the personnel department. Managers and supervisors should not maintain separate files in their desks. Let employees see their personnel files by contacting the personnel department and viewing the file in the department with the personnel manager present.

When changes occur in any of the following categories, the personnel manager should be notified so the changes can be reflected promptly in the employee's pay and benefits:

- Name
- Address
- Telephone number
- Marital status
- Number of dependents
- Beneficiaries

Following is a clause regarding personnel files that you should consider putting in your personnel policy:

> The company: (1) collects, uses, and retains only that personnel information which is required for business or legal reasons; (2) provides each employee with a chance to make sure that what is in his/her personnel record is correct; (3) restricts the internal availability of personnel information to those with a valid business need to know; (4) releases personnel information outside only with employee approval, except to verify employment or to satisfy legitimate investigatory or legal needs. All records concerning your employment with the company are company property and will be maintained by the company. You may review those records or files which are maintained on you, including your personnel file, at any time. Requests to review your records should be made to the personnel manager.

Much of personnel recordkeeping is done because it is required by federal or state regulations. We keep records of people who are hired, promoted, and terminated for EEO purposes. OSHA files are required, and we have to fill out OSHA Form 200 when an employee is hurt on the job. Most of the personnel records are retained in the employee's personnel file. These files should be maintained in a special room in locked file cabinets. There is a privacy issue surrounding employee files, and only the personnel manager and the immediate supervisor should have access to the files. There are times when another supervisor or executive may have a "need-to-know" reason for seeing an employee file, but generally the files should be treated in a confidential manner with restricted access.

Responding to Telephone Requests for Information on an Employee

Information on employees including addresses, telephone numbers, salaries, and so on should not be given out over the telephone. If a bank needs to verify salary for a home loan, for example, the form should come to the personnel department in writing and there should be a statement on the form signed by the employee giving the employer permission to provide that information.

NEW HIRE REPORTING MANDATORY

The Personal Responsibility and Work Opportunity Reconciliation Act of 1996 (welfare reform bill) required in part that all states have a mandatory new hire reporting program in place by October 1, 1997. States which already had such a program had until October 1, 1988 to meet minimum federal requirements. The report must include, at minimum, the employee's name, address and Social Security number, and the employer's name, address and federal employer identification number. The states may add additional fields, such as date of hire or birth. Employers may report by W-4 an equivalent form, by paper, magnetic media, or electronic transmission. Employers must also make the information available to employment security agencies for use in reducing unemployment compensation fraud.

EMPLOYEE INFORMATION AND RECORDKEEPING REQUIREMENTS

The following chart provides general recordkeeping requirements in seven major personnel functional areas.

INFORMATION TO INCLUDE IN THE PERSONNEL FILE

- Application
- Resume
- Post-employment form
- Letter of confirmation
- Personnel data sheet
- Employee handbook acknowledgment form
- Performance appraisals
- Computer printouts showing all activity on the employee
- Forms on leave of absence
- Any correspondence regarding pay, leaves, and performance
- Separation notice and termination information

Manager's Tip

There should be no medical information retained in the personnel file. A separate benefits file should be created for privacy reasons. The benefits file should be available only to the immediate supervisor or an executive with a valid need to know the information.

EMPLOYEE INFORMATION AND RECORDKEEPING REQUIREMENTS

Recruiting	Employment	Changes in Employment	Compensation & Benefits	Health & Safety	Discipline	Termination
1. Advertising Records application	1. Completed form completed	1. Personnel action operation showing changes	1. Established hours of reports	1. Accident & injury	1. What is your policy? documentation	1. Need to file all
2. Records of Jobs listed with an outside recruiting firm	2. Reference check form	2. Update computer records	2. How flextime works (if applicable)	2. OSHA Form 200s	2. What forms must be used, procedures followed?	2. Review copies of warning notices
3. EEO records (where you recruit minorities)	3. Immigration I-9 form properly completed	3. Benefits or compensation changes	3. Wages to be paid— how time cards are handled	3. Worker's compensation forms	3. Are there progressive steps in carrying out discipline?	3. Completed supervisor's checklist for termination
4. Applicant log	4. Bond forms (if required)	4. If a job was opened internally file job bid forms	4. Exempt or non-exempt is overtime paid?		4. Does the employee have the opportunity to respond to disciplinary notices?	4. Has employee returned all company property?
5. Applicant files (by job category then date)	5. W-4 form	5. Payroll notifications	5. Provide information on pay periods		5. Records retained where and for how long? These records should be maintained in a separate file.	5. If it is a voluntary termination? Be sure employee signs voluntary separation form.
6. Record of internal job bids received for any open position	6. Set up personnel file		6. Review payroll deductions		6. Has supervisor treated employee fairly?	6. Will employee be eligible to collect unemployment compensation?
	7. Enter on computer via personnel status form		7. How are garnishments handled?			
			8. When and how do pay raises occur?			
			9. Maintain benefits records in a separate file			

PAYROLL PROCEDURES AND RELEVANT STATUTES

Salaries represent a major element in the cost structure of most businesses. The largest single expense incurred by some service businesses may be the compensation paid to employees. Many different regulations relate to your company's payroll expense.

Payroll accounting procedures are influenced significantly by state and federal statutes. These laws levy taxes based on payroll amounts, establish remittance and reporting requirements for employers, and establish minimum standards for wages paid and hours worked.

Federal Insurance Contributions Act

In the mid-1930s, the federal government enacted a national Social Security program to provide a continuing source of income during retirement. The program has been expanded several times since then, one example being the enactment of the Medicare program providing hospital and medical insurance for persons 65 years of age and older. Today, in addition to health insurance benefits for eligible people, Social Security provides monthly payments to workers and their dependents when a worker retires, is disabled, or dies.

Monthly benefit payments and hospital insurance protection under Medicare are financed by taxes on employees, their employers, and self-employed people. Approximately nine out of ten employed persons in the United States currently have Social Security protection through this process. Medical insurance under Medicare is financed by premiums paid by persons who enroll for this protection and from the general revenue of the federal government. The Federal Insurance Contributions Act (FICA) establishes taxes levied on both employee and employer. The schedule of tax rates and the amount of earnings subject to the tax are amended from time to time.

FICA tax applies to wages paid to employees during a calendar year, up to a certain amount per employee. The amount of earnings subject to the FICA tax is adjusted yearly for changes in the Consumer Price Index. Near the end of each year, the Social Security Administration announces the earnings base for the following year. The employee's tax is deducted from each paycheck by the employer. The employer and the employee are taxed at the same rate.

Federal Unemployment Tax Act

The Federal Unemployment Tax Act (FUTA) is also part of the federal Social Security program. The states and the national Social Security Administration work together in a joint unemployment insurance program. FUTA raises funds to help finance administration of the unemployment compensation programs operated by the states. Generally, funds collected under this act are not paid out as unemployment compensation benefits, but are used to pay administrative costs at the federal and state levels. In times of high unemployment, however, the federal government may appropriate funds from its general revenue to provide extended unemployment benefits.

FUTA generates funds through a payroll tax levied on employers. however, employers are entitled to a credit against this tax for unemployment taxes paid to the state.

The amount due on federal unemployment insurance taxes must be reviewed quarterly. If undeposited taxes exceed $100 at the end of any of the first three quarters of a year, a deposit must be made in a Federal Reserve bank or authorized commercial bank during the first month of each quarter. If the amount due is $100 or less, no deposit is necessary. By January 31, each employer must file Form 940, Employer's Annual Federal Unemployment Tax Return, for the preceding year. If the annual tax reported on Form 940, less deposits made, exceeds $100, the entire amount due must be deposited by January 31. If this amount is $100 or less, it may either be deposited or remitted with Form 940.

State Unemployment Compensation Taxes

Benefit payments to compensate individuals for wages lost during unemployment are handled through unemployment compensation programs administered by each state. Generally, a worker who becomes unemployed through no fault of his or her own, who is able to work, and who is available for work is eligible for unemployment benefits. The duration and amount of benefits typically depend on the worker's length of employment and average wage during a previous base period.

The funds for unemployment benefits are generated in most states by a payroll tax levied on employers. In a few states, the employee must also contribute. Because of the credit allowed against the FUTA tax, states often establish their unemployment tax rate for new employers at 5.4 percent of the first $7,000 of wages paid each employee. However, the rate may vary over time according to an employer's experience rating. Employers with records of stable employment may pay less than the basic rate. An employer with a favorable experience rating who pays less than the basic rate is still entitled to the maximum 5.4 percent credit against the federal unemployment tax.

FICA, FUTA, and state unemployment taxes are levied on certain maximum amounts of payroll. Throughout the calendar year, employers must be aware of the fact that a greater amount of each period's wages may no longer be subject to one or more of these taxes.

The filing and payment requirements for unemployment compensation taxes vary among the states. Often, however, employers must pay the taxes when they file quarterly reports. Some states require payments more frequently, sometimes monthly, if the taxes owed by an employer exceeds a set level.

Federal Income Tax Withholding : W - 4

As an employer you are required to withhold federal income taxes from wages and salaries paid to employees. The amount of income tax withheld from each employee is based on the amount of the employee's wages, the employee's marital status, and the number of withholding allowances to which the employee is entitled. When first employed, each employee reports marital status, Social Security number, and number of withholding allowances to the employer on Form W-4. Employees file new W-4s if withholding allowances or marital status change. Employees are entitled to each of the withholding allowances for which they qualify, including one for the employee, one for his or her spouse, and one for each dependent. Additional allowances may be claimed if the employee or spouse is age 65 or older. Blind employees may also claim one or more additional allowances based on expected excessive itemized deductions on their annual income tax return.

Employers usually use the government's wage-bracket tables to determine the amount of federal income taxes to withhold from each employee. These tables indicate the amounts to withhold at different wage levels for different numbers of withholding allowances.

Alternatively, employers may use the percentage method, which is especially useful when no wage-bracket tables pertain to the length of the payroll period in question. Both the wage-bracket tables and the percentage method incorporate a graduated system of withholding. That is, the withholding rates increase as the earnings subject to withholding increase.

State Income Tax Withholding

Most states now have an income tax that is withheld by employers. Payroll procedures for withholding state income taxes are similar to those for withholding federal income taxes. Taxes related to payroll amounts may be levied on the employee, the employer, or both.

Employee or Independent Contractor?

Salaries and wages paid to employees provide the basis for withholding taxes and levying payroll taxes on the employer. Independent contractors are not subject to the supervision and control of another party (the employer). The following elements establish the existence of an employer-employee relationship: (1) the employer has the power to discharge the worker; (2) the employer sets the work hours for the worker; and (3) the employer furnishes a place to work. An independent contractor, on the other hand, may also perform services for a business firm, but that firm does not have the legal right to direct and control the methods used by the person. Independent contractors are in business for themselves; examples include some accountants, lawyers, and physicians.

Remittance and Reporting Requirements

The legislation levying taxes on payroll amounts also specifies the procedures for remitting those taxes to the government and establishes the reports an employer must file. A good system of payroll accounting ensures that these payments are made and reports are filed on time.

FICA Taxes and Federal Income Taxes

Employer remittance and reporting requirements are the same for both employer's and employee's FICA taxes and federal income taxes withheld, because these taxes are combined for payment and reporting purposes. Generally, remittances are deposited in a

Federal Reserve bank or authorized commercial bank. The specific remittance requirements vary depending on the combined dollar amount of the taxes. An employer has three banking days to make a deposit if the unpaid taxes are at least $3,000 by the 3rd, 7th, 11th, 15th, 19th, 22nd, 25th, or last day of the month. At the end of any month, undeposited taxes of $500–$3,000 must be deposited within 15 days. If the undeposited taxes are less than $500 at the end of a calendar quarter, the amount must be deposited within one month (or paid with the employer's quarterly tax return).

Each quarter, employers file an Employer's Quarterly Federal Tax Return, Form 941, with the Internal Revenue Service. On this form, the employer schedules a record of its liability for FICA taxes and withheld income taxes throughout the quarter and reports its deposits of these taxes.

By January 31, an employer must give each employee two copies of Form W-2, Wage and Tax Statement, which specifies the employee's total wages paid, the federal income taxes withheld, the wages subject to FICA tax, and the FICA tax withheld for the preceding calendar year.

Fair Labor Standards Act

The Fair Labor Standards Act establishes minimum wage, overtime pay, and equal pay standards for employees covered by the act and sets recordkeeping requirements for their employers. The act's coverage has been amended several times since its passage in 1938. Its provisions now extend, with certain exemptions, to employees directly or indirectly engaged in interstate commerce and to domestic service workers. Executive, administrative, and professional employees are exempt from the act's minimum wage and overtime provisions. A covered employee must be paid an amount equal to at least $1 \frac{1}{2}$ times the employee's regular pay rate for every hour over 40 worked in a week. Some states such as the state of California require payment of overtime for over 8 hours worked in a day. Check the laws in your state.

Equal Pay Act of 1963

Under the Equal Pay Act of 1963, employers may not discriminate on the basis of sex in the rates paid to men and women employees performing equal work on jobs demanding equal skill, effort, and responsibility and having similar working conditions. The equal pay provisions also provide that employers must eliminate illegal pay differentials by a means other than reducing employee pay rates. The law does permit wage differentials between men and women when due to a job-related factor other than sex, such as a difference based on a bona fide merit system, or a point factor job evaluation system.

Employers are required under the law to maintain a detailed record of each employee's wage and hours, including the hour and day the employee's work week begins, the regular hourly rate of pay, the total overtime pay for any week in which more than 40 hours are worked, the deductions from and additions to wages, and the employee's total wages paid each period. The law does not prescribe any particular form for these records. The payroll records maintained in a typical payroll accounting system contain much of this information, which is also needed to comply with other laws and regulations.

Other Payroll Deductions

In addition to FICA taxes, federal income taxes, and state and local income taxes, other items may be deducted from an employee's gross earnings in arriving at the net take-home pay for the period. Each additional deduction must be authorized by the employee. Often this is done individually, although in some instances the union contract provides the authorization needed by the employer. Examples of these items are payments for:

- Union dues
- Premiums on life, accident, hospital, surgical care, major medical insurance, 401(K) plan
- Loan from employee's credit union
- U.S. savings bonds
- Contributions to charitable organizations

Payroll Records

The nature of a company's payroll records and procedures depends on the size of the work force and the degree to which the recordkeeping is automated. In some form, however, two records are basic to most payroll systems—the payroll register and individual employee earnings records.

The Payroll Register

The payroll register, prepared each pay period, lists the company's complete payroll in detail. Each employee's earnings and deductions for the period are contained in the payroll register.

An employee receives an amount equal to gross earnings less total deductions for the pay period. These net earnings are shown in the payment section of the payroll register, along with the number of the check issued by the company in payment of the wages.

Individual Employee Earnings Record

Employers maintain an individual earnings record for each employee. This record contains much of the information needed for the employer to comply with the various taxation and reporting requirements established by law.

The individual earnings record contains the details on earnings and deductions shown on the payroll register. in addition, the cumulative gross earnings alerts the employer when an employee's yearly earnings have exceeded the maximum amounts to which the FICA and unemployment taxes apply.

Employers prepare Form W-2, the wage and tax statement sent to every employee each year, from the individual employee earnings records. although Form W-2 is sent only once and covers an entire year, employers typically provide employees with an earnings statement each pay period, detailing the earnings and deductions for that period. These earnings statements may be a detachable portion of the employee's paycheck or may be enclosed as a separate document with the paycheck.

In order to ensure your company is complying with all federal, state, and local pay regulations, you should hire a qualified personnel/payroll person to maintain records and manage the payroll function. These regulations change from year to year and it is a good idea to have your accountant regularly review changes in state and federal regulations and tax laws.

PAY TERMINOLOGY AND DEFINITIONS

AUTOMATIC PAY INCREASES/GENERAL ADJUSTMENTS. Some organizations have automatic pay increases at specified intervals. These organizations have a fixed-rate type of pay structure. This results in employees in certain job classifications with the same number of years of service to the organization earning the same salary. This is typical of the civil service.

BASE-RATE STRUCTURE. An organization that has no type of compensation other than pay shows only a base pay structure. If there are additional forms of compensation, they may be reflected in total compensation. Many companies pay bonuses at certain levels, and it's important when making external comparisons through surveys to be sure you compare base pay to base pay, and that the bonuses and other perks are listed separately.

BENCHMARK JOBS. When using a point method of measuring jobs, evaluations of a selected group of representative jobs help to clarify various factors and establish a framework for evaluating and comparing jobs throughout the organization. If you are installing a job evaluation system from scratch, establishing benchmark jobs saves time, effort, and cost by providing points of comparison throughout the organization. Benchmark jobs should be easy to define, non controversial, and representative of the organization in general.

BONUS. A bonus can be almost anything other than base pay or perks. Most bonuses are cash, usually determined at the end of the fiscal year after profit and loss statements are completed. Other bonus payments might be in the form of company stock, stock options, and so on.

CALL-BACK PAY. This is hourly pay guaranteed for a certain minimum number of hours when an hourly worker is called to work at a time other than the ordinary shift.

CALL-IN PAY. This is hourly pay guaranteed for a specified number of hours if the worker is called to work on a day that is not an ordinary workday.

CAREER LADDERS. These are successive promotional steps in an occupational or professional area that allow movement up through the organization. There is normally at least a 15 percent increase in pay between each step.

CAREER PLANNING. Job descriptions and performance appraisals form the basis for planned career development in most organizations and include identifying needed skills and abilities for higher level jobs and scheduling the training needed to prepare for those jobs.

CENTRALIZED/DECENTRALIZED COMPENSATION PROGRAM. A centralized salary program is designed, implemented, and administered at the corporate level. A centralized compensation program is less complex, easier, and less costly to administer in one location. The main characteristic is its uniformity throughout the organization—it can address the diverse needs of separate groups, but it has the same overall guidelines. A centralized compensation effort provides more control over internal equity and uniform administration. A company that has union contracts may decentralize hourly pay. Hourly pay administration will follow union contract provisions and can follow administrative guidelines without regard for the type of company organization.

COMPA-RATIO. The compa-ratio is a person's current salary as a percentage of the midpoint of their salary range.

COMPENSATION SURVEY. Companies that wish to compare their salary ranges and actual pay practices participate in compensation surveys. The surveys include companies in their industry and their location. It is important to compare actual benchmark jobs when using the data of any survey. When participating in a compensation survey, it's a good idea to have a third party collect the data and produce the survey so that raw data are not exchanged. There might be antitrust implications.

COMPRESSION. Compression is the narrowing of pay differentials between employees who should be paid at varying levels. Three of the most common situations where compression can occur are:

- Subordinate vs. supervisor
- New hire vs. senior employee
- Superior performer vs. average performer

The obvious problems associated with inequities caused by salary compression are poor morale and performance, unwillingness to accept promotions, and higher turnover.

COLA. An increase based on measure of cost of living (nationally) used in union contracts.

COST-OF-LIVING ALLOWANCES OR GEOGRAPHIC DIFFERENTIALS. Some corporations pay cost-of-living allowances to employees they ask to relocate to areas of this country or overseas where the cost of living is significantly higher than the cost of living at their current location.

DEFERRED COMPENSATION PLAN. This is compensation awarded to an employee where payment is deferred. Deferred compensation is usually in the form of cash or stock. Some plans require purchase by the employee and might be (1) employee savings plans, (2) stock purchase plans, or (3) stock options. Some plans that do not require purchase by the employee are (1) stock bonuses, (2) profit-sharing plans, and (3) deferred cash compensation. Deferred compensation plans are desirable because of their tax advantages.

EQUITY.   There are two main kinds of equity, internal and external. The perceptions that employees have of equity are so varied that they are difficult to define. Equity seems to exist as an individual perception that is influenced by a variety of factors, a perceived sense of rewards. Equity is seen by most people as the balance between output and the pay received for the job done. It is also a perception that persons are paid fairly within their work group, their total organization, and externally compared to other companies in the same industry.

EXEMPT EMPLOYEES.   Exempt employees are salaried and hold managerial, supervisory, administrative, professional, or sales positions. They are exempt from the overtime provisions of the Fair Labor Standards Act.

INCENTIVES.   Incentives are frequently part of an executive's total compensation package. Incentives may include such items as added compensation, commissions, bonus plans, prizes, awards, stock options, and profit sharing.

MATURITY CURVE DATA.   Maturity curve data are a comparison of pay levels with years of experience. We traditionally look at technical people like scientists and engineers in relation to the number of years since receiving their degrees. This kind of analysis is a normal characteristic of most engineering salary surveys. Maturity curve data are not normally found in other salary surveys, but are available from professional organizations.

MERIT INCREASES.   A merit increase system rewards employees for job performance and ties job performance to the percentage increase in pay.

NONEXEMPT EMPLOYEES.   Nonexempt employees are hourly paid employees who are paid overtime for working more than 40 hours in a week. The tests that determine whether a job is exempt or nonexempt are set out in the Fair Labor Standards Act.

REPORT-IN PAY.   This is hourly pay guaranteed when work is called off because of something like bad weather or machine breakdown.

SALARY BUDGET.   The human resource manager normally prepares a budget for the organization's pay increases. Personnel and payroll policies and the company's total financial philosophy are taken into account. The formal budget is normally established after a survey of the external competitive situation and a review of the company's resources and financial condition.

RECORD RETENTION REQUIREMENTS

Personnel recordkeeping is an important function in any company. It is regulated by the federal government, and when not carried on adequately it's an area where a company is vulnerable to litigation. It's a good idea to review federal recordkeeping requirements every year or so to ensure your compliance. The following table lists most federal record retention requirements.

Record	Period of Retention	Statutes
Advertisements Regarding Job Openings, Promotions, Training Programs or Overtime Work	One Year	Age Discrimination in Employment Act 29 CFR 1627.3 and 29 CFR 1627.4
Affirmative Action Compliance Programs (Federal contractors, sub-contractors) Written affirmative action programs, including required workforce analysis and utilization evaluation. Records and documents on nature and use of tests, validations of tests, and test results as required.	Not specified. When the Labor Department's Office of Federal Contract Compliance Programs audits organizations, they may request records from current year and the previous year.	Executive Order 11246 41 CFR 60
Age Records Date of Birth, if under 19	Three Years	Fair Labor Standards Act 29 CFR 516 Walsh-Healey Act 41 CFR 50.201
Date of Birth	Three Years	Age Discrimination in Employment Act, 29 CFR 1627.3
Americans with Disabilities Act—Employer Records Same employer record retention requirements as the Civil Rights Act of 1964 as Amended, Title VII. Following the Title VII requirements (along with the requirements of other acts which afford protection from employment discrimination such as the Age Discrimination Act, Immigration Reform & Control Act, Vietnam Veterans Readjustment Assistance Act, Vocational Rehabilitation Act) is considered a helpful defense against an ADA discrimination charge.		
Applicant identification / Flow Logs According to the Office of Federal Contract Compliance Programs (OFCCP), an internal audit and reporting system designed to monitor the progress of an affirmative action program should include applicant flow records. Such a record should contain the name of the applicant, date of application, race, sex, referral source, job applied for, interview information, and disposition of the application (hired, rejected and on what basis, no openings, and so forth). The highest year of school completed and pre-employment test results might also be of interest to the OFCCP. Such records must be kept separate from the files or records used by the employer in making hiring decisions.	Not specified.	Title VII 29 CFR 1607.4
	Not specified. When the Labor Department's Office of Federal Contract Compliance Programs audits organizations, they may request records from current year and the previous year.	Executive Order 11246 41 CFR 60

Record	Period of Retention	Statutes
Application, Resumes or Other Replies to Job Advertisements, Including Temporary Positions	One Year One year from date record was made or human resource action was taken, whichever is later.	Age Discrimination in Employment Act 29 CFR 1627.4 Title VII 29 CFR 1602.14
Apprenticeship Selection and Programs For apprenticeship programs: • chronological list of names and addresses of all applicants, dates of application, sex and minority-group identification, or file of written applications containing same information; other records pertaining to apprenticeship applicants, for example, test papers, interview records, and	Two years from date application was received or period of successful applicant's apprenticeship, whichever is later.	Title VII 29 CFR 1602.20
• any other records made solely for completing report EEO-2 or similar reports.	One year from the due date of the report.	Title VII 29 CFR 1602.20
Bloodborne Pathogens/Infectious Material Standard Protects employees who may be occupationally exposed to blood or other infectious materials. • Written exposure control plan. • Medical records. • Training records.	Not specified. Must be available to workers and kept current. Duration of employment + thirty years Three Years	Occupational Safety and Health Act 29 CFR 1910.1030
Child Labor Provisions—Age Certificates	Employers may protect themselves from unintentional violation of the child labor provisions by keeping on file an employment or age certificate for each minor to show that the minor is the minimum age for the job. Certificates issued under most State laws are acceptable for purposes of the Act.	Fair Labor Standards Act 29 CFR 570.5
Citizenship or Authorization to Work Immigration and Naturalization Services Form I-9 (Employment Eligibility Verification form) for **all** employees hired after November 6, 1986.	Three years from date of hire or one year after separation, whichever is later. (Minimum of three years.)	Immigration Reform Control Act 8 CFR 274A.2

Record	Period of Retention	Statutes
Demotion Records	One Year	Age Discrimination in Employment Act 29 CFR 1627.3 Title VII 29 CFR 1690².14
Discrimination or Enforcement Charges • Personnel records relevant to charge of discrimination or enforcement against employer, including records relating to charging party and to all other employees holding positions similar or sought after, such as application forms, test papers or performance documentation.	Until final disposition of charge or action.	Age Discrimination in Employment Act 29 CFR 1602.20 Title VII, 29 CFR 1602.14 Americans with Disabilities Act 29 CFR 1602.14 Executive Order 11246 41 CFR 60
• Minimum Wage and Overtime Charges	Two Year Minimum. However, Department of Labor may request records back three years.	Fair Labor Standards Act 29 CFR 516
• Also see: — Citizenship or Authorization to Work — Handicapped Applicant & Employee Complaints — Insurance / Welfare and Pension / Retirement Plans — Labor Organizations & Employer Records — Occupational Injuries & Illnesses — Payroll—Basis on which Wages are Paid — Physical / Medical — Polygraph Test — Veterans—Hiring Records — Veterans—Military Leave		Immigration Reform and Control Act ADA & Vocational Rehabilitation Act of 1973 Empl. Retirement Income Security Act Landrum-Griffin Act Occupational Safety and Health Act Equal Pay Act OSHA, ADEA, ADA and FMLA Employee Polygraph Protection Act Vietnam Veterans Readjustment Assistance Act Vietnam Veterans Readjustment Assistance Act
Drug Testing Records (Required by Dept. of Transportation) • Breath alcohol test with results of .02 or higher • Positive controlled substances tests • Documentation of refusals to test • Calibration documentation • Evaluation and referrals • Copy of calendar year summary	5 years	Omnibus Transportation Employee Testing Act of 1991 Federal Aviation Administration (FAA) 14 CFR Part 121 (Appendix to Subpart J) Federal Highway Administration (FHWA) 49 CFR 382.401 Federal Railroad Administration (FRA) 49 CFR Part 219 (Appendix to Subpart J)

Record	Period of Retention	Statutes
Drug Testing Records, Continued • Information on the alcohol and controlled substances collection process • Information on training	Two Years	Federal Transit Administration (FTA) 49 CFR Part 653.71 Research and Special Programs Administration (RSPA)
• Negative and canceled controlled substances test results • Alcohol test results of less than .02 alcohol concentration	One Year	49 CFR 199.27
Earnings Per Week	Three Years	Age Discrimination in Employment Act 29 CFR 1627.3 Fair Labor Standards Act 29 CFR 516
Employer Information Report For employers with 100 or more employees, a copy of the EEO-1 Form (Employer Information Report) must be kept.	A copy of the most current report filed for each reporting unit must always be kept at each unit or at company or divisional headquarters.	Title VII 29 CFR 1602.7
Employment Contracts Individual Employment Contracts (where contracts or agreements are not in writing, a written memorandum summarizing the terms) include collective bargaining agreements, plans and trusts.	Three Years	Fair Labor Standards Act 29 CFR 516
Employment Tax Records	Four Years	Internal Revenue Code 26 CFR 31.6001-1
Family And Medical Leave Act (FMLA) Employer Records **Leave Under FMLA—Exempt Employees** If employees are not subject to FLSA's recordkeeping regulations for purposes of minimum wage or overtime compliance, an employer need not keep a record of actual hours worked provided that: • Eligibility for FMLA leave is presumed for any employee who has been employed for at least 12 months. • A written record is maintained as to the agreement between the employer and employee regarding reduced or intermittent leave and the employee's normal schedule or average hours.	Three Years No particular order or form of records is required.	Family and Medical Leave Act 29 CFR 825.110 29 CFR 825.206 29 CFR 825.500

Record	Period of Retention	Statutes
Leave Under FMLA—Non-exempt Employees Employers shall keep records pertaining to their obligations under the Act in accordance with the recordkeeping requirement of the Fair Labor Standard Act (FLSA). Records kept must disclose the following: • Basic payroll identifying employee data (name, address, and occupation), rate or basis of pay and terms of compensation, daily and weekly hours worked per pay period, additions to or deductions from wages, total compensation paid. • Dates FMLA leave is taken. • Hours of the leave if FMLA is taken in increments. • Copies of employee notices of leave furnished to the employer and copies of all general and specific notices given to employees. • Documents describing employee benefits or employer policies and practices regarding the taking of paid and unpaid leaves. • Premium payments of employee benefits. • Records of any dispute between the employer and an employee regarding designation of leave as FMLA leave.	Three Years No particular order or form of records is required.	Family and Medical Leave Act 29 CFR 825.500 29 CFR 825.110 29 CFR 516
Garnishment Documents NOTE: The terms of some state garnishment laws are more protective of the employee than the provisions of the Federal law.	Federal garnishment laws are enforced under the Fair Labor Standards Act. Refer to Payroll Records—Additions or Deductions from Wages Paid.	Fair Labor Standards Act 29 CFR 516
Group Health Insurance Coverage After Certain Qualifying Events Employers need records showing covered employees and their spouses and dependents: • have received written notice of continuing group health insurance and COBRA rights, • whether the employee and his or her spouse and dependents elected or rejected coverage.	Not specified by regulations	Internal Revenue Code Sec. 4980 B (f)(6) ERISA Sections 606 (1) and 502 (c)(1)

Record	Period of Retention	Statutes
Hazardous Materials Exposure Records of any personal or environmental monitoring of exposure to hazardous materials.	Thirty years	Occupational Safety and Health Act 29 CFR 1910.1200
Records of "significant adverse reactions" to health or the environment that may indicate "long-lasting or irreversible damage," "partial or complete impairment of bodily functions," "impairment of normal activities which is experienced by all or most of the persons exposed at one time," and "impairment of normal activities which is experienced each time an individual is exposed." Records must contain original allegation: abstract of allegation, including name and address of plant site that received allegation, date allegation received, implicated substance, description of alleger, description of alleged health effects, results of any self-initiated investigation of allegation, and copies of any other required reports or records relating to allegation.	Thirty years for records of significant adverse reactions to employees' health; five years for all other allegations, including environmental or consumer charges; thirty years for employee health-related allegations arising from any employment related exposure.	Toxic Substances Control Act from Environmental Protection Agency—applies primarily to chemical manufacturers. 40 CFR 717
Hiring Records	One year from date record made or personnel action taken, whichever is later.	Title VII 9 CFR 1602.14
Homeworker Programs Payroll or other record specifying date on which work given out to or begun by each industrial homeworker and amount of such work; date on which work turned in by worker, and amount of work; kind of articles worked on and operations performed; piece rates paid; hours worked on each lot of work turned in.	Not specified. (Upon request, all records must be made available for inspection and transcription by Wage-Hour Division administrators.)	Fair Labor Standards Act—Homeworker Regulations 29 CFR 516.31
Name and address of each agent, distributor, or contractor through whom homework is distributed or collected, and name and address of each homeworker to whom homework is distributed or from whom homework is collected by the agent, distributor, or contractor.	Not specified. (Upon request, all records must be made available for inspection and transcription by Wage-Hour Division administrators.)	Homeworker Regulations 29 CFR 516.31

Record	Period of Retention	Statutes
Homeworker Programs, Continued Homeworker handbook in which each homeworker records daily and weekly hours worked, piece work information, and business-related expenses.	At least two years after the handbook is filled completely or the homeworker is terminated. Employers must "keep and preserve" handbook as submitted by each homeworker and, upon request, make the handbook available for inspection by the Wage-Hour Division of the Labor Department. The handbook must include a statement signed by the employer attesting to the accuracy of the entries.	Homeworker Regulations 29 CFR 516.31
Insurance / Welfare and Pension / Retirement Plans • Benefit plan descriptions. • Records providing the basis for all required plan descriptions and reports necessary to certify the information including vouchers, worksheets, receipts, and applicable resolutions.	Full period that plan or system is in effect, plus one year after termination of the plan. Not less than six years after filing date of documents.	Age Discrimination in Employment Act 29 CFR 1627.3 Employee Retirement Income Security Act 29 CFR 2520.101-1 thru 2520.104b-30
Job Orders Submitted to Employment Agency or Union	One Year	Age Discrimination in Employment Act 29 CFR 1627.3
Labor Organization and Employer Records Employers are subject to certain annual reporting requirements which include filed reports showing: any loans to a union/union official or representative; agreements with or payments to any labor relations consultant, worker or other individual for the purpose of persuading employees about their union sentiments; and any expenditures to obtain information about the activities of employees or a union in connection with a labor dispute.	Documents to support the accuracy of required reports must be retained for at least five years from filing the report.	Labor Management Reporting and Disclosure Act of 1959 29 CFR 405.9
Layoff Selection	One Year One year from date record made or personnel action taken, whichever is later.	Age Discrimination in Employment Act 29 CFR 1627.3 Title VII 29 CFR 1602.14

Record	Period of Retention	Statutes
Material Safety Data Sheets (MSDS) • Employers must have a MSDS on file for each hazardous chemical they use and ensure copies are readily accessible to employees in their work area.	No specific time—must be maintained in a current fashion.	Occupational Safety and Health Act 29 CFR 1910.1200
• Employer must keep records of chemicals used, where they were used and for how long.	Thirty Years	Occupational Safety and Health Act 29 CFR 1910.1200
Occupational Injuries and Illnesses "Log and Summary of Occupational Injuries and Illnesses"—OSHA Form 200. Job-related injuries and illnesses must be recorded within six days of their occurrence.	Five years following the end of the year to which records relate.	Occupational Safety and Health Act 29 CFR 1904.2
"Supplementary Record of Occupational Injuries and Illnesses"—OSHA Form 101. Provides details on each recordable injury and illness.	Five years following the end of the year to which records relate.	Occupational Safety an Health Act 29 CFR 1904.4
Older Workers Benefit Protection Act—Employer Records Same employer record retention requirements as Age Discrimination in Employment Act (ADEA).	No specific requirement. Keeping waivers forever is considered a helpful defense against an ADEA waiver of rights discrimination charge.	Older Workers Benefit Protection Act 29 CFR 1627.3 and 1627.4 29 CFR 1602.20
Waiver of Age Discrimination in Employment Act rights.		
Order, Shipping, and Billing Records From the last date of entry, the originals or true copies of all customer orders or invoices received, incoming or outgoing shipping or delivery records, as well as all bills of lading and all billings to customers (not including individual sales slips, cash register tapes or the like) which the employer retains or makes in the usual course of business operations.	Two Years	Fair Labor Standards Act 29 CFR 516
Payroll Records-Additions or Deductions from Wages Paid All records used by the employer in determining additions to or deductions from wages paid.	Three Years	Fair Labor Standards Act 29 CFR 516

Record	Period of Retention	Statutes
Payroll Records for Age Discrimination in Employment Act Payroll or other records containing each employee's name, address, date of birth, occupation, rate of pay, and compensation earned per week.	Three Years	Age Discrimination in Employment Act 29 CFR 1627.3
Payroll Records—Basis on which Wages Are Paid • The basis on which wages are paid must be documented in sufficient detail to permit calculation for each pay period. The records may include payment of wages, wage rates, job evaluations, merit and incentive programs and seniority systems. • The basic reason for these records is to give the Wage-Hour Division an indication on whether or not sex discrimination exists. • Although there is no specific form furnished by the Wage-Hour Division for calculation of the benefit costs, the data necessary to calculate these costs should be readily available to Wage-Hour audit personnel.	Two Years	Equal Pay Act 29 CFR 516
Payroll Records for Davis-Bacon Act & Service Contract Act (Federal contractors, sub-contractors) Payroll records listing name, address, social security number, job classification, rate of pay, daily and weekly number of hours worked, deductions made, and actual wages paid.	Three Years after completion of contract	Davis-Bacon Act 29 CFR 5.1 and 5.5 Service Contract Act 29 CFR 4.6
Payroll Records for FLSA—Exempt Employees (*Bona fide* executive, administrative, professional and outside sales employees.) • Name in full of employee (as used for social security record purposes) and identifying number or symbol, if such is used on payroll records. • Home address, including zip code. • Date of birth, if under 19 years of age. • Sex and Occupation • Time of day and day of week on which employee's work week begins, if this varies between employees; otherwise a single notation for the entire establishment will suffice. • Total wages paid each pay period. • Dates of payment and pay period covered.	Three Years Records of hours worked is recommended for Department of Labor Wage and Hour audits.	Fair Labor Standards Act 29 CFR 516

Record	Period of Retention	Statutes
Payroll Records for FLSA—Non-Exempt Employees All required for Exempt Employees plus: • Regular hourly rate of pay for any week when overtime is worked and overtime compensation is due. (May be in the form of vouchers or other payment data.) • Daily hours worked and total hours worked each workweek. (Workday may be any consecutive 24-hour period and workweek is any fixed and regularly recurring period of seven consecutive days.) • Total daily or weekly straight-time earnings or wages due for hours worked during the workday or workweek. • Total premium pay for overtime hours. This amount excludes the straight-time earnings for overtime hours recorded under the above item. • Total additions to or deductions from wages paid each pay period including employee purchase orders or wage assignments. Also, in individual employee records, the dates, amounts, and nature of the items which make up the total additions and deductions.	Three Years	Fair Labor Standards Act 29 CFR 516
Payroll Records for Title VII Rates of pay or other terms of compensation.	One year from date record made or personnel action taken, whichever is later.	Title VII 29 CFR 1602.14
Payroll Records for Walsh-Healey Act (Federal contractors, sub-contractors) Basic employment and earning records, wage-rate tables, and work-time schedules. Employment records, including name, address, sex, occupation, date of birth of each employee under 19 years of age, and wage-hour records, complete with identifying number of contract on which each employee is working.	Two years from date of last entry or last effective date, whichever is later. Three years from date of last entry.	Walsh-Healey Act 41 CFR 50.201 Walsh-Healey Act 41 CFR 50.201
Physical/Medical Records Under ADEA and ADA Results of physical examinations considered in connection *with personnel action.*	One Year	Age Discrimination in Employment Act 29 CFR 1627.3 Americans with Disabilities Act 29 CFR 1630.14

Record	Period of Retention	Statutes
Physical / Medical Records Under FMLA Records and documents including an FMLA leave request relating to medical certifications, recertification or medical histories of employees or employees' family members, shall be maintained in separate files/records and be treated as confidential medical records, except that: • Supervisors and managers may be informed regarding necessary restrictions and accommodations, not the nature of the condition. • First aid and safety personnel may be informed (when appropriate) if the employee may/might require emergency treatment. • Government officials investigating compliance with FMLA shall be provided relevant information.	Three Years No particular order or form of records is required.	Family Medical Leave Act 29 CFR 825.500
Physical / Medical Records Under OSHA Complete and accurate records of all medical examinations *required by OSHA law.*	Duration of employment, plus 30 years unless a specific OSHA standard provides a different time period.	Occupational Safety and Health Act 29 CFR 1910.2
Plant Closing or Mass Layoff Notice A 60-day advance notice before a plant closing or mass layoff.	Not specified by regulation. Enforcement action is through the courts.	Worker Adjustment and Retraining Notification Act 20 CFR 639.3(a)
Polygraph Test Polygraph investigation of a workplace theft or other incident or activity resulting in economic loss to the employer. A copy of statement provided to employees setting forth specific incident or activity under investigation and basis for testing.	Three years from date polygraph test is conducted or from date examination is requested, whichever is later.	Employee Polygraph Protection Act 29 CFR 801.30
Polygraph investigation of criminal or other misconduct involving, or potentially involving, loss or injury to the manufacture, distribution or dispensing of controlled substances. Records specifically identifying the loss or injury in question and the nature of the employee's access to person or property being investigated.	Three years from date polygraph test is conducted or from date examination is requested, whichever is later.	Employee Polygraph Protection Act 29 CFR 801.30

Record	Period of Retention	Statutes
Polygraph Test Continued Copy of notice provided to polygraph examiner identifying persons to be examined. Copies of all opinions, reports, charts, written questions, lists, and other records relating to employee polygraph tests (for example, records of number of examinations conducted each day, records specifying duration of each test period) that have been furnished to the employer by the polygraph examiner.	Three years from date polygraph test is conducted or from date examination is requested, whichever is later. Three years from date polygraph test is conducted or from date examination is requested, whichever is later.	Employee Polygraph Protection Act 29 CFR 801.30 Employee Polygraph Protection Act 29 CFR 801.30
Promotion Records or Notices	One year from date record made or personnel action taken, whichever is later. One Year	Title VII 29 CFR 1602.14 Age Discrimination in Employment Act 29 CFR 1627.3
Recall Selection	One Year	Age Discrimination in Employment Act 29 CFR 1627.3
Sales and Purchase Records A record of: (1) total dollar volume of sales or business, and (2) total volume of goods purchased or received during such periods (weekly, monthly, quarterly, and so on) and in such forms as the employer maintains in the ordinary course of business.	Three Years	Fair Labor Standards Act 29 CFR 516.5
Seniority or Merit Rating Systems	For the full period the plan or system is in effect, plus one year.	Age Discrimination in Employment Act 29 CFR 1627.3
Termination Records	One year from date record made or personnel action taken, whichever is later. One Year	Title VII 29 CFR 1602.14 Age Discrimination in Employment Act 29 CFR 1627.3

Record	Period of Retention	Statutes
Test Records • Tests used in connection with employer administered aptitude or other employment test. • Tests—Federal Contractors & Sub-contractors. Records and documents on nature and use of tests, validations of tests, and test results as required.	One Year Not specified. When the Labor Dept.'s Office of Federal Contract Compliance Programs audits organizations, they request records from current and previous year.	Age Discrimination in Employment Act 29 CFR 1627.3 Title VII 29 CFR 1607.4 Executive Order 11246 41 CFR 60
Time Worked Records All basic time and earnings cards or sheets and work production sheets of individuals where all or part of the employee's earnings are determined.	At least two years.	Fair Labor Standards Act 29 CFR 516
Training Selection	One Year 29 CFR 1627.3 One year from date record made or personnel action taken, whichever is later.	Age Discrimination in Employment Act Title VII 29 CFR 1602.14
Transfer Records	One Year 29 CFR 1627.3 One year from date record made or personnel action taken, whichever is later.	Age Discrimination in Employment Act Title VII 29 CFR 1602.14
Veterans—Hiring Records Organizations with federal contracts or subcontracts of $10,000 or more must file an annual report—Form VETS-100—that lists, by job category and hiring location, the number of Vietnam-era and disabled veterans hired during a 12-month period. The data are used to determine whether employers are fulfilling their affirmative action obligations, as well as the legal requirement to list job vacancies with the Job Service.	One Year	Veterans Readjustment Assistance Act 61 CFR 250
Veterans—Military Leave Organizations must grant leaves of absence to perform military obligations. Service limits are set on the amount of time an employee may spend in active duty and still be eligible for re-employment. Employees are re-employed to their former position or a position of like status and pay with seniority and vacation as if they had not taken a military leave.	Not specified by regulations. The service limit on the time an employee may spend in active duty and still be eligible for re-employment can be up to five years.	Uniformed Services Employment and Reemployment Rights Act Sec. 4311 and 4312

Record	Period of Retention	Statutes
Vocational Rehabilitation Act—Handicapped Applicant & Employee Records		
• (Federal contractors, sub-contractors) For handicapped applicants and employees, complete and accurate employment records are required. The Department of Labor suggests that this requirement may be met by annotating the application or personnel form for the handicapped employee or applicant to indicate each vacancy, promotion, and training program for which he or she was considered, including a statement of reasons for any rejection that compares the handicapped individual's qualifications to those of the person selected. Also, any accommodations actually undertaken should be attached.	One Year	Vocational Rehabilitation Act 41 CFR 60.741.52
• Complaints under the Vocational Rehabilitation Act	One Year	Vocational Rehabilitation Act 41 CFR 60.741.52
Wage-Rate Tables		
All tables or schedules (from their last effective date) of the employer which provide the piece rates or other rates used in computing straight-time earnings, wages, or salary, or overtime pay computation.	Two years. However, Department of Labor may request records back three years.	Fair Labor Standard Act 29 CFR 516

NOTE: This list is not all-inclusive and is subject to change when new regulations are passed.

MAINTAINING CONTROL OF STAFFING LEVELS

It is difficult to maintain control over the numbers of people hired in any organization. There are a couple of simple ways to do it on a monthly basis:

1. Draw-up an organization chart for each of your current departments. Put everyone on the chart with their salaries and titles. Add up the total salaries by department and put that figure at the top of the form. A sample form appears on the next page. Adapt the form to your particular needs. The first chart you complete for each of your departments can be the starting point for the approved budget.

Prepare a cover page to accompany all the charts. It should provide data on the entire organization showing number of positions and total salaries.

Update the charts as people are hired and terminated.

To control staffing, state that when anyone is added to the charts after a certain date (when staffing has been approved), managers must complete an employment requisition form (see sample).

Maintain employment requisitions that have been approved and the updated organization charts as your control system.

2. You can control staffing levels and hiring by approving an overall budget each year for every department. Use the form, Monthly Staff Level Report, that follows. Adapt the form to your specific needs. Require anything over the approved budget to be approved by the president.

MONTHLY PAYROLL TREND

Using a Lotus 123 or Excel spreadsheet, produce a monthly payroll trend report for all your business locations. See sample report which follows.

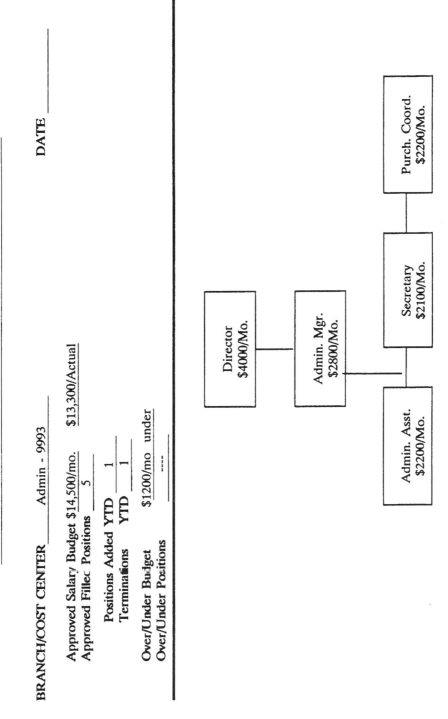

ORGANIZATIONAL CHART - EMPLOYEE STAFFING

BRANCH/COST CENTER _____ Admin - 9993 _____   DATE _____

Approved Salary Budget $14,500/mo. $13,300/Actual
Approved Filled Positions _____ 5 _____

Positions Added YTD _____ 1 _____
Terminations   YTD _____ 1 _____

Over/Under Budget $1200/mo under
Over/Under Positions   ----

Director
$4000/Mo.

Admin. Mgr.
$2800/Mo.

Admin. Asst.
$2200/Mo.

Secretary
$2100/Mo.

Purch. Coord.
$2200/Mo.

1 PT Clerical
$6/Hr.

MONTHLY STAFF LEVEL REPORT

Department _____   Month of _____   Year _____

Department	Staff Level			Total Staff Level* Prior Month	Total Staff Level* Current Month	Total Staff Level* Current Month (last year)	Current Budgeted Levels	Variance (Current Month Budget Minus Current Month Actual)
	Exempt	Nonexempt	Vacancies					
Administration	2	3	--	5	5	4	13.3	+1200
Marketing	4	5	--	9	9	7	30.0	+4000
Production	3	90	2	93	94	92	150.0	+30.0
Data Processing	2	4	--	6	6	5	90.0	+15.0
Totals	11	102	2	118	118	117	283.3	+50.0

*Including Vacancies

MONTHLY PAYROLL TREND
XYZ COMPANY

	12/31/95 Head Count				03/31/96 Head Count				04/30/96 Head Count			
	Overhead	Capitalized	Sales	Total	Overhead	Capitalized	Sales	Total	Overhead	Capitalized	Sales	Total
New York	120	83	60	263	136	75	64	275	143	76	65	284
Mid-Atlantic Division												
Maryland	14	38	48	100	14	43	46	103	13	40	50	103
Virginia	57	56	56	169	56	54	57	167	56	54	56	166
Total Mid-Atlantic Division	71	94	104	269	70	97	103	270	69	94	106	269
California Division												
Northern California	19	16	19	54	17	16	18	51	17	15	18	50
Southern California	30	22	26	78	30	23	25	78	33	22	26	81
Total California Division	49	38	45	132	47	39	43	129	50	37	44	131
Arizona Division												
Phoenix	28	31	36	95	29	30	36	95	27	32	33	92
Tucson	12	8	20	40	13	8	14	35	13	8	14	35
Total Arizona Division	40	39	56	135	42	38	50	130	40	40	47	127
Nevada	4	4	3	11	26	9	12	47	25	9	12	46
XYZ Corporate	80	0	0	80	84	0	0	84	82	0	0	82
American Mortgage, Inc.	132	0	0	132	134	0	0	134	140	0	0	140
Financial Companies, Inc.	21	0	0	21	20	0	0	20	20	0	0	20
Total All Divisions	517	258	268	1043	559	258	272	1089	569	256	274	1099

12/31/95
Active Division Difference YTD 20
Inactive Divisions Difference YTD (101)
All Divisions Difference YTD (81)
(All) Difference Current Month (7)

03/31/96
Active Divisions Difference YTD 46
All Divisions Difference YTD 46
(All) Difference Current Month 1

04/30/96
Active Divisions Difference YTD 56
All Divisions Difference YTD 56
(All) Difference Current Month 10

HOW TO FIGURE RECRUITING AND SELECTION COSTS

The cost to hire is probably one of the most difficult indices to develop because there are both tangible and intangible cost factors. There are two categories to be concerned with: those that can be measured (tangible), and those that cannot be measured (intangible). Intangible factors can create as significant an impact upon the efficiency and organization of the corporation as the measurable costs.

TANGIBLE COSTS INCLUDE:
- Advertising
- Employment agency fees
- Publications used in recruiting
- Medical examinations for selection
- Security, credit, and reference checks
- Personnel department overhead (office space, personnel staff compensation, and so on)
- Telephone calls
- Stationery and other office supplies
- Interviewing costs
- Relocation costs
- Data processing costs
- Related clerical costs
- Other recruitment costs
- Testing equipment and material costs

INTANGIBLE COSTS INCLUDE:
- Disorientation of the department
- Disruption of morale
- Increase in employee complaints
- Reduced management efficiency
- Reduced morale
- Generally lower productivity
- The stimulation of additional turnover
- Overhiring in order to maintain an average work force

Some items we might include as intangible on closer examination might be determined to be tangible costs. Depending on the industry, they might include more on-the-job accidents, higher scrap rates, additional overtime, larger human resource staff in order to handle replacement needs, and so on.

Following is a sample cost-to-hire computation:

XYZ COMPANY
SAMPLE COST-TO-HIRE COMPUTATION

Search and Selection

Advertising	$ 1,884.00
Employee handbooks	248.60
Medical examinations	525.00
Security, credit, reference checks	1,350.00
Personnel department overhead	27,393.11
Interviewing costs	1,847.80
Relocation	40,000.00
Telephone	436.00
Subtotal	$73,684.51

Assignment and Placement

Personnel department overhead	$12,898.85
Administrative expenses	706.00
Follow-up telephone calls	172.00
Stationery and other supplies (incl. data processing forms)	1,263.00
New employee orientation costs	1,505.00
Subtotal	$16,544.85

Training

Training department overhead	$27,129.00
Follow-up telephone calls	272.00
Makeup pay during training period	20,400.00
Subtotal	$47,801.00

Retention

Publications (holiday/birthday cards, employee newsletters)	$ 2,830.00
Professional expenses	4,500.00
Increased benefits	14,856.00
Personnel department overhead	12,898.85
Miscellaneous costs	3,165.50
Subtotal	$38,250.35

Terminations

Outplacement fees	$ 4,000.00
Follow-up telephone calls	72.00
Stationery and other supplies	1,126.00
Lost production	23,828.00
Subtotal	$29,026.00

Summary Analysis—Cost to Hire

It cost XYZ Company:

$73,684.51 to find and relocate people

16,544.85 to assign and place them

47,801.00 to train them

38,250.35 to retain them

29,026.00 to terminate them

FREQUENTLY USED PERSONNEL CALCULATIONS, FORMULAS, AND TABLES

Figuring a Salaried Employee's Hourly Pay

Figure 40 hours worked in a week × 52 weeks in a year = 2080 hours. 24 pay periods divided into 2080 hours = a factor of .011538.

Multiply the employee's semi-monthly salary by a factor of .011538 to get the hourly rate.

Example: The semi-monthly salary is $2500.00.

$2500.00 × .011538 = $28.85 hourly rate.

Figuring Absenteeism

$$\frac{\text{Number of person days lost through job absence during period}}{\text{Average number of employees x number of work days}} \times 100$$

The rate can be computed based on the number of hours instead of days. In a study of 143 organizations the absentee rate ranged from 1.8% to 11.4%, with the average being 4%.

Figuring Turnover

$$\frac{\text{Number of employee separations during the month}}{\text{Total number of employees at midmonth}} \times 100$$

SAMPLE HUMAN RESOURCES CALCULATIONS AND REPORTS

Using the following formula, turnover is calculated quarterly on a calendar year basis. To derive a quarterly figure, the firm needs, first of all, to keep track of the number of employees and the number of terminations for each month during the quarter.

Job Functions to Be Measured

In this sample calculation, the formula is kept simple and workable by limiting the number of individual departments/job functions for which turnover will be calculated. The number of employees and terminations will be reported for the following departments:

SINGLE-FAMILY RESIDENTIAL PRODUCTION: Includes loan officers, both salaried and commissioned, loan processors, branch managers, underwriters, closers, and other functions.

SINGLE-FAMILY RESIDENTIAL SERVICING/LOAN ADMINISTRATION: Includes employees who perform functions in cashiering, remitting, hazard insurance, property taxes, customer service, payoffs, assumptions, collections, foreclosures, and REOs. Excludes employees who perform functions in servicing acquisitions, loan setup, or personal insurance.

ALL OTHER DEPARTMENTS: Includes marketing and administration departments. Both exempt and non-exempt positions are included in the employee count. Full-time employees are counted as one employee, part-time employees as one-half person. We included part-time employees because they often constitute a significant element of the real estate company's work force. Employees on leaves of absence, such as maternity leave, are counted.

Measuring Terminations

Both voluntary and involuntary terminations are included in counting terminations. For example, voluntary terminations such as resignations and retirements are included. Involuntary terminations include workers who are fired but not laid off. Layoffs can constitute a significant percentage of involuntary terminations; however, they should not be included in the calculation because they may artificially inflate the amount of turnover in the firm for a given year. Unlike involuntary terminations which represent an expense to the company because the position must be refilled, layoffs represent a reduction in cost, since these positions are presumably not to be refilled. However, because of their overall impact on the industry, the firm may want to do a separate calculation on the percentage of layoffs. For purposes of this example, terminations are not broken down into voluntary/involuntary categories.

Turnover Report

The following formula has been developed to be used in conjunction with a turnover report. The numbered examples below correspond to the numbers on the report.

EXAMPLE 1: TURNOVER BY QUARTER Divide the number of terminations for the quarter by the average number of employees. Average number of employees is derived by adding the number of employees for the quarter and dividing by 3 to determine the percentage of turnover for that quarter.

Example: 24 terminations in Residential Production divided by 291 average employees for that department = 3.4% turnover in Residential Production for the first quarter.

EXAMPLE 2: TURNOVER ANNUALIZED BY QUARTER   Divide the percentage of turnover for the quarter (according to Example 1 above) by 3 (the number of months in the quarter) to determine the average per month percentage of turnover.

Example: The total percentage of turnover for the second quarter for all departments was 5.2%. This figure divided by 3 equals 1.7%.

Multiply the average per month percent of turnover by 12 to derive the annualized percentage of turnover for the quarter.

Example: 1.7% × 12 = 20.8%

EXAMPLE 3: YEAR-TO-DATE TURNOVER   Add the average number of employees for each quarter and divide by the number of quarters to derive the year-to-date number of employees.

Example: 579 (first quarter) + 598 (second quarter) = 1,177 employees for the first two quarters. 1,177 divided by 2 equals 588.

Add the number of terminations for each quarter to derive the year-to-date number of terminations.

Example: 24 (first quarter) + 31 (second quarter) = 55 terminations for the first two quarters.

Divide the year-to-date number of terminations by the year-to-date average number of employees to derive the year-to-date percentage of turnover.

Example: 55 (terminations for the first two quarters) divided by 588 (year-to-date average number of employees) = 9.35% (year-to-date percentage of turnover).

Divide year-to-date percentage of turnover by six (number of months in first two quarters).

Example: 9.35% divided by 6 = 1.56% (annualized quarterly turnover).

Multiply annualized quarterly turnover by 12 to derive annualized yearly turnover.

Example: 1.56% × 12 = 18.7%

EXAMPLE 4: ANNUALIZED YEAR-TO-DATE TURNOVER   Divide the year-to-date percentage of turnover by the number of months included to derive the year-to-date average monthly turnover.

Example: 16.1% (year-to-date percentage of turnover for the first three quarters) divided by 9 (number of months for first three quarters) = 1.8% (year-to-date average monthly turnover).

Multiply the year-to-date average monthly turnover by 12 to derive the annualized year-to- date percentage of turnover.

Example: 1.8% (year-to-date average monthly turnover) by 12 = 21.6% (annualized year-to-date percentage of turnover).

EXAMPLE 5: YEAR-END TURNOVER   Divide the total average number of employees for each quarter by 4 (number of quarters in the year) to derive the average number of employees for the year.

Example: 2,373 (total average number of employees for 4 quarters) divided by 4 = 593 (average number of employees for year).

Divide the total number of terminations for the year by the average number of employees for the year to derive the percentage of year-end turnover.

Example: 114 (total number of terminations for the year) divided by 593 (average number of employees for the year) = 19.2% (percentage of turnover for the year).

Note
_____

This Department of Labor table will save you time in computing hours worked and overtime.

COEFFICIENT TABLE FOR COMPUTING EXTRA HALF-TIME FOR OVERTIME

This table may be used for computing overtime on piecework, bonuses, commissions or fixed salaries for varying hours. Refer to Part 778 of Title 29 of the CFR for guidance regarding when the coefficient method is applicable.

This form has been prepared for use by employers who may find the coefficient table to be a time saver when computing the extra half time for hours worked over 40 in a workweek.

Hours	Even	1/4	1/2	3/4	1/10	2/10	3/10	4/10	6/10	7/10	8/10	9/10
40		0.003	0.006	0.009	0.0012	0.0025	0.0037	0.0049	0.0074	0.0086	0.0098	0.0110
41	0.012	.015	.018	.021	.0134	.0146	.0157	.0169	.0192	.0204	.0215	.0227
42	.024	.027	.029	.032	.0249	.0261	.0272	.0283	.0305	.0316	.0327	.0338
43	.035	.038	.040	.043	.0360	.0370	.0381	.0392	.0413	.0423	.0434	.0444
44	.045	.048	.051	.053	.0465	.0475	.0485	.0495	.0516	.0526	.0536	.0546
45	.056	.058	.060	.063	.0565	.0575	.0585	.0595	.0614	.0624	.0633	.0643
46	.065	.068	.070	.072	.0662	.0671	.0680	.0690	.0708	.0717	.0726	.0736
47	.074	.077	.079	.081	.0754	.0763	.0772	.0781	.0798	.0807	.0816	.0825
48	.083	.085	.088	.090	.0842	.0851	.0859	.0868	.0885	.0893	.0902	.0910
49	.092	.094	.096	.098	.0927	.0935	.0943	.0951	.0968	.0976	.0984	.0992
50	.100	.102	.104	.106	.1008	.1016	.1024	.1032	.1047	.1055	.1063	.1071
51	.108	.110	.112	.114	.1086	.1094	.1101	.1109	.1124	.1132	.1139	.1146
52	.115	.117	.119	.121	.1161	.1169	.1176	.1183	.1198	.1205	.1212	.1219
53	.123	.124	.126	.128	.1234	.1241	.1248	.1255	.1269	.1276	.1283	.1289
54	.130	.131	.133	.135	.1303	.1310	.1317	.1324	.1337	.1344	.1350	.1357
55	.136	.138	.140	.141	.1370	.1377	.1383	.1390	.1403	.1409	.1416	.1422
56	.143	.144	.146	.148	.1435	.1441	.1448	.1454	.1466	.1473	.1479	.1485
57	.149	.151	.152	.154	.1497	.1503	.1510	.1516	.1528	.1534	.1540	.1546
58	.155	.157	.158	.160	.1558	.1564	.1569	.1575	.1587	.1593	.1599	.1604
59	.161	.162	.164	.165	.1616	.1622	.1627	.1633	.1644	.1650	.1656	.1661
60	.167	.168	.169	.171	.1672	.1678	.1683	.1689	.1700	.1705	.1711	.1716
61	.172	.173	.175	.176	.1727	.1732	.1737	.1743	.1753	.1759	.1764	.1769
62	.177	.179	.180	.181	.1779	.1785	.1790	.1795	.1805	.1810	.1815	.1820
63	.183	.184	.185	.186	.1830	.1835	.1840	.1845	.1855	.1860	.1865	.1870
64	.188	.189	.190	.191	.1880	.1885	.1890	.1894	.1904	.1909	.1914	.1918
65	.192	.193	.195	.196	.1928	.1933	.1937	.1942	.1951	.1956	.1960	.1965
66	.197	.198	.199	.200	.1974	.1979	.1983	.1988	.1997	.2001	.2006	.2010
67	.201	.203	.204	.205	.2019	.2024	.2028	.2033	.2041	.2046	.2050	.2054
68	.206	.207	.208	.209	.2063	.2067	.2072	.2076	.2085	.2089	.2093	.2097
69	.210	.211	.212	.213	.2106	.2110	.2114	.2118	.2126	.2131	.2135	.2139
70	.214	.215	.216	.217	.2147	.2151	.2155	.2159	.2167	.2171	.2175	.2179
71	.218	.219	.220	.221	.2187	.2191	.2195	.2199	.2207	.2211	.2214	.2218
72	.222	.223	.224	.225	.2226	.2230	.2234	.2238	.2245	.2249	.2253	.2257
73	.226	.227	.228	.229	.2264	.2268	.2271	.2275	.2283	.2286	.2290	.2294
74	.230	.231	.232	.232	.2301	.2305	.2308	.2312	.2319	.2323	.2326	.2330
75	.233	.234	.235	.236	.2337	.2340	.2344	.2347	.2354	.2358	.2361	.2365
76	.237	.238	.239	.239	.2372	.2375	.2379	.2382	.2389	.2392	.2396	.2399
77	.240	.241	.242	.243	.2406	.2409	.2413	.2416	.2423	.2426	.2429	.2433
78	.244	.244	.245	.246	.2439	.2442	.2446	.2449	.2455	.2459	.2462	.2465
79	.247	.248	.249	.249	.2472	.2475	.2478	.2481	.2487	.2491	.2494	.2497
80	.250	.251	.252	.252	.2503	.2506	.2509	.2512	.2519	.2522	.2525	.2528
81	.253	.254	.255	.255	.2534	.2537	.2540	.2543	.2549	.2552	.2555	.2558
82	.256	.257	.257	.258	.2564	.2567	.2570	.2573	.2579	.2582	.2585	.2587
83	.259	.260	.261	.261	.2593	.2596	.2599	.2602	.2608	.2611	.2613	.2616
84	.262	.263	.263	.264	.2622	.2625	.2628	.2630	.2636	.2639	.2642	.2644
85	.265	.265	.266	.267	.2650	.2653	.2655	.2658	.2664	.2666	.2669	.2672

TO CONVERT INTO WEEKLY EQUIVALENT: Multiply SEMIMONTHLY salary by 0.4615; MONTHLY salary by 0.2308; ANNUAL salary by 0.01923.

TO CONVERT INTO STRAIGHT-TIME HOURLY EQUIVALENT FOR 40 HOURS: Multiply WEEKLY salary by 0.025; SEMIMONTHLY by 0.01154; MONTHLY salary by 0.00577; ANNUAL by 0.00048.

TO CONVERT INTO TIME AND ONE-HALF HOURLY RATE BASED ON 40 HOUR WEEK: Multiply WEEKLY salary by 0.0375; SEMIMONTHLY by 0.0173; MONTHLY salary by 0.00866; ANNUAL by 0.000721.

CAUTION: Be sure straight-time earnings are not below legal minimum.

INSTRUCTIONS

<u>General.</u> In determining the extra half-time that is due for overtime pay after 40 hours, the method of calculation commonly used is to divide the straight-time earnings by the total number of hours worked and multiply the result by the number of overtime hours divided by two. For instance, the

Computation for 48 hours would be $\dfrac{Earnings}{48} \times \dfrac{8}{2}$; for 50 hours, $\dfrac{Earnings}{50} \times \dfrac{10}{2}$; for 47 ¾ hours,

$\dfrac{Earnings}{47 ¾} \times \dfrac{7 ¾}{2}$. The table on the reverse side contains the decimal equivalents of the fraction,

$\dfrac{O.T. \ Hours}{Total \ Hr. \ X \ 2.}$

For example, the decimal for 48 hours is $\dfrac{8}{48 \times 2} = \dfrac{1}{12} = .083$; for 50 hours it is $\dfrac{10}{50 \times 2} = \dfrac{1}{10} = .1$;

and for 47 ¾ hours $\dfrac{7 ¾}{47 ¾ \times 2} = \dfrac{7.75}{95.5} = .081.$

<u>How to use:</u> (a) Multiply the straight-time earnings for an overtime week by the applicable decimal and the result will be the extra half-time due. Thus, by using the decimals in the table (on the reverse side) the computations performed are, in effect, exactly the same as if the equivalent fractions were used, with the advantage of having eliminated the long division necessitated by the fractions. For example:

    (1). A pieceworker earns varying wages each week. In a 43 9/10 hour week he earned $153.65 straight-time. The coefficient for 43 9/10 hours is .0444. .0444 X $153.65 = $6.82, additional half-time due. $153.65 + $6.82 = $160.47, the pieceworker's total pay for the week.

    (2). Jones is paid a weekly salary of $180.25. He worked 51½ hours. The coefficient for 51½ hours is .112. .112 X $180.25 = $20.19. $180.25 + $20.19 = $200.44, Jones total pay for the week.

(b) The decimal table can also be used effectively when back wages are due because of additions to wages (such as a weekly bonus) that were not included in the regular rate in computing overtime. For example:

    (1). An employee worked 48 hours and received a production bonus of $9.60 which was not included in the regular rate. Thus, $9.60 X .083 = $0.80, the additional half-time due on the bonus.

    (2). Jones in the same week (example (a), (2) above) received a production bonus of $25.00. .112 X $25.00 = $2.80, the additional half-time due on the bonus. $180.25 + $20.19 + $25.00 + $2.80 = $228.24, Jones' total earnings. A further short-cut (combining (a), (2), and (b), (2)) would be: $180.25 + $25.00 = $205.25 X .112 = $22.99 + $205.25 = $228.24, Jones' total earnings.

(c) <u>Short-cuts For Computing Back Wages.</u> When both the overtime hours and the earnings vary, individual weekly computations must be made. However, if an employee is paid at a constant hourly rate, time can be saved by adding the unpaid overtime hours during the period and multiplying the total by one-half the hourly rate. When the weekly hours vary and the straight-time earnings are constant, add the decimals for the overtime weeks and multiply the total by the earnings for 1 week. When the weekly hours are constant but the earnings vary, add the earnings for the overtime weeks and multiply the total by the decimal for 1 week. For example:

VARYING HOURS—CONSTANT EARNINGS			CONSTANT HOURS—VARYING EARNINGS	
Hours	**Decimal**	**Earnings**	**Hours**	**Earnings**
42	0.024	$180.25	47	$164.50
43	.035	180.25	47	159.80
46	.065	180.25	47	162.15
	.124 x $180.25 = $22.35		$486.45 x .074 = $36.00	

AUDITING THE HR FUNCTION

In order to ensure that you have the major elements of the Human Resources function in place and in compliance with state and federal regulations, you may need to complete an HR practices audit. This is the most effective way to ensure compliance with legal standards and government regulations and provides an opportunity to view personnel practices. The following checklist for an HR audit will help you ask some meaningful questions in reviewing your HR function. It is not an all-inclusive audit list but will raise significant issues that your organization should review on a regular basis.

_____ Review all of the federal regulations, state EEO laws and record retention requirements in this book on pages 106–119, 185–188, and 190–195 for compliance.

_____ Review current policies, procedures and your employee handbook to ensure they comply with all federal and state regulations. Have an attorney review them in light of current laws and court cases.

_____ How are applicants handled. Do all applicants receive a response. What is the applicant flow process. How are job offers made. Verbally or in writing. Review any letters that go to applicants and to new hires to ensure they do not unintentionally commit the company to actions or benefits that are not intended.

_____ Look into the procedures for handling recruiting and interviewing. Have interviewers been trained so they know how to conduct interviews legally. Is there a procedure for encouraging current employees to apply for open positions.

_____ How does the new employee orientation work. Is there sufficient time given to ensuring new employees know company policies and procedures and how their department operates. Have all employees completed the proper forms and have they signed the "employment-at-will" form. Does the company have a 90-day Introductory Period. Do not use the term "Probationary Period."

_____ Review all forms used in the human resources function. Make sure they are up-to-date and that they do not commit the company to elements of employment that are not intended.

_____ Take an in-depth look at your compensation program. Do you have a formal program and is it working to the benefit of both the company and your employees. You should have formal job descriptions, a specific job evaluation plan and established salary ranges that are competitive and enable you to retain your best employees at all levels of the organization.

_____ Review all of your benefit programs. Are they working both for the company and for employees. Do an age-based analysis to target your benefits to the broad base of employees. For example, if your employee base is older, you may want to provide more retirement benefits than with a primarily younger workforce who may want more immediate benefits such as child care vouchers, etc.

_____ How does the company ensure that all benefits reporting requirements like the federal 5500's are completed correctly and on time. If you have a 401(k) is it being effectively administered and are documents including plan loans and rollovers being completed correctly and timely.

_____ Does the company issue an annual benefits statement for employees and do you hold annual benefits meetings with all employees. How are open enrollments handled. What type and how many complaints do you receive from employees regarding administrative problems. How quickly and effectively does your human resources department respond.

_____ What formal employee complaint procedures are in effect and how are they managed. Does the company have discipline and discharge procedures and are managers trained on how to handle these important issues.

_____ How are Unemployment Compensation and Worker's Compensation issues managed. Are appropriate procedures in place and is reporting regularly monitored.

_____ What safety policies and procedures are in place. Who is responsible for safety and for accident reporting.

_____ Does the company have an affirmative action program. Are you a government contractor. Are there pending EEO charges against the company. If so, who is handling them.

_____ What type of training is currently being done. Is it done inside or outside of the company. Is there training for all employee levels. Is more training needed. Do you have a tuition refund program. If so, is it working effectively to help retain your best employees.

_____ How are personnel files maintained. Do you have specific procedures for handling and storing personnel files. You should maintain personnel files and benefit files separately. Who has access to personnel files and benefit files. Access should be kept on a "need to know" basis. Be aware of privacy issues.

3

REGULATORY COMPLIANCE

- Key Federal Statutes Affecting Employment, Termination, EEO, Compensation, and Benefits
- Fair Labor Standards Act (FLSA)
- Federal Guidelines on Affirmative Action
- Affirmative Action Plans
- Drug-Free Workplace Act of 1988
- Making the Decision About Having a Drug and Alcohol Testing Policy
- Drug and Alcohol Testing
- Employee Polygraph Protection Act
- What to Do When a Wage-Hour Investigator Calls to Announce a Visit
- Do You Use Independent Contractors? The IRS May Not Think So
- What You Need to Know About the Consolidated Omnibus Budget Reconciliation Act (COBRA)
- Employers Who Have Medical Plans Must Provide Notice of COBRA Amendments
- Posters Required by Federal Statute
- Termination Requirements by State
- State by State Analysis of EEO Laws
- Complying with the Immigration Reform and Control Act of 1986
- The Objective of Workers' Compensation
- What to Do About Workers' Comp Costs
- Worker's Comp Checklist
- Unemployment Compensation
- Personal Privacy and Employee Rights
- ADA Compliance Checklist and Sample Accommodation Letter
- Family and Medical Leave Act and Certification Form
- What You Should Know About an Employee Returning to Work Under the Family Medical Leave Act

REGULATORY COMPLIANCE

Today every organization has to be concerned with federal and state regulatory compliance in the area of personnel administration and human resource management. Since the 1980s the federal administrations have been strongly pro-business, but there have also been more new laws affecting business than at any other time in our history.

All this legislation regulates how we do business, how we and our employees are taxed, how we manage employees, what benefits we must provide, and how long we must provide them. Federal legislation is sometimes difficult to find out about and to understand. Many small business owners don't even know exactly what laws pertain to them, or where to go to get valid information.

The list that follows provides an easy-to-read non-"legalese" list of key federal regulations that pertain to the hiring, managing, and termination of employees. It is not a complete list because nearly every month new legislation is passed that impacts how we do business.

Complying with federal regulations is not easy. Furthermore, it can be expensive and time-consuming. Most business people need help at one time or another from attorneys or consultants who have background and experience in human resource management.

KEY FEDERAL STATUTES AFFECTING EMPLOYMENT, TERMINATION, EEO, COMPENSATION, AND BENEFITS

Following is a brief overview of key regulations that relate to the human resource management function.

Title VII of the Civil Rights Act of 1964, Including Equal Employment Opportunity Act of 1972

Prohibits job discrimination based on race, color, religion, sex, national origin, age, and handicap pertaining to hiring, promotion, demotion, transfer, layoff, termination, compensation and benefits, and selection for training for those individuals in protected classes. Protected classes are defined as individuals over age 40, females, Black, Hispanic (Latin American, Mexican, Puerto Rican), Asian, Pacific Islander, Oriental, American Indian, Native American, and Alaskan Native.

1980 Sexual Harassment Guidelines Were Added to Title VII of the Civil Rights Act

Prohibits harassment and provides that an employer is responsible for the acts of its agents and supervisory employees with respect to sexual harassment

Executive Orders 11246, 11375, 11141, and 12067; Title 41 of Code of Federal Registry; Section 503 of the Rehabilitation Act of 1973

Pertains to federal government employees, federal contractors and subcontractors. Provides equal opportunity to all qualified persons; prohibits discrimination based on race, creed, color, national origin, handicap, sex and age; and other equal employment opportunity guidelines.

Age Discrimination in Employment Act of 1967, Amended in 1978 and 1986 (ADEA)

Prohibits job discrimination based on age for individuals over age 40, regarding hiring, promotion, demotion, transfer, layoff, termination, compensation, and benefits,

Section 402 of the Vietnam Era Veterans Readjustment Assistance Act of 1974

Section 402 relates to the Vietnam veteran's equal employment opportunity. It requires affirmative action in hiring qualified Vietnam Era vets for government contractors with contracts of $10,000 or more.

Immigration Reform and Control Act of 1986

Prohibits hiring of individuals who are not legal residents of the U.S. or who do not have legal certification to be employed in the U.S. Requires proof of citizenship.

Freedom of Information and Privacy Act of 1974

Applies to most federal government agencies as well as private businesses and state and local governments which contract with federal agencies. Provides certain safeguards for an individual against an invasion of privacy. Pertains to required record keeping, and access to and disclosure of records.

Fair Labor Standards Act of 1938, Amended in 1966 (FLSA)

Wage and hour law. Establishes minimum wage, maximum hours, overtime pay, equal pay, and child labor standards, unless an exemption applies (for example, for executives, administrative staff, salespersons, and others).

Equal Pay Act of 1963 (Amendment to Fair Labor Standards Act)

Provides for equal pay for females and males for work of an equal skill, effort, and responsibility, and performed under similar working conditions (excludes differences based upon longevity, merit, production, or any basis other than sex).

Rehabilitation Act of 1973

Designed to promote the employment of people with handicaps by banning discrimination.

Pregnancy Discrimination Act of 1978

Establishes the eligibility for pregnancy-related benefits, including health insurance, disability income plans, and leaves of absence, on equal terms with other disabilities.

Employee Retirement Income Security Act of 1974 (ERISA)

Provides standards for employers' funding and vesting of employee benefits and pension plans.

Health Maintenance Organization Act of 1973 (HMO)

Provides for health maintenance organizations (HMOs) in the U.S. There are now 120 qualified HMOs in the U.S.

HMO Act Amendments

In 1988, the HMO Act had its first significant amendments affecting employer-HMO relationships since initial passage. These amendments affect only federally qualified HMOs. The amendments include: nondiscriminatory employer contributions, a new rate setting method, disclosure of calculations, a self-referral option, and repeal of dual choice in 1995.

Omnibus Budget Reconciliation Act of 1986

Pertains to pension participation and taxation.

Consolidated Omnibus Budget Reconciliation Act of 1986 (COBRA)

Covers continuation of health and dental insurance benefits to employees and their dependents at group rates upon the employees' termination from an employer, if employee pays premiums.

Occupational Safety and Health Act of 1970 (OSHA)

Pertains to providing a safe and healthy workplace, and provides guidelines to follow and forms that must be completed when an accident occurs. In addition, under new Hazard Communication Standards, OSHA requires every workplace in the country to identify and list hazardous substances on the premises and train employees how to use them.

Tax Reform Act of 1986

Revision of the U.S. tax law. Changes the way benefits are taxed and the levels at which workers and employers are taxed. The Act contains changes to compensation and benefit provisions of the Internal Revenue Code.

Technical and Miscellaneous Revenue Act

Provides corrections and changes to the Tax Reform Act of 1986. Contains numerous changes to compensation and benefit provisions of the Internal Revenue Code. Reduced the penalty for violation of COBRA among other things. There are revisions in the area of healthcare, cafeteria plans, dependent care, and educational assistance.

Worker Adjustment and Retraining Notification Act

Requires employers of 100 or more full-time workers to give 60 days' advance notice of closings or major layoffs. Became effective February 4, 1989. Impacts employers who are closing a facility or an operating unit with 50 or more workers, or who will lay off from 50 to 499 employees.

Polygraph Protection Act

In 1988, Congress passed the Employee Polygraph Protection Act which prohibits most private employers from using lie detector examinations either for pre-employment screening or for screening during the course of a worker's employment.

The Americans with Disabilities Act of 1990

The legislation prohibits employment discrimination of the disabled by businesses with fifteen or more employees (although the limit is actually twenty-five employees for two years). The Bill guarantees 43 million disabled Americans, including AIDS victims, rights to employment, transportation, and the use of restaurants and other businesses.

Drug-Free Workplace Act of 1988

Relates to federal contractors with contracts of $25,000 or more, mandating they provide a drug-free workplace. Contractor must post notices and establish an awareness program.

Resource Conservation and Recovery Act (RCRA)

Provides regulations and guidelines for all businesses in the U.S. regarding the handling of hazardous waste. Oversight of this Act is conducted by the Environmental Protection Agency (EPA). The EPA now requires organizations generating even small quantities of hazardous waste to train all workers to be thoroughly familiar with waste handling and emergency procedures.

Trade and Competitiveness Act of 1988

Provides programs to companies and their workers to help industries hurt by foreign competition to retrain their workers through the Job Training Partnership Act.

Family and Medical Leave Act of 1993

The Family and Medical Leave Act of 1993 (FMLA) provides up to 12 weeks of leave for the care of a newborn or newly adopted child, or for personal or family illness, with the guarantee of their regular or an equivalent job upon return to work. To be eligible, employees must be employed for at least 12 months, and have provided 1,250 hours of service during the 12 months before the leave is requested. An employee must first use any accumulated sick leave and vacation time when taking FMLA. The balance of the time after the employee uses all sick leave and vacation time will be unpaid. The total amount of this leave can be only 12 weeks. A FMLA Leave of Absence Form must be completed and approved. The Company should pay their portion of the employee's medical benefits while an employee is on an approved FMLA.

Small Business Job Protection Act of 1996

The Small Business Job Protection Act (SBJPA) became law on August 20, 1996. This law increased the minimum wage to $4.75 per hour October 1, 1996 and to $5.15 per hour September 1, 1997. The Act also contains a number of provisions that affect the administration and design of benefit plans. Major changes:

- Allow tax-exempt non governmental employers to offer 401(k) plans.
- Reinstate the tax exclusion for employer-provided educational assistance.
- Make available a $5,000 tax credit for qualified adoption expenses, or a $5,000 income exclusion for employer-reimbursed adoption expenses.
- Modify the rules for determining whether a worker is an employee or independent contractor for employment tax purposes.

Health Insurance Portability and Accountability Act of 1996

The changes made by the Health Insurance Portability and Accountability Act (HIPAA) are generally effective for plan years beginning after June 30, 1997. The new law applies equally to insured and self-insured employer group health plans, as well as to HMOs offered by employers. State and local government plans may elect to have certain provisions of the Act not apply to them.

The following provisions of the Act have the greatest impact on employers:

- Restrictions on basing eligibility or premiums on health-related factors.
- Restrictions on the duration of preexisting condition exclusions.
- Requirement that employers and insurance companies provide certification of coverage periods.
- Guaranteed availability and renewability of health coverage.
- Expansion of COBRA health care continuation coverage.
- Favorable tax treatment of long-term care insurance and accelerated death benefits.
- Phase out of the loan interest deduction for corporate-owned life insurance.

The Personal Liability and Work Opportunity Act of 1996 (Welfare Reform)

This Act includes a number of changes that tighten the Earned Income Tax Credit. Employers who take a tax credit for hiring a person off welfare must comply with the tax provisions of this regulation. In addition, the Act requires a mandatory new hire reporting program effective October 1, 1997.

The Newborns' and Mothers' Health Protection Act of 1996

This Act is effective January 1, 1998, and covers any employer that has a group health plan either insured or self-insured. The Act prohibits group health plans from restricting hospital stays for childbirth to less than a 48-hour minimum stay for a normal delivery and a 96-hour stay for a cesarean delivery. In addition, the plan may not require prior authorization to qualify for the 48 or 96-hour minimum stay.

The Mental Health Parity Act of 1996

This Act is effective January 1, 1998, and covers employers with 50 or more employees. The new parity requirement applies to benefits furnished on or after September 30, 2001. The Act provides that group health plans that offer mental health coverage may not set annual or lifetime limits for mental health coverage that are more restrictive than those for medical and surgical coverage.

State Laws

State laws cover virtually all of the above areas, plus:

WORKERS' COMPENSATION ACTS Provide workers' compensation benefits for job-related injuries, death, and disease, regardless of whether the employer or employee was at fault. Benefits provided through insurance paid for and provided by the employer. Employee gives up the right to sue the employer in turn for compensation through the employer-provided insurance.

EMPLOYMENT SECURITY ACTS   Provide for payment of unemployment compensation to individuals who have been separated from their jobs due to no fault of their own.

Labor Relations Laws

COMMON LAW AFFECTING EMPLOYMENT
Employment-at-Will
Wrongful Discharge
Constructive Discharge

Important

If you have more questions about these laws or you are contacted by a federal agency regarding an investigation you should retain an attorney versed in the specific law under which you are being investigated.

[handwritten note: COMPLY TO Law That is "MOST" Burdensome]

FAIR LABOR STANDARDS ACT (FLSA)

The Fair Labor Standards Act (FLSA) was originally enacted by Congress in 1938. Its basic intent was to ensure that the number of jobs paying a minimum wage made maximum use of the available labor force. The minimum wage on October 1, 1996 was $4.75 per hour; on September 1, 1997 it increases to $5.15 per hour. The Act sets forth legal standards concerning minimum wages, hours of work, overtime pay, equal pay, use of child labor, and record keeping that must be complied with by those employers covered by the Act. To create the needed incentive for employers to hire a maximum number of employees, Congress established an employer penalty for working employees more than the established 40 hour work week by adding the requirement that an overtime premium rate must be paid above the 40 hours worked in any week. We should note that there is overlapping jurisdiction between the federal and various state wage and hour laws. In order to comply with both laws an employer needs to comply with whichever law is most burdensome to it. For example, if the state minimum wage is $3.50 per hour and the federal minimum wage is $5.15 per hour, an employer covered by both laws must pay $5.15 per hour in order to comply with both laws. Likewise, if the state law requires payment of time and one-half after 8 hours in a day (which is the case in California), while the federal law requires time and one-half after 8 hours, assuming the employer was covered by both laws. Again, whichever law is the most burdensome to an employer is the law that must be adhered to. Check your State's overtime regulations.

The FLSA is administered and enforced by the Department of Labor, Wage and Hour Division of the Employment Standards Administration through its 10 regions. Each region has area offices in most metropolitan locations where claims are received, investigated, hearings conducted, and determinations made. Regional offices coordinate regulatory matters with the division concerning rules, regulations, and interpretations of the Act. Typically, it is the area office that conducts periodic audits of employer payroll records to determine compliance with the Act, and such audits can be either scheduled activities of a routine nature or in response to an industry or employer pattern of complaints by employees.

Complaints can be registered, and claims filed, by employees within two years from the date an event covered by the Act occurred. This statute of limitation can be extended to three years in cases where it can be demonstrated that the employer's action was a willful violation of the Act, meaning that the employer knew about the law but chose to ignore it for the purpose of imposing a detrimental effect on the employee (e.g., refusal to pay overtime wages due the employee). Where the employer is found to have unwittingly violated or otherwise not complied with the provisions of the Act, a hearing or investigative officer will normally only require that the employer pay whatever is due the employee, and may additionally impose a small fine on the employer for the violation. However, wage claims that are lost by employers in court often carry the costs of back pay, liquidated damages (equal to the amount of back pay), and attorney fees.

Who Is Covered Under FLSA?

The original Act was made to apply to private and nonprofit sector employers and their employees. However, amendments brought employees of hospitals, nursing homes, public schools, and local transit operations within the minimum wage and overtime provisions of the FLSA, and in 1985 the U.S. Supreme Court decision brought all public employees under coverage of the Act. While some of these various employees have special conditions in their application to the FLSA, it has now become easier to designate who is *not* covered than those who are. Those who are *not* covered by the FLSA are:

- Boards of Directors
- Legal Advisors
- Independent contractors
- Bona Fide Volunteers

- Elected Officials
- Official's Staff Members
- Political Appointees
- Prison Laborers

Every other employed person is covered by the Act as either exempt or nonexempt, meaning they are ineligible for overtime pay if classified as exempt or eligible if nonexempt. A third category is those employees who have special conditions associated with their employment wages and hours. Fundamentally then, every covered employee should fall into one of these three categories:

EXEMPT EMPLOYEES	NONEXEMPT EMPLOYEES	SPECIAL CONDITION EMPLOYEES
• Executive	• Hourly	• Law Enforcement
• Administrative	• Piecework	• Fire Fighters
• Professional		• School Personnel
• Outside Sales (Commissioned)		• Hospital and Nursing Home Staff
• Seasonal Recreation Employees		

Which Jobs Are Exempt or Nonexempt?

The easiest way to determine which jobs are either exempt or nonexempt is to first establish which jobs in your organization are exempt in accordance with *both* federal and state definitions. Why? Because there are going to be fewer exempt jobs in any organization compared to the number of nonexempt jobs. Such was the intent of Congress based on their original goal of enticing employers to hire as many workers as their payrolls could absorb. To achieve that end, the criteria for employees considered exempt from the overtime provisions had to be limited. That defined limitation came in the form of two independent tests, one or the other of which must be used by employers to determine whether or not a specific job is exempt or nonexempt.

These tests are referred to as the "long and short tests." The long test provides detail on the job's duties, responsibilities, authorities, obligations, and minimum *salary*. The long test also measures the employee's duties on a weekly basis; therefore the determination of exempt or nonexempt status can likewise be seen as a weekly event. Conversely, the short test requires fewer conditions associated with the employee's duties and responsibilities, but requires a higher minimum salary for the employee to be considered exempt. Moreover, under the short test employees do not lose their exemption if they perform nonexempt work in some weeks as long as their work overall is exempt. The following excerpt from the exempt definitions contained in 29 C.F.R. Part 541 should help you make determinations of which of your jobs, and therefore employees, are exempt. All other employees will thereby be nonexempt unless they meet other exempt or special conditions, which may require more than cursory research on your part. In any case, you should bear in mind that it is the job contents and conditions that determine its exempt or nonexempt status, not the employee, the job title, or mere preferences of management.

Executive Employees

An employee who meets *either* the "long test" or the "short test" as specified below is considered exempt.

LONG TEST FOR EXECUTIVE EMPLOYEES   An executive employee must meet *all* of the following requirements in order to he exempt from the FLSA minimum wage and overtime provisions:

1. *Duties:* Primarily management of the agency, department, or subdivision.
2. *Supervision:* Customarily and regularly directs two or more other employees.
3. *Authority:* Possesses the power to hire or fire employees, or whose suggestions are given substantial weight in such decisions, including promotions.
4. *Discretion:* Customarily and regularly exercises discretionary power.
5. *Work Responsibility:* Does not devote more than 20 percent of his or her hours in a workweek to the performance of activities not closely related to items (1) through (4).
6. *Compensation:* Is paid not less than $155 per week exclusive of board, lodging, or other facilities.

SHORT TEST FOR EXECUTIVE EMPLOYEES An executive must meet *all* of the following requirements to he exempt:

1. *Compensation:* Is paid not less than $250 per week exclusive of board, lodging, or other facilities.
2. *Duties:* Primarily management of the agency, department, or subdivision.
3. *Supervision:* Customarily and regularly directs 2 or more other employees.

DEFINING AN EXECUTIVE EMPLOYEE The regulations provide some guidance as to the application of the executive exemption test. For example, managerial and supervisory functions are described in the following manner:

Interviewing, selecting, and training of employees; setting and adjusting their rates of pay and hours of work; directing their work; maintaining their production or sales records for use in supervision or control; appraising their productivity and efficiency for the purpose of recommending promotions or other changes in their status; handling their complaints and grievances and disciplining them when necessary; planning the work; determining the techniques to be used; apportioning the work among the workers; determining the type of materials, supplies, machinery or tools to he used or merchandise to he bought, stocked, and sold; controlling the flow and distribution of materials or merchandise and supplies; providing for the safety of the men and the property.

The "primary duty" requirement for management is generally, though not always, a 50 percent test. In some cases, the employee can therefore spend less than 50 percent of his or her time on management and still qualify for the executive exemption.

The words "customarily and regularly" regarding the exercise of discretion signify a greater frequency than occasional, but less than constant.

Administrative Employees

An employee who meets *either* the "long test" or the "short test" for administrators is exempt.

LONG TEST FOR ADMINISTRATIVE EMPLOYEES An administrative employee must meet *all* of the following requirements in order to be exempt from the FLSA minimum wage and overtime provisions:

1. *Duties:* Primarily consist of either-
   a. non-manual or office work directly related to management policies or general business operations; or
   b. performance of administrative functions in an educational establishment in work related to academic instruction or training.
2. *Discretion:* Customarily and regularly exercises discretion and independent judgment.
3. *Supervision:*
   a. regularly and directly assists a person employed in an executive or administrative capacity; or

    b. performs under only general supervision work requiring special training, experience, or knowledge, or

    c. executes special assignments and tasks under only general supervision.

4. *Work Responsibility:* Does not devote more than 20 percent of work time to activities not directly or closely related to performance of administrative work.

5. *Compensation:* Is paid not less than $155 per week exclusive of board, lodging, or other facilities.

SHORT TEST FOR ADMINISTRATIVE EMPLOYEES An administrative employee must meet *all* of the following requirements to be exempt:

1. *Compensation:* Is paid at least $250 per week exclusive of board, lodging, or other facilities.

2. *Duties:* Primary performance of office or non-manual work directly related to management policies or general business operations, or the performance of functions in the administration of an educational establishment, or a department or subdivision thereof, in work directly related to the academic instruction or training.

3. *Responsibilities:* Primary duty *includes* work requiring the exercise of discretion and independent judgment.

DEFINING AN ADMINISTRATIVE EMPLOYEE The regulations provide some guidance as to the application of the administrative exemption test. For example, the phrase "directly related to management policies or general business operations" can include: advising management, planning, negotiation, representing the organization, consulting, safety direction, wage rate analysis, and systems analysis in computers.

Similar to the executive exemption, the "primary duty" requirement is not necessarily a 50 percent test.

Professional Employees

An employee who meets *either* the "long test" or the "short test" for professionals under the FLSA is exempt.

LONG TEST FOR PROFESSIONAL EMPLOYEES A professional employee must meet *all* of the following requirements to be exempt from the FLSA minimum wage and overtime provisions:

1. *Duties:* Primarily work requiring—

    a. advanced learning acquired by a prolonged course of specialized intellectual instruction as distinguished from general academic education, apprenticeships, or routine training; or

    b. original or creative work depending primarily on invention, imagination, or talent; or

    c. teaching, tutoring, instructing, or lecturing for a school system or educational institution.

2. *Discretion:* Work requiring the consistent exercise of discretion and judgment.

3. *Work Product:* Predominantly intellectual and varied in character and which cannot be standardized in relation to a given period of time.

4. *Work Responsibility:* Must devote not more than 20 percent of his or her hours to activities not essential, part of, or necessarily incident to the work.

5. *Compensation:* Is paid not less than $170 per week exclusive of board, lodging, or other facilities.

Short Test for Professional Employees   A professional employee must meet *all* of the following requirements to be exempt:

1. *Compensation:* Is paid not less than $250 per week exclusive of board, lodging, or other facilities.

2. *Duties:* Primarily consist of performing work requiring advanced learning or work as a teacher.

3. *Discretion:* Must include work that requires the consistent exercise of discretion and judgment or work requiring invention, imagination, or talent in a recognized field of artistic endeavor.

Defining a Professional Employee   The regulations provide some guidance as to the application of the professional exemption test.

The "primary duty" requirement is, by reference, the same as for executives and administrators. Professional work is not purely mechanical or routine, since it involves discretion. "Predominantly intellectual" means that the job is varied and not routine mental, mechanical, manual, or physical work. In order for routine work to be exempt, it should be an essential part of and necessarily incident to the professional work.

Other General Exemptions

There are numerous other general exemptions from the minimum wage and overtime provisions of the FLSA. Employers interested in exploring the prospect of whether or not specific positions in their employ are exempt under these definitions should consult with authoritative legal counsel based on the regulations noted.

- Amusement or recreational establishment employees
- Agricultural employees
- Retail and service establishment
- Certain retail or service establishment employees
- Certain domestic service workers, baby-sitters, and companions
- Outside sales representatives
- Fishing and offshore seafood processing
- Small newspapers and weeklies
- Seamen on foreign vessels

Partial exemptions from only the FLSA overtime provisions—not the minimum wage requirements—have been granted for other occupations, including:

- Employees of interstate motor carriers, railroads, and air carriers
- On-shore seafood processing
- Seamen
- Taxi drivers
- Certain employees of auto dealers
- Movie theater employees
- Certain forestry employees

FEDERAL GUIDELINES ON AFFIRMATIVE ACTION

The following guidelines on Affirmative Action for federal contractors were established by Executive Order 11246.

EXEMPTION:　Companies that do less than $10,000 in business with the federal government per year. Covered employers must:

- refrain from discriminating against any employee or job applicant because of race, color, religion, sex, or national origin;
- take affirmative action to ensure that applicants are employed and employees are treated during their employment without regard to race, color, religion, sex, or national origin (the obligation extends to working conditions and facilities such as restrooms, as well as hiring, firing, promotions, and compensations);
- state in all solicitations or advertisements that all qualified applicants will receive consideration without regard to race, color, religion, sex, or national origin;
- advise each labor union with which they deal of their commitments under the order;
- include the obligations under the order in every subcontract or purchase order, unless specifically exempted;
- comply with all provisions of the order and the rules and regulations issued; furnish all information and reports required; permit access to books, records and accounts for the purpose of investigation to ascertain compliance; and
- file regular compliance reports describing hiring and employment practices.

The mandatory starting point for affirmative action programs is analysis of areas in which the employer may be under utilizing "protected" persons. The employer must consider at least the following factors:

- minority population of the labor area surrounding the facility;
- size of the minority unemployment force in the labor area;
- percentage of minority workforce as compared with the total workforce in the immediate area;

- general availability of minorities having requisite skills in the immediate labor area;

- availability of minorities having requisite skills in an area in which the employer can reasonably recruit;

- availability of promotable minority employees within the employer's organization;

- anticipated expansion, contraction, and turnover in the labor force;

- existence of training institutions capable of training minorities in the requisite skills; and

- degree of training the employer is reasonably able to undertake to make all job classes available to minorities.

SEX-BIASED GUIDELINES: In addition to its affirmative action guidelines, the OFCCP issued a special set of guidelines on sex discrimination. These guidelines prohibit employers from:

- making any distinction based on sex in employment opportunities, wages, hours, and other conditions;

- advertising for workers in newspaper columns headed "male" and "female" unless sex is a bona fide occupational qualification for the job;

- relying on state protective laws to justify denying a female employee the right to any job that she is qualified to perform; and

- denying employment to women with young children or making a distinction between married and unmarried persons, unless the distinctions are applied to both sexes.

The guidelines also specify that covered employers take affirmative action to recruit women to apply for jobs from which they have been previously excluded.

AFFIRMATIVE ACTION PLANS

The intent of affirmative action plans initiated by the federal government has been to accord preferential treatment in recruitment, hiring, promotion and development to groups against whom discrimination might have been practiced in the past. The federal government has applied affirmative action plan standards primarily to organizations that are government contractors, however, all organizations should consider the basics of an affirmative action plan in the recruiting, placement and promotion of employees.

Since the inception of the government's affirmative action policy, its goal has been given various interpretations. For example:

- Changing management attitudes toward underrepresented groups.

- Removing discriminatory obstacles that work to the disadvantage of underrepresented groups.

- Recruiting groups that are underrepresented in the employer's workforce.

- According preferential treatment in hiring and promotion decisions to underrepresented groups.

The most controversial interpretation, and the one that continues to be constantly litigated, is that pertaining to preferential treatment. The controversial nature of the preferential treatment aspects of affirmative action may be judged from major civil court rulings by the United States Supreme Court in 1989. They are: Richmond v. Croson, Price Waterhouse v. Hopkins, Wards Cove Packing v. Atonio and Patterson v. McClean Credit Union. I won't go into the details of these cases, but the rulings have been viewed by some observers as "judicial revisionism" while other people note that "old cases have no degree of finality" and that affirmative action was not intended to last forever, but was intended to jump start the machinery of tolerance and reason, after which the government's heavy hand could be removed.

New law suits can be anticipated, since the court has widened the right to fight affirmative action plans. In fact in 2000, in a decision that threatened hundreds of affirmative action programs in California, the California State Supreme Court ruled that government agencies can no longer limit recruitment efforts to women and minorities. In the State of Washington voters have also struck down preferences in hiring.

For 30 years the American legal system has gone here-and-there-and-everywhere with affirmative action plans and other aspects of anti-discrimination law. The main problem with affirmative action plans is their complexity. In the spirit of trying to simplify the mystique surrounding these plans, I am providing the following guidelines you could follow if you are charged with the responsibility of implementing an affirmative action plan in your organization.

Affirmative action plans contain the following components:

Policy Statement. The heart of an affirmative action plan is the policy statement issued by executive management indicating intent to provide equal opportunity for all persons who apply for employment or who are employed regardless of race, creed, color, gender, national origin or age.

Responsibility. Responsibility for administering the affirmative action plan is delegated to the organization's management group. The Human Resources executive is also responsible for the plan. The major functions of this responsibility include gathering and disseminating information on affirmative action, maintaining internal and external relationships in matters affecting affirmative action, designing, implementing and coordinating the affirmative action plan and maintaining an information system to administer affirmative action plans effectively and in a timely manner.

Communication. The affirmative action plan includes the systematic communication of system plans and procedures to people and agencies within and outside of the organization. Design and use of formal communication channels which serve to enforce the organization's decision on the affirmative action plan.

Workforce Analysis. Another step in developing the system's affirmative action plan is analyzing the composition of the workforce with respect to balance in the number and percentage of minority, and male/female personnel currently employed. The analysis should also include disabled employees in the current workforce. Current employees should be viewed in terms of their levels and position classifications. This step is actually institutional self-evaluation of the extent to which, and the location in which, there are imbalances or discriminatory practices in existing positions within the organizational structure.

Goals and Timetables. This is an important element of the plan for organizations that are government contractors. If the company is not a government contractor management may review and make a decision on the use of goals and timetables. The goals and timetables indicate when and how the company intends to achieve affirmative action goals.

Note
_____

This is the element of an affirmative action plan that draws the most controversy. If your workforce analysis shows that the company has indeed hired and promoted minorities and women in numbers that reflect affirmative action, the goals and timetables may not be as critical as they will be if your company does not have a track record in this area.

Linkage with Human Resources Processes. The human resources processes represent means by which the affirmative action plan is implemented. Plans, policies, and procedures are of little consequence unless minorities and women are recruited, not discriminated against in the selection process, placed in positions where their talents can be utilized, and provided with development opportunities to become highly effective in present positions as well as proficient enough to warrant promotion to positions of greater responsibility and opportunity. These same processes should be in place for people with disabilities.

Plan Control. Like all major business plan, an affirmative action plan must be monitored to determine whether it is proceeding according to plan. Controlling the plan involves developing and maintaining an information system that provides accurate and detailed records on the progress made in achieving hiring and promotion goals. Executive management of the organization has the responsibility of ensuring that the affirmative action plan is developed, implemented and carried out over time in an effective manner.

Here are a few questions that you should be able to answer affirmatively as you review your organization's affirmative action plan.

- Are hiring decisions made without regard to sex, race, national origin, age, or religion, and by using bona fide occupational qualifications?
- Are prerequisites to employment and promotion valid indicators of success in the specific jobs for which they are used?
- Is there a legitimate business necessity for policies that adversely affect certain classes of employees?
- Are questions used in job interviews directly related to the candidate's ability to perform the job.
- Are hiring, promotion, compensation, and job-assignment decisions based on considerations that relate to qualifications, merit, and performance rather than stereotypic assumptions?
- Is pregnancy treated like any other temporary disability in terms of sick leave, seniority, and disability benefits?
- Have reasonable accommodations been made to enable qualified handicapped employees to perform adequately?

- Have precautions been taken to ensure that current practices do not perpetuate the effects of past discrimination?

- Are employment policies and internal grievance procedures well publicized to all employees?

DRUG-FREE WORKPLACE ACT OF 1988

The Drug-Free Workplace Act presented here is a guideline for federal contracts. However, most companies today must consider setting up policies that relate to control of drugs on the job. Referring to the federal regulations will help you write and implement drug control policies for your company.

SEC. 5151. SHORT TITLE.

This subtitle may be cited as the "Drug-Free Workplace Act of 1988."

(41 USC 701)

SEC. 5152. DRUG-FREE WORKPLACE REQUIREMENTS FOR FEDERAL CONTRACTORS.

(a) DRUG-FREE WORKPLACE REQUIREMENT.—

(1) REQUIREMENT FOR PERSONS OTHER THAN INDIVIDUALS.—No person, other than an individual, shall be considered a responsible source, under the meaning of such term as defined in section 4(8) of the Office of Federal Procurement Policy Act (41 U.S.C. 403(8)), for the purposes of being awarded a contract for the procurement of any property or services of a value of $25,000 or more from any Federal agency unless such person has certified to the contracting agency that it will provide a drug-free workplace by—

(A) publishing a statement notifying employees that the unlawful manufacture, distribution, dispensation, possession, or use of a controlled substance is prohibited in the person's workplace and specifying the actions that will be taken against employees for violations of such prohibition;

(B) establishing a drug-free awareness program to inform employees about—

(i) the dangers of drug abuse in the workplace;

(ii) the person's policy of maintaining a drug free workplace;

(iii) any available drug counseling, rehabilitation, and employee assistance programs; and

(iv) the penalties that may be imposed upon employees for drug abuse violations;

(C) making it a requirement that each employee to be engaged in the performance of such contract be given a copy of the statement required by sub-paragraph (A);

(D) notifying the employee in the statement required by sub-paragraph (A), that as a condition of employment on such contract, the employee will—

(i) abide by the terms of the statement; and

(ii) notify the employer of any criminal drug statute conviction for a violation occurring in the workplace no later than 5 days after such conviction;

(E) notifying the contracting agency within 10 days after receiving notice under sub-paragraph (D)(ii) from an employee or otherwise receiving actual notice of such conviction;

(F) imposing a sanction on, or requiring the satisfactory participation in a drug abuse assistance or rehabilitation program by, any employee who is so convicted, as required by section 5154; and

(G) making a good faith effort to continue to maintain a drug-free workplace through implementation of subparagraphs (A), (B), (C), (D), (E), and (F).

(2) REQUIREMENT FOR INDIVIDUALS.—No Federal agency shall enter into a contract with an individual unless such contract includes a certification by the individual that the individual will not engage in the unlawful manufacture, distribution, dispensation, possession, or use of a controlled substance in the performance of the contract.

(b) SUSPENSION, TERMINATION, OR DEBARMENT OF THE CONTRACTOR—

(1) GROUNDS FOR SUSPENSION, TERMINATION, OR DEBARMENT.—Each contract awarded by a Federal agency shall be subject to suspension of payments under the contract or termination of the contract, or both, and the contractor thereunder or the individual who entered the contract with the Federal agency, as applicable, shall be subject to suspension or debarment in accordance with the requirements of this section if the head of the agency determines that—

(A) the contractor or individual has made a false certification under subsection (a);

(B) the contractor violates such certification by failing to carry out the requirements of subparagraph (A), (B), (C), (D), (E), or (F)of subsection (a)(1); or

(C) such a number of employees of such contractor have been convicted of violations of criminal drug statutes for violations occurring in the workplace as to indicate that the contractor has failed to make a good faith effort to provide a drug-free work place as required by subsection (a).

(2) CONDUCT OF SUSPENSION, TERMINATION, AND DEBARMENT PROCEEDINGS.—(A) If a contracting officer determines, in writing, that cause for suspension of payments, termination, or suspension or debarment exists, an appropriate action shall be initiated by a contracting officer of the agency, to be conducted by the agency concerned in accordance with the Federal Acquisition Regulation and applicable agency procedures.

(B) The Federal Acquisition Regulation shall be revised to include rules for conducting suspension and debarment proceedings under this subsection, including rules providing notice, opportunity to respond in writing or in person, and such other procedures as may be necessary to provide a full and fair proceeding to a contractor or individual in such proceeding.

(3) EFFECT OF DEBARMENT.—Upon issuance of any final decision under this subsection requiring debarment of a contractor or individual, such contractor or individual shall be ineligible for award of any contract by any Federal agency, and for par-

ticipation in any future procurement by any Federal agency, for a period specified in the decision, not to exceed 5 years.

MAKING THE DECISION ABOUT HAVING A DRUG AND ALCOHOL TESTING POLICY

The decision to implement a drug and alcohol testing policy is an important one and should be made only after much thought and deliberation. The following material should be thoroughly reviewed by management and by your company attorney as you move toward implementation of such a policy.

DRUG AND ALCOHOL TESTING

The numerous laws and government regulations mandating drug-control policies, as well as the rapidly developing case law on the effect of drug and alcohol testing policies on individual rights, leave employers in an unsettling position with respect to their policies. Whether an employer should develop a workforce drug and alcohol control program depends on a number of variables. Is the employer a private or public employer? Is it a federal contractor, and if so, with what federal agency? Is the workforce covered by a collective bargaining agreement? As a practical matter, is a drug and alcohol testing policy needed, and what impact will it have on both operational efficiencies and employee morale? Should the policy cover only drugs or only alcohol or both? And the list of questions goes on.

Guidelines for Developing a Program

While no uniform drug and alcohol abuse policy can fit all employers, the following guidelines can be tailored to fit your company's specific needs:

1. Demonstrate the need for a testing program.
2. Define the objectives of the testing program:
   - the obligation to maintain a safe workplace;
   - the prevention of potential negligence liability;
   - the basis for discipline; and/or
   - consistency in handling substance-abuse problems.
3. Define the reasons for considering a testing program. Is the desire to implement a testing program a response to an existing problem, or is it intended as a long-term, preventative measure? The reasons for the program may help determine the type of screening needed:
   - pre-employment testing?
   - for cause testing;
   - post-accident testing; and/or
   - random testing.

4. Document the relationship between job performance, health and safety, and drug or alcohol usage. Consider the following factors as they exist in the workplace:

   • What is the nature of the job as it relates to safety risks?

   • Is the level of supervision such that abuse might be detected by a supervisor or is testing the only means of determining fitness for duty?

   • Is there evidence of drug or alcohol usage on the job?

   • Is there a need for a deterrent?

   • Is there a need for confirmation of the supervisor's observations?

5. Develop the organization's drug- and alcohol-abuse policy.

6. State the purpose of the policy.

7. State the policy regarding the use, possession, sale, manufacture, distribution, dispensation and reporting to work with illegal drugs or alcohol in the employee's system.

8. Determine whether the employer is subject to any statutory or regulatory drug-free workplace initiatives or the duty to bargain over a drug and alcohol policy with a labor organization, and consider the other potential legal implications of the policy.

9. State the policy on the relationship between the organization and law enforcement agencies. Will drug-related activities be reported to the police?

10. State the testing policy, including:

    • Who will be screened?

    • When will employees or applicants be subject to testing?

    • What will happen if an employee or an applicant refuses testing?

    • What drugs are to be included in the testing and what are the tests cutoff limits?

    • What will be the policy on the confidentiality of test results?

    • What action will be taken against an employee or job applicant who has confirmed positive test results?

    • Will an Employee Assistance Program (EAP) be implemented to rehabilitate drug or alcohol abusers? Employers have no legal obligation to pay the cost of rehabilitating employees. It may be a good business policy to retain valuable employees where possible, through counseling for drug or alcohol abuse problems.

11. Present the drug and alcohol abuse policy to a competent advisor for review.

12. Conduct management and supervisor training.

13. Inform all employees and job applicants of the organization's drug and alcohol abuse policy.

14. Present the policy in a health and safety context rather than a disciplinary context. Emphasize the objective of the policy is to improve employee health and promote a safer work environment.

15. Distribute a written copy of the policy to all employees. Obtain a signed acknowledgement from all employees that they have read and understand the policy.

16. Include the policy in all future employment contracts.

17. Include appropriate notations in your employment ads.

18. If the policy includes the testing of existing employees, advise employees in advance that testing will be a routine part of their employment as well as a condition of employment.

19. Inform employees of your EAP if you have one.

20. Select a quality vendor of testing services. Considerations should include:
    * Is the laboratory certified?
    * Are scientifically-acceptable testing methods employed?
    * Is a positive test confirmed by an analytically different method?
    * Are quality-control procedures employed?
    * Will the laboratory provide expert testimony?
    * Are proper chain-of-custody forms utilized to protect the integrity of the sample?
    * Are positive specimens retained by the lab, and for how long?
    * Which drugs are included in a drug screen, and what are the detection limits?
    * Are the personnel performing the test qualified?
    * Can the supplier handle a decentralized program with consistent quality?

21. Ensure that at least one responsible HR staff member is familiar with the details of the testing program, including basic laboratory terminology.

22. Implement and enforce the drug and alcohol abuse policy.

23. Ensure that all results of the testing program are included in the employer's existing record protection program and will remain confidential. It is recommended that test results not be maintained in personnel files, because individuals who have no need to know may have access to the personnel files. Accordingly, information on an employee's drug or alcohol problems should only be released on a need-to-know basis.

If you are considering a drug and alcohol control program, you should realize that substance abuse is a complex problem. No action, particularly when it comes to drug and alcohol testing, is entirely guaranteed against legal challenge. On the other hand, companies do have the right to ensure a safe work environment and hire competent workers free from the effects of substance abuse. The issues are complicated, but many companies are taking action to deal with the problem. You should consult with an attorney to explore reasonable ways of implementing methods for reducing or preventing drug and alcohol abuse, including drug and alcohol testing.

EMPLOYEE POLYGRAPH PROTECTION ACT

You are required by law to post a notice about the Employee Polygraph Protection Act on your premises where applicants and employees can see it. Following is a sample of the poster. You can order it from the U. S. Department of Labor, Employment Standards Administration, Wage and Hour Division, Washington, DC 20210.

NOTICE
EMPLOYEE POLYGRAPHY
PROTECTION ACT

The employee Polygraph Protection Act prohibits most private employers from using lie detector tests either for pre-employment screening or during the course of employment.

PROHIBITIONS

Employers are generally prohibited from requiring or requesting any employee or job applicant to take a lie detector test, and from discharging, discipline, or discriminating against an employee or prospective employee for refusing to take a test or for exercising other rights under the ACL.

EXEMPTIONS*

Federal, State and local governments are not affected by the law. Also, the law does not apply to tests given by the Federal Government to certain private individuals engaged in national security related activities.

The Act permits polygraph (a kind of lie detector) tests to be administered in the private sector, subject to restrictions, to certain prospective employees of security service firms (armored car, alarm, and guard), and of pharmaceutical manufacturers, distributors and dispensers.

The Act also permits polygraph testing, subject to restrictions, of certain employees of private firms who are reasonably suspected of involvement in a workplace incident (theft, embezzlement, etc.) that resulted in economic loss to the employer.

EXAMINEE RIGHTS

Where polygraph tests are permitted, they are subject to numerous strict standards concerning the conduct and length of the test. Examinees have a number of specific rights, including the right to a written notice before testing, the right to refuse or discontinue a test, and the right not to have test results disclosed to unauthorized persons.

ENFORCEMENT

The Secretary of Labor may bring court actions to restrain violations and assess civil penalties up to $10,000 against violators. Employers or job applicants may also bring their own court actions.

ADDITIONAL INFORMATION

Additional information may be obtained, and complaints of violations may be filed, at local offices of the Wage and Hour Division, which are listed in the telephone directory under U.S. Government, Department of Labor, Employment Standards Administration.

**THE LAW REQUIRES EMPLOYERS TO DISPLAY THIS POSTER
WHERE EMPLOYEES AND JOB APPLICANTS CAN READILY SEE IT.**

*The law does not preempt any provision of any State or local law or any collective bargaining agreement which is more restrictive with respect to lie detector tests.

U.S. Department of Labor
Employment Standards Administration
Wage and Hour Division
Washington, DC 20210

WHAT TO DO WHEN A WAGE-HOUR INVESTIGATOR CALLS TO ANNOUNCE A VISIT

It doesn't happen very often, and when it does it is usually because an ex-employee has filed a complaint with the Wage-Hour Division of the U.S. Department of Labor. The most frequent complaints are about a company's procedures for payment of overtime.

Most people in companies today understand that the Fair Labor Standards Act requires business to pay overtime to all hourly non-exempt employees at the rate of time-and-one-half for all hours worked in excess of 40 in a week. If you are not doing that you are in violation of the law. There is also a lot of misunderstanding about what constitutes an exempt or non-exempt position. The Fair Labor Standards Act thoroughly covers this issue. There are specific criteria for executive, administrative, professional and outside sales people that you should become familiar with.

When the investigator calls, it is normal procedure to give a few days' notice of the visit and at that time there is usually an indication of what the investigator wants to see. It is usually the time cards for a specific department and for a certain period of time.

It is common for a company to be in violation of the Fair Labor Standards Act at one time or another. The violation is usually unintentional, and occurs because the employer is unfamiliar with the duties or the working hours of a specific employee somewhere in the organization. Another common violation occurs when you don't know the actual hours being worked by all of the employees.

An employee could work a half hour overtime everyday and not record that time on the time card. Everything is fine until the employee gets upset about something, quits, and goes to the Labor Department to complain about not being paid the overtime.

Also, when an investigator from the Labor Department comes to your place of business to investigate a wage claim, he/she will ask to review your Immigration I-9 forms to see if you have a form on every employee and that it is completed correctly. Do not file I-9 forms in the personnel files. File them in a separate file. You can then hand that file to an investigator without providing the full personnel file. Fines can be significant for not having I-9's or not having them properly completed.

Most Wage and Hour Investigators are pleasant people who are just doing their job, but you should assume that they are there for investigative purposes and that normally they do not have your company's welfare foremost in their minds. Investigators are paid to find violations.

Treat the investigator with courtesy and honor all reasonable requests. Indicate you have nothing to hide, and it is your desire to comply with the Act. Do not, however, volunteer any documents or information that is not specifically requested. It's not in your best interest to help the investigator support conclusions that may be detrimental to your business. The authority of the Wage and Hour Division is very broad however, and no useful purpose can be served by objecting to the investigator viewing or copying any data which is relevant to the payment of wages including overtime or the proper completion of Immigration I-9 forms. Once again, only provide data the investigator asks for, do not provide entire payroll computer printouts or any information that is not requested. The investigator has no right to remove data from your premises, but can copy the information at your site.

Find an empty room or office and put the investigator there to look at the requested information. Hopefully the investigator will find "no cause" for the complaint and in that event, may just call you and say no violation was found and therefore the investigation is closed. If there is a problem, however, the investigator may ask for a meeting to discuss the violation.

If there are violations, you should seek competent advice. Don't just accept a determination without fully considering all facts. Have your legal counsel review your rights. Without competent advice the company could incur a liability for unpaid wages.

Page 163 contains a sample letter to the Wage Hour Division of the Department of Labor regarding a claim. If you need to write such a letter, revise this one to fit your needs.

DO YOU USE INDEPENDENT CONTRACTORS?
THE IRS MAY NOT THINK SO

In the past ten years there has been an enormous increase in the number of people who decide to be their own boss, and become an independent contractor. For young, growing businesses, hiring an independent contractor who is not on the payroll full time and doesn't have a benefits package but who offers quality service, can be very appealing.

However, this growth of independent contractors into the marketplace has not gone unnoticed by the IRS—especially because of the ease in which companies can classify full-time employees as "independent contractors," and avoid withholding federal income taxes or paying social security (FICA) taxes. In light of this, the IRS has taken a strict view of what it means to employ an independent contractor.

The IRS concluded a nationwide program aimed at identifying employers who misclassify their employees as "independent contractors." Over 9,000 delinquent employment tax returns have been filed, and tax assessments have been issued to 92 percent of those employers selected for examination.

If you have employees, you are required to withhold federal income tax from their wages (including bonuses). You may also have to withhold and pay social security (FICA) taxes. If you do not withhold these taxes, you may be subject to a penalty equal to the amount of the tax.

Work Status

Generally the relationship of employer and employee exists when the employer has the right to control and direct the individual who performs the services, not only as to the results but also as to the details and means by which that result is accomplished. Understand that it isn't necessary for the employer to actually direct or control the employee—only that the employer has the right to do so. The following is a list of factors the IRS would use to determine whether an employer/employee relationship exists:

- Doing the work on the employer's premises, which might indicate control, especially when the work could be done elsewhere.

- The establishment of set hours of work by the employer.
- The furnishing of tools or materials by the employer.
- The existence of a continuing relationship.
- Payment by the employer of the worker's business and travel expenses.

How can you determine that an individual working for you is an independent contractor? An independent contractor would match the following criteria:

The workers:

- Ordinarily uses his or her own methods and receives no training from the purchaser of services.
- Has made a significant investment in facilities he or she uses in performing services.
- Is in a position to realize a profit or suffer a loss as a result of services provided.
- Services are available to the general public.
- Is usually responsible to complete a specific job or is legally obligated to make good for failure to complete a job.

The description of a job is immaterial when an employer and employee relationship exists as listed above. So, superintendents, managers and other supervisory personnel are employees. Generally, an officer of a corporation is an employee of the corporation but a director may not be. However, an officer of a corporation who does not perform any services is not considered to be an employee of the corporation.

The Revenue Act of 1978 permits a taxpayer to treat a worker as other than an employee, under certain circumstances, without incurring employment tax liabilities. This is only available if certain conditions are met:

- The employer did not treat the worker as an employee and for all periods after December 31, 1978, all federal tax returns (1099's), were filed on a consistent basis, and
- The employer has a reasonable basis for treating the worker as not being an employee.

Penalties

If you withhold income and social security taxes from an employee, but do not pay them to the IRS, you may be subject to a penalty of 100% of the tax. If you are the person responsible for the collection and payment of withholding taxes, you can be subject to this penalty even if you are not an officer.

A 10% penalty is charged when taxes are deposited late or when they are mailed to the IRS offices rather than the authorized depositories or Federal Reserve Banks.

For each month a return is not filed, there is a penalty of 5% of the tax. The maximum penalty is 25%.

Due to the substantial penalties, it is important that you document whether a worker is an employee or an independent contractor. It is also important that you are consistent in your practices.

WHAT YOU NEED TO KNOW ABOUT THE CONSOLIDATED OMNIBUS BUDGET RECONCILIATION ACT (COBRA)

COBRA significantly changed the way employers handle benefits when an employee terminates. Following is an overview of COBRA regulations with sample letters you should send employees. The first letter that follows should be given to all *new* employees.

The Consolidated Omnibus Budget Reconciliation Act of 1986 (COBRA) requires employers with twenty or more employees to give employees and dependents who are covered by an employer-sponsored healthcare plan the option to continue their health plan coverage at group rates for substantial periods of time after certain "qualifying events" that would otherwise result in an employee's or dependent's loss of coverage. An employee has a right to choose continuation coverage if he or she loses group health coverage because of a reduction of hours of employment or the termination of employment (for reasons other than gross misconduct).

Such continuation coverage is for an 18-month period. The spouse of an employee covered by a group health plan has the right to choose continuation coverage for three years, if the employee dies, if the employee's employment is terminated (for reasons other than gross misconduct) or the employee's hours of employment are reduced, if the spouse and the employee are divorced or legally separated, or if the employee becomes eligible for Medicare. Likewise, a dependent child of an employee covered by a group health plan has the right to continue coverage for a three-year period if the employee dies, if the employee's employment is terminated (for reasons other than gross misconduct) or the employee's hours of employment are reduced, if the parents are divorced or legally separated, if the employee becomes eligible for Medicare, or if the dependent ceases to be a "dependent child" under the terms of the group health plan.

The employee or dependent has sixty days from the date he or she would otherwise lose health plan coverage to exercise the continuation coverage option. If continuation coverage is selected, the employee or dependent must pay for the coverage (at group health plan rates). This law applies to group health plans for plan years beginning on or after July 1, 1986, except for plans maintained pursuant to collective bargaining agreements. In the case of collectively bargained plans, COBRA does not apply to plan years beginning before the later of (a) the date on which the last collective bargaining agreement relating to the plan terminates, or (b) January 1, 1987.

COBRA does impose significant administrative and recordkeeping burdens on employers, because employers are required to notify employees and their spouses (if any) who are covered by healthcare plans that they will have the option to continue healthcare insurance coverage after a qualifying event occurs. COBRA also requires employers to notify each employee and his or her spouse as soon as they are covered by the employer-sponsored plan that the option to continue healthcare coverage will be available following a qualifying event. Employers also must notify their plan administrators that qualifying events have occurred within thirty days after such qualifying events occur. The employee or dependent is responsible for giving notice of a divorce, legal separation, or a dependent child's loss of coverage.

It is imperative that employers comply with the requirements of COBRA. Among other penalties, a covered employer who fails to provide a required healthcare continu-

SAMPLE LETTER TO REPRESENTATIVE OF WAGE AND HOUR DIVISION ON THE DEPARTMENT OF LABOR REGARDING CLAIM

Mr. Jonathan Wright   Date _____
Wage and Hour Division
Department of Labor
1800 Sherman Street
Denver, CO 80203

RE: Claim No. 478265 Jennie Welsh

Dear Mr. Wright:

In response to your request for information on our hours of work, we provide the following work schedules:

> *Day Shift*
> 8:00 A.M. to 5:00 P.M.
> One hour paid for lunch

> *Night Shift*
> 5:00 P.M. to 2:00 A.M.
> Onc hour paid for dinncr

We have investigated the claim by Mrs. Jennie Welsh. She feels that she should be paid for overtime because she reported to work 15 minutes early every day and took only one-half hour for lunch for a period of three months, commencing July 5 and ending October 7.

Our investigation shows that Mrs. Welsh did in fact work these hours. They were not her regularly scheduled hours, however, and she completed her time cards as having worked 8:00 a.m. to 5:00 p.m. each day with a one-hour lunch period.

Mrs. Welsh's supervisor substantiates her claim. It is not company policy to allow employees to change their work schedules. However, because her supervisor allowed the altered schedule, we feel an obligation to reimburse Mrs. Welsh for the overtime of three hours and forty-five minutes per week for the three-month period.

We have instituted an audit of our procedures and payroll records to ensure that other employees have not participated in similar practices. If you need further information or explanation of the claim, please give me a call at (303) 222-1111.

Sincerely,

Walter Reed
Director, Human Resources

ation option will be denied a tax deduction for the expenses it incurs in maintaining all of its group health plans.

Also, employers with twenty or more employees must offer active employees and their spouses age 65 and over the same health insurance coverage that they offer younger workers. The employer plan must be the employee's or spouse's primary plan unless the employee or his or her spouse elects to be covered only by Medicare. Before the enactment of COBRA, this requirement did not apply to persons over age 70.

Following are several sample letters to employees which you can use to comply with COBRA regulations. (See pages 166–178.)

EMPLOYERS WHO HAVE MEDICAL PLANS MUST PROVIDE NOTICE OF COBRA AMENDMENTS

Rules governing continuation of health care coverage, as initiated by the *Consolidated Omnibus Budget Reconciliation Act of 1986* (COBRA), have been amended. Employers must notify COBRA beneficiaries of some of the changes. The *Public Health Services Act* and ERISA also contain continuation coverage provisions that were similarly amended. This article refers to the continuation coverage laws collectively as COBRA.

Two recent laws amended COBRA: the *Small Business Job Protection Act* and the *Health Insurance Portability and Accountability Act* (HIPAA). The *Small Business Job Protection Act* clarified COBRA's multiple qualifying event rule regarding Medicare entitlement. Previously, it had appeared that if Medicare entitlement of a covered employee was a second qualifying event for a COBRA beneficiary, COBRA coverage would continue for another 36 months for any qualified beneficiary who was a spouse or dependent of the covered employee. The new law clarifies that the intention was to provide 36 months total coverage from the date of the initial qualifying event (i.e., termination of employment or reduction in hours) for the covered spouse and dependents—not an additional 36 months. This provision is effective retroactively for plan years beginning after December 31, 1989.

HIPAA amended several COBRA provisions, and the amendments become effective January 1, 1997, regardless of when the qualifying even occurred. The amendments

- Clarify that the 11-month extension of coverage for disabled qualified beneficiaries is not limited to former employees. The extension is available to any qualified beneficiary who is disabled.

- Change the law to allow the 11-month extension of coverage for qualified beneficiaries who are determined by the Social Security Administration to have been disabled on the date of the qualifying event (i.e., termination of employment or reduction in hours) or within the first 60 days of COBRA coverage. Currently, qualified beneficiaries must be disabled on the date of the qualifying event.

- Change the definition of qualified beneficiary to include a child born to, or placed for adoption with, the covered employee during the period of COBRA coverage. Currently, children born or placed for adoption during this period can be added to a qualified beneficiary's coverage, but are not considered qualified beneficiaries.

- Allow termination of COBRA coverage when the qualified beneficiary receives new group health coverage that does not contain any preexisting condition exclusions or limitations (other than those that do not apply or are satisfied due to HIPAA's preexisting condition provisions). This change is intended to coordinate with HIPAA's new limits on preexisting conditions.

Note: Because these regulations change frequently, you should check with your carrier once a year to make sure all COBRA communications are up-to-date and correct.

SAMPLE COBRA LETTER TO EMPLOYEES
SUMMARY OF RIGHTS AND OBLIGATIONS REGARDING
CONTINUATION OF GROUP HEALTH PLAN COVERAGE

TO: Employees of XYZ Company

FROM: Director Human Resources

DATE:

SUBJECT: Continuation of coverage under the group health plan
               maintained by the Employer (the Plan)

**IT IS IMPORTANT THAT ALL COVERED INDIVIDUALS TAKE THE TIME TO
READ THIS NOTICE CAREFULLY AND BE FAMILIAR WITH ITS CONTENTS.**

The Consolidated Omnibus Budget Reconciliation Act (COBRA) requires that the
employer offer to employees, their spouses and dependents the opportunity for temporary extension of health (medical and dental) coverage called "continuation coverage"
where coverage under the Plan would otherwise end due to certain specific events (listed below).

To Whom Does This Continuation Apply?

Continuation of coverage under a group health plan may be elected for the following
Qualifying Events:

Qualifying Events for Covered Employee—If you are an employee of the XYZ Company
and covered by the Company's medical and/or dental coverage, you may have the right
to elect continuation coverage if you lose your group health coverage because of a termination of your employment or a reduction in your hours of employment.

Qualifying Events for Covered Spouse—If you are the spouse of an employee of XYZ
Company and covered by the Company's medical and/or dental coverage, you may have
the right to elect continuation coverage for yourself if you lose group health coverage
under the Plan for any of the following reasons:

1. A termination of your spouse's employment or reduction in your spouse's hours of
   employment with XYZ Company;
2. The death of your spouse;
3. Divorce or legal separation from your spouse; or
4. Your spouse becomes entitled to Medicare.

Qualifying Events for Covered Dependent Children—If you are the covered dependent
child of an employee covered by the Company's medical and/or dental coverage, you
may have the right to elect continuation coverage for yourself if you lose group health
coverage for any of the following reasons:

1. A termination of a parent's employment or reduction in the employee's hours of employment with XYZ Company;

2. The death of a parent employed by XYZ Company;

3. Parent's divorce or legal separation;

4. The parent employed by XYZ Company becomes entitled to Medicare;

5. You cease to be a "dependent child" under the XYZ Company Plan (i.e., you are between the ages of 19 and 25 and are no longer a full-time student, or you are over the age of 25 irrespective of whether or not you are a full-time student).

Rights similar to those described above may apply to retirees, spouses, and dependents if the employer commences a bankruptcy proceeding and these individuals lose coverage within one year of one or one year after the bankruptcy filing.

The taking of leave under the Family & Medical Leave Act does not constitute a qualifying event under COBRA.

What Is the Election Period and Coverage?

The employee or a family member has the responsibility to inform the Company/Plan administrator via enrollment/change form of a divorce, legal separation, or a child losing dependent status under the company's medical and/or dental coverage within 60 days of the date of the event or the date on which coverage would end under the Plan because of the event, whichever is later.

When the employer is notified that one of these events has happened, you will be notified that you have the right to choose continuation coverage. You have at least 60 days from the date you would lose coverage because of one of the events described above to inform the employer that you want continuation coverage.

If you do not choose continuation coverage within the 60-day election period, your opportunity to elect group health insurance coverage will end.

If a qualified beneficiary elects continuation coverage and pays the applicable premium, the employer will provide the qualified beneficiary with coverage that is identical to the coverage provided under the Plan to similarly situated employees and/or covered dependents.

For What Period of Time May the Coverages Be Continued?

1. **18 Months of Continued Coverage**

   If the event causing the loss of coverage is a termination of employment or a reduction in work hours, each qualified beneficiary will have the opportunity to continue coverage for 18 months from the date of the qualifying event.

2. **29 Months of Continued Coverage**

   Continuation of coverage can be extended to 29 months if a qualified beneficiary is disabled in accordance with the provisions of the Social Security Act at the time of the covered employee's termination of employment or reduction of hours. The extension to 29 months is available only if the qualified beneficiary provides notice of the determination of his or her disability under the Social Security Act within the 18-month period after the qualified event. The notice must be given within 60 days after the date of the disability determination to the employer. The employer must also be notified of any final determination that the qualified beneficiary is no longer disabled.

3. **36 Months of Continued Coverage**

   If the event causing the loss of coverage was the death of the employee, divorce, legal separation, or a dependent child ceasing to be a dependent child under the XYZ Company's medical and/or dental plan, each qualified beneficiary will have the opportunity to continue coverage *up to 36 months* from the date of the qualifying event.

Secondary Events—An extension of the 18-month continuation period can occur, if *during the 18 months* of continuation coverage, a secondary event takes place (divorce, legal separation, death, Medicare entitlement, or a dependent child ceasing to be a dependent). If a secondary event does take place, then the 18 months of continuation coverage can be extended to 36 months from the original qualifying event.
If a secondary event occurs, it is the responsibility of the qualified beneficiary to notify the employer. In no event, however, will continuation coverage last beyond 36 months from the date of the event that originally made the qualified beneficiary eligible for continuation coverage.

Medicare Entitlement—There is a special rule for Medicare entitlement. If a covered employee has an 18-month qualifying event and becomes entitled to Medicare during that period, the continuation coverage period for qualified beneficiaries (i.e., spouse less than 65 years old) other than the covered employee will be terminated 36 months from the date the covered employee becomes entitled to Medicare.

Under What Circumstances May Coverage Under This Continuation Be Terminated?

The law provides that *if elected and paid for,* continuation coverage may end prior to the maximum continuation period for any of the following reasons:

1. XYZ Company ceases to provide any group health plan to any of its employees;
2. Any required premium for continuation coverage is not paid in a timely manner;
3. An employee is covered under another group health plan that does not contain any exclusion or limitation with respect to any preexisting condition of such beneficiary;
4. A qualified beneficiary becomes entitled to Medicare (Medicare eligibility terminates coverage only for the Medicare-eligible individual)
5. A qualified beneficiary extended continuation coverage to 29 months due to a Social Security disability and a final determination has been made that the qualified beneficiary is no longer disabled;
6. A qualified beneficiary notifies the employer that they wish to cancel continuation coverage.

When Must a Decision to Continue Be Made?

A covered employee, spouse, or dependent has 60 days from the date coverage would otherwise terminate or the date the election notice is sent to you, whichever date is later.

How and to Whom Are Premium Payments Made?

For the first premium payment, you have 45 days from the date you elect to continue coverage to pay the retroactive premium. Thereafter, your premiums are payable on the first of each month. There is a grace period of 30 days for the regularly scheduled monthly premiums. If your payment is not received within this time basis, your insurance will be canceled. No statements will be sent.

Important Notifications Required by an Employee, Spouse, and Dependent

The employee, spouse, or other family member has the responsibility to inform the employer of a divorce, legal separation, or a child losing dependent status under the XYZ Company's medical and/or dental coverage. This notification must be made within 60 days from whichever date is later, the date of the event or the date on which coverage would be lost because of the event. Please check with the human resource department for procedures to follow in making this notification. *If this notification is not completed in a timely manner, then rights to continuation coverage may be forfeited.*

Notification of Address Change

To ensure that all covered individuals receive information properly and efficiently, it is important that you notify the employer of any address change as soon as possible. Failure on your part to do so may result in delayed notifications or a loss of continuation coverage options.

Eligibility, Premiums, and Potential Conversion Rights

A qualified beneficiary does not have to show that they are insurable to elect continuation coverage. The XYZ Company however, reserves the right to verify eligibility status and terminate continuation coverage retroactively if you are determined to be ineligible or if there has been a material misrepresentation of the facts. A qualified beneficiary may have to pay all of the applicable premium plus a 2% administration charge for continuation coverage. These premiums may be adjusted in the future if the applicable premium amount changes. In addition, if continuation coverage is extended from 18 months to 29 months due to a Social Security disability, the XYZ Company can charge up to 150% of the applicable premium during the extended coverage period. There is a grace period of 30 days for the regularly scheduled monthly premiums.

Any Questions?

If any covered individual does not understand any part of this summary notice or has questions regarding the information or your obligations, please contact the Director of Human Resources at (303) 919-9990.

SAMPLE LETTER TO BE SENT TO THOSE FORMER EMPLOYEES
CURRENTLY ON COBRA AND THOSE EMPLOYEES WHO WILL
GO ON COBRA AFTER JANUARY 1, 1997

Date _____

Mr. John Doe
123 Street
City, State 00000

Subject: Changes In Group Health Plan Continuation Coverage

Dear Mr. Doe:

As you may be aware, On August 21, 1996, President Clinton signed into law the Health Insurance Portability and Accountability Act of 1996. While there were many provisions that will relate to Acme Company's group health plan in the future, there are a few changes that have taken effect as of January 1, 1997. These changes are noted below;

- Under the current rules, Qualified Beneficiaries disabled (as determined by the Social Security Administration) *on the date of a Qualifying Event* resulting from a termination of employment or reduction in working hours may be entitled to a total of 29 months of continuation coverage, rather' than the normal 18 months. Under the new law, if the Qualified Beneficiary is determined to have been disabled *at any time during the first 60 days of* continuation coverage, they are entitled to a total of 29 months of coverage.

- Under the current rules, children acquired after the date of any Qualifying Event (newborn or adopted) may have been eligible for coverage, *but not as a Qualified Beneficiary.* Under' the new rules' all newborns and adopted children must be eligible to be added to continuation coverage within XX days, and are considered to be *a Qualified Beneficiary* if enrolled.

In addition, the Small Business Job Protection Act recently clarified COBRA's multiple qualifying event rules as follows:

- Under' the current law, if Medicare Entitlement was a second Qualifying Event, the actual language of the law permitted 36 months *additional coverage.* Under the new law, this has been clarified to permit a *total of 36 months* for both Qualifying Events. This change is retroactively effective to January 1, 1990.

To assist you in understanding the group health plan coverage continuation provision, we are enclosing a copy of the rules that apply to the group health plan's coverage continuation provision that has been updated to reflect the changes in the law. Please take the time to read it carefully. If you have question:, please contact the Human Resources Department.

Sincerely,

GROUP HEALTH PLAN
COVERAGE CONTINUATION NOTICE

On April 7, 1986, a federal law called COBRA was enacted requiring that most employers sponsoring group health plans offer covered employees and their covered spouses and dependent children the opportunity' for a temporary extension of health coverage (called "continuation coverage") at group rates. This coverage is available in certain instances (called "qualifying events"), where coverage under the plan would otherwise end. This notice is intended to inform you, in a summary, of your rights and obligations under the continuation coverage provisions of the law. *Both you and your spouse should take the time to read this notice carefully.*

If you are an employee of (*employers name*) covered by (*group health plan name*) you have a right to choose this continuation coverage if you lose your group health coverage because of a reduction in your work hours or the termination of your employment (for reasons other than gross misconduct on your part).

If you are the spouse of an employee covered by (*group health plan name*), you have the right to choose continuation coverage for yourself if you lose group health plan coverage under (*group health plan name*) for any of the following reasons:

(1)   Death of your spouse;
(2)   A termination of your spouse's employment (for reasons other than gross misconduct) or reduction in your spouse's hours of employment;
(3)   Divorce or legal separation from your spouse;
(4)   Your spouse becomes entitled to Medicare;

In the case of a dependent child of an employee covered by (*group health care name*), he or she has the right to continuation coverage if group health plan coverage under (*group health plan name*) is lost for any of the reasons listed above for a spouse or if his/her coverage under the plan terminates because s/he no longer qualifies as a dependent under the terms of the plan.

Under COBRA, the employee or a covered spouse or dependent child have the responsibility to inform the (*group health plan name*) Administrator of a divorce, a legal separation or a child losing dependent status under (*group health plan name*) within 60 days of the event or the date on which coverage would end with the plan because of the event. (*Name of employer*) has the responsibility to notify the Plan Administrator of the employee's death, termination, reduction in hours of employment or Medicare entitlement. Similar rights may apply to certain retirees and their spouses and dependent children if your employer commences a bankruptcy proceeding and these individuals lose coverage.

When the Plan Administrator is notified that one of these events has happened, the Plan Administrator will in turn notify you that you have the right to choose continuous coverage. Under COBRA, you have at least 60 days from the later of the date you would lose coverage because of one of the events described above or the date you are sent notice about your right to continued coverage to inform the Plan Administrator that you want continuation coverage. There is one exception, however. If you waive continuation coverage, you may revoke your waiver at any time before your 60-day election period ends, but, in that case, your continuation coverage begins on the date your waiver is revoked (it will not include coverage for the period between the date your regular plan coverage ends and the date your waiver is revoked).

Each affected individual may make his or her own decision when choosing continuation coverage. Unless the covered employee's election of continuation coverage says otherwise, that election will also cover his or her' spouse and/or dependent children who would also be losing coverage. If a spouse elects coverage, the spouse election will (unless otherwise stated) also cover the employee and dependent children who would also be losing coverage.

If you do not choose continuation coverage within the 60-day period, your group health plan coverage will end.

If you choose continuation coverage, (*name of employer*) is required to give you coverage which, as of the time coverage is being provided, is identical to the coverage provided under the plan to similarly situated employees or spouse or dependent child who have not experienced a qualifying event. The law requires that you be afforded the opportunity to maintain continuation coverage for up to 36 months unless you lost group health plan coverage because of a termination of employment or reduction in hours. In that case, the maximum continuation coverage period is 18 months. This 18-month period is extended to 36 months if other events (such as death, divorce, legal separation, Medicare entitlement, or a child is no longer a dependent) occur during that 18-month period.

In the case of qualifying events that are termination of employment or reduction of hours, the 18 months of continued coverage may be extended to 29 months. To receive their extended coverage, an individual must be determined to have been disabled (for Social Security disability purposes) on the date of the original qualifying event, or during the first 60 days of continuation coverage, and notify the Plan Administrator of that determination within 60 days of receipt and within the original 18-month period. The affected individual must also notify the Plan Administrator within 30 days of any final determination that the individual is no longer disabled. In no event will continuation coverage last beyond 36 months from the date of the first event that originally made a qualified beneficiary eligible to elect coverage.

However, the law also provides that continuation coverage may be discontinued before the end of the maximum period for any of the following five reasons:

(1)   (*Name of employer*) no longer provides group health plan coverage to any of its employees;

(2)   The premium for the continuation coverage is not paid on time;

(3)   The qualified beneficiary becomes covered under another group health plan that does not contain any exclusion or limitation with respect to any pre-existing condition he/she may have or is prohibited from enforcing the exclusion or limitation;

(4)   The qualified beneficiary becomes entitled to Medicare;

(5)   The qualified beneficiary's coverage was extended to 29 months due to disability and there has been a final determination that he/she is no longer disabled. In that case' continuation coverage will end on the first day of the month that begins more than 30 days after the date of the final determination that the individual is no longer disabled.

You do not have to show that you are insurable to choose continuation coverage. To receive continuation coverage, you must pay the full cost of the monthly premium plus a two percent administrative charge. If you experience a qualifying event, you will be notified about the premium rates and the due dates for payments. If you or a covered spouse or dependent child qualifies for extended continuation coverage as a disabled individual, 150 percent of the all cost of the monthly premium must be paid for the 19th through 29 months of the coverage. There is a grace period of at least 30 days for payment of the regularly scheduled premium. You have 45 days from the date you initially elect coverage to make your first payment. The law also requires that if; at the end of the 18-month or 36-month coverage continuation period, you must be allowed to enroll in an individual conversion health plan if offered under (*group health plan name*) at that time.

If you have questions about COBRA, contact (*Plan Administrator's name, business address, and phone*). Also, if you have changed marital status, or you or your spouse have changed addresses, please notify(*Plan Administrator*) at the above address.

SAMPLE COBRA NOTICE TO TERMINATING EMPLOYEE

Dear _____,

The Consolidated Omnibus Budget Reconciliation Act of 1986 required that employers offer certain categories of individuals the opportunity to continue in the employers group health insurance plan within sixty (60) days of becoming eligible. Coverage may continue for eighteen (18) or thirty-six (36) months depending upon category of eligibility.

Who is covered	Situation	Duration of coverage
1. Employee	Termination other than for "gross misconduct"; reduction in hours	18 months
2. Family members	Death of employee	36 months
3. Spouse	Divorce or legal separation from employee	36 months
4. Dependent child	For a child who ceases to be a dependent under terms of the health plan	36 months
5. Spouse	Employee reaches age 65 and makes Medicare primary health insurer	36 months

The cost to you is $_____. It is your responsibility to remit each month's premium to the Human Resources Manager no later than the first of each month. Failure to do so will result in cancellation of coverage.

_____I decline coverage

_____I elect coverage   _____ Monthly premium: _____

_____Category applies to me

Please print name of individual(s) covered.

_____   _____

_____   _____

_____   _____

_____   _____
Date   Signature

Sample COBRA Letter to Terminating Employee or Dependent

Mr. Eldon Johns   _____Date
32981 Harbor Street
Boston, MA 02215

Dear Eldon:

You are eligible to receive healthcare coverage from Putman Power Products Corporation as a result of the Consolidated Omnibus Budget Reconciliation Act (COBRA).

The regulation affects former employees, including retirees and dependents of employees whose coverage under our healthcare program has stopped.

Under this law, you may purchase the same medical, dental, and prescription drug coverage provided to current employees for up to 18 months. The attached sheet summarizes the items covered by the medical plan.

Your monthly cost is $_____ for individual coverage and $_____ for family coverage. This is equal to the company s cost of providing the same coverage to each of our current employees. You are not required to furnish proof of insurability to receive this coverage.

If you accept the coverage, you must complete, sign, and mail the enclosed application form to our Human Resources Department within 60 days of receipt of this letter. The premium is due within 45 days of your application for coverage and may be paid monthly or in a single payment. Your payments should also be mailed to the Human Resources Department.

Healthcare benefits under this program will stop automatically at the end of the 18-month period, or sooner if you stop making the payments, become covered under another employer's healthcare plan, or become eligible for Medicare. It could also stop if for some reason our company discontinued the employee healthcare plan.

Your dependent children automatically receive the same medical coverage as you if you choose to participate. They will have an opportunity to apply for the individual coverage for themselves when they no longer qualify as your dependents. This happens when they reach age 19, when they are no longer full-time students, or sooner if they get married.

If you fail to apply for coverage within 60 days of receiving this letter, or fail to send your first premium payment within 45 days of enrolling, you will forfeit your right to coverage under the healthcare plan.

If you have any questions about the program or the provision of the law, please write or call me at (212) 555-8931.

Sincerely,

Fred J. Corbin
Human Resources Manager

SAMPLE ALTERNATIVE COBRA LETTER TO EMPLOYEES

Date _____

Dear Employee:

You and your eligible dependents may continue participation in the firm's group medical and dental plans even though certain events occur which would otherwise cause loss of coverage. This continued coverage is provided by the Consolidated Omnibus Budget Reconciliation Act (COBRA), a federal law enacted on April 7, 1986. This notice is intended to inform you of your rights and obligations under the continuation coverage provisions of the new law.

How the Law Will Apply:

1. Your coverage can be extended up to 18 months if one of the following "qualifying events" occurs:

   • Your employment with the firm terminates for any reason (including voluntary resignation or retirement) other than gross misconduct.

   • Your working hours are reduced to a level at which you would no longer be eligible for coverage.

2. Coverage for your eligible dependents can be extended up to 36 months if one of the following "qualifying events" occurs:

   • They are covered under the plans and you die while still employed.

   • You or your spouse become legally separated or divorced.

   • A dependent child reaches maximum age for coverage.

   • Your spouse or dependents are under age 65 when you become eligible for Medicare and are no longer an active employee.

The Full 18- or 36-Month Extension Will Not Apply If:

• All employer-provided medical or dental plans are terminated.

• You do not pay your required premium in a timely manner.

• You or your dependents become (an employee) covered by any other group medical and/or dental plan.

• Your former spouse remarries and becomes covered under another group medical and/or dental plan.

• A dependent becomes eligible for Medicare (Medicare eligibility terminates coverage only for the Medicare-eligible individual).

How to Obtain This Continuation Coverage

You or a family member must notify the plan administrator in the event of a divorce or legal separation, or if a child loses dependent status under the Plan. You must notify the plan administrator of the employee's death, termination of employment, reduction of hours, or Medicare eligibility. The plan administrator will, within fourteen days of receiving notification, inform you or the dependent of the right to choose continuation coverage. You do not have to show that you are insurable to choose continuation coverage. Please note that prompt notification is extremely important. You will have at least sixty days from the date you would otherwise lose coverage to inform the plan administrator is you want continuation coverage. If you do not elect continuation coverage, your group health plan coverage will end.

Your Cost for Continuation Coverage

You will be charged the full cost of coverage under the group plan in which you are enrolled. We will no longer pay a portion of it. You will also pay a 2 percent administrative charge. (Note: This may still be less expensive and provide better coverage than an individual health policy.)

You may pay for the continuation coverage on a monthly basis. You must make your first payment within forty-five days after the date you elect the continuation of this coverage. Subsequent payments must be made to the Human Resources Manager by _____.

This Does Not Affect Your Normal Conversion Privilege

You will still have the option to convert your group coverage to individual coverage. If you first elect continuation coverage under our group plan(s), your election period to convert to an individual policy will be the last 180 days of your continuation coverage. If you *do not wish* to continue coverage under the group plan(s), you must make your conversion election for individual coverage within thirty days of the date your regular group health coverage ends. The new continuation coverage option under our plan *does not* apply to life insurance. If you wish to convert your group life insurance to individual life insurance, you must elect to do so within thirty days of the date your regular group life insurance coverage ends.

If you have any questions about either the conversion option or the continuation coverage option, please call or write:

(Insert name of your carrier)

Also, if you have changed marital status, or you or your spouse have changed addresses, please notify the plan administrator at the above addresses.

Sincerely,

Scott Macon
Human Resources Director

WAIVER LETTER

(Be sure an employee who elects *not* to take COBRA coverage signs
a Waiver Letter like this one)

Date

XYZ Company
Human Resources Department
Denver, Co. 80237

RE: Waiver of Right to Continue Benefits under COBRA Continuation

Dear Plan Administrator:

I have received the notification of the right to continue certain covered benefits for myself and my covered dependents, if any, and the cost computation form.

At this time, the undersigned Principal Qualified Beneficiary waives the right to purchase the continuation coverage. Family coverage, if provided, is also waived by signature of my spouse, if any in the space provided below.

In waiving this coverage, I (we) hereby acknowledge that at the end of the election period which is _____, my (our) decision will be final and irrevocable.

Sincerely,

_____
Signature of Employee

_____
Signature of Spouse

POSTERS REQUIRED BY FEDERAL STATUTE

There are several posters required by federal regulations. Those posters, the statute, the posting requirement, and the office listing where they can be ordered are all provided on the attached sheets. Also attached is a sample Equal Employment Opportunity Policy statement and poster that should be posted on the same bulletin board as the other required posters.

Some states also require the company to identify regular paydays. If your state requires that posting you can use a small card to list your paydays, and post on your bulletin boards. The simplest way to ensure you have all the posters required by your particular state, as well as all required federal posters, is to order them from the G. Neil Companies, P.O. Box 450939, Sunrise, FL 33345. (800) 999-9111. Otherwise, you have to call the various federal and state offices and order each set individually. If you want to do that, following are some of the numbers you will need.

TERMINATION PAY REQUIREMENTS BY STATE

WHEN YOU MUST PAY A DEPARTING EMPLOYEE

STATE	FIRED EMPLOYEE	QUITTING EMPLOYEE
Alaska	Within 3 working days	Within 3 working days
Arizona	Next payday or within 3 working days	Next regular payday
Arkansas	Date of discharge	Next regular payday
California	Within 72 hours	Within 72 hours
Colorado	At time of discharge	Next regular payday
Connecticut	Next business day	Next regular payday
Delaware	Next regular payday	Next regular payday
D.C.	Next working day	Next working day
Florida	—	—
Georgia	—	—
Hawaii	Next working day	Next regular payday
Idaho	Next regular payday	Next regular payday
Illinois	Next regular payday	Next regular payday
Indiana	Next regular payday	Next regular payday
Iowa	Next regular payday	Next regular payday
Kansas	Next regular payday	Next regular payday
Kentucky	Next regular payday	Next regular payday
Louisiana	Within 3 days of separation	Within 3 days of separation
Maine	Next regular payday	Next regular payday
Maryland	Next regular payday	Next regular payday
Massachusetts	Day of discharge	Next regular payday

STATE	FIRED EMPLOYEE	QUITTING EMPLOYEE
Michigan	Day of discharge	Day leaving
Minnesota	Within 24 hours of demand	Within 5 days
Mississippi	—	—
Missouri	Day of discharge	Day leaving
Montana	Immediately	Within 3 days
Nebraska	Day of discharge	Next regular payday
Nevada	Immediately	Within 24 hours of demand
New Hampshire	Within 72 hours	Next regular payday
New Jersey	Next regular payday	Next regular payday
New Mexico	Within 5 days of discharge	Next regular payday
New York	Next regular payday	Next regular payday
North Carolina	Next regular payday	Next regular payday
North Dakota	Within 24 hours	Next regular payday
Ohio	—	—
Oklahoma	Next regular payday	—
Oregon	Immediately	Within 2 working days
Pennsylvania	Next regular payday	Next regular payday
Rhode Island	Within 24 hours	Next regular payday
South Carolina	Generally within 48 hours	Next regular payday
South Dakota	Within 5 days	Next regular payday
Tennessee	—	—
Texas	On 6 days demand	On 6 days demand
Utah	Within 24 hours	Within 72 hours
Vermont	Within 72 hours	Next regular payday
Virginia	Next regular payday	Next regular payday
Washington	Next regular payday	Next regular payday
West Virginia	Within 72 hours	Next regular payday
Wisconsin	Within 3 days	Within 15 days
Wyoming	Within 24 hours	Within 72 hours

Government Addresses and Phone Numbers

REGIONAL INFORMATION OFFICES-DEPARTMENT OF LABOR

138W 424 Trapelo Rd., Boston, MA 02135 1515

Broadway, New York, NY 10036

3535 Market St., Philadelphia, PA 19104

1371 Peachtree St. NE, Atlanta, GA 30309

230 S. Dearborn St., Chicago, IL 60604

555 Griffin Sq. Bldg., Dallas, TX 75202

911 Walnut St., Kansas City, MO 64106

1961 Stout St., Denver, CO 80294

450 Golden Gate Ave., San Francisco, CA 94102

909 First Ave., Seattle, WA 98174

REGIONAL OFFICES-OCCUPATIONAL SAFETY AND HEALTH ADMINISTRATION

16–18 North St., 1 Dock Sq., Boston, MA 02109

1515 Broadway, Rm. 3445, New York, NY 10036

3535 Market St., Philadelphia, PA 19104

1375 Peachtree St. NE, Atlanta, GA 30367

230 S. Dearborn St., Chicago, IL 60604

555 Griffin Sq. Bldg., Griffin & Young Sts., Dallas, TX 75202

911 Walnut St., Kansas City, MO 64106

Federal Bldg., 1961 Stout St., Denver, CO 80294

Federal Office Bldg., 450 Golden Gate Ave., San Francisco, CA 94102

Federal Office Bldg., 909 First Ave., Seattle, WA 98174

Equal Employment Opportunity Commission
2401 "E" Street N.W.
Washington, DC 20506

U. S. Department of Labor
Employment Standards Administration
Wage and Hour Division
Washington, DC 20210

U. S. Department of Justice
Immigration and Naturalization Service
425 "I" Street N.W.
Washington, DC 20536

Equal Employment Opportunity Commission Field Offices

Albuquerque, 505 Marquette, NW, Suite 1515, Albuquerque, NM 87101

Atlanta, 75 Piedmont Ave., NE, 10th Flr., Atlanta, GA

Baltimore, 109 Market Pl., Suite 4000, Baltimore, MD 21202

Birmingham, 2121 Eighth Ave., North, Birmingham, AL 35203

Boston, 150 Causeway St., Suite 1000, Boston, MA 02114

Buffalo, 210 Franklin St., Rm. 503, Buffalo, NY 14202

Charlotte, 1301 East Morehead, Charlotte, NC 28204

Chicago, 536 So. Clark St., Rm. 240, Chicago, IL 60605

Cincinnati, 550 Main St., Rm. 7015, Cincinnati, OH 45202

Cleveland, 1375 Euclid Ave., 6th Flr., Cleveland, OH 44115

Dallas, 1900 Pacific, 13th Flr., Dallas, TX 75201

Denver, 1531 Stout St., 6th Flr., Denver, CO 80202

Detroit, 660 Woodward Ave., Suite 600, Detroit, MI 48226

El Paso, 109 No. Oregon St., Suite 1112, El Paso, TX 79901

Fresno, 1313 P St., Suite 103, Fresno, CA 93721

Greensboro, 324 West Market St., Rm. B 27, Greensboro, NC 27402

Greenville, 7 North Laurens St., Suite 1001, Greenville, SC 29601

Houston, 405 Main St., 6th Flr., Houston, TX 77002

Indianapolis, 46 East Ohio St., Rm. 456, Indianapolis, IN 46204

Jackson, 100 West Capitol St., Suite 721, Jackson, MS 39269

Kansas City, 911 Walnut, 10th Flr., Kansas City, MO 64106

Little Rock, 320 West Capitol, Little Rock, AR 72201

Los Angeles, 3255 Wilshire Blvd., 9th Flr., Los Angeles, CA 90010

Louisville, 601 W. Broadway, Rm. 104, Louisville, KY 40202

Memphis, 1407 Union Ave., Suite 502, Memphis, TN 38104

Miami, 300 Biscayne Blvd. Way, Suite 414, Miami, FL 33131

Milwaukee, 342 North Water St., Rm. 612, Milwaukee, WI 53202

Minneapolis, 12 South Sixth St., Suite 1110, Minneapolis, MN 55402

Nashville, 404 James Robertson Pky., Suite 1820, Nashville, TN 37219

Newark, 744 Broad St., Rm. 502, Newark, NJ 07102

New Orleans, 600 South Street, New Orleans, LA 70130

New York, 90 Church St., Rm. 1501, New York, NY 10007

Norfolk, 200 Granby Mall, Rm. 412, Norfolk, VA 23510

Oakland, 1515 Clay St., Rm. 640, Oakland, CA 94612

Oklahoma City, 50 Penn Pl., Suite 504, Oklahoma City, OK 73118

Philadelphia, 127 North Fourth St., Suite 300, Philadelphia, PA 19106

Phoenlx, 135 No. Second Ave., 4th Flr., Phoenix, AZ 85003

Pittsburgh, 1000 Liberty Ave., Rm. 2038A, Pittsburgh, PA 15222

Raleigh, 414 Fayetteville St., 2nd Flr., Raleigh, NC 27601

Richmond, 400 North Eighth St., Rm. 6213, Richmond, VA 23240

San Antonio, 727 East Durango, Suite B-601, San Antonio, TX 78206

San Diego, 880 Front St., Rm. 4521, San Diego, CA 92188

San Francisco, 10 United Nations Plaza, 4th Flr., San Francisco, CA 94102

San Jose, 84 West Santa Clara Ave., Rm. 300, San Jose, CA 95113

Equal Employment Opportunity is...

THE LAW

Private Employment, State and Local Government, Educational Institutions

Race, Color, Religion, Sex, National Origin

Title VII of the Civil Rights Act of 1964, as amended, prohibits discrimination in hiring, promotion, discharge, pay, fringe benefits, and other aspects of employment, on the basis of race, color, religion, sex or national origin.

Applicants to and employees of most private employers, State and local governments and public or private educational institutions are protected. Employment agencies, labor unions and apprenticeship programs also are covered.

Age

The Age Discrimination in Employment Act of 1967, as amended, prohibits age discrimination and protects applicants and employees aged 40-70 from discrimination in hiring, promotion, discharge, pay, fringe benefits and other aspects of employment. The law covers most private employers, State and local governments, educational institutions, employment agencies and labor organizations.

Sex (wages)

In addition to the sex discrimination prohibited by Title VII of the Civil Rights Act (see above) The Equal Pay Act of 1963, as amended, prohibits sex discrimination in payment of wages to women and men performing substantially equal work in the same establishment. The law covers most private employers, State and local governments and educational institutions. Labor organizations cannot cause employers to violate the law. Many employers not covered by Title VII, because of size, are covered by the Equal Pay Act.

If you believe that you have been discriminated against under any of the above laws, you should immediately contact

The U.S. Equal Employment Opportunity Commission
2401 "E" Street, N.W.
Washington, D.C. 20506
or an EEOC District Office
listed in most telephone
directories under U.S. Government.

Employers holding Federal contracts or subcontracts

Race, Color, Religion, Sex, National Origin

Executive Order 11246, as amended, prohibits job discrimination on the basis of race, color, religion, sex or national origin, and requires affirmative action to ensure equality of opportunity in all aspects of employment.

Handicap

Section 503 of the Rehabilitation Act of 1973, as amended, prohibits job discrimination because of handicap and requires affirmative action to employ and advance in employment qualified handicapped individuals who, with reasonable accommodation, can perform the functions of a job.

Vietnam Era and Disabled Veterans

Section 402 of the Vietnam Era Veterans Readjustment Assistance Act of 1974 prohibits job discrimination and requires affirmative action to employ and advance in employment qualified Vietnam era veterans and qualified disabled veterans.

Applicants to and employees of companies with a Federal government contract or subcontract are protected under the authorities above. Any person who believes a contractor has violated its nondiscrimination or affirmative action obligations under Executive Order 11246, as amended, Section 503 of the Rehabilitation Act or Section 402 of the Vietnam Era Veterans Readjustment Assistance Act should contact immediately

 The Office of Federal Contract Compliance Programs (OFCCP)
Employment Standards
Administration
U.S. Department of Labor
200 Constitution Avenue, N.W.
Washington, D.C. 20210
or an OFCCP regional or area office listed in most telephone directories under U.S. Government, Department of Labor

Programs or activities receiving Federal financial assistance

Handicap

Section 504 of the Rehabilitation Act of 1973, as amended, prohibits employment discrimination on the basis of handicap in any program or activity which receives Federal financial assistance. Discrimination is prohibited in all aspects of employment against handicapped persons who, with reasonable accommodation, can perform the essential functions of a job.

Race, Color, National Origin

In addition to the protection of Title VII of the Civil Rights Act of 1964, Title VI of the Civil Rights Act prohibits discrimination on the basis of race, color or national origin in programs or activities receiving Federal financial assistance. Employment discrimination is covered by Title VI if the primary objective of the financial assistance is provision of employment, or where employment discrimination causes or may cause discrimination in providing services under such programs.

If you believe you have been discriminated against in a program which receives Federal assistance, you should immediately contact the Federal agency providing such assistance.

Don't Forget...
Equal Employment Opportunity is the Law!

EQUAL EMPLOYMENT OPPORTUNITY POLICY

(Company Name)

It is the ongoing policy of _____ and all individual locations to afford equal employment opportunity to qualified individuals regardless of their race, color, religion, sex, national origin, age, physical or mental handicap, veteran status, or because he or she is a disabled veteran, and to conform to applicable laws and regulations. In keeping with the intent of this policy, the Company will adhere strictly to the following personnel practices:

       Recruitment, hiring and promotion of individuals in all job classifications will be conducted without regard to race, color, religion, national origin, age, sex, physical or mental handicap, veteran status, or because he or she is a disabled veteran, except where a bona fide occupational qualification exists.

       Employment decisions will be made in such a manner as to further the principle of equal employment opportunity.

       Promotional decisions will be made in accordance with the principles of equal employment opportunity through the use of valid job-related criteria.

       All other personnel actions such as compensation, benefits, transfers, training and development, educational assistance, and social and recreational programs will be administered without regard to race, color, religion, national origin, age, sex, physical or mental handicap, veteran status, or because he or she is a disabled veteran, except where a bona fide occupational qualification exists.

       Thorough and documented analyses of all personnel actions will be conducted to insure compliance with the concept of equal opportunity.

Overall responsibility for the development and execution of our Affirmative Action Program is delegated to _____ as EEO/AAP Coordinator. The EEO/AAP Coordinator will provide the president of _____ with quarterly and special activity and progress reports.

\

_____   _____
Date   President

Key Federal Regulations
Relating to the Human Resources Function

STATUTE	COVERAGE	BASIC REQUIREMENTS	POSTING PROVISION	ORDER POSTERS FROM
Fair Labor Standards Act (FLSA)	Employers engaged in interstate commerce	Pay minimum hourly rate and 1 1/2 hourly rate after 40 hours per week. Contains child labor restrictions; equal pay coverage	Minimum wage postings in conspicuous places to permit employees to readily observe on way to or from work	U.S. Department of Labor - WH Publication 1088 *
Walsh-Healey Act	Establishments engaged on a government contract exceeding $10,000	Pay minimum hourly rate at 1 1/2 hours after 40 hours per week; also contains health and safety requirements and a notation on fringe benefits	In sufficient number of places to permit employees to observe on way to or from work (WH 99:832)	U.S. Department of Labor - Publication WH 99:832 *
Davis-Bacon Act	Employers on public construction contracts exceeding $2,000	Pay minimum wages found by Labor Secretary to be prevailing in the area	Minimum wage to be paid, posted in prominent and easily accessible place at work site	U.S. Department of Labor *
Civil Rights Act of 1964 (Title VII)	Employers of 15 or more employees and engaged in interstate commerce	No job discrimination based on race, color, creed, religion, sex or national origin	In conspicuous places where notices to employees and job applicants will be seen. Bilingual postings required	EEOC *
Executive Order 11246, as amended	Federal government contractors and subcontractors; contractors under federally-assisted construction contracts	No job discrimination based on race, color, creed, religion, national origin or sex	In conspicuous places available to employees, job applicants and union representatives	U.S. Department of Labor *
Age Discrimination in Employment Act (ADEA)	Employers of 20 or more employees and engaged in interstate commerce	No job discrimination based on age 40 to 70	In prominent and accessible places where readily observable by employees, job applicants and union representatives	EEOC *
Pregnancy Discrimination Act of 1978 (PDA)	All employers	Requires that women employees "affected by pregnancy, childbirth, or related medical conditions" be treated the same as other employees with medical disabilities in terms of leave and pay	Cover in personnel policy manuals and employee handbooks	N/A *
Occupational Safety and Health Act (OSHA)	Employers engaged in interstate commerce; effective Jan. 1, 1983, the following industries are exempt: retail trade, finance, insurance and real estate, and services	Employers must furnish employees a place of employment free from recognized hazards that might cause serious injury or death. Employers must comply with the specific safety and health standards issued by the Dept. of Labor. Employees must comply with safety and health standards, rules, regulations and orders issued under the Act	OSHA Form 200 posted in a conspicuous place in each establishment. Includes injury and illness totals for previous year; must be posted for 30 days annually during the month of February	OSHA *

STATUTE	COVERAGE	BASIC REQUIREMENTS	POSTING PROVISION	ORDER POSTERS FROM
Rehabilitation Act of 1973	Federal government contractors and subcontractors (with a contract of $2,500 or more)	Take affirmative action to employ and advance in employment qualified handicapped persons	Display ADA Poster effective July 26, 1992	U.S. Department of Labor *
Vietnam Era Veterans' Readjustment Act of 1974	Federal government contractors and subcontractors (with a contract of $10,000 or more)	Take affirmative action to employ and advance in employment qualified Vietnam era veterans	Display poster or notice in conspicuous places available to employees and job applicants	EEOC *
Employee Polygraph Protection Act	All employers. Act exempts federal, state and local government employees	Employers prohibited from requiring or requesting employees or job applicants to take a lie detector test	Display poster in conspicuous places available to employees and job applicants	U.S. Department of Labor *
Drug Free Workplace Law	Federal contractors with contracts of $25,000 or more and Federal grantees	Certify to the contracting or granting agencies that they maintain a drug-free workplace by publishing and administering specific drug-free workplace policies and drug-awareness programs	Post company drug-free workplace notice and cover in personnel policy manuals and employee handbooks	Company-generated notice *
Worker Adjustment and Retraining Notification (WARN)	Any employer that employs 100 or more employees excluding part-time workers	Notice of plant closings and mass layoffs required	Notice must be posted for 60 days in advance of the layoff or plant closing	Company-generated notice *
Immigration Reform and Control Act of 1986 (IRCA)	Law says you should hire only American citizens and aliens who are authorized to work in the U.S.	Verify employment eligibility and complete and retain Form I-9	Display poster obtained from INS	U.S. Department of Justice Immigration and Naturalization Service (INS) *
The Immigration Act of 1990	Counterpart to the Immigration Reform and Control Act of 1986 - Can hire only those authorized to work in the U.S. Covers new areas including workers of "distinguished merit" and employer-sponsored visas	Verify employment eligibility and complete and retain Form I-9	Display poster obtained from INS	U.S. Department of Justice Immigration and Naturalization Service (INS) *
Older Worker's Protection Act of 1990	Changes the Age Discrimination Act (ADEA)	Centers on two important issues: severance and early retirement. Tightens the rules on waivers (giving up the right to sue in exchange for an enhanced retirement package).	Same as ADEA	EEOC *

STATUTE	COVERAGE	BASIC REQUIREMENTS	POSTING PROVISION	ORDER POSTERS FROM
Americans With Disabilities Act of 1990 (ADA)	Employers of 25 or more, effective July 26, 1992. Employers of 15 or more, effective July 26, 1994. For employment section only	Employers may not discriminate against an individual with a disability in hiring or promotion if the person is otherwise qualified for the job The Act also covers public transportation and public accommodations and these sections have different effective dates	Display poster of ADA employment and promotion regulations effective July 26, 1992	U.S. Department of Justice Civil Rights Division Coordination and Review Section (Implementation and Enforcement by EEOC) *
The Civil Rights Act of 1991 (CRA)	Basically restores Title VII by overruling five major court cases and strengthens the "disparate impact" theory Under the new Act, an employer must demonstrate that educational requirements, physical requirements, etc. are job related and consistent with business necessity Expands the scope and amount of monetary relief available to employment discrimination plaintiffs	Same as Title VII	Same as Title VII	EEOC *
The Family and Medical Leave Act of 1993	The law applies to all employers with more than 50 employees. It defines eligible employees as those who have been employed for at least 12 months and who have provided at least 1250 hours of service during the 12 months before the leave was requested. The law provides up to 12 weeks of unpaid leave during any 12-month period. The employee must be guaranteed the same or equivalent job on return to work, and the employers must continue to pay their portion of medical benefits during the leave.	A covered employer must provide 12 weeks of unpaid leave if the employee provides appropriate documentation substantiating the need for the leave.	Cover in Manuals and Handbooks and post notices as required.	*
The Illegal Immigration Reform and Immigrant Responsibility Act of 1996 Effective September 30, 1996	The Act's changes are designed to streamline the verification process and reduce the I-9 verification burden on employers.	New programs when finalized will provide for confirmation of employment status through telephone or electronic communication. The Immigration and Naturalization Service and the Social Security Administration are required to establish reliable and secure methods to confirm inquiries from employers.	Cover in Manuals and Handbooks and post notices as required.	*

STATUTE	COVERAGE	BASIC REQUIREMENTS	POSTING PROVISIONS	ORDER POSTERS FROM
Small Business Job Protection Act of 1996	$5.15 hour as of September 1, 1997. Extends tax-exempt status of employer-paid educational assistance. Establishes new roles for handling tip income tax credits. Establishes safe harbor non-discrimination rules for 401(k) plans. Creates savings incentive match plans for employees of small businesses.	Employers must pay minimum wage and comply to all new provisions of the Act.	Cover in Manuals and Handbooks and post notices as required.	*
The Health Insurance and Portability Act of 1996	Creates test program for tax-favored medical savings accounts (MSAS). Treats costs of long-term care services and some long-term care insurance as medical expenses for tax purposes. Imposes portability requirements on group health care plans. Includes several other general provisions.	Employers must comply with the portability and other tax related requirements.	Cover in Medical Plan documents and post notices as required.	*
The Personal Liability and Work Opportunity Act of 1996 (the Welfare Act)	Includes a number of changes that tighten the Earned Income Tax Credit. Mandatory new hire reporting program, effective October 1, 1997.	Employers who take a tax credit must comply with new tax provisions of the Act. All employees.	None	*
The Newborns' and Mothers' Health Protection Act of 1996 (Effective after January 1, 1998)	Covers any employer that has a group health plan (insured or self-insured).	The Act prohibits group health plans from restricting hospital stays for childbirth to less than a 48-hour minimum stay for a normal delivery and a 96-hour stay for a cesarean delivery. In addition, the plan may not require prior authorization to qualify for the 48-hour or 96-hour minimum stay.	Cover in medical plan documents.	*
The Mental Health Parity Act of 1996 (Effective January 1, 1998)	Covers employers with 50 or more employees. The new parity requirement will not apply to benefits furnished on or after September 30, 2001.	The Act provides that group health plans that offer mental health coverage may not set annual or lifetime limits for mental health coverage that are more restrictive than those for medical and surgical coverage.	Cover in medical plan documents.	*

* All state and federal posters may be ordered from the G. Neil Companies 1-800-999-9111.
NOTE: The minimum wage may be different in states like California where the minimum wage went to $6.25/hour 1/01/01 and to $6.75/hour in 1/01/02. January 1, 2001

STATE BY STATE ANALYSIS OF EEO LAWS

Following is a matrix of EEO laws by state. Because these regulations change from time to time, it is a good idea to check with the appropriate state regulatory agency if you have questions on the EEO laws and feel there may have been recent changes.

EEO LAWS BY STATE

State	EEO Law	Persons Protected	Enforcement Agency
Alabama	No comprehensive fair employment law.	State budget forbids discrimination based on sex or race in state employment.	
	Handicapped Discrimination in State Employment	Protects those with physical disabilities.	
Alaska	Human Rights Law	Race, color, religion, national origin, sex, age, physical or mental disability, changes in marital status, pregnancy or parenthood.	Alaska Commission for Human Rights
Arizona	Civil Rights Act	Race, color, religion, sex, age (at least 40), handicap or national origin.	Arizona Civil Rights Division
Arkansas	Civil Rights Act	Race, religion, ancestry, or national origin, gender (including pregnancy, childbirth or related medical conditions), or sensory, mental or physical disability.	Arkansas Department of Labor.
	Age discrimination in Public Employment	Public employees over 40 years old.	
California	Fair Employment & Housing Act	Race, religious creed, color, age (40 or over), national origin, ancestry, physical disability, or mental disability, medical condition, marital status or sex (including pregnancy, childbirth or related conditions).	Fair Employment & Housing Commission
	Sexual Orientation Bias Law	Sexual orientation.	
Colorado	Anti-Discrimination Act	Disability (physical & mental), race, creed, color, sex, age (over 40 & under 70), national origin, ancestry, lawful activity away from workplace during nonworking hours.	Colorado Civil Rights Commission
Connecticut	Human Rights and Opportunities	Race, color, religious creed, age, sex (including pregnancy or child-bearing capacity), marital status, national origin, ancestry, present or past history of mental disorder, mental retardation, physical disability, learning disability or sexual orientation.	Connecticut Commission on Human Rights and Opportunities
	Smokers' Rights Laws	Legal users of tobacco	
Delaware	Fair Employment Practices Act	Race, marital status, color, age (between 40 & 70), religion, sex or national origin	Delaware Department of Labor
District of Columbia	Human Rights Act	Race, color, religion, national origin, age (18 and older), sex (including pregnancy, childbirth or related conditions), marital status, personal appearance, sexual orientation, family responsibilities, disability, matriculation, political affiliation, source of income, place of business or residence.	Department of Homan Rights and Minority Business Development
	Smokers' Rights Law	Legal users of tobacco.	

State	EEO Law	Persons Protected	Enforcement Agency
Florida	Civil Human Rights Act	Race, color, religion, sex, national origin, age, handicap, or mental status.	Florida Commission in Human Relations
Georgia	Fair Employment Practices Act	Prohibits discrimination in public employment on the basis of race, color, religion, national origin, sex, handicap or age (between 40 & 70).	Commission on Equal Opportunity
	Equal Employment for Persons with Disabilities Code	Physical or mental disabilities.	
	Age Discrimination Act	Age (over 40 and under 70)	
Hawaii	Fair Employment Practices Law	Race, sex (including pregnancy, childbirth or related medical conditions), sexual orientation, age, religion, color, ancestry, handicapped status, marital status, arrest & court records, garnishments against employees, bankruptcy, work injury.	Hawaii Civil Rights Commission
Idaho	Fair Employment Practices Act	Race, color, religion, sex, national origin, age (40 and over) or handicap.	Idaho Commission on Human Rights
Illinois	Human Rights Act	Race, color, religion, national origin, citizenship status, ancestry, age (at least 40), sex (including sexual harassment), marital status, a determinable physical or mental handicap unrelated to ability to perform a particular job, military status, unfavorable discharge from military service, expunged, sealed or impounded arrest or criminal records.	Illinois Department of Human Rights
	Smokers' Rights Law	Legal users of tobacco.	
Indiana	Civil Rights Law	Race, religion, color, sex, disability, national origin, or ancestry.	Indiana Civil Rights Commission
	Indiana Age Discrimination Act	Age (over 40 and under 70).	
	Smokers' rights Law	Legal users of tobacco.	
Iowa	Civil Rights Act	Age (over 18), race, creed, color, sex (including pregnancy, childbirth and related conditions), national origin, religion, or disability.	Iowa Civil Rights Commission
Kansas	Act Against Discrimination	Race, religion, color, sex, disability, national origin, or ancestry.	Kansas Human Rights Commission
	Age Discrimination in Employment Act	Age (over 18).	
Kentucky	Civil Rights Act	Familial status, race, color, religion, national origin, sex (including pregnancy, childbirth and related conditions), age (over 40) and disability or legal users of tobacco.	Kentucky Human Rights Commission
	Discrimination Against Physically Handicapped	Disabled persons, those infected with AIDS or HIV.	

State	EEO Law	Persons Protected	Enforcement Agency
Louisiana	Fair Employment Practices Act	Race, color, religion, sex, disability, national origin.	Louisiana Commission on Human Rights Law
	Smokers' Rights Law	Legal users of tobacco.	
	Age Discrimination Law	Age (over 40 and under 70).	
	Civil Rights Act for Handicapped Persons	Those with physical or mental disabilities.	
Maine	Human Rights Act	Race, color, sex, physical or mental disability, religion, age, ancestry or national origin.	Maine Human Rights Commission
	Smokers' Rights Law	Legal users of tobacco.	
Maryland	Fair Employment Practices Act	Race, color, religion, sex, age, national origin, marital status, or physical or mental handicap unrelated to job performance (including HIV infection).	Maryland Human Relations Commission
Massachusetts	Fair Employment Practices Act	Race, color, religious creed, national origin, age (40 or older), sex (excluding sexual harassment), sexual orientation (excluding pedophilia), ancestry, physical or mental handicap.	Massachusetts Commission Against Discrimination.
Michigan	Discrimination in State Employment Law	Political affiliation, race, color, national origin, sex, religion, age or handicap.	Michigan Department of Civil Rights
	Handicapped Discrimination in State Employment Law	Physical disabilities such as blindness or deafness unless the disability affects performance.	
	Smokers' Rights Law	Legal users of tobacco.	
Minnesota	Human Rights Act	Political affiliation, race, color, religion, national origin, sex, marital status, status with regard to public assistance, membership or activity in a local commission, disability, sexual orientation or age.	Minnesota Department of Human Rights
	Smokers' Rights Law	Legal users of tobacco	
	Age Discrimination Law	Age	
Mississippi	Discrimination in State Employment Law	Political affiliation, race, color, national origin, sex, religion, age or handicap.	Mississippi State Personnel Board
	Handicapped Discrimination In State Employment Law	Physical disabilities such as blindness or deafness unless the disability affects performance.	
	Smokers' Rights Law	Legal users of tobacco.	

State	EEO Law	Persons Protected	Enforcement Agency
Missouri	Civil Rights Act	Race, color, religion, national origin, sex, ancestry, age (over 40 and under 70) or handicap.	Missouri Commission on Human Rights
	Smokers' Rights Law	Legal users of tobacco.	
	AIDS Act	Those infected with HIV or AIDS.	
Montana	Human Rights Act	Race, creed, religion, marital status, color, sex, physical or mental handicap, age or national origin.	Montana Human Rights Commission
	Smokers' Rights Law	Legal users of tobacco.	
Nebraska	Fair Employment Practices Act	Race, color, religion, sex (including sexual harassment and pregnancy, childbirth or related medical conditions), disability, marital status or national origin.	Nebraska Equal Opportunity Commission
Nevada	Age Discrimination Law	Age (over 40 and under 70).	Nevada Equal Rights Commission
	Fair Employment Practices Act	Race, color, religion, national origin, sex, age, disability, smokers.	
New Hampshire	Law Against Discrimination	Age, race, sex, color, marital status, physical or mental disability, religious creed or national origin.	New Hampshire Commission for Human Rights
	Smokers' Rights Law	Legal users of tobacco.	
New Jersey	Law Against Discrimination	Race, creed, color, national origin, ancestry, age (over 40 and under 70), marital status, affectional or sexual orientation, sex, atypical hereditary cellular or blood trait, genetic information, refusal to submit to a genetic test or make the results available to an employer, liability for service in the Armed Forces, physical or mental handicap unrelated to job performance (including infection with HIV or AIDS), familial status.	New Jersey Division on Civil Rights
	Smokers' Rights law	Legal users of tobacco.	
New Mexico	Human Rights Act	Race, age, religion, color, national origin, ancestry, sex, physical or mental disability, or serious medical condition.	New Mexico Human Rights Commission
	Employee Privacy Act	Legal users of tobacco.	
New York	Human Rights Act	Age (18 or older), race, creed, color, national origin, sex, disability, genetic predisposition or carrier status, or marital status.	New York Division on Human Rights
	Smokers' Rights Law	Legal users of tobacco.	
North Carolina	Equal Employment Practices Act	Race, religion, color, national origin, age, sex or handicap.	North Carolina Human Relations Commission
	Smokers' Rights Law	Legal users of tobacco.	
	Communicable Disease Law	Those infected with HIV.	

State	EEO Law	Persons Protected	Enforcement Agency
North Dakota	Human Rights Act Age Discrimination Act	Race, color, religion, sex (including sexual harassment and pregnancy, childbirth or related medical conditions), national origin, age, physical or mental handicap, status with respect to marriage or public assistance or participation in lawful activities off the employer's premises during nonworking hours. Age.	
Ohio	Fair Employment Practice Law	Race, color, religion, national origin, handicap, age, ancestry, sex (including pregnancy, childbirth or related medical conditions).	Ohio Civil Rights Commission
Oklahoma	Age Discrimination law Anti-Discrimination Act Smokers' Rights Law	Age (40 or over). Race, color, religion, sex, national origin, age, handicap. Legal users of tobacco.	Oklahoma Human Rights Commission
Oregon	Fair Employment Practices Act Smokers' Rights Law	Race, religion, color, sex (including pregnancy, childbirth or related medical conditions), marital status, national origin, age over 18, a juvenile record that has been expunged or disability. Legal users of tobacco.	Bureau of Labor & Industries
Pennsylvania	Human Relations Act	Race, color, familial status, religious creed, ancestry, age, sex, national origin, or non-job related disability.	Pennsylvania Human Relations Act
Rhode Island	Fair Employment Practices Act Smokers' Rights Law	Race or color, sex, sexual orientation, religion, disability, age or country of ancestral origin. Legal users of tobacco.	Rhode Island Commission for Human Rights
South Carolina	Human Affairs Law Handicapped Bill of Rights Smokers' Rights Law	Race, religion, color, national origin, age (over 40) or sex. Legal users of tobacco.	South Carolina Human Affairs Commission
South Dakota	Human Relations Act Smokers' Rights Law	Race, color, creed, religion, sex, ancestry, disability or national origin. Legal users of tobacco.	South Dakota Division of Human Rights.
Tennessee	ANT-Discrimination Act Smokers' Rights Law	Race, creed, color, religion, sex, age (40 or older) or national origin. Legal users of tobacco.	Tennessee Human Rights Commission
Texas	Employment Discrimination Law	Race, color, disability, religion, sex (including pregnancy, childbirth or related medical conditions), national origin, or age (40 or older).	Texas Commission of Human Rights

State	EEO Law	Persons Protected	Enforcement Agency
Utah	Antidiscrimination Act	Race, color, sex (including pregnancy, childbirth or related medical conditions), religion, national origin, handicap or age (40 or older).	Utah Antidiscrimination Division of the Industrial Commission State Human Rights Commission
Vermont	Fair Employment Practices Act	Race, color, religion, ancestry, national origin, sex (including sexual harassment), sexual orientation, place of birth, age (18 years or older) or physical or mental condition, individuals who have tested positive for HIV.	Civil Rights Commission of the Vermont Attorney General's Office
Virginia	Human Rights Act	Race, color, religion, national origin, sex, (including pregnancy, childbirth or related medical conditions), age, marital status, disability.	Council of Human Rights Governor's Office
	Public Employees' Smoking Law	Legal state employee users of tobacco.	
Washington	Law Against Discrimination in Employment	Age (40 or older), sex, marital status, race, creed, color, national origin (including ancestry), presence of any sensory, mental or physical disability.	Washington State Human Rights Commission
West Virginia	Human Rights Act	Race, religion, color, national origin, ancestry, sex, age (40 or older), blindness or other handicap.	West Virginia Human Rights Commission
	Smokers' Rights Law	Legal users of tobacco.	
Wisconsin	Fair Employment Act	Age (over 40), race, creed, color, handicap, marital status, sex (including sexual harassment and pregnancy, childbirth or related medical conditions), national origin, ancestry, sexual orientation, arrest or conviction record, service in the armed forces, genetic testing, and the use or nonuse of lawful products off employer's premises during nonworking hours.	Department of Industry, Labor and Human Relations
Wyoming	Fair Employment Practices Act of 1965	Handicap, race, color, creed, sex, age (over 40 and under 70), national origin, ancestry, legal users of tobacco.	Wyoming Fair Employment Commission

January 2001

COMPLYING WITH THE IMMIGRATION REFORM
AND CONTROL ACT OF 1986

Most companies are required to verify the work authorization and identity of all employees and applicants for employment. The Form I-9 must be completed for every new employee, and the forms must be retained for at least three years.

Methods by which the personnel department can verify applicant eligibility are provided on the Form I-9.

Some business people don't think they will ever be audited and have not taken the time and effort to verify work authorization. Donald Russell, Director of the Denver INS Office for the three-state area encompassing Colorado, Wyoming, and Utah says that more than a dozen companies within that district were cited in one year and more than thirty companies have been audited and are awaiting review.

The fines are substantial. An Aspen company that owns two restaurants was fined $52,500 after knowingly hiring three illegal workers and having more than 100 paperwork violations.

Although INS does carry out spot inspections, most of their information about violators comes from tips from disgruntled employees or other informants.

It makes good economic sense to comply with federal law in this area. Don't take a chance by violating the documentation laws.

Manager's Tip

Purchase a large expandable alphabetical file and keep your I-9 forms in it. If an inspector comes in and asks to review your I-9s you don't have to go through all the personnel files pulling them out. Also Department of Labor, Wage and Hour inspectors coming into your company to investigate a complaint on wage and hour violations may ask to review your I-9 files while there.

What You Need to Know About the Immigration Law and Completion of the Immigration Form I-9

If you employ persons to perform labor or services in return for wages or other pay, you must complete Form I-9 for:

PERSONS HIRED AFTER MAY 31, 1987   For these employees, you must complete a Form I-9 within three business days of the date of the hire. If you employ the person for less than three days, you must complete the Form I-9 before the end of the employee's first working day.

PERSONS HIRED BETWEEN NOVEMBER 7, 1986 AND MAY 31, 1987   For these employees, you must complete Form I-9 before September 1, 1987.

Note:

If you employ people for domestic work in your private home on a regular basis, these requirements also apply to you.

You *do not* need to complete Form I-9 for:

- Persons hired before November 7, 1986
- Persons hired after November 6, 1986, who left your employment before June 1, 1987
- Persons you employ for domestic work in a private home on an intermittent or sporadic basis
- Persons who provide labor to you who are employed by a contractor providing contract services (employee leasing)
- Persons who are independent contractors.

Persons who are self-employed do not need to complete Form I-9.

Note:

Congress is still considering major Immigration Law reform. Changes in the law may take place after publication of this book. Contact the U. S. Department of Justice, Immigration and Naturalization Service for current regulations.

March 20, 1996 was the deadline for immigrants with "green cards" (Form I-l 51) issued before 1979 to apply for a new card.

The replacement cards, issued by the Immigration and Naturalization Service, are pink and must be renewed every 10 years. The applications take six to eight months to process, and new cards are mailed to applicants.

You should be aware of the following:

- For employees hired *before* March 20, 1996—Employers *do not* have to reverify employment eligibility for those employees who used a green card issued before 1979 to establish employment eligibility on the I-9 Form.
- For employees hired *after* March 20, 1996—The original green cards *may not* be used as documentation to establish employment eligibility on the I-9 Form.

U.S. Department of Justice
Immigration and Naturalization Service

OMB No. 1115-0136
Employment Eligibility Verification

Please read Instructions carefully before completing this form. The Instructions must be available during completion of this form. ANTI-DISCRIMINATION NOTICE. It is illegal to discriminate against work eligible individuals. Employers CANNOT specify which document(s) they will accept from an employee. The refusal to hire an individual because of a future expiration date may also constitute illegal discrimination.

Section 1. Employee Information and Verification. To be completed and signed by employee at the time employment begins

Print Name: Last	First	Middle Initial	Maiden Name

Address (Street Name and Number)		Apt. #	Date of Birth (month/day/year)

City	State	Zip Code	Social Security #

I am aware that federal law provides for imprisonment and/or fines for false statements or use of false documents in connection with the completion of this form.	I attest, under penalty of perjury, that I am (check one of the following): ☐ A citizen or national of the United States ☐ A Lawful Permanent Resident (Alien # A _____) ☐ An alien authorized to work until ___/___/___ (Alien # or Admission # _____)

Employee's Signature	Date (month/day/year)

Preparer and/or Translator Certification. *(To be completed and signed if Section 1 is prepared by a person other than the employee.) I attest, under penalty of perjury, that I have assisted in the completion of this form and that to the best of my knowledge the information is true and correct.*

Preparer's/Translator's Signature	Print Name

Address (Street Name and Number, City, State, Zip Code)	Date (month/day/year)

Section 2. Employer Review and Verification. To be completed and signed by employer. Examine one document from List A OR examine one document from List B and one from List C as listed on the reverse of this form and record the title, number and expiration date, if any, of the document(s)

List A	OR	List B	AND	List C
Document title: _____		_____		_____
Issuing authority: _____		_____		_____
Document #: _____		_____		_____
Expiration Date (if any): __/__/__		__/__/__		__/__/__
Document #: _____				
Expiration Date (if any): __/__/__				

CERTIFICATION - I attest, under penalty of perjury, that I have examined the document(s) presented by the above-named employee, that the above-listed document(s) appear to be genuine and to relate to the employee named, that the employee began employment on (month/day/year) __/__/__ and that to the best of my knowledge the employee is eligible to work in the United States. (State employment agencies may omit the date the employee began employment).

Signature of Employer or Authorized Representative	Print Name	Title

Business or Organization Name	Address (Street Name and Number, City, State, Zip Code)	Date (month/day/year)

Section 3. Updating and Reverification. To be completed and signed by employer

A. New Name (if applicable)	B. Date of rehire (month/day/year) (if applicable)

C. If employee's previous grant of work authorization has expired, provide the information below for the document that establishes current employment eligibility.

Document Title: _____   Document #: _____   Expiration Date (if any): ___/___/___

I attest, under penalty of perjury, that to the best of my knowledge, this employee is eligible to work in the United States, and if the employee presented document(s), the document(s) I have examined appear to be genuine and to relate to the individual.

Signature of Employer or Authorized Representative	Date (month/day/year)

Form I-9 (Rev. 11-21-91) N

LISTS OF ACCEPTABLE DOCUMENTS

LIST A		LIST B		LIST C
Documents that Establish Both Identity and Employment Eligibility	**OR**	**Documents that Establish Identity**	**AND**	**Documents that Establish Employment Eligibility**

LIST A — Documents that Establish Both Identity and Employment Eligibility

1. U.S. Passport (unexpired or expired)
2. Certificate of U.S. Citizenship (INS Form N-560 or N-561)
3. Certificate of Naturalization (INS Form N-550 or N-570)
4. Unexpired foreign passport, with I-551 stamp or attached INS Form I-94 indicating unexpired employment authorization
5. Alien Registration Receipt Card with photograph (INS Form I-151 or I-551)
6. Unexpired Temporary Resident Card (INS Form I-688)
7. Unexpired Employment Authorization Card (INS Form I-688A)
8. Unexpired Reentry Permit (INS Form I-327)
9. Unexpired Refugee Travel Document (INS Form I-571)
10. Unexpired Employment Authorization Document issued by the INS which contains a photograph (INS Form I-688B)

OR

LIST B — Documents that Establish Identity

1. Driver's license or ID card issued by a state or outlying possession of the United States provided it contains a photograph or information such as name, date of birth, sex, height, eye color, and address
2. ID card issued by federal, state, or local government agencies or entities provided it contains a photograph or information such as name, date of birth, sex, height, eye color, and address
3. School ID card with a photograph
4. Voter's registration card
5. U.S. Military card or draft record
6. Military dependent's ID card
7. U.S. Coast Guard Merchant Mariner Card
8. Native American tribal document
9. Driver's license issued by a Canadian government authority

For persons under age 18 who are unable to present a document listed above:

10. School record or report card
11. Clinic, doctor, or hospital record
12. Day-care or nursery school record

AND

LIST C — Documents that Establish Employment Eligibility

1. U.S. social security card issued by the Social Security Administration (other than a card stating it is not valid for employment)
2. Certification of Birth Abroad issued by the Department of State (Form FS-545 or Form DS-1350)
3. Original or certified copy of a birth certificate issued by a state, county, municipal authority or outlying possession of the United States bearing an official seal
4. Native American tribal document
5. U.S. Citizen ID Card (INS Form I-197)
6. ID Card for use of Resident Citizen in the United States (INS Form I-179)
7. Unexpired employment authorization document issued by the INS (other than those listed under List A)

Illustrations of many of these documents appear in Part 8 of the Handbook for Employers (M-274)

Form I-9 (Rev. 11-21-91) N

QUESTIONS AND ANSWERS ABOUT I-9 IMMIGRATION FORMS

Q. Where can I get the Form I-9?

A. There are three copies of the Form I-9 in this book. You can photocopy the forms. You may obtain a limited number of copies from INS, or you may order them in bulk from the Superintendent of Documents at the following address:

> Superintendent of Documents
> U.S. Government Printing Office
> Washington, D.C. 20402
> Tel. (202) 783-3238

Q. Do United States citizens need to prove they are eligible to work?

A. Yes. While United States citizens are automatically eligible for employment, they too must provide the required documents and complete the Form I-9.

Q. Do I need to complete an I-9 for everyone who applies for a job with my company?

A. No. You need to complete I-9s only for people you actually hire. For purposes of the new law, a person is "hired" when he or she begins to work for you.

Q. Do I need to fill out an I-9 for independent contractors or their employees?

A. No. For example, if you contract with another company to provide temporary secretarial services, you do not have to complete I-9s for that company's employees. The other company is responsible for completing the I-9s for its own employees. However, you must not knowingly use contract labor to circumvent the law against hiring unauthorized workers.

Q. What do I do when an employee's work authorization expires?

A. You will need to update the I-9 if you want to continue employing the person. At that time, the employee must present a document that either shows an extension of employment eligibility or that is a new grant of work authorization. If the employee cannot produce such a document, that person is no longer eligible to work. Continuing to employ that person is a violation of the law, even if the employee was previously authorized to work.

Q. As an employer, do I have to fill out all the I-9s myself?

A. No, you may designate someone to fill out the form for you such as a personnel officer, foreman, agent, or anyone else acting in your interest. However, you are still responsible for compliance with the law.

Q. When I review the identity and work authorization documents, should I make photocopies of them?

A. The law does not require you to photocopy documents. However, if you wish to make photocopies, you must retain them with the I-9. Photocopies must not be used for any other purpose.

Q.   **What are the requirements for retaining the I-9?**

A.   You must retain the form for at least three years. If you employ the person for more than three years, you must retain the form for one year after the person leaves your employment.

Q.   **Will I get any advance notice if an INS or DOL officer wishes to inspect my I-9s?**

A.   Yes. The officer will give you at least three days' advance notice before the inspection. He or she will not need to show you a subpoena or warrant at that time. Failure to provide the I-9s for inspection could result in civil penalties.

Q.   **What happens if I do everything the new law requires and INS discovers that one of my employees is not actually authorized to work?**

A.   Unless the government can show that you had actual knowledge of the illegal status of the employee, you will have an affirmative defense against the imposition of employer sanctions penalties if you have done the following things:

- had employees fill out their part of the I-9 when they started to work;
- checked the required documents (they should appear to be genuine and to relate to the individual);
- properly completed the I-9;
- retained the form for the specified time; and
- presented the form upon request to an INS or Department of Labor Officer. You will receive at least three days' advance notice.

Q.   **May I specify which documents I will accept for verification?**

A.   No. You must accept any document or combination of documents listed on the I-9 that appear to be genuine.

Q.   **What should I do if the person I hire is unable to provide the required documents within three days?**

A.   If an employee is unable to provide the required document or documents within three days he or she must at least produce a receipt showing that he or she has applied for the document. The employee must produce the document itself within twenty-one days of the hire.

Q.   **What is my responsibility concerning the authenticity of documents?**

A.   You should examine the documents. If they appear to be genuine on their face and relate to the person, you should accept them. If on their face the documents do not appear to be genuine or relate to the person, you should not accept them. In addition, if the work authorization documents carry restrictions, you should abide by them.

Where to Get More Information on Immigration Law and Obtain the I-9 Forms

You may obtain information from one of the following local INS offices. Direct your letter to the attention of the *Employer Relations Officer.*

ALABAMA

75 Spring Street S.W.
Atlanta, GA 30303

ALASKA

701 "C" Street, Room D-25 1
Lock Box 16
Anchorage, AK 99513

ARIZONA

230 North First Avenue
Phoenix, AZ 85025

ARKANSAS

701 Loyola Avenue, Room T-8005
New Orleans, LA 70113

CALIFORNIA

300 North Los Angeles Street
Los Angeles, CA 90012

880 Front Street
San Diego, CA 92188

630 Sansome Street
San Francisco, CA 94111

COLORADO

1787 Federal Building
1961 Stout Street
Denver, CO 80202

CONNECTICUT

JFK Federal Building
Government Center
Boston, MA 02203

DELAWARE

601 Market Street
Room 1321, U.S. Courthouse
Philadelphia, PA 19106

DISTRICT OF COLUMBIA

4420 North Fairfax Drive
Arlington, VA 22203

FLORIDA

7880 Biscayne Boulevard
Miami, FL 33138

GEORGIA

75 Spring Street S.W.
Atlanta, GA 30303

GUAM

595 Ala Moana Boulevard
Honolulu, HI 96813

HAWAII

595 Ala Moana Boulevard
Honolulu, HI 96813

IDAHO

Federal Building, Room 512
310 South Park, Drawer 10036
Helena, MT 59626-0036

INDIANA

219 South Dearborn Street
Chicago, IL 60604

IOWA

Federal Building, Room 1008
106 South 15th Street
Omaha, NE 68102

KANSAS

9747 North Conant Avenue
Kansas City, MO 64153

KENTUCKY

701 Loyola Avenue, Room T-8005
New Orleans, LA 70113

LOUISIANA

701 Loyola Avenue, Room T-8005
New Orleans, LA 70113

MAINE

P.O. Box 578, Downtown Station
Portland, ME 04112

MARYLAND

101 West Lombard Street
Baltimore, MD 21201

MASSACHUSETTS

JFK Federal Building
Government Center
Boston, MA 02203

MICHIGAN

333 Mount Elliott Street
Detroit, MI 48207

MINNESOTA

927 Main Post Office Building
St. Paul, MN 55101

MISSISSIPPI

701 Loyola Avenue, Room T-8005
New Orleans, LA 70113

MISSOURI

9747 North Conant Avenue
Kansas City, MO 64153

MONTANA

Federal Building, Room 512
310 South Park, Drawer 10036
Helena, MT 59626-0036

NEBRASKA

Federal Building, Room 1008
106 South 15th Street
Omaha, NE 68102

NEVADA

230 North First Avenue
Phoenix, AZ 85025

NEW HAMPSHIRE

JFK Federal Building
Government Center
Boston, MA 02203

NEW JERSEY

970 Broad Street
Newark, NJ 07102

NEW MEXICO

343 U.S. Courthouse
P.O. Box 9398
El Paso, TX 79984

NEW YORK

68 Court Street
Buffalo, NY 14202

26 Federal Plaza
New York, NY 10278

NORTH CAROLINA

75 Spring Street S.W.
Atlanta, GA 30303

NORTH DAKOTA

927 Main Post Office Building
St. Paul, MN 55101

OHIO
1240 East 9th Street, Room 1917
Cleveland, OH 44199

OKLAHOMA
Federal Building, Room 6A 21
1100 Commerce Street
Dallas, TX 75242

OREGON
511 N.W. Broadway
Portland, OR 97209

PENNSYLVANIA
601 Market Street
Room 1321, U.S. Courthouse
Philadelphia, PA 19106

PUERTO RICO
GPO Box 5068
San Juan, Puerto Rico 00936

RHODE ISLAND
JFK Federal Building
Government Center
Boston, MA 02203

SOUTH CAROLINA
75 Spring Street S.W.
Atlanta, GA 30303

SOUTH DAKOTA
927 Main Post Office Building
St. Paul, MN 55101

TENNESSEE
701 Loyola Avenue, Room T-8005
New Orleans, LA 70113

TEXAS
Federal Building, Room 6A 21
1100 Commerce Street
Dallas, TX 75242

P.O. Box 9398
El Paso, TX 79984

2102 Teege Road
Harlingen, TX 78550

2627 Caroline Street
Houston, TX 77004

727 East Durango, Suite A301
San Antonio, TX 78206

UTAH
1787 Federal Building
1961 Stout Street
Denver, CO 80202

VERMONT
P.O. Box 578, Downtown Station
Portland, ME 04112

VIRGINIA
4420 North Fairfax Drive
Arlington, VA 22203

VIRGIN ISLANDS
GPO Box 5068
San Juan, Puerto Rico 00936

WASHINGTON
815 Airport Way South
Seattle, WA 98134

WEST VIRGINIA
601 Market Street
Room 1321, U.S. Courthouse
Philadelphia, PA 19106

WISCONSIN
219 South Dearborn Street
Chicago, IL 60604

WYOMING
1787 Federal Building
1961 Stout Street
Denver, CO 80202

THE OBJECTIVE OF WORKERS' COMPENSATION

When accidents happen at work, employers are required to ensure an employee is provided with income protection and medical care.

Workers' compensation is designed to protect employees who suffer work-related injuries or illnesses. Each state governs its own workers' compensation program. Specific benefits vary by state.

The objectives of workers' compensation are:

- To provide income and medical benefits to victims of work-related injuries or illnesses.

- To provide rehabilitation so that injured parties may again become gainfully employed.

- To encourage employer interest in workplace safety and accident/illness prevention.

Standard Workers' Compensation Exemptions

Most states cover all employees under workers' compensation, however, some states exempt the following:

Municipal government employees or certain categories of government employees such as police officers, firefighters, etc. These employees are usually covered by a special program. Family members working for a family-owned business, religious organizations, or members of the clergy, domestic workers working in private homes, volunteers, self-employed people and agricultural workers.

Injuries/Illnesses Covered By Workers' Compensation

The exact definition of a work-related injury or illness varies by state. Generally, work-related injuries/illnesses are covered as follows:

Specific injury/illness:	Resulting from an incident or exposure in the workplace that causes an injury or illness. For example, if an employee injures his or her back lifting a box at work, that is a specific injury.
Cumulative injury/illness:	Caused by repetitive activities extending over a period of time. Carpal tunnel syndrome and stress disorders are examples of cumulative injuries/illnesses.

Some states provide for exclusions from coverage for work-related injury/illness that occur under special circumstances, such as, injuries suffered while under the influence of drugs or alcohol in violation of company policy. Check with your workers' compensation insurance carrier to determine exclusions allowed in your state.

In addition to injuries sustained on the job, most state laws hold employers liable for injuries "arising out of and in the course of employment." Such activities might include an employer sponsored softball game or a bowling league. For example: Employers should be careful to ensure that employees are not pressured to participate in these activities. To avoid liability, employers should emphasize the voluntary nature of such activities, and have employees sign "informed consent" forms which acknowledge their voluntary participation. Check with your workers' compensation carrier regarding such activities.

Covered Benefits

Generally workers' compensation benefits include:

Medical Expenses:	Coverage for medical treatment (including diagnostic testing, doctor visits, surgery, physical therapy or chiropractic treatment, hospitalization, and prescriptions) for injuries or illnesses sustained during the course of employment.
Temporary Total Disability:	Provides income benefits while the person is restricted from work due to his or her work-related injury/illness.
	The employee's average wage during the pre-injury period is used in the formula to calculate the cash benefits paid by the workers' compensation system.
Permanent Partial Disability:	Provides benefits for expected income loss due to a person's permanent partial disability arising from a work-related injury or illness, when the person cannot return to work.
Permanent Total Disability:	Provides benefits for workers who have permanent work-related injuries that are totally disabling (with respect to his or her occupation).
Rehabilitation:	Provides funds for educational and training expenses, as well as temporary total disability income during retraining when a person cannot return to his or her usual and customary occupation as a result of his or her work-related injury/illness.
Death Benefits:	When a work-related accident or exposure results in death, the employee's spouse or dependent children are usually eligible for death/survivor benefits. These may be in the form of a lump-sum payment (for example, a life insurance benefit), or a monthly payment for a specified period of time, for example, monthly payment to dependent children until high school or college graduation.

Check the law in your state to determine the types of benefits available to your employees.

Work-Related Injury/Illness Liability

Workers' compensation is intended to be an *exclusive remedy* program. This means that (1) employers accept full responsibility for the injuries/illnesses incurred by their employees arising out of, and in the course of their employment, and (2) employees accept the benefits prescribed by the state in lieu of suing employers for other damages. However, under some circumstances, employees may still sue the employer or other parties for work-related injuries/illnesses for liability in tort. The premise for these claims can be gross negligence or *intentional acts* on the part of the employer. Negligence claims may include:

Employer negligence—Where it can be demonstrated that the employer knowingly allowed a safety hazard to exist that was likely to result in an injury/illness.

Fellow employee—Suits against a fellow employee who the injured party believes caused the injury/illness through his or her intentional acts.

Contractors—Suits against contractors or subcontractors working in the place of employment whose actions caused the injury/illness.

Manufacturers—Suits against manufacturers on whose equipment the employee sustained the injury, or manufacturers of hazardous substances.

Failure to Carry Workers' Compensation Insurance

When state law requires employers to carry workers' compensation insurance coverage, liability for failure to carry insurance can be extensive. Again, specific liabilities/penalties are defined by your state's laws. However, typical liabilities/penalties include:

- The employee is still entitled to benefits as though the employer had insurance coverage. Such benefits are paid directly by the employer.

- The injured employee may bring a civil lawsuit against the uninsured employer. Since the employer is in violation of state law, negligence and, therefore, liability may be presumed.

- The uninsured employer may be subject to regulatory agency fines and penalties, both civil and criminal.

Requirements

While requirements vary by state, employers are generally required to:

- Post a visible notice advising employees of their rights under workers' compensation laws.

- Provide employees with the name of the employer's workers' compensation insurance carrier.

- Take accident reports, and submit claim forms for workers' compensation insurance benefits on behalf of employees.

- Notify the insurance carrier of workplace accidents on a timely basis. Most states have claim reporting deadline requirements and assess penalties for late filing. Exceptions may be made if records are kept off site.

- Report a death or serious injury to the appropriate agency (i.e., OSHA) by phone, fax or telegram within 24 hours.

- Maintain an OSHA 200 log of reportable workplace injuries and post it annually (February).

- Cooperate with workers' compensation insurance carriers investigating claims for benefits.
- Protect employees who file or support a claim for workers' compensation insurance benefits from any form of discrimination or retaliation related to the claim.

Financing of Workers' Compensation

Risk financing is the manner in which an organization finances its obligation to remedy workers' compensation claims.

There are basically three types of risk financing:

1. Assumption of risk, (self-insured or self-funded).
2. Transfer of risk, using a contract or leased employee.
3. Purchase of indemnity insurance.

Self-Insurance

Self-insurance programs involve the decision to retain risk rather than to insure it, and requires a formalized plan and a system to pay losses as they occur. Accurate loss data records of claims funding and other claims costs must be maintained. Depending on state regulations, a formal self-insurance program may be funded on a "pay as you go" basis from operating cash balances, through systematic payments into a special reserve fund, or through loan instruments such as letters of credit.

Third-Party Contracting

Some employers choose to transfer risk by contracting with a third party. In this case people are provided on a temporary basis to an employer, and the third parry agency is responsible for providing workers' compensation coverage. Or an employer may retain the services of an independent contractor who is typically not covered by workers' compensation coverage.

Purchasing Insurance Coverage

The most common approach to workers' compensation coverage is to purchase insurance. Forty-four states allow an employer to choose its workers' compensation carrier, the remaining six states below require employers to insure via monopolistic state compensation funds:

Nevada
North Dakota
Ohio
Washington
West Virginia
Wyoming

The following states offer the employer the choice of insuring through a private carrier or the state fund:

Arizona	Minnesota
California	Montana
Colorado	New York
Hawaii	Oklahoma
Idaho	Oregon
Louisiana	Pennsylvania
Maine	Tennessee
Maryland	Texas
Michigan	Utah

Reform of the Workers' Compensation System

Recently some states have enacted workers' compensation insurance reforms, including: revised reporting and record keeping requirements; redefined benefit levels; toll-free telephone numbers for reporting safety and health hazards; revised funding arrangements; fraud protection provisions designed to protect employers and the workers' compensation system against fraudulent claims; additional categories of work-related injuries/illnesses including HIV/AIDS, carpal tunnel syndrome, stress or psychological disorders, and prolonged exposure to chemicals or toxins such as radon or electromagnetic exposures.

Manager's Tip

The workers' compensation system should never be used to get rid of an unwanted employee. The practice is illegal and can increase costs for every employer in the system. Employers must be aware of the consequences of taking such action and avoid retaliatory discharge of an employee. The employer who engages in this practice is subject to severe fines as well as civil lawsuits at both the state and federal levels.

WHAT TO DO ABOUT WORKERS' COMP COSTS

HR managers can save money by focusing on safety and showing concern for injured employees. The Workers' Compensation (WC) system is socking it to companies and companies are looking for ways to cut these costs. The average cost of a Workers' Comp claim has tripled in the last ten years, exceeding $19,000 per claim. A Fortune 500 company can easily pay out $50 to $100 million a year in WC claims. Small companies also have a difficult time. They often can't afford to self-insure as many large companies can and their insurance premiums took annual double-digit jumps through most of the 1990's.

The U.S. economy as a whole is feeling the pain. Workers' Comp premiums are tied to a company's payroll, rising as employees are added and salaries increase. For several years now, reform of the WC system has been near the top of the legislative agenda in many states. Business groups have been lobbying intensively for ways to slow the growth in benefits and for other structural changes that only lawmakers can put in place. These bills, however, are crawling through the legislative process at a slow pace. In the meantime, HR managers can effect dramatic cost savings on their own by focusing on safety and the care of injured employees. Here are some things you can do to cut your WC costs:

- Communicate with workers. Show concern over an injury and don't let the employee become an adversary. When you do costs soar.
- Watch for careless managers. One company pays Workers' Comp claims out of a corporate pool. When you establish monetary rewards you will see a tremendous decrease in accidents.
- Get employees back to work fast. Employees usually get bored and want to get back to work. The Weyerhaeuser Corporation has formalized its return to work program with task banks. Each department is responsible for finding assignments that an impaired person can handle.
- Find out what's causing the injuries. Track them and get rid of the problems. Do whatever you need to do to cut down on injuries. More training, more safety initiatives may need to be provided.

A small issue that does have costly implications if not addressed, is the situation where an employee is hurt on the job and just goes to his own doctor and runs up substantial bills that aren't always necessary. You can curtail this cost if you have each employee sign a Workers' Comp Verification Form when they are hired. This form tells the employee that if they are hurt on the job they **must** go to a company designated physician. If they don't go to the company designated physician, they agree that you can charge them for the services. See form that follows.

(Company Name Goes Here)

WORKERS' COMPENSATION
EMPLOYEE VERIFICATION FORM

I have been notified by my employer of the procedure to follow in the event I incur work-related injury or illness. I understand that my employer has designated the
_____ as the primary provider for all work-related injuries and illnesses. I understand that if do not receive my medical care for work-related injuries and illnesses from the _____
I may be financially responsible for that care. See attached list of locations and phone numbers.

I have been informed that authorization is required from my employer before I access medical care for non-emergency work related injuries and illnesses.

_____   _____

Name of Employee (Please Print)   Location

_____   _____

Signature of Employee   Date

_____   _____

Signature of Human Resources Manager   Date

WORKER'S COMP CHECKLIST

Following is a checklist of actions you can take to further reduce your Worker's Comp (WC) costs:

1. Conduct research and document your organization's WC costs. Pay particular attention to your experience since the last time WC costs began to increase. The last cycle can give you a good indication of what to expect.

2. In your research, establish what strategies were previously used to contain costs. Reevaluate those strategies. Find out what other similar companies are doing. Look at benchmarks in your industry and establish new WC policies to contain costs.

3. Make sure you have an effective safety program in place. You may want to hire an outside safety consultant to review your policies and safety procedures to make sure they are adequate and effective. Your insurance carrier can recommend a consultant.

4. Put someone in charge of coordinating WC claims and nonoccupational disability claims in order to eliminate duplicate claims and assure employees receive timely assistance.

5. Review and update your claims reporting system in order to reduce administrative costs.

6. Assign responsiblity for monitoring claims performance monthly. Hopefully you will spot cost increases before they become a problem.

7. You might start charging WC costs to departments so managers understand that their WC costs have a direct impact on the bottom line.

8. Train managers so they know how to respond when an employee sustains a work related injury. Workers are more likely to return to work promptly when they know their bosses care. Stay in touch with injured employees—communicate.

9. Treat employees well. Positive treatment boosts productivity and is a good way to control WC costs. Satisfied employees are less likely to file phony WC claims.

10. Talk to your insurance broker and your WC carrier to ensure the insurance arrangement you have is best suited to your organization's current needs and get involved at the legislative level to ensure WC costs are contained.

Workplace Injuries Under FMLA and ADA

It used to be that an employer's only concern about a workplace injury was whether or not the injury would result in a compensable workers' compensation claim, but now employers have to view every workplace injury not only as a potential workers' compensation claim, but also as a potential Americans With Disabilities Act (ADA) or Family and Medical Leave Act (FMLA) claim.

Because of the potential expense in an ADA action or FMLA leave request, employers need to reconsider how to manage injuries which have occurred in the workplace to minimize their exposure. This includes providing alternative work arrangements for injured employees who continue employment. The ultimate goal is to return employees to work as soon as possible. In addition, employers should concentrate on methods to minimize exposure to workplace injuries.

DIRECTORY OF STATE WORKERS' COMPENSATION OFFICES

Employment Standards Administration
Office of State Liaison and Legislative Analysis
Division of State Workers' Compensation Programs

ALABAMA
Workmen's Compensation
Division of Workmen's Compensation
Department of Industrial Relations
Industrial Relations Building
Montgomery, Alabama 36130
(205) 261-2868

ALASKA
Workmen's Compensation Division
Department of Labor
Post Office Box 1149
Juneau, Alaska 99802
(907) 465-2790

ARIZONA
Workmen's Compensation Division
Industrial Commission
Post Office Box 19070
1601 West Jefferson Street
Phoenix, Arizona 85005
(602) 255-4661

ARKANSAS
Workmen's Compensation Commission
Justice Building
State Capitol Grounds
Little Rock, Arkansas 72201
(501) 372-3930

CALIFORNIA
Division of Industrial Accidents
Department of Industrial Relations
525 Golden Gate Avenue, 6th Floor
San Francisco, California 94102
(415) 557-3542

COLORADO
Division of Labor
Department of Labor and Employment
1313 Sherman Street
Denver, Colorado 80203
(303) 866-2782

CONNECTICUT
Workers' Compensation Commission
1890 Dixwell Avenue
Hamden, Connecticut 06514
(203) 789-7783, 579-6235

DELAWARE
Industrial Accident Board
Carvel State Office Building, 6th Floor
820 North French Street
Wilmington, Delaware 19801
(302) 571-2884

DISTRICT OF COLUMBIA
Department Director for Labor Standards
D.C. Department of Employment Services
1200 Upshur Street, N.W.
Washington, D.C. 20011
(202) 576-7100

FLORIDA
Division of Workers' Compensation
Department of Labor and Employment Security
Suite 201, Ashley Building
1321 Executive Center Drive, East
Tallahassee, Florida 32301
(904) 488-2514

GEORGIA
Board of Workers' Compensation
Suite 1000, South Tower
One CNN Center
Atlanta, Georgia 30303–2705
(404) 656-3875

HAWAII
Disability Compensation Division
Department of Labor and Industrial Relations
Post Office Box 3769
830 Punchbowl Street
Honolulu, Hawaii 96813
(808) 548-5414

IDAHO
Industrial Commission
317 Main Street
Boise, Idaho 83720
(208) 334-6000

ILLINOIS
Industrial Commission
100 West Randolph Street, 8th Floor
Chicago, Illinois 60601
(312) 793-6500

INDIANA
Industrial Board of Indiana
Room 601, State Office Building
100 North Senate Avenue
Indianapolis, Indiana 46204
  (317) 232-3808

IOWA
Workers' Compensation Service
Department of Employment Services
1000 East Grand
Des Moines, Iowa 50319
  (505) 281-5934

KANSAS
Division of Workers' Compensation
Landon State office Building
900 W.W. Jackson Room 651-S
Topeka, Kansas 66612
  (913) 296-344l

KENTUCKY
Workmen's Compensation Board
Department of Labor
127 South Building
Highway 127
Frankfort, Kentucky 40601
  (502) 564-5550

LOUISIANA
Department of Labor
Office of Workers' Compensation
910 N. Bon Marche Drive
Baton Rouge, Louisiana 70806
  (504) 925-7211

MAINE
Workers' Compensation Commission
Deering Building, Station 27
Augusta, Maine 04333
  (207) 289-3751

MARYLAND
Workmen's Compensation Commission
6 North Liberty Street
Baltimore, Maryland 21201
  (301) 333-4775 or
toll free 1-800-492-0470

MASSACHUSETTS
Industrial Accident Board
100 Cambridge Street
Boston, Massachusetts 02202
  (617) 727-4900

MICHIGAN
Bureau of Workers' Disability Compensation
Department of Labor
309 North Washington
Post Office Box 30016
Lansing, Michigan 48909
  (517) 373-3490

MINNESOTA
Division of Workers' Compensation
Department of Labor and Industry
Space Center, Fifth Floor
444 Lafayette Road
St. Paul, Minnesota 55101
  (612) 296-6490

MISSISSIPPI
Workmen's Compensation Commission
1428 Lakeland Drive
Post Office Box 5300
Jackson, Mississippi 39216
  (601) 987-4200

MISSOURI
Division of Workers' Compensation
Post Office Box 58
Jefferson City, Missouri 65102
  (314) 751-4231

MONTANA
Division of Workers' Compensation
Department of Labor and Industry
Five South Last Chance Gulch
Helena, Montana 59601
  (406) 444-6500

NEBRASKA
Workmen's Compensation Court
State Capitol, Post Office Box 94967
Lincoln, Nebraska 68509–4967
  (402) 471-2568

NEVADA
State Industrial Insurance System
515 East Musser Street
Carson City, Nevada 89714
  (702) 885-5284

NEW HAMPSHIRE
Workmen's Compensation Division
Department of Labor
19 Pillsbury Street
Concord, New Hampshire 03301
  (603) 271-3176, 271-3171

NEW JERSEY
Department of Labor
Division of Workers' Compensation
C.N. 381
Trenton, New Jersey 0862
  (609) 292-2414

NEW MEXICO
Workers' Compensation Division
P.O. Box 27198
Albuquerque, New Mexico 87125-7198
  (505) 841-8787

NEW YORK
Workers' Compensation Board
180 Livingston Street
Brooklyn, New York 11248
  (718) 802-6934

NORTH CAROLINA
North Carolina Industrial Commission
Dobbs Building
430 North Salisbury Street
Raleigh, North Carolina 27611
  (919) 733-4820

NORTH DAKOTA
Workmen's Compensation Bureau
Russel Building
4007 North State Street
Bismarck, North Dakota 58501
  (701) 224-2700

OHIO
Bureau of Workers' Compensation
246 North High Street
Columbus, Ohio 43215
  (614) 466-2950 or toll free
1-800-282-9536

OKLAHOMA
State Industrial Court
1915 N. Stiles
Oklahoma City, Oklahoma 73105
  (405) 557-7600

OREGON
Workmen's Compensation Department
201 Labor and Industries Building
Salem, Oregon 97310
  (503) 378-3304

PENNSYLVANIA
Bureau of Workers' Compensation
3607 Derry Street
Harrisburg, Pennsylvania 17111
  (717) 783-5421

PUERTO RICO
Chairperson
Industrial Commission
G. P. O. Box 4466
San Juan, Puerto Rico 00936
  (809) 781-7576

RHODE ISLAND
Department of Workers' Compensation
P.O. Box 3500
610 Manton Avenue
Providence, Rhode Island 02909
  (401) 272-0700

SOUTH CAROLINA
Workers' Compensation Commission
1612 Marion Street
P.O. Box 1715
Columbia, South Carolina 29202–1715
  (803) 758-3498

SOUTH DAKOTA
Division of Labor and Management
Department of Labor
700 North Illinois Street
Pierre, South Dakota 57501
  (605) 773-3681

TENNESSEE
Division of Workers' Compensation
Department of Labor
501 Union Building, Second Floor
Nashville, Tennessee 37219
  (615) 741-2395

TEXAS
Industrial Accident Board
200 East Riverside Drive, First Floor
Austin, Texas 78704–1287
  (512) 448-7900

UTAH
Workmen's Compensation Division
Industrial Commission
160 East 3rd South
P.O. Box 45580
Salt Lake City, Utah 84145
  (801) 530-6800

VERMONT
Department of Labor and Industry
Five Court Street, 3rd Floor
Montpelier, Vermont 05602
  (802) 828-2286

VIRGINIA
Industrial Commission
Post Office Box 1794
Richmond, Virginia 23214
  (804) 257-8600 or toll free
1-800-552-4007

WASHINGTON
Department of Labor and Industry
General Administration Building
Mail Stop AX-3 I
Olympia, Washington 98504
  (206) 753-6307

WISCONSIN
Workers' Compensation Division
Department of Industry, Labor and Human Relations
201 East Washington Avenue
Post Office Box 7901
Madison, Wisconsin 53707
  (608) 266-6827

VIRGIN ISLANDS
Division of Workmen's Compensation
Department of Labor
Post Office Box 890
Christiansted
St. Croix, Virgin Islands 00820
  (809) 775-5747

WEST VIRGINIA
Workers' Compensation Fund
601 Morris Street
Charleston, West Virginia 25301
  (304) 348-2580

WYOMING
Workmen's Compensation Department
122 West 25th Street
Herschler Building
Cheyenne, Wyoming 82002–0700
  (307) 777-7441

CANADA—FEDERAL

ALBERTA
Workmen's Compensation Board
9912–l07th Street
Post Office Box 2415
Edmonton, Alberta T5J 2S5
  (403) 427-1100

BRITISH COLUMBIA
Workers' Compensation Board
6951 Westminster Highway
Richmond, British Columbia V7C 1C6
  (604) 273-2266

MANITOBA
Workers' Compensation Board
333 Maryland Street
Winnipeg, Manitoba R3G 1M2
  (204) 786-5471

NEW BRUNSWICK
Workers' Compensation Board
Post Office Box 160
Saint John. New Brunswick E2L 3X9
  (506) 652-2250

NEWFOUNDLAND
Workers' Compensation Board
P.O. Box 9000
Station B
St. John's, Newfoundland A1A 3B8
  (709) 754-2940

NOVA SCOTIA
Workers' Compensation Board
Post Office Box 1150
Halifax, Nova Scotia B3J 2Y2
  (2-7341)

ONTARIO
Honorable Chairman
Workers' Compensation Board
Two Bloor Street, East
Toronto, Ontario M4W 3C3
  (416) 965-8880

PRINCE EDWARD ISLAND
Workers' Compensation Board
60 Belvedere Avenue
Post Office Box 757
Charlottetown, Prince Edward Island
  C1A 7L7

QUEBEC
Workers' Compensation Board
524 Rue Bourdages
Post Office Box 1200
Postal Terminal, Quebec GIK 7E2
   (418) 643-5964

SASKATCHEWAN
Workers' Compensation Board
1840 Lorne Street
Reginia, Saskatchewan 54P 2L8
   (306) 565-4379

YUKON
Workers' Compensation Board
4114 4th Avenue
Suite 300
Whitehorse, Yukon Y1A 4N7

NORTHWEST TERRITORIES
Workers' Compensation Board
P.O. Box 8888
Yellowknife, Northwest Territories X1A 2R6
   (403) 873-7484

UNEMPLOYMENT COMPENSATION

Unemployment compensation is another legally required benefit that was established years ago as part of the Social Security Act of 1935. Each state operates its own unemployment compensation system, and regulations differ significantly from state to state.

Employers finance this benefit by paying a percentage tax on their total payrolls to state and federal unemployment compensation funds. When an employee is out of work and is actively looking for employment, he or she normally receives up to 26 weeks of pay, at the rate of 50 percent to 80 percent of normal pay. In most states employees may collect unemployment benefits only if they are involuntarily terminated, and they must use up any vacation and severance pay before they can start collecting.

Contact your local unemployment compensation office for details and a copy of your state's regulations.

Curbing Unemployment Compensation Costs

Unemployment Compensation costs can be one of the most expensive elements of doing business. If you aren't familiar with the laws in the states in which you do business, and don't have the time to monitor this activity, you may want to use an outside organization to report terminations, administer claims, and closely monitor fees and costs. These outside companies more than pay for themselves in dollars saved through effective administration. There are several companies nationwide that do this type of administration. One such company is The Frick Company, 2675 Scott Avenue, St. Louis, MO 63103; 1 (314) 535-3999.

PERSONAL PRIVACY AND EMPLOYEE RIGHTS

Personal Privacy Versus the Computer and the HRIS

As more and more personal information on employees is entered into the corporate computer, legal and ethical issues are being raised. In fact, human resource executives, academic experts, congressional committees, and business people have all expressed concern that the use of computers to gather personal information about people may outpace the legal safeguards.

In America, the two most significant gatherers of information on people are the federal government and the individual's employer. Federal laws provide protections against governmental abuses under the concepts of constitutional rights, due process, equal opportunity, individual rights, and safety. Also, government falls under public scrutiny, especially by the press and the television media. The laws that provide safeguards and legal restrictions on government information, however, do not regulate private employers.

Employers can gather all the information on employees they want. There are no controls over employer record keeping, virtually no legal limits on the information that an employer may gather, and no limits on the disclosure of that information to others.

Laws have been passed in some states stating that employees have a right to see their personnel files and may request the company change any information that is in error.

Medical records are another major concern of employees. Even though a doctor takes the Hippocratic Oath, agreeing not to disclose medical information on patients, third party payments and personnel data banks make confidentiality impossible.

Most human resource people can tell horror stories about medical information being used to make a decision on an employee's suitability for promotion. Most human resource people will tell employees not to use medical benefits to pay for psychotherapy if they want to move up in an organization. This is certainly a privacy and an ethical issue that will be challenged in the future.

Employees sign away their rights to privacy when, for example, they sign a medical claims form that says, "I authorize any licensed physician, medical practitioner or other person to disclose information." When you hurriedly sign this statement, you may not realize it, but you are knowingly granting access to any and all medical information in your personnel file.

The issue of personal privacy versus the corporate computer is heating up and employees are beginning to question the invasion of privacy threat of personnel data systems.

Three Steps to Avoid Invasion of Privacy Lawsuits

It is absolutely essential today to implement corporate privacy policy guidelines. There are three steps you can take to implement workable guidelines and avoid costly litigation in the privacy area.

1. Publish a privacy policy or statement regarding your computer system. Include such areas as controls on operating practices, access of data subjects, and usage control by data subjects. This statement should cover both the system's impact on individual employee privacy and the effect of privacy regulations on the system.

2. Construct a comprehensive privacy plan for all computer systems. A plan will ensure that all necessary privacy controls are integrated into the design of the system. For an existing system, the plan should cover changes in programs, equipment, and procedures.

3. Train employees who work in data systems and in human resources how to handle personal information on employees. Make your privacy policies and procedures well known to all operating personnel and to all employees.

Employees who work with personal information on employees should understand the legal and ethical considerations of employee privacy. Also, employees want to know how their personal information is being treated; because of past abuses, many employees do not trust their employer to maintain confidentiality over personal information. Smart corporate management is open and above-board with employees-telling them exactly what is maintained, where and how it is maintained, and they communicate privacy policies openly to employees.

Privacy and Home Based Employees

Many employees are working at home using computers and telephones. Television used to be just a device for bringing news and entertainment into the home, but now people hook up their televisions to computers, cable systems, and telephones and are creating new technology called interactive home media, *hometech,* or telecommuting.

Cable is primarily used today for commercial programming, but cable companies are exploring new services that will transform cable into a tremendous network of data available on a daily basis. We will be able to receive electronically stored news, classified ads, yellow pages, weather reports, and stock quotations, and perform interactive transactions such as banking, shopping, making airline reservations, and even have remote medical diagnosis. There will also be monitoring of home security, energy use, opinion polling, and special communications for home workers.

All of this tremendous technical capability also creates privacy dangers that have been largely overlooked. Our old traditional concepts of individual privacy do not account for the new realities of interactive home media.

As more employees choose to work at home and as more companies provide these arrangements, human resource managers must take responsibility in addressing the important issues of both personal privacy and corporate security.

Protecting the Privacy of Computerized Personnel Records

Most automated personnel systems have protections and safeguards built in, but many human resource information systems that were developed years ago contain information that is contrary to privacy and affirmative action regulations today. You must ensure that the HRIS is cleansed of old, obsolete data. An automated personnel records audit is one way of doing this.

Every change that goes into the system should trigger a profile printout that is given to the employee in order to allow updating and cleansing of wrong information on a regular basis.

There has been an increased use in the last few years of HRIS data in court cases. Most of the time it is used in discrimination cases. Plaintiffs can gain access to the HRIS data through legal processes and attempt to use the data to prove discrimination. The data from computerized systems may be given more credence by a jury and may, therefore, be difficult to rebut.

In the case of *Adams v. Dan River Mills, Inc.,* a case involving alleged racially discriminatory employment practices, the court ordered the defendant, Dan River, to supply the plaintiff with a computerized master payroll file, as well as printouts for the W-2 forms of defendant's employees. The court reasoned:

> The plaintiffs stated that they need the current computer cards or tapes and the W-2 printouts in order to prepare accurate, up-to-date statistics which will be relevant to determining whether or not discriminatory practices have occurred. Furthermore, the plaintiffs contend that the use of this computerized data is the most inexpensive and reliable method which can be used since making the necessary studies with human labor is not only extremely time-consuming and expensive, but also is more susceptible to error.
>
> Because of the accuracy and inexpensiveness of producing the requested documents in the case at the bar, this court sees no reason why the defendant should not be required to produce the computer cards or tapes and the W-2 printouts to the plaintiff.

A plaintiff's attorney can use inaccuracies in a computerized system to weaken a company's defense against an employment discrimination claim. It could also be embarrassing for the human resource department to be the focal point in a lawsuit where the employee-related database they designed, developed, and maintained becomes a helpful tool for a plaintiff.

It becomes more obvious every day how important the management of the human resources information system is. The responsibility transcends just the departmental personnel files.

AN ADA CHECKLIST FOR EMPLOYERS

The company has long supported equal opportunities for people with disabilities. We support the goals of the Americans with Disabilities Act of 1990 (ADA) because we believe it reflects sound human resource and business practices.

Although this checklist is not intended to be a definitive document on ADA compliance, a "No" answer indicates an area that you may need to examine for improvement.

HUMAN RESOURCE POLICIES:

		YES	NO
1.	Have you communicated to all employees your company's policy and commitment to employment and reasonable accommodation for qualified applicants and employees with disabilities?	❏	❏
2.	Have training sessions and/or information been made available to current supervisors and managers regarding their ADA responsibilities?	❏	❏
3.	Is there a process in place to identify the need for reasonable accommodations and other ADA requirements when employees become disabled?	❏	❏
4.	Is a system in place to maintain confidential medical and health information separately from personnel files?	❏	❏
5.	Do you provide the same opportunities of employment to all employees in the same job classification, e.g. compensation, benefits, promotion, training, etc.?	❏	❏
6.	Have you posted notices regarding the individual rights of employees under the ADA?	❏	❏

INTERVIEWING AND HIRING:

		YES	NO
7.	Is your application/interviewing process fully accessible to *all* job applicants?	❏	❏
8.	Have job applications been checked for prohibited questions related to health, disability or workers' comp history, and have interviewers been advised not to ask questions of this nature?	❏	❏
9.	Do job descriptions within your company identify the essential functions necessary to perform the job?	❏	❏
10.	Do employment tests and procedures for taking the tests accurately assess only the necessary skills and aptitudes required to perform the essential job functions?	❏	❏
11.	Are all employer-requested physicals conducted only after a conditional job offer is tendered, and are they required of *all* applicants in that job category?	❏	❏
12.	Do your post-offer physicals assess only the candidate's ability to perform the essential functions of the offered position? The results of post-offer physicals cannot be used to discriminate against a qualified individual on the basis of disability.	❏	❏
13.	Are requirements for "reasonable accommodations" understood to be a necessary part of the process when considering an applicant?	❏	❏
14.	Are managers most likely to be involved with reasonable accommodations aware of the best approach with a disabled person? Have competent external resources been identified that can be used when needed?	❏	❏

OTHER POLICIES:

		YES	NO
15.	Have you notified all professional search organizations with whom you have contracts of your intention to fully comply with the ADA?	❏	❏
16.	Do employees with disabilities have equal access to break rooms, cafeterias, and other facilities (on-site/off-site) provided by you?	❏	❏
17.	Have you ensured that your company meets its obligations under the Public Accommodations title of the ADA?	❏	❏

SAMPLE ADA ACCOMMODATION LETTER

Date

ADDRESS

Dear Mr./Mrs.:

Thank you for applying for the position of _____ at XYZ Company. We had a number of qualified applicants for the position and have chosen another candidate who met all of the qualifications for the position. After speaking with your contact person, we ascertained that because of your hearing disability you are not able to use a regular telephone or an amplifier on a regular telephone.

The job description for this position states that the physical qualifications for the job require "a normal range of hearing and vision." Frequent telephone discussions with clients, contractors and vendors are an integral part of this job. (See attached job description.)

With your experience we feel you could perform some of the essential job functions, but one of the most important functions is use of a telephone. The Company would be willing to make an accommodation for you if you could use an amplifier on our telephone, but the cost of a special telephone system would create an undue financial hardship on the Company and an administrative burden we're not able to accommodate.

We thank you for contacting us and applying for the position, and wish you luck in your job search.

Sincerely,

Human Resources Manager
XYZ Company

FAMILY AND MEDICAL LEAVE ACT OF 1993

FMLA requires covered employers to provide up to 12 weeks of unpaid, job-protected leave to "eligible" employees for certain family and medical reasons. Employees are eligible if they have worked for a covered employer for at least one year, and for 1,250 hours over the previous 12 months, and if there are at least 50 employees within 75 miles.

REASONS FOR UNPAID LEAVE: Unpaid leave must be granted for *any* of the following reasons:

- to care for the employee's child after birth, or placement for adoption or foster care;
- to care for the employee's spouse, son or daughter, or parent, who has a serious health condition; or
- for a serious health condition that makes the employee unable to perform the employee's job.

At the employee's or employer's option, certain kinds of *paid* leave may be substituted for unpaid leave.

ADVANCE NOTICE AND MEDICAL CERTIFICATION: The employee may be required to provide advance leave notice and medical certification. Taking of leave may be denied if requirements are not met.

- The employee ordinarily must provide 30 days advance notice when the leave is "foreseeable."
- An employer may require medical certification to support a request for leave because of a serious health condition, and may require second or third opinions (at the employer's expense) and a fitness for duty report to return to work.

JOB BENEFITS AND PROTECTION:

- For the duration of FMLA leave, the employer must maintain the employee's health coverage under any "group health plan."
- Upon return from FMLA leave, most employees must be restored to their original or equivalent positions with equivalent pay, benefits, and other employment terms.
- The use of FMLA leave cannot result in the loss of any employment benefit that accrued prior to the start of an employee's leave.

UNLAWFUL ACTS BY EMPLOYERS: FMLA makes it unlawful for any employer to:

- interfere with, restrain, or deny the exercise of any right provided under FMLA;
- discharge or discriminate against any person for opposing any practice made unlawful by FMLA or for involvement in any proceeding under or relating to FMLA.

ENFORCEMENT:

- The U.S. Department of Labor is authorized to investigate and resolve complaints of violations.
- An eligible employee may bring a civil action against an employer for violations.

FMLA does not affect any Federal or State law prohibiting discrimination, or supersede any State or local law or collective bargaining agreement which provides greater family or medical leave rights.

FOR ADDITIONAL INFORMATION: Contact the nearest office of the Wage and Hour Division, listed in most telephone directories under U.S. Government, Department of Labor.

U.S. Department of Labor, Employment Standards Administration
Wage and Hour Division, Washington, DC 20210

WH Publication 1420
June 1993

CERTIFICATION OF PHYSICIAN
UNDER THE FAMILY AND MEDICAL LEAVE ACT OF 1993

1. Employee's Name:	2. Patient's Name (If other than employee):

3. Diagnosis _____
_____
_____
_____

4. Date condition commenced:	5. Probable duration of condition:

6. Regimen of treatment to be prescribed (Indicate number of visits, general nature and duration of treatment, including referral to other provider of health services. Include schedule of visits or treatment if it is medically necessary for the employee to be off work on an intermittent basis or to work less than the employee's normal schedule of hours per day or days per week):

   a. By Physician: _____
_____
_____

   b. By another provider of health services, if referred by Physician: _____
_____
_____
_____

IF THIS CERTIFICATION RELATES TO CARE FOR AN EMPLOYEE'S SERIOUSLY-ILL FAMILY MEMBER, SKIP ITEMS 7, 8 AND 9 AND PROCEED TO ITEMS 10 THROUGH 14 ON REVERSE SIDE. OTHERWISE CONTINUE BELOW.

Check Yes or No in the boxes below, as appropriate:

    Yes No

7. ❏   ❏   Is inpatient hospitalization of the employee required?

8. ❏   ❏   Is employee able to perform work of any kind? (If "No" skip Item 9.)

9. ❏   ❏   Is employee able to perform the functions of employee's position? (Answer after reviewing statement from employer of essential functions of employee's position, or, if none provided, after discussing with employee.)

15. Signature of Physician:	16. Date:

17. Type of Practice (Field of Specialization, if any):

FOR CERTIFICATION RELATING TO CARE FOR THE EMPLOYEE'S SERIOUSLY-ILL FAMILY MEMBER, COMPLETE ITEMS 10 THROUGH 14 BELOW AS THEY APPLY TO THE FAMILY MEMBER AND PROCEED TO ITEM 15 ON REVERSE SIDE.

	Yes	No	
10.	❑	❑	Is inpatient hospitalization of the family member (patient) required?
11.	❑	❑	Does (or will) the patient require assistance for basic medical, hygiene, nutritional needs, safety or transportation?
12.	❑	❑	After review of the employee's signed statement (See Item 14 below), is the employee's presence necessary or would it be beneficial for the care of the patient? (This may include psychological comfort.)

13. Estimate the period of time care is needed or the employee's presence would be beneficial:

ITEM 14 TO BE COMPLETED BY THE EMPLOYEE NEEDING FAMILY LEAVE.

14. When Family Leave is needed to care for a seriously-ill family member, the employee shall state the care he or she will provide and an estimate of the time period during which this care will be provided, including a schedule if leave is to be taken intermittently or on a reduced leave schedule:

_____

_____

_____

Employee Signature: Date:

Company/Division/Location:

WHAT YOU SHOULD KNOW ABOUT AN EMPLOYEE RETURNING TO WORK UNDER THE FAMILY MEDICAL LEAVE ACT

Significant issues must be addressed when an employee returns from family or medical leave. This is, one of the most difficult issues, as well as one of the most important ones to manage under the Family and Medical Leave Act (FMLA). Here are the answers to some of the most frequently asked questions about the FMLA.

A Key FMLA Issue

The Act states that employees are entitled to be returned to either the *same position* they had when they began their FMLA leave or to an *equivalent position*, with *equivalent benefits, pay and other terms and conditions of employment*, so long as they are *ready to return to work*. There are special rules for *key employees*, and for *recovering benefit costs* for workers who do not return to work.

What Does "Same Position" Really Mean?

Although the idea is a difficult one, an employer can deny an employee reinstatement if it can show that the employee would not have been employed at the time reinstatement is requested. The U.S. Department of Labor has given employers several examples of when reinstatement is not required.

IN CASE OF A LAYOFF: If the employee would have been laid off during the FMLA leave period, the employee would not be entitled to reinstatement if she still would have been laid off at the time reinstatement is sought.

IN THE CASE OF THE TERMINATION OF A SHIFT: If a shift has been eliminated, the employee would not be entitled to return to work that shift. However, if the shift still exists and is only being filled by another employee, the original employee is entitled to be restored to the shift.

IN THE CASE OF A TERM OR PROJECT EMPLOYEE: If an employee was hired for a specific term or to perform a specific project, the employer has no obligation to reinstate the employee if the term or project has been completed and the employer would not have otherwise continued to employ the employee.

IN THE CASE OF A CONCURRENT WORKERS' COMPENSATION LEAVE THAT EXTENDS PAST 12 WEEKS: If an employee has been on workers' compensation leave during which FMLA leave was taken concurrently, and is unable to return to work after the 12 weeks of FMLA leave has expired, the employee loses the protection and benefits of FMLA.

WHAT IF THE EMPLOYEE HAS BEEN REPLACED? Even if the employee has been replaced or the employee's position has been restructured to accommodate the employee's absence, the employee is still entitled to be reinstated.

WHAT IF THE EMPLOYEE'S LEAVE HAS EXCEEDED THE 12-WEEK MAXIMUM? Once an employee has exhausted the entitlement to 12 weeks of FMLA leave in a 12-month period, FMLA benefits and protections end. Therefore, if an employee does not return to work within 12 weeks, the employee is not entitled to reinstatement under FMLA.

WHAT IF THE EMPLOYEE CAN NO LONGER PERFORM THE JOB? If the employee is no longer able to perform an essential function of the position because of a serious health condition (an illness, injury, impairment, or physical or mental condition that involves either inpatient care or continuing treatment by a health care provider), the employee has no right under FMLA to be reinstated to another position they can perform. However, if the employee qualifies for protection under the American with Disabilities Act of 1990 (ADA) and can perform the essential functions of the position with a "reasonable accommodation," the employer must reinstate the employee if it can accommodate the employee without undue hardship. If the same employee is unable to perform the essential functions of the position even with a reasonable accommodation, the ADA may require the employer to make other reasonable accommodations, such as offering to transfer the employee to a vacant position or working a part-time schedule.

CAN YOU REQUIRE AN EMPLOYEE RETURN TO MODIFIED OR LIGHT DUTY? An employer cannot require that an employee with a serious health condition return to work in a modified or light duty position. Rather, an employee on FMLA leave may reject an employer's offer to return to work to perform light duty or different work of which the employee is capable.

WHAT IS "EQUIVALENT POSITION"? The Department of Labor states that an equivalent position is one that is virtually identical to the employee's former position in terms of pay, benefits and working conditions, including privileges, prerequisites and status. It must involve the same or substantially similar duties and responsibilities, which must entail substantially equivalent skill, effort, responsibility, and authority.

DEFINE "EQUIVALENT PAY"? Equivalent pay means that an employee is entitled to:

Unconditional pay increases which occurred while the employee was on leave (such as cost of living increases).

The same or equivalent pay premiums, such as shift differentials.

The same opportunity for regular overtime that existed for the employee's former position.

Non-performance based bonuses, such as for safety and perfect attendance, if the employee had met the required goals before beginning FMLA leave.

Performance based bonuses, such as exceeding monthly production goals, to the extent such bonuses are provided to other employees taking paid or unpaid leave for reasons other than FMLA.

Unless it is the employer's policy or practice to do so for employees on regular leave without pay, an employer who provides salary increases based on seniority or length of service may exclude the time the employee used for FMLA leave for purposes of calculating the increase.

DEFINE EQUIVALENT BENEFITS? The term "benefits" includes all benefits provided to employees by the employer (such as all forms of insurance, sick and annual leave, educational benefits and pensions) regardless of whether such benefits are provided by practice or written policy. An employee returning from FMLA leave is entitled to resume their benefits in the same manner and at the same level as provided when the leave began, unless the employee elects otherwise. However, the employee's benefits are subject to the same changes affecting the entire work force that occurred while they were out on FMLA leave.

DOES AN EMPLOYEE ACCRUE SENIORITY WHILE ON FMLA? An employee is not entitled to accrue seniority while on FMLA leave.

DOES AN EMPLOYEE LOSE ACCRUED BENEFITS WHILE ON FMLA? An employee does not lose accrued benefits while on FMLA leave. Benefits accrued at the time the leave began (e.g. paid vacation, sick or personal leave to the extent not substituted for FMLA leave) must be available to the employee upon their return to work.

DOES FMLA AFFECT AN EMPLOYEE'S PENSION OR RETIREMENT PLANS? Any period of unpaid FMLA leave may not be treated as or counted toward a break in service for purposes of vesting and eligibility to participate in pension or other retirement plans. Moreover, if the retirement plan requires that the employee be employed on a specific date to be credited with a year of service for purposes of participating or vesting in the plan, an employee on unpaid FMLA leave on that date shall be deemed to have been employed on that date. However, unpaid FMLA leave periods need not be treated as periods of employment service for other retirement plan purposes such as benefit accrual, vesting and eligibility to participate.

DEFINE EQUIVALENT TERMS AND CONDITIONS OF EMPLOYMENT? Equivalent terms and conditions of employment mean that the employee is entitled to:

> Be reinstated to the same work location or one that is geographically close. If the employee's original work location is closed while the employee was on FMLA leave, the employee must be afforded the same transfer options as all other employees.

> Return to the same work shift or to the same or an equivalent work schedule.

> The same or equivalent opportunity for bonuses, profit-sharing, and other similar discretionary and non-discretionary payments as the employee's original position.

IS THE EMPLOYEE READY? CERTIFYING FITNESS FOR DUTY An employer may adopt a uniformly-applied policy or practice that requires all similarly-situated employees who take FMLA leave due to their own serious health condition to obtain and present certification from the employee's health care provider that the employee is fit to return to work. An employer must inform the employee if a fitness for duty certification will be required at the commencement of the leave.

WHAT ACTION CAN AN EMPLOYER TAKE WHEN AN EMPLOYEE DOES NOT PROVIDE A FITNESS FOR DUTY CERTIFICATION? An employer may delay restoration to employment until an employee submits the required fitness for duty certification unless it failed to provide proper notice that such certification would be required when the leave commenced. If the employer provided the required notice and an employee refuses to provide the certification, the employee may be terminated.

DOES THE EMPLOYEE PAY FOR THE FITNESS FOR DUTY CERTIFICATION? Yes, the cost of the certification is borne by the employee.

DOES THE FITNESS FOR DUTY CERTIFICATION HAVE ANY LIMITATIONS? Yes, there are important limitations regarding fitness for duty certifications:

No information other than a simple statement of an employee's ability to return to work can be requested.

No second or third fitness for duty certifications may be required.

No fitness for duty certification may be required from an employee on intermittent leave.

If State or local law or the terms of a collective bargaining agreement create standards or conditions for an employee's return to work, those provisions shall be applied. Accordingly, if an employee qualifies as disabled under the Americans with Disabilities Act, fitness for duty examinations must be job-related and consistent with business necessity. In cases where the Americans with Disabilities Act apply, the certification is limited to whether the employee can perform the essential functions of the job.

CAN AN EMPLOYER DENY A JOB TO A "KEY EMPLOYEE"? An employer may deny job reinstatement to "key employees' if the denial is necessary to prevent "substantial and grievous economic injury" to the operations of the employer.

DEFINE "KEY EMPLOYEE". Key employees are salaried employees who are eligible for FMLA protection and are among the highest paid 10% of all the employees employed by the employer within 75 miles of the employee's workplace.

ARE KEY EMPLOYEES TREATED DIFFERENTLY? An employer may deny job reinstatement to a key employee if the denial is necessary to prevent substantial and grievous economic injury to the operations of the employer. Because key employees can be denied reinstatement for economic reasons, they have different rights than other employees. For instance, the employer must give key employees written notice at the time FMLA leave is requested that the employee will not be reinstated if the employer determines that to do so will cause the employer's operations substantial and grievous economic injury. Even after receiving notice that reinstatement will result in a substantial and grievous economic injury to the employer, the key employee is still entitled to request reinstatement. The employer must then again determine whether it will suffer substantial and grievous economic injury if it reinstates the key employee. If the employer determines it cannot reinstate the key employee, the employer must notify the employee in writing (in person or by certified mail) of the denial of restoration.

IS THERE A TEST FOR SUBSTANTIAL ECONOMIC INJURY? There is no precise test for determining the level of economic hardship or injury to the employer which must be sustained before a key employee can be safely denied reinstatement. However, the Department of Labor has provided two examples of qualifying events: 1) when reinstatement of a key employee would threaten the economic viability of the employer's operation; and 2) a lesser injury which will cause substantial long-term economic injury. Employers familiar with the Americans with Disabilities Act should note that Department of Labor regulations specifically state that FMLA's substantial and grievous economic injury standard is different and more stringent than that Act's undue hardship standard.

CAN AN EMPLOYER RECOVER THE COSTS OF HEALTH INSURANCE PREMIUMS FROM THE EMPLOYEE? As a general rule, if an employee does not return to work after exhausting their FMLA leave entitlement, an employer may recover its share of health plan premiums paid during unpaid FMLA leave. An employer may not recover the costs of health plan premiums if the reason the employee does not return to work is one of the following reasons:

> The continuation, recurrence, or onset of a serious health condition of the employee or the employee's family member which would otherwise qualify the employee to FMLA leave.

> Circumstances beyond the employee's control, such as: caring for a family relative not otherwise covered by FMLA who has a serious health condition, the employee is laid off while on leave or the employee is a key employee who was not reinstated.

> An employee on temporary disability or workers' compensation leave.

CAN AN EMPLOYER RECOVER THE COSTS OF OTHER BENEFIT PREMIUMS FROM AN EMPLOYEE? An employer may elect to continue other employee benefits (e.g. life insurance or disability insurance) by paying the employee's share of the premiums while the employee is on unpaid FMLA leave. An employer may do this to ensure that the employee will have equivalent benefits upon their return. Regardless of whether the employee returns to work at the conclusion of their leave, the employer is entitled to recover the costs it incurred for paying the employee's share of the premiums.

DEFINE WHEN AN EMPLOYEE HAS "RETURNED TO WORK." An employee who returns to work for at least 30 calendar days is considered to have returned to work. The one exception to this rule is if an employee transitions directly from the FMLA leave or within the 30 day period to retirement. In those cases the employee is deemed to have returned to work.

CAN AN EMPLOYER RECOVER THE COST OF PREMIUMS? An employer can use two methods for recovering the cost of premiums from non-returning employees:

> Deduct the costs of the premiums from any sums due to the employee (e.g., unpaid wages, vacation pay, profit sharing, etc.) provided such deductions do not violate Federal or State wage and hour laws.

> Initiate a legal action.

This information should assist you in resolving the many difficult issues that arise when an employee returns to work under the Family Medical Leave Act.

4

EMPLOYEE COMMUNICATIONS

- Making the Personal Connection Is Important to Your Company's Success

- 25 Management/Employee Communications Channels You Can Implement in Your Company

- Communicating Through Corporate Intranets

- How to Start an Employee Newsletter

- Sample Employee Handbook

- Employee Handbook Acknowledgment Form

Employee Communications

MAKING THE PERSONAL CONNECTION IS IMPORTANT TO YOUR COMPANY'S SUCCESS

Don't rely too heavily on impersonal forms of employee communications if you want the most productive and successful organization possible. The changing makeup of today's workforce is a major contributor to the need for more frequent and personal employee/management communications. The dramatic forces that have been affecting business in the last five years-intense restructuring, mergers and acquisitions, deregulation, global competition, the switch to a service economy-have all had a huge impact on employees and on human resource management. It is becoming more obvious every day that employee communications and a hands-on, positive attitude are needed to successfully manage the diverse workforce of the 1990s.

25 MANAGEMENT/EMPLOYEE COMMUNICATIONS CHANNELS YOU CAN IMPLEMENT IN YOUR COMPANY:

1. *Multi-level staff meetings* where workers and supervisors at all levels participate and where their input is sought and used.

2. *Face-to-face communications* every day through walk-arounds and regular non threatening employee contact.

3. *Frequent informational letters and memos* telling everyone at every level what the company is doing and how current projects are going.

4. *Committees and task forces* that address current issues and problems on a participative basis.

5. *Discussion groups* where there are regular forums, both structured and unstructured, to discuss current issues and company problems, reading discussion groups on topics such as "In Search of Excellence," or "Getting to Yes" (learning how to negotiate).

6. *Employee mass meetings* when there is something of substance to discuss.

7. *Training programs* to address the needs of workers at every level. There may be basic literacy training or more difficult skill building workshops for supervisors on coaching and developing subordinates.

8. *Employee newsletter* published once a month that contains information about the company and employees. Use pictures of employees and company events.

233

9. *Bulletin boards* for company information and for employee use in selling items or letting each other know about special events.

10. *Social programs,* picnics, Christmas parties, tailgate parties in football season, covered dish lunches where everyone brings the food of their ancestral country (this idea helps foster positive relations with today's diverse workforce).

11. *Athletic programs:* bowling leagues, softball teams. The relaxed atmosphere can create positive communication networks.

12. We are entering an era where the family will once again be the center of activity for many people. Plan *family nights* or a Saturday now and then where you open your plant or offices and let employees bring their children to see where they work. Serve refreshments and encourage the families to linger and get acquainted.

13. *Employee attitude surveys* to give you an idea what employees are thinking and to test the climate. You might want to use an outside consultant to do the survey for you. If you do a survey be sure to give the employees the results and tell them what you intend to do if the survey shows improvements are needed.

14. *Feedback sessions.* If your survey shows that you have some problem areas, it's a good idea to have some small group feedback and discussion sessions. It's a mistake to bury problems. You need to get them out in the open and discuss them.

15. *Brown-bag lunches,* lunch hour movies and mini-seminars. Have local speakers with interesting topics or hobbies come in and talk to employees. Many people will do this free of charge.

16. *Annual report to employees* showing how the company is doing and discussing company benefits and any other human resource items.

17. Run *contests for employees* occasionally. Set sales goals, or build contests around attendance or safety records.

18. Give *service awards* and have service awards dinners for employees at 1 year, 3 years, 5 years, 10 years, and so on.

19. Have an *arts and crafts week.* Let employees bring their artwork or crafts and provide a room for display. Let them sell their items during lunch hours and after work.

20. Start an *employee speakers bureau.* Invite someone from a local speakers group like Toastmasters to come to your offices or plant and help start the group.

21. *Suggestion system* or suggestion box. Give an award each month for the best suggestion. Encourage employees to offer ideas for improving their jobs or increasing production or sales.

22. Once a year *ask each department to prepare an overview* of their department and what they do, for the entire company. This fosters a sense of pride in employees and increases basic knowledge for everyone in the organization.

23. Start an *in-house audio tape library* that employees can use to increase their individual skills. Let them check out tapes and listen to them while commuting to and

from work. Tapes could be on improving listening skills or learning how to negotiate. There are hundreds of good subjects. Make audio tapes on the company's history or products.

24. Provide *safety training and classes on CPR or first aid.* Do the training in small groups so that employees learn to work together as a team and to communicate with each other. Design the groups so that participants are from different departments.

25. Start *noontime walking/jogging groups* from different departments in the spring, summer, and fall. It's not only a good idea health-wise, it promotes cross-departmental communications.

Check the chapter on checklists for more ideas on developing new communications programs.

COMMUNICATING THROUGH CORPORATE INTRANETS

Company bulletin boards have gone high-tech. Employers are using internal web sites that help employees communicate within the company and also take care of personal business. General Electric has a site where workers can buy discounted appliances. Texas Instruments lets employees use its site to hire a concierge. On AT&T's intranet, employees can make changes to their 401(k) accounts.

Until recently the corporate intranet was mostly a no-frills affair. Now, 80 percent of companies use their intranet as the primary method for delivering human resources services and communicating with employees worldwide, up from 50 percent just two years ago. According to a survey conducted by Watson Wyatt Worldwide.

In this global workplace where employees are scattered around the world, companies need to stay in touch and they need ways to communicate in a hurry. A company intranet is the answer.

After General Electric revamped its intranet, the number of hits jumped from a couple of thousand a week to 10 million a week. Employees can create a personalized page where they can read industry-specific news or check on their benefits. They also can download tax forms and review benefits information. An online marketplace offers discounts on GE appliances, Dell computers and other company products.

AT&T has an intranet where workers can manage benefits, check their 401(k) plans and make investment changes. Company news is updated daily.

Hallmark Cards in Kansas City posts the cafeteria menu, employee newsletter and job-training resources on the intranet. Employees at all levels use the intranet to stay informed on Company affairs.

Texas Instruments is rolling out a program that will let new hires access the intranet before their first day on the job, getting them up to speed before they start. The site includes a concierge service that will plan vacations and run errands, and it provides access to pick doctors from their health plan.

The wave of the future is to get company news online. It improves services to employees and enhances employee communication.

HOW TO START AN EMPLOYEE NEWSLETTER

Starting an employee newsletter is a challenging assignment. In order for any publication to be successful, it must be attractive and informative for today's wide range of workers.

Readership surveys show that internal publications are the primary source of information for most employees and that the contents of most company newsletters are reliable, accurate, and believable. A survey conducted by the International Association of Business Communicators and Towers, Perrin, Forster and Crosby, of 45,000 personnel at forty organizations in the United States and Canada indicates that a high percentage of people (89 percent) find employee publications believable.

The first thing to do is to define the scope and format of the newsletter. Then establish a budget and a time line for publication.

Newsletter Startup Checklist

❏ Establish the scope of the newsletter. (Is it a total company information tool, or merely an anniversary, birthday, safety award type of publication?)

❏ Establish format (tabloid, newsletter).

❏ Decide on frequency of publication (monthly, quarterly).

❏ Decide on basic contents.

❏ Establish a budget.

❏ Evaluate and decide on the time restrictions of current staff. Will a new person be hired to produce the newsletter?

❏ What outside resources will you use (writers, graphic artists, printers)?

❏ If outside printers are to be used, get three or four quotes on production costs.

❏ Will the publication have to appeal to local employees only, or is there a national or international readership?

❏ Who will have editorial control of the contents? Who will produce the newsletter?

❏ What will be the distribution, and who has distribution control?

❏ How will you measure the newsletter's effectiveness over time?

It's a good idea to set up a news-gathering network from key areas of the business. Ask for volunteers to be reporters, and build a backlog of articles and fillers to have on hand for times when current events are slow. It's also a good idea for the person who does the newsletter to understand design, photography, graphics, and reproduction. Most printers will help in this area.

In planning the newsletter, think about how readability will be measured. How will you determine what employees want to read? What will be the style of the publication? Who will have the editorial and distribution control?

Writing for Your Audience

CASE IN POINT   Linda Brown got a job editing a company newsletter and launched the publication quickly and efficiently, publishing the first issue within her first three weeks on the job. Instead of her first issue being a hit, however, it was a flop! She used the experiences she had gained from her previous employer, not taking the time to assess her new readership. Her previous employer had an older employee population and management that insisted on a formal style. Her writing and graphics followed the formal format she had used before, but the readers in her new company were younger and the company style was more informal. What was accepted and appreciated in her previous company was not accepted at all by her new readers. It is difficult to regroup and gain credibility for a newsletter if you start off on the wrong foot, so audience identification is an important element when starting an employee newsletter.

SAMPLE EMPLOYEE HANDBOOK

There are pros and cons to having an employee handbook, but most executives and attorneys today feel that a handbook that provides employees with uniform policies and procedures is an important management tool. In a survey of over 600 companies that use handbooks and policy manuals a majority of executives said that among other things, manuals and handbooks pay for themselves by making things work better and eliminating the constant need to interpret "what the policies and procedures are around here."

The key is consistency of treatment, and without set policies and procedures everyone in the company tends to interpret things their own way. A free-wheeling management style tends to get companies into trouble.

The old handbooks and policy manuals tended to be long and full of "legalese." They sounded dry and intimidating. The new, more acceptable style is to keep manuals short and to the point, written in a less formal style. Limit a policy or a procedure to one or two paragraphs and keep the wording simple.

The following model employee handbook may be too brief for your needs. If it is, adapt it to fit your organization.

Manager's Tip

The difference between an employee handbook and a personnel policy manual is *purpose*. The handbook tells employees what procedures to follow and what their benefits are. The personnel policy manual is primarily for supervisors, to help them know and understand the policies in order to manage consistently. The policy manual is a management guide.

Employee Handbook

Date

THIS HANDBOOK SUPERSEDES ALL PREVIOUS HANDBOOKS ISSUED BY THE COMPANY OR ANY OF ITS SUBSIDIARIES

Manager's Tip

Always date your employee handbook and *always* include the above wording. You will need to revise this handbook to fit your policies, procedures, and benefits.

EMPLOYEE GUIDELINES

This handbook provides guidelines related to appropriate handling of matters concerning personnel policies and procedures of _____.
These guidelines are for informational purposes and are not intended to be a legal document or an employment contract. Questions regarding the guidelines should be directed to your immediate supervisor, or to the Human Resources Department. The Company reserves the right to change, modify, suspend, interpret or cancel, in whole or in part, any personnel policy, guideline or practice at any time without advance notice.

AT-WILL EMPLOYMENT RELATIONSHIP

This handbook is not intended to create or constitute an expressed or implied contract between the Company and any one or all of its employees. The Company or the employee may terminate the employment relationship at any time, without prior notice. The Company may terminate an employee for any or no reason with or without the use of progressive discipline. This is called "At-Will employment." apart from the policy of At-will employment and those policies required by law, the Company may change its policies or practices at any time without prior notice.

Note:

Use the elements of this handbook that best fit your company needs, however, always use the above paragraphs to reinforce the at-will relationship. You may wish to have your attorney review your handbook before you distribute it to employees.

CONTENTS

INTRODUCTION
- Your Company
  - Confidential Information and External Communications
  - Code of Conduct
  - Harassment
  - Employees with Disabilities

YOUR JOB
- Introductory Period
- Hours of Work and Overtime
- Attendance
- Absence
- Rest Periods
- Administration
- Scheduling
- Civic Duties
- Jury Duty
- Leaves of Absence
  - Family and Medical Leave
  - Maternity Leave of Absence
  - Military Leave of Absence
  - National Guard
  - Bereavement
  - Absence for Occupational Disabilities
  - Personal Leave of Absence Without Pay
  - Sick Leave

YOUR PAY
- Pay Periods
- Performance Appraisals and Raises
- Overtime

YOUR BENEFITS
- Benefits and Services
- Recognized Holidays
- Holiday Pay
- Vacations

YOUR SAFETY
- Safety
- In Case of Injury
- Security Procedures

JOB OPPORTUNITIES

EMPLOYEE RELATIONS POLICY

NON-VIOLENCE POLICY

PROBLEMS . . . HOW TO SOLVE THEM
- Termination

WHAT ELSE YOU NEED TO KNOW
- Appearance and Attire
- Bulletin Boards
- Business Mileage Reimbursement
- Business Travel
- Inclement Weather Procedures
- Pay For Lost Time Due to Inclement Weather
- Smoking
- Solicitation and Distribution
- Suggestions
- Miscellaneous

OVERVIEW OF EMPLOYEE BENEFITS

ACKNOWLEDGMENT AND RECEIPT OF EMPLOYEE HANDBOOK

INTRODUCTION

We believe that our employees play a major role in our Company's success. We seek to create an atmosphere within the Company that will allow all employees to feel a genuine sense of accomplishment. At no time will we knowingly permit discrimination toward an employee because of age, sex, race, color, religion, national origin, disability, sexual orientation or for any other unlawful reason.

We believe that both the Company and its individual employees should be good citizens. We seek to fulfill our obligations toward our government and toward the community in which we work. We encourage our employees to play a positive role in community endeavors.

Through the contribution of our employees and the recognition of their efforts, we believe that the Company can achieve a level of performance which will provide each of us with a sense of pride. We hope you will enjoy working for our Company. We have established some guidelines to help maintain the harmonious working relationships we feel are important.

YOUR COMPANY

(Put information about your Company here.)

Confidential Information and External Communications

How the Company is perceived by its business associates, the media, legislators, regulatory agencies, special interest groups, and the general public is a direct result of the external communications activities carried out by our management and employees. These external relations have a significant impact on our business. In order to present the best image of the Company, it is important that the messages we communicate are consistent with Company philosophy, policies and procedures.

Serious problems could be created for the Company by unauthorized disclosure of internal information about the Company, whether for the purpose of facilitating improper trading in the Company's stock or otherwise. Company personnel should not discuss internal Company matters or developments with anyone outside of the Company, except as required in the performance of regular job duties.

If you are unsure as to what information is confidential, please consult with your supervisor or the Corporate Compliance Department. *Outside inquiries regarding Company business should be referred to the President.*

The President serves as an information channel for news media and for any person or organization outside the Company. He is responsible for approval of press releases, responding to media inquiries, and coordinating interviews with the media.

Code of Conduct

The Company has a Corporate Code of Conduct that relates to business ethics and conflicts of interest, among other things. The Code is provided to each employee at the time of hire. All employees are required to read the Code, to attend a meeting or watch a video tape that explains the Code in depth, and then to sign an Annual Certification and Compliance Questionnaire. Questions relating to the Corporate Code of Conduct, or possible violations of its provisions, should be referred to the Corporate Compliance Department.

Harassment

Harassment of any employee in the workplace, based on a person's race, color, sex, religion, national Origin, age, disability or sexual orientation, is unlawful. We fully support equal employment opportunity and will not tolerate discriminatory harassment of its employees. Discriminatory conduct which is sufficiently severe or pervasive as to alter the conditions of employment and which creates an intimidating, hostile, or abusive work environment will be considered harassment pursuant to this policy.

Sexual harassment includes unwelcome sexual advances, requests for sexual favors, sexually degrading or suggestive communications or statements, and other verbal, visual or physical conduct of a sexual nature. No supervisor shall threaten or insinuate, either explicitly or implicitly, that an employee's submission to or rejection of sexual advances will affect the employee's employment, evaluation, wages, advancement, assigned duties or any other term or condition of employment or career development.

Any employee who feels that he/she or someone else is a victim of harassment, including but not limited to any of the conduct listed above, by any employee, customer, client or any other person in connection with his or her employment should report the concern immediately to their supervisor, a member of senior management, or the Director of Human Resources. All complaints will be investigated promptly in as confidential a manner as possible and appropriate corrective or disciplinary action will be taken where warranted.

Any employee who is determined, after investigation, to have engaged in harassment in violation of this policy will be subject to immediate disciplinary action, up to and including discharge.

Employees with Disabilities

The Americans with Disabilities Act of 1990, as amended, prohibits discrimination on the basis of disability, and protects qualified applicants and employees with disabilities from discrimination in hiring, promotion, discharge, pay, job training, fringe benefits, and other terms and conditions of employment. The law also requires that covered entities provide qualified applicants and employees with disabilities, as defined by the Act, with appropriate reasonable accommodation, if such accommodation does not impose an undue hardship. If you believe that you have been discriminated against based upon disability, you should contact your supervisor or the Human Resources Department immediately. If you believe you have a qualifying disability and require some reasonable accommodation, also contact your immediate supervisor or the Human Resources Department.

YOUR JOB

Introductory Period

There is a 90-day introductory period for all new employees and employees who accept a transfer into a new job. All employees, regardless of status or duration of employment, are required to meet and maintain Company standards for job performance and behavior. Either the employee or the Company may end the employment relationship at will at any time during or after the introductory period, with or without reason or advance notice. Completion of the introductory period does not guarantee employment for any specific period of time. As stated previously, we are an "At-Will" employer.

Benefits go into effect the first day of the month following three months of employment. information regarding benefits will be provided at the New Employee Orientation session.

Hours of Work and Overtime

Work Week—The regular or normal work week consists of 40 hours and begins with the period beginning 12:00 A.M. Monday and ending 168 consecutive hours later on the following Sunday.

Work Day—The normal work day for the Company consists of eight hours, excluding lunch periods. Normal hours of business in Denver are 8:30 A.M. to 5:30 P.M. Field locations may have different business hours. Lunch periods are set by each department or subsidiary and may be dictated by the laws in the varying states in which we operate.

Work Schedules—Work schedules will be established based upon business needs and objectives and are subject to change at management's request. Employees will be notified in advance of changes in work hours or work schedules.

Overtime—All overtime work must be approved in advance by your supervisor.

Nothing in these guidelines should be assumed to be a guarantee of employment for any number of hours or period of time.

Attendance

You are an essential member of our team . . . and teamwork is the heart of our business. It is important that employees be prompt and regular in attendance. If you are unable to report to work on time because of circumstances beyond your control, you should notify your supervisor as soon as possible on the day you will be absent.

Absence

The Company and your co-workers depend on you. The success of the Company is dependent on everyone doing their job. When you are absent, it is difficult to fill your shoes. If you need to be away from work, your supervisor must be given advance notice so the vacancy can be filled with a minimum of inconvenience to the operation and to your fellow employees.

If your absence will be longer than one day, your supervisor must be given an expected date of return. Should this date change, notify your supervisor at once. The Company may require medical certification for any absence. When returning to work after an illness of five days or more, a written medical release from your doctor may be required. The Company reserves the right to request a doctor's statement or require the employee to be examined by a physician of the Company's choice. If you are given a conditional medical release, the doctor must state what the conditions of the partial release are and specify any job limitations.

In cases of serious personal illness or other situations in which advance notice is impossible, notify your supervisor as soon as you can. A member of your immediate family may, if necessary, fulfill this obligation.

Tardiness or absenteeism which is considered by the Company to be excessive may result in disciplinary action, up to and including termination. An absence for a period of three consecutive work days without contacting your supervisor to request a leave of absence could be a considered voluntary termination of employment.

Rest Periods

The Company provides one paid 10-minute break each morning and one paid 10-minute break in the afternoon. Employees who take additional breaks must punch out on the time clock because additional breaks are not paid. Excessive absence from the job during the work day results in lost productivity and could result in an unfavorable performance evaluation or disciplinary action, including termination. Each supervisor establishes the break schedule based on the needs of his or her department, and applicable state regulations.

Administration

Non-exempt employees must record all hours by submitting a time card or time sheet to their supervisor for approval. Time cards with discrepancies must be corrected prior to each pay period.

Employees must record any vacation, sick pay, personal pay, jury duty, bereavement leaves or any other absence on an Employee Absence Report Form. Your supervisor or the Human Resources Department has these forms.

It is the manager's responsibility to ensure that their employees record all hours correctly on their time cards.

Scheduling

As the need arises, managers may schedule work days and hours that differ from the standard work days and hours described above. Occasionally, a flex-time schedule may be granted by a manager if the schedule is arranged in advance in writing and benefits the Company as well as the employee. This type of schedule is only for short-term use in order to address a specific employee need. Lunch periods are scheduled by managers. Advance approval of the manager is required when overtime is to be worked or any change in scheduled hours is required.

Civic Duties

It is Company policy to allow employees reasonable time off without loss of pay to attend to civic duties, such as court appearances on behalf of the Company, voting, witness or jury duty. You may be asked to provide documentary proof of such summons. Your supervisor can provide more information.

Jury Duty

The Company recognizes jury duty as a civic responsibility of everyone. When summoned for jury duty, you are granted leave to perform your duty as a juror. If you are excused from jury duty during your regular work hours, we expect you to report to work promptly.

You will receive regular pay for the first five days of jury duty if you were scheduled to work and you submit a juror service certificate.

NOTE: Jury pay varies from state to state. Check with your supervisor for jury pay at your location.

Leaves of Absence

For an unpaid leave of absence of more than 10 days, written application must be made on a Leave of Absence Form and must have the department manager's approval.

Family and Medical Leave: The Company will comply with The Family and Medical Leave Act of 1993 which became affective August 6, 1993, by providing up to 12 weeks of leave in a 12-month period with the guarantee of the same or an equivalent job upon return to work. Family or medical leave may be taken to care for a newborn or newly adopted child, for your own personal illness, or to care for an immediate family member who is seriously ill. To be eligible, you must be employed for at least 12 months, and have provided 1,250 hours of service during the 12 months before the leave is requested. No more than 12 weeks of Family or Medical Leave may be taken within a 12 month period (measured backward from the beginning of the leave).

If you do not meet the eligibility requirements for a family or medical leave, but need time off because of your medical condition, the Company may grant up to four weeks of unpaid leave, but job reinstatement is not guaranteed.

If the leave is for your own serious medical condition, you must first use your accumulated sick leave; thereafter, or after a 15-day waiting period, you may be paid through the Company's Short-Term Disability program, if eligible. If the leave is to care for the birth or placement of a child, or is to care for a seriously ill family member, you will be paid any accrued vacation time, then accrued sick time, and thereafter your leave would be without pay.

A Leave of Absence Request Form must be completed and approved in advance. The Company will pay their portion of your medical benefits while on an approved Family or Medical Leave. Contact the Human Resources Department in Denver for further details regarding a Family or Medical Leave of Absence.

Maternity Leave of Absence: Maternity leave is the same as medical and family leave, and benefits are the same. Maternity leave is compensated in the same manner as any medical disability.

Military Leave of Absence: Any regular full-time employee of the Company who enters active duty in the armed forces of the United States will be granted a military leave of absence without pay.

Active military service entered directly from Company employment may result from:

- Being drafted
- Being ordered to active duty, or active duty for training when on reserve status.

An individual returning from military service will be rehired into the former position or into a job of similar status and like pay if the following eligibility criteria are met:

- The individual presents to the company a copy of a certificate of satisfactory completion of military service.
- Application for re-employment is made within 90 days of discharge or from hospitalization continuing after discharge for a period of not more than one year.
- The individual is able to perform the duties of the former or similar position.

National Guard: Any regular, full-time employee, employed seven months or longer, who is a member of a reserve component of the armed forces of the United States, or a member of the National Guard or Air National Guard, will be granted an unpaid two-week leave of absence for annual training duty or for emergency National Guard duty at the call of a state governor. A leave of absence without pay may be granted for any additional time needed to complete annual training or emergency duty.

Bereavement: In the event of the death of an immediate family member (spouse, mother, father, siblings, children, grandparents or grandchildren and in-laws), the employee may take up to three consecutive days' paid leave. If the employee must travel out of state, an additional two days may be granted for travel time.

Employees should notify their supervisor immediately upon learning of the death so proper arrangements can be made during the employee's absence. Should additional time be needed and approval is granted by the supervisor, the employee may take vacation time or floating holiday. The employee must make the appropriate notation on the time card.

Absence for Occupational Disabilities: An employee who must be away from work due to a work-related illness or injury will fall under the guidelines of the Family and Medical Leave Act. If the employee is unable to return to work within 12 weeks, he/she may be given additional leave under the worker's compensation statutes of the state in which the employee is working. The leave will be unpaid by the Company, and the Company will not pay the employer's portion of the medical insurance premium, while the employee is out and receiving workers' compensation benefits.

If the employee has a work-related injury but can continue to work, time off for medical appointments will be paid by the Company.

Personal Leave of Absence Without Pay: The Company may make provisions for a personal leave of absence without pay for an employee who needs more than one month's time off work for a valid reason other than those covered by the above paragraphs. The maximum leave that may be granted is six months.

When an unpaid personal leave of absence is granted, it is given on an individual basis and at the discretion of management, taking into consideration the purpose of the leave, the employee's work record, and the needs of the Company at that particular time. An employee must exhaust all earned unused vacation before an unpaid personal leave will be authorized.

You must be classified as a regular full-time employee and have completed six months of continuous service prior to the effective date of the unpaid personal leave, and you must complete a Leave of Absence Form and have it approved by your supervisor and submit it to the Human Resources Department.

The Company cannot guarantee reinstatement to the former position or to a position with like status and pay, except in the case of Family and Medical Leave or Military Leave. In these two instances, an employee's job or an equivalent job for which the employee is qualified is guaranteed by federal law.

Employees who are on any approved unpaid leave of absence other than a Family or Medical Leave, which is mandated by state and/or federal law, must pay their own medical, life and dental insurance premiums if they wish to keep their insurance in force while they are gone. Additionally, it should be noted that when an employee who is on an authorized Family Care/Medical Leave mandated by state and/federal law, the Company will pay its portion of medical benefits for a period not to exceed 12 work weeks.

Sick Leave: All regular full-time employees earn 6.67 hours of sick time per month beginning the first day of the month following date of hire. Regular part-time employees who are normally scheduled to work at least 30 hours per week will receive a pro-rated amount. The eligibility requirements for regular part-time employees are the same as for regular full-time employees. *NOTE:* Change these numbers to fit your plan.

Up to five sick days per year may be used to care for an ill immediate family member.

For each three full days of accrued sick leave in excess of 30 days, the employee will be eligible for one day of vacation. At the employee's anniversary date, any unused "excess" sick leave for the prior year will automatically convert to vacation days at a rate of 3 sick days to 1 vacation day.

An employee should make the appropriate notation for sick pay on their time card or on an Employee Absence Report Form. Where required, attach the doctor's certification to the Form.

Unused sick time is not paid upon termination, except for unused excess sick time which has automatically converted to vacation days.

YOUR PAY

Pay Periods

Pay days are on the 15th and the last day of each month. If pay day falls on a holiday or weekend, you will be paid on the last working day preceding the holiday or weekend. Please endorse your check and cash or deposit it within 30 days. If you would like direct deposit of your paycheck, your supervisor or payroll administrator can provide the appropriate forms.

Performance Appraisals and Raises

Performance is appraised once a year, usually in July. Raises are not guaranteed but are at management's discretion and based on, among other things, management's assessment for job performance and the Company's operating results.

Overtime

Non-exempt employees are paid one and one-half times their base rate for all hours in excess of 40 hours worked in a week. If you are a regular full-time employee and are asked to work on a Company-recognized holiday you will receive double time for all hours worked on that holiday. Overtime laws vary by state. Ask your supervisor for details for your specific location.

YOUR BENEFITS

Benefits and Services

As an employee, you will have an opportunity to participate in our many fine benefits programs. A summary of the Company's benefit plans is set forth in the Overview of Employee Benefits in this Employee Handbook.

Recognized Holidays

We normally observe nine paid holidays per year as follows: New Year's Day, Memorial Day, Independence Day, Labor Day, Thanksgiving Day, day after Thanksgiving Day, Christmas Day, one floating holiday, and the employee's birthday. The birthday holiday may be taken within 30 days of your birthday. An unused floating holiday or birthday holiday may not be carried forward from year to year, and only the current year's days will be paid on termination.

Holiday Pay

Regular full-time and part-time employees who are regularly scheduled to work a minimum of thirty (30) hours per week are eligible for holiday pay. To be eligible for holiday pay you must be at work on the scheduled workday before and after a holiday, unless you are on a paid leave of absence, vacation, or are ill. New employees will be eligible for holiday pay after the first day worked.

If your supervisor feels that you have sufficient justification to be off the day before or after a holiday, your absence may be excused and payment of holiday pay will be approved. Written approval must be furnished to the payroll department. Some Company positions, including regular part-time employees, receive prorated holiday pay.

Vacations

The Company provides a paid vacation benefit to regular full-time and part-time employees who regularly work a minimum of thirty (30) hours per week. Vacation time is prorated for part-time employees who regularly work more than 30 hours per week. A Vacation Request Form must be completed and approved by your supervisor in advance. Each year on your anniversary date, the Company provides the following vacation:

- 2 weeks after 1 year
- 3 weeks after 5 years
- 4 weeks after 10 years

In some states, such as California, vacation benefits accrue immediately when the person is hired. Ask your supervisor about vacation accrual at your location. Earned, unused vacation is paid upon termination.

YOUR SAFETY

Safety

Your safety is a concern. We make every reasonable effort to provide you with a safe place to work. We want you to be safe on the job as well as off. Don't take chances. When you think safety, you make things safe for yourself and your fellow employees. If an accident occurs on the job, notify your supervisor immediately. You must complete a First Report of Injury form and give it to your supervisor as soon as you are able but in any case within 48 hours. If immediate medical assistance is required and you cannot reach your supervisor, call 911. Unsafe conditions or employee conduct which jeopardizes your safety or the safety of others should be reported immediately to your supervisor or other management personnel. Such reports will be investigated and appropriate action will be taken, including disciplinary action, where appropriate.

In Case of Injury

If you are injured on the job in the normal course of your employment, you are directed to report the injury to your supervisor and Human Resources Department immediately, and to seek medical attention from our Health Care Facility. In a life or limb threatening emergency, call 911 and then notify your supervisor immediately. All job site injuries must be reported within 48 hours, or as per state law. If on the day of your work-related injury, you are, in the opinion of your supervisor, unable to work the remainder of the day, you will be compensated. Check with your supervisor for information on reporting accidents and obtaining medical assistance at your specific location.

Security Procedures

Each company location has its own set of security procedures. Ask your supervisor for specific information.

Whenever the office fire alarm sounds or there is a bomb threat, everyone in the building is to calmly proceed to the nearest stairway exit and vacate the building. *Never attempt to enter an elevator during an emergency fire alert.*

When leaving your work areas, you are asked to take your personal wallets and purses with you for security reasons. Each supervisor is to check their area to ensure that all personnel have evacuated.

JOB OPPORTUNITIES

In an attempt to advise employees of job opportunities within the Company, each Division and the Corporate office may post weekly bulletins announcing job vacancies at their specific locations. If you meet the minimum qualifications and would like to be considered for a posted job, contact a Human Resources Representative for a Job Bid form and further information. Following is the Job Line number for our employees: _____.

You must be in a position for six months before asking to be considered for a new job, and you must not be on a performance improvement plan or disciplinary action.

Jobs posted are not necessarily reserved or held exclusively for current employees. The Company reserves the right to hire the candidate that it determines in it's discretion is best suited for the job, and to promote, demote, increase or decrease wages, or take any other actions concerning the terms and conditions of employment without cause or reason and without notice.

Employee Relations Policy

We hope that your work experience will be rewarding. The Company provides equal opportunity to all applicants and employees regardless of race, color, religion, national origin, sex, age, disability or sexual orientation.

Non-Violence Policy

Our Company strives to provide a safe workplace for employees. We know that we cannot guarantee our facilities will not be targeted by a person or persons who are driven to violence. This can unfortunately happen in any company no matter what precautions are taken. However, we have established a non-violence policy in the hope that we can minimize the risk of personal injury to employees on our property.

Unacceptable Conduct

Threats, threatening language, or any other acts of aggression or violence made toward or by any Company employee will not be tolerated. For the purposes of this policy, a threat includes any verbal or physical harassment or abuse, attempts to intimidate or to cause fear in others, menacing gestures, bringing weapons to the workplace, stalking, or any other hostile, aggressive, injurious or destructive actions undertaken for the purpose of intimidation.

Procedures for Reporting a Threat

All potentially dangerous situations including threats by co-workers should be reported immediately to the Manager of Human Resources, or to any other member of management with whom you feel comfortable. Reports of threats may be made anonymously. All threats will be promptly investigated. No employee will be subject to retaliation, intimidation or discipline as a result of reporting a threat in good faith under this policy.

If an investigation confirms that a threat of a violent act or violence itself has occurred, the Company will take appropriate corrective action with regard to the offending employee.

If you are the victim of a threat made by an outside party, please follow the steps detailed in this policy. It is important for us to be aware of potential danger in our workplace. We appreciate your cooperation and although we cannot guarantee that no violence will ever occur on our property, we will be responsive to all reports and take appropriate action when such reports are received.

Problems: How to Solve Them

We hope all employees share a feeling of pride in the Company, and that your spirit of cooperation and enthusiasm in working for the good of the Company will be apparent in all your relations. We realize however that valid differences occasionally arise. Here is how to handle these differences.

The following complaint procedures have been established. *These procedures may be used by current employees or by terminating employees.*

Step1—Employee discusses the complaint or problem with immediate supervisor. It is expected that every effort will be made to resolve the complaint in a fair and amicable manner at this level.

Step 2—If the employee is not satisfied with this attempt to resolve the complaint or a response (written or verbal) is not received within ten working days, the employee may discuss the matter with the next management level.

Step 3—If the problem still has not been resolved within another ten days at the second level, a formal written complaint may be directed to the President. A determination by the President is final.

At any time, the employee may contact the Director of Human Resources for assistance in resolving a problem.

The Company may impose counseling or disciplinary action which, in its judgment, most effectively addresses the problem. You will be advised of such actions should they occur.

We hope it will not be necessary to discipline or discharge employees. There may be times however, when it becomes necessary to formally correct the performance of individuals and, in some cases, termination could occur. The Company reserves the right to make these decisions, including the right to terminate an employee at any time for any or no reason, with or without use of progressive discipline or performance improvement plans.

Termination

If it is your intent to resign from employment, two weeks' notice should be provided to the Company. The Company will appreciate the opportunity to make arrangements to cover the vacancy created by your leaving.

WHAT ELSE YOU NEED TO KNOW

Appearance and Attire

Our public image is directly dependent on our staff, individually and collectively. People are inclined to judge organizations by the people who represent them. The personal appearance, quality of service and positive attitude of all of our employees are essential to creating and maintaining a favorable public image.

Attire should be conservative, in good taste and promote a business-like professional attitude and image in keeping with your specific job. The best "rule of thumb" is to dress for the position you fill and the people you serve. The Company reserves the right to insist that employees who serve our clients and customers dress professionally. The Company will comply with any state statutes which apply to employee dress codes in states in which we do business.

The Company specifies certain days as casual dress days, however, even on casual days, attire must be in good taste. Managers will be notified of these special days in advance.

Bulletin Boards

To keep you informed, the Company provides bulletin boards in the lunch rooms at every work site. No material may be posted or removed from bulletin boards `without the approval of the Director of Human Resources.

All applicable federal and state employment laws must remain posted at each location.

Business Mileage Reimbursement

Unless you are already provided an auto allowance, you will be compensated for mileage on the use of your personal car for Company business at the current rate allowed by the Internal Revenue Service. Your supervisor or the Human Resources Department has special forms for this purpose.

Business Travel

If you are required to travel out of town to conduct the Company's business, we will pay for your necessary expenditures. Your supervisor will let you know the appropriate procedures for business travel.

Inclement Weather Procedures

Employees should listen to radio stations or call their supervisor to learn if the offices will be closed when the weather is bad. Employees at other field locations should also check with their supervisor for inclement weather procedures.

Pay for Lost Time Due to Inclement Weather

- If the Company closes the office, employees will be paid for the hours they missed but were scheduled to work that day.

- If the office is open but attendance "optional," employees who do not work will not be paid for their time off unless they make up the lost time during that same week or use a vacation day.

- If the office is open for business as usual, employees who do not work must use vacation time in order to be paid for the time off, or take the time off without pay.

Smoking

The Company and all its subsidiaries do not allow smoking in any facility.

Solicitation and Distribution

Out of respect for the private lives of our employees and our desire to receive the full benefit of your productivity, no person who is not an employee of this Company (except commercial sales people calling on the Company) may come onto the property at any time to solicit for any cause or to distribute material of any kind for any purpose without permission.

Employees may not engage in solicitation or in the distribution of materials of any type for any purpose during working time on Company property, except for that which is necessary to carry out their assigned job duties. However, employees may engage in solicitation during their non-working time and may participate in the distribution of materials on their non-working time in non-working areas as long as standards of neatness are maintained.

An employee is not to enter or remain in work areas except during scheduled working time and a reasonable time before or after scheduled work, or when working scheduled overtime. If an employee wants to enter those working areas at any other time for a legitimate reason, permission must be secured.

Suggestions

The exchange of ideas within our organization is considered by management to be an asset and is strongly encouraged. Your thoughts concerning ways of increasing productivity, improving the quality of our work products, our projects, safety, and other related matters are welcome. Address your suggestions to the president of the company.

Miscellaneous

Information regarding employee parking, building access, and facilities may be obtained from your supervisor.

SAMPLE OVERVIEW OF EMPLOYEE BENEFITS

This is a sample summary of the employee benefits. See official plan documents for more detailed information in your company.

Benefit	Description	Eligibility
Holiday Pay	Nine paid holidays per year, as follows: • New Year's Day • Memorial Day • Independence Day • Labor Day • Thanksgiving Day • Day after Thanksgiving • Christmas Day • Employee's Birthday (must be used within 30 days of birthday) • 1 Floating Holiday If a holiday falls on a Saturday, it will be observed the preceding Friday; if a holiday falls on a Sunday, it will be observed the next Monday. Holiday pay is pro-rated for eligible part-time employees.	Regular full-time or part-time employees. Must be on a paid status to be eligible for holiday pay.
Sick Pay	Employees earn ten days of paid sick time per year (6.67 hours per month for full-time employees), up to a maximum accrual of 30 days (240 hours). Sick pay is pro-rated for eligible part-time employees. Five days of sick time per year may be used to care for an ill family member. Sick time accrued in excess of 30 days is converted to vacation time, at the rate of one day of vacation for each three full days of sick time.	Accrual begins first of month after hire date for regular full-time and part-time employees who are scheduled to work a minimum of 30 hours per week.

Vacation Pay	Vacation pay is earned on employee's anniversary date,* and is based on years of continuous service:
	   2 weeks after 1 year
	   3 weeks after 7 years
	   4 weeks after 12 years
	Vacation time must be scheduled ahead of time and be approved by supervisor; it may be used in increments of half-days. Unused vacation time will carry over from year to year. Vacation pay is pro-rated for eligible part-time employees.
	(*California employees accrue vacation immediately, based on state law.)
		Regular full-time or part-time employees scheduled to work a minimum of 30 hours per week; upon completion of one full year of service.

Other Paid Time Off	*Bereavement Leave*—Pay will be granted for up to three days leave in the event of death of immediate family member (spouse, mother, father, siblings, children, grandparents, grandchildren and in-laws). Two additional days off may be granted for out-of-state travel. *Jury Duty*—Employees who miss work while performing jury duty will receive the time off with pay for up to a maximum of 30 days, upon submission of proof of jury service.	Regular full-time and part-time employees scheduled to work a minimum of 30 hours per week.
Medical insurance	Eligible employees may choose one of the two following plans. Cost of health insurance coverage is shared between employer and employee; premiums are deducted from semi-monthly pay. *Designated Provider Program (DPP):* Covered individuals choose a primary care physician (PCP) who will manage all health care needs. Preventive care is stressed. **If PCP and In-Network Used:** • No annual deductible; • No limitations on treatment for pre-existing conditions; • $10 co-pay for doctor's office visit; • $50 for outpatient surgery; • $200 co-pay for hospitalization; • $5 co-pay for generic Prescription drugs from participating pharmacies (supply of 30 days or less); maintenance drugs may be purchased through the mail at discount.	First of month following three months of employment for regular full-time or part-time employees scheduled to work a minimum of 30 hours per week. Common-law marriages are not recognized in the states of Arizona, California and Virginia. Subject to change in state legislation. May apply for benefits during open enrollment (October 1st of each year).

Benefit	Description	Eligibility
Medical Insurance, *continued*	**If Non-Network Provider Used:** • $400 per person annual deductible/$800 per family; • Employee pays 30% of covered charges, up to a maximum of $3,400 per person/$6,800 per family (including deductible); • After maximum out of-pocket expenses are met, covered services are paid at 100%; • Preventive care not covered; • 30% co-insurance for prescription drugs, subject to deductible. *Preferred Provider Organization (PPO)* **If Network Provider Used:** • No annual deductible; • $10 per Doctor office visit; • 10% per hospitalization; • Limited preventive care coverage Is provided. **If Non-Network Provider Used:** • $200 per person annual deductible/$400 per family; • Employee pays 30% of covered charges, up to maximum of $1,500 per person/$3,000 per family (including deductible); • After maximum out of-pocket expenses have been paid, covered services are paid at 100%; • $5 co-pay for generic prescription drugs; $20 co-pay for brand-name drugs.	
Dental Insurance	Employees may select one of the following dental plans. Cost of dental insurance coverage is deducted from employee's semi-monthly pay: *U.S. Dental* (pre-paid plan): • Must choose dentist within the U.S. Dental Plan network; • $5 co-payment for office visits; • **Basic preventive and diagnostic services** are paid at no charge to employee; • **Restorative services** are provided at no charge or at minimal co-payments; • **Extensive services** are provided at reduced fees • **Orthodontic services** are offered at reduced fees. *Unilife Dental Plan* (traditional indemnity plan): • Free choice of dentist; • **Preventive procedures** are paid at 100%; • **Restorative procedures** are paid at 80% after the annual deductible of $50 per person has been met; • **Major services** are reimbursed at 50% after the annual deductible of $50 per person has been met; are not available during the first year on the plan; • **Orthodontia services** are available for children after the third year. Are reimbursed at 50% after the lifetime deductible of $50 has been paid; • Maximum annual dental benefit of $750 for first year, $1,000 for second year, and $1,500 per year thereafter.	First of month following three months of employment, for regular full-time or part-time employees scheduled to work a minimum of 30 hours per week. May apply for benefits during open enrollment (October 1st of each year). Common-law marriages are not recognized in the states of Arizona, California and Virginia. Subject to change in state legislation.
Life Insurance and Accidental Death and Dismemberment Insurance	Available as part of Health Insurance package. Company provides $20,000 of life insurance and $20,000 of accident insurance for each eligible employee enrolled in the health insurance plan. scheduled to work a minimum of 30 hours per week.	First of month following three months of employment, for regular full-time or part-time employees

Benefit	Description	Eligibility
Voluntary Term Group Life Insurance Plan	Employee may purchase coverage up to five times base annual pay (maximum $300,000), in increments of $10,000 for self and spouse. Employee may purchase coverage for eligible children, in increments of $2,500, up to $10,000 maximum. $30,000 guarantee issue available if application is made within 30 days of employment. Reduced rates available for non-smokers.	Regular full-time or part-time employees scheduled to work a minimum of 30 hours per week. No waiting period; coverage begins first of the month after payroll deductions begin. Common-law marriages are not recognized in the states of Arizona, California and Virginia. Subject to change in state legislation.
Short Term Disability	Employees who miss more than 15 days of work due to an illness or injury may receive up to 60% of weekly base pay, to maximum of $500 per week. Benefits end after 150 days away from work, at which time the long term disability benefits may apply.	First of month following three months of employment for regular employees scheduled to work a minimum of 30 hours per week.
Long Term Disability	Employees who miss more than 150 consecutive work days because of an illness or injury may receive up to 60% of their base monthly earnings, up to a maximum of $4,000 per month, through the long term disability program.	First of month following three months of employment for regular employees scheduled to work a minimum of 30 hours per week.
401k Plan	Employee may contribute 1–15% of base pay to retirement account on pre-tax basis, up to statutory limits. Company matching is determined on a year-to-year basis, based on company earnings. Employee has six investment options for contributions.	First of quarter following one full year of employment, for regular full-time employees.

ACKNOWLEDGMENT AND RECEIPT
OF EMPLOYEE HANDBOOK

This employee handbook published (*Date*) supersedes all previous employee handbooks.

I have received a copy of the employee handbook. I understand that I am to read and become familiar with the contents. If I have questions, I understand that I should talk to my Supervisor or the Director of Human Resources.

Further, I understand that:

This handbook is not intended to, nor does it create promises or representations of continued employment. Every employee has an at-will relationship with the Company. This means that I am free to resign my employment at any time, just as the Company is free to terminate my employment, for any or no reason, with or without cause or the use of progressive discipline, at any time.

This handbook represents a summary of the more important company guidelines at the time of publication, and is not intended to be all inclusive. In all instances, the benefit plan texts, trust documents and master contracts, as appropriate, are the governing documents. The employee handbook, personnel policies, benefit plan texts, any trust agreements, or master contracts are not employment contracts.

Apart from our policy of *At-Will* employment and those policies required by law, the Company may change its policies or practices at any time without prior notice. I understand the Company may terminate an employee at any time with or without notice.

Further, I understand that this document will become a part of my personnel file.

_____   _____
Employee Name (Please Print)   Location/Department

_____   _____
Signature   Date

5

PERSONNEL POLICIES

- Keys to Successful Implementation of Personnel Policies
- Checklist for Personnel Policy Manual
- Fifteen Ways to Communicate Your Policies
- Personnel Policy Manual Key Instructions
- Sample Personnel Policy Manual
- E-Mail, Internet & Other Electronic Information Resources

Personnel Policies

Most organizations today, even small ones, need a set of personnel policies and guidelines. Set policies help managers and supervisors to evenhandedly manage the workforce. This helps the company avoid costly litigation brought by people who feel they were not treated fairly. You don't need a policy to regulate every single event that might occur. What you do need are policies to cover difficult personnel areas like discipline and termination. Policy manuals are for the use of supervisory personnel only, to aid in day-to-day management of their people.

KEYS TO SUCCESSFUL IMPLEMENTATION OF PERSONNEL POLICIES

Planning is the key to success when writing and implementing a personnel policy manual.

Before Implementation

1. Ask potentially affected department heads to choose a representative to aid in the determination of need, shaping, structure, and implementation of the proposed policy or procedure.
2. Involve representatives from affected departments in all phases.
3. Explore the reasons for the change—advantages and disadvantages—with representatives of affected departments.
4. Evaluate potential alternatives in content and structure with representatives.
5. Determine whether a trial period and subsequent fine-tuning are appropriate.
6. Plan and organize the implementation or revision to ensure smooth transition through clear advance communication and training.

After Implementation

1. Have the representatives from each affected department oversee and monitor the success of the transition and post-transition phases.
2. Any problem areas that cross departmental lines should be addressed by the committee of representatives.
3. Problems that lie within one department only should be addressed by the representative, department head, and policy initiator.

4. A formal survey throughout affected departments might be conducted six months after implementation in order to assess the workability and success of the newly implemented policy or procedure.

Manager's Tip

Ask yourself the following questions:

Does everyone affected clearly know the policy or procedure?

Is the policy or procedure set up to produce the desired result?

Are the skills that are necessary for successful administration found or developed in those who will need them?

Does the policy and procedures manual contain the current information?

CHECKLIST FOR PERSONNEL POLICY MANUAL

Use the following checklist when writing a personnel policy manual. Issues such as clarity, format, tone, and style should be addressed before you start the process.

Review for Clarity, Readability, and Understand Ability

❑ Review each policy for clarity, readability, and understand ability.

❑ Consider the education and training levels of the entire work force.

❑ Eliminate all ambiguities.

❑ Review handbook to ensure that all significant terms are used consistently and correctly.

❑ If a significant portion of the work force speaks a language other than English, consider (1) preparing the entire handbook in the foreign language, or (2) including a provision in the handbook that is written in the foreign language and that informs employees where they can obtain assistance if they have difficulty translating or understanding any policies.

Issues Regarding Style and Tone: Formal vs. Informal Tone

FORMAL

❑ References to employees in the third person rather than as "you."

❑ Less personal tone.

❑ Emphasis on professionalism.

INFORMAL

❑ References to "you" rather than third person or "the employee."

❑ Emphasis on brevity.

❑ Use of cartoons and pictures.

❑ Avoid too much detail.

❑ Avoid legal and technical terminology.

❑ Tone "folksy" rather than "you're in the army now."

❑ Watch level—don't "talk down" to employees.

Considerations

❑ Size of work force.

❑ Composition of work force.

❑ Average education levels of employees.

❑ Ability of employees to read and understand English.

❑ Occupations covered by the handbook.

❑ Industry practices and customs.

❑ Practices in the same geographical area.

❑ The impression the employer wishes to convey.

❑ The nature of the work environment.

Gender References

❑ Check for consistency in all references to gender.

❑ Don't use "he," "she," or "he/she." Change to a plural pronoun and use "employees" or "they."

❑ Avoid references to gender by use of the second person "you" or gender-neutral terms such as "the employee" or "an individual."

Areas Where Inconsistencies Are Frequently Found

❑ References to gender.

❑ References to employee classifications should be consistent and accurate (permanent employees, full-time employees, and regular full-time employees).

❑ The term used to describe the employer should be used consistently throughout the manual without switching from one term to another.

❑ A handbook should use numbers consistently. A common practice is to spell out numbers from one to one hundred and use numerals from 101 on. Make exceptions where spelling out numbers would be cumbersome, such as for measurements (40 hours; 5 feet). Many practices are "correct"; the important thing is to be precise and consistent.

FIFTEEN WAYS TO COMMUNICATE YOUR POLICIES

If policies and procedures are not communicated frequently and in a manner that your current work force will accept, they will not be followed or used properly. In addition, any communication program must stay current with changing business conditions.

Following are fifteen ways to communicate with employees:

1. Conduct one-on-one communication between supervisor and employee at least once a month, quarterly, and at the yearly performance review.

2. Publish employee newsletters, articles, and stories about employees who are actively supporting the company and its business plans.

3. Use the media. Show films and slides on topics of current interest. Use video to train employees and for special programs.

4. Have programs during the lunch period, where speakers come in to speak on a variety of subjects pertinent to your business and industry. The company may donate 30 minutes extra if the program helps employees on their jobs, and the investment may be well worth the cost.

5. Some organizations, like U.S. Homes, have started monthly discussion group programs, aimed at managers and professionals. This is used as a management development tool. A particular book will be chosen, all participants read the book, and then a vice- president leads a discussion group on the merits of the principles set out in the book.

6. Sometimes, when companies are going through a particularly difficult time, a question box or telephone hotline will encourage dialogue. The employee doesn't have to give a name. Guarantee a response to all reasonable questions within a few days. You can reply through a special newsletter to all employees. If you do have a question box or hotline, it's important to reply in timely fashion, and you and your top management must agree to be open and honest or these avenues won't work well.

7. Create a communications task force to identify communication problems and suggest solutions. The task force should include people from a variety of functions and all levels in the company. People have more ownership in programs they or their peers help create.

8. To communicate policies and procedures in your own department, route the policy book throughout the department and ask each employee to read it.

9. Put an extra copy of the policy manual in your library or in the personnel office, where employees can check it out if they want.

10. Implement an orientation program for families so they understand the company, its products, its policies, and the office or plant facilities.

11. Publish an annual report to employees and their families, updating them not only on employee benefit statements, but also on the company's business plans and accomplishments.

12. Use athletic activities and health programs as avenues for employee communication.

13. Start an employee speakers' bureau. Give employees training in public speaking, and select topics that would be of benefit to the company as well as topics the employees choose.

14. If you have extra space that can be used occasionally, have an employee crafts fair where employees can sell their crafts.

15. Set up closed circuit TV/VHF programs to inform employees about important management meetings, and pass on specific information employees may read.

PERSONNEL POLICY MANUAL KEY INSTRUCTIONS

The policies in the following model personnel policy manual are purposely brief. Review them and rework them to fit your needs. Once you get them on your computer, rework them as the need arises, and keep them current with changes in your organization. You may not need every policy in this manual. Don't create more work for yourself than necessary by having policies that aren't needed.

Having a personnel policy manual will save you and your supervisors and managers untold time spent attempting to define policy verbally everyday throughout the company. Having written policies ensures consistency of treatment and will help you avoid unnecessary litigation. Have your attorney review your manual before implementation.

Use someone on your staff or a personnel consultant to implement the manual. Be sure to let your department heads review all policies, and ask for their input if you want them to be proactive in implementation.

Note

This personnel policy manual is a sample format. All policies and procedures must conform to the laws in the state in which it will be used and should be reviewed by an attorney familiar with labor and personnel laws prior to being installed.

Manager's Tip

Instead of using "Personnel Policies and Procedures," you may prefer to call them "Personnel Guidelines." There are two schools of thought: One says, "Make them hard and fast policies." The other says, "They should only be guidelines; let managers manage the company." It's a matter of style, but whether "policies" or "guidelines," they must be administered evenhandedly.

Sample

Personnel
Policy Manual

Note

Use the policies that fit your needs; you may not need every policy that is in this sample manual. Rewrite the policies to be company-specific. Then have your attorney review your manual before you print, distribute, and implement.

PERSONNEL POLICIES AND PROCEDURES

This manual is designed as a statement of policy and outline of procedures and guidelines for supervisors to aid in the proper handling of matters concerning company personnel.

The policies and procedures set forth in this manual apply to all employees of _____ Company. However, this manual is not to be interpreted as a legal document or an employment contract. Policies contained herein are only summaries and are not all-inclusive. Managers must still manage day-to-day activities and make policy decisions where there are, at times, no strict guidelines.

Questions regarding these policies and procedures should be directed to _____.

The company reserves the right to alter, change, add to, or delete any of these policies or procedures at any time without notice.

CONTENTS

- Absenteeism
- Advertising, Help Wanted
- Appearance and Attire
- Benefits
- Bulletin Boards
- Catastrophic Illness
- Complaint Procedure
- Confidentiality Agreement
- Disability
- Disciplinary Action and Warning Notices
- Drugs at Work
- Educational Assistance Program
- Emergency Procedures
- Employee Handbook and Agreement
- Employment of Spouse
- Equal Employment Opportunity
- Employee Assistance Program
- Exit Interviews
- External Communications
- Evaluation Period
- Funeral—Time Off
- Garnishments
- Gifts and Gratuities
- Harassment
- Hiring Procedures
- Holidays
- Hours of Work
- Immigration Reform and Control Act Compliance
- Job Descriptions
- Job Posting
- Jury Duty
- Layoff
- Leaves of Absence

- Lunch and Rest Periods
- Maternity Leave of Absence
- Moonlighting
- Orientation, New Employee
- Overtime
- Paydays
- Personnel Records
- Performance Appraisal
- Personal Time Off
- Professional Memberships
- Promotions
- Recreation Activities
- References
- Rehire
- Reinstatement of Benefits
- Relocation
- Safety and Health
- Salary Administration
- Security
- Separation Pay
- Service Awards
- Sick Time
- Smoking Policy
- Suggestion Program
- Signing Authority
- Temporary and Part-Time Employees
- Terminations
- Time Off with Pay
- Unemployment Compensation
- Veterans Reporting Requirements
- Voting
- Work Hours
- Vacation
- Work Rules
- Workers' Compensation

ABSENTEEISM

Because each employee is an essential member of our team and teamwork is important, we expect employees to be prompt and regular in attendance.

Employees who are unable to report to work on time because of circumstances beyond their control (including illness) are expected to notify their manager within a reasonable period of time on the morning of the absence.

If the absence is going to be longer than one day, the manager should be given an expected date of return. When an employee is returning to work after an illness of over five working days, a medical release from the doctor may be requested.

An absence for a period of three consecutive days without contacting a supervisor or the Personnel Department may be considered justification for termination.

A form is available for use in tracking employee attendance. If it becomes necessary to terminate an employee for absenteeism, the absentee record is an important part of the termination documentation.

ADVERTISING, HELP WANTED

All help-wanted ads should be processed through the Personnel Department using the Help-Wanted Ad form. This will help the company make a uniform presentation in all print media. When an opening occurs and an ad is to be placed, the supervisor should draft the ad so that it contains the appropriate job specifications. The supervisor should send the ad copy to Personnel along with an employment requisition.

APPEARANCE AND ATTIRE

Our public image is directly dependent on our staff, individually and collectively. People are inclined to judge organizations by the people who represent them. The personal appearance, quality of service, and positive attitude of all of our employees are essential to creating and maintaining a favorable public image.

Attire should be conservative, in good taste, and promote a businesslike professional attitude and image in keeping with each specific job. Extreme forms of dress, hairstyle, or makeup are not acceptable. The best rule of thumb is to dress for the position you fill and the people you serve.

Manager's Tip
_____

You can only require a specific dress code where the job justifies it. For example, someone who meets the public everyday can be required to dress in more business-oriented attire than a warehouse clerk who doesn't interact with customers.

BENEFITS

New Hire Benefits

The company provides medical and life insurance plans, all of which are described in separate brochures. All regular full-time employees are eligible to participate in these benefits after they have passed the 90-day evaluation period.

As employees become eligible, all necessary information will be provided to them.

Benefits Upon Termination

Comprehensive Omnibus Budget Reconciliation Act (COBRA)

On April 7, 1986, Congress enacted the Comprehensive Omnibus Budget Reconciliation Act (COBRA) which requires that most employers sponsoring group health plans offer employees and their families the opportunity for a temporary extension of health coverage (called "continuation coverage") at group rates in certain instances where coverage under the plan would otherwise end.

Effective January 1, 1987, employees covered by the company's group health plan have a right to choose continuation coverage should they lose their group health coverage because of (1) reduction in hours of employment or (2) termination of employment (for reasons other than gross misconduct on the employee's part).

A spouse or dependent of an employee covered by the company health plan has the right to choose continuation coverage if group health coverage under this plan is also for any of the following reasons:

1. The death of a spouse/parent;
2. A termination of a spouse's/parent's employment (for reasons other than gross misconduct) or reduction in a spouse's/parent's hours of employment;
3. Divorce or legal separation from a spouse/of parent;
4. Dependent ceases to be a dependent child as provided by the plan; or
5. Spouse/parent becomes eligible for Medicare.

Under COBRA, the employee or a family member has the responsibility to inform the personnel department of a divorce, legal separation, a child losing dependent status, Medicare eligibility, or death of an employee covered by the company's group health plan within 14 days of the event.

When the Personnel Department is notified that one of these events has happened, we will notify employees of their right to choose continuation coverage. Under COBRA, the person has at least 60 days from the date coverage would be lost because of one of the events described above to inform the Personnel Department that continuation coverage is desired. If continuation coverage is not chosen, the group health insurance coverage will end.

When continuation coverage is chosen, the company is required to provide coverage which is identical to the coverage provided under the plan to similarly situated employees or family members. The new law requires that employees be afforded the opportunity to maintain continuation coverage for three years unless group health coverage was lost because of a termination of employment or reduction in hours. In that case, the required continuation coverage period is 18 months. However, the new law also provides that continuation coverage may be cut short for any of the following five reasons:

1. The company no longer provides group health coverage to any of its employees;
2. The premium for continuation coverage is not paid;
3. The employee becomes an employee covered under another group health plan;
4. The employee becomes eligible for medicare; or
5. The insured is divorced from a covered employee and subsequently remarries and is covered under the new spouse's group health plan.

The law allows the employer to charge the employee the full premium for the insurance. It also provides that, at the end of the 18-month or three-year continuation coverage period, the employee must be allowed to enroll in an individual conversion health plan provided under the company's group health plan.

BULLETIN BOARDS

Organizational bulletins announcing the names of newly hired employees, promotions, internal reorganizations, and other pertinent staff data will be posted on all bulletin boards along with other items of interest to employees.

Items intended for placement on bulletin boards must be approved and distributed by the personnel department. (Unless the company has a union: in that case, the union may post bulletins.)

Manager's Tip

Don't allow employees or outsiders to post things on your company bulletin boards without your permission. Have a separate bulletin board (maybe in the lunch room) for items "For Sale" and other employee generated notices.

CATASTROPHIC ILLNESS

The company recognizes that employees with life-threatening illnesses, including but not limited to cancer, heart disease, and AIDS, may wish to continue to engage in as many of their normal pursuits as their condition allows, including work. As long as these employees are able to meet acceptable performance standards, and medical evidence indicates that their conditions are not a threat to themselves or others, managers should be sensitive to their conditions and ensure that they are treated consistently with other employees. At the same time, the company has an obligation to provide a safe work environment for all employees. Every precaution should be taken to ensure that an employee's condition does not present a health or safety threat to other employees. Consistent with this concern for employees with life-threatening illnesses, the company offers the following resources available through the personnel department:

- Management and employee education and information on terminal illness and specific life-threatening illnesses

- Referral to agencies and organizations which offer supportive services for people with life-threatening illnesses

- Benefit consultation to assist employees in effectively managing health, leave, and other benefits

Guidelines

When dealing with situations involving employees with life-threatening illnesses, managers should:

1. Remember that an employee's health condition is personal and confidential. Reasonable precautions should be taken to protect information regarding an employee's health condition.

2. Contact the personnel department if you believe that you or other employees need information about terminal illnesses or a specific life-threatening illness, or if you need further guidance in managing a situation that involves an employee with a life-threatening illness.

3. Contact the personnel department if you have any concern about the possible contagious nature of an employee's illness.

4. Contact the personnel department to determine whether a statement should be obtained from the employee's attending physician to the effect that continued right to require an examination by a medical doctor appointed by the company.

5. If warranted, make reasonable accommodation for employees with life-threatening illnesses consistent with the business needs of the division/unit.

6. Make a reasonable attempt to transfer employees with life-threatening illnesses who request a transfer and are experiencing undue emotional stress.

7. Be sensitive and responsive to co-workers' concerns and emphasize employee education available through the personnel department.

8. No special consideration should be given beyond normal transfer requests for employees who feel threatened by a co-worker's life-threatening illness.

9. Be sensitive to the fact that continued employment for an employee with a life-threatening illness may sometimes be therapeutically important in the remission or recovery process or may help to prolong that employee's life.

10. Employees should be encouraged to seek assistance from established community support groups for medical treatment and counseling services. Information on these can be requested through the personnel department.

Manager's Tip

You may or may not want a catastrophic illness policy. Some attorneys say yes, some say no. The consensus of human resource people today, however, is that you should be prepared to deal with major illnesses and have the policy in place.

COMPLAINT PROCEDURE

Good employee-employer relationships can exist only if employees believe they have been treated equitably and fairly within the management policies, procedures, and actions which influence this relationship. It is recognized that there are occasions when honest differences of opinion can occur regarding the interpretation and application of policies, procedures, and actions.

The following procedure is established to provide an effective and acceptable means for employees to bring problems and complaints to the attention of management.

Procedure

Step 1—Employee discusses the complaint or problem with immediate supervisor. It is expected that every effort will be made to resolve the complaint in a fair and amicable manner at this level.

Step 2—If the employee is not satisfied with this attempt to resolve the complaint or a response (written or oral) is not received within ten working days, the employee may discuss the matter with the next management level.

Step 3—If the problem still has not been resolved to the employee's satisfaction within another ten days at the second level, a formal written complaint may be directed to the president. A determination by the president is final.

Documentation

It is understood that any employee who elects to use the employee complaint procedure will be treated courteously and that the case will be handled confidentially at all times. An employee will not be subject to discourteous action or reproach in any form due to use of the complaint procedure.

A complaint documentation file will not become part of an employee's regular personnel file. Complaint documentation will be maintained in a separate file and used only as a basis for recommending changes in management procedures.

Only those members of management with a "need to know" and who are in the employee's chain of command may have access to complaint procedures documentation.

Manager's Tip

This is an important labor relations policy that every company should have. If there is no safe way for employees to file legitimate complaints they will go to outside third parties for assistance.

CONFIDENTIALITY AGREEMENT

Policy I

It is the company policy that an Agreement of Confidentiality be signed by all employees. Please read and sign this agreement and return it to the Personnel Department.

AGREEMENT OF CONFIDENTIALITY

As a condition of employment I understand that I will from time to time be engaged in work on projects that are proprietary and confidential. Because I may have access to or control over various confidential documents, I hereby agree that I will not in any manner reveal or divulge proprietary information to any person outside the company during or after my term of employment.

_____
Signature of Employee

_____
Date

Manager's Tip

This agreement may or may not hold up in court. However, the consensus is that you may have a better chance of prosecuting a former employee who gives away proprietary information if you have a signed agreement of confidentiality.

DISABILITY

The company has a short-term disability plan. Use of the plan requires a doctor's statement, and works as follows:

Short-Term Disability. Covers illness or injury of seven days or more.

Accrual. One day after 90 days of employment, then one day per month thereafter through the first full calendar year, to a maximum of ten days accrual per year. You can accumulate up to 65 days maximum.

Long-Term Disability. Long term disability (after 90 days) can be purchased separately by employees from the company's current insurance broker.

Manager's Tip

This policy should be tailored to your specific needs and your company's budget. Few small companies can afford disability pay, so you may not need this policy.

DISCIPLINARY ACTION AND WARNING NOTICES

Open communications between management and employees and the establishment of a friendly, cooperative work atmosphere go a long way toward eliminating serious disciplinary problems. If, however, disciplinary problems do arise, supervisors and man-

agers should make every effort to ensure that employees have a thorough understanding of company policies and an awareness of what is expected in the area of job
performance.

The purpose of this policy is to provide for progressive, evenhanded disciplinary
action. Application of these guidelines must be consistent and equitable so that all
employees receive like treatment for similar offenses.

These procedures are meant to assist managers in determining a proper course
of action when discipline is needed. They are guidelines, not a substitute for common
sense. Documentation of all verbal and written warnings is important in order to avoid
the situation of an employee being discharged with no written proof of progressive discipline. In most cases, it is advisable to give an employee at least one documented verbal warning and one written warning before termination.

Warning Notices

A minimum of two weeks and a maximum of 60 days is suggested as a guideline for
determining the length of time between warnings. The warning should be specific in
describing what improvement is needed. Copies of the warning should be provided to
the employee and to the personnel department.

> **Verbal Warning.** Before a written warning is issued, a verbal warning may be
> given to the employee. A copy or text of the verbal warning should be placed in
> the employee's personnel file.

> **Written Warning.** If improvement is not made within the time period granted in
> earlier warning, it will be necessary to issue a written warning. Copies of written
> warnings must be furnished to the personnel department and to the employee. If
> the employee fails to improve by the date given on the warning, other disciplinary
> action, including suspension or termination, may result.

> **Following the Issuance of a Written Warning.** There should be consultations
> with the employee to check on progress and improvement in the problem area.
> These consultations should be accurately documented as to the dates and out-
> come of the meetings. These meetings with employees should be positive and
> intended to help the employee improve in the job.

Repeat Offenses

The procedures described above need not be followed if the employee repeats an
offense for which warning has previously been given (in the preceding twelve months).
In this case, the employee's supervisor should use discretion in determining the proper course of action. There should be consultation with the next level of management
and with the personnel department to determine what actions should be taken.

Records Retention

Records of verbal or written warnings may be removed from an employee's file after
the employee has improved behavior in the problem area to the satisfaction of the man-

ager. Employees should not be unduly penalized in future years for past difficulties and problems. Some human resources people prefer to keep copies or warnings in a separate file, not in the employee's regular personnel file.

If, in the opinion of the company an infraction is serious enough, any and all steps can be bypassed and discharge may occur.

Manager's Tip

This is an area where you must be honest, nondiscriminatory, and evenhanded in policy administration. If you list infractions in your policy you should include a statement that the list is meant for illustrative purposes and is not all-inclusive.

DRUGS AT WORK

The company will not tolerate the use of alcohol, intoxicants, or illegal drugs at work. An employee found in possession of illegal drugs, using drugs or alcohol at work, or under the influence of alcohol or illegal drugs at work will receive one written warning. The second instance will be grounds for termination.

If there is any doubt about the employee's alcohol or drug use on the job, the company will require a test. The company will help employees who are addicted to alcohol or drugs by referring them to our Employee Assistance Program (EAP). A one-time referral will be paid for by the company. An employee who is referred to our EAP for drug or alcohol rehabilitation must enter the program and stay in it the prescribed time period as a condition of continued employment.

Our company's drug testing policy is aimed at stopping drug abuse through rehabilitation.

Manager's Tip

The kind of drug policy you write will depend on the goals you want to achieve. It is a good idea to have a human resource consultant or attorney help you write your policy. The policy should fit your particular needs and reflect your attitude toward drug abuse. Most experts today feel you cannot just fire an employee for drug abuse before trying to help them through rehabilitation. This is one area where you need some expert advice.

EDUCATIONAL ASSISTANCE PROGRAM

We recognize that the educational development of employees is important to the company's success, and we encourage employees to engage in personal development activities. For that reason, this policy is established to provide an opportunity for all employees to obtain additional education or training in order to increase their competence in their present jobs and to prepare for advancement in the future.

Eligibility

This policy applies to all regular, full-time employees provided their plan of study does not interfere with their work schedule. In addition, the eligible participant must have completed six months of continuous service before starting the course. The maximum course load should be limited to six credit hours at any one time.

Employees already entitled to educational aid extended by a governmental agency (e.g., Veteran's Administration), private agencies, foundations, scholarships, or other such programs may be exempt from this plan. In those cases where such outside aid does not fully cover tuition or other expenses, the company may reimburse the employee for any differences covered by our plan if the employee meets all other requirements. The course must be business-related and approved by the supervisor. After successful completion of the approved course, an employee must submit receipts for tuition and books required for the course, and the company will reimburse the employee for those expenses. Successful completion will be defined as obtaining a grade of C or better.

EMERGENCY PROCEDURES

The company has the following emergency procedures in place in case of crisis:

FIRE:

BOMB THREAT:

TERRORIST OR CRAZED PERSON ENTERING THE BUILDING:

MEDIA CRISIS:

OTHER:

Manager's Tip

Every company should try to identify the types of crisis that might occur and what procedures employees should follow in the case of each crisis. We are living in a time when crisis is commonplace; advance planning can save lives and considerable expense. The company should maintain current records that contain an emergency contact and next of kin on each employee.

EMPLOYEE HANDBOOK AND AGREEMENT

It is company policy to provide each employee with an employee handbook setting out key company policies and procedures. This employee handbook should not be considered as an employment contract or a guarantee of employment. Each employee must sign an Employee Agreement that specifically states he or she realizes that neither the employee handbook nor the personnel policy manual constitutes an express or implied contract or assurance of continued employment, or that just cause is required for termination. (See Employee Agreement attached.)

The employee handbook should contain the date it was issued and further state that all previous editions are superseded by the current publication.

EMPLOYEE AGREEMENT

This employee handbook and the personnel policy manual describe only the highlights of the company policies, procedures, and benefits. In all instances the official benefit plan texts, trust agreements, and master contracts as appropriate are the governing documents. Your employee handbook is not to be interpreted as a legal document or an employment contract. Employment with the company is at the sole discretion of the company and may be terminated with or without cause at any time for any reason. Nothing in this handbook or in the personnel policy manual constitutes an express or implied contract or assurance of continued employment, or that just cause is required for termination.

Understood and Agreed:

_____
(Employee's Signature)

_____
Date

Manager's Tip
_____

This employee agreement is to be signed and returned to the personnel department to be placed in the employee's personnel file when an employee handbook is provided to the employee. Note that in the past some courts have ruled that employee handbooks may be considered employment contracts.

EMPLOYMENT OF SPOUSE

It is company policy not to discriminate in employment and personnel actions with respect to employees, prospective employees, and applicants on the basis of marital status. No employee, prospective employee, or applicant will be denied employment or benefits of employment solely on the basis of marital status. However, the company retains the right to:

- Refuse to place one spouse under the direct supervision of the other spouse where there is the potential for creating an adverse impact on supervision, safety, or morale.
- Refuse to place both spouses in the same department, division, or facility where there is the potential for creating an adverse effect on supervision, safety, security, or morale, or conflict of interest.

The company will allow the transfer of spouses between departments in order to accommodate married employees.

Manager's Tip

Policies on nepotism or restriction on the employment of relatives are almost a thing of the past. Employees are taking these cases to court and winning, so you may not want this policy.

EQUAL EMPLOYMENT OPPORTUNITY

It is the intent of the company to establish by policy our commitment to afford equal employment opportunity to qualified individuals regardless of their race, color, religion, sex, national origin, age, physical or mental handicap, or veteran status and to conform with the content and spirit of applicable Equal Opportunity and Affirmative Action laws and regulations. This policy is intended to apply to those actions related to both employees and applicants for employment.

Guidelines

In keeping with the intent of this policy, the company will adhere strictly to the following practices:

- Recruitment, hiring, and promotion of individuals in all job classifications will be conducted without regard to race, color, religion, national origin, age, sex, physical or mental handicap, or veteran status, except where a bona fide occupational qualification exists.
- Employment and promotional decisions will be made in such a manner as to further the principle of equal employment opportunity when possible, based upon selection criteria that are job related.

Implementation

Overall responsibility for the development and execution of our affirmative action program and equal opportunity compliance is the responsibility of our managers; however, the day-to-day administration of the program is the responsibility of the equal opportunity coordinator. The equal opportunity coordinator will provide the president with quarterly and special activity and progress reports. Our Affirmative Action Plan is available in the personnel department for review by all employees.

Recordkeeping

In order to fulfill recordkeeping requirements, applicant and hire logs should be maintained by each office that interviews and hires employees.

Manager's Tip

Reserve the right to fill the job with the most qualified person. EEO policy should include information as to which company official is responsible for enforcement of the policy.

To Be Posted on the Employee Bulletin Boards and Included in the Employee Handbook and Personnel Policy Material

EQUAL EMPLOYMENT OPPORTUNITY POLICY

It is the policy of _____ to afford equal employment opportunity to qualified individuals regardless of their race, color, religion, sex, national origin, age, physical or mental handicap, or veteran status, and will conform to all applicable state and federal laws and regulations. In keeping with the intent of this policy, the Company will adhere to the following personnel practices:

- Recruitment, hiring and promotion of individuals in all job classifications will be conducted without regard to race, color, religion, national origin, age, sex, physical or mental handicap, or veteran status, except where a bona fide occupational qualification exists. All employment decisions will be made in such a manner as to further the principle of equal employment opportunity.

- Promotional decisions will be made in accordance with the principles of equal employment opportunity through the use of valid job related criteria.

- All other personnel actions such as compensation, benefits, transfers, promotions, training and development, educational assistance and social and recreational programs will be administered without regard to race, color, religion, national origin, age, sex or physical or mental handicap, or veteran status, except where a bona fide occupational qualification exists.

Overall responsibility for the development and execution of our Affirmative Action Program is delegated to _____ as EEO/AAP Coordinator. The EEO/AAP Coordinator will provide the president with regular EEO activity reports.

_____
Date

_____
President

E-MAIL, INTERNET & OTHER ELECTRONIC INFORMATION RESOURCES

Most organizations feel the need to have an e-mail, Internet and general computer usage policy for employees, temporary workers and independent contractors. If you decide on a policy, you will want to orient employees and all newly hired personnel to the policy, why it is needed and how it is enforced. Then you ask employees to read the policy and sign a statement saying that they understand it and agree to abide by it. The signed policy statement should be added to the employee's personnel file. Following is a sample policy and statement form. Review and revise them to fit your company's requirements.

Policy

The Company provides computers, computer files, software and electronic mail (e-mail) systems to assist you in completing your job. This equipment and any other informational storage or retrieval services (including the Internet) provided by the company are owned by the company and are to be used for business purposes only. Use of these services for personal reasons is prohibited.

The Company reserves the right to enter, search and monitor the computer files or e-mail of any employee, without advance notice. Such action may be taken for business purposes such as investigating theft, disclosure of confidential business or proprietary information, personal abuse of the system or monitoring workflow or productivity.

It is illegal and therefore against company policy to load unlicensed or unauthorized software on the company's computers. To do so could interfere with the operation of licensed software and breach the software license agreement.

This policy applies to all employees, temporary workers, independent contractors, and all individuals who use the Company's electronic information resources.

Failure to follow this policy and/or any personal or inappropriate use of the Company computer and electronic services may result in disciplinary action up to and including termination of employment.

EMPLOYEE AGREEMENT

_____
(Company Name)

E-Mail, Internet, & Other Computer Services Policy

I have read this Company policy, and I understand and agree to comply with the terms of the policy. Further I understand that violation of this policy may result in disciplinary action and/or termination of employment.

_____
Printed Name

_____
Signature

_____
Date

EMPLOYEE ASSISTANCE PROGRAM

The company has an outside employee assistance program (EAP) which is available for use by employees who have alcohol or drug abuse problems, or serious personal problems they cannot cope with. To use the program you can either contact your manager to get permission to seek outside help through the EAP, or if you have a substance abuse problem you can call the EAP directly without fear of losing your job. The number is _____.

For further information on the EAP contact the personnel department. The EAP is provided by the company to assist troubled employees in seeking help to keep their jobs.

Manager's Tip

You can make use of the EAP mandatory if you have reason to think the employee has an alcohol or drug problem. Excessive absenteeism and poor performance are reasons to insist the employee get help. You may want to make use of the EAP a condition of employment. Be sure you have used progressive discipline and counseling and are being fair with the employee.

EXIT INTERVIEWS

It is company policy to conduct exit interviews for terminating employees. The interview is conducted in the personnel department. Its purpose is to enable the company to identify conditions which may contribute to terminations and to formalize the reason for termination for unemployment compensation purposes.

Pertinent comments made by terminating employees will be discussed with appropriate management personnel in order to improve and update our policies and procedures.

When employees voluntarily terminate, they will be asked to sign a separation form stating the reason for terminating and that it is a voluntary termination. See attached separation form.

Manager's Tip

The reason you need the separation form signed is so that if employees try to collect unemployment when they terminate voluntarily you can send the signed form to the unemployment commission to show the terminations were voluntary. This can save a lot of money on your unemployment compensation account.

EXTERNAL COMMUNICATIONS

How the Company is perceived by its clients, business associates, the media, legislators, regulatory agencies, special interest groups, and the general public is a direct result of the external communications activities carried out by our management and employees. These external relations have a significant impact on our business.

In order to present the best image of the Company, it is important that the messages we communicate are consistent with our philosophy, policies and procedures. Before discussing confidential or sensitive information with anyone outside of the Company, questions regarding what constitutes confidential or sensitive information or Company confidential information should also be discussed with your supervisor.

The President serves as the information channel for news media and is responsible for approval of all press releases, responding to media inquiries, and coordinating interviews with the media.

EVALUATION PERIOD

The evaluation period is the time allowed all newly hired employees to demonstrate their qualifications for the job. The evaluation period for all employees is up to 90 days. However, passing the evaluation period is not a guarantee of future employment. At the end of the 90-day evaluation period, employees will be formally evaluated by management.

The following regulations apply to new employees during the time their status is being evaluated:

- The employee is eligible for all benefits as defined and outlined in the Employee Benefits Statement.
- Employees may be transferred or promoted within their organizational unit.
- Previous employees must satisfy the evaluation requirements upon rehire.
- The company reserves the right to hire and fire at will.

Manager's Tip

Evaluation period used to be called the probationary period before courts ruled that there is somehow an implicit agreement that one becomes a permanent employee after passing the probationary period.

Also, we now use the term regular employment rather than permanent employment because the word permanent implied that the employee was promised permanent employment.

In a non-union company there is really no need for an evaluation period any more because employee's rights are protected from the first day of employment. Most companies like the idea of such a period, however, because supervisors will pay more attention to the employee's performance during the initial months on the job and decide not to retain poor performers.

It's a good idea to use the words "up to 90 days" rather than "the first 90 days," because some organizations have interpreted the latter to be a guarantee of employment for the maximum number of days, regardless of how poorly the employee is performing.

FUNERAL-TIME OFF

See "Time Off With Pay"

GARNISHMENTS

Employees are expected to conduct their personal financial affairs in such a manner that the company will not be served by garnishments. Garnishment refers to any legal procedure through which the earnings of an individual are required to be withheld for payment of a debt. However, under the Federal Consumer Credit Protection Act as well as the laws of some states, employers are prohibited from discharging employees as a result of a garnishment.

Guidelines

Contested Garnishments
In the case of contested garnishments (particularly false claims), employees are entitled to resist garnishments by every legal means, and this policy may not be used to force them to settle against their will. However, unless a court release is obtained within legally prescribed time limits, the company must remit the required amount to the court.

Wages Subject to Garnishment
Only disposable earnings are subject to garnishment. Disposable earnings are defined as that part of an employee's earnings remaining after all legally required deductions.

All disposable earnings owed to the employee on the date and time of the garnishment is received are to be used in determining the amount to be sent to the court. This includes checks written but not yet mailed.

In addition to regular pay, the Internal Revenue Service has legislative authority to levy paid time off, floating holidays, and vacation that has accrued but has not been taken.

Calculating and Processing Garnishments
Garnishment actions will be calculated and processed in accordance with applicable federal and state laws and regulations and will be handled by the accounting department.

GIFTS AND GRATUITIES

No employee shall accept, receive, or benefit from any gift, gratuity, present, property, or service of any kind or nature regardless of value, which may be directly or indirectly offered as a result of, or in anticipation of, an employee's position or performance of duties with the company. Exceptions include:

- Unsolicited advertising or promotional materials of nominal intrinsic value such as pens and calendars
- Awards for meritorious civic service contributions
- Unsolicited consumable items that are donated to an entire work group during holidays and are consumed on the premises

Harassment

The company will not tolerate any form of harassment including sexual harassment or hazing. A supervisor who harasses or solicits favors (including sexual favors) from an unwilling subordinate in return for promotions, increased wages, continuance of the job, or any similar promise will be terminated.

Likewise, unwelcome sexual propositions between employees may also constitute sexual harassment and will not be tolerated.

If an employee feels he or she is being harassed and cannot for whatever reason discuss the problem with the appropriate supervisor or manager, a discussion should take place between the employee and the Personnel Manager. A second option would be to use the Employee Assistance Program hotline. The number is _____.

A report of sexual or other harassment will be treated seriously, and a thorough investigation will be conducted. An employee who files a complaint will be treated fairly and courteously at all times.

Hiring Procedures

All positions must be approved prior to being filled, and it is the company's policy to coordinate all hiring with the Personnel Department.

When a replacement or additional regular full-time employee is needed, you must complete a requisition for help. If it is a new position for which there is no job description, a standard Job Description Form must be completed. Please forward these forms to the Personnel Department along with information on any advertising you plan to do. Once the proper salary grade has been assigned and the necessary approvals are granted, you may start the interviewing process. Sample forms for new hires are attached.

Before you hire you must complete:

- Requisition for Help
- Job Description

After you hire you must complete:

- Application
- W-4

Holidays

We recognize certain days of religious and historic importance as approved paid holidays. These are:

New Year's Day	Labor Day
Memorial Day	Thanksgiving (2)
Independence Day	Christmas (2)

Eligibility

All regular full-time and regular part-time employees are eligible for paid holidays.

Rules

Employees must be at work on their scheduled workdays before and after a holiday in order to receive holiday pay unless on:

- Paid leave of absence
- Long-term disability
- Vacation

Note:

If a paid holiday occurs during a vacation, an additional day may be added to the vacation period to compensate for that holiday.

An employee's manager may approve an employee's being off on a scheduled workday before or after a holiday. In this case the employee will receive holiday pay.

When a holiday falls on Saturday, it is observed the preceding Friday. When a holiday falls on Sunday, it is observed the following Monday.

HOURS OF WORK

Work Hours

Work hours are 8:00 A.M. to 5:00 P.M., Monday through Friday. Flex-time hours may be established at the supervisor's discretion within the time frame of 7:30 A.M. to 5:30 P.M.

Lunch Period

(Check state wage and hour laws to determine your policy.)

Break Period

No official break period is established. However, the company will permit brief, occasional breaks when needed by an employee and upon approval of the supervisor. (Check your state laws on this policy also.)

Compensation

Employees will be paid their regular base rate of pay for 40 hours worked in a week. Overtime worked in excess of these hours will be paid at time and one-half the regular rate. Overtime will be paid within the same pay period in which it is worked. Salaried employees are not paid overtime but may occasionally receive compensatory time. Compensatory time must be taken in the same pay period in which it is worked. Lunch periods are not paid, but breaks, if taken according to policy, are paid.

Scheduling

As the need arises, supervisors may schedule work days and hours that differ from the standard set forth above. Flex-time may be granted by supervisors if the schedule is arranged with the employee. Lunch periods are scheduled by supervisors. Advance approval of the supervisor is required when overtime is to be worked or any change in scheduled hours is required.

Time Records

Nonexempt employees are required to complete time cards reflecting the exact time worked.

Responsibility

Supervisors are responsible for scheduling work hours that will provide maximum coverage of the department during the regular work day. At the same time, needs of the employee should be given consideration. Flexibility of the hours worked will be at the discretion of the supervisor. When overtime is necessary, employees are required to work as requested; however, advance notice should be given.

Employees may receive written warnings for abuse of the work schedule. Repeated abuse as determined by the supervisor could result in termination.

IMMIGRATION REFORM AND CONTROL ACT COMPLIANCE

It is company policy to conform to the Immigration Reform and Control Act of 1986. We are required to verify the work authorization, identity, and citizenship of all employees and applicants for employment who are hired. Government Form I-9 must be completed on every new employee and the forms must be retained in the personnel department.

Employer Review and Verification

Following are the methods by which the Personnel Department will verify documents:

> Examine one document from those in List A and check the correct box, or examine one document from List B and one from List C and check the correct boxes. Provide the Document Identification Number and Expiration Date for the document checked in that column.

List A-Identity and Employment Eligibility

- United States passport
- Certificate of Naturalization
- Unexpired foreign passport with attached employment authorization
- Alien Registration Card with photograph

Document Identification # _____

Expiration Date (if any) _____

List B-Identity

- A state driver's license or I.D. card with a photograph, or information, including name, sex, date of birth, height, weight, and color of eyes.

  Specify state _____
- U.S. Military Card
- Other (Specify document and issuing authority)

_____

Document Identification # _____

Expiration Date (if any) _____

List C-Employment Eligibility

- Original Social Security Number Card (other than a card stating it is not valid for employment)
- A birth certificate issued by state, county, or municipal authority bearing a seal or other certification.
- Unexpired INS Employment Authorization

  Specify Form _____

  Document Identification # _____

  Expiration Date (if any) _____

Manager's Tip

Independent contractors who work with the company from time-to-time are not required to complete I-9 forms. I-9 forms must be retained for three years after the date of hire, or for one year after the date of termination.

U.S. Department of Justice
Immigration and Naturalization Service

OMB No. 1115-0136
Employment Eligibility Verification

Please read instructions carefully before completing this form. The instructions must be available during completion of this form. **ANTI-DISCRIMINATION NOTICE.** It is illegal to discriminate against work eligible individuals. Employers **CANNOT specify which document(s) they will accept from an employee. The refusal to hire an individual because of a future expiration date may also constitute illegal discrimination.**

Section 1. Employee Information and Verification. To be completed and signed by employee at the time employment begins

Print Name: Last	First	Middle Initial	Maiden Name
Address (Street Name and Number)		Apt. #	Date of Birth (month/day/year)
City	State	Zip Code	Social Security #

I am aware that federal law provides for imprisonment and/or fines for false statements or use of false documents in connection with the completion of this form.

attest, under penalty of perjury, that I am (check one of the following):
- ☐ A citizen or national of the United States
- ☐ A Lawful Permanent Resident (Alien # A _____)
- ☐ An alien authorized to work until ___/___/___
(Alien # or Admission # _____)

Employee's Signature

Date (month/day/year)

Preparer and/or Translator Certification. (To be completed and signed if Section 1 is prepared by a person other than the employee.) I attest, under penalty of perjury, that I have assisted in the completion of this form and that to the best of my knowledge the information is true and correct.

Preparer's/Translator's Signature	Print Name
Address (Street Name and Number, City, State, Zip Code)	Date (month/day/year)

Section 2. Employer Review and Verification. To be completed and signed by employer. Examine one document from List A OR examine one document from List B **and** one from List C as listed on the reverse of this form and record the title, number and expiration date, if any, of

	List A	OR	List B		List C
Document title:					
Issuing authority:					
Document #:					
Expiration Date (if any):	___/___/___		___/___/		___/___/___
Document #:					
Expiration Date (if any):	___/___/				

CERTIFICATION - I attest, under penalty of perjury, that have examined the document(s) presented by the above-named employee, that the above-listed document(s) appear to be genuine and to relate to the employee named, that the employee began employment on (month/day/year) ___/___/___ and that to the best of my knowledge the employee is eligible to work in the United States. (State employment agencies may omit the date the employee began employment).

Signature of Employer or Authorized Representative	Print Name	Title
Business or Organization Name	Address (Street Name and Number, City, State, Zip Code)	Date (month/day/year)

Section 3. Updating and Reverification. To be completed and signed by employer

A. New Name (if applicable)	B. Date of rehire (month/day/year) (if applicable)

C. If employee's previous grant of work authorization has expired, provide the information below for the document that establishes current employment eligibility.

Document Title: _____ Document #: _____ Expiration Date (if any): ___/___/

I attest, under penalty of perjury, that to the best of my knowledge, this employee is eligible to work in the United States, and if the employee presented document(s), the document(s) I have examined appear to be genuine and to relate to the individual.

Signature of Employer or Authorized Representative	Date (month/day/year)

Form I-9 (Rev. 11-21-91) N

LISTS OF ACCEPTABLE DOCUMENTS

LIST A		LIST B		LIST C
Documents that Establish Both Identity and Employment Eligibility	**OR**	**Documents that Establish Identity**	**AND**	**Documents that Establish Employment Eligibility**

LIST A — Documents that Establish Both Identity and Employment Eligibility

1. U.S. Passport (unexpired or expired)

2. Certificate of U.S. Citizenship *(INS Form N-560 or N-561)*

3. Certificate of Naturalization *(INS Form N-550 or N-570)*

4. Unexpired foreign passport, with *I-551 stamp* or attached *INS Form I-94* indicating unexpired employment authorization

5. Alien Registration Receipt Card with photograph *(INS Form I-151 or I-551)*

6. Unexpired Temporary Resident Card *(INS Form I-688)*

7. Unexpired Employment Authorization Card *(INS Form I-688A)*

8. Unexpired Reentry Permit *(INS Form I-327)*

9. Unexpired Refugee Travel Document *(INS Form I-571)*

10. Unexpired Employment Authorization Document issued by the INS which contains a photograph *(INS Form I-688B)*

OR

LIST B — Documents that Establish Identity

1. Driver's license or ID card issued by a state or outlying possession of the United States provided it contains a photograph or information such as name, date of birth, sex, height, eye color, and address

2. ID card issued by federal, state, or local government agencies or entities provided it contains a photograph or information such as name, date of birth, sex, height, eye color, and address

3. School ID card with a photograph

4. Voter's registration card

5. U.S. Military card or draft record

6. Military dependent's ID card

7. U.S. Coast Guard Merchant Mariner Card

8. Native American tribal document

9. Driver's license issued by a Canadian government authority

For persons under age 18 who are unable to present a document listed above:

10. School record or report card

11. Clinic, doctor, or hospital record

12. Day-care or nursery school record

AND

LIST C — Documents that Establish Employment Eligibility

1. U.S. social security card issued by the Social Security Administration *(other than a card stating it is not valid for employment)*

2. Certification of Birth Abroad issued by the Department of State *(Form FS-545 or Form DS-1350)*

3. Original or certified copy of a birth certificate issued by a state, county, municipal authority or outlying possession of the United States bearing an official seal

4. Native American tribal document

5. U.S. Citizen ID Card *(INS Form I-197)*

6. ID Card for use of Resident Citizen in the United States *(INS Form I-179)*

7. Unexpired employment authorization document issued by the INS *(other than those listed under List A)*

Illustrations of many of these documents appear in Part 8 of the Handbook for Employers (M-274)

Form I-9 (Rev. 11-21-91) N

JOB POSTING

Policy 1

The company is generally committed to providing promotional opportunities to employees who have demonstrated exemplary job progress and self-motivation. In an attempt to advise employees of job openings, bulletins will be posted announcing job vacancies as the need arises. Employees who meet the standards and are interested in being considered for posted jobs should contact the Personnel Manager for an application and further information about the job. Those employees selected for consideration of a posted job will be contacted by the Personnel Manager and will receive an interview.

Jobs posted are not necessarily reserved or held exclusively for current employees. The company may concurrently advertise or otherwise recruit qualified persons in the appropriate labor market, and may, at its discretion, hire from outside the company. The company reserves the right to hire the most qualified person for the job.

Policy 2

It is the policy of the Company to post all open positions for a period of five working days and to entertain bids from current employees before we go outside the company to fill a position. Jobs are posted up through manager level.

The only exception to this policy will be situations where an internal department candidate is being groomed and developed to fill a higher level position through promotion. In that instance the job will not be posted if the employee is ready for promotion.

Samples of job postings are attached to this policy.

Manager's Tip

A few years ago, it was unthinkable to post open positions in a nonunion salaried environment. But over the past few years, with Equal Employment Opportunity, the need for companies to maximize their human resources, and increasing concern for individual career progression, job posting has become quite common.

Here are some pros and cons of posting open positions:

Pros
- Fewer employees look for new jobs or transfers because they find suitable jobs through the posting system.
- The program makes upward mobility easier.
- It creates better morale by making employees aware of open positions.
- Employees have more control over career progression.
- It assists with affirmative action programs.
- It affords better use of the human resources.

Cons
- The program lengthens the process of filling jobs.
- It creates a chain reaction, and more jobs have to be filled.
- Employees who don't get jobs require counseling and may become disgruntled.

Job Posting Form

Date _____

POSITION ANNOUNCEMENT

The _____ Corporation is recruiting for the following position:

TITLE:	**HUMAN RESOURCE SECRETARY**
REPORTS TO:	Human Resource Director
SUMMARY OF DUTIES:	Provides secretarial support and coordinates a variety of human resource activities including screening applicant inquiries, scheduling meetings and interviews, processing benefit paperwork. Responsible for maintaining confidential employee records and files.

REQUIREMENTS:

EDUCATION:	High school diploma or equivalent. Some college or business courses preferred.
EXPERIENCE:	Two years of secretarial experience preferably in a human resource department.
SKILLS:	Ability to type 60 w.p.m. on a word processor. Knowledge of Word Perfect preferred. Strong organizational skills, good grammar, and spelling competency. Must have ability to communicate with a variety of people, work independently, and maintain strict confidence of personnel information.

CLOSING DATE: _____

Interested applicants should submit an application form and letter of interest to: Employment Manager, (list address and phone).

THE _____ CORPORATION IS AN EQUAL OPPORTUNITY EMPLOYER

JOB BID FORM

Name _____   Date _____

Current Department _____

Current Supervisor _____

Job Applying for_____   Dept. _____

Your qualifications for the job: _____

_____

_____

_____

_____

Other qualifications such as degrees, licenses, etc.

_____

_____

_____

_____

_____
Employee Signature

TO BE COMPLETED BY PERSONNEL DEPARTMENT

Date employee was interviewed_____

Did this employee get the job? _____ yes _____ no

Why didn't employee get the job _____

_____

Has employee's supervisor been notified?_____

Has employee been notified? _____

_____
Personnel Representative

Jury Duty

See "Time Off with Pay."

Layoff

It is company policy to avoid layoffs when possible. It may, however, be necessary from time-to-time when there are adverse business conditions to lay people off or to eliminate jobs.

In the event of either a layoff or job elimination, the company reserves the right to retain those employees with the best performance rather than those with the most seniority. If jobs are to be eliminated they will be those jobs the company least needs to effectively run the remaining operations. The company will take performance, job importance, and seniority into consideration in a layoff, but retains the right to make the final decision based on business and economic needs and will not provide bumping or recall rights to employees who are terminated.

The company will comply with the Worker Adjustment and Retraining Notification Act that became effective on February 4, 1989. We do employ more than 100 full-time workers and therefore will give 60 days advance notice of facility closings or major layoffs as follows:

- When closing a facility or discontinuing an operating unit with 50 or more workers;
- When laying off 50–499 workers (and these workers comprise at least 33 percent of the total work force at a single site of employment); or
- When laying off 500 or more workers at a single site of employment.

Notice will be provided as follows:

- To each employee to be laid off or, if represented by a union or unions, to the employee's union representatives. Notice will be mailed to the employee's last known address.
- We will mail notice to the local government's chief elected official.

Manager's Tip

Bumping refers to letting an employee bump a lower level or less tenured employee down the line out of their job. Recall relates to calling a laid-off employee back to work when business picks up rather than hiring a new employee. You want to reserve the right to make those decisions.

Leaves of Absence

Personal leaves of absence for reasons other than civic duties, military duty, or work-related injury/illness are granted on an individual basis at the sole discretion of the company, but always taking into consideration the purpose of the leave, the employee's work record, and the needs of the company at that particular time. A personal leave of absence may be granted as a result of illness, accident, pregnancy, or for any other reason of a personal nature not specifically covered under other policies. The leave must be approved by the employee's supervisor and department manager.

All personal leaves are without pay unless otherwise approved by the employee's supervisor and department manager. The company does not normally guarantee reinstatement to the former position or to a position with like status and pay. However, if work loads permit, the position may be held open if the employee's supervisor and department manager approve. This concession must be made in writing and requires personnel department approval.

Upon return from the approved leave, if no prior guarantee of reinstatement has been made, every effort will be made to reinstate the employee in a comparable position. If reinstatement is impossible, the returning employee will have continuous service rights, so long as the employee follows the rules and procedures outlined in this policy, and meets the eligibility requirements of company benefit plans.

Length of Leave

This policy applies to requests for time off from work exceeding one month. Approved time off from work for a period of one month or less for a reason other than active military or reserve duty will be considered an excused absence. The maximum personal leave granted under this policy is six months.

Family and Medical Leave Act

The Family and Medical Leave Act of 1993 provides that eligible employees may take up to 12 work weeks of unpaid leave within a prescribed 12 month period for the care of a newborn or newly adopted child, or for the serious health condition of the employee or the employee's spouse, son, daughter or parent. To be eligible, employees must be employed for a total of 12 months, and have provided 1,250 hours of service during the previous 12 month period. No more than 12 work weeks of Family or Medical Leave may be taken within a 12 month period (measured backwards from the beginning of the leave), except where applicable state law requires otherwise. In all instances the company should comply with applicable federal and state law.

If an employee does not meet the eligibility requirements for a Family or Medical Leave but needs time of because of his/her own medical condition, the company should grant up to four weeks of unpaid leave; however, job reinstatement does not need to be guaranteed.

If the leave is for an employee's serious medical condition, the employee should first exhaust any accrued sick leave. If the leave is related to the birth or placement of a child, or is to care for a seriously ill family member, the employee should be paid any accrued vacation time, then accrued sick pay, and, thereafter, the remainder of the leave would be without pay. (Note: In California, a female employee on a pregnancy disability leave will have the option of substituting accrued vacation leave, but shall not be required to use her vacation time.)

The employee should be required to provide medical certification to support a request for leave based upon a serious health condition and may require second and third opinions, at the company's expense. Medical certification for returning to work will be required upon the employee's return to work from a leave based upon a serious medical condition.

The company will require certification from the health care provider if the leave is to take care of a child, parent or spouse who has a serious health condition. If the company grants a leave, the employee should be reinstated to the same or comparable job at the end of the leave subject to any defense the company may assert under law. The company should pay its portion of the employee's medical benefits while the employee is on an approved Family or Medical Leave. The employee must pay his or her portion of the premium during the leave period. If the employee fails to return to work after the expiration of the leave, the company may seek to recover from the employee the insurance premiums it paid during the leave period.

Where the Family or Medical Leave is foreseeable, the employee should notify the company no less than thirty days prior to the commencement of the leave. Intermittent or reduced leaves may be permitted in some circumstances. Your supervisor or the Human Resources Department can provide more information. A Leave of Absence Request Form must be completed and approved in advance.

Pregnancy Medical Disability Leave: Pregnancy leave is treated as a Family and Medical Leave, and benefits are the same, except where state law requires additional leave be granted. (Example: State of California requires the company to provide a maximum of 88 work days in addition to the 12 work weeks.) The company should comply with the laws of each state in which it does business. Maternity leave should be compensated in the same manner as any medical disability.

Military Leave

The company will pay the difference between the employee's regular rate of pay and their military pay for a period of up to ten working days for summer military duty. The company will grant leaves of absence for longer periods of military duty in accordance with the Veterans Re-employment Act. See the personnel department for details of the law.

Medical Leave (Not FMLA)

The company may grant a medical leave of absence for an employee if all of their sick leave has been used. (Some companies have short-term and long-term disability policies. Write this policy to fit your company benefits.) A doctor's certificate may be required before an employee may return to work after a medical leave.

When an employee is on a medical leave the company will continue payment of medical insurance benefits. Employees on a medical leave will retain their seniority and benefit eligibility rights.

Benefit Status While on Personal Leave of Absence

The company does not provide benefit coverage for employees while on an unpaid, nonmedical leave of over 30 days. The employee can, however, make arrangements to pay for their medical coverage while on an approved leave. Failure to return from an approved leave may result in the employee's termination.

Manager's Tip

Maternity leave regulations require that employers provide employees on maternity leave the same benefits they provide to workers on any type of disability leave.

The Veterans Reemployment Rights Act requires that employees be granted a leave of absence to perform military obligations. No employee should be denied retention of employment or any promotion because of military obligations. Employees on a military leave of absence are entitled to participate in insurance and other benefits offered by the employer to the same extent as employees granted other types of leave. Employers are not required to pay employees who are on active duty in the armed forces.

Upon completion of military service, employees must be restored to their former position or a position of like seniority, status, and pay. This assumes that the employees are still qualified to perform the duties of the former position and that they make an application for reemployment within 90 days after discharge from military service 31 days after reserve service.

Seniority status, pay, and vacations must be credited as if the employee had not been absent. Employers may not require employees to use earned vacation for summer encampment or military training call-ups (Veterans Reemployment Rights Act).

A simple sentence stating that "veteran reemployment rights are determined by law" may be all that is required in an employee handbook or policy manual.

Review this entire policy carefully and change it to fit your company's needs. If in doubt about how your specific policy should be written, have a labor attorney help you with it.

CERTIFICATION OF PHYSICIAN UNDER THE FAMILY AND MEDICAL LEAVE ACT OF 1993

1. Employee's Name:	2. Patient's Name (If other than employee):

3. Diagnosis _____
_____
_____
_____

4. Date condition commenced:	5. Probable duration of condition:

6. Regimen of treatment to be prescribed (Indicate number of visits, general nature and duration of treatment, including referral to other provider of health services. Include schedule of visits or treatment if it is medically necessary for the employee to be off work on an intermittent basis or to work less than the employee's normal schedule of hours per day or days per week):

    a. By Physician: _____
_____
_____

    b. By another provider of health services, if referred by Physician: _____
_____
_____
_____

IF THIS CERTIFICATION RELATES TO CARE FOR AN EMPLOYEE'S SERIOUSLY-ILL FAMILY MEMBER, SKIP ITEMS 7, 8 AND 9 AND PROCEED TO ITEMS 10 THROUGH 14 ON REVERSE SIDE. OTHERWISE CONTINUE BELOW.

Check Yes or No in the boxes below, as appropriate:

    Yes No

7. ❏   ❏   Is inpatient hospitalization of the employee required?

8. ❏   ❏   Is employee able to perform work of any kind? (If "No" skip Item 9.)

9. ❏   ❏   Is employee able to perform the functions of employee's position? (Answer after reviewing statement from employer of essential functions of employee's position, or, if none provided, after discussing with employee.)

15. Signature of Physician:	16. Date:

17. Type of Practice (Field of Specialization, if any):

FOR CERTIFICATION RELATING TO CARE FOR THE EMPLOYEE'S SERIOUSLY-ILL FAMILY MEMBER, COMPLETE ITEMS 10 THROUGH 14 BELOW AS THEY APPLY TO THE FAMILY MEMBER AND PROCEED TO ITEM 15 ON REVERSE SIDE.

	Yes	No	
10.	❑	❑	Is inpatient hospitalization of the family member (patient) required?
11.	❑	❑	Does (or will) the patient require assistance for basic medical, hygiene, nutritional needs, safety or transportation?
12.	❑	❑	After review of the employee's signed statement (See Item 14 below), is the employee's presence necessary or would it be beneficial for the care of the patient? (This may include psychological comfort.)

13. Estimate the period of time care is needed or the employee's presence would be beneficial:

ITEM 14 TO BE COMPLETED BY THE EMPLOYEE NEEDING FAMILY LEAVE.

14. When Family Leave is needed to care for a seriously-ill family member, the employee shall state the care he or she will provide and an estimate of the time period during which this care will be provided, including a schedule if leave is to be taken intermittently or on a reduced leave schedule:

_____

_____

_____

Employee Signature:	Date:

Company/Division/Location:

LEAVE REQUEST/RETURN FROM LEAVE FORM

Date _____

Employee's
Name _____

Social Security
Number _____

Job Title _____

Date Hired _____

LEAVE REQUEST

REASON FOR LEAVE:

  ( ) Personal disability   ( ) Family illness (name) _____

  ( ) Military   ( ) Family death (name) _____

  ( ) Training conference   ( ) Other (explain) _____

  ( ) Compensatory time off   _____

  ( ) Jury duty   _____

LEAVE REQUESTED:

                                  A.M.   Total number of

From: Date _____ Time _____ P.M.   hours requested: _____

                                  A.M.   Total number of

To: Date _____ Time _____ P.M.   days requested: _____

Regular Work Shift: _____

_____

Employee Signature: _____ Date: _____

- -

I recommend that this   ( ) With pay
leave be approved: ( ) Without pay

Authorized Signature: _____ Date: _____

RETURN FROM LEAVE

ABSENT:

                                A.M.

From: Date _____ Time _____ P.M.   Total number of

                                A.M.   working days absent: _____

To: Date _____ Time _____ P.M.

  ( ) Excused/warranted

  ( ) Not excused/not warranted (explain) _____

EMPLOYEE:

  ( ) Resumed part-time work

  ( ) Resumed full-time work

  ( ) Resumed modified duty (explain) _____

  ( ) Other (explain) _____

Affirmed by: _____ Date: _____

LUNCH AND REST PERIODS

See "Hours of Work."

MATERNITY LEAVE OF ABSENCE

See "Family Medical Leave Act."

MOONLIGHTING

For some time it has been company policy that employees be asked not to hold second jobs or to "moonlight" outside the organization.

Because many of the states in which we operate have laws that make it illegal to prohibit employees from engaging in lawful occupations wherever and whenever they see fit, our policy on moonlighting has been changed.

We still do not allow executives, managers, and officers of the company to hold second jobs, but we do not put such restrictions on hourly nonexempt personnel.

ORIENTATION, NEW EMPLOYEE

It is company policy to provide each new employee with a thorough orientation to the company and its policies and procedures.

Following are a number of the areas that will be covered in the orientation:

- Introduction to the company
- Discussion of organizational structure, key employees, office locations
- Review of policies, procedures, and the employee handbook
- Review of benefits and signing of all necessary forms
- Introduction to managers and co-workers

OVERTIME

All hourly nonexempt employees who are requested to work overtime will be paid time and one-half for all hours worked in excess of 40 in a work week. Overtime must be approved in advance by the appropriate supervisor. Salaried exempt employees who work exceptional amounts of overtime may occasionally receive compensatory time off. If a salaried employee takes compensatory time they must take it in the same period in which it is worked.

Vacation, holidays, and sick pay will not be treated as hours worked in the calculation of overtime.

PAYDAYS

The pay period at the company is Monday through Sunday and paydays are Thursdays. When a payday falls on a holiday, employees will be paid on the last workday before the holiday.

The company posts on all bulletin boards a notice of our regular paydays and the time and place of payment.

Manager's Tip

Some states require companies to post this information on their bulletin boards.

PERSONNEL RECORDS

Employee personnel records are maintained in the Personnel Department. Managers and supervisors should not maintain separate files in their desks.

When changes occur in any of the following categories, please notify the Personnel Department so that they can be reflected promptly in the handling of your pay benefits:

- Name
- Address
- Telephone number
- Marital status
- Number of dependents
- Beneficiaries
- Educational progress

The Personnel Department: (1) collects, uses, and retains only that personnel information which is required for business or legal reasons; (2) restricts the internal availability of personnel information to those with a business need to know; (3) releases personnel information outside the company only with employee approval, except to verify employment or to satisfy legitimate investigatory or legal requirements. All records concerning employment are company property and are maintained in the Personnel Department. Employees may review their personnel file. Requests to view the records should be made to the Personnel Manager.

PERFORMANCE APPRAISAL

It is company policy to conduct performance reviews with all employees once a year. The appraisal is intended to be an employee development activity to assist and motivate employees to attain their maximum potential.

The objectives of the program are:

- To motivate and guide employees toward greater self-development and improved performance by discussing significant strengths and areas needing improvement in a positive, constructive manner
- To provide an objective and uniform means for supervisors to make merit salary determinations based on an assessment of employee performance
- To identify training needs and succession planning activities
- To provide a record of employee progress

The appraisal will be conducted by the employee's immediate supervisor and reviewed by the department manager.

PERSONAL TIME OFF

The company recognizes that occasionally employees need personal time off. If you do need some time off for personal reasons, it may be granted at the discretion of your manager. However, it will be without pay unless you have paid vacation days coming. Employees should give advance notice if possible in order to allow adequate scheduling in their department. Personal time off without pay is granted at the discretion of the company taking into account departmental work loads and responsibilities.

Manager's Tip

More companies are providing some paid personal time off in order to help families cope with sick children or conduct personal business that can't be done on weekends.

PROFESSIONAL MEMBERSHIPS

It is the policy of the company to provide memberships in professional and technical organizations for employees. We feel these memberships aid employees in doing their jobs and provide professional growth opportunities.

Eligibility

Only regular full-time employees are eligible for company-sponsored or company-paid memberships in professional or technical organizations. These memberships will be determined by the position held by the employee, the need for the membership from a business standpoint, and the benefits to be derived by the Company.

Company-Sponsored Memberships

Company-sponsored memberships are those in which the company is responsible for acquiring the membership, paying directly for all costs of the membership. This type of membership is transferable and is the sole property of the Company.

Approval

All memberships paid by the company require the approval of the president. At least annually, a list of employee memberships will be prepared for the president's approval.

Number of Memberships

Employees are expected to limit their professional memberships so that they may participate actively and therefore benefit fully from each membership.

PROMOTIONS

It is company policy to promote current employees rather than hiring from outside the company whenever possible. The purpose of our in-house training and development programs is to help employees experience their full potential.

Guidelines

When position vacancies occur, supervisors will assist the Personnel Department in determining whether there are eligible candidates within the company. Candidates for promotion will be selected on the basis of their qualifications and work records without regard to age, sex, race, color, religion, mental or physical handicap, or national origin. The standards will apply to all employees.

Service with the company may be a factor considered in the process of selecting a candidate for promotion. However, it will not be the deciding factor when determining which candidate is chosen. Promotions will always be based on ability, potential, and actual performance.

The company reserves the right to hire or promote at its discretion and in its best interests.

RECREATION ACTIVITIES

It is the intent of the company to encourage social and recreational activities which will assist in maintaining good working relationships among our employees and with other members of the community. To this end, management will give consideration to requests for modest financial assistance to such programs, provided that participation is open to all employees.

Eligibility for Financial Support

Determination of activities to be sponsored will be made on the basis of overall employee interest and cost to the company. As a general practice, it is desirable that the cost of such activities be shared with the participating employees.

In the best interest of employees, sponsorship will generally be limited to activities in which only our employees participate. In the event there is an insufficient number of participants to complete a roster, remaining positions may be filled by persons outside the company. If during the program or season, however, there are additional employees interested in participating, outside team members will be replaced unless otherwise restricted by program or association regulations.

Grants for financial assistance may be made for the following items:

1. Entry fees and other pertinent and reasonable association charges.
2. Cost for uniforms or other athletic equipment. These costs will be shared with employees.

Approval Procedures

Employees who wish to start or participate in a program should first consult with their immediate supervisor.

Requests for financial assistance for recreational activities should be made in writing to the Personnel Manager, stating the activity, participants' names, association charges or entry fees, projected total shared costs for uniforms, equipment, or both, and the requested company contribution.

Waiver of Liability

The company, its officers, and management assume no liability for the actions of participants while participating in company supported recreational activities, including a reasonable period of time preceding and following such activity, or for policies of the association, except as expressly set forth as company policy or benefits (for example, medical insurance programs for employees). Employees participating in recreational activities will be asked to sign a waiver of liability.

WAIVER OF LIABILITY

I, (Employee Name) hereby release (Company Name) from any and all liability connected with my participation in company recreational activities. I acknowledge that I am participating in these activities on my own time and of my own choice.

_____
Employee

_____
Date

_____
Witness

References

It is the policy of the company to verify the facts and information which applicants furnish regarding their qualifications. The Personnel Manager is authorized to do this by telephone or with a reference letter. Applicants release employer from all liability when they sign our application for employment. Employment reference procedures are as follows:

- A reference check may be made by telephone. In this case, the details are recorded and retained in the employee's personnel file.
- Reference letters may be mailed to selected employers listed on the application.
- An individual will not be hired prior to verification of previous employment.
- Falsification of information on an employee's application may be considered cause for discharge.
- A verification of college degrees is always conducted.

It is the policy of the company to Cooperate with other businesses requesting information regarding previous employment of an individual as follows: The Personnel Manager is authorized to reply to telephone inquiries by verifying dates of employment and termination and job titles only. Salaries are not verified by telephone. Employment verification information for home loans and so forth, may be obtained upon written request to the Personnel Manager. No one in the company is authorized to provide personal references on former employees.

Manager's Tip

There has been a flurry of lawsuits in the past few years in which employers gave references on past employees and were later sued for slander because the person giving the information said something negative about the former employee. When the employee didn't get the new job, and heard about the past employer's comments, he brought suit against the company. Be careful of what information you provide on former employees.

Rehire

The company may, at its discretion, rehire former employees. It will do so only after a thorough review of the employee's past personnel records and only by approval of the appropriate vice-president or the CEO.

The guidelines for reinstating the employee's benefits and seniority are as follows:

- Reinstatement of benefits and seniority may take place if the employee was gone from the company one year or less and is at the discretion of the employee's manager and the appropriate departmental vice-president.
- Employees will not be given credit for vacation pay or pension accruals during the time they were gone. The employee will start earning credit toward vacation and other benefits again on date of rehire.

Sample Letter Regarding Rehire and Reinstatement of Benefits

Ms. Kathleen Kane
1918 North Parkway
Colorado Springs, Co 80906

Dear Kathleen:

We appreciate your responding to our recent advertisement for an insurance administrator and letting us know that you would like to come back to work for American Insurance Company.

We have discussed your return with Jane Ackerman, Human Resources Director, and she agrees that according to our personnel policies you can be reinstated to your old position. Because your lapse in employment was less than one year we have agreed to treat it as a leave of absence and not as a termination and rehire for the purpose of computing your future vacation and retirement benefits.

Our rehire policy states that employee benefits can be reinstated if the time an employee is gone from the Company is less than one year.

It is our policy, however, to require a signed agreement before you can be reinstated. That agreement is attached to this letter. Please sign the agreement and bring it to work when you return on December 9.

We are pleased that you are coming back to work for American Insurance Company.

Sincerely,

John L. Macon
Vice-President, Administration

Enclosure: Agreement

ACKNOWLEDGMENT AND AGREEMENT

This Acknowledgment and Agreement is made by and between American Insurance Company ("the Company") and Kathleen Kane ("Kane").

RECITALS

1. Kane was employed with the Company from June 20, 1979 until May 1, 1989, at which time she terminated her employment.

2. Kane became reemployed with the Company on December 9, 1989, and has worked continually with the Company or its subsidiaries since that time.

3. Kane desires to have her lapse of employment (May 1, 1989 to December 9, 1989) be treated as a leave of absence and not as a termination and rehire for the purposes of future vacation and retirement benefits.

4. The Company is willing to treat such lapse in employment as a leave of absence for said purposes upon certain conditions, as enumerated below.

AGREEMENT

The Company and Kane agree and/or acknowledge as follows:

1. Kane acknowledges that as of this date, she knows of no claim which she may have against the Company or any of its subsidiaries, agents, or employees under any common law rights or under Title VII of the Civil Rights Act of 1964 (42 U.S.C. Sec. 2000 et seq.), the Colorado Fair Employment Act found under C.R.S. 24-34-401 et seq., or the Age Discrimination and Employment Act of 1967 (29 U.S.C. Sec. 621 et seq.), and, to the fullest extent possible hereby releases and holds the Company, its agents, employees, and subsidiaries, harmless from any and all liabilities and claims which she may have against such parties at the present time.

2. For its part, the Company shall treat the lapse of employment (May 1, 1989 through December 9, 1989) as a leave of absence for purposes of future computation of retirement and vacation privileges.

3. Kane acknowledges that she makes no claim for any benefits whatsoever which may have accrued to her during the lapse of employment (including but not limited to vacation pay, benefits, retirement contributions, and health insurance coverage).

ALL OF WHICH IS DATED THIS 9TH DAY OF DECEMBER, 1989

_____
Kathleen Kane
AMERICAN INSURANCE COMPANY

By: _____
John K. Smith

RELOCATION

It is the policy of the company to pay the reasonable expenses incurred by employees as a result of a transfer from one location to another, when such transfer is made for the benefit of the company. Specific benefits will be finalized with the employee's manager and the Personnel Department and will be put in writing. A copy of the approved relocation benefits memorandum will be placed in the employee's personnel file.

SAFETY AND HEALTH

The company is concerned about the safety and health of all of its employees and will strive to maintain the highest level of personal safety for employees.

We will make every effort to provide working conditions that are as healthy and safe as possible, and employees are expected to be equally conscientious about workplace safety, including using proper work methods and reporting potential hazards. Unsafe work conditions in any work area that might result in an accident should be reported immediately to a supervisor. The company's safety policy and practices will be strictly enforced including possible termination of employees found to be willfully negligent in the safe performance of their jobs.

If an employee is injured in connection with employment, regardless of severity of the injury, the employee must immediately notify the supervisor, who will see to necessary medical attention and complete required reports. In any case of serious injury, employees will receive prompt medical attention followed by the filing of necessary reports.

General Safety Rules

The following general safety rules apply in all company work places. Each work unit may prepare separate safety rules applicable to the specific nature of work in their area but not in conflict with these rules.

- No employee will be assigned to work under unsafe conditions or with unsafe tools or equipment. In the event that such a condition develops, it will be immediately reported to the supervisor, who will determine and initiate corrective action if necessary.
- Employees should pay strict attention to their work. Practical joking and horseplay will not be tolerated.
- Warning signs and signals posted to point out dangerous conditions are to be obeyed by employees.
- Employees will not take shortcuts through or over dangerous places.
- Extreme caution should be exercised by employees operating any type of power equipment.
- Employees should not jump from truck beds, platforms, fences, or other elevated places unless absolutely necessary to the performance of duty.

- Because of the hazard inherent in running, employees should refrain from running unless it is absolutely necessary to the performance of duty.

- Employees will use safety equipment appropriate to the job, such as safety glasses, gloves, toe guards, and hard hats.

- Employees will avoid wearing loose clothing and jewelry while working on or near equipment and machines.

- All accidents, regardless of severity, personal or vehicular, are to be reported immediately to the supervisor.

- Operators and passengers in a business vehicle equipped with seat belts must wear them when the vehicle is in operation, and all employees operating vehicles will observe all local traffic laws.

- In all work situations, safeguards as required by state and federal Safety Orders are provided in the Personnel Department.

Manager's Tip

Tailor these rules to your particular organization. Enlist the help of supervisors and managers from all departments to ensure they meet your company's specific needs.

SALARY ADMINISTRATION

It is company practice to pay an equitable salary competitive with that paid by other companies in our field and our location and commensurate with the value of service performed. A salary range is set for each position according to the level of responsibility relative to similar positions in other business environments.

Your specific salary level within that range is determined primarily by your performance on the job. Appropriate salary adjustments may occasionally be made within the assigned range for each job. The size and frequency of such salary adjustments are based on careful evaluation of your job performance in your present assignment and on the financial ability of the company to make pay adjustments.

Performance reviews are given once a year. All promotions and merit increases are based on performance.

Your salary is a confidential matter between you and the company and is not a topic for discussion with anyone other than your manager. You may be assured, however, that all personnel who have similar responsibilities are paid within the same salary range. Salaries will vary somewhat within any salary range based upon length of service, ability, and performance.

SECURITY

Today, violence in the workplace is a very real concern. The security of the company, its facilities, and employee property are important. We ask that our employees be vigilant in their work areas and make sure that unauthorized people are not wandering around unattended. Employees should keep purses and other personal items in drawers where they are not readily accessible. Keys to offices and combinations to company safes should be protected. If you see unauthorized people in your work area, please call a security guard.

Computer security is of special concern and all employees are asked to strictly adhere to computer security guidelines.

Manager's Tip

It is important to write security guidelines to fit the specific needs of each individual organization. Consider the following:

- Size of company
- Location
- Type of business
- Number of employees
- Industry needs
- Union or non-union

Draft a policy you think will fit your needs and then run it by the managers in each key functional area for their input before you finalize it.

SECURITY CHECKLIST

❏ Screen applicants for potential security risks: Use a company such as Filofax or Avert. Check with previous employers.

❏ Provide policies and procedures for terminating employees caught stealing company or employee property.

❏ Hire a security guard on staff or on an occasional contract basis to check on security of buildings, equipment, parking lots, and so forth.

❏ Install an alarm system to protect facilities.

❏ Mark company equipment and property for theft prevention and recovery.

❏ Perform a regular inventory of equipment and supplies. Put someone in charge of issuing supplies and make that person responsible for them.

❏ Depending on company size, value of equipment, and building access, require employee identification badges.

❏ Provide procedures for monitoring visitors entering your facilities. Require visitors to sign in and out and require that they wear identification badges while on the premises.

❏ Provide written instructions to receptionists on how to handle crisis situations such as a person entering the buildings with a gun. Provide emergency numbers.

❏ Establish a formal evacuation plan for fire, bomb threats, terrorist situations, shootings, and the like.

❏ Develop written security guidelines for bomb threats.

❏ Develop a community relations program. Work with local community leaders and create a "good citizen" public image in the immediate area of the facility. Get to know local officials. Locate closest police station.

❏ Provide emergency first aid stations in several locations and post first aid information in accessible areas. Include fire, police, and ambulance numbers.

❏ Communicate company security policies and procedures to employees.

❏ If there is a high incidence of theft, consider hiring an undercover detective service.

❏ Analyze computer security. Establish guidelines for computer entry.

❏ Audit cash flow and other monetary procedures.

❏ If there is an area of significant loss, form a risk management committee to review the problem.

❏ Maintain emergency phone numbers on all employees in the central location in each facility.

SEPARATION PAY

When jobs are eliminated or the company must undergo a reduction in force, it is our policy to provide separation pay to those employees being terminated. The company will provide one week of separation pay for each year of service up to a maximum of 12 weeks.

Separation pay is designed for situations where an individual's job has been eliminated or the employee is being laid off. It does not apply to discharges, resignations, retirements, or situations where the company has been acquired, merged, or ceases to operate.

Manager's Tip

Eligibility for separation pay can be granted across the board or can be based on any of the following:

- Length of service
- Management position vs. nonmanagement position
- Level of salary
- Company's ability to pay

Many companies have eliminated separation or severance pay when they are experiencing adverse economic conditions.

SERVICE AWARDS

The company recognizes employees for longevity of service at five-year intervals, as follows:

   1 year award—Company pin
   3 year award—Desk Set with scissors and letter opener
   5 year award—Gold Cross pen and pencil set
   10 year award—Clock-radio with employee's name on a small plate in the front
   15 year award—VCR
   20 year award—Color television set

Annual Presentation of Awards

The presentation of service awards will be made at a time and date set by the president.

SICK TIME

You are granted up to 40 hours per year sick time. Sick time is a privilege extended by the company to prevent inconvenience or the hardship in loss of pay when an employee is ill. This time may be used for family medical appointments or illness. When possible, you are requested to schedule doctor's appointments with a minimum of inconvenience to your department. Illness should be reported during the first hour of absence. Sick time can be taken only after the 90-day evaluation period, although accrual is retroactive to the beginning of employment. We hope you will use this time only when needed. Sick time not used will be paid in cash on December 10 of each year and may not be carried over from year to year. Unused sick time is not paid upon termination.

SMOKING POLICY

As a result of the changing attitudes of employees and the fact that a majority of current employees do not smoke, the company has taken action at this time to install a no-smoking policy. A variety of national reports, including one from the Surgeon General's office, verify the fact that smoking is a serious health hazard to smokers and to non-smokers who work around smokers.

   Smoking is not permitted in any of our buildings except in private offices and in certain designated smoking areas. We wish to be considerate of both nonsmokers and smokers and to fairly address issues surrounding this no-smoking policy. Any employee who wishes to discuss the policy may do so at any time by contacting the personnel manager.

We are confident that implementation of this policy will go smoothly. We will all try to remain sensitive to the needs of both smokers and nonsmokers in order to maintain a caring attitude toward one another.

If problems arise as a result of this policy, a task force of employees, both smokers and nonsmokers, will be convened to arbitrate and resolve the issues.

Manager's Tip

This policy or any policy you end up using may create as many problems as it resolves. Smoking issues are very emotional. You can expect further state and local regulations and more litigation from both smokers and nonsmokers. The key is to try and meet the needs of both smoking and nonsmoking employees.

SUGGESTION PROGRAM

The company provides an employee suggestion box in the lunch room. We welcome employee suggestions. We are all working to better ourselves and the company, and employee suggestions are one way of helping us all achieve our goals.

When an employee signs the suggestion form and asks for a response, a reply will be provided within five working days of receipt.

If an employee has suggestions to help the company or their department but does not wish to sign the form no response can be given. However, if the suggestion results in positive change we will make note of that change in the company newsletter.

SIGNING AUTHORITY

It's the company's intent that those employees in management positions have sufficient authority to carry out the responsibilities required of each position. However, it's also necessary that the president be informed as to the extent of obligations to which the company is being committed.

The company assumes no responsibility or liability for any financial obligation that has been executed by an employee who is not an approved officer of the company.

Whenever it is deemed necessary that the company be committed by means of a space or equipment lease to an extent greater than $250, appropriate review is required. Capital expenditures over $250 also require executive review. That review will include having legal counsel review and approve of the general terms and conditions of the document. Further, the manager should send to the office of the president a written explanation of why the equipment, space, or capital expenditure is needed, the terms and conditions of the obligation, and the approval of the head of the division. If no further discussion is necessary, the president will initial the memorandum, sign the required legal documents, and return the package to the originator so that the transaction can proceed.

When the purchase or lease of equipment or other capital expenditures are anticipated, the Purchasing Department must be involved. The items may be available from storage or from a vendor with whom a price has been negotiated based on the company's purchasing volume.

This policy also covers all employee compensation arrangements. Salaries are determined by the evaluation of job description, job evaluation, and the company's ability to pay. All commission, incentive, or bonus arrangements must be reviewed by the Personnel Manager and approved by the president of the parent company before a commitment is made.

Any violation of this policy may be considered cause for disciplinary action or termination. The company reserves the right to take any action necessary to recover costs and expenses that may be incurred in the case of violation of this policy.

Signing Authority (Alternative Policy)

It is the company's intent that those employees in management positions have sufficient authority to effectively carry out their required responsibilities. However, it is also necessary that the president and chief financial officer of the Company be informed of the obligations to which the company is being committed. Therefore, we have approved two levels of authority as follows:

	Approval Authority	Dollar Commitment
LEVEL II	Branch Managers Department Heads	Up to $500.00
LEVEL 1	President and CEO Chief Financial Officer	Anything over $500.00

Any contract that the company is considering entering into must be reviewed and approved by our legal counsel.

When the purchase or lease of equipment or other relevant capital expenditures are anticipated, the Purchasing Department should become involved. The item may be available from our storage areas or from a vendor with whom a price has been negotiated based on the company's total buying volume.

This policy also covers all employee compensation arrangements including new hires, promotions, raises, advances, and bonus agreements. Violation of this policy may be cause for termination. The company reserves the right to take any action necessary to recover costs and expenses that may be incurred in the case of a violation of this policy.

Temporary and Part-Time Employees

Temporary Part-Time Employees

Temporary part-time employees are needed from time to time to perform a variety of duties. Temporary part-time employees may be obtained by running an ad or by using a temporary service. Call the Personnel Department for assistance in obtaining temporary help.

Temporary part-time employees do not receive company benefits and should not be on the company payroll for long periods of time.

Regular Part-Time Employees

Regular part-time employees are sometimes added to the payroll. The schedule of a regular part-time employee should not be more than 30 hours per week. If a regular part-time employee works at least 30 hours per week for an extended period, the employee may be eligible for some company benefits. Employees who work over 1,000 hours must receive pension benefits according to ERISA regulations.

TERMINATIONS

When termination of an employee is indicated, it is the responsibility of the supervisor to follow the procedures set forth in this policy. The maintenance of accurate records and a thorough investigation of the reasons for termination are necessary to ensure fair compliance with Equal Employment Opportunity guidelines and to determine the employee's eligibility for unemployment Compensation. In order to document the exact reason for a voluntary termination, an exit interview should be done and a separation form completed. Please send all records of terminated employees and termination forms to the Personnel Department as soon as possible.

The rules and procedures for handling terminations vary according to the voluntary or involuntary nature of the termination, the length of the employee's service, and the general circumstances surrounding the termination. These rules do not apply to temporary employees, since they can be terminated without notice and are not eligible for the benefits afforded permanent full-time employees until they have worked 1,000 hours. All terminations should be reviewed by the Personnel Manager.

General Rules

Resignation notice period will be two weeks only, regardless of length of service. An extension of this two-week period will require appropriate management level approval.

Failure to report for three consecutive days may be grounds for voluntary termination. The terminated employees are ineligible for rehire, unless there are extenuating circumstances, in which case the Personnel Manager should be consulted.

Termination Procedures

Supervisor collects all company property (keys, credit cards, books, equipment) as directed in the Personnel Manual. All terminating employees will receive a letter advising them of their insurance conversion rights, including letters required by government regulation under COBRA.

Voluntary Terminations

All forms associated with a voluntary termination must be received in Accounting within twenty-four hours after the employee gives notice. The employee's final check will be provided on the next normal payday, unless the employee requests it sooner.

   The time card must be transmitted to Accounting on the employee's final day. An exit interview will be conducted on all voluntary terminations, and a separation form will be completed.

Involuntary Terminations

All forms associated with an involuntary termination should be processed in advance so the employee can be given the last paycheck at the time of termination. Employees being involuntarily terminated must be paid immediately.

TIME OFF WITH PAY

Funeral Leave

Up to three days of paid leave may be given to an employee for the purpose of attending the funeral of a member of the immediate family. Immediate family is defined as spouse, children, parents, and siblings (grand, step, and in-laws included). Additional time, if needed, must be arranged through the supervisor and reviewed by the Personnel Department. Time off to attend the funeral of someone other than a relative may be arranged with the employee's supervisor.

Jury Duty

The company will continue the employee's regular rate of pay for jury service up to a maximum of ten days. Proof of service must be submitted.

Voting Time

NOTE: Write this policy in accordance with the laws in your state.

UNEMPLOYMENT COMPENSATION

The company is a covered employer and pays taxes for unemployment insurance purposes in this state. An employee who is separated from the company may be entitled to unemployment insurance benefits, if certain requirements (prescribed by the state) are met. Employee information regarding state unemployment insurance benefits is posted on company bulletin boards and is available in the Personnel Department. It is the responsibility of supervisors, managers, and the human resources personnel to ensure that an exit interview and a separation form are completed on terminating employees in order to determine whether a terminating employee is eligible for unemployment compensation.

Manager's Tip

When the termination is voluntary and the employee signs the separation form, the form can be sent to the Unemployment Compensation Department if the employee tries later to file for unemployment. A person may collect unemployment only when termination is involuntary.

VETERANS REPORTING REQUIREMENTS

Employed veterans must be reported to the Department of Labor by all companies doing business with the federal government. The report is VETS-100, and it must include the total number of new employees hired during the year, the number of disabled veterans, and the number of veterans with service during the Vietnam War, their job categories and place of hire. The company complies with this federal reporting requirement.

VOTING

See "Time Off with Pay."

WORK HOURS

See "Hours of Work."

VACATION

All regular full-time employees who have completed the 90-day evaluation period earn vacation as follows:

    2 weeks after 1 year

    3 weeks after 5 years

    4 weeks after 10 years

If an employee desires to take a week's vacation before it is earned, this can be granted with supervisor's approval. A form must be signed by employees stating that if they quit before the vacation is earned, the pay will be withheld from the last check. (See attached form.) Accrued unused vacation is payable on termination.

Employees must take earned vacation each year or forfeit it. Unused vacation may not be carried over or paid. Occasional exceptions to this policy may be approved by the supervisor. However, the company feels employees need time off the job for rest and relaxation.

Manager's Tip

You can design your own vacation policy, but keep it as simple as possible.

MEMO TO: Payroll Department When Taking Unearned Vacation

I have requested that I be allowed to take _____ days of vacation from _____ to _____. These days are unearned and I agree that if I quit before this vacation time is earned, the company is authorized to withhold the unearned pay from my final check.

_____

Employee Signature

_____

Date

_____

Supervisor Signature

_____

Date

WORK RULES

Any group of people working together must honor rules for their common good and safety and maintain a consistent standard of action for all. Therefore, some rules have been established to protect employee rights against arbitrary actions by others. They are intended not to restrict, but to provide a uniform policy upon which to base actions and decisions.

The severity of any problem at work will determine whether verbal or written warning, suspension, or termination is appropriate. In most cases, before a written warning is issued a verbal warning will be given to the employee. If improvement is not made within the time period granted in earlier warnings, it will be necessary to issue a written warning. Copies will be furnished to the Personnel Department and to the employee. If the employee fails to improve by the date given on the warning or suspension, termination of employment could result.

Upon notification by the manager, the Personnel Department will remove records of verbal or written warnings from an employee's personnel file after the employee has improved in the problem area to the satisfaction of the manager. We feel employees should not be unduly penalized in future years for past difficulties.

The following work rules apply to employees while on company property. Violation of the rules may be grounds for termination:

1. Theft, vandalism, or careless destruction of company property, or property belonging to a fellow employee is prohibited.

2. Drinking, using, possessing, or selling intoxicants, narcotics, or illegal drugs on company property is prohibited.

3. Use or possession of firearms is prohibited.

4. Making fraudulent statements on employment applications or job records is prohibited.

5. Performing work of a personal nature on company time is prohibited.

6. Employees may not solicit for any purpose or sell anything during working hours or in work areas unless specifically authorized by their supervisor.

7. Gambling during working time or on company property is prohibited.

8. Insubordination or willful disregard of a supervisor's instructions is prohibited.

9. Fighting on company property is prohibited.

10. Excessive absenteeism is grounds for dismissal.

11. Failure to observe proper work schedules with regard to starting times, meal times, and quitting times, is prohibited.

The above list of work rules is not all-inclusive and may be amended at any time without notice.

WORKERS' COMPENSATION

In accordance with applicable state laws and regulations, certain employees are eligible for workers' compensation benefits. These benefits are available in the event of an accident or illness resulting from an employee's occupation and which requires medical treatment, hospitalization, or loss of work time.

Promptness in reporting an injury cannot be overemphasized. In the event of an accident or illness resulting from a covered employee's occupation, the company must complete a report of the accident or illness. This report will assist in the determination of any liability.

Workers' compensation bulletins are posted on bulletin boards throughout the company, and forms are available in the Personnel Department.

Reporting Requirements

It is the joint responsibility of covered employees and their supervisors to report any job- related injury or illness. Each worksite will comply with local and state regulations concerning the recording and filing of information on covered employee injuries and illnesses. State laws and regulations vary to the extent that no attempt will be made in this policy to define the various regulations.

Definition of Covered Employees"

Employees in most occupational classifications, are eligible for benefits under the applicable state worker's compensations laws and regulations.

Manager's Tip

Be sure to check on the worker's compensation law in your state and write your policy to conform.

6

COMPENSATION
AND BENEFITS

- How Compensation Programs Are Changing
- Designing and Evaluating Your Compensation Program
- Compensation Program Evaluation Checklist
- Job Descriptions and Job Evaluations: How to Choose the Best System for Your Company
- The DOs and DON'Ts of Writing Job Descriptions
- Understanding "Essential Job" Functions Under the Americans with Disabilities Act (ADA)
- Sample Statements That Can Be Used in Job Descriptions to Describe Physical and Mental Demands
- Sample Job Descriptions
- The Three Most Common Methods of Job Evaluation
- Making Job Evaluation Simple but Effective
- Model of Wage Grades and Rates for a Small Company
- Sample Job Descriptions
- Sample Salary Program
- Pay for Performance and Performance Management
- Employee Benefits
- Glossary of Benefits Terms
- Work and Family Benefits
- Examples of Employee Benefits

COMPENSATION AND BENEFITS

Most compensation programs are taking on a new look today. The entire area of compensation and benefits is changing dramatically in the U.S. The key terms are *flexible* and *multiple compensation strategies*. Pay-for-performance is in, and most companies are moving away from a single policy or pay line and one compensation system for the whole company.

More businesses are using one-time lump-sum pay increases that don't increase base pay, and many factories are going to all-salaried plants. Some companies are moving to two-tier wage programs and a variety of new pay structures. They are not all working well, but the idea is that companies are trying all types of new programs.

HOW COMPENSATION PROGRAMS ARE CHANGING

Here are eleven items to consider when developing your strategies for new salary programs.

1. Consider developing and implementing plans that marry compensation systems to company goals. Find more tangible ways of linking employee productivity goals to corporate profits and thereby actualizing pay-for-performance objectives.

2. The move to multiple-compensation objectives allows a company to save in some areas by putting that money into programs that will provide a better return on investment. For example: an organization might announce its intention to move to a third quartile pay level in hard-to-fill technical jobs but remain at first quartile pay levels in staff jobs where the first quartile is externally competitive.

3. Many companies have moved to multiple policy lines in salary programs. For example, there may be one policy line for hourly nonexempt employees, another for salaried exempt professionals, and still a third for executives.

4. There is a trend to salaried manufacturing plants. Some companies feel productivity increases at salaried plants. Dow Chemical, TRW, Rockwell International, and Dana Corp. have all tried this concept. Companies still pay overtime to workers, but they have eliminated time clocks and treat all levels of employees as salaried, attempting to increase self-worth and self-esteem.

5. Many organizations are developing innovative pay-for-performance programs and taking them seriously. More union contracts are linking scheduled pay increases to specific measurable productivity improvements. Even the teaching profession has experienced new incentive programs. One school board links pay to performance

by paying salary incentives of up to $7,000 based on measurable performance improvements.

6. Deferred compensation is becoming more popular. Management employees and professionals who have the option more and more prefer to defer taking pay increases until retirement.

7. Gain sharing is replacing profit sharing in many organizations. Gain sharing is more of an industrial engineering approach that supports the idea of affordability and makes sense in many businesses.

8. Comparable worth claims are becoming more frequent as more women enter the workforce. This emotional issue will continue to plague companies that employ large numbers of low-paid female workers. Be sure new programs are designed with this in mind.

9. High-tech industries are often more innovative in terms of pay, benefits, and perks. These differences will begin to run over into other industries, like the information and service industries, as more high tech people cross over to work for service and information companies.

10. More companies are considering implementing lump sum pay increases that don't increase base pay. The auto, aerospace, and insurance industries already have plans in effect. One-time lump sum pay increases need not increase base pay, which has been accelerating at any incredible rate in some industries.

11. There is a move by many organizations to two-tier pay in labor contracts. American Airlines claims it has saved over $100 million per year with its two-tier contract. Labor unions and employees do not approve of two-tier contracts that penalize new workers by paying them much less than long-term employees doing the same job, but companies that have two-tier pay programs say they have gone to them out of necessity to remain in business.

What is most obvious today is that compensation programs are no longer market driven. The key issue is affordability. The whole compensation and benefit scene is a collage of changing, innovative thought and programming.

DESIGNING AND EVALUATING YOUR COMPENSATION PROGRAM

It is almost easier to design a new salary program than to reevaluate or revise your current one to fit your changing needs. Whether designing a new plan or revising an old one, you need a checklist or an audit procedure to identify your specific compensation needs. You must look internally and externally at all the issues, problems, and opportunities you face.

Compensation Program Evaluation Checklist

If you have not performed a thorough audit of compensation before, here is a fairly standard procedure to use with tips on completing the project so that the information obtained will be most relevant to your actual compensation picture.

Answer the following questions:

❏ Who are your competitors and what will your competitive posture be? What is your current position?

❏ What is your company's preferred mix of pay? How does base salary compare with bonuses, benefits, and other components? If your salaries appear to be "low," it may be because your fringe benefits package is so expensive. In many companies benefits are costing 37 percent to 40 percent of payroll, and management cannot afford to increase base pay and still provide benefits.

❏ How could you better relate salary to individual effort and good performance? Can you set performance standards in most jobs, and then relate pay incentives to productivity gains?

❏ What emphasis should you give to performance rather than seniority or cost of living (COLA) increases? Most companies are putting more emphasis on productivity and pay for performance, and in most cases have eliminated COLAs altogether.

❏ Should you change from a profit sharing program to a gain sharing plan? This is more of an industrial engineering approach, but it works well in many companies. You will need some help from experts in the compensation industry to research and design a plan that will fit your specific needs. Companies like the Hay Group in Philadelphia, or Hewitt Associates in Lincolnshire, Ill. can be very helpful.

❏ Have you looked seriously at market conditions for your industry, your region, and your specific business? Many businesses today can't afford to have market-driven compensation programs. Affordability is the key issue.

❏ Do you pay attention to practices of your industry? Should the same policies apply to all locations? If your company has been involved in mergers and acquisitions, your overall policies probably need a critical review. Check with human resource directors in similar organizations and with your industry associations to ensure your practices are competitive.

❏ Do you need a change in the policy itself, or do you just need to update a policy that is basically sound? By reviewing your policies on a regular basis, you may find policies that cost you money could be eliminated as times change.

❏ Review your relocation and transfer practices. Consider the real necessity of assignments to high-cost living either in the United States or overseas if you have international operations.

❏ Overseas employee policies need review. Some companies are changing policies that were set up for United States expatriates in favor of using local nationals whenever possible to eliminate the high cost of relocation of American employees. Relocation is an expensive issue.

Job Description

- ❏ Are there current job descriptions for every job? Job descriptions should be revised as jobs change.
- ❏ Do descriptions support job evaluations, provide guides for selection and recruiting, meet EEO and other legal requirements? Do they stress job content?
- ❏ Who writes your job descriptions? Is the person trained? Do you know what the job really entails?
- ❏ Are descriptions reviewed by higher management?
- ❏ Do you have a regular updating schedule so that if the job is split or downsized the job descriptions and job evaluations are revised?

Job Evaluation

- ❏ Are the job evaluation (JE) factors appropriate to the tests to which your program is likely to be subjected?
- ❏ Are factors defined sufficiently and have you looked at relationships?
- ❏ Are evaluators trained and knowledgeable? Watch out for a "down bias" in ratings of jobs that are held by minorities and women.
- ❏ Do employees have an appeal mechanism if they don't agree with the evaluation? Most employee handbooks provide an employee complaint procedure. Be sure you have one.
- ❏ What does it cost to administer? Some plans are so complex that there are unreasonable costs to administer the plans. If your plan is too complex, review and simplify it to cut costs of administration. If you don't have time to do it, hire a consultant to assist you with the project.
- ❏ Is your plan market-oriented or job/content-oriented? Can you defend a market-based approach? Job evaluation plans that are market-oriented have been ruled in some courts to be discriminatory against women. It is best to use a specific job/content-oriented evaluation program to avoid charges of sex or pay discrimination.

Salary Structure

- ❏ Check compa-ratios: Where are the majority of your jobs placed within your salary ranges? Are compa-ratios very low or very high? Extremes can be a danger signal. Compute compa-ratio by dividing employees' current salary by the salary midpoint. A compa-ratio of 80 percent places employees at minimum of the salary range, 100 percent at midpoint, and 120 percent at maximum of range.
- ❏ Check internal relationships. Watch for signs of compression. Particularly watch where this problem is arising—in hourly operations or in professional categories?

❏ Has the plan been kept up to date with the minimum wage and wage-hour regulations?

❏ Do you review geographic and industry differentials regularly to ensure the plan is competitive?

❏ Do you pay shift differentials? Are they competitive in your industry?

❏ Are survey sources still relevant? Periodically review and evaluate sources. If you feel survey data are weak, consider starting a new survey group to compare relevant data.

❏ Check communications: How much do you tell employees about the plan, and how good a job do you do? Do you get feedback from employees on your plan?

Policies

❏ Check written policies on hiring, promotion, transfers. Do the same rules apply to individuals in all departments?

❏ How good are merit guide rules? Have they flattened out so that, in effect, most people are getting "average" raises, thus turning your "merit" program into a longevity system?

❏ What basis are you using for making these individual determinations: merit? performance? cost of living? a combination? What proportion of the raise is allocable to each factor?

❏ Measure whether your program is in fact doing what your policy says. Do this by going back to increases that were given and see how they check out against the employees' performance. Can you defend your choices?

❏ If your system is truly performance-related, do you follow through to check performance ratings?

❏ What is your timing for giving raises: annual, semiannual? Is this policy working well?

❏ When individuals are promoted, are promotional raises substantial enough to reward them for their extra effort and responsibility?

❏ Do promotional raises get all the employees into the range of the new job? Check to see that women employees are treated the same as males in promotional increase percentages. In some companies women always fall below the range after a promotion and men always fall above. This should not be allowed to happen.

❏ Do you periodically check policies and philosophical objectives to be sure your practices and procedures are on target?

After you've completed the checklist you will have covered most of the issues facing you when you design your plan. If you are a small organization you will not need as sophisticated a plan as you would if you employed over 300 people. For example, if you are a small company (fewer than 100 people), you can use the short form job description.

Also, you can use the simplified job grade system rather than the more difficult and time-consuming point factor evaluation system. Samples of these plans follow.

JOB DESCRIPTIONS AND JOB EVALUATIONS: HOW TO CHOOSE THE BEST SYSTEM FOR YOUR COMPANY

Job descriptions and job evaluations are the underpinnings of an effective compensation program. If you are a mid-size or large organization you need to create a program that includes in-depth job descriptions and a point-factor job evaluation program that will hold up in case of litigation. If you are a small company, the long job descriptions and point-factor evaluation process may not be necessary.

The job description is the most important document in the compensation program. Ask yourself three important questions before you begin to write the job description:

1. How will the job descriptions be used?
2. What kind of job descriptions do you want, long or short forms?
3. Are you capable of maintaining updates on an ongoing basis?

Preparing Job Descriptions

The first step in preparing your job descriptions is the collection of data. This should be done systematically, by gathering important facts about the job. There are four key data elements: skill requirements, effort, responsibility, and working conditions.

In order to include all of the key data elements, follow these seven steps:

1. *Principal job duties and responsibilities.* Determine and record any function that takes up 5 percent or more of the employee's time.
2. *Output.* Determine what results are expected by the job, quantitative and qualitative.
3. *Reporting relationships.* Determine all reporting relationships, upward and downward. Include an accurate and current organizational chart.
4. *Skill requirements.* Determine all skill, ability, or training requirements, including formal education (degree), specialized training (certification), specialized skills (licensing), and amount of experience.
5. *Effort.* Include the physical and mental effort required to perform the job.
6. *Responsibilities.* Determine and record in detail how much independent judgment is allowed and used, the impact of the job on the organization, whether the job has responsibility for the supervision of others, and whether it has responsibility for policy design and administration.
7. *Working conditions.* Include any unpleasant or dangerous working conditions, travel required (determine percentage of time), or abnormal working times or workdays.

Methods of Collecting Data

There are several methods available to the job analyst collecting the key data elements for job descriptions. Interviews are often conducted on a one-to-one basis with the job incumbent. This method produces high-quality data but is very expensive. It is most suitable for collecting data on senior management jobs. Direct observation also produces high-quality data. But it's time-consuming and methods-oriented, slanted to the incumbent's way of doing things. This method is recommended for use with short-cycle, production-type jobs.

The fastest and least expensive method of data collection is the questionnaire. It's also considered the best general-purpose method. If possible, have the entire group of employees that hold the job fill out the questionnaire at the same time. This gives a fuller picture of how the job is performed and doesn't damage morale by singling out employees to be surveyed.

When the data collection is completed and you begin to write the job descriptions, remember to:

- Keep in mind the primary use of the job description (compensation, legal defense).
- Make sure all personnel jargon is removed.
- Review the description in light of legal requirements.

Job Descriptions and the Law

To help make sure job descriptions won't run afoul of the law, remember to focus on job content, not the incumbent. Keep your descriptions up to date with periodic review. Do an immediate follow-up when job duties change. Keep your records accurate. Don't include unreasonable requirements or expectations. Some specific tips are as follows:

- Make sure your job descriptions don't include such phrases as, "This job requires a young, aggressive . . . or, "a training position for a recent college graduate." Such statements in your job descriptions could get you into trouble under the Age Discrimination in Employment Act.

- Keep educational and experience requirements job-related. The EEOC considers such requirements to be employment "tests," and they are subject to the uniform guidelines on testing. Requirements that aren't job-related can get you into trouble under Title VII of the Civil Rights Act.

- Make sure your job descriptions' references to health requirements, working conditions, and effort are proper and accurate. Job descriptions that don't fully explain physical activities won't help you if you're charged with violating the Rehabilitation Act.

- When developing your wage and salary programs, use only complete and accurate descriptions of job content. When the content of two or more jobs is similar, grade and range should be similar.

THE DOS AND DON'TS OF WRITING JOB DESCRIPTIONS

No one likes to write job descriptions, but here are some guidelines and some DOs and DON'Ts that can speed the process.

DOs

- Focus on job content—the essential job functions, not extraneous information.
- List only the requirements that are necessary now; you can focus on expectations when the employee has mastered the current job.
- Keep education and experience job related. This is essential for regulatory reasons, but it also ensures the incumbent has the background to succeed in the position.
- Describe physical and mental requirements and working conditions. Medical group practices do not have the demanding physical or working conditions of a mining operation, but every job has some critical environmental factors. For example, a clerical position may require sitting at a switchboard/reception desk most of the day, or at a word processor. Working conditions may be stressful, such as in an emergency outpatient clinic.
- Keep records of job analysis information. You will want to refer to them when you begin your next revision cycle or in case of equal employment opportunity (EEO) action.
- Build flexibility into the job description. Ensure that it is a true position description which is tailored to fit the job incumbent.
- Allow an opportunity to broaden job responsibilities. Again, turning the job description into a position description provides the means for developing the employee through increased responsibility.
- Use job descriptions that focus on results. For example, instead of the duty being typing, it should be typing and completing the letter to company standards. Use results-oriented language.

DON'Ts

- Don't focus on the incumbent. The job analysis and job description are about the job, not the person.
- Don't list desirable requirements. List necessary requirements.
- Don't use potentially discriminatory methods or terminology. Avoid possible discrimination with wording that adversely impacts someone regarding race, age, gender, handicap, veteran status, or religion. Unfortunately, job descriptions are a way in which unintended bias and resistance to change may perpetuate unfair employment and pay practices.
- Don't be vague. Job descriptions must be as specific as possible.
- Don't detail every activity of the job holder. A job description is a list of tasks for which the employee is responsible.

- Don't make them too long. Although the job description includes much information, present it as briefly as possible. An outline format works well.

- Don't use the common phrase that ends so many job descriptions, "and other tasks as assigned." This phrase kills the intent of a well-developed job description—to precisely define the content and requirements of an employee's work. By using the phrase, the employee is subject to demands that may affect successful job performance. A better phrase is "and other tasks as negotiated." This implies that the employee and supervisor communicate about new job needs and prioritize workload.

Tips

- Rank order essential job functions. Put the most important first, followed by the less important and lastly by occasional duties so the employee is clear about priorities.

- Develop a graphic representation of job duties showing priority duties, with the amount of time allocated for duties. The total should add up to 100 percent. However, ensure every job picture includes room for occasional duties and contingencies. For example, 10 percent of time is allocated for extra, unexpected duties. See the sample "Job picture" found in the Appendix at the back of this handbook.

- Provide an organizational chart that shows where this position fits into the "big picture." This graphic also helps reporting structure, interpersonal relationships and the overall thrust of the organization. See the sample "Organizational chart" found in the Appendix at the back of this handbook.

- Use action verbs when writing duty descriptions. See the "Standard action verbs for job descriptions" found in the Appendix at the back of this handbook.

- Avoid sexist language, such as using only masculine terms like "he," "him," etc. Preferably, construct sentences so that pronouns are not required. If necessary, use "he/she," "they/them" or neutral/genderless words. Do not specifically state or generally infer that certain jobs are "male" or "female" jobs.

- Use quantitative words. The employee should be given a frame of reference as a performance measure. For example, must type 40 words per minute or must lift 50 pounds.

- Avoid ambiguous words. Be as clear as possible. For example, instead of saying "handles files," say, "sets up files according to the organization's procedures, pulls and refiles files daily, and makes new files as needed."

- Avoid brand name/proprietary words unless critical to the duty. If the employee is expected to do general photocopying, say so instead of "xeroxing," unless you have a complex Xerox machine that requires specific experience.

- Limit the use of the word "may"; it is a vague word. Instead, say what you mean. For example, "Periodically the employee substitutes for the receptionist." Don't say "may substitute."

UNDERSTANDING "ESSENTIAL JOB" FUNCTIONS UNDER THE AMERICANS WITH DISABILITIES ACT (ADA)

The term "essential functions" means the fundamental job duties of the position the individual with a disability holds or desires. According to the Regulations, a job function may be considered essential for any of several reasons, including but not limited to the following:

- the function may be essential because the reason the position exists is to perform that function;
- the function may be essential because of the limited number of employees available among whom the performance of that job function can be distributed; and/or
- the function may be highly specialized so that the incumbent in the position is hired for his or her expertise or ability to perform the particular function.

The Guidelines state that, once it is determined that the individual who holds the position is actually required to perform the function the employer asserts is an essential function, the inquiry will then center around whether removing the function would fundamentally alter that position. The Regulations list several kinds of evidence that are relevant to determining whether a particular job function is essential. These factors include, but are not limited to:

- the employer's judgment as to which functions are essential
- written job descriptions prepared before advertising or interviewing applicants for the job
- the amount of time spent on the job performing the function
- the consequences of not requiring the incumbent to perform the function
- the terms of a collective bargaining agreement
- the work experience of past incumbents in the job and/or
- the current work experience of incumbents in similar jobs.

Consideration is given to the employer's judgment as to what functions of the job are essential as a matter of business necessity and, if an employer has prepared a written job description before advertising or interviewing applicants for the job, the description will be considered as evidence of the essential functions of the job.

SAMPLE STATEMENTS THAT CAN BE USED IN JOB DESCRIPTIONS TO DESCRIBE PHYSICAL AND MENTAL DEMANDS

Typical Physical Demands

- Requires prolonged sitting, some bending, stooping, and stretching. Requires eye–hand coordination and manual dexterity sufficient to operate a keyboard, photocopier, telephone, calculator, and other office equipment. Requires normal range of hearing and vision to record, prepare and communicate appropriate reports. Requires lifting boxes up to 50 pounds. Requires dexterity and data entry skills.

- Requires prolonged standing, bending, stooping, and stretching. Requires occasional lifting up to 75 pounds. Requires exposure to machines, chemicals, and solvents. Requires manual dexterity and eye–hand coordination for data input. Must be able to operate simple to complex and heavy duty machinery. Requires normal range of hearing and vision.

- Requires frequent sitting, standing, bending, or stooping for prolonged periods. Requires lifting up to 75 pounds. Requires vision correctable to within the normal range and to operation of fork-lift and heavy equipment. Requires working in areas which are not ventilated or air-conditioned. Requires eye–hand coordination sufficient to operate machinery such as a truck or fork-lift Requires full range of body motion including handling and lifting, manual and finger dexterity and eye–hand coordination. Requires standing and walking for extensive periods of time. Occasionally lifts and carries items weighing up to 50 pounds. Requires corrected vision and hearing to normal range. Requires working under stressful conditions or working irregular hours.

- Frequent mobility and/or sitting required for extended periods of time. Some bending and stooping required. Requires occasional lifting up to 50 pounds of boxes or paper. Requires manual dexterity to operate computer keyboard, calculator, copier machine, and other office equipment. Requires eyesight correctable to 20/20 to read numbers, reports, and computer terminals. Requires hearing within normal range for telephone use. Occasional high stress work may require dealing with customers/clients.

- Requires sitting, standing, bending, and reaching. May require lifting up to 50 pounds. Requires manual dexterity sufficient to operate standard office machines such as computers, fax machines, calculators, the telephone, and other office equipment. Requires normal range of hearing and vision.

- Requires sitting, standing and bending and a normal range of hearing and vision.

Typical Mental Demands

- Must understand vague and implicit instructions, and react favorably in all work situations. Must be mentally adaptable and flexible in dealing with a variety of people. Is frequently called upon to handle difficult situations.

- Must be able to deal with a variety of emotions and frustrations in making business decisions. Emotional stability and personal maturity are important attributes in this position.

- Must be able to analyze many variables and choose the most effective course of action for the organization at any given point in time. Must handle novel and diverse work problems on a daily basis.

- Must be able to communicate providing verbal feedback in a professional manner. Must be able to analyze causes of interpersonal conflict and resolve complex communications issues (i.e., undefined roles, objectives, and information gaps).

- Must be able to resolve problems, handle conflict, and make effective decisions under pressure. Must have a long attention span in order to listen to people, perceive the *real* problems, and bring issues to a successful conclusion.

- Must be able to accurately code data, must be knowledgeable in office procedures, and able to answer questions in a professional and friendly manner. Must be able to balance accounts and compile computer reports. Requires public contact and excellent interpersonal skills. Must be able to make effective decisions in manager's absence.

- Ability to give, receive, and analyze information, formulate work plans, prepare written materials, and articulate goals and action plans. Must understand people and be able to communicate effectively with them.

- Ability to receive and analyze data and input into the computer.

- Ability to do simple math calculations, input data into the computer, and analyze data as requested.

Equipment to Be Used

- Must be able to operate computer and other office machines such as fax, calculator, telephone, and so on.

Working Conditions

- May be required to work some overtime. Works in typical office setting.

Manager's Tip

You may mix the descriptions on these two pages or add information as needed.

Sample Job Description

JOB TITLE:	Human Resources Director	**FLSA STATUS:** Exempt
JOB CODE:	409	**DATE:**
DIVISION:	Human Resources	**REVISION NO.:**
REPORTS TO:	President & CEO	**REVISION DATE:**

POSITION SUMMARY:

This position is responsible to the President and CEO for the direction, coordination and overall management of the Human Resource (HR) function. The Director must identify, plan and implement strategic objectives for the HR Department including an annual human resource plan, to ensure the organization's overall effectiveness. The Director is responsible for recruiting, employment, affirmative action, compensation, benefits, labor relations, management training and development, as well as employee relations and communications. This responsibility includes ensuring compliance with all federal, state and local government regulations as they relate to the human resources function.

ESSENTIAL JOB FUNCTIONS:

- Responsible for the implementation and ongoing maintenance of all human resource policies and procedures.

- Responsible for recruiting and employment to ensure positions are filled in a timely manner.

- Develop and implement compensation programs within the budget guidelines of the Company. Ensure that the program includes objective and defensible elements for job evaluation, and an employee salary program that includes internal fairness and external competitiveness in our industry.

- Provide guidance and expertise to employees and management in resolving personnel problems.

- Provide leadership with regard to the Company's Affirmative Action Program. Manage the implementation of the Americans with Disabilities Act and The Civil Rights Act, guidelines to ensure that these programs are implemented and reviewed annually, and that all supervisors receive the information and training needed in order to comply with all government regulations pertaining to the human resources function.

- Maintain current working knowledge of benefit laws and IRS requirements to ensure the Company's compliance. Maintain benefit programs for the Company. Manage the benefits function in an effective manner to ensure timely resolution of benefit claims and employee benefits problems.

- Develop, implement and conduct management or other human resources related training programs to ensure the organization is up-to-date on management techniques, and that professionals (CPAs, Attorneys, and so on) can maintain their credentials.

- Ensure compliance with all regulatory and legal requirements.

- Manage human resources administrative functions including personnel files, an applicant tracking system and all other personnel actions and administrative responsibilities of the HR function.

- Design and implement employee communication programs in order to ensure ongoing, positive up and down communications throughout the organization.

THIS JOB DESCRIPTION DOES NOT CONSTITUTE A CONTRACT FOR EMPLOYMENT

JOB TITLE: Human Resources Director
DATE:
PAGE 2 of 3

ESSENTIAL JOB FUNCTIONS: (cont'd)

- Manage the human resources of the organization in an effective manner, institutionalizing positive human resources procedures and policies, thus assisting in the prevention of litigation or costly labor relations problems.
- Delegate responsibility to appropriate staff members to ensure that the day-to-day human resource functions are carried out. Personally manage the human resources staff members who are responsible for the administrative areas of the Human Resources Department.
- Responsible for encouraging the growth of the human resources staff

JOB REQUIREMENTS:

EDUCATION: Bachelor's Degree in Business or Human Resource Management, or ten years experience in human resource management.

EXPERIENCE: A minimum of ten years of successful human resource experience in developing, implementing and managing HR programs, benefit contract negotiations, compensation programs, familiarity with governmental regulations and complex organizational structures, as well as training and development.

SKILLS: Strong leadership, management and organizational skills, as well as understanding of multi-disciplinary programs. An ability to integrate and harmonize diversified functions, including the administrative function. Effective consultative skills as well as executive and managerial skills. Understanding, influencing and serving others are important attributes in this position. The ability to select, develop and motivate people and create a positive work environment. The ability to resolve human resource problems quickly and effectively, and determining appropriate courses of action for the organization in the human resources area. Must display a high degree of emotional maturity while keeping difficult situations in proper perspective. Must be flexible and have well-developed interpersonal skills. Must excel in personal interactions with the human resources staff and employees at all levels of the Company.

SUPERVISORY RESPONSIBILITIES:

Supervise the human resources staff.

EQUIPMENT TO BE USED:

Must be able to operate computer and other office machines such as fax, calculator, telephone, and so on.

TYPICAL PHYSICAL DEMANDS:

Requires sitting, standing, bending and reaching. May require lifting up to 50 pounds. Requires manual dexterity sufficient to operate standard office machines such as computers, fax machines, calculators, the telephone and other office equipment. Requires normal range of hearing and vision.

THIS JOB DESCRIPTION DOES NOT CONSTITUTE A CONTRACT FOR EMPLOYMENT

JOB TITLE: Human Resources Director
DATE:
PAGE 3 of 3

TYPICAL MENTAL DEMANDS:

Must be able to analyze many variables and choose the most effective course of action for the organization at any given point in time. Must handle novel and diverse work problems on a daily basis. Personal maturity is an important attribute. Must be able to resolve problems, handle conflict and make effective decisions under pressure. Must have a long attention span in order to listen to people, perceive the *real* problems and bring issues to a successful conclusion. Must relate and interact with people at all levels in the Company.

WORKING CONDITIONS:

Occasionally called upon to work overtime or odd schedules. Works in a typical office setting.

REVIEWED BY: _____

DATE: _____

THIS JOB DESCRIPTION DOES NOT CONSTITUTE A CONTRACT FOR EMPLOYMENT

THE THREE MOST COMMON METHODS OF JOB EVALUATION

The classification method of job evaluation is used by most civil service systems. Before the jobs are evaluated, a decision is made as to the number of pay grades that are needed, and then job descriptions are written for each class of jobs in the structure.

The ranking method of job evaluation is one of the easier methods. A list of jobs to be evaluated is established, and the jobs are then ranked in relation to each other on an overall basis. The overall judgment is made on the value of each job in relation to all other jobs on the list. This method works best in smaller companies.

The point method of job evaluation reviews three or four job factors that are common to all the jobs being evaluated and then rates each job in relation to each factor on a numerical scale. Points are given for each factor, looking at the degree to which the job possesses each factor. There are usually four or five factors reviewed. They might be education, know-how, safety, responsibility for budgeted dollars, management skills, and so on. The points are added, and a total point factor is assigned to each job. Jobs are then related to each other on the basis of the total point scores, and total points can be related to wage and salary ranges. To arrive at a salary range, points usually apply to a dollar formula, which will place the job at a particular place on a salary policy line. For example:

Job points = 500

Policy line formula = $50 per point + $10,000

Multiply through, and you get a salary range midpoint of $35,000 for a job worth 500 points.

If the measured worth of a job fits an established job grade schedule, a range of point totals (for example, 401 to 500 points) could be assigned a specific salary grade (for example, a grade 12 in a 20-grade system).

MAKING JOB EVALUATION SIMPLE BUT EFFECTIVE

There seems to be a trend today of hiring qualified compensation people and implementing your own salary programs in-house. One area, however, where we do see outside consultants used most in human resource management is the area of job evaluation. Consultants in this area are expensive, but there are good reasons for considering an outside expert:

- Trial and error is an expensive way to attempt to install a salary program. The errors can cost more than the consultant.
- The consultant can devote full time to the project, and if there are time constraints this is a real plus.
- Top management's commitment is essential to the successful installation of a job evaluation program, and executives may be more amenable to an outside expert with prestige in the field.
- You can utilize the expert to the fullest in the job evaluation process by seeing that your staff is trained as the installation is implemented.

- The consultant should provide an operating guide for use of the system, and cooperation between your staff and the consultant can ensure that the program and the guide are tailored specifically to your company.

The fact that the consultant is an impartial third party should aid the installation. One of the foremost consultants in the job evaluation field today is the Hay Group of Philadelphia, Pennsylvania. They install the Hay Guide Chart Profile method of job evaluation, which is popular in many larger organizations throughout the country. There are many other proprietary systems available.

The Hay Guide Chart Profile Method of Job Evaluation

The two key elements for measuring job content under the Hay Guide Chart Profile method are (1) a thorough understanding of the content of the job to be measured, and (2) the comparison of one job with another in order to determine the relative value.

It's almost impossible to measure an entire job against another entire job, so elements that are present in all jobs are measured. These elements are:

- *Know-how.* The sum total of all knowledge and skills, however acquired, needed for satisfactory job performance.
- *Problem solving.* The amount of original thinking required by the job for analyzing, evaluating, creating, reasoning, and arriving at conclusions.
- *Accountability.* The person's responsibility for actions and for the consequences of those actions.

The most important aspect of the Hay job evaluation method is understanding the job. This understanding usually comes from the job description, so it's important that the job description be current and complete and captures the essence of the job—what it's expected to accomplish, why it's needed, what results are to be achieved, and so on.

Whether you use the Hay job evaluation or another system of your own design, there are several essential elements to consider.

Essential Elements of Job Evaluation

Job evaluation (JE) is a systematic method for comparing jobs in an organization to determine a reasonable and effective order or hierarchy. A good job evaluation program will give you an accurate measure of differences in accountabilities and duties of the jobs in your company so that reasonable salary differentials can be made between them.

Performance is irrelevant to job evaluation. It is not meant to judge the performance of the employee being observed. Its purpose is to measure *what* is done, not *how well* one particular person performs.

The goal of JE is to offer a solution to the basic management problem of pay inequity. When employees feel there is no logical connection between their compensation and their jobs, dissatisfaction and poor performance can easily result. Job evaluation works on the premise that a basic pattern controls the wage relationships between jobs in every company. JE helps you discover what that pattern is, and it produces an *explain-*

able system for comparing the relative worth of similar or widely differing jobs—routine, observable jobs with easily defined tasks, as well as jobs requiring the performance of non observable, highly cognitive tasks.

The following are important goals and benefits of a sound job evaluation program as reported by Prentice-Hall in their *Compensation Service:*

- To simplify and make rational the relatively chaotic wage structure likely to result from chance, custom, and individual biases; to eliminate favoritism and discrimination.

- To justify existing pay rates and relationships between jobs (internal equity).

- To provide a factual guideline for judging the relevance of job applicants' backgrounds to available jobs.

- To aid performance review. (Only by knowing what the job consists of can the quality of performance be measured.)

- To attract and hold capable employees by setting pay in line with rates for comparable jobs in other firms (external equity).

- To provide work incentives and boost morale. (Only by studying jobs can you recognize superior performance.)

- For unionized firms, to provide a rational basis for setting negotiated rates.

- For non unionized firms, to remove a common cause of low morale and dissatisfaction when employees perceive an inequity exists. If there is a perception of inequity, it might encourage unionization drives.

- To safeguard a company's prerogative to grant salary increases during periods of government wage control (incomes policy).

- To develop a policy of equal pay for equal work consistent with federal law.

How can you determine whether your firm is in sufficient need of a JE plan to justify a large commitment in capital and manpower? Here are some rules of thumb that may help you decide:

- *How large is your company?* If your CEO can't have personal knowledge of all the jobs in the organization, salary decisions must be delegated to others. Job evaluation will keep these decisions objective, consistent, and justifiable. Many JE experts feel that the critical point is somewhere between 500 and 1,000 employees. However, many smaller offices and manufacturing firms install programs covering only 50 or 100 people. It depends on the complexity of the organization and the jobs.

- *How fast is your firm growing?* Regardless of size, you may need a JE plan because of your company's growth or expansion. If former organizational patterns, recruiting techniques, or pay practices are no longer applicable, a JE program can provide a flexible system in which to grow.

- *Are you having a recruiting or turnover problem?* If you find your company is attracting low-quality job applicants or losing many employees, your pay rates may be to blame. Inconsistencies in pay, both internal (among jobs in your organization) and external (when compared with your competitors), may be the culprits.

- *How is employee morale?* Even if recruiting or turnover problems haven't materialized, productivity and costs can be adversely affected if employees are dissatisfied with existing pay relationships.

If your answers to these questions indicate that you need a formal program, your next step is to make all of the top decision-makers in your organization share your awareness.

The decision to undertake a job evaluation program must be arrived at by the top operating officers of the firm without undue sales pressure from you and with full knowledge of all that is involved. The initiator of the program, whether a personnel executive or some other manager, should never try to minimize the costs of the JE program. A lack of honesty at this state can undermine the program later. The plan will cost money, it will take managers and staff away from their normal duties, and it will interfere with the operating routine of the workers. To indicate otherwise, either directly or indirectly, in an effort to sell the program is unwise. The decision to install a JE program must be made with the full knowledge by all concerned that there will be inconveniences. The job of the initiator is to show that the benefits of the plan will far outweigh any temporary annoyances. The formation of a top management committee to approve the establishment of the JE plan can be of great help in gaining acceptance of the concept. Participation in the plan should begin at this level and continue downward throughout the organization.

If your company has a compensation specialist, he or she can be invaluable in the early stages of the plan. The compensation department will be intimately involved with the plan and can offer strong support to the claim that the plan will be soundly administered after its installation.

Manager's Tip

The point factor job-evaluation system has had the most success for companies that have become involved in litigation. There are many good books on job evaluation, including the Prentice-Hall *Compensation* publication, which is published monthly; the Society for Human Resource Management Handbook, *Motivation and Commitment,* Volume II, published by the Bureau of National Affairs, Inc., Washington, D.C. 20037, and *Recruitment and Retention* published by AMACOM Books.

MODEL OF WAGE GRADES AND RATES FOR A SMALL COMPANY

If your company is small, you needn't go to the time and expense of completing a lengthy job evaluation program. The simplest way for you to proceed is to create a job grade system, such as the following:

Grade	Job Title
1	Courier, Mail Clerk, Accounting Clerk III
2	Accounting Clerk II, Typist, Data Entry II, Payroll Clerk
3	Secretary, Accounting Clerk 1, Data Entry 1, Purchasing Expediter

Note: Your grade structure should run to the top salary level, usually vice president

Then you need to create wage ranges, for example:

Grade	Min	Mid	Max
1	$5.75/hr.	$7.20/hr.	$8.65/hr.
2	$6.75	$8.45	$10.15
3	$7.75	$9.70	$11.65

This is a simple but effective way to establish grades and pay ranges.

If there is not a local salary survey group that provides wage information on a regular basis, you can do your own survey by calling other companies in your industry and asking them to participate in a survey. Then share the information.

Manager's Tip

Be careful when exchanging raw salary data. It could be misconstrued as "wage fixing." It's a good idea to use an outside consultant to gather the data and provide it to the group.

Sample Job Description

Position:
Accounting Assistant

Basic Function:
Assists Accounting Manager in a variety of functional accounting activities. Performs a number of ongoing responsibilities in accordance with standard accounting procedures under general supervision and guidance.

Dimensions:
Provides accounting assistance to:
(1)   Accounting Manager
(1)   Internal Auditor
(1)   Sales Manager -FP
(6)   Data Entry Operators

Principal Accountabilities:
  1) Preparation of ROA for Data Entry
  2) Weekly Sales & Margin Analysis on PC
  3) Income Statement Account Reconciliations
  4) Administrative and Clerical Activities for General Accounting Department
  5) Bank Statement Reconciliation

Incumbent needs good analytical skills and knowledge of computer systems

Principal Interactions:
Inside the Company: 90 People
Outside the Company: 10 banks, finance companies, customers

Knowledge/Education Requirements:
Bookkeeping/accounting background—Bachelors degree helpful but not mandatory
3 years experience

Level of Authority:
No supervisory responsibilities.

Reports to:
Accounting Manager

Typical Physical Demands:
Requires prolonged sitting, some bending and stooping. Manual dexterity sufficient to operate a computer keyboard and calculator. Requires normal range of hearing and vision. Must be able to lift up to 40 pounds.

Note

You may wish to use some of these job descriptions as samples in your own organization. Change them to fit your needs. Ask your employees for input. The job description can't be written in a vacuum if it is to be a valuable tool.

*Job Description**

JOB TITLE: President

DATE:

Position Description

Under policy direction of the Board of Directors, performs a wide range of difficult to complex management activities related to finances and accounting, marketing and promotion of services, staffing and personnel operations, and discretionary activities that serve to support effective business operations. Uses considerable independent judgment in decisions that influence operations. Advises and assists the Board of Directors in planning, policy, and operations matters.

Responsibilities

1. Directs the development and implementation of corporate goals, objectives, policies, and procedures; directs and ensures proper coordination of all administrative affairs; prepares and submits to the Board of Directors reports of finances, staffing, programs, and other administrative activities; prepares agenda and documents, attends and participates in Board of Director meetings to receive general direction.

2. Develops and implements organizational and program plans; researches applicable laws, pending legislation, and regulations; prepares reports, correspondence, memos, records, and forms; evaluates activities and interacts with representatives of comparable firms; develops and prepares forms, records, charts, and other operational materials, and implements operations systems to achieve effective workloads and workflow.

---

*This job specification should not be construed to imply that these requirements are the exclusive standards of the position. Incumbents may be required to follow any other instructions, and to perform any other related duties, as may be required.

3. Directs and carries out the marketing plan and supervises the sales force to ensure annual marketing objectives are achieved.

4. Prepares and delivers formal presentations before various public and private concerns; attends meetings, conferences, and seminars requiring periodic to frequent commute travel.

5. Secures the services and products of outside sources such as business insurance, security systems, vehicles and equipment, office supplies and furnishings, and legal or other advisory/support services.

6. Performs immediate supervision of department heads and key support staff, and maintains official records.

7. Works with the Controller to prepare the annual budget and approves subsequent modifications and transfers; monitors and evaluates accounting systems, audits of accounts, and internal control methods; establishes the method and means of determining fiscal accountability; reviews and approves accounts payable, payroll, and other financial warrants, requisitions, purchase orders, receipts, and records or reports.

8. Works with the Human Resource Director to develop personnel policies and procedures. Reviews job specifications, performance, and disciplinary determinations; conducts staff meetings and wage surveys and initiates wage increases based on performance; hears and resolves complaints and grievances as necessary.

Employment Standards

Education/Experience: Any combination of education and experience that would provide the required skill and knowledge for successful performance would be qualifying. Typical qualifications would be equivalent to a master or bachelor degree from an accredited college or university with major coursework in business management and five years experience performing responsible general administrative work.

Knowledge of: Principles and practices of business management and marketing including personnel practices and employment laws, program budgeting, general accounting, and fiscal management practices; office procedures and business operating systems; and the appropriate methods and means of dealing with human behavior in a variety of business circumstances.

Skill at: Communicating effectively, verbally and in writing, in a diverse range of audiences and settings; persuasion and negotiation of conflicts and problems; assessing operational, program, staffing, and fiscal needs; interpreting legal documents and government regulations; evaluating fiscal and financial reports, forms, and data; analyzing complex written documents; identifying and resolving administrative problems; working long and irregular hours, and under pressure conditions; delegating responsibility and achieving results through subordinates; and maintaining order in an environment of changing priorities.

Job Description

JOB TITLE: Controller

DATE:

Position Description

Under general direction of the President, oversees the operations in connection with financial matters including accounts receivable and payable, payroll, and auditing; trains and supervises department staff; develops and initiates systems, policies, and procedures for transacting financial matters; and ensures that the financial system is accurate, efficient, and in accordance with professional accounting practices and governmental regulations.

Responsibilities

1. Develops and implements the Accounting Department's goals, policies, procedures, methods, projects, and controls.

2. Directs accounting activities including maintenance of general ledgers, analysis of computer-generated data, and review of payroll records.

3. Prepares monthly reports as required by state and federal regulations, profit-loss statements, annual corporate tax returns, and special financial reports, studies, and analyses.

4. Develops and maintains internal audit control system; develops and administers the cash management program.

5. Provides data, reports, and other information to assist in the preparation of the annual budget.

6. Forecasts revenues, expenditures, and year-end balance.

7. Plans, designs, implements, and modifies the data processing system.

8. Prepares and revises the fiscal operations procedure manual.

9. Coordinates with other departments concerning short- and long-range fiscal needs and plans.

10. Responds to requests for information.

11. Supervises daily accounting operations, especially the verification and signing of payroll and cash disbursements.

12. Selects, trains, supervises, and evaluates accounting staff.

Employment Standards

Education/Experience: Any combination of education and experience that would provide the required skill and knowledge for successful performance would be qualifying. Typical qualifications would be equivalent to:

1. Possession of a bachelor degree in accounting or business administration with an accounting concentration from an accredited college or university; and

2. Four years of progressively responsible experience in accounting, of which two years were in a supervisory capacity.

---

*This job specification should not be construed to imply that these requirements are the exclusive standards of the position. Incumbents may be required to follow any other instructions, and to perform any other related duties, as may be required.

Knowledge of: Principles, practices, and methods of accounting and auditing; principles and practices of financial administration including budgeting and reporting; modern office practices, procedures, methods, and equipment; modern principles and practices in operations procedures and data processing; application of data processing in the maintenance of accounting records and financial administration; budget preparation, program analyses, and revenue forecasting; principles and practices of organization, administration, budget, and management; and reports accounting practices required by state and federal regulations.

Skill at: Planning, coordinating, and directing a complex financial operation; developing, revising, and installing accounting systems and procedures; interpreting and applying appropriate laws and regulations; preparing various financial statements, reports, and analyses; communicating clearly and concisely orally and in writing; selecting, supervising, training, and evaluating assigned staff.

Desirable Qualifications: Possession of a Certified Professional Accountant (CPA) certificate.

*Job Description**

JOB TITLE: Human Resource Director

DATE:

Position Description

Responsible for the management of the Human Resource and Employee Relations function which includes recruiting, employment, affirmative action, compensation, benefits, labor relations, management training and development, and employee communications. Responsible for ensuring compliance with all federal, state, and local laws and regulations as they relate to the personnel function.

Responsibilities

1. Responsible for human resource planning and staffing. Seeing that the company has the people they need in the required positions in a timely manner.

2. The Human Resource Director must work closely with the Deputy Director for Administrative Services and the other deputy directors to manage the human resource and employee relations functions to ensure the maximum productivity within the corporation's budget limitations. This means keeping jobs filled and employees motivated through the corporation's compensation, benefits, and communications activities.

3. Develop and implement competitive compensation program within the budget restrictions of the company. Ensure the program includes objective and defensible elements for job evaluation and a salary program that includes internal fairness and external competitiveness in our industry.

---

*This job specification should not be construed to imply that these requirements are the exclusive standards of the position. Incumbents may be required to follow any other instructions, and to perform any other related duties, as may be required.

4. Maintain competitive benefit programs for the company. Manage the day-to-day benefits activity throughout the organization in current manner. Ensure timely resolution of benefits claims and employee requests. Maintain current working knowledge of benefits laws and IRS requirements to ensure the company compliance with laws and regulations regarding benefits.

5. Work closely with other directors to develop needed management or other business-related training programs. For example, the Human Resource Director should be able to design, implement, and personally conduct such training programs for supervisors as "How To Hire, Discipline, and Terminate Employees in Order to Avoid Unnecessary Litigation."

6. The Human Resource Director must be able to design and implement employee communications programs in order to ensure on-going, positive up and down communications throughout the organization.

7. Manage the development and implementation of the company's affirmative action program. Ensure the program is updated annually and that all supervisors and directors receive the training they need to comply with the spirit and the letter of the company's affirmative action program. Provide leadership to conduct AAP recruiting activity to ensure women, minorities, and ethnic groups are represented in the company's workforce pursuant to the objectives of the AAP.

8. Maintain a current working knowledge of all state, federal, and local laws as they pertain to the Human Resource function in order to ensure compliance in a timely manner.

9. Maintain all personnel policies, procedures, and employee handbooks in a current manner. Write and rewrite policies as needed. The policies and procedures are meant to assist supervisors and directors in getting their jobs done as quickly and as efficiently as possible. Therefore, the personnel policies should assist in that process, not delay it.

10. Provide guidance and expertise to employees, supervisors, directors, deputy directors, and the executive director in the management of the total human resources of the organization in a positive, flexible, and competent manner.

11. Responsible for encouraging the growth and development of the human resource staff.

Employment Standards

Education/Experience: Bachelor degree in business or human resource management. Applicant must have minimum of five years of human resource management experience.

Knowledge of: Principles and practices of effective human resources management and personnel administration.
Skill at: Strong managerial experience in the HR field. Strong human relations skills.

Job Description*

JOB TITLE: Branch Manager

DATE:

Position Description

Under general direction performs a wide range of difficult to complex administrative activities; coordinates and directs operations and personnel so as to ensure efficient and profitable operations; uses independent judgment within the framework of established policies and objectives in decisions affecting branch activities; makes recommendations and assists in the formulation of branch objectives, policies, and plans.

Responsibilities

1. Plans, examines, analyzes, and evaluates branch operations.
2. Prepares reports and records for management review.
3. Evaluates current procedures, practices, and precedents for accomplishing branch activities and functions.
4. Identifies and resolves operational problems; develops and implements alternative methods for work improvement.
5. Coordinates branch activities with interrelated activities of other branches or departments for optimum efficiency and economy.
6. Prepares periodic budget estimates and reports.
7. Orders supplies and equipment as needed.
8. Reviews branch audit reports to ensure operational efficiency and quality control.
9. Develops relationships with customers, businesses, and community and civic organizations to promote goodwill and generate new business.
10. Directs and coordinates, through subordinate personnel, branch activities and functions, utilizing knowledge of established policies, procedures and practices.
11. Initiates personnel actions such as recruitments, selections, transfers, promotions, and disciplinary or dismissal measures.
12. Resolves work grievances or submits unsettled grievances to next in chain of command for action; prepares work schedules; assigns or delegates responsibilities.
13. Gives work directives, resolves problems, and sets deadlines to ensure completion of branch operational functions.
14. Interprets and disseminates policy to workers and evaluates employee performance.

Employment Standards

Education/Experience: Any combination of education and experience that would provide the required skill and knowledge for successful performance would be qualifying. Typical qualifications would be equivalent to:

1. Possession of a bachelors degree in business administration with a management or financial concentration from an accredited college or university; and

---

*This job specification should not be construed to imply that these requirements are the exclusive standards of the position. Incumbents may be required to follow any other instructions, and to perform any other related duties, as may be required.

2. Three years of progressively responsible business experience of which two years were in a supervisory and planning capacity.

Knowledge of: Principles, practices, and methods of accounting and financial administration including budgeting, auditing, reporting, and quantitative analysis skills; modern principles and practices of organization, administration, budget, and management; financial and personnel reports and practices required by state and federal regulations.

Skill at: Planning, coordinating, and directing varied and complex administrative operations; speaking clearly and effectively; writing legibly and effectively; collecting, analyzing, and interpreting data from a wide variety of sources and taking appropriate action; selecting, supervising, training, and evaluating employees.

*Job Description**

JOB TITLE: Data Processing Manager

DATE:

Position Description

Under general supervision plans, coordinates, controls, supervises, and participates in the provision of activities and services relating to information system design, programming and documentation, data processing operations, and data communications; provides highly technical and responsible staff assistance.

Responsibilities

1. Participates in the development and implementation of goals, objectives, policies, and priorities for the Data Processing Department.

2. Plans, coordinates, and manages the activities involved in the study of problems, the development and analysis of alternative solutions, and the programming, testing, implementation, computer processing, procedures, and forms design of the selected solutions.

3. Establishes work standards, assigns schedules, reviews staff work, directs training, and interprets policies, purposes, and goals to subordinates; administers all work rules, disciplinary actions, and employment practices.

4. Establishes and maintains production schedules and records, consults with manufacturers' representatives to define equipment and software needs; prepares requests for proposals, reviews and evaluates proposals.

5. Prepares and administers the division budget.

6. Orders necessary data processing supplies and materials.

7. Assists other department managers and staff in using computers and computer software.

Employment Standards

Education/Experience: Any combination of education and experience that would provide the required skill and knowledge for successful performance would be qualifying. Typical qualifications would be equivalent to:

---

*This job specification should not be construed to imply that these requirements are the exclusive standards of the position. Incumbents may be required to follow any other instructions, and to perform any other related duties, as may be required.

1. Possession of a bachelor degree in business administration or computer science from an accredited college or university; and

2. Three years of increasingly responsible experience in computer operations, programming, and system development and design of which two years were in a supervisory capacity.

Knowledge of: Principles and techniques of systems analysis and programming; operating principles, methods, and practices of computers and related equipment. Must know the company's programming language, principles of organization, administration, budget, and personnel management.

Skill at: Planning, organizing, assigning, supervising, and reviewing data processing activities and services; designing systems and performing necessary programming and documentation; establishing and maintaining production schedules; operating computer equipment; communicating clearly and concisely, orally and in writing; selecting, supervising, training, and evaluating assigned staff.

*Job Description**

JOB TITLE: General Duties and Responsibilities of Supervisors

DATE:

The functions of individual office, plant, and general supervisors vary widely. There are a number of duties and responsibilities, however, which are common to most supervisors. Some of the more common ones are listed below:

1. Plans and schedules the work of a section, department, or organization for the most effective utilization of employees, equipment, and material within budgetary, cost, and quality standards.

2. Estimates manpower requirements. Requisitions and selects qualified employees necessary to perform work.

3. Assigns employees to jobs. Instructs them in proper performance of work and familiarizes them with company rules and regulations.

4. Maintains discipline of employees under their supervision in accordance with established rules and regulations. Initiates appropriate disciplinary action.

5. Assumes responsibility for the proper application of established employee relations and wage and salary administration policies, safety and health regulations, and union agreements.

6. Initiates action and approves or recommends approval of promotions, merit increases, transfers, leaves of absence, and other personnel changes.

7. Coordinates the functions performed under his/her supervision with those performed under other supervision.

8. Arranges for proper maintenance of machines, equipment, and facilities for which they are responsible.

9. Prepares reports concerning departmental activities.

---

*This job specification should not be construed to imply that these requirements are the exclusive standards of the position. Incumbents may be required to follow any other instructions, and to perform any other related duties, as may be required.

*Job Description**

JOB TITLE: Accountant

DATE:

Position Description

Under general supervision performs a variety of professional accounting work; compiles, prepares, and maintains financial data and records ensuring that all financial data are recorded in accordance with generally accepted accounting principles and consistent with established policy and procedures.

Responsibilities

1. Performs professional accounting work in accordance with prescribed accounting system and generally accepted principles of accounting. Establishes and maintains accounts.
2. Prepares monthly journal entries and accounting corrections to ensure accurate accounting records; and checks general ledger from books of detail entries.
3. Assists in the preparation, analysis, and review of estimates of revenues, reimbursements, expenditures, fund conditions, or other proprietary and budgetary accounts.
4. Analyzes and verifies financial reports and statements, accounts, and records of expenditures and revenues.
5. Assists with the preparation of accounting and management control reports. Prepares and files all necessary state and federal reports.
6. Handles asset transfers among activities.
7. Organizes, directs, and controls the retention of historical accounting and legal records, ensuring that all information is safely stored and available on short notice.

Employment Standards

Education/Experience: Any combination of education and experience that would provide the required skill and knowledge for successful performance would be qualifying. Typical qualifications would be equivalent to:

1. Possession of a bachelor degree in accounting or business administration from an accredited college or university; and
2. Two years of professional accounting experience.

Knowledge of: Principles, practices, and methods of modern accounting and auditing; principles and practices of financial administration including reporting; modern office practices, procedures, methods, and accounting equipment.

Skill at: Examining and verifying financial documents and reports; developing accounting procedures and forms; working independently from general instructions; communicating clearly and concisely, orally and in writing; assisting in supervision and training of clerical personnel.

---

*This job specification should not be construed to imply that these requirements are the exclusive standards of the position. Incumbents may be required to follow any other instructions, and to perform any other related duties, as may be required.

Job Description*
_____

JOB TITLE: Executive Secretary

DATE:

Position Description

Under general supervision, performs a variety of complex, responsible, and confidential secretarial and administrative duties requiring a thorough knowledge of organizational procedures and precedents; supervises office clerical staff; provides clerical assistance to designated staff members, and performs related work as required. This position requires the ability to work independently, exercising judgment and initiative.

Responsibilities

1. Screens visitors, telephone calls, and mail directed to the appropriate executive.
2. Independently responds to letters and general correspondence of a routine nature; responds to complaints and requests for information.
3. Assists in preparation of routine personnel, budget, payroll, and purchasing reports.
4. Researches, compiles, and analyzes data for special projects; prepares routine reports.
5. Maintains appointment schedules and calendars; makes travel arrangements; arranges meetings: assists in agenda preparation, gathers information, and contacts meeting participants.
6. Trains, supervises, assigns duties to, and evaluates subordinates; provides clerical assistance to designated staff members.
7. Takes and transcribes dictation from shorthand notes or dictaphone recordings.
8. Takes, edits, and types meeting minutes and distributes copies.

Employment Standards

Education/Experience: Any combination of education and experience that would provide the required skill and knowledge for successful performance would be qualifying. Typical qualifications would be equivalent to:

1. High school diploma.
2. Graduation from an accredited business school or two years of college.
3. Three years of increasingly responsible secretarial and clerical experience.

Knowledge of: Correct English usage, grammar, spelling, and punctuation; modern office methods and procedures, equipment, and filing systems; business letter and report writing techniques; proofreading; statistical and recordkeeping principles and procedures; principles of supervision, training, and performance evaluation.

_____
*This job specification should not be construed to imply that these requirements are the exclusive standards of the position. Incumbents may be required to follow any other instructions, and to perform any other related duties, as may be required.

Skill at: Performing responsible secretarial and clerical work requiring independent judgment with speed and accuracy; learning, interpreting, and applying organizational policies, laws, rules, and regulations; taking responsibility for the compilation and organization of reports; composing correspondence on own initiative; typing accurately from a clear copy at a speed of 65 words per minute; taking dictation at a speed of 100 words per minute and transcribing it accurately; making arithmetic calculations with speed and accuracy; meeting the public tactfully and courteously and answering questions in person and over the telephone; communicating effectively with all segments of the community.

Desirable Qualifications: Fundamental accounting or bookkeeping knowledge plus good interpersonal skills.

*Job Description**

JOB TITLE: Receptionist

DATE:

Position Description

Under general supervision operates a multi-line telephone console, gives routine information to the public; greets the public; performs routine clerical work such as typing, filing, and mail processing; performs related work as required.

Responsibilities

1. Receives calls and gives information to callers, screens and routes calls to appropriate destination. Obtains and records caller's name, time of call, nature of business, and person called upon.
2. Greets visitors, staff, and others in a professional and courteous manner. Ascertains nature of business and directs visitors or callers to appropriate department or person.
3. Types reports, business correspondence, memos, schedules, and other statistical and financial data. Adds and checks columns of figures; checks and tabulates simple statistical or accounting data.
4. Maintains various files, listings, and records.
5. Reads and routes incoming mail; prepares outgoing mail; maintains records of long distance calls; may schedule appointments.
6. Operates office machines, including calculator, copy machine, and computer.

Employment Standards

Education/Experience: Any combination of education and experience that would provide the required skill and knowledge for successful performance would be qualifying. Typical qualifications would be equivalent to:

1. Sufficient formal or informal education to assure the ability to write well, to use simple business math at a level required for successful job performance.

---

*This job specification should not be construed to imply that these requirements are the exclusive standards of the position. Incumbents may be required to follow any other instructions, and to perform any other related duties, as may be required.

2. One year of work experience in an organization performing duties comparable to a telephone switchboard operator and/or general clerk/typist.

3. Graduation from an accredited business school with courses in business practices and typing.

Knowledge of: Operation of a multi-line telephone console; correct English usage, spelling, grammar, and punctuation; office practices, procedures, and equipment.

Skill at: Operating a multi-line telephone console; performing routine clerical work; learning to operate office appliances and learning office methods, rules, and policies; understanding and carrying out verbal and written directions; typing at a speed of not less than 40 words per minute from clear copy; making arithmetic calculations; maintaining working relations with staff and public; recognizing and maintaining confidentiality of work materials as appropriate; working independently in the absence of supervision.

Desirable Qualifications: Excellent interpersonal skills.

MODEL SALARY PROGRAM

The following sample salary program can be adapted to fit your actual needs. You may not want to use all the formal wording and written explanation. If not, simplify it and make it work for you. The idea is to get across to employees that you have a formal plan, that it is internally equitable and externally competitive, and this is how it works.

If you don't have someone on staff who can write and implement a salary program for you, seek outside assistance from a human resources consultant or a compensation consultant.

Today's workers are more vocal and more active in wanting to know exactly how their company benefits and compensation programs work and that they are fair. This type of formal program needs to be well thought out, easy to understand, and fair and equitable in its implementation.

Salary Program

(Company Name)

EFFECTIVE _____ (Date)

CONTENTS

- Background and Objectives of the Salary Program
- Internal Fairness and External Competitiveness
- Position Descriptions
- Position Evaluation
- Pay for Performance
- Performance Appraisal
- Summary
- Sample Salary Grades and Positions List

BACKGROUND AND OBJECTIVES OF THE SALARY PROGRAM

_____
(Company Name)

Broad Objectives of the Program

The company's salary program is part of the organization's total management activity and helps attain the following overall management objectives:

- Attract and retain qualified people
- Provide incentive for performance by rewarding performance on the basis of results achieved
- Ensure equitable compensation regardless of sex, race, or handicap

Specific Program Objectives

The program is designed and administered to fulfill these specific salary program objectives:

Internal Fairness. This assures fair salary treatment in line with your position and the effectiveness of your performance.

External Competitiveness. The salary structure is maintained at a competitive level in the job market in which we hire.

Pay for Performance. The program provides the means for recognizing and rewarding individual performance.

Centralized Program Administration. The salary program is administered under overall company management guidelines.

Flexible Program Management. The salary program is flexible enough to be easily adapted to organizational change. It is responsive not only to internal organizational change but also to changes in the job market.

INTERNAL FAIRNESS AND EXTERNAL COMPETITIVENESS

It is our intention that your salary be fair for the position you hold and your performance in it. We also consider its value with respect to other positions in our organization.

The salary program achieves internal fairness and external competitiveness through four basic and interacting devices:

- Position descriptions
- Position evaluation
- Actual pay practice
- Outside market information

POSITION DESCRIPTIONS

Preparation and Structure

A position description exists for each individual job in the organization. The descriptions were developed using information gathered from the people performing the jobs and from their supervisors. Each job incumbent and supervisor then reviewed and approved the descriptions. Our position descriptions include eight key elements of a job.

Basic Function.   This includes a brief description of the job.

Dimensions.   The purpose of this information is to show who the position assists and who it impacts on a daily basis and, when applicable, its budget impact.

Principal Accountabilities.   This is a list of the end results the position is expected to produce. Accountabilities identify what the job is held accountable for, not how it is accomplished. The pay-for-performance philosophy emphasizes achieving results, not generating activity.

Human Relations and Other Skills.   This describes the level of interpersonal skills needed to reach positive, long-term results.

Principal Interactions.   Describes the main internal and external interactions.

Knowledge, Education, and Experience.   This is a statement of the basic knowledge, education, and experience needed to perform the job.

Level of Authority.   This shows levels of responsibility, including supervision and budget authority.

Reports to.   Shows the level of the job in the organization.

The total position description is concerned only with position content and end results, not the qualifications of the incumbent.

Uses of Position Descriptions

Position descriptions serve a number of useful purposes, including the following:

Position Evaluation

Organization Analysis.   Position descriptions contain valuable information for study and analysis of operating needs and organization structure and design.

Communication.   Your description serves as the basis for you and your immediate supervisor to reach a common understanding of your position. This is useful in day-to-day activities and for the long-range planning of your performance.

Performance Management and Pay for Performance.   The content of the job description, and specifically the accountabilities, are vital ingredients in planning and measuring your job performance for both pay for performance and performance management.

Access to Position Descriptions

Every employee should receive a copy of the current position description from his/her supervisor.

POSITION EVALUATION

Purpose and Method

The purpose of position evaluations is to relate the value of your position to other positions in the organization and to job market data. While positions can be evaluated in many ways, the company uses a point factor method to provide an objective means of measuring position content. An experienced job evaluation consultant performed the evaluations. The job is evaluated, not the person who holds it. The evaluator considers what the position actually is, as described in the position description, not what it should be or might become in the future.

The evaluation of the job is accomplished using the following criteria:

- Knowledge—What the individual in the position needs to know to perform satisfactorily.

- Ability to solve—What thinking is required to perform the job.

- Accountability—What the position contributes toward achieving the goals of the organization, including fiscal responsibility.

- Human relations and other skills—What level of interpersonal skills are needed to influence positive long-term results.

Other evaluation considerations are: knowledge, education, experience, and level of authority.

Outside Salary Surveys

Determining external competitiveness at the outset of a compensation study and maintaining it once a compensation program has been implemented require an effective methodology to determine:

- What current salary levels are
- What the job market actually is at any point in time

Our primary source of information on the external job market is from other similar organizations. Other surveys are also used. In combination, these surveys enable us to compare our salary structure with positions of equivalent value.

At least once each year, we review our salary structure both internally and against current marketplace data. Any adjustments necessary to maintain internal fairness and external competitiveness are then made.

PAY FOR PERFORMANCE

The Salary Range

The company's salary range achieves internal fairness through:

- Preparation of accurate position descriptions
- Evaluation of those positions
- Analysis of actual salaries being paid

The company's salary range achieves external competitiveness through:

- Use of outside salary surveys to ensure our knowledge of competitive pay practices
- Establishment of salary ranges that represent our desired salary policy

In general terms, the minimum of the salary range is an appropriate pay zone for the performance level of learners or newcomers to a position. The area between the minimum and the midpoint is a pay zone for a level of good, solid job performance.

The salary program is linked to merit. It does not provide a system of regular, periodic, or automatic increases in which, rigidly and mechanically, an individual moves from minimum to maximum over a specified period of years and at a specified rate.

A fully adequate level of performance is the good, solid performance that is desired and, in fact, expected of any employee.

Merit Increases

The company pays for performance in two ways:

- Through merit increases, which are salary increases within the salary range of the position you now hold, based on your job performance level
- Through promotions to positions of greater responsibility

Our main concern here is merit increases, since these are the most directly related to our salary program policy.

Your performance is appraised at least annually by your immediate supervisor through the performance appraisal system, with your active participation. It is by means of this system that the level of your performance is determined for granting merit increases.

Raises are also based on the organization's ability to provide increases based on its profits and expenses, productivity, and overall financial condition.

PERFORMANCE APPRAISAL

The Performance Appraisal System

Under our performance appraisal system, your performance is appraised at least annually by your supervisor to:

- Determine your performance level as the basis for identifying performance improvement needs
- Permit you and your supervisor to discuss past performance and plan your future performance on the basis of your needs and the organization's expectations

Performance appraisal is therefore an important activity in the total salary administration process. It involves you and your immediate supervisor discussing your performance and determining how you might make it even better in the coming year. Improved performance is ultimately reflected in a higher salary.

SUMMARY

The company's salary program has been carefully developed and aims to do the following:

- Assure that a proper relationship is maintained between the salary for your position and the salary of other positions within the organization. This is accomplished through carefully and jointly prepared position descriptions and the evaluation of each position against uniform criteria.
- Establish a salary range for your job which compares favorably with the salary range of other similar organizations in our area.
- Provide salary opportunity tied to the level of your performance. Your efforts and successes are recognized with pay directly related to performance.
- Assist you in attaining your best performance by involving you and your immediate supervisor in the performance appraisal system. In the final analysis, good salary administration must rest with the immediate supervisor. This plan provides a means for effectively discharging that responsibility.
- Facilitate fair but flexible management of the program throughout the organization.

(SAMPLE GRADES FOR A LEGAL CENTER)

SALARY PROGRAM
GRADES AND POSITIONS LIST

Effective _____

	Grade	Position title
Nonexempt	1	Clerk
	2	Administrative Assistant
Exempt	3	Financial Manager
		Office Manager
		Ombudsman Specialist
	4	Paralegal
		Program Specialist
		Director of Development
	5	Legal Services Developer
	6	State Ombudsman
	7	Senior Attorney
	8	Supervising Attorney
	9	Executive Director
		Director Legal Services

PAY FOR PERFORMANCE AND PERFORMANCE MANAGEMENT

Most organizations today feel they can only pay for effective performance on the job. Few businesspeople can afford to pay employees just for showing up and filling a desk or a spot on a production line eight hours a day. Pay-for-performance programs are fairly easy to initiate and certainly have an impact on the bottom line.

The following information will help you start a pay-for-performance program, including how to set goals and objectives and how to give constructive feedback in a performance appraisal meeting. A sample appraisal form is also provided.

Manager's Tip

Without a human resource/personnel background, you may need to hire a personnel consultant to help you set up your pay-for-performance program. Once you establish your program and train your supervisors and managers they can manage it over time.

Ten Keys to an Effective Pay-for-Performance Program

1. Total commitment from top management.
2. A thoughtful and complete plan of action.
3. A timetable for installation and follow-through.
4. A budget for a pay-for-performance program (not the usual merit budget).
5. Specific, objective criteria for each job (identified by including the employee in the process). Establish key result areas (KRAs).
6. KRAs tie the employees' job objectives and achievements to the organization's overall strategic plans. (Linking the employee's bottom line to the organization's bottom line.)
7. A performance management program that includes performance appraisals and ongoing performance feedback throughout the organization.
8. A plan that provides up and down communications on the program and measures supervisor and employee acceptance on an ongoing basis.
9. A system to monitor the program through periodic, ongoing reports, on the program and how well it's working, including measures of productivity. You can track increases or decreases in productivity by shift, by floor, by department, etc. Some measures may be:
   - Increase in number of clients served/units produced
   - Decreases in complaints
   - Less staff needed per shift
   - Decrease in turnover
   - Long-term achievement of organizational goals
10. A feeling on the part of both the employees and management that your mutual goals are being attained.

Manager's Tip
_____

A normal merit budget for increases may be anywhere from 3 percent to 5 percent. In a pay-for-performance program you need perhaps 7 percent to 10 percent for increases in order to differentiate between levels of performance. The top performers should get a much larger increase than the fully adequate or even above-average performers.

How to Start . . .

First, decide what effective job performance is. Start by establishing key results areas (KRAs) for each job. Review the job description and update it to reflect true job content.

Then, agree on a plan to achieve the KRAs. The plan is the appraisal form itself. The form is completed by the supervisor and the employee at the beginning of each year. It is the yearly "Action Plan" agreed upon by both parties.

The management group must decide what it can afford to pay for achievement (achieving the KRAs). In some organizations, performance appraisal programs and pay raises are purposely not given at the same time. However, in a pay-for-performance program both events must occur simultaneously in order to achieve your goals. The pay increase range needs to be broad enough to take into account good, excellent, and outstanding performers—probably a range of 5 percent to 15 percent.

Remember, it's important to tie the employee's performance objectives to the organization's overall objectives.

EXAMPLE:

Organizational Objective: Increase same family usage of our facility when a hospital stay is required.

Employee Objective: Raise patient satisfaction through better individual service.

How will you know when your objective is achieved?

Organization: When there is an increase in the hospital's repeat business.

Employee: When there is an increase in repeat business and patient comments and feedback are positive.

What Is Meant by Goals?

The appraisal process starts when the employee and supervisor reach a mutual understanding of what needs to be accomplished. If expectations are not clearly stated, mutually understood, and presented in measurable terms, performance will be difficult to evaluate.

Goals are methods by which job expectations can be established. Those responsible for performance appraisals need a good understanding of goals and how to use them during the appraisal process.

A goal is a statement of results which are to be achieved. Goals describe:

1. Conditions that will exist when the desired outcome has been accomplished;
2. A time frame during which the outcome is to be completed; and
3. Resources the organization is willing to commit to achieve the desired result.

Goals should be challenging but achievable and established with the participation of those responsible for meeting them. Here is an example:

> "To increase the flow of invoices through the Accounting Department to a minimum of 150 per day by June 1. The total cost increase to accomplish this should not exceed $750."

Once a goal is accomplished, a new goal can be established to emphasize the next set of desired results.

Setting Objectives

The following steps will help you set and reach your objectives:

- Review sources for setting objectives:
    - —Organization plans, objectives, strategies
    - —Key results areas
    - —Job descriptions
    - —Discussion with subordinates
    - —Previous performance plan and objectives
- List all objectives which can be established within each of the key results areas.
- Review the list with the employee to clarify meaning, priority, and preliminary thoughts on specific objectives.
- Develop one or more draft objectives, including those of a continuing and project nature for each key results area.
- Set a rough action plan for each objective.
- Make modifications.
- Develop a detailed action plan for each objective.
- Carry out action plans.
- Periodically review plans and results.

Setting objectives is a two-way process. It involves both the employee and the supervisor. If all the objectives are set by the supervisor with no input from the employee, results will be disappointing.

Management by Objectives (MBO)

Management by objective contains four key elements:

JOB REVIEW AND AGREEMENT   The employee and the supervisor review the job description and key elements of the employee's job.

DEVELOPMENT OF PERFORMANCE STANDARDS   Specific standards of performance are mutually agreed upon. This phase identifies a satisfactory level of performance that is specific and measurable.

Setting Objectives Objectives are established by the employee in conjunction with, and guided by, the supervisor.

Ongoing Performance Discussions The employee and the supervisor use the objectives as a base for continuing discussions about the employee's performance. Although a formal review session may be scheduled, the employee and the supervisor do not necessarily wait until the appointed time for a performance discussion. Objectives may be modified and progress discussed at any time during the year.

Appraisal Benefits

Use Appraisal For:	What You Learn—Issues Identified
Staffing:	
Recruitment	Identifying current needs
Selection	Criteria for selection
Placement	Current placement data
Transfer	Individual skills for new assignment
Promotion	Identifying outstanding performers
Termination	Identifying inadequate performers
Human resource inventory	Skill and succession data
Rewarding:	
Benefits	Flexibility
Salary structure	Compensation inadequacies
Merit	Comparative data on performance
Intrinsic	Motivation through objective-selling, feedback, and participation
Changing:	
Organizational climate	Appraisee evaluation
Organizational structure	Reorganization data
Management styles	Identify need for change
Policies	Feedback
Communication	Feedback
Developing:	
Rotating	Judgments on learning
Training	Identifying individual development needs
Counseling	Career planning-performance evaluation

The Appraisal Interview

Once appraisals have been completed on employees, it is important that they be communicated. The results should be discussed with employees so they have a clear understanding of how they stand in the eyes of the immediate supervisor and the organization. The emphasis in the appraisal interview should be on counseling and developing, not on "telling" the employee what the rating is.

The appraisal interview presents both an opportunity and a difficult situation. It is an emotional experience for the supervisor and for the employee. The supervisor must communicate both praise and constructive criticism. A major concern is how to emphasize the positive and still discuss improvements that are needed. Following are some ideas for the appraisal interview:

Do	Don't
• Prepare in advance	• "Lecture" the employee
• Focus on performance and development	• Mix performance appraisal and salary or promotion issues
• Be specific about reasons for ratings	• Concentrate on the negative
• Decide on specific steps to be taken for improvement	• Do all the talking
• Consider your role in the subordinate's performance	• Be overly critical or "harp" on a failing
• Reinforce the behavior you want	• Feel it's necessary that you agree on everything
• Focus on the future performance	• Compare the employee to others

Constructive Feedback

The key to an effective performance appraisal interview lies in the ability of the supervisor to listen and to give constructive feedback. Following are eleven characteristics of positive feedback:

1. It is *descriptive* rather than evaluative. By describing one's own reactions, it leaves the individual free to use it or not to use it as he sees fit. By avoiding evaluative language, it reduces the need for the individual to respond defensively.

2. It is *specific* rather than general. To be told that one is "dominating" will probably not be as useful as to be told that "in the conversation that just took place, you did not appear to be listening to what others were saying."

3. It is focused on *behavior* rather than on our perceptions. Thus we might say that a person "talked more than anyone else in this meeting" rather than "the person is a loud-mouth."

4. It takes into account the *needs of both the receiver and the giver of feedback*. Feedback can be destructive when it serves only our own needs and fails to consider the needs of the person on the receiving end. We too often give feedback because it makes us feel better or gives us a psychological advantage. It is directed toward behavior which the receiver can do something about. Frustration is only increased when a person is reminded of some shortcoming over which the person has no control.

5. It is directed toward *behavior which the receiver can do something about*. Frustration is only increased when a person is reminded of some shortcoming over which the person has no control.

6. It is *solicited* rather than imposed. Feedback is most useful when the receiver actively seeks it.

7. It is *well-timed.* In general, feedback is most useful at the earliest opportunity after the given behavior. Feedback presented at an inappropriate time may do more harm than good.

8. It involves *sharing of information,* rather than giving advice. By sharing information, we leave people free to decide in accordance with their own goals and needs. When we give advice we tell them what to do and to some degree take away their freedom to decide for themselves.

9. It considers the *amount of information the receiver can use* rather than the amount we would like to give. When we give more than can be used, we are often satisfying some need of our own rather than helping the other person.

10. It concerns *what is said and done, or how,* not why. The "why" takes us from the observable to the inferred and involves assumptions regarding motive or intent. Telling people what their motives or intentions are tends to alienate them. It does not contribute to learning or development.

11. It is *checked to ensure clear communication.* One way of doing this is to ask the receiver to elaborate on what you've said to ensure the message is clear.

List of Phrases for Use with Performance Appraisals

COMMUNICATION SKILLS

Communicates effectively with credibility and confidence.

Excels in interpersonal communications and interactions.

Effectively communicates objectives, ideas, and concepts.

Communicates confidence with peers, subordinates, and superiors.

Conveys a positive impression which reflects favorably with the public.

Encourages open communications to achieve mutual understanding.

COMPETENCY

Combines technical competence with dependability and loyalty.

Is professionally competent.

Effectively applies skills and abilities to the position.

Demonstrates strong personal competence on the job.

COST MANAGEMENT

Effectively controls costs through the judicious use of personnel, materials, and equipment.

Projects and follows through with realistic budget data.

Displays sound judgment in managing and controlling expenses.

Ensures expenditures are in the best interests of the company.

Monitors budget variances and makes appropriate adjustments.

PERFORMANCE
APPRAISAL WORKSHEET

CONFIDENTIAL

EMPLOYEE NAME		REPORT OF PERFORMANCE FROM TO	
DATE OF THIS REPORT	POSITION TITLE	TIME IN THIS CLASSIFICATION YRS_____ MOS_____	EMPLOYMENT DATE

INSTRUCTIONS

- All employees should be appraised at least annually.
- Review employee's work performance for the entire period; refrain from basing judgment on recent events or isolated incidents only.
- Consider the employee on the basis of the standards you expect to be met for the job. Place a check by the area you feel best describes the employee's performance since the last appraisal.
- REASON MUST BE GIVEN FOR EACH FACTOR TO SUBSTANTIATE AREA CHECKED

QUALITY OF WORK—Consider standard of workmanship, accuracy, neatness, skill, thoroughness, economy of materials, organization of job.

☐ FULLY MEETS JOB   ☐ UNSATISFACTORY   ☐ MEETS MINIMUM   ☐ EXCEEDS JOB
  REQUIREMENTS   DOES NOT MEET   REQUIREMENTS   REQUIREMENTS
                             MINIMUM REQUIREMENTS

Reason: _____
_____
_____

VOLUME OF WORK—Consider use of time, the volume of work accomplished and ability to meet schedules, under normal conditions

☐ DOES NOT MEET JOB   ☐ EXCEEDS JOB   ☐ MEETS MINIMUM   ☐ FULLY MEETS
  REQUIREMENTS   REQUIREMENTS   JOB REQUIREMENTS   JOB REQUIREMENTS

Reason: _____
_____
_____

ADAPTABILITY—Consider ability to meet changing conditions and situations, ease with which the employee learns new duties and assignments.

☐ IMPROVEMENT   ☐ SATISFACTORY   ☐ OUTSTANDING   ☐ VERY GOOD
  NEEDED

Reason: _____
_____
_____

JUDGMENT—Consider ability to evaluate relative merit of ideas or facts and arrive at sound conclusions, ability to decide correct course of action when a choice can be made.

☐ VERY GOOD   ☐ NEEDS MUCH   ☐ SATISFACTORY   ☐ OUTSTANDING
                            IMPROVEMENT

Reason: _____
_____
_____

JOB KNOWLEDGE AND SKILL—Consider understanding of job procedures and methods, ability to acquire necessary skills, expertness in doing assigned tasks and utilization of work experience.

☐ FULLY MEETS JOB   ☐ IMPROVEMENT   ☐ MEETS MINIMUM   ☐ EXCEEDS JOB
  REQUIREMENTS   NEEDED   JOB REQUIREMENTS   REQUIREMENTS

Reason: _____
_____
_____

ATTITUDE–Consider cooperation with supervisor and co-workers; receptiveness to suggestions and constructive criticisms; attitude toward company; enthusiasm in attempts to improve performance.

☐ EXCEEDS JOB
REQUIREMENTS
☐ FULLY MEETS
JOB REQUIREMENTS
☐ MEETS MINIMUM
JOB REQUIREMENTS
☐ IMPROVEMENT
NEEDED

Reason: _____
_____
_____

TEAM EFFORT–LEADERSHIP–Consider ability to inspire teamwork, enthusiasm to work towards a common objective, desire to assume responsibility, ability to originate or develop ideas and get things started.

☐ DOES NOT MEET
JOB REQUIREMENTS
☐ EXCEEDS JOB
REQUIREMENTS
☐ MEETS MINIMUM
JOB REQUIREMENTS
☐ FULLY MEETS
JOB REQUIREMENTS

Reason: _____
_____
_____

EMPLOYEE'S COMMENTS AND SELF-EVALUATION REMARKS
_____
_____
_____

PRESENT STATUS–NEEDS–PLAN OF ACTION

OVERALL EFFECTIVENESS–Considering the amount of experience on present job, check the rating which most nearly describes *total* current performance.

☐ EXCEEDS
JOB REQUIREMENTS
☐ DOES NOT MEET
JOB REQUIREMENTS
☐ FULLY MEETS
JOB REQUIREMENTS
☐ MEETS MINIMUM
JOB REQUIREMENTS

WHAT ASPECTS OF PERFORMANCE, IF NOT IMPROVED, MIGHT HINDER FUTURE DEVELOPMENT OR CAUSE DIFFICULTY IN PRESENT CLASSIFICATION (WEAKNESSES OF EMPLOYEE)?
_____
_____

WHAT ARE GREATEST STRENGTHS OF EMPLOYEE: _____
_____

Forward completed performance appraisal to designated approval authority before reviewing with subject employee. After appraisal is approved, review contents of appraisal with subject employee and complete section concerning specific plans to improve performance. Have employee sign the form and then forward original appraisal to the HR Department — retain copy for your files. Give copy to employee.

GIVE SPECIFIC PLANS YOU AND YOUR EMPLOYEE HAVE MADE TO IMPROVE WORK PERFORMANCE

_____
_____
_____

EVALUATED BY:_____ TITLE:_____ DATE:_____

APPROVED:_____ TITLE:_____ DATE:_____

EMPLOYEE'S COMMENTS AND SIGNATURE _____
(Does not necessarily indicate concurrence) TITLE:_____ DATE:_____

CREATIVITY

Demonstrates creative ability in managing the department.

Excels in creative thinking and effective problem solving.

Creates satisfying solutions while conforming to organizational policies.

Originates, develops, and implements constructive ideas.

Encourages an environment for creative excellence.

Initiates fresh ideas.

DELEGATING

Delegates to maximize organizational strengths.

Recognizes the importance of working through subordinates.

Delegates with clearly defined responsibility and authority.

Delegates to motivate subordinates.

DEPENDABILITY

Consistently accurate and dependable.

Consistently achieves results when confronted with major responsibilities and limited resources.

Can be counted on to achieve results in difficult circumstances.

A self-starter who displays a strong personal commitment to successfully completing projects.

DEVELOPMENT

Excels in selecting and developing potential talent.

Deals effectively with different levels of employees.

Effectively plans for future career development and accomplishment.

Successfully demonstrates ability to develop employees.

Inspires subordinates to reach their fullest potential.

Encourages employees to acquire appropriate skills and knowledge.

GOALS AND OBJECTIVES

Effectively implements departmental goals and objectives.

Excels in formulating and achieving goals and action plans.

Sets, obtains, and manages organizational goals.

Formulates realistic objectives.

Establishes relevant objectives and performance standards.

Excels in planning, forecasting, and determining courses of action.

Leadership

Projects self-confidence, authority, and enthusiasm.

Demonstrates natural leadership ability.

Displays the strengths of an exceptional leader.

Inspires confidence and respect.

Effectively uses power and influence.

Inspires the cooperation and confidence of others.

Promotes harmony and teamwork.

Loyalty and Dedication

Places organizational interests ahead of personal goals.

Is committed to organizational goals.

Displays a high degree of honesty, loyalty, and integrity.

Management Ability

Is effective at planning, organizing, motivating, and controlling resources.

Displays the qualities that make a manager effective on the job.

Recognizes the difference between managing and doing.

Excels at resolving interdepartmental conflicts.

Effectively manages change.

Maximizes the use of company resources.

Uses personnel effectively and efficiently.

Maturity

Displays a high degree of emotional maturity.

Keeps situations in proper perspective.

Displays superior emotional adjustment and stability.

Mental Capacity

Understands both theoretical and practical concepts.

Thinks fast on the feet.

Uses common sense to reach workable conclusions.

Grasps the most difficult concepts.

Is alert, quick, and responsive.

Thinks logically—uses common sense.

Organization

Builds organizational effectiveness.

Maximizes organizational productivity.

Encourages organizational action.

Makes effective use of organizational resources.

Overcomes organizational blocks.

Keeps organizational levels to a minimum.

PERFORMANCE QUALITIES

Demonstrates positive self-concepts.

Turns negatives into positives.

Maintains an optimistic outlook when faced with difficulties.

Competes with confidence—extremely self-confident.

Demonstrates credibility.

PERSONALITY AND APPEARANCE

Displays natural charm and a cheerful disposition.

Is stable, patient, and steady.

Is relaxed, confident, and enjoyable to be with.

Polished and poised; displays social grace.

Uses humor constructively.

EMPLOYEE BENEFITS

Most employers, unless they are very small, provide some benefits to their employees. You are probably already providing more benefits than you realize. The following table provides an identification of various types of employee benefits companies offer.

Employee benefits are so highly regulated by the federal government that the average businessperson cannot begin to design, purchase, and install their own benefits program. It's a good idea to ask other business people you know and trust to recommend a personnel or benefits consultant to assist you in choosing a benefits package to fit your organization.

Benefit Consultants

Hewitt Associates
100 Half Day Road
Lincolnshire, IL 60015
(212) 345-7000

Watson Wyatt Worldwide
999 Eighteenth Street
Suite 2900
Denver, CO 80202
(303) 298-7878

William M. Mercer, Inc.
3500 Texas Commerce Tower
2200 Ross Avenue
Dallas, TX 75201
(214) 220-6524

Benefit Costs

Although benefits are generally not considered part of an individual's compensation for tax purposes, they do represent a significant expenditure from the organization's point of view. Every two years the U.S. Chamber of Commerce surveys a large number of industries to determine the extent of benefit payments. In the most recent survey, an employer in American industry averaged paying 39 percent of total payroll in benefits. The significance of this figure is that the average employee earns $15,191 per year and receives $5,924.49 in benefits per year. The amount of benefits provided varies significantly. An employee in the hospital industry averages $64.60 per week in benefits, while an employee in the chemical manufacturing industry receives $135.79 per week in benefits.

Because benefits are so expensive, it is important for a company that provides even a few benefits to do a good job of communicating to their employees just what is provided. Use an annual report to let employees know what you are doing for them in this area.

The key to keeping benefits costs down is to monitor usage, institute prevention and health programs, use HMOs or PPOs where possible, and install flexible benefits programs. Provide a certain dollar amount of benefits and let the employee choose the ones most needed. Don't pay for a lot of fixed benefits your employees don't need or use. Many organizations have started passing on some of the costs of providing benefits to the employees, but this practice is not well accepted. Many employees can't afford the costs of their benefits any more than the employer can.

The benefits area is a difficult one to understand, and it is highly regulated. The following glossary of benefits terms will help you deal with administrators and consultants in the field.

GLOSSARY OF BENEFITS TERMS

American Academy of Actuaries (AAA). A national association of actuaries based in Washington, D.C. Acting in an advisory capacity, the AAA formed a task force after passage of the Tax Reform Act of 1986 to study ways to value benefits under Section 89. A report produced by that task force was completed in April 1988. It presently constitutes the most thorough methodology for valuing benefits, although it lacks the force of law or regulation and has not been endorsed or approved by the Treasury Department.

Average employer-provided benefit. The total value of all employer-provided benefits received by employees under all plans being tested, divided by the total number of employees, whether or not they are covered under the plans being tested. The average benefits for highly compensated employees and non-highly compensated employees are calculated separately.

Blue Book. The general explanation of every major tax reform act that is prepared after the legislation is enacted by the Joint Committee on Taxation. Because the Blue Book is prepared after enactment of the legislation, it is not considered by courts or the Internal Revenue Service to be as authoritative as pre-enactment legislative history. However, the Blue Book frequently clarifies issues that were not adequately discussed in the legislative history and also may point out where the statute needs to be technically corrected.

Bright-line test.   Any clear standard, such as a dollar maximum on an excludable benefit or the new mathematical nondiscrimination tests of Section 89, that when applied to a given set of facts will always yield the same result. The nondiscrimination rules of prior law were vague standards that were applied differently by different employers and/or different revenue agents.

Cafeteria plan.   An employer-maintained benefit plan under which participating employees may choose between at least one taxable benefit (usually cash) and at least one nontaxable benefit. Also referred to as a "flexible benefits plan."

Cash or deferred arrangement (CODA).   A type of profit-sharing or stock bonus plan under which an employee may defer current compensation into an account on a pretax basis. Also referred to as "salary reduction" plans under Section 401(k).

Classification test.   A requirement under Section 89 that a plan must be made available to employees in a manner that does not discriminate in favor of highly paid employees.

COBRA.   The Consolidated Omnibus Budget Reconciliation Act of 1985. This law includes the federal mandate that requires employers to offer continuation health coverage to certain former employees.

"Code" or "IRC."   The Internal Revenue Code.

Comparable plan rules.   A Section 89 testing provision that involves comparing the value of coverage offered under different health plans. An employer may combine either a group of health plans or a group of health benefits that have been desegregated into separate plans, as long as the least valuable benefit available under any plan is at least 95 percent of the most valuable benefit available.

Compensation.   TAMRA modified the definition of compensation by specifying that: (1) compensation need not be determined on the basis of the plan limitation year used for qualified retirement plan purposes, and (2) the definition should not include either accrued compensation or any amounts received while the employee is not a participant in the plan.

Concentration tests.   Nondiscrimination rules that apply to cafeteria plans, dependent care plans, educational benefit plans, and group legal services plans which prohibit excessive percentages of plan benefits from being provided to employees who own five percent or more of the employer.

Conference report.   The explanation of the statutory provisions of a tax bill. The conference report is prepared by members of the House Committee on Ways and Means and the Senate Finance Committee after differences in the two versions of the bill as initially passed by the House of Representatives and the Senate have been eliminated in conference. Unlike a Blue Book, the conference report on a bill is considered by the courts and the Internal Revenue Service to establish binding precedents for interpreting vague or ambiguous statutory provisions.

Constructive receipt.   An income tax principle that requires money or property to be included in income at the time the person has an unrestricted right to receive the money or property, even if the person may decide not to actually claim the money or property until a later date.

Controlled group.   A group of corporations, each of which is at least 80 percent owned (either directly or through one or more chains of subsidiary corporations) by a common parent corporation, or by a group composed of five or fewer individuals, estates, or trusts.

Core benefits.   Generally defined as all accident and health benefits except coverage for dental, vision, psychological, and orthodontic expenses and elective cosmetic surgery (which are defined as "non-core benefits"); disability insurance; low-level non-elective medical reimbursement coverage; and health insurance plans that are funded entirely through salary reduction amounts. Section 89 does not specifically define core benefits.

Cost modification factors.   Under Section 89 as amended by TAMRA, employers may modify their actual costs (for purposes of valuing employer-provided health benefits) based on variables such as historic costs, geographic differences, demographic characteristics, utilization rates, and multiemployer plan considerations.

De minimize benefit.   A fringe benefit provided to employees or independent contractors that has a value so small as to make accounting for it unreasonable or administratively impracticable. Meals eaten at certain company cafeterias that meet special standards (including nondiscrimination rules) are classified as de minimize benefits.

Deemed family coverage.   Under TAMRA, employers may deem family coverage to be available to employees without families, if such coverage is offered to them at no charge, and the employer does not use the rule to evade the nondiscrimination rules. The rule was designed to relieve employers from the burden of determining which employees have families.

Defined benefit plan.   An employer-provided retirement plan in which employer contributions are determined by actuarial calculations based on projected benefits. Minimum contributions are required by law, and benefits are usually paid monthly.

Defined contribution plan.   An employer-provided retirement plan that involves contributions made by the employer to individual employees' accounts, usually based on compensation. Benefits are based on an employee's account balance upon retirement, and are usually paid in a lump sum.

DEFRA.   Deficit Reduction Act of 1984.

Dependent care plans.   Employer-provided assistance to employees through (1) cash reimbursements for dependent care expenses incurred by employees, (2) payments directly to daycare centers, or (3) on-premises dependent care facilities. This care must be provided to children or other dependents under age 18, or other older dependents, including spouses, who are physically or mentally unable to care for themselves, and must enable the employee to be gainfully employed.

Determination letter.   A letter from the Internal Revenue Service formally recognizing that an employee benefit plan satisfies the code requirements governing exclusion of benefits provided under the plan.

Determination year.   The current plan year.

Discriminatory excess. The amount of an employer-provided benefit that exceeds the "highest permitted benefit" under Section 89 (see below). In other words, the amount of nontaxable employer-provided benefits that would have to be purchased with after-tax employee dollars in order to pass Section 89's discrimination tests.

Disregard rule. Permits employers to disregard employees with core coverage from another employer. Under Section 89 as amended by TAMRA, employers must offer employees core coverage before they can be disregarded. TAMRA also permits employers to offer free core coverage as an alternative to collecting sworn statements.

DRG. Diagnostic Related Group.

Dual-service personnel. Unless exceptions are established in future regulations, employees who perform services for more than one line of business cannot be treated as belonging to a stand-alone line of business, but rather must be allocated among the employer's other lines of business.

EBRI. Employee Benefit Research Institute.

Elective contribution. Contributions to employee benefit plans made as a result of an employee's choice. A pre-tax elective contribution results from an employee's election under a cafeteria plan to reduce salary or forego a bonus before the compensation is received, in order that the employer would instead contribute to a welfare benefit plan selected by the employee. These pre-tax elective contributions are treated under the code as employer contributions that would not be taxable to the employee as long as the rules (such as nondiscrimination rules) governing exclusion of that benefit are satisfied. An after-tax elective contribution, by contrast, is a contribution made by an employee out of salary that has already been taxed.

Employee benefits. Under Section 89, "benefits" include accident and health plans, group term life plans, welfare benefit plans, cafeteria plans, tuition reimbursement, group legal services, dependent care, educational assistance, miscellaneous fringe benefits, employee achievement awards, and continuation of health care benefits. A qualified retirement plan is not treated as a benefit under Section 89.

Employer-provided subsidy. Health benefits other than those provided through salary reduction or elective employee contribution.

ERISA. Employee Retirement Income Security Act of l974.

ESIC codes. The Enterprise Standard Industrial Classification codes. A listing of two-digit codes contained in a manual produced by the Statistical Policy Division of the Office of Management and Budget (OMB) that could be used to help employers demonstrate the differences and similarities in their products and services for determining separate lines of business.

Excess benefit. See *Discriminatory excess.*

Excludable employees. Employees who may be excluded from Section 89's nondiscrimination tests (provided that once the exclusion categories are established, they are applied uniformly) include employees who are subject to a collective bargaining agreement, employees with less than six months of service (one year for non-core benefits), employees who work fewer than 17.5 hours per week or six months per year, employees who are under 21 during the entire plan year, and nonresident aliens with no U.S.-source income.

Exclusion reversal rules. Rules designed to prevent employers from applying any of the various employee exclusion categories unless the exclusion is applied uniformly to all employees in the excludable class. TAMRA provides that multi-employer plan entry standards that govern benefits for newly hired, part-time, seasonal, or under-age employees will not trigger these rules.

401(k) ADP/ACP tests. Mathematical nondiscrimination tests governing cash or deferred arrangements that prohibit the average compensation deferral percentages for all highly compensated employees from exceeding, by more than fixed amounts, the average deferral percentages for all non-highly compensated employees. The "compensation deferral percentage" is the contribution to the Section 401(k) plan on behalf of each employee, divided by that employee's compensation.

Family member. Under Section 89, "family members" are defined as an employee's spouse, lineal ascendants and descendants, and their spouses.

The Family Support Act. Signed into law on October 13, 1988, this law makes major changes in the nation's welfare system. These changes are financed in part by various tax provisions, including altering the present relationship between the child care credit and the dependent care exclusion as of January 1, 1989. As a result of these changes, the new law will have a major impact on the notices that employers must send to employees that describe the dependent care exclusion.

FICA. Federal Insurance Contributions Act (a.k.a. Social Security).

50-Employee test. A rule requiring that all employees must be allocated to a particular line of business or operating unit, each of which must contain at least 50 nonexcludable employees. To comply, employers may be forced to aggregate otherwise distinct, but small, lines of business with unrelated groups of employees.

Flexible benefits. See *Cafeteria plans*.

Form 5500. An IRS form covering a plan's financial activity that must be filed with an employer's tax return annually.

Former employees. TAMRA exempts employers from having to test benefits provided to employees who separated from service before 1989 with respect to benefits provided as of Dec. 3 i, 1988, and with respect to certain nondiscriminatory increases in those benefits made after Dec. 31, 1988.

Geographically separate businesses. An employer's businesses can be tested separately under the line of business rules if they are geographically separate—such as in different states or different cities.

Good faith compliance standard. In the absence of Treasury regulations, employers must make a "good faith effort" to comply with Section 89 using a reasonable interpretation based on the statute and its legislative history and considering the likely position on unclear issues that would be taken by the IRS and the courts. An employer would not be acting in good faith if he or she consistently resolves unclear issues in his or her own favor.

Grandfathered. A term used to describe individuals or entities that are exempted from a new statutory rule, most commonly using a cut-off date to determine eligibility.

Group legal services plan (GLSO).   An employee benefit that offers legal services (or reimbursement for same) to plan participants, such as divorce actions, traffic offenses, and estate planning. Congress is currently considering a retroactive extension of GLSO's nontaxable status under Code Section 120, which expired on Dec. 31, 1987.

Group term life insurance.   General life insurance (other than travel or accident insurance) provided by an employer to a group of employees under a policy carried directly or indirectly by the employer that provides insurance benefits based on uniform factors such as age, years of service, compensation, or position.

Headquarters employees.   Under Section 89, headquarters employees must be allocated for testing purposes to one line of business in accordance with the performance of their services. Thus, if a majority of a headquarters employee's services are performed for a particular line of business or operating unit, the employee must be allocated to that line of business or operating unit. Employees performing services for more than one line of business or operating unit may be allocated on a pro rata basis or to any one line of business.

Health maintenance organization (HMO).   An organization that provides a range of health care services for a specific group of individuals for a fixed periodic fee.

Helper health plans.   Under Section 89 as amended by TAMRA, plans that are outside the allowable percentage range for plan comparability can be aggregated with other plans (for purposes of passing the 80-percent benefits test), provided that each helper plan actually provides health coverage to a percentage of non-highly compensated employees that is equal to at least 80 percent of the percentage of highly compensated employees who are covered under the plan.

Highest permitted benefit.   To determine the highest permitted benefit, the nontaxable benefits of all highly compensated employees in a discriminatory plan are reduced until the plan becomes nondiscriminatory.

Highly compensated employee.   During the previous plan year, five-percent owners, employees who earned over $75,000 in compensation, employees who earned over $50,000 in compensation and were among the top-paid 20 percent of employees, and officers of the company who earned more than $30,000. Every employer must have at least one officer who is treated as a highly compensated employee. Former employees are treated as highly compensated employees if they were highly compensated at the time of separation or at any time after attaining age 55.

HII.   Health Insurance Institute.

Indemnity.   Predetermined benefits that are paid in the event of a loss covered by insurance.

Key employees.   Officers of an employer whose compensation is more than $45,000, and individuals who fall into one of three groups of highly compensated employees who hold ownership interests in the employer: (1) employees with the ten largest ownership interests (at least 0.5 percent ownership); (2) employees whose compensation is at least $150,000 and who own at least one-percent interests; and (3) employees who own at least five-percent interests.

Leased employees. Under Section 89, leased employees are treated as employees of the organization for which they provide services. A person is a "leased employee" if he or she has been performing services for a recipient employer under one or more agreements with a leasing organization for a period of at least a year (six months in the case of core health benefits), and the services provided are of a type historically performed by employees in the business field of the employer.

Look-back year. The plan year prior to the current plan year.

Line of business. See *Separate line of business.*

Lineal ascendant. For Section 89 purposes, a parent of an employee.

Lineal descendent. For Section 89 purposes, a child of an employee.

Medicare Catastrophic Coverage Act of 1988. A law passed during the 100th Congress that expands the Medicare system to include benefits for catastrophic illnesses. The controversial "maintenance of effort" provision in the law requires that employers pass on to employees most of the health insurance savings in 1989 and 1990 that may result from the Act's expansion of Medicare benefits.

Multi-employer plan. A collectively bargained defined benefit plan to which more than one employer contributes and which is administered by a joint employer/union board.

Non-core benefits. See *Core benefits.*

Nondiscriminatory terms test. Under this test, the plan being tested must not contain any provision relating to eligibility to participate that explicitly or implicitly discriminates in favor of highly compensated employees. For example, a plan that is designed to suit special needs of certain highly compensated employees violates this rule.

Nontaxable benefit. A benefit whose value is excludable from an employee's gross income for tax purposes.

Normal working hours. For purposes of classifying part-time employees, TAMRA recognizes that an employee is considered to normally work the average number of hours that were worked during the period in the testing year prior to the testing date. If the period is less than 60 days, an employee is considered to normally work either (1) the average number of hours worked during the prior testing year; or (2) if the employee did not work at least 60 days during the prior testing year, the average number of hours the employee is scheduled to work as of the testing date, during the longer of (a) the next 60 days, or (b) the period between the testing date and the end of the testing year.

OBRA. Omnibus Budget Reconciliation Act.

OMB. Office of Management and Budget.

Open-season rule. Beginning in 1990, no non-highly compensated employee can be disregarded in testing incremental family coverage separately, even if the employee's sworn statement includes single status, unless the employer informs the employee that he or she has the right, should the employee ever have a family, to elect health coverage for the family without regard to whether it is open season at the time.

Operating unit.   A business that includes all the employees necessary for the preparation of property for sale to customers, or for the provision of services to customers, such as a manufacturing plant or a beauty parlor. Operating units that meet the "geographic separateness" standard can be tested separately from each other under the line of business rules.

Permissive aggregation.   Under Section 89's comparable plan rules, health plans with different values may be aggregated (at an employer's choice) for purposes of the 80-percent alternative benefits test and the 50-percent eligibility test.

Plan permanency.   One of the requirements for plan qualification included in Section 89(k). Under this requirement, a plan must be established "with the intention of being maintained for an indefinite period of time." This rule is drawn from an existing "permanent program" requirement for qualified retirement plans. The employer may reserve the right to amend or terminate a plan. However, such abandonment of a plan within a few years after its establishment for any reason other than business necessity is considered evidence that the plan is not a permanent, bona fide program for the exclusive benefit of employees.

Plan year.   The 12-month period (or shorter period, in the case of an initial plan year) used as the fiscal year of an employee benefit plan. Typically, employees' benefit elections must be made (or changed) prior to the beginning of the plan year.

Preferred provider organization (PPO).   An arrangement to provide medical care in which an insurer or third-party payor contracts with a group of physicians to provide care at lower than customary fees in return for a predetermined volume of patients and prompt payment.

Private letter ruling (P.L.R.).   An opinion letter issued by the Internal Revenue Service in response to specific questions and factual situations presented by an individual taxpayer. While a P.L.R. can be relied upon as an authoritative ruling only by the taxpayer to whom it is issued, they are often cited by other taxpayers since they may indicate the IRS' position on a particular issue. User fees must be paid before the IRS will consider a taxpayer's request for a P.L.R.

Pro-rata allocation.   Employees who do not perform a "majority of services" for one line of business may be allocated on a proportionate basis among different lines of business.

Qualification requirements.   Under Section 89, an employee benefit plan must meet five standards or "qualification requirements": (1) the plan must be in writing; (2) employees' rights under the plan must be enforceable; (3) employees are provided with reasonable notification of their benefits; (4) the plan is maintained for the exclusive benefit of employees; and (5) the plan is intended to be maintained indefinitely. If a plan does not meet all five requirements, covered employees lose their favorable tax status.

Reasonable classification test.   When organizing a company into separate lines of business, employers must demonstrate that the plan being tested is available on an employer-wide basis. The reasonable classification test examines the facts and circumstances of each case to determine whether the plan unduly benefits highly compensated employees.

Reasonable notification. One of the requirements for plan qualification included in Section 89(k). The term "reasonable notification" is not defined in the legislative history of Section 89. However, the IRS is not likely to establish a new standard that differs from similar requirements that are already in force under the Employee Retirement Income Security Act of 1974 (ERISA). The ERISA rules allow employers to provide employees with plan notices by mail or by posting them on a bulletin board. The rules also specify what information should be provided (and/or cross-referenced) in the notice itself.

Rule of convenience. A provision in a statutory requirement that is intended to ease the administrative burden of the requirement.

Qualified benefit or plan. A general term that applies to a benefit that is provided free by the employer and meets applicable qualification requirements under tax law.

Safe harbor. A provision in a statute or regulation that exempts specific types of individuals or organizations from one or more of the statute's requirements.

Salary reduction. An election by an employee to reduce his or her salary in exchange for contribution by the employer of an equivalent sum to a cash or deferred arrangement or a cafeteria plan. Also see *Elective contribution.*

Section 89 coalition. A group of employers, employer organizations, insurance companies, and organized labor formed in the Spring of 1988 to lobby Congress for a one year delay in Section 89's effective date. The coalition proposed a series of changes in the law that were included in TAMRA.

Self-employed individuals. Under Section 89, self-employed individuals are treated as employees.

Self insurance. A group insurance program that provides benefits financed entirely by the employer through a self-insurance reserve fund, under an "administrative services only" contract, or under a retrospectively rated premium contract with a commercial carrier. Under a self-insurance program, there is no shifting of insurance risk to a commercial carrier.

Separate line of business. Under Section 89, a business entity that is part of a larger organization, has at least 50 employees, and satisfies the Treasury Department's guidelines or obtains a determination letter or private letter ruling certifying it as a separate line of business.

Separate plans. Generally, every plan that is not substantially the same is considered to be separate under Section 89. A separate health plan has one or more of the following: separate levels of coverage, separate levels of employee contribution, or different coinsurance and deductible levels. Additionally, employee-only coverage is separate from family coverage, and former employees' plans are separate from current employees' plans.

Simplified employee pension (SEP) plan. A simple form of defined contribution plan, available only to employers with twenty-five or fewer employees, in which an employer may contribute to employees' Individual Retirement Accounts under a set formula. Employees may also contribute to an SEP on a salary-reduction basis.

Single plan.   Under Section 89, two or more plans that are identical except for the employees they cover may be tested as a single plan. In addition, group term life plans that vary their coverage according to employees' compensation and identical health plans that proportionately reduce the benefits of employees who work fewer than 30 hours a week also may be tested as one plan.

Sole proprietor.   Under Section 89, a sole proprietor is treated as his or her own employer.

Special scrutiny.   If an employer cannot satisfy the general tests to prove the genuine separateness of its business lines or operating units, but nevertheless wishes to test these businesses separately under Section 89, the Internal Revenue Service will look more closely at the facts and circumstances of each particular case and issue private letter rulings, if requested, under "special scrutiny" standards to be outlined in regulations.

Statutory plan.   Any plan that includes health or group term life insurance on a mandatory basis. In addition, employers may elect to treat group legal services, educational assistance, and dependent care plans as statutory plans.

Summary plan description (SPD).   A brief, clear description of provisions in an employee benefit plan that is distributed to employees whenever a plan is adopted or amended.

Supplemental plan.   A health plan providing benefits in addition to those provided under the employer's basic health plan. In applying the permissive aggregation rules, supplemental coverage should be added to the basic coverage for valuation purposes before plans are tested for comparability.

Table I rates.   Relatively low, safe-harbor rates for valuing group term life insurance premiums under Reg. 1.79-3(d).

TAMRA.   The Technical and Miscellaneous Revenue Act of 1988 (P.L. 100-647). This law includes technical corrections to the Tax Reform Act of 1986. Substantive changes to Section 89 designed to ease the compliance burden were incorporated in the law.

Tax expenditure.   The revenue that is lost to the government as the result of a tax exemption.

Taxable year.   The fiscal year used for tax purposes. Almost all individuals use the calendar year as their taxable year.

Tax Reform Act of 1986.   One in a series of laws that modified the Internal Revenue Code. TRA 1986 added Section 89 to the Code.

TEFRA.   Tax Equity and Fiscal Responsibility Act of 1982.

Testing day.   Under Section 89 as amended by TAMRA, employers must test their plans on only one day per year (as opposed to every day under prior law). The testing day may be any day in the testing year, including the last day of the year. The date must be the same for all plans of the same type being tested together. The annual date need not be an actual date (e.g., Jan. 1) but may also be determined using a fixed method (e.g., the last day of the first two-week pay period ending in the testing year). If a testing date is not specified, the IRS assumes the testing date to be the last day of the testing year.

Testing year.   Employers may designate a common 12-month period as the testing year to be used in testing plans that may have non-uniform plan years. The testing period is subject to the same consistency requirement that applies to the testing date. In general, the testing year must be the same for all plans of the same type. Designation of a testing period may not result in any period being disregarded for purposes of Section 89. If a testing date is not specified, the IRS assumes the testing year to be the calendar year.

Top-heavy plan.   A qualified retirement plan that has accrued excessive benefits for "key employees" and meets other tests provided by Code Section 416.

Top-paid group.   The highest paid 20 percent of an employer's workforce.

"Top 100" rule.   An employee who is not among the 100 employees earning the highest compensation during a plan year will not be treated as (1) receiving compensation above $75,000; (2) receiving compensation above $50,000 and being in the "top-paid group" (see above); or (3) an officer receiving compensation above $45,000 in the plan year if he or she failed to meet one of those three criteria in the preceding plan year.

Transition period.   Under Section 89, a period of time that begins on the date an employer becomes or ceases to be a member of a controlled group or an affiliated service group and ends on the last day of the first plan year beginning after the change in status.

Tuition reduction program.   Programs under which schools provide current and retired employees (and their dependents) discounts of up to 100 percent on tuition for education below the graduate level at either the employer school, or at another educational institution covered by a student exchange agreement.

Utilization rates.   In valuing employer-provided health benefits, employers may take into account differences in the use of certain health care features that are common to different coverages. This adjustment must be made by estimating the cost of each plan with the common features as if the usage had been distributed evenly among all plans.

Valuation.   See *Valuing benefits.*

Valuing benefits.   Under Section 89, the process of determining the total value of coverage under health and group term life plans. For all other plans, the value of the employer- provided benefit is calculated.

WORK AND FAMILY BENEFITS

In a survey of 259 major U.S. employers, Hewitt Associates found that:

- 56 percent of employers offer some kind of childcare assistance to employees. Most common is dependent care spending accounts.
- 3 1 percent of employers offer elder care assistance; usually a dependent care spending account.
- 56 percent of employers offer flexible scheduling arrangements, usually a flextime program.
- Only 5 percent of employers have paid parental leave programs, but 42 percent have unpaid parental leave policies.
- 77 percent offer employee assistance programs (EAPs). EAPs are most commonly provided through an outside provider.

With the changing structure of the family and with more two-career couples, work and family benefits are becoming increasingly important.

Examples of Employee Benefits

Required Security	Voluntary Time Off	Insurance	Social and Financial	Recreational	Retirement
1. Worker's compensation	1. Birthdays	1. Medical	1. Credit union	1. Bowling league	1. Social security
2. Unemployment compensation	2. Vacation time	2. Dental	2. Profit-sharing or 401(k)	2. Company newsletter	2. Pension funds
3. Old age, survivors', and disability insurance	3. Company-subsidized travel	3. Survivor benefits	3. Company provided housing or car	3. Professional memberships	3. Early retirement
4. State disability insurance	4. Holidays	4. Accidental dismemberment insurance	4. Legal services	4. Club memberships	4. Preretirement counseling
5. Medicare hospital benefits	5. Sick pay	5. Travel accident insurance	5. Purchase discounts	5. EAP counseling	5. Retirement gratuity
6. Benefits portability	6. Military reserve	6. Group insurance	6. Stock plans	6. Company-sponsored events	6. Retirement annuity plan
	7. Election day	7. Disability insurance	7. Financial counseling	7. Childcare services	7. Benefits for retired employees
	8. Social service sabbatical	8. Life insurance	8. Moving expenses	8. Cafeteria	8. Disability retirement benefits
	9. Funeral leave	9. Misc. medical insurance	9. Tuition assistance	9. Season tickets	
	10. Jury duty pay		10. Discounts on company products	10. Service awards	

7

HANDLING DISCIPLINE AND DISCHARGE

- Performance Improvement

- Determining Discipline and Discharge Policy

- Sample Discipline Policy

- Discipline and Discharge Forms

- Sample Letters on Discipline

- Preventing Discrimination Complaints

- Policy Against Harassment

- Investigating Claims of Sexual Harassment

Handling Discipline and Discharge

Business people should take a long, serious look at the changing trend in the law relating to "employment at will." As business people, we have had a long period where we could run our own show and fire people for any reason other then causes covered by the Civil Rights Act or the Federal Labor Relations Law. For years the right to do so was unquestioned.

It's made a different story today, however, as courts in some states have ruled that statements made to employees may constitute employment contracts and can, in some cases, eliminate our ability to terminate at will.

The main issue in disciplinary action is *just cause*. It's generally held that you must have *just cause* for enforcing discipline. Just cause definitions vary, but it's a good idea to ask yourself the following questions before you terminate an employee:

- Did we adequately communicate the policy or procedure involved in the disciplinary action?

- Has the employee been warned orally, in writing, or both of the consequences of his or her action?

- Did we investigate the misconduct? Was the investigation thorough and fair?

- Has the policy or procedure that was violated been violated by other employees? Was disciplinary action taken in those cases? If so, what action was taken?

- Have we reviewed the employee's personnel record to see if this is the first time discipline has been administered?

- Is the planned discipline too tough or too light? Does the discipline fit the severity of the situation? Is it being used as a corrective/learning experience or as a punitive action?

The key to appropriate discipline is equal treatment and internal consistency.

PERFORMANCE IMPROVEMENT

Before you take disciplinary action, you may want to try a more positive approach by giving an employee a performance improvement memorandum. This sometimes works better than immediately issuing a disciplinary notice. It puts the employee on notice that you are serious when you ask for improvement in performance, and it documents that discussion. If you decide to use a performance improvement memorandum, be specific in detailing the poor performance and in listing exactly what you expect in the way of improvement. Establish a time frame for improvement and follow-up to make sure the employee is performing to established standards. A sample performance improvement memorandum follows.

MEMORANDUM

TO: Employee Name

FROM: Supervisor

DATE:

SUBJECT: Performance Improvement Plan

This memo is notification that your performance has not been acceptable for the following reasons:

    1.

    2.

    3.

    4.

You have had a verbal warning about your performance and this written warning will serve as notice that the following actions must be taken:

    1.

    2.

    3.

    4.

We expect you to perform your job requirements in a timely, professional and conscientious manner at all times.

This plan will be in effect for the next 30 days and there must be immediate and sustained improvement or further action up to and including termination could occur.

Nothing contained herein is, or shall be construed as an employment contract. Your employment with the Company has been, and if continued, remains employment-at-will.

I have received a copy of this memo on the date below:

Received

_____   _____
Employee   Date

_____   _____
Supervisor   Date

MEMORANDUM

TO: Jane Doe

FROM: John Brown

DATE: January 10th

SUBJECT: Performance Improvement Plan

This memorandum is notification that your management/supervisory performance is not acceptable for the following reason:

> Your department has experienced a great deal of turnover
> (5 people in 6 months) due to your management style.
> I have had several discussions with you over this period of time.
> Your defensiveness, arrogance and the overly critical style you
> display with your subordinates is unacceptable.

Employees have complained and have either quit or transferred to other departments in frustration over your management methods and attitudes. Other employees who have wanted to learn your function turn down the opportunity when it presents itself, because they don't want to work for you.

You are an excellent closer and technically good at that part of your job, but you are being paid to manage other employees as well, and that part of your job is not being handled in a positive manner.

You must learn to delegate and to coach and mentor your employees, creating a positive, non-threatening work environment. We are a team and each team member, no matter at what level, is important to the success of your department and our Company.

This written performance improvement plan will serve as notice that the following actions must be taken immediately:

Page 2 - Performance Improvement Plan

`1.   You must improve your managerial skills as well as your personal
      interaction and relationships with your employees and your peers.
      In order to help you do this, the Company will pay for you to attend a
      supervisory skills workshop. Please see me for the details. This
      workshop will cover the interpersonal skills that you need to learn
      in order to build trust and respect with your employees. It will also
      help you learn how to coach and develop your employees and create a
      non-threatening, more open environment in your department.

2.   Pursuant to our discussion, I also want to emphasize that our work hours
      are 8:00 AM to 5:00 PM and although management employees have some
      latitude because they normally work longer hours, you have the
      responsibility to work the hours needed to get the job done. You set
      the standard for your employees and when you rarely get to work on time
      you are not providing a positive example for your staff. We expect this
      situation to improve immediately.

This plan will be in effect for the next 60 days. There must be immediate and sustained
improvement in your management/supervisory performance or further action may be
taken up to and including termination.

Nothing contained herein is, or shall be construed as an employment contract. Your
employment with the Company has been, and if continued, remains employment at-will.

I acknowledge that I received a copy of this memorandum on the date below.

_____   _____
Employee Signature   Date   Supervisor Signature   Date

DETERMINING DISCIPLINE AND DISCHARGE POLICY

Discipline and discharge are the two toughest areas to manage in any organization. The way your supervisors and managers handle these issues will impact your bottom line.

You must have a discipline and discharge policy in order to ensure that everyone is treated fairly and that there is due process. By this we mean that employees facing discipline or discharge should be aware of the employer's conduct or performance expectations, that they have a copy of the handbook setting out the work rules and that they are given a chance to present their side of the story and defend themselves against charges of misconduct. Other issues in due process are:

- *Forewarning*—Before discipline or discharge takes place employees should be made aware of their misconduct. A series of warnings, usually one oral and one written, should be made.

- *Reasonableness of rule and penalty*—An employer should be able to show that the work rule violated by an employee is reasonable and was reasonably applied. Additionally, the penalty assessed against the employee should reflect the seriousness of the offense and be consistent with progressive discipline principles.

- *Evenhanded enforcement*—Employees who commit similar acts or cause similar problems should be subject to similar penalties.

- *Timeliness*—Discipline should be imposed in a timely manner.

SAMPLE DISCIPLINE POLICY

The following model discipline and discharge policy can be adapted to your organization. Word it to fit your needs. Be sure that your policy is reasonable and is enforced in an evenhanded manner.

If you have no other policies in your policy manual, you must have a policy and a procedure on discipline and discharge in order to avoid costly litigation.

Consider holding mandatory workshops for all your supervisors and managers to train them in your discipline policy and procedures. If you cannot conduct an in-house workshop or find a local workshop, write to the American Management Association at 135 West 50th Street, New York, New York 10020. Ask for their seminar catalog.

Sample Discipline Policy

Policy

Open communications between management and employees and the establishment of a friendly, cooperative work atmosphere go a long way toward eliminating serious disciplinary problems. If, however, disciplinary problems do arise, supervisors should make every effort to ensure that employees have a thorough understanding of company policies and an awareness of what is expected in the area of job performance.

The purpose of this policy is to provide guidelines for disciplinary action. Application of these guidelines must be consistent and equitable so that all employees receive like treatment for similar offenses.

Procedures

The procedures described below are meant to assist supervisors and managers in determining proper course of action when discipline is needed. They are guidelines, not a substitute for common sense. Documentation of all verbal and written warnings is important to avoid the situation of an employee being discharged with no written proof of earlier warnings. In most cases, it is advisable to give an employee at least one documented verbal warning and one written warning before termination.

Warnings

You should use your own judgment in determining the length of time between warnings. A minimum of thirty days and a maximum of ninety days is suggested as a guideline. The warning should be specific in describing what improvement is needed. Copies of the warning should be forwarded to the senior officer of the employee's department and to the affirmative action coordinator in the human resource department for follow-up.

1. *Verbal Warning.* Before a written warning is issued, a verbal warning may be given to the employee. This verbal warning should be recorded.
2. *Written Warning.* If improvement is not made within the time period granted in earlier warnings, it will be necessary to give a written warning. This may be done in the form of a memo. In such cases, signature of the employee acknowledges receipt of the written warning but may not indicate concurrence with the information contained in the warning. Copies of written warnings should go into the files and a copy should go to the employee. If the employee fails to improve by the date given on the warning, other disciplinary action, including termination, may result.
3. *Consultation.* Following a written warning, you should consult with the employee to check on progress and improvement in the problem area. Consultations should be documented accurately as to the dates and outcomes of the meetings.

The employee's file will be purged if after twelve months have elapsed, the employee has improved and there have been no subsequent warnings.

Consistency of Treatment

If there is one guideline that cannot be stressed enough, it is consistency and equality of treatment of all employees.

Suspension

Some companies employ progressive disciplinary procedures that include suspensions. Suspensions work best when the problem is not serious enough to warrant discharge, but the supervisor needs to take action.

Evaluation

An evaluation period (formerly called probationary period) also is utilized by some organizations to give the employee time to change behavior. The key here is to identify the best disciplinary situation for your specific organization and your work force.

The key to discipline is to make it as positive as possible, to allow the employee to retain self-respect. The objective is to correct problem behavior and, when the employee has corrected behavior, to wipe the slate clean.

Manager's Tip

Set up a tracking system to ensure that proper follow-up occurs on any disciplinary action. Follow through—if you don't, you might have to reinstitute the disciplinary procedures with a new time period.

DISCIPLINE AND DISCHARGE FORMS

When completing discipline or termination forms, you must be thorough, honest, and to the point. You must "tell it like it is" in terms of stating the facts, but eliminate judgments and blame. You may end up explaining these issues and your forms to top executives or to regulatory people such as hearing examiners or attorneys. Don't be frightened of the issues, but take them seriously and spend the time you need to complete adequate documentation.

SUPERVISOR'S CHECKLIST FOR EFFECTIVE DISCIPLINE
(COMPLETE BEFORE TAKING ACTION)

Employee's Name _____   Date _____

Length of Service _____   Department_____

INCIDENT

Employee(s) involved _____

_____

What happened?—Provide an accurate statement of what happened.

_____

_____

_____

How did it happen?

_____

_____

_____

What are the facts?—Be specific—no opinions.

_____

_____

_____

_____

Has the employee had a chance to tell his/her side of the story? . . . . ❏ Yes   ❏ No

Explain_____

_____

_____

Did you talk to the employee in private?. . . . . ❏ Yes   ❏ No

Was the employee aware of the rule or procedure? . . . . ❏ Yes   ❏ No

Was the rule published in writing and communicated to all employees?. . . . . . ❏ Yes   ❏ No

How consistently has the rule been enforced? _____

_____

What needs to be corrected?

_____

_____

_____

What has been done in similar cases?

_____

_____

_____

Has this violation been previously overlooked . . . . ❏ Yes   ❏ No

Did the employee have any previous warning . . . . ❏ Yes   ❏ No

What is the employee's past record?

_____

_____

_____

Can you back up this record with facts . . . . ❏ Yes   ❏ No

What is appropriate and justifiable discipline?

    ❏ Verbal warning

    ❏ Written warning

    ❏ Placed on probation

    ❏ Discharge

Will corrective action prevent a recurrence and encourage better performance? . . ❏ Yes   ❏ No

Which persons did you check with before taking disciplinary action?

    ❏ Your Manager   ❏ Human Resource Department   ❏ Other

    _____

    _____

FOLLOW-UP ACTION

What follow-up action is necessary?

_____

_____

_____

_____

_____

Have you recorded this incident and put a copy in the personnel file? . . . . ❏ Yes   ❏ No

DISCIPLINARY WARNING NOTICE

Employee's Name _____   Date _____

Department _____   Position/Title _____

REASON FOR NOTICE:

_____

_____

_____

ACTION TAKEN ON THIS NOTICE:

❏ Verbal Warning

❏ First Written Warning
Discussion   _____

_____

_____

NEXT STEP:

❏ Second Written Warning

❏ Termination

❏ Other (specify)   Discussion _____

_____

_____

SUPERVISOR'S COMMENTS:

_____

_____

_____

EMPLOYEE'S COMMENTS:

_____

_____

_____

_____

EMPLOYEE'S SIGNATURE _____

SUPERVISOR SIGNATURE _____

NOTE: **If, in the opinion of the Company, an infraction is serious enough, any and all steps may be bypassed and discharge may occur at any time.** A copy of this notice must be given to the employee and a copy placed in the employee's personnel file.

Employee Warning Notice

Employee Name: _____

Social Security Number: _____

Position Title: _____

Date of Warning: _____

TYPE OF PROBLEM	( ) Tardiness	( ) Quality of Work	( ) Carelessness
	( ) Absenteeism	( ) Quantity of Work	( ) Safety
	( ) Insubordination	( ) Neatness	( ) Intoxication or Drinking
	( ) Other: _____		

_____

_____

Problem Occurred on: Date _____   **WARNING**   ( ) First Date: _____
Time _____   **NOTICE:**   ( ) Second Date: _____
Place _____   ( )Final

_____

COMPANY STATEMENT	**WARNING DECISION**
1. Describe in detail what the employee has done	1. Explain in detail what the employee must do to improve performance or change behavior.
2. Cite how this interferes with work environment, employee performance, business operations or the well being of other employees.	2. Cite date that improvements are to be required.
3. Cite verbatim the rule, policy, law, standard, or regulation that was violated	3. Cite consequences if improvements are not achieved by date specified.
	APPROVED BY:_____
	TITLE: _____
	DATE: _____

Attach separate page if needed for more detailed explanations.

EMPLOYEE COMMENTS: _____

_____

_____

_____   _____
Employee's Signature   Date

_____   _____
Supervisor's Signature   Date

Manager's Tip

The Employee Consultation Form can be used for many types of consultations, not only for discipline or discharge. You may want to modify the form and use it for general employee counseling sessions.

The key issue with all of these forms is that you have documentation of discussions and warnings. You keep copies for the personnel files, and you also give copies to the employee. If you were to end up in a regulatory hearing, the first thing a hearing examiner would ask you is whether you provided the employee with a copy of the warning notice.

EMPLOYEE CONSULTATION FORM

NAME _____ Dept._____

Type of Problem _____

Date of Problem _____

First Warning

Second Warning

Third Warning

Suspension. . . . From _____ To _____ Return to Work _____

Discharge

Description of Problem: _____

_____

_____

_____

Disciplinary action to be taken: _____

_____

_____

_____

_____

Employee's statement: _____

_____

_____

_____

Signed _____   Date _____
       Supervisor

Signed _____   Date _____
       Employee
       Signature acknowledges receipt only

SEPARATION NOTICE

COMPANY NAME _____

EMPLOYEE NAME _____

SS # _____ JOB TITLE _____

DATES OF EMPLOYMENT: Start_____ Last_____ Previous dates of employment_____

WORKING HOURS_____ ___ AM PM TO_____ AM PM WORKING DAYS _____

RATE OF PAY_____ per _____ PAID OVERTIME? Yes___ No___ UNION INVOLVED? Yes___ No___

AMOUNT OF PAY GIVEN IN LIEU OF NOTICE, IF ANY _____

VOLUNTARY QUIT _____ DISCHARGED _____ LACK OF WORK ___

WHAT WAS THE FINAL CIRCUMSTANCE LEADING TO SEPARATION? _____

_____

_____

_____

WHAT OTHER CIRCUMSTANCES, IF ANY, WERE TAKEN INTO CONSIDERATION? _____

_____

_____

_____

EMPLOYEE'S COMMENTS (Continue on back) _____

_____

_____   _____
Employee's Signature   Immediate Supervisor's Signature

                                                Title: _____
Date: _____   Date:_____
                                                Phone: _____

WOULD YOU REHIRE THIS INDIVIDUAL?   _____
Yes _____   No _____   Witness

Attached are supportive documents as applicable (warning notices, application forms, doctor's statements, etc.)
This form should be completed immediately at separation time.

Note
_____
By completing this form and having the terminating employee sign it, you have documentation showing the type of termination. If the employee agrees that it is a voluntary termination, he/she may not collect unemployment compensation if it is not due on voluntary terminations under the laws of your state.

Checklist for Termination
(Attach All Termination Documentation)

Employee Name _____ Dept. _____ Date _____

Complete all areas of the form.

_____ Voluntary

_____ Involuntary

_____ With Notice

_____ Reason _____

            _____

_____ Eligible for Rehire?

_____ Vacation Pay Paid?

_____ Letter of Resignation/Separation Notice Completed

_____ License information

_____ Return of all Company property, including keys and parking
          pass, telephone codes, credit cards, personnel manual, and so
          on.

_____ Paycheck delivered to employee at time of termination

                        _____
                        Supervisor

                        _____
                        Date

Exit Interview Form

Employee Name _____   Employee Number _____

Department/Company _____

Job Title _____   Job Code _____

Termination Date _____

VOLUNTARY TERMINATION

1. Because your termination was *voluntary,* we would like to know your reasons for leaving the company.

    _____

    _____

    _____

    _____

    _____

2. Did you experience any dissatisfaction during your employment at _____? If so, please describe.

    _____

    _____

    _____

    _____

    _____

3. What recommendations would you suggest to make this a better company?

    _____

    _____

    _____

    _____

    _____

4. What did you like most about working here?

    _____

    _____

    _____

    _____

Are there any other comments—positive or negative—that you would like to make? If so, please do so in the space below. (Feel free to use the back of this form or attach another sheet.)

_____

_____

_____

_____

_____

_____

_____

_____

_____

_____

**Thank you for completing this form. Your comments will be helpful to us
in our future planning as we are constantly striving to improve in all areas.**

Please sign below:

_____   _____

Employee's Signature   Date

- -

For Human Resources Department Use Only

_____Keys and access card checked in   _____Final check given to Employee

_____Termination form presented to employee   _____Insurance conversion discussed

_____Prescription card returned

SAMPLE LETTERS ON DISCIPLINE

Letters or memos on discipline or discharge are the most difficult ones most managers have to write in the course of their jobs. The following model letters will provide you with ideas and formats to help you get started. Modify the letters to fit your specific needs. All letters come from *The Personnel Manager's Complete Model Letter Book,* by Mary Cook, Prentice Hall 1989, and are used by permission of the publisher.

Tips for Disciplinary Action or Discharge Letters

- Get the facts right and state them succinctly.
- Act on and write about first-hand information only, not hearsay.
- Get directly to the point. Don't be vague and don't get "on your soapbox."
- Provide the reasons for discipline or termination but don't agonize over the details.
- Convince the employee there is only one course of action, and help the employee to understand the reasons behind the discipline or termination.

Be careful of statements made to employees in writing. Such statements might be construed as inappropriate or even illegal and later used against your company.

DISCIPLINARY ACTION: SUSPENSION WITHOUT PAY

Date

Mr. John Simpson
60241 Green Lane
Montgomery, AL 36130

Dear John:

This letter is to inform you that you are hereby suspended from your job without pay for three working days commencing March 15. This disciplinary action is being taken based on the following facts:

- You fell asleep on your job on February 26 and left power equipment in the plant unattended for over an hour.
- This is the second such incident in 30 days.

Your conduct as described above constitutes sufficient cause for disciplinary action. In addition, you have been disciplined in the past for the same problem.

Your formal disciplinary action is:

- Suspension without pay for three consecutive working days beginning March 15.

A copy of this letter will be placed in your personnel file. You have the right to respond in writing to this information or arguments rebutting this suspension. If you choose to respond, you have until 5:00 P.M. on April 1 to do so. Your response, if any, will be given consideration. It is assumed that you have waived the right to respond if you do not take advantage of the above alternative.

The purpose of this suspension is to impress upon you the seriousness with which we regard the above violation of employment and to give you the opportunity to reflect upon your future compliance with our employment standards. One more violation of the conditions of your employment will result in termination.

Sincerely,

Karen True
Director Human Resources

DISCIPLINARY ACTION: SIX-MONTH EVALUATION

Date

Dale L. Bradley
8796 Dawn Drive
Brooklyn, NY 11210

Dear Dale:

The purpose of this letter is to describe the events that have occurred over the past several weeks which have resulted in the need for disciplinary action, and to inform you of the conduct required on your part for continued employment with ROC.

On Thursday, January 19th, you left your work assignment in Washington, D.C. without permission from your supervisor, and traveled to Miami, Florida, for personal reasons. On February 1st, you submitted your expense report to your supervisor and falsified the dates that you were on the job in Washington, D.C.

Inconsistencies between your expense report and the hotel receipt were noticed by our supervisor. When questioned about this, you admitted that you had left Washington, D.C. and then falsified the expense statement.

As we discussed, such acts of deception are unacceptable and will not be permitted by either myself or the executive management of ROC. Accordingly, I am placing you on disciplinary notice for a period of six months from the date of this letter. During this period, l will carefully monitor your work activities.

Any further incidents observed during this period that are contrary to acceptable standards of behavior could result in your dismissal.

Dale, we want you to succeed, and we hope that your acknowledgment of the seriousness of this situation will have a positive result on your future at ROC.

Sincerely,

Stanley Bishop
Human Resources Director

PREVENTING DISCRIMINATION COMPLAINTS

What do the EEOC and State Civil Rights Agencies Look for When Investigating a Discharge Complaint?

Answering that question will give you a good idea as to how discharge complaints may be prevented and defended. As you read the following questions, which must be answered in writing by employers charged with a discharge complaint, you'll realize how government agencies look at discharges yourself. Ask these questions. Can you justify the discharge? Was it fair? Was it in line with company policies? Was it in line with the way others have been treated? Can you document the reasons for the discharge? The questions asked during an investigation actually provide us with a good checklist to evaluate how tight our discharge procedures are or, on the other hand, how vulnerable we are to discrimination complaints and violations. It's better to consider these questions now than learn about the government's concerns the hard way after a complaint is filed. In the following paragraphs, the term **complainant** relates to the person filing the complaint. The **respondent** is the employer.

- *State the specific reason(s) why complainant was discharged.* Note the word "specific" in the question. Giving reasons which are vague and general will not do. Terms such as "bad attitude" or "uncooperativeness" are too general.

- *State the date and time of discharge.*

- *Explain in detail each specific act for which the complainant was discharged.* Here it will be impossible to be vague. The government will want to know about each specific act. Do you have a record of each act? Referring to it would be a lot easier and more credible than relying on your memory, especially if the acts occurred over a period of months or years.

- *For each act listed above state the name, address, race, national origin, sex and phone number of the witness(es) to the act(s) and the date(s) of the act(s).* The government will not depend solely upon your knowledge of what happened. They also want witnesses to the acts with their phone numbers so that they can be called after working hours. It's also felt that the race, national origin, and sex of the witnesses may be important, since bias may affect their observations. If witnesses are not provided, it's likely that an investigator would try to locate witnesses by obtaining a list of the complainant's coworkers.

- *Attach hereto any and all documentary evidence concerning complainant's discharge, including statements of all witnesses.* You probably realize by now that your ability to justify a discharge is important. Supplying documentary evidence will be a key part of that ability. The government is looking for witnesses' statements, performance evaluation forms, warnings and reprimands, interoffice memos and letters, production records, evidence of poor work quality, customer complaint letters, etc.

- *What explanation did complainant give the respondent for the conduct which gave rise to the discharge?* By asking this question the government is saying, "Did you give the complainant a chance to explain his or her side of the story?" Be sure you can answer yes and give details. A poor response here indicates that the company may have been unfair, since most employees will try to explain their actions before getting fired.

- ***Respondent did not accept this explanation because?*** Be able to show that you actually listened to the explanation and can demonstrate why it was not acceptable. In one actual case an employee was fired because he unfairly accused his boss of discrimination. However, the government viewed the case as an act of reprisal because at no time did the company listen in good faith to the employee's complaints and look into the charges. They simply fired him for a memo he wrote about his boss to a superior.

- ***Does the respondent have written rules and regulations which govern employees' duties and conduct? If yes, attach a copy of any such rules and regulations and indicate the provisions relied upon to justify the discharge.*** Employers will be more able to justify their actions based upon rules and regulations written before the complaint was filed, although it's impossible to have a policy covering all reasons for discharge. The government will be interested in whether the rules were followed in the complainant's case as compared with others.

- ***If no written rules and regulations are established, what are the respondent's policies with respect to the type of conduct involved in the discharge of the complainant?*** Basing a decision on an unwritten policy is a lot less credible than basing it on a written one. In its investigation the government will probably examine witnesses to determine if the unwritten policies do in fact exist.

- ***Does the respondent utilize oral warnings? If so, please state who makes such warnings and specify respondent's policy with respect to them.*** It's much more difficult to support a discharge by pointing to verbal warnings. There will likely be a disagreement over who said what. Also, it's difficult to defend a discharge without any warnings whatsoever except for extreme acts which cause an employee to be fired instantly.

- ***Does the respondent utilize written warnings? If so, please state who makes such warnings and specify respondent's policy with respect to them.*** One or more written warnings made over a period of time prior to a discharge are evidence that the complainant may have been fired for just cause. Also, if a written policy exists, the government wants to know if it was followed with the complainant or if the complainant was treated differently.

- ***Were any warnings made to the complainant? If so, please state the date, person(s) present, and the circumstances under which such warnings were made and attach copies of any record of such warnings to this interrogatory.*** How was the policy enforced? Having a written record of oral warnings makes it possible to answer this question. Having copies of written warnings makes it easy to answer. Having no written record and no copies will make it difficult to answer with credibility.

- ***If one reasons for complainant's discharge was absenteeism or tardiness, attach a copy of complainant's attendance and sick day record and specify what respondent's policy is with respect to absenteeism or tardiness.*** Provide the record of absenteeism and provide the policy. Once the complainant's attendance record is obtained an investigation will probably look at other employee records to make comparisons. Usually the discharged person will know of someone who seems to have been absent or late more often and was not discharged.

- *State the name, address, phone number, race, national origin, and sex of the person who recommended complainant's discharge. What is his job title? How long has he been in this position? How long has he been employed by respondent?* Finally, the investigation centers on you, the supervisor who recommended the discharge. If you have not been in the position long or are the opposite race or sex of the discharged person, it would be hard to justify a recommendation based on subjective argument. However, if policies have been established, their application has been uniform, and the reasoning is well documented, it's highly probable that the complaint would have been either prevented or was dropped after the investigation.

Importance of Being Uniform

How many reasons are there for justifying the firing of an employee? Ten? Twenty? It's probably impossible to list them all. And even if we could manage to write down all the possible reasons and put them into a policy, it would surely be overly rigid and unworkable. It is this fact which brings about one of the most bothersome problems confronting supervisors and the major cause of discrimination complaints relating to discharge: lack of uniformity.

Some managers make the mistake of looking at the discharge of a worker in isolation. They simply ask, "Is this person's performance or behavior such that he or she should be fired?" But from the point of view of how discrimination laws are enforced, answering this question is not enough. One must go further and wonder, "Is it fair to fire this person considering the way others have been treated for doing the same thing?" It's not enough to find out if a company rule has been violated and if that is deserving of discharge. Government agencies and the courts will assume that the "rule was applied to accomplish an illegal purpose" if a protected class member was treated differently than others in the way standards were applied. The differential treatment will be seen as unlawful.

Keep the issue of uniformity in mind at all times. Remember that fairness is a major consideration of anyone responsible for directing the actions of others. Try to take an objective look at what has happened in the past so that uniformity can be maintained. This is true not only when thinking about the reason for discharge but the manner of discharge as well.

Before recommending a discharge be able to give a "yes" answer to each of the following questions:

- Have other employees performing similarly or worse also been discharged?
- Have other employees committing similar or worse offenses also been discharged?
- Was this employee given the same amount of warnings or reprimands as other employees in similar situations?
- Was this employee given the same amount and kind of training, opportunities, and equipment as other employees in similar situations?

You should consult with your Human Resources executive to determine these answers before you make a final decision in a discipline or termination.

POLICY AGAINST HARASSMENT

The Company strictly prohibits harassment of any of our employees, applicants, suppliers or customers. Any form of harassment related to an individual's race, color, sex, gender, sexual orientation, religion, age, national origin, disability or citizenship status or other protected status is a violation of this policy and will be treated as a disciplinary matter. Harassment may take many forms, but the most common forms include:

- Offensive verbal conduct, such as remarks, comments, jokes or slurs pertaining to an individual's race, color, sex, gender, sexual orientation, religion, age, national origin, disability or citizenship status or other protected status.

- Offensive sexual remarks, sexual advances or requests for sexual favors regardless of the gender of the individuals involved.

- Offensive physical conduct, including touching, staring and blocking, regardless of the gender of the individuals involved.

- Offensive visual conduct, including the display of pictures, drawings or photographs or other communications, including e-mail, Internet programs or websites.

- Threatening reprisals for an employee's refusal to respond to requests for sexual favors or for reporting a violation of this policy.

Any violation of this policy may subject an employee to disciplinary action, up to and including termination. If you have questions about what constitutes harassing behavior or what conduct is prohibited by this policy, you should discuss them with your supervisor or your human resources representative.

Harassment of our employees in connection with their work by non-employees is also a violation of this policy. Any employee who experiences or observes any harassment of an employee by a non-employee should report such harassment to his or her supervisor. An investigation will be conducted and appropriate action will be taken.

Following are suggested procedures for investigating sexual harassment. If you do not have a policy or investigative procedures in place you may want to consult a labor attorney.

INVESTIGATING CLAIMS OF SEXUAL HARASSMENT

Every claim of sexual harassment must be immediately investigated. Your company should designate an executive or manager (usually the HR manager) to conduct the investigation and decide how the results of the investigation will be communicated to the parties involved. Following is a step-by-step guide on how the investigation might proceed.

Step 1 Interview the complainant. What does he or she say happened? (Usually the complainant is a female, but that is not always the case—in order to simplify this guide I use the term "she"). Who is named as harasser? Where and when did the incident take place? What exactly did happen? How did complainant react? When did she report the incident and to whom did she report it? Were there witnesses. Was this an isolated incident or part of a series? Has she spoken to anyone else about the incident?

Step 2   Interview the accused harasser(s). Remain objective. Assume nothing. Put every statement in writing. Remember that your notes may end up in court.

Step 3   Interview all witnesses. Be careful to phrase your questions so that you don't give any information or influence responses. For example, it's better to say, "Did you hear anyone say anything to Susan that was suggestive or made her uncomfortable?" Rather than "Did you hear Bill proposition Susan?"

Step 4   Consider the credibility of each person you talk to and weigh the evidence. Consider the reputation of each person you question and also the reputation of the alleged harasser(s). Is there any possibility that the employee is trying to make trouble for the alleged harasser? Are there previous complaints against the accused harasser? Have you investigated the charge as thoroughly as you can?

Step 5   Take action. Once you have all the facts, ask yourself if sexual harassment did occur. If you decide the accusation is without merit, write a detailed report explaining why and include the evidence to back up your findings. Have a one-on-one private meeting with the complainant and provide a copy of your report. File a copy of the investigative report in the complainant's personnel file. If your investigation revealed that harassment did occur, you have several options based on the severity of the case.

Here are some options:

Option 1   First offense - written warning to harasser(s). The warning should include a statement that sexual harassment is against company policy, and that any additional complaints will result in disciplinary action, up to discharge. The complainant should be aware of any action taken against the harasser. Follow-up is absolutely essential to make sure the harassment stops.

Option 2   Consider transferring the accused or offering a transfer to the complainant if that is something the complainant would like. Make sure if you offer a transfer to the complainant and she accepts it, that the transfer doesn't look like retaliation. The complainant must accept the transfer as a positive resolution to the harassment.

Option 3   Suspension or discharge is usually reserved for repeated offenses or a severe first offense. Make sure the punishment fits the severity of the act. Be consistent in the penalties you impose. You can't fire one manager for sexual harassment and suspend or transfer another for an identical offense.

Be sure to document the investigation and the actions taken to resolve the problem. The importance of consistency cannot be overstated. Consistency and fairness are the two most important issues.

8

SAFETY, ACCIDENT REPORTING, AND OSHA REGULATIONS

- Occupational Safety and Health Administration's Leading Violations

- Employer Obligations for Reporting Occupational Injuries and Illness Under OSHA

- Sample Guide to Accident and Injury Reporting

- Guide to Compliance with the Federal OSHA Hazard Communication Standard

- Accident Reporting Forms

- Glossary of Occupational Safety and Health Terminology

SAFETY, ACCIDENT REPORTING, AND OSHA REGULATIONS

All organizations have a responsibility to maintain a safe workplace. Some of the areas of accident prevention are proper engineering controls, preventive maintenance, and employee safety training. The following are some basic safety procedures:

- Plants and manufacturing facilities must have good preventive maintenance programs for production and other equipment.
- Supervisors should be required to inspect work areas every day. This can be an informal inspection but should be seriously carried out.
- Worker-management teams using checklists should inspect monthly or quarterly.
- Formal plant and office safety audits should be completed annually with ultimate reporting responsibility to top management.
- Management should encourage employees to report hazards and provide an avenue for them to do so.
- Training and retraining on a regular basis including employees and supervisors should be mandatory.
- Offices and plants should be clean, well designed, and controlled for noise, heat, dust, fumes, and hazardous waste.
- OSHA has toughened exposure limits on 376 toxic chemicals in the workplace. OSHA's Hazards Communication Standards require every workplace in the country to identify hazardous substances on the premises, list them, and train employees in their use. This law applies to all employers—from accountants to zookeepers.

OCCUPATIONAL SAFETY AND HEALTH ADMINISTRATION'S LEADING VIOLATIONS

The ten most common workplace OSHA violations according to Department of Labor Statistics are:

1. No posting of the OSHA notice of employer obligations.
2. No grounding of electrical equipment connected by cord and plug.
3. No machinery guards at point of operation.
4. No guards for pulleys.

5. No guards for live parts of electrical equipment.

6. No enclosures for blades of fans in use less than 7 feet above floor of working level.

7. No guards for belt, rope, and chain drives.

8. Disorderliness in aisles and passageways.

9. No guards for vertical and inclined belts.

10. Not maintaining a log and summary of job injuries and illnesses.

EMPLOYER OBLIGATIONS FOR REPORTING OCCUPATIONAL INJURIES AND ILLNESS UNDER OSHA

The Occupational Safety and Health (OSHA) Act of 1970 requires covered employers to prepare and maintain records of occupational injuries and illnesses. The Bureau of Labor Statistics of the U.S. Department of Labor is responsible for administering the recordkeeping system established by the act. The OSHA Act and record keeping regulations in 29 CFR 1904 provide specific recording and reporting requirements which comprise the framework of the OSHA recording system.

Some employers may be subject to additional record keeping and reporting requirements not covered in this report. Many specific standards and regulations of the Occupational Safety and Health Administration (OSHA) have additional requirements for the maintenance and retention of records for medical surveillance, exposure monitoring inspections, and other activities and incidents relevant to occupational safety and health, and for the reporting of certain information to employees and to OSHA. For information on these requirements employers should refer directly to the OSHA standards and regulations or contact their OSHA regional office.

Annual Survey of Occupational Injuries and Illnesses

Section 8(c)(2) of the Act requires employers to make periodic reports of deaths, injuries, and illnesses which have been recorded on the OSHA injury and illness records. This periodic reporting is accomplished through the Annual Survey of Occupational Injuries and Illnesses conducted by the Bureau of Labor Statistics.

The annual survey provides measures of the occurrence and the extent of recordable occupational injuries and illnesses. Injuries and illnesses are reported as either fatalities, lost workday cases, or nonfatal cases without lost workdays.

Measures produced by the survey include incidence rates and numbers of occupational injuries and illnesses. Incidence rates relate the numbers of injuries, illnesses, or lost workdays to a common base of exposure. They show the equivalent number of injuries and illnesses or lost workdays per 100 full-time workers. This common base enables accurate interindustry comparisons, trend analysis over time, and comparisons among firms regardless of size.

This survey is conducted on a sample basis, and firms required to submit reports of their injury and illness experience are contacted by BLS or a participating state agency.

A firm not contacted by its state agency or BLS need not file a report of its injury and illness experience. Employers should note, however, that even if they are not selected to participate in the annual survey for a given year, they must still comply with the record keeping requirements as well as with the requirements for reporting fatalities and multiple hospitalization cases.

Participants in the annual survey consist of two categories of employers: (1) employers who maintain OSHA records on a regular basis; and (2) a small, rotating sample of employers who are regularly exempt from OSHA record keeping. The survey procedure is different for these two groups of employers.

Participation of Firms Regularly Maintaining OSHA Records When employers regularly maintaining OSHA records are selected to participate in the Annual Survey of Occupational Injuries and Illnesses, they are mailed the survey questionnaire in February of the year following the reference calendar year of the survey. The survey form, the Occupational Injuries and Illnesses Survey Questionnaire, OSHA No. 200-S, requests information about the establishment(s) included in the report and the injuries and illnesses experienced during the previous year. Information for the injury and illness portion of the report form can usually be copied directly from the totals on the log and summary, OSHA Form 200, which the employer should have completed and posted in the establishment by the time the questionnaire arrives. The survey form also requests summary information about the type of business activity and number of employees and hours worked.

Participation of Normally Exempt Small Employers and Employers in Low-Hazard Industries A few regularly exempt employers (those with fewer than 11 employees and those in designated low-hazard industries) are also required to participate in the annual survey in order to produce injury and illness statistics that are comparable in coverage to the statistics published in years prior to the reference calendar year of the survey. These employers must maintain injury and illness records for the coming year.

SAMPLE GUIDE TO ACCIDENT AND INJURY REPORTING

If you are a small company with only one location, you may not need a formal guide to accident and injury reporting. However, if you have more than one location and are a fast-growing business, you may want to provide uniform guidelines so that all supervisors at all of your locations will handle injury reporting in the same manner.

Having such a guide could save money and unnecessary delay should a crisis arise. Even one single automobile or truck accident that an employee or supervisor mishandles could cost hundreds of thousands of dollars. As you grow you'll want to consider a more formal risk management program, but if you are still a small or medium-sized organization the guide that follows will be helpful. Modify the guide to fit your specific needs. Review your accident insurance policies and federal and state regulations as you rewrite this guideline to ensure you are in compliance in each area.

GUIDE TO COMPLIANCE WITH THE FEDERAL OSHA HAZARD COMMUNICATION STANDARD

Federal OSHA recently expanded the coverage of their Hazard Communication Standard (HCS). The HCS now applies to virtually all commercial workplaces where workers use or may be exposed to hazardous chemicals.

The HCS says that each employer has to prepare a written hazard communication program. The employer must make the written program available to the workers upon request, and it will probably be the first thing an OSHA inspector will want to see. Here is an outline that can serve as a checklist of the items which must be included in this program.

Responsible Person(s). Identify by job title who has duties to perform in file preparation and maintenance, in training, in labeling containers, etc.

Hazardous Chemicals List. Prepare a list of all the chemical product in your operation which could be considered hazardous. Look for label information such as "DANGER", "WARNING" or "CAUTION" and check other information on the product. The list should say where the product is stored and where it is used.

MSDS File. Prepare a file of Material Safety Data Sheets (MSDS) for the hazardous products. Request from your supplier any MSDS you do not have in the file. To be sure you cover the hazardous products, it is really a good idea to have an MSDS for every product.

Container Labels. Insure that all containers of hazardous products are marked with the name of the product as it appears on the corresponding MSDS. The container label must include appropriate hazard warnings.

Note:

This labeling requirement does not include containers filled and used by the same person during one work shift. Nevertheless, it is always good to have all containers marked to avoid mix-ups.

Non-Routine Situation. Develop plans and practices for non-routine situations where a person could be exposed to a hazardous chemical. This happens when an employee works on an occasional job such as maintenance or tank cleanouts, and also when employees of a contractor come on-site for special work.

Worker Training. Employee training must cover at least:

- Which products they use that are hazardous and what the physical and health hazards are.
- How they can tell by noting spills, smells, physical discomfort, etc. when a hazardous chemical is released in the workplace.
- What they should do to protect themselves when working with these products.
- What the MSDS is and how to get information from it.
- The details of the written program, the location and availability of the program and the MSDS file.

Any new employee must be trained before starting to work with hazardous chemicals, and any affected employee should have a training update to cover new hazardous products being introduced. It is a good idea to document these training sessions listing who was there and what was covered. Most compliance inspections will start by reviewing your records, so record keeping is important.

Guide to Accident and Injury Reporting

(COMPANY NAME)

(DATE)

CONTENTS

- Purpose
- Definitions
- General
- Accident Reporting
- Physical Examination
- Injury Report/Investigation Form
- Accident Reporting Forms

PURPOSE

The purpose of this guide is to provide a source of information for the supervisor to assist in complying with corporate policy and federal and state laws concerning the reporting of work related injuries.

DEFINITIONS

- For the purpose of this guide, a work *injury* is any injury including occupational disease and other work-connected disability which arises out of and in the course of employment.
- A *day of disability* (lost time) is any day on which an employee is unable, because of injury, to perform effectively throughout a full shift the essential functions of a regularly established job which is open and available to him/her.
- American National Standard Z16.1, Method of Recording and Measuring Work Injury Experience, shall be used as a reference in all work-related injuries or illnesses.

GENERAL

In order to comply with both workers compensation and OSHA regulations, certain forms must be completed and procedures and time guidelines followed.

ACCIDENT REPORTING

Fatality

1. Report immediately by telephone to the supervisor or the Personnel Department and to the police department where the death occurred.
2. Follow up with written report of Injury using Injury Report and Investigation Form, and the OSHA Form 200 and send copies to the Personnel Department.

Medical Treatment for Accident or Injury

- Employees will be notified by a bulletin board posting and verbally by their supervisors that injuries occurring in the course of regular employment must be immediately reported to their supervisor.

- Emergency first aid treatment will be given by a supervisor certified in first aid. It will be the duty of the supervisor providing first aid to determine whether further medical treatment is warranted.
- Injuries requiring the attention of a person qualified to administer first aid, a nurse, or physician must be reported by phone to the Personnel Department within 24 hours.
- Completion of the Injury Report, the Investigation Form, and OSHA Form 200 is required in these cases and is to be forwarded to the Personnel Department within 24 hours of injury.

PHYSICAL EXAMINATION

The following employees must be found physically fit by a company physician before being allowed to return to work:

- All employees returning to work after absence for work-related accident or injury.
- All employees returning to work after absence of 30 working days because of illness, injury, or disability regardless of cause. The Personnel Department at its discretion may require a physical examination for anyone who has been absent from work with a contagious disease.
- Employees in jobs running machinery or critical quality control equipment when returning to work after drug or alcohol abuse rehabilitation.

INJURY REPORT/INVESTIGATION FORM

Data provided on the Injury Report and Investigation Form is required for the completion of other reports and forms for workers compensation.

Procedure

The Injury Report and Investigation Form is divided into eight sections. The responsibility for completion and information required is as follows:

Section 1: The basic information is to be supplied by the supervisor, who may find it necessary to check the employee personnel file for complete and accurate information.

Section 2: This section is to be completed by the injured employee, in his or her own handwriting, describing the events and conditions contributing to the injury. If the employee is unable to write as a result of the injury an oral statement may be obtained and entered on the form by the supervisor.

Section 3: The medical disposition of the employee must be entered in this section by the supervisor or attending physician.

Section 4: After a thorough investigation of the accident and its probable cause, the supervisor completes this portion.

Section 5: The supervisor is to check the appropriate square or squares indicating the unsafe act or unsafe conditions which contributed to the accident. Company management wants to ensure that any unsafe work areas or equipment are immediately attended to and brought up to standard.

Section 6: Again, the supervisor is to show why the unsafe act or conditions existed and what steps are to be taken to correct the situation. The estimated completion date sets goals and is intended to create a commitment to remedy the situation causing the accident or injury.

Section 7: The name of the person responsible for assuring the recommended action is taken.

Section 8: The department head and personnel safety representative are to sign indicating their satisfaction that the information is complete and an effective remedy has been implemented.

Complete the form and forward to the Personnel Department within 72 hours of injury.

ACCIDENT REPORTING FORMS

The following are sample forms for use in safety reporting. Modify them to fit your specific needs. Ask your supervisors to help design the forms. They will have to use them and will be more likely to accept them if they took part in their design and implementation. It is a good idea to form a safety committee comprised mainly of supervisors. Ask them to meet on a regular basis to review safety problems and accident report forms. Keep the committee small and workable and ask for feedback to management on safety issues.

Manager's Tip

All safety and accident reports must be filled out completely and accurately. You never know when the incident might blow up into a major case costing hundreds of thousands of dollars. Your documentation then becomes all-important and directly impacts your bottom-line. Insist that your supervisors be thorough in creating documentation records and maintaining files.

INJURY REPORT AND INVESTIGATION FORM

1

DATE: _____ OFFICE: _____ STATE: _____

EMPLOYEE'S NAME: _____ AGE: _____ DATE OF BIRTH: _____ ____ SEX: M F

ADDRESS: _____ SOC. SEC. NO. _____

DATE OF INJURY: _____ TIME: _____ DATE INJURY REPORTED: _____

DEPARTMENT ASSIGNED: _____ SUPERVISOR'S NAME: _____

DATE HIRED: _____ LENGTH OF TIME ON PRESENT JOB: _____

2

DID YOU HAVE AN INJURY IN THE COURSE OF YOUR EMPLOYMENT?   YES: _____ NO: _____

DESCRIBE HOW ACCIDENT OCCURRED: (WHAT, HOW, OBJECT OR SUBSTANCE INVOLVED) _____

_____

_____

_____

_____

_____

_____ EMPLOYEE'S SIGNATURE: _____ DATE: _____

3

DISPOSITION	YES	NO
DISABLING INJURY:		
SENT TO HOSPITAL		
SENT TO COMPANY DOCTOR		
RETURN TO REGULAR JOB		
RETURN TO LIGHT DUTY JOB		
RECORDABLE ON OSHA FORM 100		

ESTIMATED DAYS OF DISABILITY: _____

DATE TO RETURN TO WORK: _____

INITIAL MEDICAL DIAGNOSIS: _____

_____

IF HOSPITALIZED, NAME & ADDRESS OF HOSPITAL:

_____

_____

BODY PART INJURED

☐ EYE
☐ HEAD
☐ CHEST
☐ BACK
☐ ABDOMEN
☐ ARM
☐ HAND - FINGER
☐ LEG
☐ FOOT - TOE
☐ RESPIRATORY SYSTEM
☐ _____

TYPE OF INJURY

☐ LACERATION
☐ ABRASION
☐ PUNCTURE
☐ BURN
☐ FRACTURE
☐ STRAIN - SPRAIN
☐ AMPUTATION
☐ FOREIGN BODY
☐ HERNIA
☐ CONTUSION
☐ _____

ATTENDING PHYSICIAN OR MEDICAL ATTENTION: _____

4

SUPERVISOR'S DESCRIPTION OF ACCIDENT AFTER INVESTIGATION: (Note if employee was wearing required personal protective equipment)

_____

_____

_____

_____

8

_____	SUPERVISOR'S SIGNATURE DATE
EMPLOYEE RELATIONS (Signature) DATE	FUNCTIONAL HEAD (Signature) DATE

ALL ACCIDENTS ARE THE RESULT OF UNSAFE ACTS AND/OR UNSAFE CONDITIONS.
INVESTIGATE THOROUGHLY AND CHECK THE APPROPRIATE CAUSES BELOW.

YES	NO	UNSAFE ACT	UNSAFE CONDITION	YES	
		LACK OF SKILL OR KNOWLEDGE	IMPROPER MATERIAL STORAGE		
		UNSAFE ACT OF OTHER	CONGESTION - LACK OF SPACE		
		PHYSICAL LIMITATION OR MENTAL ATTITUDE	IMPROPER AND/OR WORN TOOLS AND EQUIPMENT		
		FAILURE TO USE PROPER TOOLS OR EQUIPMENT	UNSAFE DESIGN AND/OR CONSTRUCTION		
		FAILURE TO WEAR PERSONAL PROTECTIVE EQUIPMENT	UNSAFE CONDITION OF MACHINE		
		UNAWARE OF HAZARDS	IMPROPER GUARDING		
		SHORT CUT TO SAVE TIME OR EFFORT	IMPROPER JOB PROCEDURE		
		UNSAFE MATERIAL HANDLING	UNSAFE FLOORS, RAMPS, STAIRWAYS		
		OTHER:	IMPROPER LIGHTING		
			OTHER:		

5

WHAT WAS DONE UNSAFELY?   WHAT UNSAFE CONDITION EXISTED?

WHY WAS IT DONE THAT WAY?   WHY DID THESE CONDITIONS EXIST?

6

HOW WILL WE CONTROL THE ABOVE?   HOW WILL WE CORRECT THESE CONDITIONS?

ESTIMATED COMPLETION DATE: ESTIMATED COMPLETION DATE:

WHO WILL ASSUME RESPONSIBILITY FOR CONTROL?   WHO WILL ASSUME RESPONSIBILITY FOR CORRECTION?
BE SPECIFIC: BE SPECIFIC:

7

U.S. Department of Labor

For Calendar Year 19 _____   Page _____ of _____

Company Name

Establishment Name

Establishment Address

Form Approved
O.M.B. No. 44R 1453

Extent of and Outcome of INJURY						Type, Extent of, and Outcome of ILLNESS												
Fatalities	Nonfatal Injuries					Type of Illness								Fatalities	Nonfatal Illnesses			
Injury Related	Injuries With Lost Workdays				Injuries Without Lost Workdays	CHECK Only One Column for Each Illness *(See other side of form for terminations or permanent transfers.)*								Illness Related	Illnesses With Lost Workdays			Illnesses Without Lost Workdays
Enter DATE of death. Mo./day/yr.	Enter a CHECK if injury involves days away from work, or days of restricted work activity, or both.	Enter a CHECK if injury involves days away from work.	Enter number of DAYS away from work.	Enter number of DAYS of restricted work activity.	Enter a CHECK if no entry was made in columns 1 or 2 but the injury is recordable as defined above.	Occupational skin diseases or disorders	Dust diseases of the lungs	Respiratory conditions due to toxic agents	Poisoning (systemic effects of toxic materials)	Disorders due to physical agents	Disorders associated with repeated trauma	All other occupational illnesses		Enter DATE of death. Mo./day/yr.	Enter a CHECK if illness involves days away from work, or days of restricted work activity, or both.	Enter a CHECK if illness involves days away from work.	Enter number of DAYS away from work.	Enter number of DAYS of restricted work activity.	Enter a CHECK if no entry was made in columns 8 or 9.
(1)	(2)	(3)	(4)	(5)	(6)	(a)	(b)	(c)	(d)	(e)	(f)	(g)	(8)	(9)	(10)	(11)	(12)	(13)
										(7)								

INJURIES   ILLNESSES

Certification of Annual Summary Totals By _____ Title _____ Date _____

FOLD

OSHA No. 200   **POST ONLY THIS PORTION OF THE LAST PAGE NO LATER THAN FEBRUARY 1.**

Bureau of Labor Statistics
Log and Summary of Occupational
Injuries and Illnesses

NOTE:	This form is required by Public Law 91-596 and must be kept in the establishment for 5 years. Failure to maintain and post can result in the issuance of citations and assessment of penalties. *(See posting requirements on the other side of form.)*			RECORDABLE CASES: You are required to record information about every occupational death; every nonfatal occupational illness; and those nonfatal occupational injuries which involve one or more of the following: loss of consciousness, restriction of work or motion, transfer to another job, or medical treatment (other than first aid). *(See definitions on the other side of form.)*	

Case or File Number	Date of Injury or Onset of Illness	Employee's Name	Occupation	Department	Description of Injury or Illness
Enter a nondupli-cating number which will facilitate com-parisons with supple-mentary records.	Enter Mo./day.	Enter first name or initial, middle initial, last name.	Enter regular job title, not activity employee was per-forming when injured or at onset of illness. In the absence of a formal title, enter a brief description of the employee's duties.	Enter department in which the employee is regularly employed or a description of normal workplace to which employee is assigned, even though temporarily working in another depart-ment at the time of injury or illness.	Enter a brief description of the injury or illness and indicate the part or parts of body affected. Typical entries for this column might be: Amputation of 1st joint right forefinger; Strain of lower back; Contact dermatitis on both hands; Electrocution—body.
(A)	(B)	(C)	(D)	(E)	(F)
					PREVIOUS PAGE TOTALS ➔
					TOTALS (Instructions on other side of form) ➔

OSHA No. 200

Instructions for OSHA No. 200

I. **Log and Summary of Occupational Injuries and Illnesses**

Each employer who is subject to the recordkeeping requirements of the Occupational Safety and Health Act of 1970 must maintain for each establishment a log of all recordable occupational injuries and illnesses. This form (OSHA No. 200) may be used for that purpose. A substitute for the OSHA No. 200 is acceptable if it is as detailed, easily readable, and understandable as the OSHA No. 200.

Enter each recordable case on the log within six (6) workdays after learning of its occurrence. Although other records must be maintained at the establishment to which they refer, it is possible to prepare and maintain the log at another location, using data processing equipment if desired. If the log is prepared elsewhere, a copy updated to within 45 calendar days must be present at all times in the establishment.

Logs must be maintained and retained for five (5) years following the end of the calendar year to which they relate. Logs must be available (normally at the establishment) for inspection and copying by representatives of the Department of Labor, or the Department of Health, Education and Welfare, or States accorded jurisdiction under the Act.

II. **Changes in Extent of or Outcome of Injury or Illness**

If, during the 5-year period the log must be retained, there is a change in an extent and outcome of an injury or illness which affects entries in columns 1, 2, 6, 8, 9, or 13, the first entry should be lined out and a new entry made. For example, if an injured employee at first required only medical treatment but later lost workdays away from work, the check in column 6 should be lined out, and checks entered in columns 2 and 3 and the number of lost workdays entered in column 4.

In another example, if an employee with an occupational illness lost workdays, returned to work, and then died of the illness, the entries in columns 9 and 10 should be lined out and the date of death entered in column 8.

The entire entry for an injury or illness should be lined out if later found to be nonrecordable. For example: an injury or illness which is later determined not to be work related, or which was initially thought to involve medical treatment but later was determined to have involved only first aid.

III. **Posting Requirements**

A copy of the totals and information following the fold line of the last page for the year must be posted at each establishment in the place or places where notices to employees are customarily posted. This copy must be posted no later than *February 1 and must remain in place until March 1*.

Even though there were no injuries or illnesses during the year, zeros must be entered on the totals line, and the form posted.

The person responsible for the *annual summary totals* shall certify that the **totals are true** and complete by signing at the bottom of the form.

IV. **Instructions for Completing Log and Summary of Occupational Injuries and Illnesses**

Column A — CASE OR FILE NUMBER. Self-explanatory.

Column B — DATE OF INJURY OR ONSET OF ILLNESS.

For occupational injuries, enter the date of the work accident which resulted in injury. For occupational illnesses, enter the date of initial diagnosis of illness, or, if absence from work occurred before diagnosis, enter the first day of the absence attributable to the illness which was later diagnosed or recognized.

Columns
C through F — Self-explanatory.

Columns
1 and 8 — INJURY OR ILLNESS-RELATED DEATHS.
Self-explanatory.

Columns
2 and 9 — INJURIES OR ILLNESSES WITH LOST WORKDAYS.
Self-explanatory.

Any injury which involves days away from work, or days of restricted work activity, or both must be recorded since it always involves one or more of the criteria for recordability.

Columns
3 and 10 — INJURIES OR ILLNESSES INVOLVING DAYS AWAY FROM WORK. Self-explanatory.

Columns
4 and 11 — LOST WORKDAYS––DAYS AWAY FROM WORK.

Enter the number of workdays (consecutive or not) on which the employee would have worked but could not because of occupational injury or illness. The number of lost workdays should not include the day of injury or onset of illness or any days on which the employee would not have worked even though able to work.

NOTE: For employees not having a regularly scheduled shift, such as certain truck drivers, construction workers, farm labor, casual labor, part-time employees, etc., it may be necessary to estimate the number of lost workdays. Estimates of lost workdays shall be based on prior work history of the employee AND days worked by employees, not ill or injured, working in the department and/or occupation of the ill or injured employee.

Columns
5 and 12 — LOST WORKDAYS––DAYS OF RESTRICTED WORK ACTIVITY.

Enter the number of workdays (consecutive or not) on which because of injury or illness:
(1) the employee was assigned to another job on a temporary basis, or
(2) the employee worked at a permanent job less than full time, or
(3) the employee worked at a permanently assigned job but could not perform all duties normally connected with it.

The number of lost workdays should not include the day of injury or onset of illness or any days on which the employee would not have worked even though able to work.

Columns
6 and 13 — INJURIES OR ILLNESSES WITHOUT LOST WORKDAYS. Self-explanatory.

Columns 7a
through 7g — TYPE OF ILLNESS.
Enter a check in only *one* column for each illness.

TERMINATION OR PERMANENT TRANSFER—Place an asterisk to the right of the entry in columns 7a through 7g (type of illness) which represented a termination of employment or permanent transfer.

V. Totals

Add number of entries in columns 1 and 8.
Add number of checks in columns 2, 3, 6, 7, 9, 10, and 13.
Add number of days in columns 4, 5, 11, and 12.
Totals are to be generated for each column at the end of each page and at the end of each year. *Only* the yearly totals are required for posting.

If an employee's loss of workdays is continuing at the time the totals are summarized, estimate the number of future workdays the employee will lose and add that estimate to the workdays already lost and include this figure in the annual totals. No further entries are to be made with respect to such cases in the next year's log.

VI. Definitions

OCCUPATIONAL INJURY is any injury such as a cut, fracture, sprain, amputation, etc., which results from a work accident or from an exposure involving a single incident in the work environment.
NOTE: Conditions resulting from animal bites, such as insect or snake bites or from one-time exposure to chemicals, are considered to be injuries.

OCCUPATIONAL ILLNESS of an employee is any abnormal condition or disorder, other than one resulting from an occupational injury, caused by exposure to environmental factors associated with employment. It includes acute and chronic illnesses or diseases which may be caused by inhalation, absorption, ingestion, or direct contact.

The following listing gives the categories of occupational illnesses and disorders that will be utilized for the purpose of classifying recordable illnesses. For purposes of information, examples of each category are given. These are typical examples, however, and are not to be considered the complete listing of the types of illnesses and disorders that are to be counted under each category.

7a. Occupational Skin Diseases or Disorders
Examples: Contact dermatitis, eczema, or rash caused by primary irritants and sensitizers or poisonous plants; oil acne; chrome ulcers; chemical burns or inflammations; etc.

7b. Dust Diseases of the Lungs (Pneumoconioses)
Examples: Silicosis, asbestosis, coal worker's pneumoconiosis, byssinosis, siderosis, and other pneumoconioses.

7c. Respiratory Conditions Due to Toxic Agents
Examples: Pneumonitis, pharyngitis, rhinitis or acute congestion due to chemicals, dusts, gases, or fumes; farmer's lung; etc.

7d. Poisoning (Systemic Effect of Toxic Materials)
Examples: Poisoning by lead, mercury, cadmium, arsenic, or other metals; poisoning by carbon monoxide, hydrogen sulfide, or other gases; poisoning by benzol, carbon tetrachloride, or other organic solvents; poisoning by insecticide sprays such as parathion, lead arsenate; poisoning by other chemicals such as formaldehyde, plastics, and resins; etc.

7e. Disorders Due to Physical Agents (Other than Toxic Materials)
Examples: Heatstroke, sunstroke, heat exhaustion, and other effects of environmental heat; freezing, frostbite, and effects of exposure to low temperatures; caisson disease; effects of ionizing radiation (isotopes, X-rays, radium); effects of nonionizing radiation (welding flash, ultraviolet rays, microwaves, sunburn); etc.

7f. Disorders Associated With Repeated Trauma
Examples: Noise-induced hearing loss; synovitis, tenosynovitis, and bursitis; Raynaud's phenomena; and other conditions due to repeated motion, vibration, or pressure.

7g. All Other Occupational Illnesses
Examples: Anthrax, brucellosis, infectious hepatitis, malignant and benign tumors, food poisoning, histoplasmosis, coccidioidomycosis, etc.

MEDICAL TREATMENT includes treatment (other than first aid) administered by a physician or by registered professional personnel under the standing orders of a physician. Medical treatment does NOT include first-aid treatment (one-time treatment and subsequent observation of minor scratches, cuts, burns, splinters, and so forth, which do not ordinarily require medical care) even though provided by a physician or registered professional personnel.

ESTABLISHMENT: A single physical location where business is conducted or where services or industrial operations are performed (for example: a factory, mill, store, hotel, restaurant, movie theater, farm, ranch, bank, sales office, warehouse, or central administrative office). Where distinctly separate activities are performed at a single physical location, such as construction activities operated from the same physical location as a lumber yard, each activity shall be treated as a separate establishment.

For firms engaged in activities which may be physically dispersed, such as agriculture; construction; transportation; communications; and electric, gas, and sanitary services, records may be maintained at a place to which employees report each day.

Records for personnel who do not primarily report or work at a single establishment, such as traveling salesmen, technicians, engineers, etc., shall be maintained at the location from which they are paid or the base from which personnel operate to carry out their activities.

WORK ENVIRONMENT is comprised of the physical location, equipment, materials processed or used, and the kinds of operations performed in the course of an employee's work, whether on or off the employer's premises

ACCIDENT/INJURY REPORT

Supervisor must complete report and return to the Human Resource Department within 24 hours.

Name: _____   SSN: _____ - _____ - _____

Date of Accident: Day_____ Mo._____ Yr._____

Time of Accident: _____am/pm

Place of Accident: _____

Witnesses: (if any)   First Aid Given? _____Yes _____No

Name _____   By Whom? _____

Address: _____   Hospitalized? _____Yes _____No

_____   Physician: _____

Phone No.: _____

Nature and extent of injuries: _____

_____

How did accident/injury occur? (Be specific; use extra sheet if necessary): _____

_____

_____

Job or activity engaged in at time of injury (Be specific): _____

_____

_____

Describe any unsafe conditions, methods or practices related to the accident: _____

_____

_____

_____   _____

Employee's Signature   Date

_____   _____

Supervisor's Signature   Date

_____   _____

Department/Company   Location

SUPERVISOR'S REPORT OF ACCIDENT INVESTIGATION
CONFIDENTIAL REPORT—FOR CORPORATE USE ONLY

Injured Employee _____ Date of This Report _____

Job Title _____ Dept _____ Age _____ Sex _____ Length of Employment _____

Date and Time of Accident _____ Exact Location _____

Description of Accident (Detail what employee was doing and what tools, equipment, structures, or fixtures were involved). _____

_____

_____

_____

_____

_____

_____

_____

Nature of Injuries _____

_____

Was report to supervisor of first aid given immediately? _____ Explain _____

_____

_____

Check accident causes on this report; Comment Fully (Use back of this sheet if you need more space).

_____

_____

_____

_____

_____

_____

_____

_____

_____

What should be done, and by whom to prevent recurrence of this type of accident in the future? _____

_____

_____

_____

Supervisor's Signature _____ Date _____
Comments By Department Head or Safety Manager _____

_____

_____

_____

_____

XYZ COMPANY

```
┌─────────────────────────────────────┐
│  Workers' Compensation              │
│  Employee Verification Form         │
└─────────────────────────────────────┘
```

I have been notified by my employer of the procedure to follow in the event I incur a work-related injury or illness. I understand that my employer has designated _____ medical centers as primary providers for all work related injuries and illnesses. I understand that if I do not receive my medical care for work-related injuries and illnesses from _____ medical centers, I may be financially responsible for that care. See attached maps for _____ medical center locations.

I have been informed that authorization is required from my employer before I access medical care for non-emergency, work-related injuries and illnesses.

_____
Name of Employee (Please Print)

_____   _____
Signature of Employee   Date

_____   _____
Signature of Human Resources Administrator   Date

QUARTERLY SAFETY
PERFORMANCE RECORD

For the Period: _____

LOCATION	CURRENT QUARTER			YEAR-TO-DATE			LATEST NATIONAL RATES
	HOURS WORKED	LOST WORK DAY INJURIES	INCIDENCE RATE	HOURS WORKED	LOST WORK DAY INJURIES	INCIDENCE RATE	
TOTALS							
REMARKS	INCIDENCE RATE LOST WORK DAY INJ =		No. OF CASES x 200,000 / HRS. WORKED				

GLOSSARY OF OCCUPATIONAL SAFETY
AND HEALTH TERMINOLOGY

The following glossary of occupational safety and health terminology is provided as a quick reference for supervisors, managers, and others who must complete safety records or deal with OSHA officials. Most business people today need a basic understanding of safety and health language.

Annual summary.   Consists of a copy of the occupational injury and illness totals for the year from the OSHA No. 200, and the following information: The calendar year covered; company name; establishment address; certification signature, title, and date.

Annual survey.   Each year, BLS conducts an annual survey of occupational injuries and illnesses to produce national statistics. The OSHA injury and illness records maintained by employers in their establishments serve as the basis for this survey.

Bureau of Labor Statistics (BLS).   The Bureau of Labor Statistics is the agency responsible for administering and maintaining the OSHA record keeping system and for collecting, compiling, and analyzing work injury and illness statistics.

Certification.   The person who supervises the preparation of the Log and Summary of Occupational Injuries and Illnesses, OSHA No. 200, certifies that it is true and complete by signing the last page of, or by appending a statement to that effect to, the annual summary.

Cooperative program.   A program jointly conducted by the states and the federal government to collect occupational injury and illness statistics.

Employee.   One who is employed in the business of his or her employer affecting commerce.

Employee representative.   Anyone designated by the employee for the purpose of gaining access to the employer's log of occupational injuries and illnesses.

Employer.   Any person engaged in a business affecting commerce who has employees.

Establishment.   A single physical location where business is conducted or where services or industrial operations are performed; the place where the employees report for work, operate from, or from which they are paid.

Exposure.   The reasonable likelihood that a worker is or was subject to some effect, influence, or safety hazard; or in contact with a hazardous chemical or physical agent at a sufficient concentration and duration to produce an illness.

Federal Register.   The official source of information and notification on OSHA's proposed rule making, standards, regulations, and other official matters, including amendments, corrections, insertions, or deletions.

First aid.   Any one-time treatment and subsequent observation of minor scratches, cuts, burns, splinters, and so forth, which do not ordinarily require medical care. Such treatment and observation are considered first aid even though provided by a physician or registered professional personnel.

First report of injury.   A workers compensation form which may qualify as a substitute for the supplementary record, OSHA No. 101.

Incidence rate.   The number of injuries, illnesses, or lost workdays related to a common exposure base of 100 full-time workers. The common exposure base enables one to make accurate interindustry comparisons, trend analysis over time, or comparisons among firms regardless of size. This rate is calculated as:

$$N/EH \times 200,000$$

where:

N   =   number of injuries and/or illnesses or lost workdays

EH   =   total hours worked by all employees during calendar year

200,000   =   base for 100 full-time equivalent workers (working 40 hours per week, 50 weeks per year).

Log and Summary (OSHA No. 200).   The OSHA record keeping form used to list injuries and illnesses and to note the extent of each case.

Lost workday cases.   Cases which involve days away from work or days of restricted work activity, or both.

Lost workdays.   The number of workdays (consecutive or not), beyond the day of injury or onset of illness, the employee was away from work or limited to restricted work activity because of an occupational injury or illness.

1. *Lost workdays—away from work.* The number of workdays (consecutive or not) on which the employee would have worked but could not because of occupational injury or illness.

2. *Lost workdays—restricted work activity.* The number of workdays (consecutive or not) on which, because of injury or illness: (1) the employee was assigned to another job on a temporary basis; (2) the employee worked at a permanent job less than full time; or (3) the employee worked at a permanently assigned job but could not perform all duties normally connected with it.

   The number of days away from work or days of restricted work activity does not include the day of injury or onset of illness or any days on which the employee would not have worked even though able to work.

Low-hazard industries.   Selected industries in retail trade; finance, insurance, and real estate; and services which are regularly exempt from OSHA record keeping. To be included in this exemption, an industry must fall within an SIC not targeted for general schedule inspections and must have an average lost workday case injury rate for a designated 3-year measurement period at or below 75 percent of the U.S. private sector average rate.

Medical treatment.   Includes treatment of injuries administered by physicians, registered professional personnel, or lay persons (i.e., nonmedical personnel). Medical treatment does not include first aid treatment (one-time treatment and subsequent observation of minor scratches, cuts, burns, splinters, and so forth, which do not ordinarily require medical care) even though provided by a physician or registered professional personnel.

Occupational illness. Any abnormal condition or disorder, other than one resulting from an occupational injury, caused by exposure to environmental factors associated with employment. May include acute and chronic illnesses or diseases which may be caused by inhalation, absorption, ingestion, or direct contact. The following categories should be used by employers to classify recordable occupational illnesses on the log in the columns indicated:

Column 7a. Occupational skin diseases or disorders

Examples: Contact dermatitis, eczema, or rash caused by primary irritants and sensitizers or poisonous plants; oil acne; chrome ulcers; chemical burns or inflammations

Column 7b. Dust diseases of the lungs (pneumoconioses)

Examples: Silicosis, asbestosis, and other asbestos-related diseases, coal worker's pneumoconiosis, byssinosis, siderosis, and other pneumoconioses

Column 7c. Respiratory conditions due to toxic agents

Examples: Pneumonitis, pharyngitis, rhinitis or acute congestion due to chemicals, dusts, gases, or fumes; farmer's lung

Column 7d. Poisoning (systemic effects of toxic materials)

Examples: Poisoning by lead, mercury, cadmium, arsenic, or other metals; poisoning by carbon monoxide, hydrogen sulfide, or other gases; poisoning by benzol, carbon tetrachloride, or other organic solvents; poisoning by insecticide sprays such as parathion, lead arsenate; poisoning by other chemicals such as formaldehyde, plastics, and resins

Column 7e. Disorders due to physical agents (other than toxic materials)

Examples: Heatstroke, sunstroke, heat exhaustion, and other effects of environmental heat; freezing, frostbite, and effects of exposure to low temperatures; caisson disease; effects of ionizing radiation (isotopes, X-rays, radium); effects of non ionizing radiation (welding flash, ultra-violet rays, microwaves, sunburn)

Column 7f. Disorders associated with repeated trauma

Examples: Noise-induced hearing loss; synovitis, tenosynovitis, and bursitis; Raynaud's phenomena; and other conditions due to repeated motion, vibration, or pressure

Column 7g. All other occupational illnesses

Examples: Anthrax, brucellosis, infectious hepatitis, malignant and benign tumors, food poisoning, histoplasmosis, coccidioidomycosis

Occupational injury. Any injury such as a cut, fracture, sprain, or amputation which results from a work accident or from a single instantaneous exposure in the work environment. Note: Conditions resulting from animal bites, such as insect or snake bites, and from one-time exposure to chemicals are considered to be injuries.

Occupational injuries and illnesses, extent and outcome. All recordable occupational injuries and illnesses resulting in either:

1. Fatalities, regardless of the time between the injury, or the length of illness, and death;

2. Lost workday cases, other than fatalities, that result in lost workdays; or

3. Nonfatal cases without lost workdays.

Occupational Safety and Health Administration (OSHA). OSHA is responsible for developing, implementing, and enforcing safety and health standards and regulations. OSHA works with employers and employees to foster effective safety and health programs which reduce workplace hazards.

Posting. The annual summary of occupational injuries and illnesses must be posted at each establishment by February 1 and remain in place until March 1 to provide employees with the record of their establishment's injury and illness experience for the previous calendar year.

Premises, employer's. Consist of the employer's total establishment; they include the primary work facility and other areas in the employer's domain such as company storage facilities, cafeterias, and restrooms.

Recordable cases. All work-related deaths and illnesses, and those work-related injuries which result in: loss of consciousness, restriction of work or motion, transfer to another job, or require medical treatment beyond first aid.

Record keeping system. Refers to the nationwide system for recording and reporting occupational injuries and illnesses mandated by the Occupational Safety and Health Act of 1970 and implemented by Title 29, Code of Federal Regulations, Part 1904. This system is the only source of national statistics on job-related injuries and illnesses for the private sector.

Regularly exempt employers. Employers regularly exempt from OSHA record keeping include: (1) all employers with no more than 10 full- or part-time employees at any one time in the previous calendar year; and (2) all employers in retail trade; finance, insurance, and real estate; and services industries; i.e., SICs 52-89 (except building materials and garden supplies, SIC 52; general merchandise and food stores, SICs 53 and 54; hotels and other lodging places, SIC 70; repair services, SICs 75 and 76; amusement and recreation services, SIC 79; and health services, SIC 80). (Note: Some state safety and health laws may require these employers to keep OSHA records.)

Report form. Refers to survey form OSHA No. 200-S which is completed and returned by the surveyed reporting unit.

Restriction of work or motion. Occurs when the employee, because of the result of a job-related injury or illness, is physically or mentally unable to perform all or any part of his or her normal assignment during all or any part of the workday or shift.

Single dose (prescription medication). The measured quantity of a therapeutic agent to be taken at one time.

Small employers. Employers with no more than 10 full-time and/or part-time employees among all the establishments of their firm at any one time during the previous calendar year.

Standard Industrial Classification (SIC). A classification system developed by the Office of Management and Budget, Executive Office of the President, for use in the classification of establishments by type of activity in which engaged. Each establishment is assigned an industry code for its major activity which is determined by the product manufactured or service rendered. Establishments may be classified in 2-, 3-, or 4- digit industries according to the degree of information available.

State (when mentioned alone). Refers to a state of the United States, the District of Columbia, and U.S. territories and jurisdictions.

State agency. State agency administering the OSHA record keeping and reporting system. Many states cooperate directly with BLS in administering the OSHA record keeping and reporting programs. Some states have their own safety and health laws which may impose additional obligations.

Supplementary Record (OSHA No. 101). The form (or equivalent) on which additional information is recorded for each injury and illness entered on the log.

Title 29 of the Code of Federal Regulations, Parts 1900–1999. The parts of the Code of Federal Regulations which contain OSHA regulations.

Volunteers. Workers who are not considered to be employees under the act when they serve of their own free will without compensation.

Work environment. Consists of the employer's premises and other locations where employees are engaged in work-related activities or are present as a condition of their employment. The work environment includes not only physical locations, but also the equipment or materials used by the employee during the course of his or her work.

Workers' compensation systems. State systems that provide medical benefits and/or indemnity compensation to victims of work-related injuries and illnesses.

9

LABOR RELATIONS

- Key Issues In Labor Relations

- Questions and Answers on Retaining Union-Free Status

- What You Should Know About Plant Closings and Layoffs/Sample Labor Relations Letters

- Arbitration of Employment Disputes

- Outsourcing HR Functions

LABOR RELATIONS

The pros and cons of unionization will be debated forever. Whether you are pro-union or against unions is immaterial, what you need to determine in your particular business venture is whether you think your company needs union representation. Most business people feel that they do not need an outside third party telling them how to run their company. However, if employees perceive that they are not being treated fairly, or paid a competitive wage, they may seek third party representation and they have that right.

KEY ISSUES IN LABOR RELATIONS

When does a company need labor relations assistance? When should a small company that is growing formalize personnel policies? When does a company need someone assigned full time to personnel administration and human resource management? There's no simple answer to these questions but the following list will assist any businessperson in determining when a formal human resource management program is needed. When you start asking yourself if you need full-time personnel assistance or an HRM consultant do the following:

Systematically review the current policies (written or unwritten) that are followed in the organization. Are there frequent problems with any of the policies?

- Review the cost of carrying out your policies and procedures. Are the costs reasonable?
- The largest costs of doing business for most small organizations (fewer than 150 people) are employee costs. Review the costs of hiring, retaining, and replacing employees.
- Can existing policies be modified or strengthened by putting them in writing and distributing them to the employees? If they were in writing, would they save managers time from constantly interpreting policy?
- Are policies and current practices consistent with federal, state, and local laws and regulations?
- Are processes available so that employees clearly understand what is expected of them and how they are doing in meeting those expectations?
- What are the lines of up-and-down communication in the organization? Are they open and working? How do you know?
- Do you have a healthy labor relations climate, or do you have ongoing problems?

- Can you use an HR consultant on a part-time basis or do you need a full-time HR manager on staff?

If you do not have a human resource manager, perhaps it is time to hire one. Ask yourself these questions:

1. Is human resource leadership needed?
2. Is authority to make personnel decisions so diffused that it is perceived as unfair and unequal across the company?
3. Are personnel decisions either too inflexible or too loose?
4. Is effective manpower planning done? Do you have the people you need when you need them?
5. Are people receiving the training they need?
6. Are jobs filled from within, including promotions? Is there effective succession planning? Are open jobs posted, or does the company always go outside to fill jobs? If so, employee morale could be affected.
7. Do you have a lot of EEO charges? If so, in which departments and in which jobs? EEO charges can be an indication of human resource problems that should be resolved before they go too far.
8. Are you complying with all state and federal regulations?

These are just some of the questions that should be answered when considering whether to install a full human resource department or to hire a human resource professional. Keep in mind that you may not need a full-time HR manager on staff. Many small and mid-size companies use a personnel consultant part time until they get big enough, (about 250 to 300 employees) to have a full-time person.

QUESTIONS AND ANSWERS ON RETAINING UNION-FREE STATUS

Q.   What does it really mean to a company to remain union-free?

A.   It means the company maintains full control of its operations. It means the human resource function can be administered in an open environment, with direct communication with employees and without third-party intervention.

Q.   What is the key element in remaining union-free?

A.   There are many things that foster a union-free environment, but probably the most important is competitive pay. We've all seen the articles that say pay is far down on the list of priorities for employees, but pay is very important. There are naturally other things that make an employee happy in the job, including:

- Good communications up and down in the company
- Job enrichment
- Participatory management
- A fair and impartial supervisor

- Pleasant work and working conditions
- Good pay and benefits

Q. How far can a company go in saying a union could do more harm than good?

A. It used to be that you walked a fine line between what was permissible and what was not permissible. You needed to be as strong as you could be in saying that a union may not do employees as much good as it claimed, but on the other hand, if you went too far, you ran the risk of having your statements viewed by the National Labor Relations Board as threats, and the company could be ordered to bargain on the grounds that a fair election could not be held. In June 1982, the Board began to announce policy-changing decisions that have affected basic rules of labor law. For example, the National Labor Relations Board will not rule at all now on whether campaign statements made by either side were accurate or inaccurate. The NLRB will continue, however, to set elections aside if:

- Either side uses threats, promises, or the like which interfere with employees' free choice.
- Either side uses a forgery that leaves voting employees unable to tell whether what they are reading is propaganda.
- Official NLRB documents are altered so it appears the board itself is endorsing one side or the other.

The decision that brought about this NLRB change was *The Midland National Life Insurance Company* decision on August 4, 1982.

Another significant decision of the NLRB in 1982 was the *Materials Research* decision, which held that all employees, union or nonunion, have the right to bring help to a meeting or interview that the employee fears may end in discipline. It is incumbent on the employee to ask permission to bring someone to the meeting; however, management has no obligation to advise the employee of the right to help.

What to Do and What Not to Do When the Union Organizer Demands Recognition

A union gains the right to represent your employees:

1. by a secret ballot election conducted by the labor board;
2. by voluntary recognition; or
3. by board-ordered recognition.

In any case, you are required to bargain in good faith with the union over wages, hours, and other terms and conditions of employment.

The union has a right to demand recognition in an appropriate bargaining unit as long as a majority of your employees has signed authorization cards. You have a right to demand a labor board election if you have a good-faith doubt that the union represents a majority of your employees in a unit appropriate for bargaining.

Even when a union does represent a majority of your employees and even when you have a good-faith doubt of its majority, the union can file refusal to bargain charges against you, and the NLRB will order you to bargain without an election if management takes steps to undermine or destroy the union majority by threats or promises to your employees or by committing unfair labor practices that tend to undermine the union's majority.

A union that wants to organize or unionize a group of employees usually tries to persuade the employees to sign authorization cards or a petition. If 30 percent of the employees in an appropriate bargaining unit sign such cards or petitions, the union may petition the National Labor Relations Board for a secret-ballot election in which all eligible employees in the group or unit may vote on whether they want to be represented by the union. However, if more than 50 percent of the employees sign cards or a petition, the union may demand immediate recognition and bargaining from the employer without having to file a petition and prove its majority status in the secret-ballot election. The employer may be forced to accede to this demand and to bargain with the union without an election if the employer makes the wrong move and commits unfair labor practices when the first union contact is made.

A union that has obtained signed authorization cards or a petition from a majority of the employees sometimes demands both recognition and bargaining from the employer and files a petition for an election. Even if the union loses the election, it then may seek an order from the NLRB requiring the employer to recognize and bargain with the union. Thus, the employer's actions after receiving a demand for bargaining must be carefully planned even if the union has also filed a petition for an election.

Once a union has obtained signed authorization cards or a petition from a majority of the employees in an appropriate unit, it almost always will make a demand on the employer for immediate recognition and bargaining. This demand may or may not be a prelude to or be accompanied by the filing of a petition for an election with the NLRB. However, in either case, the manner in which the demand is presented to the employer may vary. It may be by (1) letter, (2) telegram, (3) telephone, (4) personal visit by union representatives, or (5) a combination of these methods.

If and when a demand for recognition is made in person by a union organizer, *do not:*

- Ask to see the cards.
- Look at any lists of employees.
- Discuss, look at, review, count, or accept any cards or even flip through them if they are handed to you or deposited on your desk.
- Review or comment upon any offered document that may be or purports to be a labor agreement.
- Look at, discuss, or review any writing or paper they may attempt to hand you or deposit on your desk.
- Refuse to talk to or meet with union representatives if they are already in your presence.
- Poll or interview your employees to ascertain whether they signed cards.
- Engage in objectionable conduct that may tend to undermine the union's majority.
- Threaten employees, directly or by implication.
- Make promises, directly or by implication.
- interrogate employees about union activities or the union campaign.

When a demand is made, *do:*

- Arrange to have a witness with you if at all possible. There is no need to have a secretary present to record or transcribe what was said during the visit.

- Remain calm and dignified. Keep your cool.

- Ask questions. You run the show, and if you have difficulty, ask them to leave and not return until they can act courteously and in a businesslike manner. Be a good listener! Do not engage in small talk about matters having nothing to do with the purpose of the visit. Do not talk about children, sports, hunting, fishing, the weather, or the state of the nation. The less said, the better. Keep the meeting short.

- When the union representatives identify themselves, either get their calling cards or, carefully and specifically, in their presence, put down their names, addresses, and exactly who it is they claim to represent.

- Ask them to state their business. Obtain, but do not give, information. If and when they claim in any form to represent your employees, state clearly, "I have good-faith doubt that your union does, in fact, represent an uncoerced majority of our employees in an appropriate bargaining unit."

If the union organizer suggests that you agree on a professor, federal mediator, or someone like that to check the cards for the purpose of verifying the union's majority, stand firm on the ground that you believe justice would be better served by utilizing the orderly processes of the governmental agency set up to handle them and to make the necessary determinations.

Should the cards be put on your desk or thrown at you in leaving, you should have someone witness that you put them in an envelope at the moment and sealed them without looking at them.

On receipt of any letter, answer the letter in a reasonable period of time. The letter should state your "good-faith doubt that the union does, in fact, represent an uncoerced majority of the employees in a unit appropriate for bargaining."

Q. What are employee, management, and union rights?

A. Employee rights include:

- The right to form and join a union.
- The right to vote the way they want.
- The right to vote join or not join a union.

Management rights include:

- The right to wage a campaign and to talk about union negatives.
- The right to run your own business.
- The right of free speech.
- The right to answer false and misleading charges.

Union rights include:

- The right to organize and make promises.
- The right to bring charges against the employer. The right to picket for a certain period of time.

Labor relations is a difficult and highly regulated area of human resource management. If you are having labor problems it is a good idea to retain a labor attorney.

There are also excellent consulting groups around the U.S. that provide labor relations assistance. One such organization is Mountain States Employers Council in Denver, Colorado, 303-839-5177.

WHAT YOU SHOULD KNOW ABOUT PLANT CLOSINGS AND LAYOFFS/SAMPLE LABOR RELATIONS LETTERS

The Worker Adjustment and Retraining Notification Act requires employers of 100 or more full-time workers to give 60 days advance notice of closings or major layoffs. It became effective in February 1989, and impacts employers who are closing a facility or an operating unit with 50 or more workers, or who will be laying off over 50 employees. Please note that there is a layoff checklist in the checklist section of this book.

The following letters and memos are provided to give you a start at writing documents regarding layoffs and reductions in force. You should modify them to fit your specific needs.

LETTER TO BRANCH PERSONNEL MANAGER ON PREPARING FOR A LAYOFF

Date

Ms. Gwen Chavez
Personnel Manager
The Aimes Company
1839W. 19th Avenue
Chicago, IL 89000

Dear Gwen:

I am following up on our telephone conversation regarding the impending layoff at our Los Angeles facility.

Layoffs are certainly unpleasant, but if you prepare ahead of time and account for all contingencies in advance, you can manage a smooth transition.

The following are items to consider when preparing for a layoff:

- How many people will be involved?
- What departments are involved?
- What will be the layoff criteria? Performance, seniority, job elimination? If it is a job elimination, it may be a reduction in force, rather than a layoff, which means there may be no recall rights involved.
- Prepare a layoff policy, stating criteria decided upon and what regular pay, severance, and vacation pay will be paid.
- Determine how much advance notice will be given.
- Before a reduction in force, some companies poll employees to determine whether anyone wishes to quit voluntarily. If any employees do, the company gives them severance pay.
- Ask employees of retirement age if they wish to take early retirement and receive severance pay.
- Decide when the layoff notice is given whether employees will be allowed time to look for a job before the layoff date.
- Develop a seniority list.
- Review lists of company property held by employees who will be laid off.
- Draft letters from management to employees regarding the layoff.
- Prepare a press release. Send it to the newspapers after employees have been notified.
- Have appropriate benefits people make arrangements regarding medical and life insurance coverage. Review pension plans if you have such benefits. Provide insurance conversion forms and send COBRA notifications.
- Prepare an information sheet to hand out to employees regarding what benefits they will have and for how long.
- Decide on the amount of severance and unused vacation that will be paid to each employee.
- Prepare an out placement program that includes workshops in writing a resume and interviewing.
- Provide employees with information on how to collect unemployment insurance.
- Contact employers in the area to find out if they have any employment opportunities.

A layoff or reduction in force is never pleasant, but if you have a game plan it makes the whole effort much easier.

Sincerely,

Fred K. Adams
Director, Human Resources

MEMO TO EMPLOYEES REGARDING A REDUCTION IN FORCE

Date

TO: All Salt Lake City Employees

FROM: Raymond C. Davidson
President, Davidson Corporation

SUBJ: REDUCTION IN FORCE

You will recall that a very stringent cost-improvement program was implemented at Davidson Corporation with the expectation that the economy would recover by midyear. Unfortunately, that has not occurred, and the economic outlook continues to be uncertain.

Therefore, it is necessary at this time to take a most difficult step and reduce the number of our employees. The reduction in force will take place immediately, and affected employees at the Salt Lake City operation will be informed by their managers.

Terminated employees will be paid through September and will receive severance pay according to their years of service. We have made arrangements to provide medical and hospitalization coverage for these employees through October and will provide job counseling and assistance in preparing résumés.

Any questions concerning these actions should be directed to your immediate manager or to the Human Resources Department.

We expect market conditions to improve and hope that the remaining organization will permit us to fully meet the demands of these expected improvements. It is important to note that this is a permanent reduction in force, not a temporary layoff situation.

We are sorry to be losing many good employees and wish you the best of luck in finding new positions. The company will be providing out placement services including resume preparation classes. Ask your manager about these benefits.

In addition, you will be receiving a letter in the next few days telling you about your medical benefits and the costs of continuation for the next 18 months.

If you have other questions, please ask your immediate supervisor.

LETTER TO EMPLOYEE REGARDING A REDUCTION IN WORKFORCE

Date

Mr. Fred L. Fine
14390 32nd Avenue
Los Angeles, CA 90031

Dear Fred:

Due to current economic conditions and our inability to finalize several of our current projects on a timely basis, we have found it necessary to have a reduction in force, and we are terminating your employment effective October 8. The company agrees to pay you, however, for an additional 30 days through November 7; all unused and accrued vacation; and severance pay at the rate of two weeks for each year of service up to a maximum of 26 weeks.

You understand and agree that this severance payment is in lieu of all other payments and benefits due you as a result of your employment at Macro-Software Company and its affiliate companies except those payments and benefits specifically identified in this letter.

In addition to termination pay, severance pay, and vacation pay, the company will pay your medical insurance coverage through December. All other benefits cease October 8. You will have the right to continue medical coverage at your own expense for an additional 18 months.

The company is also prepared to provide job search counseling and resume assistance to those employees who request it. Please notify us no later than October 15 if you wish to receive these services.

A letter reviewing specific details of your particular benefits and severance pay will be mailed to your home on October 10.

We wish you the best of luck in your future career endeavors.

Sincerely,

Fred K. Adams
Director, Human Resources

LETTER OF NOTIFICATION OF LAYOFF

Date

Ms. Julie Waltham
250 Mt. Aubum Street
Cambridge, MA 02138

Dear Julie:

Due to current economic conditions and our inability to finalize on a timely basis several new projects, we have found it necessary to have a reduction in force, and we are terminating your employment, effective Friday, July 30. However, in view of your ten years of service to the Company, we agree to pay you an additional 30 days through August 31, plus all unused accrued vacation, and severance pay as follows:

Unused vacation	$1,000
Severance pay = one week's pay for each year of service	$5,000
Total	$6,000

You will receive all severance and vacation pay in one check on Friday, July 30.

You understand and agree that this severance payment is in lieu of all other payments and benefits due you as a result of your employment by Webster-Stone Company and its parent or affiliate companies, except those payments and benefits specifically identified in this letter.

You will receive your normal pay checks on August 5 and August 20, and your final check for August on September 5. Normal direct deposit procedures will apply for the August 5 check if you have already chosen that option. For other people, it will be sent to their homes. Please complete the attached instruction to Payroll for the checks of August 20 and September 5. If applicable, make sure your final time card is filled out, signed, and forwarded to Payroll immediately.

In addition to termination pay, severance pay, and vacation pay, the Company will pay your medical insurance coverage for the months of August and September. All other benefits will cease as of July 30.

The Company is also prepared to provide out placement assistance to those individuals who request it. Please contact Ruth Span, ext. 2902, by August 6 to participate in our out placement service.

For more specific details on your benefit coverage, refer to the attached summary. If you have any questions, please contact me.

Sincerely,

Linden Blue
Vice-President, Human Resources

Attachments

Read and accepted:

_____   _____
Employee Signature   Date

Letter of Termination—Reduction in Force

Date

Mr. Kenneth W. Long
537 Washakie Avenue
Rockville, MD 20852

Dear Kenneth:

Please be advised that we are terminating your employment, effective February 15 due to a need to reduce our workforce. In view of your year of service to the Company we agree to pay you the following severance:

Regular wages		$1,116.76
Vacation (none—already taken in November)		
Severance Pay		$1.030.77
		$2,147.53
Less:	FIT	-632.05
	FICA	-143.88
	Savings Bond	-25.00
Net:		$1,346.60

If you desire, you may continue your medical insurance coverage at your expense under COBRA regulations. The choice to continue must be made within sixty days of your termination. If it is your desire to continue coverage, contact Mary Bell in the benefits office for additional information.

You understand and agree that this severance payment is in lieu of all other payments and benefits due you as a result of your employment by RMSE and its parent or affiliate companies.

Sincerely,

Myrna Browne
Personnel Manager

Read and accepted:

_____   _____
Kenneth W. Long   Date

ARBITRATION OF EMPLOYMENT DISPUTES

In the last few years, employers have seen a number of employment laws passed, including the Americans with Disabilities Act, Family and Medical Leave Act, Small Business Job Protection Act, and the Health Insurance Portability and Accountability Act. In addition to these relatively new laws, there has been unprecedented litigation activity related to Title VII claims, the Age Discrimination in Employment Act, state discrimination laws, and a number of common law claims. Compounding this problem for companies is the fact that, in addition to the enormous number of cases being filed by disgruntled ex-employees, juries seem to be awarding larger and larger damage amounts to plaintiffs in these cases.

More often today, employers are seeking alternatives to the slow and very expensive process of litigation. The attraction of alternative dispute resolution (ADR) has been tempting employers for some time. One of the dispute methods thought to be a viable and preferable alternative to litigation is binding arbitration. Only recently, however, have the courts provided much guidance as to the effectiveness and legitimacy of arbitration.

In 1991, the Supreme Court issued a landmark decision in *Gilmer v. Interstate Johnson Lane Corp.* This case and those that have followed have profoundly affected the resolution of employment law disputes. In light of these cases, many employers are turning to binding arbitration in an effort to avoid costly litigation. Although many questions remain unanswered by the Supreme Court, a substantial body of law is developing in lower courts that suggests arbitration may provide a viable alternative to litigation.

OUTSOURCING HR FUNCTIONS

Given the complexity, cost, and highly regulated nature of the Human Resources (HR) function, thousands of companies have started to outsource some of their HR activities. For companies, large or small, using outside service providers to process payroll and administer benefit programs is more efficient and less costly than handling these highly regulated functions in-house. Companies are constantly looking for ways to cut general and administrative (G&A) costs, and outsourcing Payroll and Benefits is one way.

As you search for answers to your questions about outsourcing you will find that there are many options. Depending on the specific HR activity you will consider outsourcing, the following options are available.

Partial HR outsourcing. Depending on the specific HR activity you plan to outsource (staffing, payroll, benefits, etc.), you may find it more cost effective to retain some activities and outsource others.

Example

Benefits Administration. You may find it most effective for your company to outsource claims administration and retain employee communications of outsource 401(k) open enrollment meetings and retain day-to-day 401(k) administration. These are all questions you will want answered when you look into outsourcing. Each organization has its strengths and weaknesses and therefore specific issues to consider.

Outsourcing via Time Sharing. Many companies use a vendor on a timesharing basis. In this situation you share systems time and equipment, and the vendor furnishes the technical staff. The idea of having HR become a business partner focusing on the business operation and letting an outside service provider handle the detailed administrative support functions when it makes economic sense.

Example

Payroll Administration. Some companies use a vendor such as ADP to process their payroll. Thousands of companies around the country have ADP process payroll on a timesharing basis.

What Happens When You Look for Service Providers

When you look for an outside vendor, you have a wide array of potential service providers. The key to success after you locate vendors is in checking their credentials and doing a good job of interviewing and choosing the one you think will do the best job in your particular business environment. Then it's important that you establish timelines and mechanisms to monitor services on an on-going basis.

Because the HR function is so highly regulated, it is important to review a service provider's track record in legal compliance including record keeping, reporting and handling difficult issues such as medical leaves, sexual harassment, and Worker's Compensation issues. Reducing the compliance burden may allow small companies to offer better benefits to remaining employees, thereby attracting a stronger pool of talented and skilled workers.

Hewitt Associates in Lincolnshire, Illinois, an international compensation and benefits consulting firm that has become one of the largest multi-service benefits outsourcing providers in the United States, supports the benefits administration for nearly 9 million people nationwide. Hewitt has conducted a survey on HR outsourcing.

Employer Experience in HR Outsourcing

93% of employers in the Hewitt survey currently outsource some part of their HR activities, and another 4% are considering outsourcing. Only 1% said they considered outsourcing, but decided against it. None of the employers outsource all HR activities.

Of the employers that indicated their companies' outsourcing programs were very effective in meeting their strategic business goals, nearly all (85%) responded their companies' overall business performance either met or was above expectations for the last 3 years.

Company's Overall Business Performance

	% of Employers
Significantly above expectations	21%
Above expectations	31%
Met expectations	33%
Below expectations	15%
	100%

What Are Companies Outsourcing?

Employee benefit functions are the most frequently outsourced HR functions with 95% of companies outsourcing at least a portion of health and group benefits activities. Claims payment is the function most commonly outsourced (89% of employers), followed by disability management (58%) and health care data analysis (56%). In addition to health benefits, 91% outsource a portion of their defined contribution plan activities and 68% of employers outsource at least one part of the defined benefit plan activities. Outsourcing doesn't stop with group benefits, however. Other areas of human resources being outsourced include organizational development (58%), direct compensation (56%), and expatriate administration (33%).

The nature of Human Resources as we know it has been changing for the past 20 years and the outsourcing trend is the latest in the function's evolution according to Scott Peterson, a benefits administration consultant at Hewitt Associates. HR has gone from being Personnel Administrators in the 1980s and 1990s to being Management Advisors and Implementers in the 2000s. Today, with the rapid changes in market economies, corporate needs and employee motivations, the focus is on being more of a strategic business partner leading change in an organization. Outsourcing some of the more routine administrative HR functions allows HR managers to focus on the more strategic needs of their companies.

There are some advantages and disadvantages to HR outsourcing:

Advantages: using an outside vendor does cost money initially, but it often provides a better quality of service at less cost than hiring someone to perform the activity in-house. It also minimizes staff time which would otherwise be devoted to time-consuming HR benefits activities and lets a company focus on its primary business mission. Reducing the compliance burden associated with staffing, payroll, benefits administration, provides a company with the opportunity to pay for additional benefits for remaining staff and possibly attract more skilled and experienced workers.

Disadvantages: Despite the many benefits of HR outsourcing, there are some potential disadvantages. Use of an outside service provider means loss of daily control of the function and the possibility of lower quality of service if service is not regularly monitored. In the HR function, when you pick a bad vendor you can have an employee morale problem, if paychecks are late or benefits administration is not up to par. It can also cost millions if employment laws are violated and repercussions fall back on the company. Just because you outsource a function doesn't mean you don't have to manage and regularly monitor vendor services.

The key to successful outsourcing is in finding more advantages than disadvantages in your specific outsourcing project.

Guidelines for Starting an HR Outsourcing Activity

You need a decision-making process when you start thinking about outsourcing any part of the HR function. The process should be a formal one with specific steps to follow:

- Appoint an internal committee of four to six individuals from different corporate functions such as HR, Finance, Tax, Legal, etc. This committee should review all outsourcing decisions.

- The HR executive should be the committee chairperson, and should take on the responsibility of initiating outsourcing research, information, and Request for Proposals (RFPs) to vendors. The Committee should identify specific criteria for choosing an outside service provider, using the company's HR philosophy, the core HRE competencies, and the needs of both employees and management in the functions that are to be outsourced.

- Develop the criteria for evaluating vendors. The committee should identify 5 to 6 criteria for outsourcing each specific HR activity, using both qualitative and quantitative factors. Weigh each factor and produce a list to use when evaluating vendors.

- The committee should review information provided by outside vendors against the criteria established by the committee for each activity that is to be outsourced. A resource directory of vendors in various HR functions appears in the back of this book. The Society for Human Resource Management has additional vendor sources. Contact 1-800-283-SHRM for The Human Resource Network. Also, you can contact your local SHRM Chapter on resources. After this research is completed, a final list of vendors is chosen and the RFPs are prepared and sent to the vendors on the list.

- The RFP process is an important one. The RFP needs to include the company's criteria for outsourcing the payroll or benefits function. A well-thought out RFP can speed the process for choosing the right vendor.

- When choosing a vendor, the company should look at the vendor's reputation, financial stability, location, the credentials of the vendor representatives, and the vendor's ability to meet the company's business needs.

- After the vendors receive the RFPs, they will review your criteria and decide whether or not they can provide the functions, activities, technology and people you require. They will decide if they want to respond, and if so, will send their responses by the deadline you have established. Be sure to ask for the number of copies of the RFP you need for each committee member. The RFP responses will be too lengthy to recopy. When the company receives the vendor response to the RFPs, the committee should review them against predetermined criteria, choosing the closest fit and the ones with the most to offer the company. Price will be one factor.

- The top 2 or 3 vendors should be invited to meet the committee and make a formal presentation. It's important that the committee personally screen the vendors to ensure a "fit" with the company. The HR executive especially wants to ensure compatibility between the HR staff, and other individuals in the company with whom the vendor representatives will interact on a daily basis.

- The final vendor selection should be made with the definition and scope of the particular HR project in mind. This process can be intense and is crucial to the success of the project. The entire evaluation process can take up to six weeks. The company should develop an integrated information management strategy that connects all the items to be done and enables the HR executive to implement the project, communicating with HR staff, and employees throughout the company in order to support and enhance the function to be outsourced.

- The Committee should establish a monitoring plan and an ongoing oversight effort to ensure regulatory compliance.

From the outset of the vendor relationship, a company must educate the vendor and the HR staff on the reasons for outsourcing and develop a program to regularly monitor the relationship including the quantity and quality of the services being provided. The company should schedule appointments to review the vendor's records, making sure to request and save copies of any legally required materials and reports. Some companies even have their auditors audit vendor records or have a third party review records and federally mandated reports. Ongoing monitoring of any outsourcing relationship is critical to overall success.

Defining the Work to Be Performed and Writing a Request for Proposal (RFP)

The RFP process is a challenge for both parties. When done correctly it provides the information you need to make an informed, and hopefully, a successful decision, as to which company/vendor is best suited to perform the outsourcing function for your organization. Because so much time is spent by vendors responding to RFPs, and by companies requesting information through the RFP process, both parties need to provide their information in an effective, succinct, and straight-forward format containing enough information to be meaningful, but not so much that you have to wade through tons of superfluous verbiage and company propaganda.

A vendor's pet peeve with RFPs is that the requests frequently come to them in a confusing format, poorly worded, and with questions that have little relevance. They are often written by people who don't understand the process. Sometimes a company will hire a consultant and pay that consultant by the word which results in a huge document with more words and fluff than substance.

On the other side, companies complain that vendors respond with stacks and stacks of company information and fluff that provides few answers or substantive information on which to base a valid outsourcing decision.

The answer to the problems of both parties is to ensure that the information asked for and the information provided relates directly to the issues at hand. The company should ask for specific information pertaining directly to the function to be outsourced. The vendor should provide exactly the information that is requested, and a minimum of company information. Only enough to let the requesting company know that the vendor is reputable and is doing the same type of outsourcing successfully for other clients. The vendor should provide the names, a contact and the telephone number of at least three client-companies that can be used as references. If the vendor sees that the requesting company has not asked a pertinent question that needs to be addressed, the vendor should provide that information and point out its relevancy.

A model RFP should consist of an introduction and background information on the company, and a group of questions in defined areas that are relevant to the particular HR function to be outsourced. Following is an example of what a good RFP should include:

Standard RFP

- Your company background, type of firm, number of employees, locations, etc.

- Requirements and expectations. Type of plan to be outsourced, such as a 401(k) plan, providing a summary plan document.

- Vendor company profile and detailed information about the company.

- Record keeping and administration. Systems and reporting capabilities, information on the vendor representatives who will be assigned to the account, their background and references, and service information.

- Communication and education. The vendor's communication capabilities, including the technology to be used, and a discussion of the proposed employee education meetings.

- Technology. Interactive voice response systems, on-line access, and kiosks.

- Conversion and Implementation. How the conversion will take place, a discussion of the people who will carry out the conversion project schedule.

- Servicing. What type of consulting advice and plan design assistance will be provided.

- Reporting. What periodic reports will be furnished.

- Compliance assistance. Will the vendor provide an initial compliance review and preparation of necessary reports.

- Investments. Funds offered, fund performance history and the assets the vendor already has under management.

- Trustee services. Reporting capabilities, check processing, and a copy of the trust agreement.

- Fees. Bundled or unbundled, asset or participant base and a sample of the vendor's service contract.

The service provider should be able to take the RFP and formulate a matrix based on each section of the document, using it to analyze the responses. For specific RFPs or for further information and a sample RFP, see *Outsourcing HR Functions*, ISBN 0-8144-0419-7, by Mary F. Cook, AMACOM Books. 1-800-262-9699.

10

PERSONNEL LETTERS AND MEMOS

- Letter to Applicant Confirming Employment Offer
- Replies to Applicants
- Applicant Rejection Letter
- Sample ADA Accommodation Letter
- Letter Requesting Employment Verification
- New Employee Welcome
- New Employee Orientation Schedule
- Orientation Schedule
- Employee Secrecy Agreement
- Confidentiality Agreement
- Letter to New Employee Regarding Conflict of Interest
- Letter Regarding Rehire and Reinstatement of Benefits
- Job Sharing Proposal
- Confirmation of Transfer Decision
- To Employee Regarding Request for a Leave of Absence
- Letter to Branch Manager on Use of Independent Contractors
- To Employees Informing of an Impending Layoff
- Notification of Layoff
- Letter to Employees Regarding Notice of Plant Closing
- To All Employees Regarding Company Relocation
- Letter Informing Employee of Being Placed on 30-Day Performance Improvement Plan
- Unacceptable Work Performance—Must Improve

continued,

- Letter Informing Employee of Disciplinary Action
- Letter to Employee Regarding Suspension Without Pay
- Written Warning for Excessive Absenteeism
- Letter to Employee on Termination for Excessive Absenteeism
- Termination for Theft of Company Property
- To Employee With a Substance Abuse Problem
- Letter to Employee on Termination for Intoxication on the Job
- Memorandum to All Employees Regarding Drug Testing
- Department Managers on Turnover Analysis
- Request for Additional Salary Budget
- Reviewing Company Policy on Salary Increases When Employee Is on Leave of Absence
- To Employee Regarding Company Privacy Policy
- To Human Resources Manager Regarding Employee Privacy
- Letter to Personnel Manager Regarding Corporate Procedures for Employees Wishing to File a Complaint
- Memorandum to Division Manager Regarding Sexual Harassment
- To Manager Regarding Sexual Harassment Complaint
- To Employee Regarding Her Sexual Harassment Complaint
- To EEOC Regarding Allegation of Age Discrimination Charge
- To Employees Covering Annual Report of Employee Benefit Plans
- Letter Questioning Claims Processing Time
- Letter to Employee Requesting 401(k) Hardship Withdrawal
- Memorandum to Employees Announcing a New Company Benefit
- Confirming Company Participation in Support of Employee Bowling League
- To Employees Regarding United Way Drive
- Sample COBRA Letter to Employees: Summary of Rights and Obligations Regarding Continuation of Group Health Plan Coverage
- Sample COBRA Letter to Terminating Employee or Dependent
- Sample Alternative COBRA Letter to Employees
- Condolences on Death of Employee's Spouse

LETTER TO APPLICANT CONFIRMING EMPLOYMENT OFFER

Date

Mr. Scott Lever
2109 South Hoyt Way
Albuquerque, NM 87197

Dear Mr. Lever:

Thank you for giving us the opportunity to discuss a professional position with our firm. It was a pleasure meeting you and discussing your personal and professional goals and the ways in which employment with our firm might help you achieve them.

We take great pleasure in welcoming our employment offer to you as an assistant on our professional accounting staff. Your starting salary will be $3,000 per month. In addition, you will be compensated for overtime hours as an accounting staff person. The agreed upon starting date is July 6.

I believe that the dedication and ability you have shown in preparing for the accounting profession will start you on the right foot, and with your ongoing commitment, will allow you to achieve your goals. We do let all new employees know that we are an "at will" employer and either the employee or the employer may terminate the employment relationship at any time with or without prior notice.

Again, we're delighted that you have accepted our employment offer and we look forward to seeing you in July. In the interim, if you have any questions please feel free to call us.

Sincerely,

Karen West
Human Resource Manager

REPLIES TO APPLICANTS

Date

Mr. Stephen L. Lipscomb
380 South Corona
Albuquerque, NM 87108

Dear Mr. Lipscomb:

Thank you for your inquiry regarding our advertisement for a plant manager.

Although we are impressed with your abilities and accomplishments, we have filled the position with another candidate whose experience is better suited to our current needs. The information you submitted will be retained for one year, and you will be contacted if an appropriate position becomes available within that time.

Your interest in New Mexico Equipment Company is very much appreciated.

Sincerely,

Ruth L. Aspen
Employment Manager

Replies to Applicants

Date

Mr. Daniel M. Norton
10840 Foothill Road
Golden, CO 80401

Dear Mr. Norton:

Thank you for your inquiry regarding employment opportunities with the Brown Construction Company.

Unfortunately, we do not anticipate any openings for construction workers at the time you expect to graduate. However, the information that you submitted will be retained for one year, and you will be contacted should an appropriate position open within that time.

Your interest in our company is appreciated, and we wish you success in your job search.

Sincerely,

James C. Wade
Human Resources Manager

Replies to Applicants

Date

Mr. R. O. Hibler
639 North Miller Drive
Salt Lake City, UT 84120

Dear Mr. Hibler:

Your letter to Mr. James C. Smith, president of Rocky Mountain Energy Company, regarding employment opportunities with our company has been referred to me for response.

Your skills and background are impressive; however, at this time we do not have an open position that would fit your qualifications. We will keep your résumé on file and will contact you if an appropriate position should become available.

In the meantime, another possibility might be our corporate audit staff. If you are interested, you may contact or send your résumé to Mr. Charles Billing, Assistant Controller, Lancaster Corporation, 1416 Gilpin Street, Omaha, Nebraska 68179.

Sincerely,

Andrew E. James
Human Resources Manager

Applicant Rejection Letter

Date _____

Dear _____:

Thank you for your response to our recent advertisement for the position of _____
_____.

We appreciated the opportunity to review your credentials and were pleased that you are interested in employment with the _____ Company.

We have narrowed our search to those few applicants who have the specific qualifications and experience we need for this position. Although your credentials do not specifically meet our current needs, we will retain your résumé for six months in the event that an appropriate career opportunity becomes available.

Thanks again for your interest. We wish you the best of luck in your job search.

Sincerely,

Vice President
Human Resources

SAMPLE ADA ACCOMMODATION LETTER

DATE

ADDRESS

Dear Mr./Mrs. _____:

Thank you for applying for the position of _____ at XYZ Company. We had a number of qualified applicants for the position and have chosen another candidate who met all of the qualifications for the position. After speaking with your contact person, we ascertained that because of your hearing disability you are not able to use a regular telephone or an amplifier on a regular telephone.

The job description for this position states that the physical qualifications for the job require "a normal range of hearing and vision." Frequent telephone discussions with clients, contractors, and vendors are an integral part of this job (see attached job description).

With your experience we feel you could perform some of the essential job functions, but one of the most important functions is use of a telephone. The Company would be willing to make an accommodation for you if you could use an amplifier on our telephone, but the cost of a special telephone system would create an undue financial hardship on the Company and an administrative burden we're not able to accommodate.

We thank you for contacting us and applying for the position and wish you luck in your job search.

Sincerely,

Human Resources Manager
XYZ Company

LETTER REQUESTING EMPLOYMENT VERIFICATION

Date

Mr. John Smith
Personnel Director
Financial Services Corporation
815 16th Street NW
Washington, DC 20006

Ref: Employment Verification
Carol L. Mills

Dear Mr. Smith:

The person identified above is being considered for employment and has signed our employment application form authorizing this inquiry. We would appreciate a statement of your experiences with this person when she was employed by your company. Please provide the information requested on the bottom of this letter and return the letter to us in the enclosed self-addressed stamped envelope at your earliest convenience. Your reply will be held in strict confidence. We sincerely appreciate your cooperation and will reciprocate with employment information on your applicants should the need arise.

Sincerely,

John Watson
Velcare Corporation

CONFIDENTIAL

Applicant Name and Address: _____

_____

Name and Location of Former Company: _____

_____

Dates Employed: _____

General Work Record: _____

NEW EMPLOYEE WELCOME

Date

Ms. Joan Garcia
13150 Walnut Street
Glendale, CA 91201

Dear Joan:

Welcome to Lincoln Energy Corporation. We are looking forward to working with you and hope you will enjoy your part-time position with our company. You'll want to review the enclosed *Things to Know* guidelines.

Lincoln is the mineral resources exploration and development subsidiary of the National Energy Corporation. Other subsidiaries of National are Overland Industries and Front Range Technology Corporation.

Our organization is highly integrated and comprised of many departments, including exploration, engineering, land acquisition, human resources, accounting, data processing, drafting, marketing, law, and mineral economics. As a result, a variety of challenging opportunities are offered to those who have the skills and desire to fill our positions.

We try to provide challenging opportunities for growth for our full-time employees, and as these full-time positions become available we welcome your application for employment. Should you decide to seek permanent employment at the Lincoln Energy Corporation, you may contact our Human resources department and a staff member will be pleased to discuss career opportunities with you.

Sincerely,

John Swenson
Director of Human Resources
Enc.: *Things to Know*

NEW EMPLOYEE ORIENTATION SCHEDULE

Date

Mr. James C. Maddox
342 Magnolia Street
Denver, CO 80202

Dear Jim:

I am enclosing a copy of the orientation schedule for your first week of employment at Rocky Mountain Energy Company.

The orientation program has been developed to assist you in learning about the Employee Relations Department and our current projects as quickly as possible.

We are looking forward to working with you and to making your first week on the job productive and enjoyable.

Welcome to the company, and to the employee relations group.

Sincerely,

Mary F. Cook
Director, Employee Relations

ORIENTATION SCHEDULE

James C. Maddox

April 11, 19XX (Monday)

8:15–10:00		New Employee Orientation
10:00–11:00	Larry White	Review of current Organizational Development activities
11:45	John King	Lunch
1:30–2:30	Mary Cook	Review of current Employee Relations activities
2:30–3:30	John King	Overview of Recruiting, Employment, and Affirmative Action program
3:30–5:00	Dick Brown	Overview of Compensation, Benefits, Approval Package processes, etc.

April 12, 19XX (Tuesday)

8:30–noon	(Auditorium)	Attend Managers' Administrative Overview presentation
Noon	(Open)	Lunch
2:00–4:30	Mary Cook	Introductions around the company

April 13, 19XX (Wednesday)

8:30–10:30	Mary Cook	Discussion of Succession Planning and Management Development
11:45	Dan Smith	Lunch
1:30-2:30	Dan Smith	Review of Training and Management Development programs planned for 19XX to 19XX
2:30–5:00	(Open)	

NEW EMPLOYEE ORIENTATION

NOTE: All employees must attend an orientation session.

Employee's Name: _____ SSN: _____

Job Title: _____ Dept.: _____ Date: _____

HUMAN RESOURCES DEPARTMENT: The information checked below has been given or explained to the employee.

Compensation and Benefits

- Time sheet/card ( )
- Payroll procedures ( )
- Insurance Program Booklet ( )
- Voice Booklet ( )
- Educational Assistance ( )
- Credit Union ( )
- Stock Purchase Plan ( )
- Savings Bond Plan ( )
- Sick Benefits—A&S— ( )
  Limitations, and so on

Leaves, Promotions, and Transfers

- Performance Evaluations ( )
- Promotions ( )
- Transfers ( )
- Vacations ( )
- Holidays ( )
- Absences—Tardiness ( )
- Jury Duty ( )
- Leaves of Absence—
  Maternity—Medical &
  Family, and so on ( )

General

- Code of Conduct ( )
- Employee Handbook ( )
- Complaints and Grievance
  Procedures ( )
- I.D. or Entrance Card ( )
- Introduction to the Department ( )
- Parking Facilities ( )
- Safety Guidelines ( )
- First Aid and Requirements
  for Reporting Injury ( )
- Bulletin Boards/Company Events ( )
- Voluntary Resignation Notice ( )
- Termination Procedures ( )

SUPERVISOR: The following is a checklist of information necessary to orient the new employee to the job in your department. Please check off each point as you discuss it with the employee and return to the Human Resources Department to be placed in the employee's personnel file.

Welcome the New Employee

- Review copy of employee's application. Be familiar with employee's   ( )
  experience, training, and education.
- Review job description with employee, including the duties, responsibilities,   ( )
  and working relationships.
- Discuss with the employee the unit organization and the department   ( )
  division organization. Explain the function of your department/division
  as related to the total organization and how the employee fits in.
- Confirm that employee has a copy of employee handbook, and has read   ( )
  and understands it.

Introduce Employee to Co-Workers

- Indicate to each co-worker the new employee's position.   ( )
- Explain the functions of each person as you introduce the new employee. ( )

Show New Employee Around the Facility

- Tour the department, plant, or company.   ( )
- Explain where lavatories, coffee areas, and parking facilities are located.   ( )
- Explain the various departments within the organization.   ( )

Introduce the New Employee to Job

- Insure that new employee's working area, equipment, tools and supplies   ( )
  are prepared and available.
- Explain the levels of supervision within the department.   ( )
- Provide new employee with necessary or required training.   ( )
- Explain use of: Telephone (personal/company calls)   ( )
                    Copy machines   ( )
                    Company vehicles   ( )
                    Mail procedures   ( )
                    Supply procedures   ( )
                    Personal expense reimbursement   ( )
- Explain hours of work/overtime/call-in procedures.   ( )
- Give new employee department telephone number.   ( )
- Review location of department's first aid equipment.   ( )
- Explain housekeeping responsibilities.   ( )

Future Follow-Up

- Set date and time within one week to cover any questions or concerns ( )
of the new employee.

_____

Supervisor's Signature

_____

Employee's Signature

_____

Supervisor's Title

_____

Date

_____

Department

_____

Date

Note: Return this form to the Human Resources Department.

MEMO TO MANAGEMENT PERSONNEL
REGARDING EMPLOYEE SECRECY AGREEMENT

DATE: _____

TO: All Management Personnel

FROM: Jonathan A. Magneson
             Chief Executive Officer

SUBJ: EMPLOYEE SECRECY AGREEMENT

Because of the highly confidential and proprietary nature of our products, as of January 1 we will require that an employee secrecy agreement be signed by all employees currently employed and by those hired after the above date. Following is a copy of this agreement. If you have any questions regarding this new policy please contact me directly (extension 5108).

EMPLOYEE SECRECY AGREEMENT

I, _____, am an employee of _____ Company. As part of my duties, I have access to trade secrets of my employer such as _____. All knowledge and information I gain from these trade secrets as well as the trade secrets themselves, including all unpatented inventions, designs, know-how, trade secrets, technical information and data, specifications, blueprints, transparencies, test data, and additions, modifications, and improvements thereon which are revealed to me shall for all time and for all purposes be regarded by me as strictly confidential and held in trust by me. I will not reveal or disclose the trade secrets to any other person, firm, corporation, company, or entity now or at any time in the future unless my employer instructs me to do so in writing. This secrecy protection will continue even if I no longer am employed by _____. I understand that if I reveal the trade secrets to unauthorized persons I personally may be subject to penalties and lawsuits for injunctive relief and money damages as well as possible criminal charges by my employer.

I acknowledge that I have read and understood the contents of this Agreement and freely sign it with the intent to be legally bound hereby.

_____   _____

EMPLOYEE SIGNATURE   DATE

_____   _____

WITNESS   DATE

Confidentiality Agreement

The nature of services provided by the (*organization's name here*) requires that information be handled in a private, confidential manner.

Information about our business or our employees or clients will not be released to people or agencies outside the company without our written consent; the only exceptions to this policy will be to follow legal or regulatory guidelines. All memoranda, notes, reports, or other documents will remain part of the company's confidential records.

Personal or identifying information about our employees (such as names, addresses, phone numbers or salaries) will not be released to people not authorized by the nature of their duties to receive such information, without the consent of management and the employee.

I agree to abide by this Confidentiality Agreement.

_____

Name

_____

Witness

_____

Date

Manager's Tip
_____

This form can be used for organizations that have goods or services of a proprietary nature, but it doesn't fit all situations. Adjust accordingly, or have it reviewed by legal counsel.

LETTER TO NEW EMPLOYEE REGARDING CONFLICT OF INTEREST

Date

Mr. Marvin Williams
1023 Fourteenth Street
West Chester, PA 19382

Dear Marvin:

During the course of your employment with Johnston Services, Inc. you will meet and come in contact with many of the company's clients.

As a tenet of your faith in and loyalty to the firm, and as part of our employment arrangement with you, kindly sign, date, and return to us the enclosed copy of this letter thereby indicating that:

In the event you leave our employment for any reason whatsoever and within a period of two (2) years from the date on which your employment is terminated you serve a client of Johnston Services, Inc. in your individual capacity, as partner or stockholder in another firm, or an employee of another individual or firm, or in any other manner in a professional capacity (the character of such services being similar to those services previously rendered to such a client or clients by Johnston Services, Inc.), you will pay to Johnston Services, Inc. an amount (determined on the accrual basis) equal to the latest year's fee earned by Johnston Services, Inc. from such client or clients. For purposes of the foregoing, clients of Johnston Services, Inc. are defined to include those for whom services have been performed by Johnston Services, Inc. within the twelve month period immediately preceding the date on which your employment terminated.

Payment of any sums due, shall be made in four (4) quarterly installments, the first payment being due on the day that the initial service is rendered to the client, with a quarterly installment due on the corresponding day of every third (3rd) month thereafter until the sum is paid in full.

Very truly yours,

Robert Jones
Vice President Human Resources

Acknowledged and agreed to in full:

_____   _____
Signature   Date

LETTER REGARDING REHIRE AND REINSTATEMENT OF BENEFITS

Date

Ms. Kathleen Kane
1918 North Parkway
Colorado Springs, CO 80906

Dear Kathleen:

We appreciate your responding to our recent advertisement for an insurance administrator and letting us know that you would like to come back to work for American Insurance Company.

We have discussed your return with Jane Ackerman, Human Resources Director, and she agrees that according to our personnel policies you can be reinstated to your old position. Because your lapse in employment was less than one year, we have agreed to treat it as a leave of absence and not as a termination and rehire for the purpose of computing your future vacation and retirement benefits.

Our rehire policy states that employee benefits can be reinstated if the time an employee is gone from the Company is less one year. It is our policy, however, to require a signed agreement before you can be reinstated. This agreement is attached to this letter. Please sign the agreement and bring it to work when you return December 9.

We are pleased that you are coming back to work for American Insurance Company.

Sincerely,

John L. Macon
Vice-President, Administration

Encl. Agreement

JOB SHARING PROPOSAL

Date

Mr. L. M. Yates
Vice-President
Harding-Snelling, Inc.
399 Sherman Avenue
Palo Alto, CA 94306

Dear Larry:

Some companies have started using a concept of job design that takes advantage of complementary skills of more than one employee to carry out a specific job function. We have implemented this job-sharing concept for various reasons. Through job sharing we can accommodate the needs of a valued employee or employees, as well as provide added know-how for selected high-demand jobs as in the data processing field.

It is recommended that two candidates fill the position of Data Technician in the Evaluation Department. These two candidates are Debra Johnson and Gloria Mooton. They have expressed their desire to move from the full-time to regular part-time status. Both people have the technical expertise the company needs.

Should the position of Data Technician be shared by these two individuals on a part-time basis, each would work twenty-four hours per week. It is expected that both the quality and quantity of work output will be met, if not improved.

The position involves the collation of large amounts of data into a sensible, workable system. It is, at times, a tedious function that calls for the transferring of data collected in the field onto the computer, and then updating and correcting the computer files on a continuing basis. Over the past two years, the tasks of the technician have grown tremendously. The additional eight hours of work per week, along with the reduced hours per day per individual (six) should increase productivity and improve work flow efficiency.

The scheduling of overlapping hours and the fact that Gloria and Debbie both have good communication skills will assist them in attaining the needed additional coordination that will be required to effectively do the job. There is an anticipated increase in employee benefit costs, because the company will have to furnish benefits for two people instead of one person, but I feel the benefits outweigh the added costs.

We will monitor the effectiveness of this new job-sharing arrangement and keep you apprised.

Sincerely,

Linda M. Lancer
Personnel Manager

CONFIRMATION OF TRANSFER DECISION

Date

Mr. John L. Duncan
10120 West 20th Avenue
Chicago, IL 60602
Dear John:

This letter will confirm our offer to you of a transfer to our California facility at Santa Clara.

The transfer will include the following benefits:

Salary increase from $4,200 per month to $4,900 per month.

Company car—your choice of any mid-size model to be picked up on your arrival at our facility on November 28.

A relocation bonus of $3,000 to cover any out-of-pocket expenses.

Full relocation benefits, including buy-out of your current home through Trans America Relocation Services and assistance in buying a new home of similar cost. You will receive a mortgage interest rate differential payment if there is an increase in the interest rate between your old loan and the new loan.

Ralph Loomis will be your transfer and relocation contact in our personnel department. Please let him know what make of car you decide on, and give him an idea of your timing on all relocation matters. You can reach him at (312) 679-4462. You can count on him to handle all matters relative to your transfer.

I know you will enjoy your new job and the location. Santa Clara is a beautiful area. If you should have any problems at all, please give me a call; we want this transfer to be a positive experience for you and your family.

Sincerely,

Ned F. Gilbert
General Manager

TO EMPLOYEE REGARDING REQUEST FOR A LEAVE OF ABSENCE

Date

Mr. John Elwood
31406 26th Street
Sunnyside, NY 11104

Dear John:

This letter is in response to your request for a six-month unpaid leave of absence for personal reasons.

I have discussed the leave with your Vice-President, Bob Lawson, and he agrees that you should be given the leave at this time in order to get your personal problems resolved. Bob is very supportive of you and your past performance in the job and wants to assist you in any way he can.

Your leave of absence will commence August 2 and end on February 1. During that time the company will hire a temporary employee to fill in for you on the job and will guarantee you the same position when you return to work.

Your benefits will continue while you are on leave, but you must send us a check each month to cover your medical plan. The check should be made out to the company in the amount of $75.35 and must be received by the tenth day of the month.

Your service date will remain the same. However, you will not earn vacation time or receive holiday pay during your absence.

If we can be of assistance to you in planning your leave or if you have any questions regarding your benefits, please call.

Sincerely,

Karen Kaiser
Personnel Manager

LETTER TO BRANCH MANAGER ON USE OF INDEPENDENT CONTRACTORS

Date

Mr. Lyle Cappers
Branch Manager
Adamson Manufacturing, Inc.
418 S. Dearborn Street
Chicago, IL 60605

Dear Lyle:

We have had problems recently with some of our outlying plant operations when they use independent contractors. As you know, the IRS takes a strict view of independent contractor arrangements.

Generally the relationship of employer and employee exists when the employer has the right to control and direct the individual who performs the services, not only as to the results but also as to the details and means by which that result is accomplished. Following is a list of factors the IRS would use to determine whether an employer/employee relationship exists, rather than an independent contractor relationship:

- Work performed on the employer's premises, which might indicate control, especially when the work could be done elsewhere.
- The establishment of set hours of work by the employer.
- The furnishing of tools or materials by the employer.
- The existence of a continuing relationship.
- Payment by the employer of the worker's business and travel expenses.

Independent contractors should meet the following criteria:

- They ordinarily use their own methods and receive no training from the purchaser of services.
- They have made a significant investment in facilities and perform services for another.
- They are in a position to realize a profit or suffer a loss as a result of their services.
- Their services are available to the general public.
- They are usually responsible to complete a specific job or are legally obligated to make good for failure to complete the job.

Lyle, please be sure that a true independent relationship exists before you contract for work at the Chicago plant. If there is any question in your mind about the contracting relationship, it is better to put the worker on our payroll and pay social security (FICA) taxes.

Please make all of your supervisors and managers aware of our concern regarding using independent contractors.

Best regards,

John L. Luger
Vice President Human Resources

TO EMPLOYEES INFORMING OF AN IMPENDING LAYOFF

DATE: _____

TO: All Employees

FROM: Bill T. Williams, President

SUBJ: IMPENDING LAYOFF

It is with great regret that I must tell you that International Computer Systems Company must lay off approximately 300 employees by the end of the year in order to avoid closing down our operation altogether. This is not a step we take lightly or without a great deal of soul searching and personal reluctance on the part of our management team.

Some of our branch offices will be closed, others will be reducing staff. The criteria for reducing staff will be performance and seniority, and no bumping of employees with less seniority will be allowed.

We hope that you understand our situation and will assist us in making these moves as fair and compassionate as possible. Detailed layoff procedures including a review of the benefits you will receive will be published at the end of the week by the Human Resource Department. We will provide assistance to employees in getting resumes updated and launching a job search. Severance pay will be one week of severance for each year of employment up to a ceiling of 26 weeks.

Out placement assistance will be provided by the Human Resource Department and will commence the week of July 15.

NOTIFICATION OF LAYOFF

Date

Ms. Cynthia Green
723 Jones Street
Cambridge, MA 02138

Dear Cynthia:

Current economic conditions and our inability to complete several projects on a timely basis have made it necessary to undergo a reduction in force. Therefore, we are terminating your employment effective Monday, January 6th. The Company agrees to pay you, however, for an additional 30 days through August 31, plus all unused accrued vacation. We will also pay severance pay at the rate of two weeks for each year of service up to a maximum of 12 weeks.

You understand and agree that this severance payment is in lieu of all other payment and benefits due you as a result of your employment by the Cambridge Company and its affiliate companies, except those payments and benefits specifically identified in this letter.

In addition to termination pay, severance pay, and Vacation pay, the Company will pay your medical insurance coverage for the months of August and September. All other benefits will cease as of July 30.

The Company is also prepared to provide out placement assistance to those individuals who request it. Please contact John Lane, ext. 415, by July 6 to participate in our out placement service.

For more specific details on your benefit coverage, refer to the attached summary. If you have any questions, please contact me.

Sincerely,

Toni Law
Vice-President, Human Resources

Attachments

Agreed and accepted:

_____   _____
Signature   Date

LETTER TO EMPLOYEES REGARDING NOTICE OF PLANT CLOSING

Date

Mr. Scott Stevens
8911 E. Bellevue Street
Bangor, ME 04652

Dear Scott:

Effective March 1, the Bangor, Maine facility will be closed. The economic downturn in our business has necessitated the plant closing at this time. This was not an easy decision to make and we are saddened at the thought of shutting down our business in Maine, thus eliminating so many jobs.

It is our desire to compensate our many loyal employees in some manner, and therefore, we have approved a severance pay package that we think will help employees through this difficult transition. The severance pay will be two weeks for each year of service up to a cciling of 26 weeks.

We are giving you 60 days' advance notice to provide an opportunity to start looking for other employment. We are contacting other companies in the area to let them know that we are closing and asking them to consider hiring our ex-employees when they have openings. Assistance will be provided in updating resumes, and workshops will be held to help employees brush up on interviewing skills.

The Company will extend paid medical benefits to all employees for 30 days after the plant closing. Further, we will make the group medical plan available to employees who want to pay for it, for another 18 months, in accordance with federal law. You will be receiving further information and correspondence regarding your employee benefits in a few weeks.

The Personnel Department has been staffed with extra people to answer questions and assist in any way they can to ease you through this difficult transition.

Sincerely,

Robert W. Wilson
Director, Human Resources

To All Employees Regarding Company Relocation

DATE: _____

TO: ALL EMPLOYEES OF THE BISHOP-FOWLER CORPORATION

FROM: Lloyd T. Campbell, President

SUBJ: COMPANY RELOCATION

It is the intent of the Bishop-Fowler Corporation to relocate our main facility from Tenafly, New Jersey to Denver, Colorado on March 1 of next year, and we feel it is important to give employees advance notice of this move.

It is also our intent to provide most employees the opportunity to relocate with us, and those employees who make the choice to move will receive paid relocation benefits. Those employees who will not be offered the opportunity to move will have 60 days' notice before termination. Employees who choose not to move with the company and those who will not be offered that opportunity will receive a severance package which will include all accrued vacation pay earned through March 1, and thirty days of severance pay.

Employees will also have the opportunity to continue their medical coverage for a period of eighteen months after the company closes in New Jersey, providing they pay the monthly premiums.

The decision to move the company was not an easy one, but the savings in facilities costs and ongoing personnel and administrative costs plus other incentives the company will receive from the move make our management believe this is a positive step for us at this time.

We wanted to give you all plenty of advance notice and the opportunity to think about your future. Further information will be forthcoming on a weekly basis commencing next week via a special relocation bulletin to be published by the Personnel Department.

LETTER INFORMING EMPLOYEE OF BEING PLACED ON
30-DAY PERFORMANCE IMPROVEMENT PLAN

Date

Ms. Linda M. Smith
1732 Simms Street
Cambridge, ME 02138

As a result of your unsatisfactory attendance during the past six months and your failure to correct your attendance problem after oral discussions and a written warning, you are now being placed on a 30-day formal evaluation, effective July 9 through August 8.

As we discussed earlier, the reason for this evaluation period is your chronic absenteeism and continual lack of punctuality. Over the past four months, you have been absent 30 days and late 12 times, ranging between 15 minutes and one hour.

The targets we agreed upon for your period of evaluation are:

1.   You will not be absent during the entire period of probation. Should absolute necessity, however, require absence, you will inform me prior to the absence, or, if an unexpected emergency arises, you will phone immediately in the morning and later give written justification of the absolute necessity for the absence; and

2.   You will not be late more than twice during the valuation period, and at no time will you be more than five minutes late.

I have scheduled a counseling session on July 20 to meet with you and to evaluate your progress during this period. Additionally, I would like to assure you that I will be available for discussions and counseling at any other time during this evaluation. I sincerely hope that this action will result in correction of this problem. Failure to correct this situation, however, will result in termination of your employment, either at the end of the evaluation period, or before that time if no positive improvement is evident during the early stages of the evaluation.

	Supervisor	Date

	Supervisor's Manager	Date

Employee's Acknowledgment Date	Personnel Manager	Date

Unacceptable Work Performance—Must Improve

Date

L. W. Winthrop
1317 Cole Blvd.
Norman, OK 73019

Dear Len:

This letter is to confirm our discussion about your unacceptable work performance. After our discussion in October, you made substantial improvement and were rated as "adequate" in January. We hoped you would continue to improve. However, your performance over the last several months has again slipped into "unacceptable."

1. Your ability to analyze a business situation and design the appropriate system continues to be a problem. You still have difficulty maintaining enough flexibility to meet the goal that has been identified. The tape review for the Olsen conversion was one example we discussed during our meeting.

   To successfully perform at the programmer/analyst level, you must produce basic detail design work and be prepared to meet your project dates in a timely fashion, without constant review by your project leader.

2. Your ability to function as an effective member of a project team is still not at an acceptable level. You seem to function best when detailed specifications are provided to you and you can work on the specifications, regardless of other activities around you, and then provide results for review. The team concept is critical to successful system development in our Company. This requires that each member of the team not only work on his or her assigned area, but also contribute to the team with suggestions and support as needed.

3. Your overall cooperation and attitude are unacceptable. You exhibit an adversary relationship with management personnel and project leaders with whom you work. The ability to communicate effectively is imperative in your continued role as a programmer/analyst.

Because of the problems mentioned above, work tasks assigned to you have been substandard for the programmer/analyst position. In many cases, the tasks that have been assigned could have been handled by a junior programmer. We hope you realize that we cannot afford to classify you as a programmer/analyst and not assign the full responsibilities associated with that position with confidence that the appropriate communication, analysis, and team effort will be provided.

Over the next three months I will closely track your performance and provide you with written performance appraisals. Clearly, it is up to you to bring your performance up to an acceptable level. Continued and sustained performance is expected, or you could be terminated.

Very truly yours,

R. A. Meade
Director, Human Resources

LETTER INFORMING EMPLOYEE OF DISCIPLINARY ACTION

Date

Dale L. Bradley
8796 Dawn Drive
Brooklyn, NY 11210

Dear Dale:

The purpose of this letter is to describe the events that have occurred over the past several weeks and which have resulted in the need for disciplinary action, and to inform you of the conduct required on your part for continued employment with ROC.

On Thursday, January 19, you left your work assignment in Washington, D.C., without the permission of your supervisor, and traveled to Miami, Florida for personal reasons. On Friday, January 20, George Long attempted to reach you at your hotel in Washington, D.C., and was told by the desk clerk that you were no longer registered. Unaware that George had tried to reach you, you subsequently called him from Miami and told him you were still on the job in Washington. Your phone call from Miami was placed a few minutes after George had called for you in Washington. On February 1, you submitted your expense report to your supervisor and falsified the dates that you were on the job in Washington, D.C.

Inconsistencies between your expense report and the hotel receipt were noticed by your supervisor. During a review of this matter, you admitted that (a) you had left Washington, D.C., on January 19; (b) you had called George Long from Miami on January 20 and told him you were on the job in Washington; and (c) you falsified your expense statement to reflect that you were in Washington, D.C., on January 20.

These recent events have resulted in the culmination of a growing concern that I have been experiencing over the past several months relative to increasingly frequent confrontations you have had with both your fellow employees and outside business contacts.

As I have discussed with you, the acts of deception attendant to the above matter, together with the incidents of confrontation, are unacceptable and will not be permitted by either myself or the executive management of ROC. Accordingly, I am placing you on disciplinary probation for a period of six months from the date of this letter. During this period, I will carefully monitor your work activities, placing particular emphasis on your interpersonal relationships with your fellow employees and outside individuals.

Any further incidents observed during this period that are contrary to acceptable standards of behavior will result in your immediate dismissal.

Dale, we want you to succeed, and we hope that your acknowledgment of the seriousness of this situation will have a positive result on your future at Rankin Oil Company.

Sincerely,

Stanley Bishop
Personnel Director

LETTER TO EMPLOYEE REGARDING SUSPENSION WITHOUT PAY

Date

Mr Kenneth Bronson
60311 Monticello Street
Montgomery, AL 36130

Dear Kenneth,

This letter is to inform you that you are hereby suspended from your job for three working days commencing December 15. This disciplinary action is being taken based on the following facts:

- You fell asleep on your job on December 3 and left safety equipment in the plant unattended for over two hours.
- This is the second such incident in 30 days.

Your conduct as described above constitutes sufficient cause for disciplinary action. In addition, you have been disciplined in the past for the same problem.

Your formal disciplinary action is:

- Suspension without pay for three consecutive working days beginning December 15.

A copy of this letter will be placed in your personnel file. You have the right to respond in writing to present information or arguments rebutting this suspension. If you choose to respond, you have until 5:00 P.M. on December 14 to do so. Your response, if any, will be considered prior to the imposition of the proposed suspension. It will be assumed that you have waived the right to respond if you do not take advantage of the above alternative.

The purpose of this suspension is to impress upon you the seriousness with which we regard the above violation of employment conditions and to give you the opportunity to reflect upon your future compliance with our employment standards. Should you continue to violate the conditions of your employment, you will be subject to termination.

Sincerely,

Linda Trice
Director, Human Resources

WRITTEN WARNING FOR EXCESSIVE ABSENTEEISM

Date

June Greet
4231 Grant Street
Omaha, NE 68131

Dear June:

This memorandum is a written warning because of your excessive absences. You must immediately improve your attendance record to acceptable standards or further discipline will result.

On several occasions I have spoken to you about your poor attendance record, and improvement was noticed for a time. However, your excessive absences always resumed. For the period covering June 2 through December 31, you were absent 36 days, excluding vacations and normal holidays. These absences are detailed below:

Days	Reason
18	Called in sick
7	Doctor's appointment
11	Personal business
36 days	Total

This is more than twice the number of absences accrued by any other Company employee during this same time period.

In our discussion on July 7, you agreed to consult with the Company nurse concerning your health and to enroll in the new Company Employee Assistance Program (EAP). Failure to enroll in the EAP or any unauthorized absences from this date on could be grounds for dismissal.

If you have problems that need discussion, please do not hesitate to talk them over with me, your supervisor or our EAP representative. We will support you in your efforts to remedy this situation, but will not tolerate further absences. If you would like to discuss this further, please call me at x370.

Sincerely,

Bill Smith
Director Human Resources

LETTER TO EMPLOYEE ON TERMINATION FOR EXCESSIVE ABSENTEEISM

Date

John W. Lawson
Route l, Box 300
Atlanta, GA 30345

Dear John,

As stated in my letter of August 10 to you, your record of absence from work has kept you from performing the full schedule of assignments for your position. I further indicated that a continuation of that pattern of absence could lead to my recommendation for your termination.

A current review of your attendance indicates that you have been absent from work for 20 out of the last 60 days since my letter of September 12.

In view of your poor attendance record, I am recommending to the Personnel Director, Jan Smith, by copy of this letter, that your employment with the company be terminated effective October 1.

Should you desire to meet with either myself or Jan Smith for the purpose of discussing this intended action, please notify us within ten working days after receipt of this letter.

Sincerely,

Fred Preston
Plant Manager

TERMINATION FOR THEFT OF COMPANY PROPERTY

Date

Mr. Larry Moody
10723 Reardon Street
Glendale, CA 91201

Dear Larry:

This letter is to inform you of my recommendation that you be terminated from your position as Purchasing Manager effective November 10.

You are hereby notified of your rights to a pre-termination meeting with the Human Resource Director prior to the effective date and your subsequent right to appeal this action.

This termination action is based upon the following facts:

- You were caught on October 10th stealing a large amount of copper tubing and trying to take the tubing from Company property in your car.

Your actions in this matter constitute a violation of Company policy, and we feel that your conduct constitutes sufficient cause for termination.

All written documents upon which this action is based are attached for your review.

You have the right to respond either orally or in writing or both in order to present information or arguments rebutting this disciplinary action and termination. If you choose to respond, you have until 5:00 P.M. on November 3 to do so. Your response, if any, will be considered prior to termination. It will be assumed that you have waived the right to respond if you do not do so by the above deadline.

Sincerely,

Lane Smith
Director Human Resources

Attachment

To Employee with a Substance Abuse Problem

Date

Mr. Steve Yates
295 Jones Avenue
Cleveland, OH 44105

Dear Steve:

I am writing to confirm our discussion yesterday and to further explain how the Employee Assistance Program (EAP) can be of benefit to you.

The EAP has proven very successful for many of our employees who at one time or another have been troubled by personal problems. Some of these problems are so serious that they affect their jobs and even their lives. I am referring to problems resulting from marital stress, financial difficulties, extreme emotional problems, as well as alcohol or drug abuse.

The objective of the EAP is to offer a method by which the Company can take *constructive* action in dealing with employees who have personal problems that make life difficult and impair their job performance. The goal is to help employees find professional assistance when it is needed because many employees are unable to cope with their problems alone.

The Company will not change job performance standards if you participate in the program. Work performed up to standard is still the basis for continued employment. And it should be understood that the EAP does not constitute any waiver of management's right to use disciplinary measures in situations where they are deemed appropriate.

Everything about this program is confidential. No records will be open to management. No records of the problems you and I have discussed will appear in your personnel file.

Steve, it is my sincere hope that you will avail yourself of this employee assistance program to its fullest extent. As we discussed, your job productivity and attendance record have been poor in the past several months. It will be your ongoing responsibility to work at resolving your problems so that they do not interfere with your job performance.

I am ready to assist you in any way I can. Please call me at (303) 872-6669.

Sincerely,

John Liggett
Director Human Resources

LETTER TO EMPLOYEE ON TERMINATION FOR INTOXICATION ON THE JOB

Date

Mr. Thomas Jones
1916 Race Street
Philadelphia, PA 19103

Dear Thomas:

This is to advise you that we are terminating your employment effective July 15. This decision is based on the incident report of June 26 submitted to me by your supervisor, John Wills, and his recommendation to terminate your employment due to your intoxication during duty hours.

As you know, the first reported occurrence of your intoxication on duty was May 10. That report was placed in your personnel file, and you were advised at that time that reoccurrence would result in a disciplinary action or possibly dismissal.

This second incident of intoxication threatened the safety of other employees and adversely affected the operational efficiency and effectiveness in your work unit.

Your final paycheck, including all forms of compensation due you, is being placed in the mail today to your home address. You may continue your medical coverage for a period of 18 months if you notify us within the next 60 days of your intent to do so and send us your check for $74.05 each month to cover your medical premiums.

Sincerely,

Larry Plummer
Vice-President, Human Resources

Warning on Internet Use

MEMO TO: John Brown

FROM: Charles Dickens
Vice President of Human Resources

DATE: January 20, 2001

SUBJ: Our Company Internet Policy and Your Internet Use

On January 18 I walked into your office and found you on your computer signed onto a pornographic web site. John, this is the second time I've had to warn you about this issue. This is a serious breach of our policy on employee use of the Internet on Company equipment and on Company time. This written warning is to tell you that if this happens again, you will be terminated.

I Acknowledge Receipt of This Warning

_____   _____

Employee Signature   Date

MEMORANDUM TO ALL EMPLOYEES REGARDING DRUG TESTING

DATE: _____

TO: All Employees

FROM: Bob Matthews
            Vice-President, Personnel

SUBJ: DRUG TESTING

As you know, our company has a comprehensive policy against the use, sale, or possession of drugs on company property. We intend to enforce this policy as strictly as possible. We have reason to believe that some employees are using drugs at work. We hope this is not the case, but we want to inform employees that when we have reason to believe an employee is taking drugs or selling drugs on our property, we plan to carry out a thorough investigation. Our investigation may include drug testing through urinalysis and may also include the use of undercover detectives from time to time. We certainly don't like the idea of resorting to such drastic measures, but if we find reasonable evidence of drug activity we will have no choice.

It is our desire to provide other avenues for employees to use in getting off drugs, rather than resorting to such serious measures as investigation and prosecution. In keeping with this desire, we have contracted with an outside Employee Assistance Program (EAP) organization. If you need help, you can call this organization and the company will pay for treatment if you stay with the program and get off drugs. This program is strictly confidential. No one in the company will know you are getting help. Getting into the program may save your job and your life. Call 555-9987.

DEPARTMENT MANAGERS ON TURNOVER ANALYSIS

DATE: _____

TO: Department Managers

FROM: Paul M. Mattrill, Personnel Manager

SUBJ: TURNOVER ANALYSIS

Attached as a matter of interest is an analysis of turnover for the first four months of this year. The 192 new hires include 61 independent contractors in the Residential Sales Division. Of the 106 terminations, 34 were independent contractors, and 76 of the people had been with the company less than two years. Although a complete turnover report is not available at this time, it appears that with the inclusion of ICs to compare with last year's figures, the rate is running near 14 percent for this period. Excluding ICs, the rate is over 17 percent.

Some points to keep in mind are:

- Some turnover is expected and is healthy.
- A conservative average training cost is $3,000 per person.
- It takes twelve to eighteen months to reach full performance on the average job.
- The company is losing more than 70 percent of its people by the time they reach two years of service.
- $3,000 × 192 = $576,000 training cost, January through April
  70 percent loss by two years = $403,200.

Proper screening and interviewing of applicants and sufficient training by knowledgeable, experienced supervisors will greatly reduce costs in this area and will make it easier to justify those costs that are necessary. The Personnel Department is here to assist you in any way we can.

REQUEST FOR ADDITIONAL SALARY BUDGET

Date

Mr. William M. Haland
Vice-President, Employee Relations
Wymore Corporation
345 Park Avenue
New York, NY 10022

Dear Bill:

As we discussed on the phone, following is an update of our request for funds to supplement our salary program in order to curtail turnover in our upper- and middle-level management staff.

Since our initial proposal on June 30, our turnover situation has continued to deteriorate. Four more managers have terminated this month, bringing the total to fifteen managers so far this year. The lack of any current major projects and the general slowdown of our business is most frequently given as a major consideration of those leaving. Of course, in almost every case, the managers leaving have accepted more responsible positions at higher salaries. Our turnover continues at one of the highest levels in our history.

To date, with few exceptions, we have been able to fill the manager vacancies internally. Our concern is that we will start losing professionals in the middle management ranks. We know that this group is also in the job market. They are also frustrated by the slowdown of activities and have been encouraged by the apparent success of the key executives who have terminated. As we noted in our initial request for supplemental funds, the actual salaries for this group have fallen behind the industry, and we do expect that we'll need a substantially larger salary budget in the coming year.

Attached is an updated list of terminations. The annualized turnover is now 18.75 percent compared to 12.5 percent for last year.

Thank you for your consideration. Please call if you need additional information.

Sincerely,

Dale L. Myers
Director, Employee Relations
Denver Division

REVIEWING COMPANY POLICY ON SALARY INCREASES
WHEN EMPLOYEE IS ON LEAVE OF ABSENCE

Date

Mr. Robert van Dorn
14310 Ralston Road
Arvada, CO 80006

Dear Bob:

In response to our phone conversation yesterday, I am setting out the company policy regarding salary increases effective while an employee is on leave of absence.

The disability policy defines earnings as "your regular rate of monthly compensation, excluding bonuses and overtime, in effect immediately before your disability begins." If a salary increase is processed to become effective during a period of paid disability, your salary continuation of LTD benefits will not be affected.

Benefit levels for life insurance, vacations, and pension will be increased on the effective date of the salary change. Thrift Plan is not affected since it is a function of pay actually received by an employee.

Please advise me if you have questions about the policy. I hope you are on the road to recovery and will be able to return to work soon.

Sincerely,

Joseph A. Gardino
Corporate Benefits Director

TO EMPLOYEE REGARDING COMPANY PRIVACY POLICY

Date

Ms. Louise W. Griego
444 Cedar Lane,
Tenneck, NJ 07666

Dear Louise:

We have had several inquiries recently regarding employee privacy—privacy of personnel files, medical records, and general employee information—so we thought it would be a good idea to let you know what our current policy is.

It is the feeling of Bob Wilson, our President, and his executive staff that all employees are entitled to know what our organizational privacy boundaries are. Following are statements that relate to our company philosophy:

We will:

- Collect information relevant solely to employment purposes and reveal how that information will be used when an employee makes a request for information.
- Explain the types of records maintained and adhere to a policy of limited internal use and external disclosure.
- Assure accuracy, relevancy, and completeness of information maintained in personnel records and provide reasonable procedures to review, clarify or amend records.
- Regularly review employment privacy practices to ensure compliance with fair information policies and legal requirements.

Personnel File Guidelines

GenCorp Industries agrees to:

- Collect and retain personal information needed only for business or legal reasons.
- Limit access to those with a "need to know."
- Limit retention to legal or useful business reasons, and conform to regulatory retention requirements.
- Provide employees who ask with the opportunity to review their personnel file.
- Limit release of information on present or former employs to dates of employment, and current or past position, or that information required by legitimate investigatory or legal need.
- Information about an employee's pay will only be released on the specific written authorization of the individual, and then only furnished in writing.

- Will maintain sensitive information such as medical files in a separate secure location and allow access only to company medical personnel.

We hope that these guidelines on the privacy of personnel records will provide our employees with a measure of comfort regarding the collection and retention of personal information.

If you have any questions regarding this policy, please give me a call or stop by my office.

Very truly yours,

John Byers
Director Human Resources

TO HUMAN RESOURCES MANAGER REGARDING EMPLOYEE PRIVACY

Date

Mr. Harvey Long
Manager, Human Resources, Eastern Division
Johnson Computer Group
10445 Newport Harbor Center
365 Thames Street
Newport, RI 02840

Dear Harvey:

I think we will go a long way toward fostering improved employee relations if the company establishes guidelines regarding employee privacy.

As the local manager of human resources, you should be the one to articulate those guidelines, but I would like to provide you with a list of items that I think should be covered.

I would like you to periodically review the following:

- The number and types of records we maintain on employees, former employees, and applicants
- The items maintained on each record
- The uses made of information in each type of record
- Any disclosures made to parties outside of the organization
- The extent to which employees are aware and informed of the uses and disclosures of information in the records maintained on them

The policies that I would like you to set up should do the following:

- Limit the collection of information about employees to that which is relevant to specific decisions
- Inform employees of the uses to be made of any such information
- Inform employees as to the type of information being maintained on them
- Adopt procedures to ensure accuracy, timeliness, and completeness of information
- Permit employees to see, copy, correct, and amend records being maintained on them
- Limit both the internal and external use and disclosure of information

After you have written the policy and procedures on employee privacy, please review them with other executives and with supervisors and managers to get their input. Then, let's get together and review the policy on employee privacy before it is implemented.

Sincerely,

Robert T. Wilson
Vice-President Corporate Human Resources

LETTER TO PERSONNEL MANAGER REGARDING CORPORATE PROCEDURES FOR EMPLOYEES WISHING TO FILE A COMPLAINT

Date

Mr. James L. Salinger
Personnel Manager
Cunningham Tool and Die Company
P.O. Box 966
Flushing, NY 11371

Dear Jim:

Due to the continuing labor activities at our Flushing facility, we feel it is necessary to institute a procedure to ensure that employee complaints are handled in a fair and timely fashion. Following is that new policy and procedure.

Policy

Good employee/employer relationships can exist only if employees believe they are being treated equitably and fairly within the management policies, procedures, and actions that influence this relationship. It is recognized that there are occasions when honest differences of opinion occur regarding the interpretation and application of policies and management actions.

The following procedure is established to provide an effective way for employees to bring problems and complaints to the attention of management, without fear of losing their jobs.

Procedure

Step 1—Employee discusses the complaint or problem with immediate supervisor. It is expected that every effort will be made to resolve the complaint in a fair and amicable manner at this level.

Step 2—If the employee is not satisfied with the first attempt to resolve the complaint and a response is not received within ten working days, the employee may discuss the matter with the department manager.

Step 3—If the problem still has not been resolved to the employee's satisfaction after the second step, a formal complaint may be directed to the director of human resources. A final determination is not made at this level. Within ten working days, the employee may take the complaint to the president of the company.

Step 4—The final decision on all employee complaints rests with the president.

Documentation and Procedure Control

A.   It is understood that any employee who makes use of the employee complaint procedure will be treated courteously and that the case will be handled confidentially at all times. An employee will not be subjected to discourteous treatment or reproach due to utilization of the complaint procedure.

B.   Under no circumstances will a documentation file become part of an employee's permanent personnel file. However, complaint procedure documentation will be maintained separately by the human resource department.

C.   Only those members of management with a need to know and who are in the employee's chain of command may have access to complaint procedure documentation.

The purpose of this policy is to encourage dialogue between employees and management, in order to resolve differences that might arise between two parties in an amicable, fair, and positive manner.

If you see any problems with this new procedure please contact me immediately. Your input is important to its implementation and success. Please make the procedure effective November 1, and let me know after the first thirty to sixty days how it is working.

Sincerely,

Leslie W. Masters
Personnel Director

MEMORANDUM TO DIVISION MANAGER REGARDING SEXUAL HARASSMENT

DATE:

TO: Peter V. Young
Division Manager, Atlanta

FROM: Jean M. Lipton
Director, Human Resources

SUBJ: COMPANY POLICY REGARDING SEXUAL HARASSMENT

We recently received a telephone call from Jan Browne regarding an allegation of sexual harassment in the Atlanta division offices.

Peter, please look into this possibility immediately, talking to all of your supervisors and managers and restating our policy on this issue to everyone in management. We will not tolerate sexual harassment.

I know that you understand the seriousness of this issue. Please be sure that our written policy is redistributed to all employees and that everyone in the Atlanta office knows the procedures for filing a complaint.

Following are my recommendations for conducting your investigation and handling the formal complaint if you do get one:

- Carefully interview employees. Obtain written statements if possible.
- Please contact our Atlanta attorneys and review the complete situation with them and get their guidance as you proceed with your investigation.
- Schedule a meeting with the alleged harasser. Interview this person and discuss the evidence obtained. Again, it is highly desirable to obtain a written statement.
- Look at the personnel records of the alleged harasser and the complainant to determine if there are any incidents that will assist in an investigation of the current complaint.
- If you find there has been harassment, consider a possible suspension pending further investigation depending on the seriousness of the situation. The terms of the suspension should require the alleged harasser to stay away from the complainant and refrain from interfering with the investigation.
- Take extreme care to preserve the confidentiality of the investigation and statements obtained. Document every step taken in this investigation.
- After consultation with our attorneys, if a final decision has been made concerning the complaint, inform those involved of your decision. Please call and bring me up to date also. You may prefer to have another management representative present during these meetings.

If you do get a formal complaint, please give me a call and provide me as well as our Atlanta attorneys with the particulars of the case. If you feel that you cannot handle the situation satisfactorily, please let me know immediately.

Please call me within the next few days to bring me up to date on your investigation.

TO MANAGER REGARDING SEXUAL HARASSMENT COMPLAINT

Date

Gary Ryan
Accounting Manager
7341 Coyne Street
Dayton, OH 45427

Dear Gary:

We have received a complaint of sexual harassment on the part of one of your supervisors. I don't have to tell you how seriously we take any complaint of harassment. I have asked John Gray, Vice President of Human Resources, to start an immediate investigation of this complaint and provide me with the details.

The employee who has been charged with harassment is Larry Brown, a supervisor in your accounting department. Beth Jones has formally complained to us about the harassment. Please proceed with caution. We don't want to falsely accuse anyone of harassment, but at the same time we must move quickly to get to the facts of this unfortunate situation.

Please cooperate fully in this investigation and proceed quickly to learn if this allegation is true. If you find there was sexual harassment, please act immediately to terminate Larry Brown. However, if you have any doubt about the allegation, please contact me. I want to stay personally involved in the resolution of this problem.

Sincerely,

Les Johnson
President

TO EMPLOYEE REGARDING HER SEXUAL HARASSMENT COMPLAINT

Date

Beth Jones
1246 Timber Lane Avenue
Dayton, OH 45427

Dear Beth:

We have received your complaint of sexual harassment on the part of your supervisor Larry Brown and want you to know that we take any complaint of harassment very seriously.

I have talked to our Accounting Manager, Gary Ryan, and our Vice President of Human Resources, Jean Smith, and followed my telephone discussion with a letter to both executives asking them to launch an immediate investigation into this matter. Please be assured that if we do find harassment has taken place we will not allow it to continue. It is our intent to provide all employees with a positive work environment.

If you wish to discuss this matter further while the investigation is taking place, please feel free to call either Jean Smith or me.

Sincerely,

Les Johnson
President

TO EEOC REGARDING ALLEGATION OF AGE DISCRIMINATION CHARGE

Date

Ms. Mary Beekman
U.S. EEOC
St. Louis District Office
84 N. Hampden
St. Louis, MO 63137
RE: Case No. 111-11-111

Dear Ms. Beekman:

In response to your letter of October 2, 19XX, Manfield Corporation presents the following information for your review in the age discrimination charge filed by Sam Jones:

Allegation	*Response*
1. I was the only plant maintenance engineer over 50 years old who was terminated.	Mr. Jones chose to retire; he was not terminated. Four other engineers over age 50 are still working for the Company.
2. My retirement pay is $40 a month less than the estimates I received four months ago.	The benefits calculation made in January included a tentative percent salary increase for all employees that management subsequently did not grant. The figures given Mr. Jones were preliminary estimates subject to final verification on the date he actually retired.
3. My performance was acceptable, but I was not offered another job.	Since Mr. Jones voluntarily elected retirement, this allegation is not relevant.

The Company denies that any act of discrimination occurred in Mr. Jones's decision to retire. If you need further information you may call me at (303) 592-4004.

Cordially,

Donna Patrick
Manager, Employee Relations

To Employees Covering Annual Report of Employee Benefit Plans

Date

Dear Fellow Employees:

As a Crossland Electronics employee, you participate in many excellent benefit plans. If you or a member of your family incurred medical expenses this past year, you are certainly aware of the value of the Medical Insurance Plan. If you have started to plan for your future financial security, you know the importance of the Pension and Savings Plans.

Chances are you are not aware of the extent of the company's cost for providing these benefits. For this reason, we are mailing under separate cover a Summary Annual Report of Employee Benefit Plans. The report is an annual statement on the financial management of certain benefits—those that are insured or have assets in the Trust Fund. In it you will find facts and figures on the following plans:

- Pension
- Life Insurance
- Medical
- Business Travel
  Accident Insurance

- Employee Stock Ownership
- Savings
- Dental
- Accidental Death and
  Dismemberment Insurance

When you consider the vital protection these plans provide, it is easy to see the importance of maintaining them on a financially sound basis. As the report shows, we can be confident that our benefits will be there when we need them. The company pays the entire cost for all these plans, except for any contributions you may make to the Savings Plan and Employee Stock Ownership Plan.

Important as these plans are, they form only part of the total benefit package. For example, you are also eligible for sick pay, long-term disability, and educational assistance. Another benefit—your yearly vacation entitlement—grows automatically with your career at Crossland.

If you have any questions on this report or any other aspect of your employee benefit program, please contact Lane K. Blake, Manager, Compensation and Benefits.

Sincerely,

Larry W. Wisner
Vice President
Human Resources

LETTER QUESTIONING CLAIMS PROCESSING TIME

                                                                        Date

Mr. Mark J. Torres
Assistant Benefits Manager
The General Life Assurance Company
   of America
136 Jones Street
Kansas City, KS 66205

Dear Mr. Torres:

I am enclosing a letter and claims log from Mrs. Jean Thompson at Electronic Data Services Corporation concerning General's claims turnaround time and unresolved claims.

We have selected a small sample of claims on the log for you to measure actual turnaround time. Please prepare a report showing date received, date paid, and number of work days required for processing.

As of May 19 we have resolved our problems with turnaround time since your last five weekly claim reports indicate that 80 percent of the claims are processed within another one to five days. Mrs. Thompson indicates a nine-work-day average for April, with a six-and-one-half-work-day average at month's end. These figures are consistent with the significant improvement in turnaround time we experienced during April.

Additionally, Mrs. Thompson indicates on the log that there are a number of claims for which no response has been received from General. Please review these claims and indicate their status to me.

In the future, we will follow up with General on any "no response" claims within twelve work days from date mailed. If this is acceptable to you, please advise me accordingly.

If you require any further information, please let me know.

Sincerely,

Harold T. Bradford
Manager, Employee Benefits

LETTER TO EMPLOYEE REQUESTING 401(K) HARDSHIP WITHDRAWAL

Date

Ms. Julie K. Hewitt
431 Prince Street
Rochester, NY 14607

Dear Julie:

This letter is in response to your request for a hardship withdrawal from your 401(k) plan with GMI Engineering, Inc. As I mentioned to you on the telephone, GMI is covered, as are all companies who have 401(k) plans, by Internal Revenue Service regulations.

On December 9, 1988, the IRS issued Notice 88-127 which clarifies certain provisions of the 401(k) regulations including those on hardship withdrawals. Under the regulations a 401(k) plan may not make a hardship distribution unless the plan established that (a) an employee has an immediate and heavy financial need, and (b) such need cannot be satisfied from other resources reasonably available to the participant. Other resources might include selling other assets, or borrowing form a bank.

Our benefits committee does not believe that obtaining a hardship withdrawal to consolidate bills would be considered a serious hardship by the IRS, and therefore, we must deny your request for the withdrawal at this time.

Sincerely,

Martha M. Frey
Benefits Manager

MEMORANDUM TO EMPLOYEES ANNOUNCING A NEW COMPANY BENEFIT

DATE: _____

TO: All Employees

FROM: Vern T. Watson
            Personnel Director

DATE: January 1

REF: NEW COMPANY BENEFIT

As you know, we are in the process of automating more and more of our administrative, technical, and engineering functions at Matheson Nugent.

In order to provide the necessary computer hardware and to encourage employees to learn how to use personal computers, we have designed the following computer purchase program:

- All employees who can show that a computer will increase productivity in their jobs may participate.

- The computers will be used mainly for work-related purposes, but will become the property of the employee after a two-year period.

- The company will approve an employee's proposal to buy a computer when it appears that the machine will pay for itself within 18 months through improved productivity.

- If the employee uses personal funds to purchase the computer, the company will lease the computer by paying a maximum of $1,000 over a 24-month period.

- Employees who don't have the entire up-front costs can borrow up to $1,000 to purchase the computer and pay the loan back over two years through payroll deduction.

- At the end of either arrangement the computer will belong to the employee. Employees may use the computers for personal business and take them home if they wish.

We hope that this program will enhance productivity and computer literacy and will be viewed as an enhancement to our company benefit program.

Confirming Company Participation
in Support of Employee Bowling League

Date

Mr. Bill Shumane
Brown Engineering Company
Box 200
Orlando, FL 32802

Dear Bill:

I'm following up on your memo and our telephone conversation with regard to the Orlando Bowling League. I have reviewed your request with management and am pleased to confirm the following support for your league:

- The company will pay the cost of shirts, with logos, and any sponsor's fees.
- It will be up to each employee to pay bowling costs and association fees.
- It is our understanding that you will have both a men's and a women's league, and that the leagues are open to all employees.

Please send a Request for Disbursement form to me for approval when you're ready. If you have any questions, don't hesitate to give me a call.

Best wishes for a winning season!

Sincerely,

David Gifford
Employee Relations Director

To Employees Regarding United Way Drive

DATE: _____

TO: All Employees

FROM: Kathy Langston, Personnel Manager

SUBJ: UNITED WAY CAMPAIGN

Recently Mr. Jefferson wrote to you about our annual United Way campaign goal of $25,000 in employee pledges. To kick off the campaign, we are holding a series of meetings on Thursday and Friday, October 1 and 2. So that we can avoid having entire departments at one meeting at one time, we have divided the company alphabetically into four groups. Please try to attend at the time indicated for the first letter of your last name. Of course, if you can't attend at that time, you are welcome to attend another session.

A–D	9:00 A.M., Thursday, October 1
E–K	10:00 A.M., Thursday, October 1
L–R	9:00 A.M., Friday, October 2
S–Z	10:00 A.M., Friday, October 2

All sessions will be held in Conference Room "A."

The meeting will consist of introductory remarks, a presentation by Norm Compton (a loaned executive from Conoco), details of the campaign, and a film about the work of the United Way.

Last year, our employees contributed $17,000, and the Company contributed $5,000 to the United Way. Attached is a breakdown of how that $22,000 may have been put to use by United Way agencies. It is a graphic illustration of how much good our dollars really can do when united with the dollars of others.

With a fair share contribution from everyone, we will surpass our $25,000 goal easily. Scoreboards will be placed at various locations in the building so that we can see how we stand.

Help us help others—so that when the campaign is over, we can say to each of you, "Thanks to YOU, it really works for all of US."

SAMPLE COBRA LETTER TO EMPLOYEES
SUMMARY OF RIGHTS AND OBLIGATIONS REGARDING
CONTINUATION OF GROUP HEALTH PLAN COVERAGE

TO: Employees of XYZ Company

FROM: Director Human Resources

DATE: xx/xx/xx

SUBJECT: Continuation of coverage under the group health plan
maintained by the Employer (the Plan)

IT IS IMPORTANT THAT ALL COVERED INDIVIDUALS TAKE THE TIME TO READ THIS NOTICE CAREFULLY AND BE FAMILIAR WITH ITS CONTENTS.

The Consolidated Omnibus Budget Reconciliation Act (COBRA) requires that the employer offer to employees, their spouses and dependents the opportunity for temporary extension of health (medical and dental) coverage called "continuation coverage" where coverage under the Plan would otherwise end due to certain specific events (listed below).

To Whom Does This Continuation Apply?

Continuation of coverage under a group health plan may be elected for the following Qualifying Events:

Qualifying Events for Covered Employee—If you are an employee of the XYZ Company and covered by the Company's medical and/or dental coverage, you may have the right to elect continuation coverage if you lose your group health coverage because of a termination of your employment or a reduction in your hours of employment.

Qualifying Events for Covered Spouse—If you are the spouse of an employee of XYZ Company and covered by the Company's medical and/or dental coverage, you may have the right to elect continuation coverage for yourself if you lose group health coverage under the Plan for any of the following reasons:

1. A termination of your spouse's employment or reduction in your spouse's hours of employment with XYZ Company;

2. The death of your spouse;

3. Divorce or legal separation from your spouse; or

4. Your spouse becomes entitled to Medicare.

Qualifying Events for Covered Dependent Children—If you are the covered dependent child of an employee covered by the Company's medical and/or dental coverage, you may have the right to elect continuation coverage for yourself if you lose group health coverage for any of the following reasons:

1. A termination of a parent's employment or reduction in the employee's hours of employment with XYZ Company;
2. The death of a parent employed by XYZ Company;
3. Parent's divorce or legal separation;
4. The parent employed by XYZ Company becomes entitled to Medicare;
5. You cease to be a "dependent child" under the XYZ Company Plan (for example, you are between the ages of 19 and 25 and are no longer a full-time student, or you are over the age of 25 irrespective of whether or not you are a full-time student).

Rights similar to those described above may apply to retirees, spouses, and dependents if the employer commences a bankruptcy proceeding and these individuals lose coverage within one year of one or one year after the bankruptcy filing.

The taking of leave under the Family & Medical Leave Act does not constitute a qualifying event under COBRA.

What Is the Election Period and Coverage?

The employee or a family member has the responsibility to inform the Company/Plan administrator via enrollment/change form of a divorce, legal separation, or a child losing dependent status under the company's medical and/or dental coverage within 60 days of the date of the event or the date on which coverage would end under the Plan because of the event, whichever is later.

When the employer is notified that one of these events has happened, you will be notified that you have the right to choose continuation coverage. You have at least 60 days from the date you would lose coverage because of one of the events described above to inform the employer that you want continuation coverage.

If you do not choose continuation coverage within the 60 day election period, your opportunity to elect group health insurance coverage will end.

If a qualified beneficiary elects continuation coverage and pays the applicable premium, the employer will provide the qualified beneficiary with coverage that is identical to the coverage provided under the Plan to similarly situated employees and/or covered dependents.

For What Period of Time May the Coverages be Continued?

1. *18 Months of Continued Coverage*

    If the event causing the loss of coverage is a termination of employment or a reduction in work hours, each qualified beneficiary will have the opportunity to continue coverage for 18 months from the date of the qualifying event.

2. *29 Months of Continued Coverage*

Continuation of coverage can be extended to 29 months if a qualified beneficiary is disabled in accordance with the provisions of the Social Security Act at the time of the covered employee's termination of employment or reduction of hours. The extension to 29 months is available only if the qualified beneficiary provides notice of the determination of his or her disability under the Social Security Act within the 18-month period after the qualified event. The notice must be given within 60 days after the date of the disability determination to the employer. The employer must also be notified of any final determination that the qualified beneficiary is no longer disabled.

3. *36 Months of Continued Coverage*

If the event causing the loss of coverage was the death of the employee, divorce, legal separation, or a dependent child ceasing to be a dependent child under the XYZ Company's medical and/or dental plan, each qualified beneficiary will have the opportunity to continue coverage *up to 36 months* from the date of the qualifying event.

Secondary Events—An extension of the 18 month continuation period can occur, if *during the 18 months* of continuation coverage, a secondary event takes place (divorce, legal separation, death, Medicare entitlement, or a dependent child ceasing to be a dependent). If a secondary event does take place, then the 18 months of continuation coverage can be extended to 36 months from the original qualifying event.

If a secondary event occurs, it is the responsibility of the qualified beneficiary to notify the employer. In no event, however, will continuation coverage last beyond 36 months from the date of the event that originally made the qualified beneficiary eligible for continuation coverage.

Medicare Entitlement—There is a special rule for Medicare entitlement. If a covered employee has an 18-month qualifying event and becomes entitled to Medicare during that period, the continuation coverage period for qualified beneficiaries (for example, spouse less than 65 years old) other than the covered employee will be terminated 36 months from the date the covered employee becomes entitled to Medicare.

Under What Circumstances May Coverage Under This Continuation Be Terminated?

The law provides that *if elected and paid for,* continuation coverage may end prior to the maximum continuation period for any of the following reasons:

1. XYZ Company ceases to provide any group health plan to any of its employees;
2. Any required premium for continuation coverage is not paid in a timely manner;
3. A qualified beneficiary becomes covered under another group health plan that does not contain nay exclusion or limitation with respect to any preexisting condition of such beneficiary;
4. A qualified beneficiary becomes entitled to Medicare;
5. A qualified beneficiary extended continuation coverage to 29 months due to a Social Security disability and a final determination has been made that the qualified beneficiary is no longer disabled;

6. A qualified beneficiary notifies the employer that they wish to cancel continuation coverage.

When Must a Decision to Continue Be Made?

A covered employee, spouse, or dependent has 60 days from the date coverage would otherwise terminate or the date the election notice is sent to you, whichever date is later.

How and to Whom Are Premium Payments Made?

For the first premium payment, you have 45 days from the date you elect to continue coverage to pay the retroactive premium. Thereafter, your premiums are payable on the first of each month. There is a grace period of 30 days for the regularly scheduled monthly premiums. If your payment is not received within this time basis, your insurance will be canceled. No statements will be sent.

Important Notifications Required by an Employee, Spouse, and Dependent

The employee, spouse, or other family member has the responsibility to inform the employer of a divorce, legal separation, or a child losing dependent status under the XYZ Company's medical and/or dental coverage. This notification must be made within 60 days from whichever date is later, the date of the event or the date on which coverage would be lost because of the event. Please check with the human resource department for procedures to follow in making this notification. *If this notification is not completed in a timely manner. then rights to continuation coverage may be forfeited.*

Notification of Address Change

To ensure that all covered individuals receive information properly and efficiently, it is important that you notify the employer of any address change as soon as possible. Failure on your part to do so may result in delayed notifications or a loss of continuation coverage options.

Eligibility, Premiums, and Potential Conversion Rights

A qualified beneficiary does not have to show that they are insurable to elect continuation coverage. The XYZ Company however, reserves the right to verify eligibility status and terminate continuation coverage retroactively if you are determined to be ineligible or if there has been a material misrepresentation of the facts. A qualified beneficiary may have to pay all of the applicable premium plus a 2% administration charge for continuation coverage. These premiums may be adjusted in the future if the applicable premium amount changes. In addition, if continuation coverage is extended from 18 months to 29 months due to a Social Security disability, the XYZ Company can charge up to 150% of the applicable premium during the extended coverage period. There is a grace period of 30 days for the regularly scheduled monthly premiums.

Any Questions?

If any covered individual does not understand any part of this summary notice or has questions regarding the information or your obligations, please contact the Director of Human Resources at (303) 919-9990.

SAMPLE COBRA LETTER TO TERMINATING EMPLOYEE OR DEPENDENT

Date

Mr. Eldon Johns
32981 Harbor Street
Boston, MA 02215

Dear Eldon:

You are eligible to receive healthcare coverage from Putman Power Products Corporation as a result of the Consolidated Omnibus Budget Reconciliation Act (COBRA).

The regulation affects former employees, including retirees and dependents of employees whose coverage under our healthcare program has stopped.

Under this law, you may purchase the same medical, dental, and prescription drug coverage provided to current employees for up to 18 months. The attached sheet summarizes the items covered by the medical plan.

Your monthly cost is $175.00 for individual coverage and $300.00 for family coverage. This is equal to the company's cost of providing the same coverage to each of our current employees. You are not required to furnish proof of insurability to receive this coverage.

If you accept the coverage, you must complete, sign, and mail the enclosed application form to our Human Resources Department within 60 days of receipt of this letter. The premium is due within 45 days of your application for coverage and may be paid monthly or in a single payment. Your payments should also be mailed to the Human Resources Department.

Healthcare benefits under this program will stop automatically at the end of the 18-month period, or sooner if you stop making the payments, become covered under another employer's healthcare plan, or become eligible for Medicare. It could also stop if for some reason our company discontinued the employee healthcare plan.

Your dependent children automatically receive the same medical coverage as you if you choose to participate. They will have an opportunity to apply for the individual coverage for themselves when they no longer qualify as your dependents. This happens when they reach age 19, when they are no longer full-time students, or sooner if they get married.

If you fail to apply for coverage within 60 days of receiving this letter, or fail to send your first premium payment within 45 days of enrolling, you will forfeit your right to coverage under the healthcare plan.

If you have any questions about the program or the provision of the law, please write or call me at (212) 555-8931.

Sincerely,

Fred J. Corbin
Human Resources Manager

SAMPLE ALTERNATIVE COBRA LETTER TO EMPLOYEES

Date

Dear Employee:

You and your eligible dependents may continue participation in the firm's group medical and dental plans even though certain events occur which would otherwise cause loss of coverage. This continued coverage is provided by the Consolidated Omnibus Budget Reconciliation Act (COBRA), a federal law enacted on April 7, 1986. This notice is intended to inform you of your rights and obligations under the continuation coverage provisions of the new law.

How the Law Will Apply:

1. Your coverage can be extended up to 18 months if one of the following (qualifying events) occurs:
   - Your employment with the firm terminates for any reason (including voluntary resignation or retirement) other than gross misconduct.
   - Your working hours are reduced to a level at which you would no longer be eligible for coverage.

2. Coverage for your eligible dependents can be extended up to 36 months if one of the following "qualifying events" occurs:
   - They are covered under the plans and you die while still employed.
   - You or your spouse become legally separated or divorced.
   - A dependent child reaches maximum age for coverage.
   - Your spouse or dependents are under age 65 when you become eligible for Medicare and are no longer an active employee.

The Full 18- or 36-Month Extension Will Not Apply If:

- All employer-provided medical or dental plans are terminated.
- You do not pay your required premium in a timely manner.
- You or your dependents become (an employee) covered by any other group medical and/or dental plan.
- Your former spouse remarries and becomes covered under another group medical and/or dental plan.
- A dependent becomes eligible for Medicare (Medicare eligibility terminates coverage only for the Medicare-eligible individual).

How to Obtain This Continuation Coverage

You or a family member must notify the plan administrator in the event of a divorce or legal separation, or if a child loses dependent status under the Plan. You must notify the plan administrator of the employee's death, termination of employment, reduction of hours, or Medicare eligibility. The plan administrator will, within fourteen days of receiving notification, inform you or the dependent of the right to choose continuation coverage. You do not have to show that you are insurable to choose continuation coverage. Please note that prompt notification is extremely important. You will have at least sixty days from the date you would otherwise lose coverage to inform the plan administrator is you want continuation coverage. If you do not elect continuation coverage, your group health plan coverage will end.

Your Cost for Continuation Coverage

You will be charged the full cost of coverage under the group plan in which you are enrolled. We will no longer pay a portion of it. You will also pay a 2 percent administrative charge. (*Note:* This may still be less expensive and provide better coverage than an individual health policy.)

You may pay for the continuation coverage on a monthly basis. You must make your first payment within forty-five days after the date you elect the continuation of this coverage. Subsequent payments must be made to the Human Resources Manager by _____ _____.

This Does Not Affect Your Normal Conversion Privilege

You will still have the option to convert your group coverage to individual coverage. If you first elect continuation coverage under our group plan(s), your election period to convert to an individual policy will be the last 180 days of your continuation coverage. If you do *not wish* to continue coverage under the group plan(s), you must make your conversion election for individual coverage within thirty days of the date your regular group health coverage ends. The new continuation coverage option under our plan does *not* apply to life insurance. If you wish to convert your group life insurance to individual life insurance, you must elect to do so within thirty days of the date your regular group life insurance coverage ends.

If you have any questions about either the conversion option or the continuation coverage option, please call or write:

(Insert name of your carrier)

Also, if you have changed marital status, or you or your spouse have changed addresses, please notify the plan administrator at the above addresses.

Sincerely,

Scott Macon
Human Resources Director

CONDOLENCES ON DEATH OF EMPLOYEE'S SPOUSE

Date

Mr. John K. Kennedy
1632 Sunset Boulevard
Los Angeles, CA 91607

Dear John:

Please accept our sincere condolences on the death of your wife. Words cannot express the sorrow we feel. We want you to know that our thoughts and prayers are with you.

If there is anything we can do to help you during this time of sorrow, please call on us.

Sincerely,

Harold M. Morrow

Personnel Manager
The Samson Company

11

PERSONNEL CHECKLISTS

- 50 Ways to Save Money in the Human Resources Area
- Employee Planning Checklist
- Checklist of Eight Uses for Temporary Help to Lower Payroll Costs
- Checklist to Use When Writing Recruiting Ads
- Applicant Interview Checklist
- Checklist of Questions You May Not Ask in an Interview
- Checklist for Use in Evaluating Interview or Appraisal Data
- New Employee Orientation Checklist
- Affirmative Action Planning Checklist
- Checklist for Investigating Sexual Harassment Complaints
- Yearly Salary Program Checklist
- Training and Development Checklist
- Checklist for Meeting Your Training Needs While Saving Money
- Checklist for Developing New Communications Programs
- Checklist and Guidelines for Using an Outside Consultant
- Human Resource Management (HRM) Merger Checklist
- Checklist and Manager's Guidelines for Handling Drug or Alcohol Problems on the Job
- Checklist for Avoiding Litigation When Terminating an Employee
- Checklist for Use in Preparing for a Layoff
- Checklist of Security Activities
- Checklist for Maintaining a Safe Workplace
- Checklist for Establishing a Complaint or Grievance Procedure
- An ADA Checklist for Employers

PERSONNEL CHECKLISTS

This chapter includes over twenty personnel checklists and a list of 50 Ways to Save Money in the Human Resource Area. Using checklists can save a lot of time. If you find yourself suddenly faced with the need to lay off employees without much advance warning and time to get ready, turn to the layoff checklist and it will help you get started in the right direction. If you are writing recruiting ads and need some help in getting started, turn to the checklist on writing classified ads. Because most business people face time restraints, these checklists can be a valuable tool.

50 WAYS TO SAVE MONEY IN THE HUMAN RESOURCES AREA

Business people are always looking for ways to retain profits. Here are 50 ways to save the valuable dollars in the Human Resources area.

1. Lease workers from an employee leasing company. It covers payroll costs and provides benefits that a small business might not be able to afford. It also handles the unemployment and workers' compensation costs and claims.

2. Use temporary help for short-term assignments. Contract with a temporary help agency and eliminate payroll and benefits costs. Try people on a temporary to permanent basis and ask the temp agency to waive their fee if you try the person and pay a fee for 90 days.

3. Try job-sharing. In an area where it is hard to find good people, you may be able to attract two experienced employees to fill one job. If you provide benefits, however, it could cost you money because you have two people on the payroll instead of one. If you consider them both part-time employees, you may not need to provide any benefits.

4. Post open jobs and recruit inside the company to avoid outside recruiting costs.

5. Ask current employees to help you recruit outside the company to fill jobs. This could also cut recruiting costs.

6. Let people work at home. This saves them transportation expenses and saves you in outlays for utilities, equipment, office furniture and so on. You may need some specific personnel policies to cover home workers.

7. If you have jobs you can't fill, you are losing money while they sit vacant. Try odd-hour scheduling. You may pick up some good, experienced people who need a second job.

529

8. Use retired workers on a project or part-time basis. They don't expect benefits because most people already have them, and most retired people have an income so they don't demand high wages.

9. If you spend the money to run a help wanted ad, set up an after-hours hotline and recorder to take calls when people are off work and can apply. This saves your staff some time.

10. Train people you already have on staff to take on one or two extra assignments. Most employees are not so busy that they can't do one or two extra things. This also can provide some added incentive to learn something new. Add to an employee's skill bank. If you have job descriptions, add a phrase at the bottom that says, "and may be expected to perform other tasks that may be assigned from time to time."

11. Consider changing the way your company is structured. Perhaps reorganizing a department can eliminate the need to add a new person.

12. Use a new employee orientation program that includes training in the new job and gets a new employee "up to speed" quickly. Many small companies put employees to work in a new job without proper indoctrination or training. Lost production costs directly affect your bottom line.

13. Review recruiting and selection costs on a regular basis to identify unnecessary expenses.

14. Be thorough in pre-employment reference checking to eliminate the possibility of hiring people who are "job hoppers," or who chronically file for workers' compensation. The costs of replacing people are much higher than you think.

15. If you are a federal contractor, periodically analyze your "impact ratio of hires to applicants by EEO category" in order to avoid litigation costs if there is an adverse impact.

16. When you set up a formal wage and salary program, eliminate as many jobs and layers of supervision as you can and still run a cost-efficient operation. Let attrition eliminate unnecessary jobs.

17. Establish a variable merit pay plan based on performance. Pay your top performers more than the people who simply show up and fill a desk.

18. Use a performance-based (as objective as you can make it) appraisal system. Weed out poor performers; they cost big dollars in lost productivity.

19. Hire a compensation consultant to help you install an income deferral program. This cuts costs of payroll and benefits.

20. If you pay your top executives a bonus, tie the bonus to company profits or sales increases.

21. Pay key executives more in the way of non-cash perks and deferred compensation.

22. To avoid costly litigation, monitor your pay practices. Be sure you don't pay men more than women in the same jobs, and that promotional increases for males and females are equitable and nondiscriminatory.

23. You can save the company money by performing a benefits needs analysis of your workforce. Don't spend money on benefits that are not needed or wanted.

24. Use a health maintenance or a preferred provider organization to cut the costs of medical benefits. Also, require a second opinion before any major surgery.

25. Ask employees to pay a portion of their medical benefits to cut costs.

26. Use careful claims administration of medical, dental, and other insurance claims, including selective audit controls of hospital bills.

27. Monitor coordination of benefits provisions to exclude double payment of the same expense.

28. Perform a training needs analysis to ensure your training dollars are spent where they are most needed, and will provide the best return on dollars spent.

29. If you do a lot of training, perform a training audit once or twice a year to see which departments and managers spend the most money . . . decide if the budget is being spent wisely.

30. If you spend a lot of money on outside training programs, bring the training in-house and use your own trainers. Once you develop your own programs, they can be used over and over again.

31. Use local colleges and universities to train in areas where the college is already teaching the programs you need.

32. Trade training programs and services with trainers in other companies. Ask the other trainers to put on the programs. Be prepared to respond when you are asked to do outside programs for other companies. Barter training to cut costs.

33. Utilize your information services people to teach classes on the PC.

34. Review governmental policies as they apply to your particular industry and your company. Be sure you have the policies you need to avoid future litigation.

35. Policies should provide control without strangling a company. They should set the conditions of employment; when they do, they save the organization money in the areas of unemployment compensation and workers compensation.

36. Have a policy that says employees must take or lose vacation pay. Vacation or sick pay that accumulates does so at an increasingly higher rate of pay as the employee receives raises.

37. Have workable discipline and discharge policies and have people who are terminating voluntarily sign a separation form. A great deal of money can be lost in unemployment compensation claims if terminations are not handled properly.

38. If some of your employees have an alcohol or drug problem, install an employee assistance program, or save money by using an outside consultant.

39. Use a lump-sum salary increase from time to time. You may not want to do this every year, but the lump-sum salary increase can be a one-time pay increase based on performance, and does not increase base pay.

40. Perform a quarterly audit/report on where human resource costs are. If you can identify where the costs are, you can usually install a program to control them.

41. Install safety rules that cut workers' compensation and high medical costs.

42. Make a concerted effort to retain a union-free status. A union costs both the employee and the employer money.

43. If you are a manufacturer, consider installing a quality control program to increase quality and productivity.

44. Institute a suggestion program that pays for suggestions that improve the way things are done in your company. Many companies have experienced substantial cost savings through suggestion systems.

45. You can save the company a great deal of money in salaries if, when you reorganize, you eliminate one or more levels of management. Most companies don't need all the levels of management they have.

46. Gain control of human resource forms. Most departments have more forms than they need. Forms do save an organization money in the long run, but too many forms are just an added cost.

47. Train people who screen and interview applicants to cut down on the time they spend by setting specific interviewing hours, and by being as specific as possible in recruiting ads so the number of people who apply will be smaller but will be better qualified.

48. Audit and review your computer costs. Do a periodic review of the number of computer reports you receive and the need for these reports. Check your computer security on a regular basis.

49. Many businesses with low skill service jobs can successfully employ disabled workers. It saves your tax dollars for support of government social programs in the long run if you employ the disabled.

50. If you add a late shift, you can hire workers who need a second income.

EMPLOYEE PLANNING CHECKLIST

The following items will assist with preparation of a comprehensive human resources plan:

❑ Prepare a current database for your human resources plan. The database is your current workforce analysis. Prepare a human resource inventory for each department that is to be included in the forecast and the plan for that particular area. Include a measure of productivity (number of projects, amount of sales, etc.). Identify the types and numbers of people to be included in the forecast.

❑ Analyze the data you have compiled. Then, review past economic objectives, productivity, and actual staffing. Review current trends and projected future demands and prepare a preliminary human resource forecast.

❑ Working with each department, review external concerns such as new technology or social and environmental issues. Make assumptions regarding the future and the impact of these changes on the forecast.

❑ Prepare the forecast for review and approval.

❑ Translate forecast numbers into position specifications. Write job descriptions. Evaluate jobs. Set salary ranges.

❏ Prepare cost estimates that include numbers of people, recruitment costs, relocation costs, and the costs of salaries, benefits, space, equipment, training, and other miscellaneous items.

❏ Review current employees against projected positions. Employees who do not meet job specifications on forecast positions are screened out.

❏ Prepare a labor market assessment.

After these eight steps have been completed, management will have the opportunity to:

1. Accept the forecast and proceed with implementation of the plan.
2. Modify the forecast as needed to meet the organization's objectives, then authorize the next step in the process.
3. Reject the forecast and repeat the process.

CHECKLIST OF EIGHT USES FOR TEMPORARY HELP TO LOWER PAYROLL COSTS

❏ Placing employees on the payroll of a temporary help service during their probationary period can minimize a company's unemployment compensation rates.

❏ Temporary help teams are a new service offered by some agencies. Teams of word processors, data processors, salespeople, and so on, can staff a whole department until permanent staffing is arranged.

❏ Mandatory retirement policies can cause an organization to lose valuable employees at a time when a particular project is crucial to the business plan. A temporary help service can assist by transferring the person to its payroll, thus easing the pressures on both the company and the employee.

❏ Before a company recruits a permanent employee for a new position, a temporary worker can be used to determine whether a valid position really exists.

❏ Consider using temporary help for one-time demands involving a special project such as product sampling, assembling an annual report, taking or doing the extensions on inventory, or a data processing conversion program, where a team of persons can go in for a short term and complete the project.

❏ Smoother transitions can be delivered when temporary workers are used during office or plant relocation as job vacancies occur.

❏ Temporaries can fill crucial spots until a hiring freeze is lifted.

❏ Sometimes exactly the right applicant comes along, but it takes a week or more to process the paperwork for authorization to hire the person. During this delay, the prospect may consider another attractive offer. If a manager can place the applicant on the job immediately, but on a temporary service firm's payroll, the problem of losing the applicant may be averted.

CHECKLIST TO USE WHEN WRITING RECRUITING ADS

A certain percentage of jobs will be filled by help-wanted ads and recruiting literature, but so many ads are sterile and boring. There is no way to know exactly how effective advertising is, even if you keep records of applicants who respond to your ads. Keep these ideas in mind when preparing an ad:

- ❏ People are attracted by class. If you can afford it, use display ads. Be sure the ads reflect the company personality.
- ❏ Use a clean-cut type style and graphics.
- ❏ The first few words need pizzazz to hook the reader and appeal to the people you want to attract. They should be printed in large type.
- ❏ Make sure your ad is placed under the appropriate job classification.
- ❏ Use your company logo if you have one.

When writing your ad, make sure you:

- ❏ List specific skills.
- ❏ List work experience required.
- ❏ State whether relocation is necessary.
- ❏ State educational requirements.
- ❏ Indicate whether the job requires regular travel.
- ❏ State whether you will train.
- ❏ Provide a good review of your overall benefit program and any other items such as "mountain location" or "mild year round climate" that you consider a benefit.

Do not include:

- ❏ References to age or sex or use any other discriminatory language.

APPLICANT INTERVIEW CHECKLIST

You have to make critical decisions based on the information you get during an interview. Because smart applicants are usually well-prepared, the information they give you may be shaded or even false. You should plan your interview strategy ahead of time. The following checklist will help:

- ❏ Be sure you know the job before you start the interview.
- ❏ Learn about the applicant in advance.
- ❏ Plan the interview in order to come away with the information you need.
- ❏ Establish a comfortable conversational style to build rapport.
- ❏ Use plain language and reveal aspects of yourself in order to give as well as get information.
- ❏ Maintain objectivity about the applicant as the interview progresses.

❏ Remain flexible and guide the conversation from general to specific and from harmless to sensitive areas.

❏ Listen. Concentrate on what the applicant is saying. Show empathy and respond appropriately.

❏ Structure the interview so that you use a variety of questioning techniques. Use more open-ended questions rather than questions that can be answered "yes" or "no."

❏ Don't ask questions that could be considered discriminatory.

❏ Give information during the interview. There should be a true one-to-one exchange.

❏ Use silence to obtain more information. If the applicant seems to run out of things to say, let the silence build up for a few seconds. The applicant probably will offer more information.

❏ If there are statements you'd like the applicant to expand on, repeat them in another way. This is called *echoing* and is an effective information-gathering technique.

❏ Watch for the "halo effect," where an interviewer permits one or two favorable traits, such as good appearance or speaking ability, to bias judgment favorably on other entirely unrelated traits. The halo effect can work in reverse, biasing the interviewer unfavorably because of one or two bad impressions.

❏ Don't talk too much. Respect the applicant's need. Exchange information.

❏ Show energy and enthusiasm. A stiff, formal interviewer will turn off most applicants.

❏ Don't try to give advice or counsel in a selection interview.

❏ Follow up hunches and unusual statements. If the applicant says, "I don't get along with certain kinds of people," you want to find out who those kinds of people are.

❏ Maintain control of the interview.

❏ Close the interview in a reasonable period of time. Close on a positive note, but don't lead an applicant on or promise anything you can't deliver.

❏ As soon as the interview is over, write down the facts and your impressions of the interview.

Sample Questions

❏ I'd like to discuss your technical experience. Tell me about your experience in the technical area.

❏ What were your major responsibilities in your last job?

❏ In your last job, what duties did you spend most of your time on?

❏ How did you feel about the progress you made with your last company?

❏ In what ways do you feel your past job developed you to take on greater responsibility?

- ❏ What are some of the reasons you had for leaving your last job?
- ❏ What were some of the things you particularly liked about your last job?
- ❏ Most jobs have pluses and minuses. What are some of the minuses in your last job?
- ❏ Did you consider your progress on the job representative of your ability? Why?
- ❏ What are some of the things your boss did that you particularly liked or disliked?
- ❏ How did your manager rate your job performance?
- ❏ What did your manager feel you did particularly well? What were major criticisms of your work?
- ❏ How do you feel about these criticisms?
- ❏ What kind of people do you like working with? What kind of people do you find most difficult to work with?
- ❏ What are some of the things in a job that are important to you? Why?
- ❏ What are some of the things you would like to avoid in a job? Why?
- ❏ How do you feel your last company treated its employees?

Unstructured (Open-Ended) Questions

- ❏ Tell me about . . .
- ❏ Would you tell me about . . . ?
- ❏ I'd be interested in knowing . . .
- ❏ How did you feel about . . . ?
- ❏ Would you explain how . . . ?
- ❏ I'm not certain I understand . . .
- ❏ Would you explain that in more detail?
- ❏ What do you mean by that?
- ❏ Tell me more about . . .
- ❏ Perhaps you could clarify . . .
- ❏ What was there about . . . that appealed to you?
- ❏ Did you have an opportunity to . . . ?

CHECKLIST OF QUESTIONS YOU MAY NOT ASK IN AN INTERVIEW

Questions seeking the following information are illegal and may not be asked of an applicant before he or she is hired:

- ❏ Date of birth
- ❏ Maiden name
- ❏ Previous married name

- ❏ Marital status
- ❏ Name of spouse
- ❏ Spouse's occupation and length of time on the job
- ❏ Spouse's place of employment
- ❏ Number of children and their ages
- ❏ Arrest record
- ❏ Convictions may be asked about, but you may not refuse employment because of a conviction, unless it is a bona fide job qualification
- ❏ Child care arrangements
- ❏ Reasons that would prevent an applicant from maintaining employment
- ❏ Ancestry
- ❏ National origin/race
- ❏ Age
- ❏ Sex
- ❏ Religion
- ❏ Affiliations with a union
- ❏ Garnishment of wages

It should be kept in mind that much of the above is the type of information necessary for personnel records and employee benefit programs. However, the information is obtained only after employment and therefore can have no bearing on the employment decision.

CHECKLIST FOR USE IN EVALUATING INTERVIEW OR APPRAISAL DATA

Consider the following personality traits of each applicant or employee being appraised. Items preceded by a minus sign are examples of unfavorable findings with respect to a given trait; those preceded by a plus sign are examples of favorable traits. The column on the right is provided for your use in rating applicants or employees.

PERSONAL FLEXIBILITY	+	–
+ Has shown an ability to handle a number of job assignments simultaneously.	☐	☐
– Personal approach reflects a tendency to be structured; tends to be a perfectionist.	☐	☐
+ Seems to like jobs involving contact with many types of people and diverse job situations.	☐	☐
+ Is flexible in personal approach.	☐	☐
– Not willing to compromise.	☐	☐

PERSONAL MATURITY   +   −

− Tends to rationalize failures.   ☐   ☐

+ Has learned to accept limitations.   ☐   ☐

− Displays chronic dissatisfaction with jobs, working conditions, peers,   ☐   ☐
  and superiors.

+ Has career goals and is optimistic about them.   ☐   ☐

+ Has mature outlook on life and work in general.   ☐   ☐

+ Understands things are not always black or white; can handle ambiguity.   ☐   ☐

EMOTIONAL STABILITY   +   −

+ Shows an ability to maintain composure in face of adversity or frustration.   ☐   ☐

+ Maintains emotional balance under trying personal circumstances.   ☐   ☐

− Has had problems with supervisors and/or peers on more than one occasion.   ☐   ☐

− Is unable to deal with others' shortcomings.   ☐   ☐

− Allows emotions to rule business decisions.   ☐   ☐

− Is abrupt with subordinates or staff employees.   ☐   ☐

ABILITY TO BE TACTFUL   +   −

+ The manner in which person phrases remarks reflects tact and consideration.   ☐   ☐

− In discussing relationships with subordinates, the person shows lack of   ☐   ☐
  sensitivity.

+ The person is a good listener.   ☐   ☐

− "Bad mouths" previous/current employer.   ☐   ☐

− Tells jokes at the expense of others.   ☐   ☐

+ Is sensitive to communication needs of others.   ☐   ☐

+ Is knowledgeable and tactful in business and social situations.   ☐   ☐

IS A TEAM PLAYER   +   −

+ The person operates successfully as a team player.   ☐   ☐

− Is strongly motivated to be the "star."   ☐   ☐

+ Seems to place the accomplishments of the group ahead of personal ego.   ☐   ☐

− Displays poor interpersonal skills and tends to be intolerant of others.   ☐   ☐

DISPLAYS FOLLOW-THROUGH   +   −

+ Once the person starts a job, seems to hang in there.   ☐   ☐

− There is indication the person starts more things than can be completed.   ☐   ☐

+ Has achieved one or more career goals.   ☐   ☐

+ Appears to follow through.   ☐   ☐

- Does not follow through.   ☐   ☐

Shows Initiative + —

+ Has demonstrated ability to operate successfully without close supervision. ☐ ☐
+ Reaches out for increasing responsibility. ☐ ☐
+ Evidence indicates the person is a self-starter. ☐ ☐
− Seems to dislike unstructured situations. ☐ ☐

Shows Assertiveness + —

+ Seems willing to take a stand on what is right. ☐ ☐
− Not sufficiently demanding of subordinates when the situation calls for it. ☐ ☐
− Seems overly concerned with the feelings of others. ☐ ☐
+ Has a positive assertive nature. ☐ ☐
− Has a negative assertive nature. ☐ ☐

Personality Traits + —

+ Personality has considerable positive impact. ☐ ☐
− Tends to be introverted. ☐ ☐
+ Has an outgoing, personable style. ☐ ☐
− Is ego-oriented and at times rude. ☐ ☐
+ Displays empathy and sensitivity. ☐ ☐
+ Understands and conforms to social graces. ☐ ☐

Is Conscientious and Loyal + —

+ Works overtime when necessary. ☐ ☐
+ Shows a conscientious nature. ☐ ☐
+ Shows a loyal nature. ☐ ☐
− Appears aloof and uncaring about management or the organization. ☐ ☐

Self-Confidence + —

+ Appraises own abilities realistically. ☐ ☐
+ General manner and style show poise. ☐ ☐
− Does not have sufficient confidence to discuss shortcomings. ☐ ☐
− Appears overconfident. ☐ ☐
− Lacks a sense of self-confidence in business dealings. ☐ ☐

Honesty and Openness

+ Is willing to give credit when credit is due. ☐ ☐
− Tends to exaggerate own accomplishments. ☐ ☐
− Stories seem to be inconsistent in terms of other statements or findings. ☐ ☐
− Brags about "pulling a fast one" or about accomplishments. ☐ ☐

+ Is willing to discuss unfavorable aspects of personal business experience. □ □
+ Is comfortable when discussing own shortcomings. □ □

TOTAL +s ___

−s ___

These categories can be used effectively to assist in evaluating an applicant or employee. Not all of them pertain to everyone, but they will get you thinking about specific qualities needed for a particular job. You may come up with other questions that better fit your own situation. Are there more pluses or minuses?

It is helpful to write a summary of your feelings immediately after the interview or performance appraisal has taken place. Concern yourself with the most important findings in terms of the person's overall qualifications.

NEW EMPLOYEE ORIENTATION CHECKLIST

Employees look to supervisors as a prime source of information about the company and working conditions. Here is a list of fifty questions which your supervisors should be able to answer for new employees.

Job/Working Conditions

❏ How long is a new employee on a temporary evaluation period?

❏ When and how should an employee report an absence from work? How long can the employee remain absent without notice before becoming subject to discharge?

❏ Is promotion determined by merit, by seniority, or by both? How can an employee find out about jobs that may be open?

❏ How is an employee's performance appraised? How frequent are performance evaluations?

❏ How does the grievance procedure work? Exactly what should an employee do when he has a grievance?

❏ What is the policy on layoffs? How long can a layoff last? What are the recall rights of the employee? Does the recalled employee retain seniority?

❏ What about physical examinations? Is an employee's health checked periodically or after an illness?

❏ Can you answer employees' questions about the company medical program? How long are lunch periods and is the employee paid for them?

❏ What eating facilities are available? When are they open? What kind of food is available?

❏ When and how long are rest periods?

❏ How does the seniority system work? Is it plant-wide, departmental, or a combination?

❏ When, where, and under what conditions can an employee smoke?

❏ On what basis is an employee penalized for being late?

❏ What is the company's system of warnings and penalties when rules are broken?

❏ How can an employee make a personal telephone call or receive an incoming call?

❏ Is an employee obliged to join the union as a condition of employment? If so, when? Does the company check off dues?

❏ How much cleanup time is permitted for workers on machines or on a production line?

Pay

❏ What are the company's overtime policies? What does it pay for work over eight hours in a day? On holidays? On Saturdays? On Sundays? Is there a meal allowance when overtime goes into the evening?

❏ Does an employee get premium pay for working afternoon and night shifts? How much?

❏ When, where, and how is an employee paid?

❏ If there's an incentive system, how does it work?

❏ If an employee reports for work and none is available, is he/she entitled to call-in pay? How much?

❏ If an employee is injured on the job and sent home, is he/she paid for a full day, a half day, or just the time he's/she's in the plant? Will he/she be given other work during convalescence, or won't he/she be permitted to resume his/her job until he's/she's completely recovered?

❏ What is the policy on severance pay?

❏ Is an employee given time off to vote?

❏ Does the company pay employees who are on jury duty?

❏ What is the policy on military leave when the employee is drafted? When he/she enlists? If he's/she's in the National Guard, does the company pay for time spent in encampment?

❏ How is vacation pay computed?

❏ What is company policy on pay increases?

❏ Does the company give periodic bonuses?

Benefits

❏ Can you explain your company's sick leave program? Is there a paid sick leave besides sickness and accident insurance? If so, how long does it last?

❏ What is the company's leave-of-absence policy?

❏ When does an employee become eligible for pension benefits? Insurance? Hospitalization benefits?

❏ What about vacations? When does a new employee become eligible for a vacation? How long is it? Are longer vacations granted as length of service increases? Can you carry over vacation time from one year to another?

❏ Does the company make loans to employees? Is there a credit union? How does it operate?

❏ Is there a company training program? Does the company sponsor any educational courses? If an employee wants to take an outside course at a college or technical school, will the company pay part or all the cost?

❏ What holidays are given during the year?

❏ Is there an employee stock-purchase plan? If so, how does it work?

❏ If there's a contributory insurance program, how much does the employee pay? The company?

❏ What's provided in the company pension plan? What are the eligibility requirements?

❏ When can an employee retire?

❏ Can you tell an employee what his pension income will be, based on his present earnings?

Miscellaneous

❏ Can you tell an employee how he/she can get news into company publications? How he/she can use the bulletin boards?

❏ Is there an employee counseling service?

❏ Do you know what employee organizations there are?

❏ How does the suggestion system operate? To whom should an employee submit an idea? Who decides if it's acceptable? How are awards calculated?

❏ Do you know how big your company is? What it makes? What the product is used for? Its annual sales? Can you give a brief outline of its history?

❏ What is your organizational culture? Your company's management style?

❏ What is your company's reputation in the community and as a corporate citizen?

AFFIRMATIVE ACTION PLANNING CHECKLIST

Affirmative action plan forms and positions statements are fairly standard today in most organizations. Title VII of the Civil Rights Act of 1964, Executive Order 11246 which applies to federal contractors and subcontractors and Revised Order No. 4 (41CFR Part 60-2) specify requirements of written programs. This checklist will help you get started with your program.

KEY ELEMENTS OF AN AFFIRMATIVE ACTION PLAN:

- ❏ Corporate policy statement
- ❏ Policy dissemination/communication
- ❏ Assignment of an EEO coordinator
- ❏ Workforce analysis
- ❏ Goals and timetables
- ❏ Development and execution of the program
- ❏ Support of community and outreach programs
- ❏ Effective auditing and reporting systems

In addition to these key elements of the plan you should:

- ❏ Develop and update the affirmative action plan annually.
- ❏ Implement affirmative action plans to include internal and external communications.
- ❏ Design and implement audit and reporting systems that will measure the effectiveness of the AAP, indicate the need for remedial action, and determine the degree to which the company's goals and objectives are being achieved.
- ❏ Identify potential and actual problems within particular departments.
- ❏ Assist management in the resolution of problems related to EEO/AAP.
- ❏ Inform management of the latest developments in the area of equal employment opportunity and on legal issues.
- ❏ Serve as liaison among the company's minority, female, and handicapped organizations and governmental compliance agencies.
- ❏ Participate in the development of goals and timetables and assist department managers with efforts to achieve the established goals.

CHECKLIST FOR INVESTIGATING SEXUAL HARASSMENT COMPLAINTS

You should take every complaint of sexual harassment seriously and investigate it thoroughly using the following step-by-step procedure:

Step 1—Notify the Human Resource Manager immediately when there is a change.

Step 2—Interview the complainant. What does he/she say happened? Who is named as harasser? Where and when did the incident take place? Were there witnesses? Was it an isolated incident or part of a series? Has he/she spoken to anyone else about the incident?

Step 3—Interview the accused harasser. Stay objective. Assume nothing. Put every statement in writing. Remember your notes may end up in court.

Step 4—Interview the witnesses. Phrase the questions so you don't give any information or influence the comments.

Step 5—Weigh all the evidence. Consider the credibility of each party based on the reputations of the employee and the alleged harasser. Is there any possibility that the employee is trying to make trouble for a supervisor? Are there previous complaints against the accused harasser? Have you investigated the charge as thoroughly as you can?

Step 6—Discuss what action to take with the Human Resource Manager or with legal counsel. Once you have all the facts, ask yourself if sexual harassment did occur. If you decide the accusation is without merit, write a detailed report explaining why and have the evidence to back it up. If harassment did occur, there are several options based on the severity of the case. The Human Resource Manager or your legal counsel will help you decide on the ultimate course of action.

Here are some options:

Option 1—First offense, written warning. It should include a statement that sexual harassment is against company policy, and that any additional complaints will result in disciplinary action, up to discharge. The complainant should be aware of any action taken against the harasser. Follow-up is absolutely essential to make sure the harassment stops.

Option 2—Consider transferring the accused or offering a transfer to the complainant. Make sure transfer of complainant is not retaliation and that the complainant accepts the transfer as a positive resolution to the problem.

Option 3—Suspension or discharge is usually reserved for repeated offenses or a severe first offense. You must be consistent in the penalties you impose. You can't fire one manager for sexual harassment and suspend another for identical offense.

YEARLY SALARY PROGRAM CHECKLIST

As you start the preparation of your next yearly salary program use this checklist to ensure review of all compensation areas.

- ❑ Identify each unit of the organization that will require a separate salary program and merit budget. For example, you may have the corporate headquarters people, salaried and hourly employees at outlying locations, and scientific or special technical people at a research facility. Each of these groups requires a separate survey and separate salary program, and the specific jobs must be correlated with the jobs in the survey in order to ensure that you are comparing apples with apples.

- ❑ Look at the company's competitive position for each group by reviewing appropriate compensation surveys.

- ❑ Review the Bureau of Labor Statistics cost-of-living changes for the past year.

❏ Review the organizational changes that have taken place during the past year to see what jobs have changed, what relationships between jobs have been altered, and how the wage structure should change as a result.

❏ Look at your local industry practice, especially if the wage surveys you use are national.

❏ Review grade, step, or career ladder adjustments.

❏ Set merit adjustments based on performance levels and monitor where employees are in their salary range.

In order to motivate and retain employees at all levels of the organization, the salary program and merit budget must be competitive, must reward performance, and must be perceived by all employees as competitive and equitable. In addition, the salary program must be flexible enough to fulfill the needs of each individual in the company.

TRAINING AND DEVELOPMENT CHECKLIST

Most organizations realize that they must pay attention to training their most valuable asset, their employees. The best employees a company has are intelligent, insightful, and talented, and they are the most difficult people to attract and retain. Here is a checklist to use to ensure you have a varied and effective training program. The program must be:

❏ an offshoot of the corporate strategic plan, the succession plan and the corporate performance appraisal program.

❏ reviewed and approved by all levels of management who will have employees involved in the program—there must be management buy-in.

❏ designed to address the needs of employees at all levels.

❏ frequently monitored and revised to stay in tune with forecasts, corporate requirements and workforce needs.

❏ designed to have an effective and up-to-date delivery system like CD-ROM, computer-based training, long-distance training, etc.

❏ cost-effective, establishing a direct link between needs requirements and costs.

❏ varied enough to maximize the talents and abilities of employees at all levels of the organization.

❏ tied-into management level planning process and ongoing weekly or monthly meeting agendas in all departments.

❏ reviewed and decisions made regarding the use of both in-house and outside training programs for each level of employee, based on individual employee needs and departmental needs.

❏ open to the idea of outsourcing certain training programs. Outsourcing has become more popular in the high-technology environment and there are thousands of companies that provide training programs.

CHECKLIST FOR MEETING YOUR TRAINING NEEDS
WHILE SAVING MONEY

Organizations are always on the lookout for ways to maximize revenues by more effectively using their employees throughout the organization. It is especially important to look for creative ways to save money and still do a good job of training and development. The following ideas will help you maximize training dollars:

❏ Conduct training programs in-house, using current staff. For example, an accounting manager can teach a course on budgeting, an employment manager or interviewer can teach a course for managers on interviewing. By allowing your staff to participate in training and development activities, you give them a growth opportunity and save training dollars.

❏ Trade services with training professionals in other companies. For example, if your trainer has expertise in communication skills, and a trainer in another company you know has expertise in time management, it's cost-effective to trade out the training time on an hour-for-hour basis rather than teaching each trainer to present a new program. Maintaining contacts with other companies in order to facilitate trades in expertise makes economic sense.

❏ Cut human resources training costs by charging outside seminars and conferences back to the department. When department managers know that outside seminar costs will show up in their budgets, they are more selective when sending employees to outside programs.

❏ Develop formal cross-training programs in-house in order to double your on-staff expertise. Include formal shadowing and mentor programs to use the expertise you already have.

❏ Use local community colleges to provide training programs. They are usually less expensive then large commercial companies.

❏ Use more video and audio cassette programs. They cost less and can be used over and over to offset initial development costs. A tape course can be taken while on the job or driving to and from work.

❏ Set up a system of formal written critiques of all courses or seminars that the company sponsors for any employee. The critique files will tell you which programs are worthwhile and which are not. This file will help you maximize the return on your investment.

❏ Check with department managers before you schedule training programs to make sure your programs will be held when the largest number of employees are available, to make the best use of the trainer's time. Classes that are not full are not cost-effective.

❏ There are thousands of films, filmstrips, and slide programs that can be borrowed free of charge from companies, associations, governmental agencies, and other sources. *The Educator's Guide to Free Films,* found in most libraries, lists many resources.

CHECKLIST FOR DEVELOPING NEW COMMUNICATIONS PROGRAMS

❏ Use video newscasts to let employees know what is going on in the company. Send them to all locations on a regular basis.

❏ Implement a program of early evening meetings once a month for discussion of specific topics or current business books. Ask the CEO or other top executive to lead the discussion groups.

❏ Try the new action-oriented bulletin boards that provide cartoons and messages on pertinent subjects.

❏ Start a newsletter or overhaul your current one. Put in more information on what the company is doing and what you expect to occur in the future.

❏ Start lunch-hour programs, brown bag lunches, etc. Have speakers on current topics. You can usually get speakers free or for small cost.

❏ Start inexpensive training programs on skills or subjects that need attention. Trade instructor skills with other companies. If you have someone who can teach stress management, trade time with an instructor in another company who can teach Spanish as a second language.

❏ Appoint committees of employees to look into new ideas, production techniques, customer service approaches, etc., used by other organizations. Have the committee report back at a brown bag lunch on their findings.

❏ Install a company hotline for one or two months. Tell employees in the newsletter you've done this and that if they have any problems or questions they can call in 24 hours a day and let the company know. If they leave their name they will receive a direct answer within a set time limit. If they don't want to leave their name you will still provide an answer in the newsletter.

❏ Have regular employee meetings where executives talk on various topics. Open the meetings to questions from employees.

❏ Provide an annual report to employees on the state of the company. Provide information on personnel and benefit programs.

❏ Have issues-management brainstorming sessions. What issues do employees think will impact the company in the next five years?

❏ Form an in-house speakers bureau. Help employees gain the skills they need to participate. Provide speakers for local community groups.

❏ Provide the mechanism for employees to volunteer to work together in the community to help those less fortunate.

❏ Hold lectures for employees on topics of current interest. Invite political candidates, interesting business people, etc., to speak to employees.

❏ Start an in-house library that includes magazines, books, and tapes on current topics and allow employees to use the materials.

❑ Start health and fitness programs and sponsor athletic events. This can be done for very little cost.

All of these ideas will foster improved communications throughout the organization by bringing employees at all levels together.

CHECKLIST AND GUIDELINES FOR USING AN OUTSIDE CONSULTANT

Ask yourself and any potential consultants the following questions:

❑ Why should I go outside the organization for assistance? Is their expertise available in-house?

❑ What about the time issue—How immediate is the need? What are the time limits of your staff or yourself?

❑ Budget considerations? Consultants may be less expensive than internal staff. They will concentrate on a specific issue or a specific problem, and some will guarantee results.

❑ Sales calls from consultants should not justify hiring someone or altering your priorities. Be careful of salespersons selling the answer to all your needs.

Assuming that you have decided to look outside the organization for expertise, here are some specific criteria for selection:

❑ Prior track record—what organizations were previously served? What topics or services were rendered? When were the services rendered? Whom can you contact at those organizations to verify results? If they can't supply these kinds of specific data, continue your search.

❑ Can you see or hear the consultant by previewing a demonstration tape? Would they consider a briefing session for a select group of managers or employees at minimal or no cost? What about an executive briefing? What would they charge for a pilot program?

❑ For persons who will be conducting programs, are they adult-centered in their teaching or seminar leading? How would they describe their presentation style? Do they encourage participation? Do they use audio-visuals? If they don't answer these questions to your satisfaction, continue looking.

❑ Are your candidates generalists or specialists? Do they have a list of topics they can consult and conduct programs on? Be wary of "can do all" types. They are probably not the people for your program.

❑ Ask for a written proposal based on what you see as your needs. Look for training objectives and outcomes in such proposals. If they can't write down what the expected outcomes are, it is doubtful that any will be realized.

HUMAN RESOURCE MANAGEMENT (HRM) MERGER CHECKLIST

❏ How many companies will be involved in the merger?

❏ Are they all in the same business? If not what other business are they in?

❏ What are the key human resource issues that must be resolved?

❏ Does each company have a separate handbook and personnel policy manual? If so, these manuals must be revised into one manual that will cover all the personnel issues that the one merged company will have. Meet with CEO and other key executives to resolve personnel policy issues before revising the manual.

❏ Review compensation plans for each company. What is the best way to bring all employees under one umbrella? Does one pay plan fit the entire group? Should it be a grade plan, or a point evaluation plan? Are there both exempt salaried employees and non-exempt hourly employees? Are there pieceworkers or incentive workers? Do any of the companies have shifts or alternative work schedules? How does management see the compensation program?

❏ Review benefits for the new company and the old companies. Can one new plan be designed that will fit everyone's needs and have a reasonable cost to the organization? Who is handling benefits? Are they planning to review all the benefit programs? Do they have the needed expertise? Should the surviving company "shop" their benefits?

❏ How are the companies handling benefits regulatory issues like COBRA and IRS or other regulatory concerns?

❏ Does the merged company have an adequate affirmative action program? Does the company have government contracts? Have any of the companies ever had a desk audit? Do the companies keep good records? Does the new company need an EEO/AAP internal audit?

❏ Do the companies being merged have training or development programs? Is there one program that is better than the others? How does management feel about training? Is specific training needed because of the merger? If so, what?

❏ Does one company need specific training the other companies don't need? If so, how will that be handled?

❏ How is recruiting and employment handled? Will all merged companies send open requisitions to one personnel person who will handle the recruiting, advertising and so forth?

❏ Does the merged company have a good personnel records or administration function? If not, what is needed?

❏ How about other regulatory concerns? Does the company comply with the Civil Rights Act, ERISA, OSHA, Immigration Law, and so forth? What specific regulatory concerns do you have?

❏ Does the company have good discipline and discharge procedures? Are the procedures being followed?

❏ Have proper safety and health policies and procedures been established? What are the key policies? Review accident reports and OSHA Form 200s records.

❏ Does the organization have security procedures for personal property, commercial property, computers, and so forth. If not, these should be drafted immediately.

❏ Does the main company now do any type of employee planning, including HR staffing reports?

❏ What types of reports are now being done in the HR area? Are they all needed? If not, what reports are needed?

❏ Does the company have a computer/HRIS system? Is it working effectively? Do the other companies have systems that will need to be merged? What will it take to merge computer systems? Is anyone in charge of HRIS? What actions must be taken?

❏ What are the other significant areas of HRM concern and activity needed to effectively complete the merger?

❏ List people/resources in the company who can assist with the merger.

CHECKLIST AND MANAGER'S GUIDELINES FOR HANDLING DRUG OR ALCOHOL PROBLEMS ON THE JOB

Even when a company has good policies and procedures and an employee assistance program (EAP) benefit, supervisors must be trained to spot problems and must know what to do when faced with an alcohol or drug problem. Following are guidelines for supervisors for discussions with employees.

❏ Make it clear that you are concerned for job performance, productivity, and attendance, and that you want to help the employee improve job performance.

❏ Remember that documented evidence of a downward trend in performance or attendance is the best tool to help a valued employee recognize a possible illness or addiction and to motivate the person to seek assistance.

❏ Behavioral problems that cause declining job performance, which the employee has been unable or unwilling to correct, will only get worse.

❏ Make it clear to the employee that the employee assistance program, if you have one, is a benefit and that assistance is available and recommended.

❏ Explain that employees must decide for themselves whether to seek assistance through the EAP. Either way, unless job performance improves, the employee's job is in jeopardy.

❏ Emphasize that all employee problems are kept completely confidential.

Don't try to diagnose the problem:

❏ Listen, but don't offer advice for solving personal problems. An employee's responsibility includes handling these situations so they do not continue to interfere with job performance. The supervisor's responsibility is to see that the employee gets professional help.

❏ Don't be misled by sympathy-evoking tactics or other seemingly acceptable excuses when they are used excessively. Insist that the employee get help.

❏ Don't moralize—right or wrong, good or bad—concerning personal behavior. It isn't your responsibility to judge. Restrict criticism to your responsibility for subordinate on-the-job performance and attendance.

❏ Don't cover up for friends. Your well-meaning but misguided kindness can lead to delay in the employee receiving needed help, and the situation, without effective intervention, will become more serious.

The key is to take action, to get help for the employee as soon as possible. There are consultants who can help companies set up employee assistance programs.

CHECKLIST FOR AVOIDING LITIGATION WHEN TERMINATING AN EMPLOYEE

❏ Be sure you use progressive and positive discipline when discipline is necessary.

❏ First give a verbal warning and then a written warning before terminating an employee.

❏ Be sure all employees understand your work rules.

❏ Have specific disciplinary procedures and make sure everyone follows them.

❏ Avoid emotional incidents where a supervisor may fire someone on the spot in a fit of anger.

❏ Don't block a terminated employee's chances to get another job—don't give negative references on a former employee.

❏ Be sure you document any actions taken against an employee in the employee's personnel file.

❏ Be sure that all discipline is handled in an evenhanded manner and is not discriminatory.

❏ Make sure employees have everything they need to do their job well.

❏ Use a termination checklist to make sure you have covered all bases before you complete a termination.

❏ If you have special concerns about a termination consult a labor relations expert or an attorney.

CHECKLIST FOR USE IN PREPARING FOR A LAYOFF

No one likes the idea of a layoff, but when faced with that possibility it helps to have a well-defined plan. An organized program also gives employees a feeling that they will be treated fairly by the company. Use the following layoff checklist:

- ❏ How many people will be involved?
- ❏ What departments are involved?
- ❏ What will be the layoff criteria? Performance, seniority, job elimination? If it's a job elimination, it may be a reduction in force, rather than a layoff, which means there may be no recall rights involved.
- ❏ Prepare a layoff policy, stating criteria decided upon and what regular pay, severance, and vacation will be paid. You should pay all unused vacation.
- ❏ Determine how much advance notice will be given.
- ❏ Before a layoff or reduction in force, some companies poll employees to determine whether anyone wishes to quit voluntarily. If employees do volunteer to quit, the company should give them the same severance pay other employees will receive.
- ❏ Ask employees who are old enough to retire if they wish to take early retirement.
- ❏ When the layoff notice is given, will employees be allowed time to look for a job before the layoff date?
- ❏ Develop a seniority list.
- ❏ Review the layoff list to see how your affirmative action plan will be affected. What percentages of minorities, women, handicapped, and people over forty are there?
- ❏ Review lists of company property held by employees who will be laid off and make provisions to get it back.
- ❏ Draft letters from management to employees regarding the layoff.
- ❏ Prepare a press release. Send it to the newspapers after employees have been notified.
- ❏ Notify corporate people if you have a corporate relationship.
- ❏ Have appropriate benefits people make arrangements regarding medical and life insurance coverage. Review pension and thrift plans if you have such benefits. Provide insurance conversion forms. Install a procedure for complying with COBRA regulations.
- ❏ Prepare an information sheet to hand out to employees regarding the benefits they will have and for how long.
- ❏ Decide on the amount of severance that will be paid to each employee. If you want employees to stay beyond a certain date, state that the severance will be paid only if employees stay through that date.
- ❏ Prepare an outplacement program that includes workshops, resume writing, and interviewing.

❏ Provide employees with information on how to collect unemployment insurance.

❏ Provide a counseling service for employees with special problems.

❏ Contact employers in the area to find out if there are any employment opportunities, and make terminating employees aware of job openings in other companies.

A layoff or reduction in force is never pleasant, but if you have a game plan it makes the whole outplacement effort much easier.

CHECKLIST OF SECURITY ACTIVITIES

Not many companies have a formal security plan, but a good plan can save a company thousands of dollars. The following checklist will help you establish a security plan.

❏ Screen applicants for potential security risks.

❏ Provide policies and procedures for terminating any employee caught stealing company property.

❏ Employ security guards on staff or on a contract basis if your organization is of a size where the need for guards is indicated.

❏ Install an alarm system to protect facilities.

❏ Mark company equipment for theft prevention and recovery purposes.

❏ Keep an up-to-date inventory of company equipment.

❏ Depending on company size, value of equipment, and building access, require employee identification badges.

❏ Provide procedures for monitoring visitors to facilities. Require visitors to sign in and out, and require that they wear identification badges while on the premises.

❏ Establish a formal evacuation plan for fire, bomb threats, and so on.

❏ Develop written security guidelines for bomb threats.

❏ Develop a community relations program. Work with local community leaders and create a "good citizen" public image in the immediate area of the facility.

❏ Provide emergency first aid equipment in several locations, and post first aid information in accessible areas. Include fire, police, and ambulance numbers.

❏ Communicate company security policies and procedures to employees.

❏ If there is a high incidence of theft, some companies employ an undercover detective service.

❏ Analyze computer security, and establish firm guidelines for access to your computer system.

❏ Audit cash flow and other monetary procedures.

❏ If there is an area of significant loss, form a risk management committee to review the problem.

CHECKLIST FOR MAINTAINING A SAFE WORKPLACE

Your first line of defense against accidents at work is an accident prevention plan. Accident prevention occurs through proper engineering controls, preventive maintenance, safety training, and training on the proper use of equipment. Use the following checklist to help prepare an accident prevention program:

❏ Encourage employees to report hazards.

❏ Be sure offices and plants are clean, well designed, and controlled for noise, heat, dust, and fumes.

❏ Maintain good preventive maintenance programs for production equipment and facilities.

❏ Have supervisors inspect work areas informally every day.

❏ Worker-management teams using checklists should inspect monthly or quarterly.

❏ Annual plant and office safety audits should be completed annually.

❏ Base safety training programs and safety checklists on specific hazard information.

❏ Make refresher safety training available on a continuing basis for all employees including supervisors.

❏ Post all required OSHA notices and any other pertinent safety bulletins and posters.

❏ Be sure all electrical equipment is grounded.

❏ Inspect to make sure that all machinery guards are in place at the point of operation.

❏ Inspect guards for pulleys.

❏ Make sure there are guards for live parts of electrical equipment.

❏ Be sure there are proper enclosures for fan blades within 7 feet of working floor level.

❏ Inspect guards for belt, rope, or chain drives.

❏ Eliminate disorderliness in aisles and passageways.

❏ Hold safety meetings on a regular basis.

❏ Maintain a log on all job injuries and illnesses.

❏ Don't let employees work around dangerous machines when they are ill.

WATCH FOR

❏ Slippery floors and walkways

❏ Tripping hazards such as piping and hoses

❏ Missing entrance and exit signs

❏ Poorly lighted stairs

❏ Loose handrails or guard rails

❏ Broken windows

❏ Dangerously piled supplies or equipment

❏ Open doors on electrical panels

❏ Leaks of steam, water, or oil

❏ Blocked aisles

❏ Blocked fire extinguishers or sprinkler heads

❏ Blocked fire doors

❏ Oily rags

❏ Evidence of smoking in nonsmoking areas

❏ Roof leaks

CHECKLIST FOR ESTABLISHING A COMPLAINT OR GRIEVANCE PROCEDURE

It is important for management of any company to resolve employee complaints quickly and effectively. Here is a checklist of questions to ask yourself before you establish an employee complaint procedure:

❏ What can be brought to management, what can be grieved?

❏ Who is ineligible to file complaints (management)? Who is eligible (management, employees, terminated employees)?

❏ What are the steps that must be followed?

❏ What are time limits on each step and who has the responsibility to take the next action?

❏ Are extension of time limits permitted?

❏ What are the consequences of failing to meet time limitations?

❏ Does grievant have the right to representation by another employee, legal counsel, or a union representative?

❏ Who has the final step in procedure?

❏ Do management representatives in the grievance process have the right to designate a substitute?

❏ What is the standard used to review the grievance (good cause, fairness, accuracy)?

❏ What is the effect of the final decision on all the parties?

AN ADA CHECKLIST FOR EMPLOYERS

The company has long supported equal opportunities for people with disabilities. We support the goals of the Americans with Disabilities Act of 1990 (ADA) because we believe it reflects sound human resource and business practices.

Although this checklist is not intended to be a definitive document on ADA compliance, a "No" answer indicates an area you may need to examine for improvement.

HUMAN RESOURCE POLICIES

YES NO

1. Have you communicated to all employees your company's policy and commitment to employment and reasonable accommodation for qualified applicants and employees with disabilities?   ❏ ❏

2. Have training sessions and/or information been made available to current supervisors and managers regarding their ADA responsibilities?   ❏ ❏

3. Is there a process in place to identify the need for reasonable accommodations and other ADA requirements when employees become disabled?   ❏ ❏

4. Is a system in place to maintain confidential medical and health information separately from personnel files?   ❏ ❏

5. Do you provide the same opportunities of employment to all employees in the same job classification (for example, compensation, benefits, promotion, training, and so on)?   ❏ ❏

6. Have you posted notices regarding the individual rights of employees under the ADA?   ❏ ❏

INTERVIEWING AND HIRING

YES NO

7. Is your application/interviewing process fully accessible to all job applicants?   ❏ ❏

8. Have job applications been checked for prohibited questions related to health, disability or workers' comp history, and have interviewers been advised not to ask questions of this nature?   ❏ ❏

9. Do job descriptions within your company identify the essential functions necessary to perform the job?   ❏ ❏

10. Do employment tests and procedures for taking the tests accurately assess only the necessary skills and aptitudes required to perform the essential job functions?   ❏ ❏

11. Are all employer-requested physicals conducted only after a conditional job offer tendered, and are they required of **all** applicants in that job category?   ❏ ❏

12. Do your post-offer physicals assess only the candidate's ability to perform the essential functions of the offered position? The results of post-offer physicals cannot be used to discriminate against a qualified individual on the basis of disability.   ❏ ❏

13. Are requirements for "reasonable accommodations" understood to be a necessary part of the process when considering an applicant?   ❏ ❏

14. Are managers most likely to be involved with reasonable accommodations aware of the best approach with a disabled person? Have-competent external resources been identified that can be used when needed?   ❏ ❏

OTHER POLICIES   YES NO

15. Have you notified all professional search organizations with whom you have contracts of your intention to fully comply with the ADA?   ❏   ❏

16. Do employees with disabilities have equal access to break rooms, cafeterias, and other facilities (on-site/off-site) provided by you?   ❏   ❏

17. Have you ensured that your company meets its obligations under the Public Accommodations title of the ADA?   ❏   ❏

12

Sample Personnel Forms

- Personnel Requisition
- Applications for Employment (English & Spanish)
- Applicant Appraisal Form
- Telephone Reference Check
- Employee Agreement (E-Mail, Internet)
- Approval of Estimated Relocation Expenses and Allowances
- Personnel Action Notice
- Payroll Time Report
- Overtime Hours Worked Report
- Employee Attendance Record
- Sample Employee Benefit Program—Plan Highlights
- Job Description Outline
- New Employee Orientation
- Employee Agreement (Employment)
- Education Verification Reference
- Employee Transfer Request
- Vacation Request Form

- Employee Absence Report Form
- Leave Request/Return from Leave Form
- Application for Funeral Leave
- Mileage Reimbursement Report
- Travel and Expense Reimbursement Request
- Performance Appraisal Worksheet
- Employee Counseling Activity Sheet
- Supervisor's Checklist and Report for Effective Discipline
- Disciplinary Warning Notice
- Employee Warning Notice
- Exit Interview Form
- Accident/Injury Report
- Supervisor's Report of Accident Investigation
- Attending Physician's Return to Work Recommendations Record
- First Aid Report Log
- Quarterly Safety Performance Record

Sample Personnel Forms

This last chapter provides a great many personnel forms. Some of these forms appeared earlier in the text of the book and some of them appear here for the first time. Remember, you should modify any form to fit your organization's specific needs.

Having these forms in one place will provide a handy resource when time is short. Just copy the form, make needed changes, and you're ready to go.

PERSONNEL REQUISITION

Job title		Department	
Salary Grade	Salary Range	Starting Salary	Date Needed by

Job Duties:

_____
_____
_____
_____
_____
_____

Job Requirements:

_____
_____
_____
_____
_____
_____
_____

Working Conditions

_____
_____
_____
_____
_____
_____
_____

Job Status

❑   Existing Position   Replacement for _____

❑   New Position   Reason Needed_____

                                          _____

❑   Full Time   ❑   Part Time   ❑   Temporary

Schedule _____

Requested by_____	Date _____
Approved by _____	Date _____
Approved by _____	Date _____

APPLICATION FOR EMPLOYMENT
An Equal Opportunity Employer

We do not discriminate on the basis of race, color, religion, national origin, sex, age, or disability. It is our intention that all qualified applicants be given equal opportunity and that selection decisions be based on job-related factors.

Each question should be fully and accurately answered. No action can be taken on this application until all questions have been answered. Use blank paper if you do not have enough room on this application. PLEASE PRINT, except for signature on back of application. In reading and answering the following questions, be aware that none of the questions are intended to imply illegal preferences or discrimination based upon non-job-related information.

Job Applied for_____ Today's Date _____

Are you seeking: Full-time ❑ Part-time ❑ Temporary ❑ employment? When could you start work? _____

Last Name	First Name	Middle Name	Telephone Number

Present Street Address	City	State	Zip Code

Are you 18 years of age or older? .... Yes ❑ No ❑
(If you are hired you may be required to submit proof of age.)

Social Security Number _____ If hired, can you furnish proof you are eligible to work in the U.S.? Yes ❑ No ❑

Have you ever applied here before?............ Yes ❑ No ❑ If yes, when? _____
Were you ever employed here?................ Yes ❑ No ❑ If yes, when? _____
Have you ever been convicted of any law violation (except a minor traffic violation)? .... Yes ❑ No ❑

    If yes, give details_____
    (A "Yes" answer does not automatically disqualify you from employment,. since the nature of the offense, date, and the job for which you are applying will also be considered.)

Are you now or do you expect to be engaged in any other business or employment? .... Yes ❑ No ❑

    If yes, please explain _____

For Driving Jobs *Only:* Do you have a valid driver's license?... Yes ❑ No ❑

    Driver's License Number _____ Class of License _____
    Have you had your driver's license suspended or revoked in the last 3 years? .... Yes ❑ No ❑

    If yes, give details: _____

List professional, trade, business or civic activities and offices held. (Exclude labor organizations and memberships which reveal race, color, religion, national origin, sex, age, disability or other protected status.) _____

LIST NAME AND ADDRESS OF SCHOOLS	Number of Years Completed	Diploma Degree Certificate	Subjects Studies
High School or GED:			
College or University:			
Vocational or Technical:			

What skills or additional training do you have that are related to the job for which you are applying? _____

What machines or equipment can you operate that are related to the job for which you are applying? _____

List names of employers in consecutive order with present or last employer listed first. Account for all periods of time including military service and any periods of unemployment. If self-employed, give firm name and supply business references.

PLEASE GIVE MONTH AND YEAR.

NAME OF EMPLOYER		JOB TITLE AND DUTIES
ADDRESS		
CITY, STATE, ZIP CODE		DATE OF EMPLOYMENT: FROM ___ TO ___
		PAY: START $ ___ FINAL $ ___
SUPERVISOR	TELEPHONE	REASON FOR LEAVING

NAME OF EMPLOYER		JOB TITLE AND DUTIES
ADDRESS		
CITY, STATE, ZIP CODE		DATE OF EMPLOYMENT: FROM ___ TO ___
		PAY: START $ ___ FINAL $ ___
SUPERVISOR	TELEPHONE	REASON FOR LEAVING

NAME OF EMPLOYER		JOB TITLE AND DUTIES
ADDRESS		
CITY, STATE, ZIP CODE		DATE OF EMPLOYMENT: FROM ___ TO ___
		PAY: START $ ___ FINAL $ ___
SUPERVISOR	TELEPHONE	REASON FOR LEAVING

NAME OF EMPLOYER		JOB TITLE AND DUTIES
ADDRESS		
CITY, STATE, ZIP CODE		DATE OF EMPLOYMENT: FROM ___ TO ___
		PAY: START $ ___ FINAL $ ___
SUPERVISOR	TELEPHONE	REASON FOR LEAVING

Have you worked under any other name? .... Yes ☐   No ☐

   If yes, give names: _____

Are you presently employed? .... Yes ☐   No ☐

   If yes, may we contact your present employer? .... Yes ☐   No ☐

Have you ever been fired from a job or asked to resign? .... Yes ☐   No ☐

   If yes, please explain: _____

Give three references, not relatives or former employers.

Name	Address	Phone

PLEASE READ EACH STATEMENT CAREFULLY BEFORE SIGNING

I certify that all information provided in this employment application is true and complete. I understand that any false information or omission may disqualify me from further consideration for employment and may result in my dismissal if discovered at a later date.

I authorize and agree to cooperate in a thorough investigation of all statements made herein and other matters relating to my background and qualifications. I understand that any investigation conducted may include a request for employment and educational history, credit reports, consumer reports, investigative consumer reports, driving record, and criminal history. I authorize any person, school, current and former employer, consumer reporting agency, and any other organization or agency to provide information relevant to such investigation and I hereby release all persons and corporations requesting or supplying information pursuant to such investigation from all liability or responsibility to me for doing so. I understand that I have the right to make a written request within a reasonable period of time for complete disclosure of the nature and scope of any investigation. I further authorize any physician or hospital to release any information which may be necessary to determine my ability to perform the job for which I am being considered or any future job in the event that I am hired.

I understand that compliance with the Company's Corporate Code of Conduct is a condition of my employment.

I understand I may be required to successfully pass a drug-screening examination. I hereby consent to a pre- and/or post-employment drug screen as a condition of my employment, if required.

I UNDERSTAND THAT THIS APPLICATION OR SUBSEQUENT EMPLOYMENT DOES NOT CREATE A CONTRACT OF EMPLOYMENT NOR GUARANTEE EMPLOYMENT FOR ANY DEFINITE PERIOD OF TIME. IF EMPLOYED, I UNDERSTAND THAT I HAVE BEEN HIRED AT THE WILL OF THE EMPLOYER AND MY EMPLOYMENT MAY BE TERMINATED AT ANY TIME, WITH OR WITHOUT CAUSE AND WITH OR WITHOUT NOTICE.

I have read, understand, and by my signature consent to these statements.

Signature: _____   Date: _____

This application for employment will remain active for a limited time. Ask the organization representative for details.

FAIR CREDIT REPORTING ACT

DISCLOSURE

The Company, when evaluating your application for employment, when deciding whether to offer you employment, when deciding whether to promote you, reassign you, or to continue your employment (if you are hired), and when making other employment-related decisions directly affecting you, may wish to obtain and use a "consumer report" about you, from a "consumer reporting agency." These terms are defined in the Fair Credit Reporting Act, 15 U.S.C.S. 1681 et seq. ("FCRA") which applies to you. As an applicant for employment or employee of our company, you are a "consumer" with rights under the FCRA.

"Consumer reporting agency" means a person or business which, for monetary fees, dues, or on a cooperative nonprofit basis, regularly assembles or evaluates consumer credit information or other information on consumers for the purpose of furnishing "consumer reports" to others.

"Consumer report" means any written, oral or other communication of any information by a consumer reporting agency bearing on a consumer's credit worthiness, credit standing, credit capacity, character, general reputation, personal characteristics, or mode of living which is used or expected to be used or collected for the purpose of serving as a factor in establishing the consumer's eligibility for, among other things, employment purposes.

If we obtain a consumer report about you, and if we intend to make an employment-related decision that adversely affects you based in whole or in part on the consumer report, you will be provided with a copy of the consumer report before the decision is made final by our Company. Any decision regarding your employment will be made by us and not by the consumer reporting agency. You are also free to contact the Federal Trade Commission about your rights under the FCRA, as a "consumer," with regard to consumer reports and consumer reporting agencies.

AUTHORIZATION FOR ___(Company Name)___
TO OBTAIN CONSUMER REPORT FOR EMPLOYMENT PURPOSES

By signing below, I hereby certify that I have read and understand *completely* the Fair Credit Reporting Act Disclosure (the "Disclosure") that has been provided to me by _____, and I hereby authorize _____ to obtain for employment purposes a consumer report and/or a motor vehicle report about me and to consider such reports when making decisions regarding my employment. I understand that I have rights under the Fair Credit Reporting Act, including the rights discussed in the above Disclosure provided to me by _____.

_____   _____

Applicant/Employee Name   Date   Witness's Name   Date

_____   _____

Signature   Signature

Un empleador que brinda igualdad de
opportunidades
SOLICITUD DE EMPLEO

Nombre: _____

Apellido   Primer Nombre   Segundo Nombre

No. de Telèfono: _____ No. de Seguridad Social: _____

Dirección Actual: _____

No.   Calle   Ciudad Estado   Código Postal

Puesto al que se postula: _____

¿Empleo a tiempo completo?   **?** Sí   **?** No
¿Empleo a tiempo parcial?   **?** Sí   **?** No

¿En qué días y horas puede usted trabajar? _____

_____

En caso de ser contratado/a, ¿cuándo puede comenzar a trabajar? _____
¿Alguna vez presentó una solicitud de empleo en nuestra compañía en el pasado?_____
_____
? Sí **?** No En caso afirmativo, ¿cuándo?_____ ¿Dónde?_____
¿Usted ha trabajado con nosotros en el pasado? **?** Sí **?** No En caso affirmativo, _____
¿Cuándo?_____ ¿Dónde?_____
¿Cómo llegó a nosotros? Publicidad **?**   Agencia de Colocaciones **?**

Empleado actual **?** Especifique el nombre: _____
Otros **?** Especificar: _____

INFORMACIÓN PERSONAL

¿Tiene usted 18 años de edad o es mayor de 18 años?   **?** Sí   **?** No

(**Nota:** La contratación podrá estar sujeta a la verificación de que usted posee la edad mínima requerida por ley.)

¿Usted cumple con los requisitos legales para trabajar en los Estados Unidos? **?** Sí   **?** No

(**Nota:** La contratación está sujeta a la verificación de que es ciudadano/a estadounidense o que posee status de inmigrante autorizado de acuerdo con la Ley de Control y Reformas de Inmigración de 1986.)

¿Alguna vez fue condenado/a por cualquier delito, exceptuando violaciones de tránsito de poca gravedad?   **?** Sí   **?** No

En caso afirmativo, especifique la naturaleza del/los delito/s, cuándo y dónde fue declarado/a culpable y la resolución del caso: _____
_____
_____

(**Nota:** No se negará *automáticamente* la contractación a los postulantes que hayan sido acusados de un delito. La naturaleza del delito, la fecha del delito, las circunstancias que lo rodearon, y la importancia del delito con respecto al/los puestos al/los que la persona se postula podrán ser tenidos en cuenta, no

**ENUMERE A CONTINUACIÓN TODOS LOS EMPLEOS
ACTUALES Y PASADOS, COMENZANDO POR EL MÀS RECIENTE**

Nombre de la Compañía	Dirección/Número de Telèfono	Empleado		Salario	
		Desde	Hasta	Inicial	Final

Describa sus tareas: Motivo por el cual dejó de trabajar:

Supervisor:

Nombre de la Compañía	Dirección/Número de Telèfono	Empleado		Salario	
		Desde	Hasta	Inicial	Final

Describa sus tareas: Motivo por el cual dejó de trabajar:

Supervisor:

Nombre de la Compañía	Dirección/Número de Telèfono	Empleado		Salario	
		Desde	Hasta	Inicial	Final

Describa sus tareas: Motivo por el cual dejó de trabajar:

Supervisor:

Nombre de la Compañía	Dirección/Número de Telèfono	Empleado		Salario	
		Desde	Hasta	Inicial	Final

Describa sus tareas: Motivo por el cual dejó de trabajar:

Supervisor:

¿Podemos ponernos en contacto con los empleadores enumerados anteriormente?_____
En caso negativo, favor indicar con cuál/es usted no desea que nos pongamos en contacto: _____

ESTUDIOS, CAPACITACIÓN Y EXPERIENCIA

Colegio	Nombre y Dirección	No. de Añós que asistió	¿Se Graduo?	Titulo obtenido o Curso que realizó
Enseñanza Primaria			Sí ☐ No ☐	
Enseñanza Secundaria			Sí ☐ No ☐	
Instituto/ Universidad			Sí ☐ No ☐	
Oficio Actividad			Sí ☐ No ☐	
Otros (Especificar)			Sí ☐ No ☐	

Responda las siguientes preguntas en caso de postularse para un *cargo administrativo:*

¿Escribe a máquina? Sí ☐ No ☐   En caso affirmativo, ¿cuántas palabras por minuto? _____

¿Tiene experiencia en el uso de computadoras? Sí ☐ No ☐   En caso affirmativo, favor explicar: ___
_____

Enumere cualquier otro aparato de oficina que usted sepa manejar: _____

¿Posee usted experiencia, capacitación o habilidades adicionales que sienta que lo/la capacitan especialmente para el/los cargo/s al/los que se postula? En caso afirmativo, favor explicar: _____
_____
_____

REFERENCIAS   **(Escriba a continuación el nombre de tres personas, que *no* sean parientes syuos y que *no* sean antiguos empleadores suyos, y a quienes conozca desde hace al menos un año.)**

Nombre: _____
Dirección: _____
                No.   Calle   Ciudad Estado   Código Postal

                                                    Número de años
No. De teléfono: _____   Que se conocen: _____
Nombre: _____
Dirección: _____
                No.   Calle   Ciudad Estado   Código postal

                                                    Número de años
No. De teléfono: _____   Que se conocen: _____
Nombre: _____
Dirección: _____
                No.   Calle   Ciudad Estado   Código postal

                                                    Número de años
No. De teléfono: _____   Que se conocen: _____
Nombre: _____
Dirección: _____
                No.   Calle   Ciudad Estado   Código postal

FAVOR LEER Y FIRMAR ABAJO

Por la presente certifico que no retuve a sabiendas ningún tipo de información que pudiera afectar en forma adversa mis posibilidades de contratación, y que mis respuestas son verdaderas y correctas, y que no poseo reserva mental alguna. Comprendo que cualquier omisión o declaración en falso de un hecho material contenido en esta solicitud, en cualquier documento utilizado para asegurar la contratación, o durante la entrevista previa a la contratación constituirá causal para que se rechace esta aplicación o para que se me despida inmediatamente en caso de que resulte contratado/a, independientemente del tiempo que haya transcurrido antes de que se descubra tal hecho.

Por la presente autorizo a   a investigar exhaustivamente mis referencias, antecedentes laborales, educación y cualquier otro asunto relacionado a mi idoneidad para el cargo y, asimismo autorizo a mis antiguos empleadores a revelar a todos y cualesquiera de mis antecedentes laborales, incluyendo informes disciplinarios y cartas de reprimenda, sin mediar notificación a mi persona de tal divulgación. Asimismo, por la presente eximo a o a mis antiguos empleadores, sus respectivos directores, funcionarios, empleados y agentes y a todas las demás personas, de todo reclamo, demanda y responsabilidad derivados o relacionados en cualquier forma con tal investigación o divulgación.

Comprendo y acepto que, en caso de ser contratado/a, mi contratación y compensación no se aplican a un período definido o determinado, sino que pueden cesar en cualquier momento, con o sin mediar causa, y con o sin mediar aviso, ya sea por decisión mía o de   Además comprendo y ningún representante de   posee autoridad alguna para celebrar ningún acuerdo de empleo por ningún plazo específico ni para realizar ninguna representación vinculante o acuerdos, ya sea en forma oral o escrita, contraviniendo lo anteriormente mencionado o aduciendo la finalidad de garantizar cualesquiera beneficios, plazos o condiciones de contratación en particular.

NOTA

Esta solicitud permanecerá vigente por noventa (90) días. Si usted no tuvo noticias de luego de noventa (90) días y aún desea ser tenido en cuenta para un empleo, deberá llenar y presentar una nueva solicitud de empleo.

_____   _____
Fecha   Firma del Postulante

COMENTARIOS ADICIONALES: _____

_____

_____

_____

_____

_____

_____

_____

_____

_____

_____

_____

AVISO A LOS POSTULANTED RESPECTO DE LOS INFORMES DE ANTECEDENTES/CONSUMO

Antes de cualquier oferta de empleo se podrá obtener un informe de consumo y/o un informe de antecedentes que incluya información respecto de su personalidad, antecedentes laborales, reputación general, antecedentes judiciales, antecedentes sobre la conducción de un vehículo motorizado, modo de vida y/o actividad crediticia y endeudamiento. Mediante una solicitud por escrito, presentada oportunamente por el Departamento de Personal de la Compañía, y dentro de un plazo de 5 (cinco) días de presentada la solicitud, se le informará a usted el nombre, la dirección y el número de teléfono del organismo informante, así como la naturaleza y el alcance del informe.

Antes de que se tome ninguna medida adversa en todo o en parte como consecuencia de la información contenida en el informe de antecedentes/consumo, se le proporcionará una copia del informe, el nombre, la dirección y el número de teléfono del organismo informante, un resumen de los derechos que usted posee según la Ley Justa para la Divulgación de Información Crediticia, así como la información adicional sobre sus derechos legales.

CONSENTIMIENTO PARA OBTENER INFORMES DE ANTECEDENTES/CONSUMO

Leí la información arriba mencionada y por el presente autorizo a la Compañía a obtener un informe de antecedentes/consumo, tal como se describió anteriormente. Comprendo que poseo el derecho de realizar una solicitud por escrito dentro de un plazo razonable para recibir información adicional y detallada sobre la naturaleza y el alcance del informe, incluyendo el nombre, la dirección y el número de teléfono del organismo informante.

_____

Firma

_____

Nombre en letra de imprenta

_____

Fecha

CONSENTIMIENTO PARA DIVULGAR INFORMACIÓN

Por favor llene la siguiente información a los efectos de identificar sus antecedentes:

Nombre (tal como figura en su licencia de conducir o documento de identidad):

En letra de imprenta: _____
Nombre   Appelido   Segundo Apellido

Indique cualesquiera otros nombres que usted haya utilizado, que no figuren en la solicitud o el curriculum vitae que presentó (Apellido de soltera, otros apellidos de casada, sobrenombres, etc.).

En letra de imprenta: _____

Enumere todas las direcciones en las que haya vivido <u>en los últimos cinco años</u> (incluya el número de calle, nombre de la calle, ciudad, estado y código postal):

Actual: _____

_____

Direcciones Anteriores   Fechas aproximadas

1. _____

2. _____

3. _____

4. _____

Número de licencia: _____ Fecha de emisión: _____
Número de seguridad social: _____ Fecha de nacimiento: _____

De conformidad con la Ley de Privacidad (5 C.E.U.A.), la Ley para la Libertad de Información y la Ley para la Justa Divulgación de Información Crediticia, expresamente autorizo a cualquier persona vinculada a cualquier institución educativa, empleador actual o pasado (incluyendo gobiernos federales/estatales/locales), cualesquiera organizaciones militares (federales o estatales), cualquier organismo para el cumplimiento de la ley (federal/estatal/local), cualquier organismo de información crediticia, cualquier institución u oficina de asistencia médica pública/privada, o cualquier persona que posea un conocimiento personal acerca de mi personalidad, antecedentes laborales, antecedentes médicos (incluyendo resultados de análisis de drogas y/o antecedentes de rehabilitación correspondientes) y modo general de vida a DIVULGAR tal información al organismo informante de mis antecedentes a los efectos de ser considerado para la contratación en un emploe. Por el presente acepto EXIMIR a   empleados, agentes y cualesquiera otras personas u otras entidades de todas y cualesquiera responsabilidad por daños de cualquier especie y naturaleza, conocidos o desconocidos, que pueden en cualquier momento recaer sobre mi persona debido a 1) que tales personas o entidades confien en la información presentada en mi solicitud de emploe, 2) que tales personas o entidades confien en la información obtenida en virtud de esta autorización, 3) el cumplimiento o cualquier intento de cumplir con esta autorización y 4) el cese de mi contratación basado en información obtenida en virtud de esta autorización. Por el presente autorizo a que una copia de esta DIVULGACIÓN sea considerada tan válida como el original.

Firma: _____ Fecha: _____

APPLICANT APPRAISAL FORM

Interview Date _____

Name of Applicant _____ Position _____

This rating form will become a part of the applicant's personnel record which may be made available to governmental compliance agencies upon request.

DO NOT FILL OUT IN THE PRESENCE OF APPLICANT Review the current job description and rate the candidate in all categories below. Comment in each section.	Outstanding	Above Average	Average	Below Average
1. *ESSENTIAL JOB FUNCTIONS*—Can the applicant perform the essential functions of this job?				
2. *EXPERIENCE*—How does previous experience relate to current opening? Consider communications and other skills such as knowledge and information and technical competence based on previous training. Review in light of the essential functions of the job.				
3. *MENTAL CAPABILITY*—Verbal ability, judgment, analytical skills, logic, decisiveness, and so on.				
4. *PHYSICAL CAPABILITY*—Can the applicant perform the physical requirements of the job?				
5. *EDUCATION/SKILLS*—Degree(s), professional licenses, registration, certifications, languages. equipment, computer skills.				
6. *GOALS AND AMBITION*—Initiative, persistence, drive, goals are well defined (as they relate to predicting success on this job).				

General comments: _____

_____

For additional comments use back of form.

Overall Appraisal:

       Outstanding _____ Above Average _____ Average _____ Below Average _____

Recommend employment for current opening: Yes _____ No _____

Future consideration: Yes _____ No _____ If yes, for _____ position

Recommendation based upon: Application Review _____ Interview _____ Telephone Contact _____ References _____

Signature of Interviewer:	Date Completed:

Telephone Reference Check

Applicant's Name _____

Company Contacted _____ Phone No._____

1. When did the applicant work for your company? From _____ To _____

2. What was the applicant's position/title? _____

3. What information can you give concerning
   Quality of work?

   _____
   _____
   _____

   Quantity of work?

   _____
   _____
   _____

   Attendance?

   _____
   _____
   _____

4. Did this person get along well with others? Yes _____ No _____

5. Why did he/she leave your company?

   _____
   _____
   _____

6. Is he/she eligible for rehire with your company? Yes _____ No _____
   If not, why? _____

   _____
   _____

Additional Comments: _____
_____
_____

Information From_____ Title _____

Reference Check Made By _____ Date _____

EMPLOYEE AGREEMENT

_____

(Company Name)

E-Mail, Internet, & Other Computer Services Policy

I have read this Company policy, and I understand and agree to comply with the terms of the policy. Further I understand that violation of this policy may result in disciplinary action and/or termination of employment.

_____

Printed Name

_____

Signature

_____

Date

Workers' Comp Form - Goes After "What to do About Workers' Comp"

(Company Name Goes Here)

**WORKERS' COMPENSATION
EMPLOYEE VERIFICATION FORM**

I have been notified by my employer of the procedure to follow in the event I incur work-related injury or illness. I understand that my employer has designated the
_____ as the primary provider for all work-related injuries and illnesses. I understand that if do not receive my medical care for work-related injuries and illnesses from the _____
I may be financially responsible for that care. See attached list of locations and phone numbers.

I have been informed that authorization is required from my employer before I access medical care for non-emergency work related injuries and illnesses.

_____   _____
Name of Employee (Please Print)   Location

_____   _____
Signature of Employee   Date

_____   _____
Signature of Human Resources Manager   Date

APPROVAL OF ESTIMATED RELOCATION EXPENSES AND ALLOWANCES

Name _____ Social Security Number _____

Account to be Charged _____ Position Title _____

Old Location _____ New Location _____

Effective Date of Hire _____ Present Residence: Own ____Rent ____

Married_____Single_____Head of Household_____Number of Dependents_____

	Estimated Cost	Actual Cost
Cost of moving household goods	_____	_____
Employee travel and lodging to new location	_____	_____
Family travel and lodging to new location	_____	_____
Househunting travel and lodging for employee and/or spouse	_____	_____
Incidental expenses	_____	_____
Federal income tax: allowance	_____	_____
Any other special items to be allowed	_____	_____

Employee's signature _____ Date _____

APPROVALS:

Department Manager _____ Date _____

Vice President _____ Date _____

Chief Financial Officer_____ Date _____

President _____ Date _____

Board (if required) _____ Date _____

Personnel Action Notice

Employee ID # _____   Team #: _____   Date _____/_____/_____

Employee Name _____   SS #: _____/_____/_____

REASON FOR SUBMITTAL: __ New Hire __ Change __ Termination   Eff. Date: _____/_____/_____
_____ Completion of Evaluation Period   _____ Performance Appraisal Attached

Birth Date: _____/_____/_____   Sex: __M __F   __Handicap
   __Caucasian   __Black   __Am. Indian   __Vietnam Era Veteran
   __Hispanic   __Asian   __Other_____   __Disabled Veteran

COMPLETE ITEMS ONLY IF CHANGED:
Address:_____

City: _____   State _____   ZIP: _____   Telephone: _____

Job Title: _____   Grade: _____

1st Division: _____   1st Location:_____   Hrs/Wk: _____

2nd Division: _____   2nd Location:_____   Hrs/Wk: _____

3rd Division: _____   3rd Location:_____   Hrs/Wk: _____
Check All That Apply:
____Full Time   ____Exempt   ____Contract
____Part Time I   ____Non-Exempt   ____Volunteer
____Part Time II   ____Supervisory   ____Student
____Temporary   ____Non-Supervisory   If not Full Time:
         Benefits: __Y   __N   Hours Per Week: _____

Salary Change   Reason for Salary Change (Check One):
____ Annual _____%   ____Merit ____Promotion ____Reclassified ____Other_____
Salary Change: From: To:
Hourly: $_____._____ $_____._____
Biweekly: $_____._____ $_____._____
Annually: $_____._____ $_____._____   Salary Authorization Signature

Signatures:
Employee: _____   Supervisor: _____

For Accounting Use Only   TERMINATION

G/L Accounts: _____ Voluntary   _____ Involuntary

G/L _____   _____%   Last Date Worked: _____/_____/_____

G/L _____   _____%   Check-Off List: __ Completed
                                                              __ Attached

Date Processed _____/_____/_____

_____ _____   _____ _____
Payroll Department Signature   Date   Supervisor's Signature   Date

                                         _____ _____
                                         Human Resources Director   Date

PLEASE RETURN ENTIRE FORM TO HUMAN RESOURCES FOR DISTRIBUTION

PAYROLL TIME REPORT

Work Unit: _____

Pay Period of _____ to: _____ , 19 ___

Date Completed: _____

Approved by: _____

Title: _____

Complete by: _____

Date: _____

Title: _____

EMPLOYEE NAME	POSITION TITLE	SOCIAL SECURITY NO./ EMPLOYEE NUMBER	DATES AND CODE*									
1.												
2.												
3.												
4.												
5.												
6.												
7.												

Examples of coded entries:

8R   - 8 hours regular
4V/4R - 4 hours vacation, 4 hours regular
4.5 SL - 4 ½ hours sick leave

8 WC - workers' comp. time
3 CTO - 3 hours comp. time
8 PD - personal disability

H - holiday
FH- floating holiday

NOTE:
Overtime is calculated on the basis of HOURS WORKED.

OVERTIME HOURS WORKED REPORT

Read instruction on reverse side before completing.

EMPLOYEE REQUEST (Employee complete, print or type)

1. Employee's name | 2. Department/Division

3. Overtime Worked | 4. Name of supervisor who gave prior approval

Date | Day

From _____ AM/PM
TIME
To _____ AM/PM

Total Hours Worked

_____ Hrs. _____ Mins.

5. Purpose for overtime (Explain)

_____

_____

_____

_____

6. Employee's Signature | Date Submitted

7. SUPERVISORY ACTION

A. Supervisor receiving report from employee credit overtime to:

( ) **COMPENSATORY TIME OFF (CTO)**   ( ) **TIME AND ONE-HALF PAY**

	Approve	Disapprove	SIGNATURE	DATE
B.				

8. CLERICAL EMPLOYEE COMPLETE | (√) Completed

A.	Verify figures. Calculate for proper overtime credit: round actual to nearest half hour, then multiply at rate specified by supervisor (ITEM 7-A).	
B.	Enter hours as calculated here: AMOUNT: _____	
C.	Enter hours (ITEM 8-B) to "Payroll Form" with "Overtime Worked" key letter "W"	
D.	File report in department file	

Instructions
Overtime Hours Worked Report

Each eligible employee must receive prior supervisory approval before overtime can be worked. This report must be submitted to the supervisor within twenty-four (24) hours after completion of the overtime. Actual overtime worked as reported by an employee will be rounded to the nearest half-hour interval by the designated clerical employee, then multiplied at the rate (straight-time or time and one-half) specified by the supervisor.

Employee Completes Items 1–6

1. & 2.   Self explanatory.

   3.   Show date and day that overtime was worked in excess of normal workday or shift. Show time period (from/to) and the total hours worked.

   4.   Show name of supervisor who gave prior approval for this overtime.

   5.   Describe in detail the purpose for the overtime. Show case or project number, type of overtime (training, court, call-back), and any other appropriate information.

   6.   Certify this report is correct by signing and dating. Submit to supervisor for action.

Department Completed Items 7 and 8

   7.   As designated by department head: First supervisor to receive report shall check appropriate box that overtime is to be credited (either compensatory time off or time and one-half), sign, date, and forward to other supervisors to review as specified, and forward to clerical employee.

   8.   Clerical employee shall process, make appropriate calculations, and file.

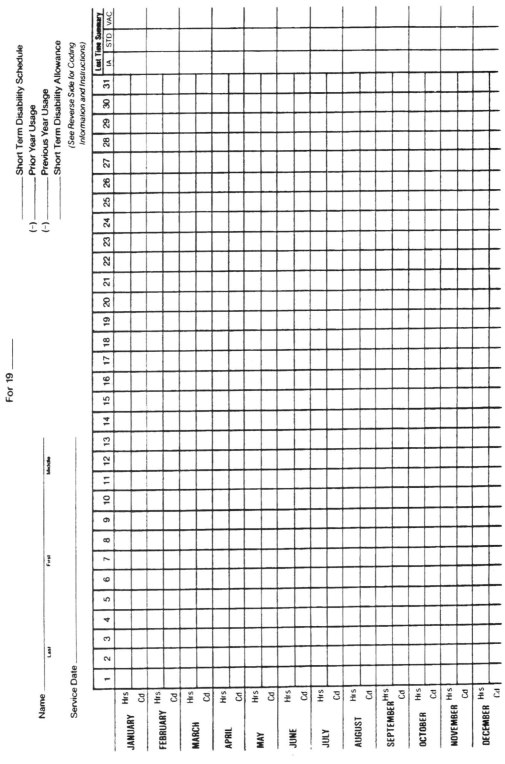

SAMPLE EMPLOYEE BENEFIT PROGRAM
Plan Highlights

PLAN	BENEFIT	ELIGIBILITY PERIOD	EMPLOYEE CONTRIBUTION
Basic Medical Insurance	• Full cost of semi-private room for 365 days • Full cost of in-hospital service • Prevailing fee surgical payments • Outpatient expenses per schedule	None	None
Major Medical Plan	• $100 calendar year deductible • 80% of covered expenses • $250,000 lifetime maximum benefits	None	None
Thrift Plan	• Employee contribution 2% minimum—6% maximum of base salary • Company matches ½ of employee contribution	1 year	Maximum of 6% of base salary
Short-Term Disability Income Plan	• Based on years of service 100% of base pay followed by 75% up to 26 weeks	6 months	None
Long-Term Disability	• 60% of base pay	2 years	None
Dental Plan	• 80% of basic services • 50% of prosthetic services • 50% of orthodontic services—$500 lifetime maximum	1st of the month following 1 year of service	None
Pension Plan	• 1 ½% of "final average earnings" for each year of service up to 30 • 1% of "final averge earnings" for each year of service 30 to 40 • Less 55% of primary social security	None	None
Life Insurance	• Noncontributory—1 × annual base pay • Contributory (optional)—1 × annual base pay	None	None 40¢ to 75¢/$1000 based on age
Educational Assistance Plan	• 100% reimbursement for approved work related courses	6 months	None
Vacation Plan	• 1 yr.—2 wks; 5 yr.—3 wks; 10 yr.—4 wks; 20 yr.—5 wks.	Per schedule	None
Holidays	• 10 per year	None	None

This sheet describes only the highlights of our benefit program for non-agreement employees. In all instances, the official plan texts, trust agreements and/or master contracts with insurance companies, as appropriate, are the governing documents.

JOB DESCRIPTION OUTLINE

JOB TITLE   STATUS:

JOB CODE: DATE:

DIVISION: REVISION NO.:

REPORTS TO: REVISION DATE:

POSITION SUMMARY:

Please provide a brief summary of the position. This information will be used for position announcements and advertisements.

PRINCIPAL ACCOUNTABILITIES:

Please make a list of job tasks stating what is done and how it's done. Begin each sentence with a verb using present tense singular. For example: <u>ANALYZE</u> financial data using spreadsheet software. <u>PREPARE</u> reports using WordPerfect 5.1 software.

THIS JOB DESCRIPTION DOES NOT CONSTITUTE A CONTRACT FOR EMPLOYMENT

JOB TITLE:
DATE:
PAGE _____ OF _____

JOB REQUIREMENTS:

EDUCATION:

List minimum acceptable educational requirements to do this job.

EXPERIENCE:

List number of years of experience in the job and specific knowledge requirements.

SKILLS:

List analytical, organizational, interpersonal, technical, managerial skills and so on.

SUPERVISORY RESPONSIBILITIES:

Please list the number of people supervised and their job titles. If you do not supervise put "none."

EQUIPMENT TO BE USED:

Please list computers, fax machines, telephones, calculators, floor waxers, power tools, fork lifts, and so on.

TYPICAL PHYSICAL DEMANDS:

Please list job requirements such as lifting, standing, sitting and so on. Try to be specific. Example: "must be able to lift 50 pounds," "must sit 7 hours a day," "must be able to drive a car."

TYPICAL MENTAL DEMANDS:

List the mental requirements of the job. Example: "must be able to do simple math calculations" or "must be able to analyze complex information."

WORKING CONDITIONS:

Please list examples such as "must work evenings and/or weekends, job requires driving _____% of the time," "works in a typical office setting," "works outside 90% of the time," and so on.

THIS JOB DESCRIPTION DOES NOT CONSTITUTE A CONTRACT FOR EMPLOYMENT

NEW EMPLOYEE ORIENTATION

NOTE: All employees must attend an orientation session.

Employee's Name: _____ SSN: _____

Job Title: _____ Dept. _____ Date: _____

HUMAN RESOURCES DEPARTMENT: The information checked below has been given or explained to the employee.

Compensation and Benefits		*Leaves. Promotions. and Transfers*	
• Time sheet/card	( )	• Performance Evaluations	( )
• Payroll procedures	( )	• Promotions	( )
• Insurance Program Booklet	( )	• Transfers	( )
• Voice Booklet	( )	• Vacations	( )
• Educational Assistance	( )	• Holidays	( )
• Credit Union	( )	• Absences—Tardiness	( )
• Stock Purchase Plan	( )	• Jury Duty	( )
• Savings Bond Plan	( )	• Leaves of Absence—	
• Sick Benefits—A&S—Limitations,		Maternity—Medical &	
and so on	( )	Family, and so on	( )

General

- Code of Conduct ( )
- Employee Handbook ( )
- Complaints and Grievance Procedures ( )
- I.D. or Entrance Card ( )
- Introduction to the Department ( )
- Parking Facilities ( )
- Safety Guidelines ( )
- First Aid and Requirements for
  Reporting Injury ( )
- Bulletin Boards/Company Events ( )
- Voluntary Resignation Notice ( )
- Termination Procedures ( )

SUPERVISOR: The following is a checklist of information necessary to orient the new employee to the job in your department. Please check off each point as you discuss it with the employee and return to the Human Resources Department to be placed in the employee's personnel file.

Welcome the New Employee

- Review copy of employee's application. Be familiar with employee's experience, training, and education.   ( )

- Review job description with employee, including the duties, responsibilities, and working relationships.   ( )

- Discuss with the employee the unit organization and the department division organization. Explain the function of your department/division as related to the total organization and how the employee fits in.   ( )

- Confirm that employee has a copy of employee handbook, and has read and understands it.   ( )

Introduce Employee to Co-Workers

- Indicate to each co-worker the new employee's position.   ( )

- Explain the functions of each person as you introduce the new employee. ( )

Show New Employee Around the Facility

- Tour the department, plant, or company.   ( )

- Explain where lavatories, coffee areas, and parking facilities are located. ( )

- Explain the various departments within the organization.   ( )

Introduce the New Employee to Job

- Insure that new employee's working area, equipment, tools and supplies are prepared and available.   ( )

- Explain the levels of supervision within the department.   ( )

- Provide new employee with necessary or required training.   ( )

- Explain use of: Telephone (personal/company calls)   ( )

                      Copy machines   ( )

                      Company vehicles   ( )

                      Mail procedures   ( )

                      Supply procedures   ( )

                      Personal expense reimbursement   ( )

- Explain hours of work—overtime—call-in procedures.   ( )

- Give new employee department telephone number.   ( )

- Review location of department's first aid equipment.   ( )

- Explain housekeeping responsibilities.   ( )

Future Follow-Up

- Set date and time within one week to cover any questions or concerns of the new Employee.   ( )

_____   _____

Supervisor's Signature   Employee's Signature

_____   _____

Supervisor's Title   Date

_____

Department

_____

Date

Note: Return this form to the Human Resources Department.

EMPLOYEE AGREEMENT

This employee handbook and the personnel policy manual describe only the highlights of the company policies, procedures, and benefits. In all instances the official benefit plan texts, trust agreements, and master contracts as appropriate are the governing documents. Your employee handbook is not to be interpreted as a legal document or an employment contract. Employment with the company is at the sole discretion of the company and may be terminated with or without cause at any time for any reason. Nothing in this handbook or in the personnel policy manual constitutes an express or implied contract or assurance of continued employment, or that just cause is required for termination.

Understood and agreed:

_____

(Employee's Signature)

_____

Date

EDUCATION VERIFICATION REFERENCE

Employer's Request for Information

The EMPLOYER will fill in the appropriate areas and send this form to the college, together with a stamped, self-addressed return envelope.

Date _____

NAME AND ADDRESS OF SCHOOL	TO BE RETURNED BY THE SCHOOL TO
	EMPLOYER _____
	EMPLOYER REPRESENTATIVE _____
ATTN: OFFICE OF THE DEAN	ADDRESS _____

REQUEST TO SCHOOL: The individual named below is being considered for employment as _____ .
(Type of position)

Applicant indicates attendance at above school. Your cooperation in furnishing the following information will expedite consideration of the applicant.

APPLICANT'S NAME AND ADDRESS			ON REGISTER OF THIS SCHOOL			
		Class	MONTH	YEAR	MONTH	YEAR
LAST (fill in)　　FIRST (fill in)		Number (1)	FROM		TO	
APPLICANT INDICATES ATTENDANCE AT THIS COLLEGE			DATE OF BIRTH AS GIVEN BY APPLICANT (FOR SCHOOL RECORD IDENTIFICATION AND VERIFICATION)			
FROM　　　　TO			MONTH	DAY		YEAR
GRADUATION DATE	TYPE OF DIPLOMA		GRADE POINT AVERAGE			
HAS APPLICATION BEEN MADE FOR ADMISSION TO GRADUATE SCHOOL OR OTHER SPECIAL SCHOOL?　　　NO ☐　　　YES ☐						

This information supplied below will be treated as confidential by the employer.

REMARKS: (AWARDS, HONORS, CLASS OFFICES HELD, ACTIVITIES)

_____

_____

_____

_____

SIGNED _____　TITLE _____　DATE _____

EMPLOYEE TRANSFER REQUEST

Date: _____

Employee's Name: _____

Position Title: _____

SSN or Employee
Payroll Number: _____

Hire Date: _____

Current Pay Rate: _____

The following transfer is requested:

	FROM (current job)	TO
Position		
Location		
Department		
Hourly Status	Full Time _____ or Part Time _____	Full Time _____ or Part Time _____ (hrs. per week)

NOTE: Separate forms must be filed for each transfer request

Employee qualifications: _____

_____

_____

_____

_____

Reasons for request: _____

_____

_____

_____

Employee Signature: _____

VACATION REQUEST FORM

Instructions for Completion: Please print when filling out this Request. All sections must be completed. Be sure to indicate the exact number of days you will be away from the office. This will enable the Human Resources Department to calculate your paycheck and attendance schedule correctly. Obtain your supervisor's approval and forward the completed request to the Payroll Department prior to the beginning of the vacation.

Employee _____   Date of Hire _____

Department _____   SSN _____ - _____ - _____

     Amount Vacation due _____   Number of Days Requested _____

     FIRST CHOICE: From _____ To _____

     SECOND CHOICE: From _____ To _____

Copy to Payroll _____

_____   _____
Employee Signature   Date

_____   _____
Supervisor Signature   Date

Please Note: Give as much advance notice as possible. In cases of conflict, the employee with the earliest request will be given priority. In cases of duplicate or similar request dates, the employee with the earliest starting date will prevail. We will try to accommodate everyone.

EMPLOYEE ABSENCE REPORT FORM

Please print when filling out this form. All sections must be completed. Forward to the Payroll Department immediately upon Supervisor's approval.

Employee's Name _____   Date _____

Social Security Number _____

Company/Department _____

Supervisor's Name _____

Dates of Absence: _____   Through _____

Reason for Absence (check one):

_____   Sick (if available)

_____   Jury Duty (attach copy of jury summons)

_____   Bereavement Leave; Relationship _____

_____   Personal Leave

_____   Other _____

_____

_____   _____

Employee's Signature   Date

_____   _____

Supervisor's Approval   Date

Return this completed form to your supervisor.

LEAVE REQUEST/RETURN FROM LEAVE FORM

Date _____

Employee's
Name _____

Social Security
Number _____

Job Title _____

Date Hired _____

LEAVE REQUEST

REASON FOR LEAVE:

( ) Personal disability

( ) Military

( ) Training conference

( ) Compensatory time off

( ) Jury duty

( ) Family illness (name) _____

( ) Family death (name) _____

( ) Other (explain) _____

_____

_____

LEAVE REQUESTED:

From: Date _____ Time _____ A.M. P.M.

Total number of
hours requested: _____

To: Date _____ Time _____ A.M. P.M.

Total number of
days requested: _____

Regular Work Shift: _____

_____

Employee Signature: _____ Date: _____

- -

I recommend that this
leave be approved:

( ) With pay
( ) Without pay

Authorized Signature: _____ Date: _____

RETURN FROM LEAVE

ABSENT:

From: Date _____ Time _____ A.M. P.M.

To: Date _____ Time _____ A.M. P.M.

Total number of
working days absent: _____

( ) Excused/warranted

( ) Not excused/not warranted (explain) _____

EMPLOYEE:

( ) Resumed part-time work

( ) Resumed full-time work

( ) Resumed modified duty (explain) _____

( ) Other (explain) _____

Affirmed by: _____ Date: _____

APPLICATION FOR FUNERAL LEAVE

DATE _____

EMPLOYEE'S NAME _____ DEPARTMENT _____

DATES OF WORK DAYS LOST _____ HOURLY RATE _____

DECEASED

NAME _____ FUNERAL DATE _____

RESIDENCE (CITY/TOWN) _____ STATE _____

BURIAL PLACE _____

RELATIONSHIP TO EMPLOYEE: (Be specific: Employee's spouse, child (including grandchild), parent (including grandparent), or sibling, and those same relatives of the employee's spouse.)

_____

_____

REMARKS _____

_____

_____

EMPLOYEE'S SIGNATURE _____

APPROVED:

SUPERVISOR _____

DEPARTMENTAL MANAGER _____

Time off without loss of straight time pay will be granted for up to three regularly scheduled working days to arrange for and attend the funeral of a member of the immediate family. Immediate family is defined as employee's spouse, child (including grandchild), parent (including grandparent), and sibling, and those same relatives of the employee's spouse.

cc: PAYROLL
    PERSONNEL

MILEAGE REIMBURSEMENT REPORT

NAME OF EMPLOYEE _____   DRIVERS LICENSE NO. _____

TYPE OF VEHICLE _____   LICENSE NUMBER _____

DEPARTMENT _____   MONTH _____

DATE	BEGINNING READING	ENDING READING	TOTAL MILEAGE	REASON FOR TRAVEL (PLACE)

TOTAL MILEAGE FOR MONTH _____ @ $0._____ per mile = $_____

Approved by: _____

Title: _____

Date: _____

TRAVEL AND EXPENSE REIMBURSEMENT REQUEST

NAME _____ DATE _____

POSITION TITLE _____

PURPOSE OF TRAVEL _____

MEAL AND LODGING EXPENSES (Attach receipts)

DATE	TYPE OF EXPENSE	LOCATION	AMOUNT

Subtotal—Meals and Lodging: $_____

TRANSPORTATION EXPENSES (Attach receipts)

1. Air fare (If paid by Company, do not claim.) $_____

2. Rontal vehicle $_____

3. Private vehicle use ($0. _____/mile) _____ miles) $_____

4. Company vehicle (actual expense only) $_____

5. Taxis and public transit $_____

Subtotal–Transportation $_____

OTHER EXPENSES (Attach Receipts)

1. Registration fees (If paid by company, do not claim.) $_____

2. Incidentals and phone calls $_____

Subtotal—Other $_____

CLAIM AMOUNT

1. Total of meals, lodging, transportation and other
   expenses $_____

2. Less amount advanced $(_____)

3. Net amount due claimant $_____

4. Net amount owed by claimant $_____

I certify this to be a true and correct statement of expenses incurred on official business.

_____
Signature of Employee

APPROVED:

_____
Signature

_____
Title

PERFORMANCE
APPRAISAL WORKSHEET

STRICTLY CONFIDENTIAL			DATE OF THIS REPORT	
EMPLOYEE NAME		REPORT OF PERFORMANCE		
		FROM TO		
DEPARTMENT	POSITION TITLE	TIME IN THIS CLASSIFICATION		EMPLOYMENT DATE
		YRS. _____ MOS. _____		

INSTRUCTIONS

1. All employees should be appraised at least annually.
2. Use in conjunction with the Merit Review Program.
3. Review employee's work performance for the entire period; refrain from basing judgment on recent events or isolated incidents only.
4. Do not allow personal feelings to govern your rating. Disregard your general impression of the employee.
5. Consider the employee on the basis of the standards you expect to be met for the job. Place a check by the area you feel best describes the employee's performance since the last appraisal.
6. REASON MUST BE GIVEN FOR EACH FACTOR TO SUBSTANTIATE AREA CHECKED

QUALITY OF WORK—Consider standard of workmanship, accuracy, neatness, skill, thoroughness, economy of materials, organization of job.

☐ FULLY MEETS JOB REQUIREMENTS   ☐ UNSATISFACTORY DOES NOT MEET MINIMUM REQUIREMENTS   ☐ MEETS MINIMUM REQUIREMENTS   ☐ EXCEEDS JOB REQUIREMENTS   ☐ OTHER (Specify)

Reason: _____

VOLUME OF WORK—Consider use of time, the volume of work accomplished and ability ot meet schedules, under normal conditions.

☐ DOES NOT MEET JOB REQUIREMENTS   ☐ EXCEEDS JOB REQUIREMENTS   ☐ MEETS MINIMUM JOB REQUIREMENTS   ☐ FULLY MEETS JOB REQUIREMENTS   ☐ OTHER (Specify)

Reason: _____

ADAPTABILITY—Consider ability to meet changing conditions and situations, ease with which the employee learns new duties and assignments.

☐ IMPROVEMENT NEEDED   ☐ SATISFACTORY   ☐ OUTSTANDING   ☐ VERY GOOD

Reason: _____

JUDGMENT—Consider ability to evaluate relative merit of ideas or facts and arrive at sound conclusions, ability to decide correct course of action when some choice can be made.

☐ VERY GOOD   ☐ NEEDS MUCH IMPROVEMENT   ☐ SATISFACTORY   ☐ OUTSTANDING

Reason: _____

JOB KNOWLEDGE AND SKILL—Consider understanding of job procedures and methods, ability to acquire necessary skills, expertness in doing assigned tasks and utilization of background for job.

☐ FULLY MEETS JOB REQUIREMENTS   ☐ IMPROVEMENT NEEDED   ☐ MEETS MINIMUM JOB REQUIREMENTS   ☐ EXCEEDS JOB REQUIREMENTS

Reason: _____

ATTITUDE—Consider coopertion with supervisor and co-workers; receptiveness to suggestions and constructive criticisms; attitude toward Company; enthusiasm in attempts to improve performance.

☐ EXCEEDS JOB REQUIREMENTS   ☐ FULLY MEETS JOB REQUIREMENTS   ☐ MEETS MINIMUM JOB REQUIREMENTS   ☐ IMPROVEMENT NEEDED

Reason: _____

_____

_____

TEAM EFFORT—LEADERSHIP—Consider ability to inspire teamwork, enthusiasm to work towards a common objective, desire to assume responsibility, ability to originate or develop ideas and get things started, ability to train others.

☐ DOES NOT MEET JOB REQUIREMENTS   ☐ EXCEEDS JOB REQUIREMENTS   ☐ MEETS MINIMUM JOB REQUIREMENTS   ☐ FULLY MEETS JOB REQUIREMENTS

Reason: _____

_____

_____

SELF-DEVELOPMENT ACTIVITIES OF THIS EMPLOYEE (To be completed during interview)

_____

_____

_____

_____

PRESENT STATUS—NEEDS—PLAN OF ACTION

OVERALL EFFECTIVENESS—Considering the amount of experience on present job, check the rating which most nearly describes *total* current performance.

☐ EXCEEDS JOB REQUIREMENTS   ☐ DOES NOT MEET JOB REQUIREMENTS   ☐ FULLY MEETS JOB REQUIREMENTS   ☐ MEETS MINIMUM JOB REQUIREMENTS

WHAT ASPECTS OF PERFORMANCE, IF NOT IMPROVED, MIGHT HINDER FUTURE DEVELOPMENT OR CAUSE DIFFICULTY IN PRESENT CLASSIFICATION (WEAKNESSES OF EMPLOYEE)?

_____

_____

WHAT ARE GREATEST STRENGTHS OF EMPLOYEE? _____

_____

Forward completed performance appraisal to designated approval authority before reviewing with subject employee. After appraisal is approved, review contents of appraisal with subject employee and complete section concerning specific plans to improve performance. Have employee sign the form and then forward original appraisal to the *Personnel Department* — retain copy for your files.

GIVE SPECIFIC PLANS YOU AND YOUR EMPLOYEE HAVE MADE TO IMPROVE WORK PERFORMANCE

_____

_____

_____

_____

EVALUATED BY:	TITLE:	DATE:
APPROVED:	TITLE:	DATE:
EMPLOYEE'S SIGNATURE (Does not necessarily indicate concurrence)	TITLE:	DATE:

EMPLOYEE COUNSELING ACTIVITY SHEET

EMPLOYEE'S NAME: _____

DATE: _____

EMPLOYEE RELATIONS STAFF MEMBER NAME: _____

Career Planning _____	Disciplinary Problems _____	
Compensation/Benefits _____	Other _____	
Job Posting _____		
EEO/AA _____	PLEASE CHECK ONE CATEGORY	

TIME IN _____   TIME OUT _____

Briefly state the problem.

Follow-up session(s), if necessary.

Results/solution: Explain the outcome of session(s).

_____
Supervisor Completing Form
(Continue on back if necessary)

SUPERVISOR'S CHECKLIST AND REPORT
FOR EFFECTIVE DISCIPLINE

This report should be completed when disciplinary action is needed and after the first verbal warning has been given to an employee. If you have any questions or concerns, telephone discussion with Personnel is encouraged.

_____   _____   _____
Employee's Name   Hire Date   Cost Center

_____   _____
Date of Incident   Incident

Give an accurate account of what happened. Be specific.

_____

_____

_____

_____

Indicate corrective steps needed.

_____

_____

_____

_____

Has employee had a chance to tell his or her side of story?   YES ☐   NO ☐

If not, why not? _____

_____

Was the employee aware of the rule or procedure?   YES ☐   NO ☐

Were instructions published in writing in a clear, understandable manner?   YES ☐   NO ☐

Was the applicable policy properly communicated?   YES ☐   NO ☐

Have you spoken previously to employee about this matter?   YES ☐   NO ☐

If so, when? _____

Has the policy been consistently enforced? YES ☐ NO ☐

Have there been other violations? YES ☐ NO ☐

If so, describe action(s) taken.

_____

_____

_____

_____

Has any previous corrective action with this employee been necessary? YES ☐ NO ☐

If so, describe briefly.

_____

_____

_____

Can you back up this record with facts? YES ☐ NO ☐

What is appropriate and justifiable discipline for this infraction? (Disciplinary action should fit the situation, discourage recurrence, and encourage better performance by employee.)

☐ Informal Warning   ☐ Formal Warning   ☐ Place on Probation

☐ Demotion   ☐ Lay-off Without Pay   ☐ Discharge

☐ Other (specify) _____

_____   _____
Date   Reporting Supervisor

THIS IS A CONFIDENTIAL RECORD THAT WILL BECOME PART OF THE EMPLOYEE'S PERSONNEL FILE. THE DISCIPLINARY WARNING NOTICE FOR THE INCIDENT WILL BE ATTACHED TO THIS REPORT.

DISCIPLINARY WARNING NOTICE

(This notice is to be completed for any disciplinary action
after the first verbal warning to employee.)

EMPLOYEE'S NAME _____ COST CENTER _____
　　　　　　　　　　　　　Last　　　　　First　　　　Init.

POSITION TITLE _____

DATE OF INCIDENT _____ INCIDENT _____

REASON FOR NOTICE:

ACTION TAKEN ON THIS NOTICE:

☐　First warning—verbal (This notice is optional.)

☐　Second warning—written　　　　　　　　☐　Suspension for _____ days

☐　Other (specify) _____

　　_____

　　_____

NEXT STEP IF INFRACTION IS REPEATED:

☐　Second warning—written　　　　　　　　☐　Suspension for _____ days

☐　Other (specify) _____

　　_____

　　_____

SUPERVISOR COMMENTS:

EMPLOYEE COMMENTS:

Signed _____　　Signed _____
　　　　　　　　　Supervisor　　　　　　　　　　　　　　　　　　Employee

Date _____　　Date _____

ORIGINAL TO BE FORWARDED TO PERSONNEL
FOR EMPLOYEE'S FILE.

EMPLOYEE WARNING NOTICE

EMPLOYEE NAME: _____

Social Security
Number: _____

POSITION TITLE: _____

Date of
Warning: _____

TYPE OF	( ) Tardiness	( ) Quality of Work	( ) Carelessness
VIOLATION	( ) Absenteeism	( ) Quantity of Work	( ) Safety
	( ) Insubordination	( ) Neatness	( ) Intoxication or Drinking
	( ) Other: _____		

Was there a witness
to the violation? _____ Witness Name: _____

VIOLATION: Date _____

VIOLATION: Time   A.M.   P.M.

PLACE VIOLATION OCCURRED: _____

WARNING NOTICE:
( ) First Date: _____
( ) Second Date: _____
( ) Final

COMPANY STATEMENT

1. Describe in detail what the employee has done.
2. Cite how this interferes with work environment, employee performance, business operations, or the well being of other employees.
3. Cite verbatim the rule, policy, law, standard, or regulation that was violated.

WARNING DECISION

1. Explain in detail what employee must do to improve performance or change behavior.
2. Cite date by which improvements must be in place.
3. Cite consequences if improvements are not achieved by date specified.

APPROVED BY: _____   TITLE: _____

DATE: _____

ATTACH SEPARATE PAGE IF NEEDED FOR DETAILED EXPLANATIONS

EMPLOYEE COMMENTS: _____

_____

_____

_____

_____

_____
Employee's Signature   Date

_____
Supervisor's Signature   Date

EXIT INTERVIEW

Employee Name: _____ Date:_____

1. What is your reason for leaving?

2. Why did you decide to seek employment elsewhere?

3. Are there any other reasons why you are leaving?

4. Was your job here the way you thought it would be after hearing it described in your hiring or promotional interview?

5. As an employee, were you given all of the information you needed to perform your job?

6. How did you feel about the quality of training you received for your job?

7. How did you feel about the supervision in your unit?

8. How did you feel about your job? Were you accomplishing something worthwhile through your job?

9. How did you feel about your rate of pay in relation to the type of work you did?

10. How did you feel about opportunities for advancement within the company?

11. What do you think of company benefits?

12. What was the most common complaint of fellow employees?

13. What were the things you liked most about working here?

14. What were the things you liked least about working here?

15. What changes would you make to make this a better place to work?

16. Would you refer friends to the company?

17. Is there anything you `would like to add about your reasons for leaving?

NOTE: Use only with voluntary terminations.

_____   _____
Employee Signature   Interviewer Signature

Accident/Injury Report

Supervisor must complete report and return to the Human Resources Department within 24 hours.

Name: _____ SSN: _____ - _____ - _____

Date of Accident: Day _____ Mo. _____ Yr. _____

Time of Accident: _____ AM/PM

Place Of Accident: _____

Witnesses: (if any)   First Aid Given? _____ Yes _____ No

Name: _____   By Whom? _____

Address: _____   Hospitalized? _____ Yes _____ No

_____   Physician: _____

Phone #: _____

Nature and extent of injuries: _____

_____

How did accident/injury occur? (Be specific; use extra sheet if necessary): _____

_____

_____

Job or activity engaged in at time of injury (Be specific):_____

_____

_____

Describe any unsafe conditions, methods or practices related to the accident: _____

_____

_____

_____   _____
Employee's Signature   Date

_____   _____
Supervisor's Signature   Date

_____   _____
Department/Company   Location

SUPERVISOR'S REPORT OF ACCIDENT INVESTIGATION
CONFIDENTIAL REPORT - FOR CORPORATE USE ONLY

Injured Employee _____ Date of This Report _____

Occupation _____ Dept. _____ Age ____ Sex ____ Length of Employment _____

Date And Time Of Accident _____ Exact Location _____

Description Of Accident (Detail what employee was doing and what tools, equipment, structures, or fixtures were involved)

_____
_____
_____
_____
_____
_____
_____
_____

Nature of Injuries _____
_____

Report To Supervisor or First Aid Delayed? _____ Why? _____
_____
_____

Check Accident Causes On Reverse Side Of This Report And Comment Fully Here _____
_____
_____
_____
_____
_____

What Should Be Done, And By Whom To Prevent Recurrence Of This Type Accident In The Future?
_____
_____
_____
_____

What Action Are You Taking To See That This Is Done? _____
_____
_____

Supervisor's Signature _____

Comments By Department Head Or Manager _____
_____
_____
_____

ATTENDING PHYSICIAN'S
RETURN TO WORK RECOMMENDATIONS RECORD

COMPANY NAME

PATIENT'S NAME (First)	(Middle Initial)	(Last)	DATE OF INJURY/ILLNESS

DIAGNOSIS

TO BE COMPLETED BY ATTENDING PHYSICIAN – PLEASE CHECK

I saw and treated this patient on _____ and:
Date

1. ☐ Recommend his/her return to work with no limitations on _____.
   Date

2. ☐ He/She may return to work capable of performing the degree of work checked below with the following limitations:

DEGREE	LIMITATIONS		
☐ **Sedentary Work.** Lifting 10 pounds maximum and occasionally lifting and/or carrying such articles as dockets, ledgers, and small tools. Although a sedentary job is defined as one which involves sitting, a certain amount of walking and standing is often necessary in carrying out job duties. Jobs are sedentary if walking and standing are required only occasionally and other sedentary criteria are met.	1. In an 8-hour work day patient may: a. Stand/Walk ☐ None ☐ 4-6 Hours ☐ 1-4 Hours ☐ 6-8 Hours b. Sit ☐ 1-3 Hours ☐ 3-5 Hours ☐ 5-8 Hours c. Drive ☐ 1-3 Hours ☐ 3-5 Hours ☐ 5-8 Hours		
☐ **Light Work.** Lifting 20 pounds maximum with frequent lifting and/or carrying of objects weighing up to 10 pounds. Even though the weight lifted may be only a negligible amount, a job is in this category when it requires walking or standing to a significant degree or when it involves sitting most of the time with a degree of pushing and pulling of arm and/or leg controls.	2. Patient may use hands for repetitive: ☐ Single Grasping ☐ Pushing & Pulling ☐ Fine Manipulation		
☐ **Medium Work.** Lifting 50 pounds maximum with frequent lifting and/or carrying of objects weighing up to 25 pounds.	3. Patient may use feet for repetitive movement as in operating foot controls: ☐ Yes ☐ No		
☐ **Heavy Work.** Lifting 100 pounds maximum with frequent lifting and/or carrying of objects weighing up to 50 pounds.	4. Patient is able to:	Frequently	Occasionally Not at all
☐ **Very Heavy Work.** Lifting objects in excess of 100 pounds with frequent lifting and/or carrying of objects weighing 50 pounds or more.	a. Bend . . . . ☐ b. Squat . . . . ☐ c. Climb . . . . ☐	☐ ☐ ☐	☐ ☐ ☐

OTHER INSTRUCTIONS AND/OR LIMITATIONS:

3. ☐ These restrictions are in effect until _____ or until patient is reevaluated on _____.
   Date   Date

4. ☐ He/She is totally incapacitated at this time. Patient will be reevaluated on _____.
   Date

PHYSICIAN'S SIGNATURE	DATE

AUTHORIZATION TO RELEASE INFORMATION

I hereby authorize my attending physician and/or hospital to release any information or copies thereof acquired in the course of my examination or treatment for the injury identified above to my employer or his representative.

PATIENT'S SIGNATURE	DATE

FIRST AID REPORT LOG*

This form is for the purpose of profiling routine occurrence of minor injuries such as small cuts and bruises which do not require medical treatment or lost work hours.

Date of Injury	Time of Injury	Name of Employee	Description of Injury or Illness (Specify part of body affected)	Injury/Illness		Treatment Administered	Administered by Whom	Injury Report Filed	
				New	Recurring			YES	NO

*Minor injuries should be recorded on the Supervisor's Report of Work Injury.

QUARTERLY SAFETY PERFORMANCE RECORD

For the Period: _____

LOCATION	CURRENT QUARTER			YEAR-TO-DATE			LATEST NATIONAL RATES
	HOURS WORKED	LOST WORK DAY INJURIES	INCIDENCE RATE	HOURS WORKED	LOST WORK DAY INJURIES	INCIDENCE RATE	
TOTALS							
REMARKS							

$$\text{INCIDENCE RATE LOST WORK DAY INJ} = \frac{\text{No. OF CASES x 200,000}}{\text{HRS. WORKED}}$$

GLOSSARY OF HUMAN RESOURCES TERMS

GLOSSARY OF COMPENSATION AND BENEFITS TERMS

Accidental Death and Dismemberment Insurance (AD&D) Insurance providing benefits in the event of loss of life, limbs, or eyesight as the result of an accident.

Accrued Benefit Under a defined contribution plan, the employee's accrued benefit is the balance in his or her plan account. (Separate accounting for each employee is required.)

Under a defined benefit plan, the employee's accrued benefit is determined under the terms of the plan. The plan formula defines the benefit commencing at normal retirement age.

Accrued Liability (Past Service Liability) The amount of liability assigned, under the actuarial method used, to years prior to the valuation date of a defined benefit plan.

Actual Compensation Percentage (ACP) One of the factors used to test 401(k) defined contribution plans for nondiscrimination. The eligible participants are divided into groups of highly compensated and non-highly compensated. Within each group, the after-tax employee contributions and the employer match for each employee is determined as a percentage of pay. These are then averaged to determine the ADP for each group. The highly compensated ADP is then compared to the non-highly compensated ADP.

Actuarial Assumptions Assumptions or estimates of future experience in those areas that will affect benefit levels and pension costs; for example, interest, pay increases, mortality, turnover (withdrawal), disability, and age at retirement.

Actuarial Cost Method A mathematical process that allocates the expected value of pension benefits to various years of an employee's career.

Actuarial Equivalent If the present value of two series of payments is equal, assuming a given interest rate and mortality table, the two series are said to be actuarially equivalent. For example, a lifetime monthly benefit of $67.60 beginning at age 60 is actually equivalent to a lifetime monthly benefit of $100 beginning at age 65.

Actuarial Gains or Losses The effect on actuarially calculated pension liabilities of deviations between actual experience and the actuarial assumptions used.

Actuarial Present Value Current worth of an amount or series of amounts payable or receivable in the future, where each such amount is discounted at an assumed rate of interest and adjusted for the probability of its payment or receipt.

Actuarial Valuation A periodic examination of a pension program to determine plan liabilities.

Actuarially Reduced Benefit Pension benefit amount payable to an employee who retires before normal retirement age. The actuarial amount reflects the longer payment period and life expectancy. (See Actuarial Equivalent.)

Actuary A person professionally trained in the technical and mathematical aspects of insurance, pensions, and related fields.

Administrative Service Contract (Administrative Service Only, ASO) An arrangement under which an insurer agrees to process claims under a group medical plan. Usually used in conjunction with a self-funded plan.

Advance Funding A payment to a defined benefit plan in advance of the date it is actually needed to provide benefits. Advance funding is one of the essential characteristics of a qualified plan.

Age Discrimination in Employment Act (ADEA) Provides protection against discriminatory treatment of workers 40 years of age and older.

Aggregate Funding Method A method of accumulating money for future payment of pension benefits whereby an actuary determines the present value of all future benefit payments, deducts from this value whatever funds may be on hand with the insurance company or trustee, and distributes the cost of the balance over the future on a reasonable basis.

Allocation Generally applicable only in a defined contribution plan in which the employer contribution is "allocated" (credited to participant accounts) under a stated allocation formula.

Amortization Paying off an interest-bearing liability by gradual reduction through a series of installments, as opposed to paying it off by one lump-sum payment.

Annual Report (Form 5500) Annual financial report of a pension benefit plan or welfare benefit plan. To be filed with the IRS.

Annuity A series of payments payable at fixed intervals of time, but usually for life. The person receiving the payment is called an annuitant. Annuity payments are usually made monthly, but can be made quarterly, semiannually, or annually.

Average Monthly Wage (AMW) or Average Indexed Monthly Earnings (AIME) For an individual, the monthly average of all pay credited for social security purposes (up to the taxable wage base each year), used to determine his or her social security benefit.

Basic Medical Benefits Name applied to insurance that reimburses hospital and doctor charges (usually at 100%) up to stipulated limits. Additional coverage can be provided by major medical insurance.

Basic Medical Plan A plan that covers hospital and surgical expenses associated with routine illness and injury.

Beneficiary The person named by the employee to receive any death payment due under an employee benefit plan.

Benefit A general term applied to any payment under the terms of an employee benefit plan.

Benefit Formula The combination of factors, such as length of service, job classification, and salary, that determines the amount of benefits to be paid under a benefit plan.

Benefit Statement Participant's individualized (usually computer-posted or laser-printed) statement, covering employer-provided benefits.

Bootleg Wages In a tight labor market, employers may pay wages above the current market rate to attract and retain skilled employees.

Break in Service Basically a calendar year, plan year, or other 12-consecutive-month period designated by a defined benefit or defined contribution plan during which an employee completes less than 501 hours of service. Alternative guidelines for determining a break in service are defined under ERISA.

Business Travel Accident Insurance Limited coverage for accidents that occur while traveling on company business. Usually covers all accidents while an employee is away from home (not merely those directly connected with travel).

Cafeteria (Flexible) Benefits A benefit plan in which employees elect the benefits they will receive within some dollar limit. Usually a common core of benefits consists of health, disability, retirement, and death benefits, plus a group of elective programs from which the employee may select. Additional coverage may be available through employee contributions.

Capitation A predetermined, fixed amount that is paid to a health care provider for each person served under the plan, without regard to the number of visits or extent of services that will be required. (The provider assumes financial risk for providing health care services.) HMOs are reimbursed on a "per capita" (capitated) basis.

Career Average Pay One definition of pay that is used as a basis for determining benefits under a defined benefit pension plan. Normally, the average of the employee's pay from date of employment to date of retirement. In some cases, the starting date for the averaging period may be the employee's eligibility date, the effective date of the plan, or the effective date of a plan amendment.

Cash Balance Pension Plan (Pension Account Plan) A retirement plan that is qualified and funded as a career average pay pension plan, but communicated to employees like a defined contribution plan, with individual employee accounts that are credited with contributions and earnings each year.

Cash or Deferred Plan (CODA) Provision under section 401(k) of the Internal Revenue Code whereby contributions may be made by employees through salary reduction such that the contribution dollars are not taxed until the money is withdrawn. Also applies to profit sharing plans where an employee may elect to take the employer contribution in current (taxable) cash or have it deferred (nontaxable) into a trust.

Certified Compensation Professional (CCP) A compensation or benefits professional who has successfully completed the certification program of the American Compensation Association.

Certified Employee Benefits Specialist (CEBS) A professional designation given to persons who pass a series of ten examinations covering the fundamental principles of the design and operation of employee benefit plans.

Claim Denial Procedure ERISA requires that SPDs explain the steps that a participant may take if a claim for a welfare or pension benefit is denied partially or wholly. Includes the participant's rights to the review of denied claims, and the time frame for the plan administrator's response.

Claim Reserve An amount set aside in a group insurance plan for both continuing and unreported claims.

Class Year Plan One in which each year's contributions vest separately. Each year's employer contributions must be 100% vested no later than the end of the fifth plan year following the plan year for which the contributions are made. After December 31, 1988, these plans were subject to the 1986 Tax Reform Act vesting rules.

Cliff Vesting Retirement plan provision under which the participant is not vested until fulfilling a certain number of years of service. After attaining the required number of years of service, the participant automatically becomes 100% vested.

Coinsurance A contract provision, frequently found in health care plans, under which both the insured person and the insurance company share the hospital and medical expenses resulting from an illness or injury in a specified ratio.

Collectively Bargained Plan A employee benefit plan maintained pursuant to a collective bargaining agreement between a union and an employer.

Comparable Worth The doctrine that men and women who perform work of the same "inherent value" should receive comparable compensation. According to this doctrine, jobs have an inherent value that can be compared across different types of jobs.

Compensation (Pay) Benefits, or contributions, are often related to pay or to pay and service. Pay may be defined to include base pay only, or base pay plus overtime, bonuses, etc. There are rules governing what definitions of pay are to be used for plan contributions and nondiscrimination testing.

Comprehensive Medical Plan A plan designed to give the protection offered by both a basic and a major medical health insurance contract. Characterized by few, if any, first dollar coverages. Often includes a deductible amount, a coinsurance feature, and high maximum benefits.

Compression A situation which occurs when the pay of lower-paid employees increases, reducing the pay differentials between different job levels. May apply either to actual pay or pay ranges.

Consolidated Omnibus Budget Reconciliation Act of 1985 (COBRA) Legislation that requires employers who offer health care plans to employees to offer continued coverage in the plans to terminated employees after certain qualifying events. Length of coverage and maximum premiums are specified by law. These requirements are known as "COBRA health care continuation."

Constructive Receipt A tax term referring to a situation in which a taxpayer is taxed on amounts he or she did not actually receive, but had the legal right to receive.

Consumer Price Index (CPI) Measurement of the relative prices of a selected group of goods and services that typify those bought by urban families at various times. Determined by the U.S. Department of Labor.

Contribution A general term used to designate any payment made by an employer or an employee to an employee benefit plan. Contributions finance benefits.

Conventional Contract Funding contract under which a premium is sent to the insurer. From this premium, the insurer pays claims, adjusts reserves, and funds its operational costs. Any surplus generally is returned to the policyholder.

Conversion Privilege The right to convert coverage from an employer-provided plan to an individual who loses eligibility for the plan.

Coordination of Benefits (COB) In cases where the same beneficiary may be covered by two or more health plans, COB ensures that the benefits paid under both plans do not total over 100% of charges. COB eliminates duplicate payments and also specifies the sequence in which coverage will be paid (the primary plan, the secondary plan, etc.)

Corporate-Owned Life Insurance (COLI) Whole life insurance or universal life insurance owned by the employer and payable to the employer, as a corporate investment. Often purchased to finance the cost of non-qualified retirement or deferred compensation benefits.

Cost-of-Living Adjustment (COLA) An across-the-board increase in wage and salary or supplemental payment designed to reflect increases in the cost of living. COLAs are sometimes included in union contracts. Generally tied to increases in price indexes published by the Bureau of Labor Statistics.

Death Benefit A general term used to designate any payment made under an employee benefit plan because of the death of an employee.

Deferred Annuity An annuity under which payments will begin at some definite future date, such as in a specified number of years or at a specified age.

Deferred Compensation A generic term that includes qualified plans, employment contracts, stock options, and other arrangements for deferred pay arrangements. The purpose of deferred compensation for employees is to defer taxation, and sometimes to obtain an opportunity for favorable investments. For employers, the purpose of deferred compensation may be to make payments contingent on continued employment, as well as to make available programs advantageous to employees.

Deferred Retirement The postponement of retirement past the age specified in the plan as the normal retirement age.

Defined Benefit Plan (Pension Plan) Any plan that is not an individual account plan. Employer contributions are figured actuarially according to a definite formula. These plans are subject to regulation by the Pension Benefit Guaranty Corporation. They are designed primarily for retirement.

Defined Contribution Plan (Individual Account Plan) Provides an individual account for each participant. Benefits are based solely on: (1) the amount contributed to the participant's account, plus (2) any income, expenses, gains and losses, and the forfeitures of other participants' accounts.

Dependents Defined by each plan. Normally the spouse and children of a covered individual. Under some plans, parents or other family members may be dependents.

Deposit Administration (DA) Contract An insurance contract under which all contributions are placed in an allocated fund that accumulates interest. When an employee retires, funds are withdrawn from the fund and are used to purchase a single, premium immediate annuity in an amount sufficient to provide the employee's benefit.

Direct Compensation As opposed to indirect compensation, all forms of compensation that involve direct and immediate payment to the individual, often including a base wage or salary payment.

Disability Retirement Benefit Periodic payment (usually monthly) made to a participant under some retirement plans if the participant is eligible and becomes totally and permanently disabled before the normal retirement date.

Discrimination Benefits or contributions that favor officers, stockholders, or highly compensated employees to a degree that is prohibited under the law. "Discrimination" may also refer to discrimination by sex, age, marital status, etc. that is prohibited by law.

Distribution Generally refers to any payouts from a retirement plan. May be in the form of a lump sum or installments.

Earnings Test A test to determine if an individual's social security benefits must be reduced because of other income. In 1990, an individual's social security benefits are reduced if earned income exceeds $9,360 (if age 65 or older and under age 70), or $6,840 (if under age 65).

Early Retirement Retirement at an age which is earlier than the age specified in the plan as the normal retirement age.

Eligibility Requirements Conditions imposed by the terms of a plan for an employee's eligibility to participate in the plan. These requirements can require an employee to complete some minimum period of service and attain some minimum age. Many plans also relate eligibility to the type of work performed by an employee, or to the nature or amount of his or her compensation.

Employee Assistance Programs (EAP) Generally, employer-sponsored programs which provide a referral source for the treatment of drug, alcohol, emotional, and financial problems that can affect job performance.

Employee Benefit Plan Under ERISA, a pension benefit plan or a welfare benefit plan maintained by an employer (or group of employers).

Employee Retirement Income Security Act of 1974 (ERISA) Also know as the Pension Reform Act. This requires that persons engaged in the administration, supervision, and management of pension monies have a fiduciary responsibility to ensure that all investment-related decisions are made: (1) with the care, skill, prudence, and diligence that a prudent man familiar with such matters would use, and (2) by diversifying the investments so as to minimize risk.

Employee Stock Ownership Plan (ESOP) A qualified stock bonus plan or money purchase plan, the assets of which are primarily invested in the sponsoring company's stock. The plan is a way for employees to share in company ownership without having to invest any of their own money. ESOPs are unique in that they can borrow money and be used as a corporate finance technique.

Entry Age Actuarial Cost Method A process that allocates pension cost on a level annual basis from the employee's assumed entry into the plan until his or her expected retirement.

Equal Employment Opportunity Commission (EEOC) A commission of the federal government charged with enforcing the provisions of the Civil Rights Act of 1964. In addition, the commission is charged with enforcing the provisions of the Equal Pay Act of 1963.(See Comparable Worth.)

Equal Pay Act of 1963 An amendment to the Fair Labor Standards Act of 1938, prohibiting pay differentials on jobs that are essentially equal in terms of skill, effort, responsibility, and working conditions, except when they are the result of bona fide seniority, merit or production-based pay systems, or any other job-related factor other than sex.

Equities An ownership of property, usually in the form of common stocks, as distinguished from fixed income-bearing securities, such as bonds or mortgages.

Equity Anything of value earned through the provision or investment of something of value. In case of compensation, an employee earns equity interest through the provision of labor on a job. So defined, equity is often used as a fairness criterion in compensation. People should be paid according to their contributions.

ERISA Excess Plan Nonqualified retirement plan with the sole purpose of making up for benefits lost from tax-qualified retirement plans because of Code Section 415 limits.

ERISA Rights Statement A statement notifying participants of their rights under ERISA. Must be included in an SPD. Acceptable language (as defined by ERISA) may be modified to suit the intended audience.

Evidence of Insurability Proof that an individual is in good health when applying for insurance, or when electing a settlement option.

Exclusive Provider Organizations (EPOs) Medical insurance arrangements in which employees must use EOP-designated providers to received coverage.

Exempt Job A job not subject to the provisions of the Fair Labor Standards Act with respect to minimum wage and overtime. Exempt employees include most professionals, administrators, executives, and outside sales representatives.

Experience Rating Method of calculating insurance rates based on a group's prior claims experience.

Extended Benefits Benefits provided for a disabled employee after coverage would normally terminate.

Extrinsic Rewards Rewards that a person receives from sources other than the job itself. They include compensation, supervision, promotions, vacations, and friendships.

Family Social Security Total benefits received by a family, including the worker, because of the worker's eligibility for social security benefits. (See Primary Insurance Amount.)

Federal Insurance Contributions Act (FICA) Legislation authorizing the payroll tax for social security.

Fee-for-Service Billing method where the health care provider charges separately for each service given.

Fiduciary One who: exercises any discretionary authority or discretionary control of the management or disposition of plan assets; renders any investment advice for a fee or other compensation; or exercises any discretionary authority or responsibility for plan administration.

Final Average Pay (FAP) One definition of "pay" that is used as a basis for determining benefit amounts under defined benefit plans. Defined as the average of the employee's pay for a relatively short period just prior to retirement. For example, the five years immediately prior to retirement, or the highest five consecutive years in the 10 or 15 years prior to retirement.

Financial Accounting Standards Board (FASB) The independent, private authority for establishing accounting principles in the United States.

Flexible Benefits (Flexible Compensation) A system of employee benefits under which an employer offers a choice to employees of types of benefits and level of coverage. There may be an allowance of flexible credits that the employee can allocate to a number of options. Usually employee contributions are paid with pre-tax dollars.

Flexible Spending Account (FSA) An arrangement under a flexible benefit plan whereby employees can choose to have money deducted from their pay on a pre-tax basis to pay for medical or dependent care benefits.

Floor Plan A tax-qualified defined benefit pension that is intended as a guarantee that the participant's accumulation under the defined contribution plan will generate at least a minimum level of retirement income. If the defined contribution plan would not generate the guaranteed minimum, the floor plan makes up the difference.

Forfeiture Amounts lost by a terminating participant because vesting requirements have not been met. In a defined benefit plan, forfeitures may be applied to reduce future employer contributions. In a profit sharing plan, forfeitures may be allocated to the accounts of remaining participants.

Forward Income Averaging A rule allowing favorable tax advantages for some lump sum distributions from tax-qualified retirement plans. After reaching 59-1/2, a participant may elect a one-time election of five-year averaging. Participants who were age 50 before January 1, 1986 can elect five- or ten-year averaging. This averaging allows employees to pay taxes on the lump sum as if it were received over five year (or ten years).

401(k) Plan Allows an employee to contribute pre-tax dollars to a qualified plan that is invested in stocks, bonds, or money market accounts. Contributions and earnings are deferred until the employee retires or leaves the company. (See Cash or Deferred Plan.)

403(b) Plan A type of tax-sheltered annuity (TSA) made available to some nonprofit organizations. Like a 401(k), this plan allows employees to contribute pre-tax dollars for investments toward retirement.

Frozen Entry Age Actuarial Cost Method A variation of Entry Age Actuarial Cost Method under which the amount initially developed as accrued liability is unchanged by deviations of future experience from assumptions.

Funded Retirement Plan A plan under which funds are set aside in advance to provide expected benefits. (See Advance Funding.)

Funding Agency An organization or individual that provides facilities for the accumulation of assets to be used for the payment of benefits under a pension plan, or an organization that provides facilities for the purchase of such benefits.

Future Service (Pension Plans) That portion of the participant's retirement benefit that relates to the period of creditable service after the effective date of the plan or after a change.

Garnishment A court order requiring the employer of a debtor to deduct a portion of the debtor's pay and to deliver it to the creditor.

Golden Handcuffs Employee benefit and related incentives linked to an individual's continued employment with an organization. Leaving the organization would forfeit the incentive. When such incentives become comparatively large compared to other incentives, the employee can no longer "afford" to leave the organization.

Golden Parachute A special financial protection plan (including cash payments and future income) for key executives in the event of an unfriendly takeover by another firm.

Group Annuity Contract A contract issued by a life insurance company that may be used as the funding instrument for a defined benefit or defined contribution plan. Forms of group annuity contracts include: Deferred Annuity, Deposit Administration, Immediate Participation Guarantee, and Guaranteed Interest.

Group Universal Life Programs (GULPs) A life insurance program that is not a group term life policy, but instead individual policies for each employee, paid with employee's after-tax contributions. Allows policyholders (employees) to vary the amount and timing of premiums, and the amount of the death benefit. Such plans provide competitive interest rates and allow buyers to accumulate tax-deferred savings. GULPs, however, do not always provide coverage for spouse and children.

Guaranteed Interest Contract (GIC) Investment contract from an insurance company, available to a defined benefit or defined contribution plan under which the interest rate is guaranteed for a fixed period of time.

Health Maintenance Organization (HMO) An organization that provides for a wide range of comprehensive care services for a specified group at a fixed periodic payment.

Highly Compensated Employee (HCE) Employee meeting the definition of a highly paid employee as defined by the Tax Reform Act of 1986.

H.R. 10 Plan SE Keogh Plan.

Immediate Participation Guarantee Contract (IPG) Variation of Deposit Administration type of contract providing immediate experience participation similar to a self-insured plan. When an employee retires, the reserves are determined to guarantee his benefit but no annuity is purchased.

Indirect Compensation Compensation in form of benefits beyond the current base salary or wage being paid. Includes such things as paid vacation, insurance contributions, and so forth.

Individual Policy Pension Plan A plan under which benefits are provided by means of level premium individual annuity or life insurance contracts issued to the trustee of a trust established by the employer. The maturity value of an employee's contract is used to provide his or her retirement benefits.

Individual Practice Associations (IPAs) A type of HMO consisting of a central administrative authority and a panel of physicians and other providers practicing individually or in small groups. Providers are usually paid on a fee-for-service or capitation basis.

Individual Retirement Accounts and Annuities (IRAs) May be established and taxpayers may fully or partially deduct contributions to these accounts from taxable income. There are no minimum contributions. Maximum contributions and deduction allowances are set by law and determined by marital status, income level, and coverage by employer-sponsored pension plans.

Insurance Cost (Imputed Income) Internal Revenue Service computed value of group life insurance benefits in excess of $50,000.

Integration of Retirement Plan Benefits The dovetailing of benefits under a private retirement plan with benefits under the Social Security Act, in such a manner that highly paid employees will receive benefits under the plan that are proportionately greater than for lower paid employees. The IRS provides extensive rules detailing allowable integration limits. (See Offset Plan and Step-Rate Plan.)

Intrinsic Rewards Rewards that are associated with the job itself, such as the opportunity to perform meaningful work, complete cycles of work, see finished products, experience variety, and receive feedback on work results.

Joint and Survivor (J&S) Options (Contingent Annuity) Pension benefit payment options that provide reduced benefits to retirees with the guarantee that a surviving beneficiary will receive a lifetime income based on a portion or all of deceased participant's benefit. Under ERISA, pension plans must offer an automatic 50% J&S method to married participants for all benefits payable as annuities.

Joint Fund (Labor-Management Funds) Retirement (and other) funds established in accordance with the Labor-Management Relations Act, which provide for balanced administrative management by both labor and employer representatives.

Keogh Plan Also known as H.R. 10 Plan. Enables self-employed individuals to contribute to tax-qualified retirement plan. May be classified as either defined contribution or defined benefit plan. For tax purposes, the individual is treated as both employer and employee.

Key Employee A plan participant who at any time during the plan year of any of the four preceding plan years is: an officer with pay greater than 150% of the Section 415 defined benefit limit (up to 50 employees or, if less, the greater of three employees or 10% of all employees); one of the 10 employees owning the largest interests in the company and having annual compensation exceeding the Section 415 defined benefit dollar limitations; a 5% owner, or a 1% owner who has annual pay of more than $150,000.

Labor-Management Relations Act of 1947 (Taft-Hartley Act) Based on the theory of equalizing the bargaining power of management with that of labor. Controls conditions under which an employer may pay any monies to a representative of his employee.

Life Annuity A series of payments that, once begun, continue throughout the remaining lifetime of the annuitant but not beyond.

Life Expectancy The average number of years (as estimated from a mortality table) that individuals may be expected to live, after attaining a specified age.

Long-term Care Medical and emotional care provided in both institutional and noninstitutional settings to people with debilitating chronic health conditions.

Lump-Sum Distribution A single payment of the actuarial equivalent of the employee's entire benefit because of the employee's death, termination of employment, or attainment of age 591/2. A lump-sum distribution may be subject to favorable tax treatment.

Margin Cushion for claim fluctuation.

Major Medical Health insurance designed to finance the expense of major illness and injuries. Characterized by: large benefit maximums ranging from $250,000 to No Limit; and an initial deductible amount.

Material Modification A summary of material modification must be filed with the DOL and distributed to participants for any change that affects a plan or a previously distributed SPD (as required by ERISA regulations).

Maximum Annual Account Addition Limitation ERISA defines a maximum annual contribution amount to be made by an employer on behalf of an employee to a defined contribution plan.

Maximum Benefit The largest benefit that may be paid under a defined benefit plan in accordance with law, even though the plan's benefit formula might produce a larger benefit if applied without limitation.

Maximum Benefit Limitation Under ERISA, the maximum annual retirement benefit permitted for an employee in a defined benefit plan.

Medicaid Federally funded medical benefit plan that is administered by the individual states for those who meet age and low-income guidelines.

Medicare Medical benefits provided under the Social Security Act once a worker reaches age 65.

Minimum Benefit Some defined benefit plans provide that a minimum amount will be paid regardless of the amount the benefit formula may yield. This minimum is usually payable only if certain service requirements are met.

Minimum Funding The minimum amount that an employer must contribute to a defined benefit, money purchase, or target benefit pension fund. If the minimum amount is not met, the IRS may impose an excise tax on the amount of the deficiency.

Minimum Premium Plan An employer and the insurance company agree that an employer will be responsible for paying all claims of a welfare benefit plan up to an agreed-upon aggregate level, with the carrier responsible for the excess.

Minimum Wage A wage level for most Americans established by Congress as part of the Fair Labor Standards Act. Beginning April 1, 1993, the minimum wage is $5.15 per hour.

Money Purchase Pension Plan A pension benefit plan under which contributions are fixed as flat amounts or as flat percentages of the employee's pay. The benefits will vary among employees depending upon factors such as age and retirement date. A type of defined contribution plan under ERISA.

Mortality Table A table showing how many members of a group, starting at a certain age, will be alive at each succeeding age. It is used to calculate the probability of dying in, or surviving through, any given period, and the value of an annuity benefit. To be appropriate for a specific group, it should be based on such common characteristics as sex, occupational group, etc.

Multiemployer Plan A plan to which two or more employers contribute according to a collective bargaining agreement with the same union. Contributions are established by a labor agreement.

Negotiated Provider Agreement (NPA) A type of preferred provider organization (PPO) that allows employees to make health insurance provisions for their specific needs. An employer can negotiate pricing and monitoring of utilization.

Noncontributory Plan An employee benefit plan to which the employer is the sole contributor.

Nonexempt Employees A classification of employees subject to the provisions of the Fair Labor Standards Act. (These employees receive compensation for overtime.)

Nonqualified Plan A defined benefit or defined contribution plan that does not meet the requirements of the Internal Revenue Code. Such plans do not receive favorable tax treatment. Reporting and disclosure rules differ from those of qualified plans.

Normal Cost The cost determined for a defined benefit pension plan, under the actuarial cost method in use, for a specific year of an employee's career.

Normal Retirement Age The time specified in a retirement plan as being the time when retirement will normally occur and when the employee will be entitled to full retirement benefits. Benefit formulas and cost calculations are usually based on the assumption that retirement will take place at normal retirement age. Normal retirement age must not be later than the latter of the participant's 65th birthday or the 10th anniversary of the date the participant began participating in the plan.

Offset Plan An integration pension benefit plan in which the benefits are reduced (offset) by part of the employee's retirement benefit provided under the Social Security Act. (See Integration of Retirement Plan Benefits.)

Old-Age Security Act (OAS) The name of the social security law in Canada. Qualified persons are entitled to benefits regardless of earnings or income. Increase in benefits are based on the CPI.

Old-Age, Survivors, Disability, and Health Insurance (OASDHI) The formal name of the federal social security program in the United States. Benefit amounts are based on a participant's earnings and income.

Open Enrollment The period during which subscribers in health benefit plans have the opportunity to select alternate health plan options. The term is also used to designate the period in which individuals may enroll in a health plan without proving good health.

Opinion No. 8 Principles adopted by the Accounting Principles Board concerning the handling of pension plan expenses in audited financial reports, such as maximum and minimum for cost accrual, treatment of gains, losses, unrealized appreciation, and disclosure of other pension plan items.

PBGC Statement Statement to be included in pension SPDs indicating that insurance of plan benefits is provided by the Pension Benefit Guaranty Corporation and the extent of coverage, or is not provided and why. Acceptable language provided by regulation.

Parity Rule A rule governing breaks in service in tax-qualified retirement plans. A right to a pension benefit can be lost if the break in service is greater than the years of vesting service the participant had accrued.

Participant An active employee who may become eligible to receive, or is receiving, benefits under an employee benefit plan.

Party-in-Interest Certain persons and entities considered to be closely related to plan interests under fiduciary responsibility provisions of ERISA.

Past Service years of service prior to the inception of the plan or prior to the employee's entry into the plan.

Pay Replacement Percent of pay that is replaced by benefits from an employee benefit plan and/or social security.

Payroll-Based Stock Ownership Plan (PAYSOP) A stock ownership plan under which an employer could take a tax credit for contributions of employer stock made to employee accounts, based on a percent of total payroll. The Tax Reform Act of 1986 eliminated the tax credit that employers received for contributions after December 31, 1986.

Pension Administrator As defined by ERISA, the person or organization (frequently the sponsor) designated by the terms of the document under which a pension or welfare plan operates.

Pension Benefit Guaranty Corporation (PBGC) Established by ERISA to provide termination insurance covering most defined benefit pension plans. Employers are required to pay annual insurance premiums to the PBGC.

Pension Plan Established and maintained by an employer (or group of employers) primarily to provide for the payment of definitely determinable benefits to employees after retirement. Also known as a defined benefit plan.

Pension Trust Established in conjunction with a pension plan to receive and invest employer and employee contributions.

Period Certain Option A life annuity which provides that payments will be made for at least a specified period, such as 5, 10, or 15 years. Any payments made after the retiree's death (but still within the specified period) would be made to a beneficiary.

Perquisite A benefit tied to a specific key or management level job. For example, a company car for personal use, free meals, financial counseling, or the use of company facilities.

Plan Administrator Under ERISA, the person or entity named to administer a pension benefit plan or welfare benefit plan.

Plan Termination Insurance Mandatory insurance provided through PBGC guaranteeing participants' "basic" retirement benefits, which are those vested under the terms of a defined benefit plan, up to certain limits. (See Pension Benefit Guaranty Corporation.)

Plan Year (Fiscal Year of Plan) Calendar, policy, or fiscal year on which the records of an employee benefit plan are kept.

Pooled Contract Funding contract under which premiums are based on many employers' claim expenses. Surpluses are not refunded.

Postponed Retirement When an employee chooses to work beyond the plan's normal retirement date. Date at which benefits must begin are regulated by law. Benefits may be increased to reflect shorter payment length.

Precertification (Predetermination, Preauthorization) Formal procedure whereby a health care provider submits a treatment plan to a third party for review before hospitalization or treatment begins. The review organization compares the proposed treatment plan against accepted standards of care.

Pre-existing Condition A physical or mental condition that existed prior to a participant's coverage in a med-ical plan. Some plans have pre-existing condition exclusions.

Preferred Provider Organization (PPO) A contracted group of physicians that provides comprehensive medical service-usually on a discounted fee-for-service basis.

Preretirement Surviving Spouse Option According to the Retirement Equity Act of 1984, this option must be offered to employees upon reaching the age of 35. Coverage pays pension plan benefits for the lifetime of a surviving spouse if a vested employee dies before retirement. The benefit amount must be equal to at least 50% of what the employee would have been entitled to if the employee had retired at the date of death.

Primary Insurance Amount (PIA) An individual's monthly benefit at age 65 under the Social Security Act. Used as a basis for determining other social security benefits. Also known as primary social security.

Profit Sharing Plan A plan under which the employer contributions are directly or indirectly related to profits. A type of defined contribution plan.

"Prudent Man" Standard Fiduciaries must carry out their duties with the care, skill, prudence, and diligence that a prudent man would use. Some states have written standards to which banks and other institutions must adhere.

Qualified Domestic Relations Order (ADRO) A legal decree that creates rights of alternate payees to qualify for retirement plan benefits. May include such things as alimony or child support.

Qualified Plan A defined benefit or defined contribution plan that the Internal Revenue Service approves as meeting the requirements of Section 401(a) of the 1986 Internal Revenue Code. Receives favorable tax treatment. For example, employer contributions are deductible as a business expense, within certain limits, and investment earnings are not subject to income tax until distributed as benefits.

Quarters of Covered Service (QCS) The number of quarters of social security coverage that have been credited to an individual and determine eligibility for social security benefits.

Rabbi Trust An irrevocable trust established by an employer to provide supplemental executive retirement benefits, deferred compensation, or similar benefit obligations. Trust assets, however, still remain subject to the claims of the employer's general creditors in the case of bankruptcy or insolvency.

Reasonable and Customary Charges A term used in many health welfare plans. Defined as the price at or below which the majority of health-care professionals of similar expertise charge for similar procedures within a specific geological area.

Recurring Clause Provision in some welfare plans specifying that recurrences of illnesses within a defined time frame will qualify as a continuation of the prior disability.

Regulations   Administrative decisions made by governmental authorities to supplement the actual law passed by Congress.

Reserves   Money retained by an insurance company or employer to fund its future liabilities.

Residential Care Facility   Facility that provides care for those unable to care for themselves due to physical, mental, or emotional conditions.

Retention   An insurer's operational cost. Includes administrative and claim processing expenses, premium taxes, and profit and risk charges.

Retirement Equity Act of 1984 (REA)   Federal law that amended ERISA. Granted greater pension equity for women and surviving spouses.

Retrospective Agreement   A device by which a promissory note is substituted for cash premium payments. The note is called only in the event of excessive claims.

Revenue Ruling   A judgment or decision by the Internal Revenue Service relative to a specific tax question.

Rollover   The movement of funds from one investment to another. To provide investment flexibility, participants can shift investment in one individual retirement plan to another without incurring any tax liability. For example, a person could roll over money from an employer's 401(k) plan into an IRA without paying a penalty tax.

"Rule of 45"   A vesting schedule using both the participant's age and years of service. The Tax Reform Act of 1986 has mandated vesting schedules for plan years beginning after December 31, 1988, which makes this obsolete.

Salary Reduction [401(k)] Arrangement   A feature of a profit sharing or stock bonus plan in which employees may elect to have the employer make payments either to the plan on their behalf or as direct cash compensation. Payments not taken in cash are not taxed until removed from the plan. Also allows contributions to be made on pre-tax salary reduction basis. A 401(k) arrangement is subject to a discrimination test that must be met in order to obtain qualifications with the IRS. Maximum contribution levels determined by law.

Savings (or Thrift) Plan   A plan to which employees contribute on a pre- or after-tax basis, usually with a supplemental contribution from the employer. Employer contributions may be related to employee's pay, employee's contribution, or profit. If the employer contribution is not contingent on profit, the plan qualifies as a money purchase pension plan; if it is contingent on profit, it qualifies as a profit sharing plan. A type of defined contribution plan.

Scheduled Plan (Indemnity Program)   A health care plan that has specific provisions for each type of care and treatment.

Section 89   Section of the Internal Revenue Code, added by the Tax Reform Act of 1986, that sets the nondiscrimination rules for health care plans and group term life insurance. Repealed in December 1989.

Section 404   Section of the 1986 Internal Revenue Code under which the contributions by an employer to a qualified plan are claimed as a deduction for federal income tax purposes.

Secular Trust   An irrevocable trust created by an employer, in which the employer makes contributions to an executive's account in the trust. Unlike a Rabbi Trust, the executive's benefits are taxed in the year in which he/she becomes vested. However, the benefit is more secure because it belongs to the executive.

Self-Administered Trusteed Plan   A retirement plan under which contributions to purchase pension benefits are paid to a trustee, generally a bank, which: (1) invests the money; (2) accumulates the earnings and interest; and (3) pays benefits to eligible employees under the terms of the retirement plan and trust agreement. This plan is administered by the employer, or by a committee appointed by the employer.

Self Funding   No insurance; employer is liable for funding all medical claims.

Self-Insured Plan   Generally a trusteed plan. The employer, in effect, insures all aspects of the medical plan, and is liable for funding all claims.

Separate Account   A fund held by an insurance company apart from its general assets. Generally used for investment of plan assets in equities or other specialized asset forms.

Service (Credited Service and Benefit Service)   Period of employment that is used as a basis for determining eligibility, vesting, and benefits. Generally a 12-month period during which an employee has met the plan's required hours of service, but ERISA also permits alternate forms of measurement.

May include all service, but may exclude years in excess of a maximum such as 30. Different benefit levels or formulas may apply to different periods of service; therefore, terms such as "past service" and "future service" may be used.

Settlement Options (Payment Options)   Alternative forms of benefits that a participant may elect in lieu of the basic form of benefit provided for in a defined benefit or defined contribution plan.

Shift Differentials   Extra pay allowance made to employees who work shifts other than a regular day shift (for example, 9 to 5, Monday through Friday), usually expressed as a percent or an additional dollar amount per hour.

Short-Term Disability Plan   A plan which covers an employee's temporary inability to perform his or her job. This may include a sickness and accident insurance program, as well as paid sick leave.

Simplified Employee Pension (SEP)   IRA to which both the employer and employee contribute. The employee must include the employer's contribution in annual income, but can take an offset deduction from his or her income. Employer contributions are governed by same rules and limits as those for self-employed plans.

Employee contributions are limited by IRA regulations.

Social Security The Social Security Act of 1935 established what has become the Federal Old-Age, Survivors, Disability, and Health Insurance System (OASDHI). The beneficiaries are workers who participate in the Social Security program, their spouses, dependent parents, and dependent children. Benefits vary according to (1) earnings of the worker, (2) length of time in the program, (3) age when benefits start, (4) age and number of recipients other than the worker, and (5) state of health of recipients other than the worker.

Social Security Option (Level Income Option) An option in some defined benefit plans. The employee may elect to receive larger plan payments before becoming eligible for social security. Once eligible for social security, plan payments are reduced to produce, as nearly as practicable, a level total annual annuity to the employee, including social security.

Split Dollar Life Insurance Individual cash value life insurance contract arranged so that the employer and employee (or beneficiary) split the death benefit. Annual premiums may be paid entirely by the employer or may be split between employer and employee.

Spouse's Benefits Payments to the surviving spouse of a deceased employee.

Statement of Account Generally applicable only under a defined contribution plan, under which the employer is required by law to provide participants with information as to the status of their accounts at least once a year.

Statement of Vested and Accrued Pension Benefit Statement required to be given vested terminations that must include amount of accrued benefit earned to date, percentage of the accrued benefit that is vested, and the amount of the accrued vested benefit.

Step-Rate Plan A form of an excess-integrated plan in which benefits are calculated by assigning different values to income above and below defined levels (i.e., Social Security wage base).

Stock Bonus Plan A defined contribution plan under which distributions are normally made in the form of employer stock. Subject to the same rules and regulations as profit sharing plans.

Stop-Loss Provision Provision in health care plan that raises the coinsurance to 100% after a certain level of benefit is paid by the plan, or an established out-of-pocket amount is paid by the participant.

Summary Annual Report (SAR) Summary, distributed to participants, of pension or welfare plan's annual financial report filed with the IRS. Supplementary explanatory material may be added to certain required information from appropriate annual report form.

Summary Plan Description (SPD) Summary of plan document required by ERISA. Distributed to plan participants and filed with the Department of Labor. ERISA defines content, style, format, and distribution procedures.

Supplemental Executive Retirement Plan (SERP) Nonqualified retirement plan for higher-paid employees. Typically in addition to a tax-qualified, broad-based pension plan.

Taft-Hartley Act See Labor-Management Relations Act of 1947.

Target Benefit Plan A defined contribution plan under which the amount of employer contributions allocated to each participant is determined under a plan formula, and on the basis of the amount necessary to provide a target benefit specified by the plan.

Tax Credit Credit against tax liability-reducing tax bill on a dollar-for-dollar basis.

Tax Deduction A deduction from taxable income. Tax is reduced because income is lowered.

Tax-Favored Benefits Designed to help employees meet special needs, these benefits are not taxed as current income. Can be divided into two types: (1) tax-deferred benefits generally include employer contributions to public and private retirement and profit sharing plans; and (2) tax-exempt benefits include employer contributions to group health and group life insurance up to $50,000, and some smaller benefits.

Tax Reduction Act (Employee) Stock Ownership Plan (TRASOP) Under this type of arrangement (Act expired at the end of 1982), an employer could take a tax credit for contributions of employer stock made to employee accounts based on qualifying capital expenditures made by the company that year.

Tax Reform Act of 1986 (TRA '86) Had a profound effect on employee benefits through overall reductions of income tax rates and provisions directly affecting benefits. Pension and welfare benefit changes aimed at producing more comparable employee benefit coverage on both ends of the compensation scale.

Tax-Sheltered Annuity (TSA) A type of annuity made available to some nonprofit organizations. Like a 401(k), it allows employees to contribute pre-tax dollars for investments toward retirement.

Taxable Wage Base The maximum amount of pay on which an individual must pay social security taxes in a given year.

Third Party Administrator (TPA) A company that administers welfare plans and generally provides services similar to those of insurance carriers.

$3,500 Rule An ERISA rule (subsequently amended by REA) that gives an employer the right to pay a participant's pension benefit in the form of a lump sum, event though the employee has not elected a lump sum. This can only be done if the conversion of the normal annuity form into a lump sum results in an amount less that $3,500.

Top-Heavy Plan A defined benefit plan under which more than 60% of total accrued benefits are for key employees, or a defined contribution plan under which the accounts of key employees comprise more than 60% of the total of all employees' accounts.

Total Disability Definition varies from plan to plan. Generally an illness or injury that prevents employees from earning wages for pay or profit or from working in a capacity for which they are qualified by education, training, or experience.

Trust Agreement An agreement between an employer and a trustee used in connection with a qualified plan. It defines the trustee's powers and duties and makes provision as to how the funds of the plan shall be invested and how payment shall be made to those who benefit under the plan. A trust agreement is always used for a noninsured plan, and may be used under some insured arrangements.

Trust Fund Plan (Trusteed Plan) A pension plan for which the funding instrument is a trust agreement.

Turnover Rate The rate at which employees terminate covered service for reasons other than death or retirement.

Unfunded Accrued Liability The excess of the accrued liability over the actuarial value of assets.

Unisex Rates Insurance rates that do not differ by sex.

Unit Credit Actuarial Cost Method A process that allocates pension cost to the year in which the benefit is earned.

Universal Life Insurance Flexible premium life insurance policy under which the policyholder may change the death benefit (with satisfactory evidence of insurability for increases) and vary the amounts or timing of premium payments. Premiums (minus expense charges) are credited to a policy account from which mortality charges are deducted and to which interest is credited at rates that may change.

Utilization Review (UR) Formal process of reviewing the quality and appropriateness of care provided. Utilization Review may be prospective (before), concurrent (during), or retroactive (after) services are provided.

Variable Annuity An annuity under which the benefit amount varies in accordance with predetermined criteria; for example, the value of the assets set aside to provide the annuity, or the Consumer Price Index.

Vesting The right to receive retirement plan benefits. An employee is 100% vested when this right is no longer contingent upon continued employment. Employee contributions are always 100% vested. Employer contributions and earnings on all contributions vest according to a schedule specified by the plan, and prescribed by law.

Vesting Schedule Tax Reform established two acceptable vesting schedules: (1) 100% vested after five years; and (2) 20% vested after three years, 20% each year thereafter until 100% vested after seven years. These rules apply to single employer plans. Multi-employer plans can still use other options (i.e., 10-year cliff vesting).

Voluntary Employee's Beneficiary Association (VEBA) A trust established to provide an employee benefit (typically health, disability, or death benefit). Also known as a "501(c)(9) trust."

W-2 Form The form a company gives an individual at year's end that reports the individual's total earnings reported to the government, and shows the total of all items withheld for various purposes, including federal, state, local and FICA taxes.

W-4 Form The form employees fill out indicating the number of allowances the employee claims for the year.

Waiver of Premium Under a group life insurance contract, a provision whereby premiums are waived in the event of total disability.

Welfare Plan (Welfare Benefit Plan) Under ERISA, a plan maintained by an employer to provide certain benefits other than retirement benefits (medical, disability, vacation plans).

Wellness Program (or Health Promotion Program) Program designed to promote good health among employees. The thought is that this will bring down absenteeism and health care costs (e.g., smoking cessation, weight loss, and stress management).

Whole Life Insurance Insurance is paid to the named beneficiary at the insured's death. Premiums may be paid for a set number of years (limited payment life) or for life (straight life). Also known as "permanent life insurance" or "cash value life insurance."

Withdrawal Liability Defined by the Multiemployer Pension Plan Amendment Act of 1980 (MPPAA). An employer who withdraws from a multiemployer plan is liable for a share of the unfunded vested benefits. Limits set by law.

Workers' Compensation Insurance Each state has its own workers' compensation law. The laws all have the goal of providing cash payment or medical care to cover health services for workers injured on the job, partial wage replacement benefits, and rehabilitation services to restore workers to their fullest economic capacity. All benefits are totally employer financed.

Year of Service Generally defined as 1,000 hours in a consecutive 12-month period. (See Service.)

GLOSSARY OF TRAINING AND DEVELOPMENT TERMS

Accelerated learning 1) Attempts to improve instruction through use of characteristics of effective instruction and teaching the learner more effective learning strategies. 2) A system of learning designed to improve rate of learning and overall retention by incorporating creative learning techniques.

Accreditation A formal process for sanction of instructional programs by an organization recognized to conduct the process.

Accreditation of prior learning (APL) Through a systematic and valid assessment process, an individual's skills and knowledge can be formally recognized and credited regardless of how, when, where, or why they were obtained. Slightly different terms are used frequently in different countries. APL is preferred in the U.K., prior learning assessment is preferred in the U.S., and recognition of prior learning is preferred in Australia.

Achievement motivation A theory mainly concerned with motivation developed by David McClelland, John Atkinson, and others. Achievement motivation attempts to measure how four factors influence achievement-oriented activity. The factors are (1) expected probability of success, (2) incentive value of success, (3) perceived difficulty of the task, and (4) intrinsic interest that the task holds for the subject.

Achievement test Measurement of learner's abilities. Achievement tests are usually used to measure existing, as opposed to newly acquired, abilities.

Adult education Learning activities engaged in by adults in either a formal or informal educational setting for the purpose of brining about change or growth. Loosely, any educational program provided for adults.

Adventure training An outdoor activity that involves physical participation, usually by team members. Adventure training activities usually have high and low challenge activities and problem-solving tasks. A particular type of adventure training is called ropes training because of its use of rope-based challenges.

American Society for Training and Development (ASTD) The largest professional society for HRD practitioners in the United States.

Application An instructional technique based on the use of knowledge and skills in real-life situations, provided in instructional settings.

Artificial intelligence (AI) A field of computer science that deals with designing computer software which can reason and solve problems. AI includes expert systems: computer programs that offer advice and form the basis of performance support systems. See expert system, job aid, and performance support system.

Assessment center Usually a process rather than a physical place, an assessment center evaluates the knowledge, skill, and attitudes of people to support their development and career and job placement.

Assessment center method A widely used formal method of data collection for evaluating the performance of individuals, involving feedback provided by a group of specially trained observers called assessors. The individuals being assessed participate in simulation exercises that enable them to demonstrate a particular skill, knowledge, or ability. The assessment center method was initiated to select foremen from among candidates and is often used to select candidates for senior level management positions. Research has validated the assessment center concept and it enjoys the confidence of a wide variety of organizations.

Baseline (performance) data Data collected before an intervention. Baseline data are useful for identifying instructional needs and comparing postinstructional improvements to preexisting conditions.

Basic skills Job-related basic skills are literacy skills (reading, writing, and speaking English) and computational skills. Basic skills programs often aim at raising learners from their preexisting level of ability to 6th- or 7th-grade level.

Behavioral objective A learning objective specifying the acquisition of a particular new behavior that the participant should be able to execute after instruction. Deals with the cognitive domain.

Behavior modeling An instructional technique used to change the behavior of learners by showing them a sample of the correct behavior. Behavior modeling is based on carefully prepared presentations showing the model or an ideal enactment of the desired behavior. Learners then try to emulate what they have seen. The total skill is usually presented before learners try out any behavior themselves. The model may be presented by video or instructors in a skit; however, the latter method may vary each time repeated. Sometimes called interactive modeling.

Behavior modification The process by which a person's particular behavior or behavior pattern is intentionally changed to some specified new behavior or behavior pattern, usually through use of external factors with reward, punishment, or recognition.

Benchmarking Evaluating one's own practices and then comparing them to another company's. Benchmarking is frequently used in the quality process.

Broadband Communications channels such as broadcast television, cable television, microwave, and satellite that are capable of carrying a wide range frequencies.

Business competencies Competencies are described in the HRD Roles and Competencies Study as having a strong management, economics, or administration base. They include business understanding, cost-benefit analysis skill, delegation skill, industry understanding, organization-behavior understanding, organization-development-theories-and-techniques understanding, organization understanding, project-management skill, and records-management skill.

Business game An instructional game based on one or more of the financial or management disciplines. Typical game objectives are to maximize profit, sales, market share, or return on investment. Learners manipulate the variables of the business and observe the effect of those changes.

Business plan A formal document that specifies the mission, vision, objectives, financial considerations, and action items which an organization has formulated to accomplish its business goals in a defined time period, usually one or more years. A business plan is often the basis for internal approval or external financing.

Buzz group A small group technique named for the buzzing sound of multiple intensive discussions. Subgroups of six or fewer participants who are part of a larger group usually all meet in the same room for a limited period of time. Each group agrees on chairperson and recorder roles. The group discusses the topic assigned, called the team task. At the end of the specified work period they report back to the whole group. Buzz groups are useful to develop agendas, react to a presentation, develop questions or points, stimulate thinking, or recommend courses of action.

Career path A structured sequence of work assignments and experiences. A career path provides employees the opportunity to participate in many aspects of a career area for the purpose of preparation for career growth. Includes detailed descriptions of interrelationships between jobs in an organization, expressed in terms of the training, education, experience, and behaviors required for movement between jobs. Used by career planners to advise an employee.

Case method An instructional technique that presents real or fictional situations or problems for learners to analyze, to discuss, and to recommend actions to be taken. It is based on the concept of discovery learning. The information given in the study realistically simulates the experience where only limited information is available. Learners are presented case information. Usually each learner determines a solution. Then groups of students discuss the problem to arrive at a group solution. Then, the entire group discusses the case.

Chaining Linking a series of discriminable responses together in a particular order. The completion of each response provides the stimulus for the next response. Chaining may involve verbal or motor responses.

Change agent In OD, any person or group responsible for initiating or implementing organizational change.

Coaching A process through which an individual supports the learning or performance improvement of another via interactive questioning and other means of active support. The coaching instructor observes the learner, provides hints, help, and feedback in a positive way as needed. Coaching is sometimes incorporated in on-the-job training.

Cognitive Outcomes based on the enhancement of knowledge and understanding of, or related to, mental processes, particularly information processing.

Cognitive development theory In developmental psychology, a theory concerned with growth in the processes of perceiving, thinking, and knowing. Swiss psychologist Jean Piaget described cognitive processes developed through four stages from early childhood to adult.

Competency-based curriculum An instructional sequence based on objectives-centered instruction.

Competency model A way of describing the requisite abilities, personal qualities, and skills needed to perform a specific job for an organization.

Composite whole brain learning group A group that is balanced in thinking and learning styles across the spectrum of mental possibilities.

Contingency Model A model of group leadership. The contingency model incorporates general predictions of leader effectiveness in selected situations based on selected scores of group leaders.

Continuing education 1) Instructional programs for adult learners that include formal degree programs and various nontraditional experiences. Programs are conducted in business, colleges and universities, government, industry, and nonprofit organizations. 2) Mandated HRD activities that individuals must engage in to retain certification, licensure, or standing. This term does not apply to the formal education or other programs required to enter the field.

Continuing education unit (CEU) A CEU is a unit of measurement based on 10 contact hours of instruction. Following an approval process, instruction conducted outside formal institutions of learning can award CEUs that may be accepted toward credit at institutions of higher education.

Cost-benefit analysis A method of evaluating the implications of alternative HRD plans. Cost-benefit analysis determines whether a project will save an amount equal to or greater than its cost and lost opportunities. A technique for assessing the relationship between results of outcomes of HRD programs and the cost required to produce them.

Cost center One financial arrangement for funding the HRD function. The cost center approach is based on the HRD department receiving a budget for all its operations. The HRD department then provides the HRD services to the organization.

Cost-effectiveness A comparative evaluation derived from the analyses of alternatives (actions, methods, approaches, equipment, support systems, team combinations, etc.) To achieve an objective. Analyses focus on the interrelated influences of cost and effectiveness in accomplishing the specific mission or objective.

Critical Incident method The identification and analysis of participant's actual experiences to better understand real problems or the role the critical incident plays in the career. The critical incident method is also known as the peak-experience approach. The participants are asked to describe the details of an incident that changed their lives. This method is used extensively in upper management or executive development programs.

Critique An analysis of a past experience or performance to enable improvement in the future.

Cultural barriers Difficulties, often unsuspected, based on the differences in the two (or more) cultural backgrounds of the parties. Identification and reduction of cultural barriers is usually the focus of cross-cultural training.

Culture 1) The unspoken pattern of values that people develop and practice unconsciously as they grow up. Culture varies significantly, even within one country. 2) In OD and HRD, unspoken patterns that guide the behavior of the people in an organization. It specifically includes attitudes and practices that are difficult to change. For example, "That's the way we do things around here."

Curriculum 1) The largest instructional component. A curriculum is made up of two or more courses. 2) A collection of formal and informal learning events that work together to support learning over time. 3) The subject areas within a specified course of study. 4) A specific plan for instruction or learning.

Custom courseware Courseware that is developed specifically for one organization. Also called custom-designed learning.

Debriefing Review and discussion of the processes and outcomes of any instructional activity. Debriefing is used after role plays and simulation games. Debriefing facilitates participants reflecting on their prior experiences, gaming insights, and sharing for mutual learning.

Decision making The process of choosing among alternatives. In a group process exercise, no best or correct answer can be validated by any means other than consensus.

Decision tree A diagram that is the basis of a technique for making choices based on the relationships and implications of one decision to others. Decision trees are often incorporated in job aids. Named because of its branching structure.

Delivery system 1) The media and other resources used to deliver instruction. 2) The equipment used to deliver a technology-based learning program.

Demonstration An instructional technique. A presentation shows a group how something works, how to perform an act, or how to use a procedure. Demonstration is an important technique in on-the-job training and behavior modeling technology.

Developer-instructor An HRD practitioner who primarily develops courseware and secondarily teaches courses.

Dialogue 1) In conferences, a session with a predesignated small group of people. Their function is to listen to a session and then engage in a conversation with the presenter in front of the audience. 2) In conferences, a conversation between two individuals in front of a large group. Dialogue presenters talk extemporaneously. Participants listen, but do not take part until after the dialogue is completed.

Distance learning An instructional method in which the instructor or facilitator is geographically separated from the learners. Also called distance education and distant learning.

Divergent thinking A nontraditional approach to problems that may produce original solutions. Divergent thinking has been described as the expansive, generative, exploratory, option-finding stage of problem solving, which seeks to understand the issue thoroughly and to identify options for solving it.

Downsizing Reductions in force. Downsizing is often used to reduce the number of employees and layers of management in an organization. Resulting lessened management opportunities result in increased scope of responsibilities and attendant training.

Dual career ladder A common pattern in organizations. One career path advances through levels of technical expertise, the other through levels of management.

Dubbing Transfer of information from one audio or visual source to another.

Educational entitlement The practice of providing funds to employees so that they can study outside the company. The term "entitlement" implies that it is a regular right to which all workers are entitled. Most countries that have educational entitlement legislation insist that the employees should not study anything directly related to the job.

Electronic blackboard A special device resembling a chalkboard. The electronic blackboard is used to transmit a blackboard-like image drawn on the device through a standard phone line to a decoding device and onto a video monitor at the receiving end. A useful system for the exchange of simple, spontaneous graphics. One method of transmitting information in distance learning.

Electronic mail Called E-mail. A means of sending text messages to individuals or groups of individuals using a computer network. The sender inputs a message to the computer via a terminal, and the receiver also uses a terminal to read and respond to messages. One method of transmitting information in distance learning.

Electronic-systems skill The HRD competency of having knowledge of functions, features, and potential applications of electronic systems for the delivery and management of HRD, such as computer-based training, teleconferencing, expert systems, interactive video, and satellite networks.

Employee educational assistance Programs that provide funding or reimbursement for employee's course or degree programs. Reimbursement ranges from partial to full and may be based on the grade earned or on the relevance of the degree work to the employee's work. A provision in the U.S. tax code under which employees are not taxed on non job related education tuition reimbursement.

Employee empowerment Giving employees the opportunity to manage themselves and make their own decisions.

Employee involvement A process that involves employees in organization decision making. Employee involvement is based on the need of leaders of the organization to know the opinions and feelings of its members and on the positive benefits of getting employee input toward, and buy-in of, organizational decisions.

Enactive model A model involving a set of appropriate actions for achieving a specific result.

Environment analysis 1) In instruction, identification of both where the instruction will occur and how the instructional materials will be used. 2) In OD, identification of the characteristics of the environment most critical to the organization. Environment analysis also predicts how those characteristics are likely to change.

Expatriate An employee who works for an extended time in a country other than the one in which citizenship is held.

Experiential learning A collective term for HRD activities based on participants' reactions to the practical activities during an exercise, as opposed to passive learning. Based on work of David Kolb, Pfeiffer and Jones' experiential learning design model portrays the process as a circle of five revolving steps: experiencing, publishing, processing, generalizing, and applying.

Expert system Programs that offer on-the-job advice to a user. Named for the origin of their information, the collected knowledge of an expert. Expert systems assist the user with taking appropriate action exactly as does a job aid. Expert systems are the principle component of performance support systems.

Facilitation 1) A process of guiding a group based on a learner-centered mode of instruction. The leader in this mode is called a facilitator. A facilitator may be considered a group member as well as leader. A facilitator contrasts with the image of a teacher as presenter of information. 2) In organizational development, the

process used by the OD practitioner to stimulate insight and learning.

Facilitator A leader of an instructional activity. Facilitator is a title for a person assisting in any learning, but is particularly applied to leaders of groups whose purpose is behavioral change.

Feedback 1) Information given to learners regarding their progress. Feedback may be immediate or delayed, oral or written, one-time or ongoing. 2) The process of verifying that communication has taken place between sender and receiver. The receiver tells the sender what is understood.

Field experience A limited assignment under real conditions. A field experience should contain specific tasks for the learners to perform that focus the learner's attention on aspects of the job, the culture, or even the language that might otherwise be overlooked.

Flow chart A graphic representation of the steps in a process, procedure, or algorithm. Widely used in technology development. Flow charting is also applicable to representing the path a product or service follows. For example, comparison charts can be drawn of both what happens and what should happen.

Focus group A facilitator-led group of six to twelve participants convened for a specific purpose, usually related to an organizational challenge, problem, or opportunity. Focus groups may meet only once or continually, depending on their character.

Forum A period of open discussion by audience participants following a panel, debate, colloquy, or speech. In a forum, participants interact with presenters under the direction of a moderator.

Games In transactional analysis, the term for the transactions with a predictable outcome. The games are the product of each of the potential combinations of the three states: parent, child, and adult. The combinations of these states in human interactions is the basis of transactional analysis.

General educational development (GED) Usually heard in its abbreviated form, the term GED is applied to tests and the high school equivalency degree that may be earned through a program of comprehensive testing in the U.S. A GED degree is often the goal of adult basic education systems.

General session Conference sessions intended for all participants. The general session usually relates directly to the theme of the conference or an aspect of it. Competing events are never scheduled at the same time as general sessions.

Generic courseware Courseware that is not specific to one organization. Generic courseware may appeal to a broader market, as opposed to custom courseware, which primarily meets the needs of one specific client or audience.

Globalization An all-encompassing concept that includes three ideas: international, multinational, and transnational. Globalization is considered the ultimate and most desirable phase in the series from domestic, export, international, multinational, transnational and global. It is generally considered to require a higher level of competence and commitment than lower states.

Global learning curve A scale to determine to what stage an organization has advanced relative to corporate globalization.

Global learning organization Any organization that both operates in at least two countries and implements the activities associated with (domestic) learning organizations, while coping with the additional complexities of the international environment.

Goal 1) An intended outcome. A goal is a broad statement of intent. 2) The end-object of an expert system.

Goal analysis A process used to identify the important components of a performance.

Goal-oriented learner A learner who uses instruction to accomplish clear-cut objectives.

Goal statement A broad description of the planned outcome of the HRD activity. The goal statement is a general expression of the expectations of the developers of the instruction.

Graphical user interface (GUI) (Pronounced gooey.) Uses of icons to represent actual objects, such as a trash can. The learner can access and manipulate these with a mouse.

Graphics Plotted points, drawn lines, and other pictures either in hard copy or on the display screen of a computer or a terminal. Graphics aid student understanding of complex items or processes, and can make an important contribution to the learning process.

Group discussion A meeting among participants in a learning event. A group discussion is typically limited in length. It provides an opportunity for participants to share information and derive a group solution to an assigned problem.

Group dynamics The methods by which a group functions as a collective whole. The give and take that occurs in all groups.

Group facilitator The HRD role of managing group discussions and group process so that individuals learn and group members feel the experience is positive.

Groupthink The situation in group facilitation, described by Irving Janis, in which group members think alike. Groupthink reinforces conformity and discourages innovation. It is caused by rigid adherence to group norms.

Halo effect When one's general impression of a person biases ratings of that person's behavior. The halo effect can distort evaluation or research.

Hardware Physical equipment. Hardware excludes the instructions to the equipment called software and the instructional software and supporting physical materials called courseware.

Helping relationship 1) A situation in which one person deploys special knowledge or skills to help another, often in the area of personal effectiveness. 2) In consulting, the ideal type relationship.

Holistic learner A person who learns by perceiving and understanding the "big picture" without dwelling on individual elements of an idea, concept, or situation. A holistic learner can see the forest as contrasted with the trees.

Homogeneous Alike, with the same or similar parts or elements. For example, learners with identical work experience.

Honorarium A token amount paid to a speaker or provider of a professional service when a market price is not feasible or appropriate. An honorarium is often a lower amount than would normally be charged for the time of the same person. Plural of honorarium is honoraria.

Hot role play A role play technique used to immediately resolve classroom issues. The participants are not given prepared instructions. The instructor reacts spontaneously to the immediate classroom dynamics. Any situation can become the content of an extemporaneous "hot" role play.

HRD activity 1) HRD activities are training, education and development. 2) Any intervention that is intended to develop an individual's or team's work-related capacity.

HRD consultant A consultant who serves as a partner with management to link HRD efforts to the organization's strategic direction and to provide various HRD services.

HRD function All instructional and administrative activities related to HRD that occur in an organization. Also, instructional activities are considered part of the HRD function, whether conducted by the HRD department or others.

Human relations training Programs designed to help people interact more effectively. Human relations training includes communications training, team building, and participative management. The term itself is less used today.

Human resource development (HRD) A concept developed by Leonard Nadler and published in Developing Human Resources. Nadler defines human resource development as organized learning experiences provided by employers within a specified period of time to bring about the possibility of performance improvement or personal growth. HRD activities are training, education, and development. HRD is differentiated from adult education in that it is focused on learning activities provided by organizations to their employees.

Human resource practice Nine areas specified in the ASTD competency study. The human resource practice areas are 1) compensation/benefits, 2) employee assistance, 3) human resource planning, 4) organization development, 5) organization/job design, 6) personnel research and information systems, 7) selection and staffing, 8) training and development, and 9) union/labor relations.

Human resources concept The philosophy that people are assets. The human resources concept maintains that the development of employees represents an investment rather than an expense.

Hypertext A program that links nonlinear text. Hypertext allows flexible, learner-directed browsing to seek additional information by moving between related documents along thematic lines without losing the context of the original inquiry. For example, the learner chooses a word such as gear. The program links to text that says, "This equipment has helical gears." Further exploration of helical is possible.

Icebreakers A climate-setting activity designed specifically to facilitate people getting to know each other and to place a group at ease for instruction.

Icon A symbol that looks like an object. An icon can represent any function or task. In icon-driven systems, the learner chooses the icon with a tactile device, such as a mouse, instead of pressing function keys or typing commands.

Imagery A method of storing information in long-term memory by generation of vivid mental visualizations. Imagery includes mental images formed from memories of sounds, touch, muscle activity, emotion or abstract concepts.

Imaginative learner A person who learns by forming mental images of things not immediately available to the senses or never wholly perceived in reality. An imaginative learner is able to confront and deal with a problem in a new way.

Imaging Imprinting in one's own mind a mental picture of improved behavior and using that vision to stimulate appropriate behaviors.

Implementation One of the phases in the ISD process. The others are analysis, design, implementation, and evaluation. Delivering the learning activities to the target population of learners in the intended environment. All instructional materials are reproduced and distributed during the implementation phase.

In-basket exercise A simple simulation technique that places the learner at a desk with realistic documents in an in-basket. The learner must process the documents, which include, but are not limited to, letters, memos, notes from the boss, records of telephone calls, appraisal forms, and routine reports which create realistic conditions. Sometimes not all documents have relevance to the goal. The participant must decide what to do with each item while taking into consideration the principles taught in the HRD program. In-basket exercises can measure decision-making or technical competence. Variations may stress wise use of time, decision-making ability, telephone calls, and instructor-simulated emergencies.

Incubation A key concept in creativity training. Incubation is the period during which one's attention is deliberately shifted away from the problem or task at hand. Solutions typically come as insight or sudden inspiration.

Individualized instruction An instructional technique in which the instruction is designed to be used by individual learners. The learner is taught only the material that is not already known, instead of taught everything in a specified curriculum as is true with traditional instruction. This is more than learners simply working on materials without regard to the activities of other learners in the same class. All individualized instruction is self-paced instruction. But not all self-paced instruction is individualized.

Indoctrination In organizational development, a change process characterized by mutual goal-setting and imbalanced power.

Infobase A database concept extended to include the means to gather information appropriate to performing tasks.

Informal A term used to describe the communication networks, norms, and status hierarchy of a group that are developed through natural processes and not necessarily sanctioned by any source of authority.

Information load The amount of information a person receives in a given situation. Information load may be overload or underload compared with the amount of information needed to function effectively.

Information processing model A representation of learning as a system. The information processing model links the environment to long-term memory through receptors, a sensory register, and short-term memory. Long- and short-term memories are linked back to the environment through a response generator.

Instructional aid Auxiliary items to support instructor-led instruction. Instructional aids stand in contrast to instructional media which present instruction. Examples of instructional aids include chalkboard, flipchart, and slides.

Instructional analysis A process that is carried out during the design of instruction to identify the presentational components necessary for the learner's mastery of complete skills. Sometimes confused with needs analysis, which is carried out during the analysis phase.

Instructional systems development (ISD) Usually heard in abbreviated form, ISD is a term for a variety of related systems that organize the development of instruction. ISD should be a deliberate and orderly, but flexible, process for planning and developing instructional programs that ensure personnel are taught in a cost-effective way the knowledge, skills, and attitudes essential for successful job performance. The phases of ISD are analysis, design, development, implementation, and evaluation. ISD depends on a description and analysis of several integral instructional factors, such as the tasks necessary for performing the job, and learning objectives. Tests are clearly stated before instruction begins, evaluation procedures are carried out to determine whether or not the objectives have been reached, and methods for revising the process are based on empirical data.

Interaction 1) A reciprocal interchange between the learner and the instructional medium. In CAI an interaction is never simply pressing a key to advance the display. A complete interaction is a question or problem, directions, expected correct and incorrect answers, and feedback for each possible answer. The interaction may be followed by branching, contributing to individualized instruction. The interactivity of courseware is sometimes judged by counting the frequency of interactions. 2) The give-and-take between participants in learning activities.

Interactive media 1) Instructional hardware that involves the viewer as a source of input to determine the content and duration of a message. Interactive media permit program material to be individualized. 2) Telecommunication channels that allow the two-way exchange of information.

Interactive videodisc (IVD) Video images linked with a computerized learning program that are learner-controlled through the use of a computer. Depending on the learner's response to a question, the learner may be shown any one of several video sequences.

Intervention 1) Any course of action taken by a change agent. Intervention is most often associated with OD. 2) Loosely, any planned change effort undertaken by HRD or activity.

ISO 9000 A set of international quality standards originated by the desire for quality standardization within the ECC.

Job analysis A process of identifying the complete set of duties that a person performs on the job. Job analysis is often combined with task analysis when instruction is needed.

Job description A formal explanation of the activities job incumbents perform at work.

Job design The process of designing how tasks will be carried out, and the authority and systems to be utilized in individual jobs.

Job enrichment The process of redesigning work to build in motivators and incorporate more positive challenges. Job enrichment is sometimes called vertical job loading. For example, it may involve changes in how the job is done, when or where one works, or with whom one works.

Job profile The competencies, outputs, and major ethical issues for a job. The job profile may include relevant issues, future demands, roles, and quality requirements. A job profile may also be prepared for a team.

Job progression ladder In career planning, career paths in which progressively higher positions in the organizational hierarchy are clearly linked and the education and experience needed to progress are stated unambiguously.

Job rotation In general, the practice of moving employees to various positions for a period of time. Job rotation

may be motivated by many reasons. For example, to reduce boredom.

Job Training Partnership Act (JTPA) Legislation enacted by the U.S. Congress in 1982 which provides funding for job training and related employment services to economically disadvantaged people who lack job skills.

Lateral thinking A concept developed by Edward de Bono to demystify the process of creative problem solving. Lateral thinking is a process of abandoning current vertical or linear progression of ideas and jumping laterally to a different starting point. Lateral thinking calls on characteristics associated with right brain hemispheric functions.

Learning organization Any organization that has a climate that accelerates individual and group learning. This concept regards the organization as a living organism, existing in its environment and having good feedback mechanisms and the ability to adapt to changes by taking timely action. Learning organizations teach their employees the critical thinking process for understanding what their organization does and why it does it. These individuals help the organization itself to learn from its mistakes as well as its success. As a result, the organization recognizes changes in its environment and adapts effectively.

Learning style Each individual's unique approach to learning. The learner's psychological traits determine how that person will perceive, interact with and respond to any environment. Specifically, the ways an individual behaves, feels, and processes information in learning situations.

Life cycle model A cost-benefit analysis model that identifies the costs of a project over its entire lifetime. In this model, phases of the life cycle are R&D, start up, operational period, and termination period.

Life cycle theory The conviction that individuals, groups, departments, and organizations progress through stages of development. Life cycle theory proposes that each stage is characterized by a central crisis that must be resolved before the individual may progress to the next stage.

Life-long learning The concept of continual learning in order to stay current with one's job.

Life planning A process of establishing goals and directions for one's entire life. These include education, family, leisure activities, spiritual development, and work. An ingredient of life planning is career planning.

Life stages Stable periods of six to eight years interspersed with difficult transitional periods of four to five years, described by Daniel Levinson in The Seasons of a Man's Life.

Literacy training Programs, similar to ESL (English as a second language), aimed at improving language skills of employees whose native language is English. These programs attempt to enable the employee to function at work and in the normal HRD programs of the organization.

Lost opportunity costs The cost of failure to conduct an HRD program. For example, the lesser amount of future revenue derived when a sales training program is not conducted.

Management by objectives (MBO) A method of articulating goals to achieve results. Tasks are resolved into smaller objectives. These add up to the whole task when completed. Management may then concentrate on the objectives to complete the larger task. The process has been called the application of the general systems theory to management.

Management by walking around (MBWA) A method of managing (improving) organizational performance. It is based on the concept that a manager who walks around the organization will learn of problems and therefore be able to resolve them. MBWA is a subject in many management development programs.

Management development The various HRD activities to assist managers in acquiring or enhancing the knowledge, skills, and values needed to be effective in their current and future managerial or supervisory leadership roles. Management development usually includes activities for employees down to first level supervisor. For example, time management sessions. This term is sometimes preferred over management training for prestige reasons.

Management involvement 1) The extensive involvement on the part of all levels of management in the HRD process. Management involvement includes taking part in the programs. 2) The extent to which management and other professionals outside the HRD department are actively engaged in the HRD process.

Mastery learning A principle of evaluating learning based on mastery of material according to a predetermined criterion. Also called criterion-referenced instruction (CRI) or performance-based instruction. This is in contrast to norm-referenced learning, in which the learner is compared to other learners instead of to a fixed standard.

Matrix-managed organization An organizational structure in which ad hoc project teams are created. Project managers use the services of employees who are regularly assigned to other divisions of the organization. Employees are commonly assigned to one or more short- or long-term projects at a time.

Media 1) In the learning sense, the delivery modes for instruction and learning. For example: text, film, audio or videotape, or ACI. Media is sometimes called AV materials. 2) In the technology sense, material that holds data. For example, magnetic media. 3) Loosely, all forms and channels used in the transmission of information.

Memory 1) An organized collection of storage elements in a technology-based instructional device into which instructions and data can be deposited and from which information can be retrieved. 2) A human being's storage mechanism for information.

Mentoring 1) A process to help people with their career development. Experienced and successful employees are matched with newer or junior employees to provide useful job and career guidance. Mentoring is often informal, but formal programs also exist. 2) A formalized process to introduce selected employees to the inner network of the organization to aid them in their career advancement.

Mission statement 1) A formal declaration of the overall goals of an organization. 2) In HRD organizations, a statement that identifies the reason for the existence of the HRD function. The mission statement should be linked to the overall mission, operations, and business of the organization.

Mixer 1) Activities designed to permit participants to get to know one another and legitimize strangers speaking to one another. Also known as warm ups, ice-breakers, and openers. 2) A device or system that combines two or more signals to feed another device or part of the audio system.

Model 1) A representation of an object, process, or phenomenon without regard to realistic appearance. 2) A standard to guide thinking and practice. 3) A full-size or scaled representation of an idea, object, process, or phenomenon. A working model has moving parts. 4) A person who helps show the product.

Module An arbitrary unit of instruction. Usually, a module is constructed to teach one specific thing and can be taught, measured, evaluated for change, or bypassed as a whole. Modules can be assembled to form complete courses and curricula.

Motivation 1) Encouragement to act in a particular manner. 2) Anything that acts to impel behavior. 3) The actuator of human behavior. The need for motivation is sometimes confused with the need for instruction because people may not be sufficiently motivated to perform a task that they actually know how to do.

Multimedia Use of any two or more instructional media together. Multimedia usually simulates person-to-person or person-to-machine dialogue. Technically, examples include any two media, such as tape-slide. In practice, this term has come to represent optical disk technology combined with computer power.

Murphy's Law General term to describe the rule "Whatever can go wrong will go wrong." Often used in specific ways within organizations to describe their business or function. For example, when the audiovisual expert assures you that you don't need to check it because it'll work fine, it won't.

Myers-Briggs, Isabel Collected data on psychological type over many years. She developed what has evolved into the modern Myers-Briggs Type Indicator.

Needs analysis A step in the analysis phase of ISD. Needs analysis is a methodical process of collecting and evaluating information about on-the-job performance to determine the learning needs of the organization's employees. Procedures used include critical incident analysis, data analysis, interviews, nominal group techniques, and questionnaires. Often, a needs analysis is limited to a specific department or job, or related to a new work practice or technology.

Negotiation skill The HRD competency of securing win-win agreements while successfully representing a special interest in a decision.

Nonverbal communication Communication based on a person's appearance, posture, style, or mannerisms. Nonverbal messages are a powerful factor in communication, especially with members of another culture.

On-line 1) In technology-based learning, information currently available for direct access. Usually implies linkage to a computer. 2) Loosely, under the control of, or connected to, a computer.

On-the-job training (OJT) OJT has been called the most common training method. The worker-learner usually performs under the supervision of someone else already qualified to do the job. OJT provides observation with guided practice in a practical situation, while learners engage in productive work.

Open communication Sending and receiving of messages by individuals or groups with few constraints. Open communication is important in the instructional setting.

Open-ended key questions Questions that cannot be answered either "yes" or "no". Open-ended key questions are used in planning instruction.

Organizational assessment A process used by military senior leaders to analyze and correlate evaluations or various functional systems, such as training, logistics, personnel, and force integration, to determine an organization's capability to accomplish its war-time mission.

Organizational audit An intensive study of an organization to determine weaknesses and potential methods of improvement.

Organizational climate Activities that establish acceptance among the learners for the learning activity. Climate setting is closely aligned with adult learning. The two components of climate are organizational climate and instructional climate.

Organizational climate survey A method of gathering data for organization analysis and organization development.

Organizational culture The principles, ideas, and pronouncements that define an organization. Four levels of organizational culture are artifacts, perspectives, values and assumptions.

Organization-change agent The HRD role of influencing and supporting changes in organization behavior.

Organization chart 1) Any chart showing the organization's formal structure. 2) A project-related chart showing the organizational relationships for a specific project.

Organization development (OD) 1) Within HRD, the field in which a long-term change effort is directed to an entire organization or some part of it, using tech-

niques from the applied behavioral sciences. 2) A planned change effort, usually long-term, directed to an entire organization or some part of it, using techniques from the applied behavioral sciences. OD is generally aimed at increasing the organization's effectiveness and health through planned interventions that help groups initiate and manage change and integrate individual desires for growth and development with organizational goals. OD strategies for producing change are called interventions.

Panel-forum A panel immediately followed by audience participation. Compared with the low audience participation of a panel, a panel-forum has increased involvement. The forum involves free and open discussion by the panel members on questions submitted by the audience.

Paradigm A mental frame of reference that affects the way people think and behave. HRD professionals are frequently tasked with getting organizations to break old paradigms to learn new methods. This is called a paradigm shift.

Pareto principle The 80/20 rule named for Vilfredo Pareto, an Italian economist. For example, 80 percent of the mistakes are made by 20 percent of the people.

Peer feedback Feedback from peers obtained by questionnaires or interviews on how participants have performed during or after an HRD program.

Peer group Any group with similar age or background.

Peer tutoring Instruction of a learner by another learner. For example, a learner who has completed instruction acts as an instructor to another learner in the skill or process to be learned. This procedure continues with each learner becoming an instructor for the next learner.

Percentile (centile or percentile rank) In statistics, points marking a distribution into 100 parts. The percentile is a score that shows approximately what percent of subjects scored below the given score.

Perception People's interpretation of what they sense. The process of information extraction. The process by which a learner receives or extracts information from the environment through experiences (sight, sound, feel, taste, or smell) and assimilates the data as facts.

Performance One of the three required parts of a Magerian learning objective. What the learners must demonstrate to prove that they have grasped the task. These action words state the main intent of the objective. The performance should match the job task, describe the simplest and most direct behavior possible, and be stated clearly.

Performance-based compensation A fee structure for a consultant's work, based on the client organization's sales or savings increasing to an agreed-upon level.

Performance-based evaluation Verification of the learner's acquisition of knowledge and skill by observing actual performance.

Performance planning Identification of a job's goals, priorities, and reward expectations. Usually accompanied by identification of training needs, performance activities, priorities, and explanations, as well as by financial compensation.

Physiological needs One of the levels of needs in Maslow's hierarchy of needs.

Pie chart A circular graph that shows relative size of categories of data. The area of the circle represents 100%. The circle is divided into sections that look like pieces of a pie. A pie chart is widely used because it is simple to interpret.

Pilot test The acquisition and analysis of data from outside the formal instructional environment to evaluate the instructional product in the operating environment. A formative evaluation step. In a pilot test, an instructional program is presented in final form to a portion of the target population.

Planned change In organizational development, a change process characterized by mutual goal-setting and equal power on both sides.

Plan of Instruction (POI) Often heard in abbreviation form P-O-I, the POI is used primarily for course planning, organization, and operation, and outlines a course broken down into lessons and modules. For every block of instruction within a course, it includes the lesson objective, learning objectives, duration of instruction, presentation plan, resources, and media support materials, and an indicator of how the student will be tested.

Positive feedback A response to an act or event that serves to encourage repetition of the same type of action. Positive feedback is given when any sign of improvement occurs.

Positive reinforcement Any favorable consequence or recognition directed at the learner. Positive reinforcement is provided upon the learner's demonstration of a desirable behavior. Learners are more likely to repeat activities for which they receive positive reinforcement.

Proactive Taking action before events make it necessary. Proactive is the opposite of reactive or waiting to take action after an external requirement forces it.

Probes In interviewing, short comments or questions to stimulate the respondent. Used to guide the interview.

Problem solving 1) Solving complex problems when there is no obvious, and possibly no single correct, answer. A problem-solving approach often requires the creative use of rules, procedures, techniques, and principles. 2) A group instruction method, based on discussion of a scenario. The small groups develop a set of proposals to solve the problem. In the large group, each proposal is critically discussed as it is presented.

Process 1) The combination of people, machine and equipment, raw materials, methods, and environment that produces a given product or service. 2) A sequence of events or actions continuously changing over time. A process usually is a progression toward a goal.

Productivity model In cost-benefit analysis, a model that measures both efficiency and effectiveness. In the productivity model, the results of matching specific learning variables resources with specific performance variables results in linked costs and outcomes.

Profit center A form of financial arrangement for the HRD function. Under that system, the HRD unit is expected to sell its services, sometimes externally. There may also be the policy that if a component of the organization can obtain the same quality service from outside the company, it is free to do so. This encourages the profit center to complete with outside suppliers.

Programmed instruction A self-instructional method in which information is presented in precisely planned steps or increments, almost always in text form. The appropriate response immediately follows each step.

Progressive disclosure A technique often used with overhead transparencies to build complexity and add dramatic effect. Progressive disclosure involves showing only one part of a visual at a time and building up to the complete visual. The most common technique is to cover the points not yet discussed with a sheet of paper-preventing the audience from seeing them until wanted. The sheet of paper is then moved to reveal each point in turn.

Prototype A working model of any learning activity.

Prototyping Developing a limited working model of a system. The purpose of prototyping is to obtain user feedback about the system before committing resources to final system development.

Psychological theory In career planning, the theory that early childhood has a critical impact on an individual's subsequent career choices. Psychological theory claims that work is really a sublimation of infantile impulse, and that occupations can be described in terms of the needs they help satisfy.

Pygmalion effect The concept, confirmed by Albert Moll's research, that one's expectations about a future event can affect the likelihood of its occurrence. The Pygmalion effect is named after a figure in Greek mythology and a play by George Bernard Shaw that became the movie *My Fair Lady*. It is a positive example of the self-fulfilling prophecy. It means that the expectation by the person in charge that an individual will do well leads to the individual actually doing well.

Quality A measure of the extent to which an element in experience meets a need, solves a problem, or adds value for someone.

Quality circles A technique for improving production quality based on the Japanese QC (quality control) circles methodology. One of several team-based techniques used in organizations' quality programs.

Quality of work life (QWL) 1) Individual and collective perception on the part of employees that relates to their total experience as a member of the organization. 2) Programs in organization focused on enhancing policies, procedures, and physical working conditions.

Question-and-answer session. At any meeting, the time set aside for audience questions. In formal presentations, question-and-answer sessions are typically scheduled at the end. Many presenters prefer to take questions whenever they occur to a learner.

Random access Refers to the ability to directly reach an information item without accessing other items. This capability is inherent in disc media. It is also a capability of a random access 35mm slide projector. Random access is usually associated with laserdisc technology.

Reality check An instructional technique to remind trainees that it may not be easy to apply the new skills learned in the presence of difficulties and obstacles.

Real time The actual time over which a learning activity operates as opposed to any simulated time scale built into its structure.

Reinforcement 1) Actions designed to reward or encourage a desired behavior; a central tenet of the theory of operant conditioning. Reinforcement of the learner's correct performance should be rewarded in order to increase the likelihood of successful performance in the future. 2) Praise or encouragement of the learner's performance. Reinforcement will strengthen the learner's interest and motivation.

Relaxation training Activities intended to help learners reduce elevations in such physiological indexes as heart rate, muscle tension, and blood pressure. Relaxation training focuses on reduction in external stimulation and focus on internal stimuli.

Relevant practice Practice of the substance of the learning objective. Relevant practice must be derived and provided for each objective. It includes any tools and equipment needed, as well as environmental requirements. Relevant practice also includes any other persons who may be required for practice to occur under realistic conditions.

Reliability The extent to which measurement results are free of unpredictable error. Tests that are reliable yield essentially the same results when readministered under different conditions.

Remedial training Instruction that provides job applicants or workers with the required entry-level knowledge and skills.

Request for proposals (RFP) A request for proposals, RFP, invites bidders to submit proposals for a project and sets forth the particulars of the requesting organization's need.

Research and development (R&D) 1) Commonly referred to in its abbreviated form, R&D is any planned effort that does not support an immediate application, customer, or product. In its best use, R&D is focused on meeting the needs of customers with new or significantly improved products and services. 2)

One of the phases of the life cycle model of cost-benefit analysis.

Resource requirements model In cost-benefit analysis, a model that identifies the relationships between costs and benefits. In this model, costs of personnel, equipment, facilities, and materials are associated with the five ISD phases: 1) analysis, 2) design, 3) development, 4) implementation, and 5) evaluation.

Response Any activity induced by a stimulus. In instruction, response designates a wide variety of behaviors. For example, a response may involve a single word, selection among alternatives (multiple choice), solution of a complex system, or manipulation of keys.

Response time The time between an entry on a computer terminal keyboard or screen and the resulting change of display. For example, the time it takes to have an answer judged by the computer system. Research shows that a response time of no more than .2 seconds is important.

Results 1) Tangible, positive changes in the organization due to training. For example, increased productivity. The results of instruction are compared to the purpose for which the instruction was originally planned. 2) A bottom line measurement. Results measures include increased production, reduced scrap, or other benefit that was management's original goal for the training program. Ideally, a financial ROI calculation can be completed.

Retention The degree to which newly acquired knowledge and skills are remembered by the learner after time has passed.

Retraining 1) Training employees to do two or more jobs as needed. 2) Learning activities to provide additional employable skills, particularly to those who have lost their jobs or whose jobs are being phased out.

Retreat A program conducted at a location that minimizes all outside communication in order to focus on a specific subject for a limited time.

Return on investment (ROI) In benefit computation, a ratio that expresses the relationship of the cost of performance value to the cost expended to achieve that value.

RIO document An objectives document used in executive development. The name is derived from its three parts: responsibilities, indicators, and objectives.

Role A set of behaviors expected of someone by virtue of job duties and status.

Role play 1) An instructional technique based on learners assuming and acting out characters other than their own. Often the players are provided with scripts of background information on which to base their participation. Learners can examine previous behavior, try out new behaviors, or experiment with behaviors that might be potentially useful. Role play is often open-ended. Both players and the audience process the completed performance. Players self-critique the role play, with support from the facilitator, and may view a videotape of the role play. 2) Practice of a newly learned or not yet mastered skill under observation. Learners are assigned their roles with specific instructions.

Sample 1) In research, a subgroup of a population. See also random sample. 2) In quality process, one or more individual events or measurements selected from the output of a process. The sample is used to identify characteristics and performance of the whole. 3) A digital recording of an analog sound.

Scenario Background information regarding the setting of an exercise. The scenario may be brief or elaborate, with many charts and plentiful background and relevant data.

Self-actualization 1) The fifty stage in Maslow's hierarchy. 2) Loosely, the highest level of functioning of which an individual is capable.

Self-awareness 1) A developmental area addressed in organizational development. Self-awareness includes personal control or power needs, need to achieve, and need for affection. 2) Loosely, a deep knowledge of oneself and one's abilities.

Self-directed learning An instructional design in which the learner takes the initiative to master predetermined material. Self-directed learning may be completed alone using self-instructional packages, or conducted with the help of others. Others may include instructors, tutors, mentors, resource people, and peers. Also called self-planned learning, self-education, self-instruction, self-study, or autonomous learning. See also andragogy, learner-centered instruction, learner-controlled instruction and self-instruction.

Self-fulfilling prophecy The principle that people tend to perform in accordance with what is expected of them. The self-fulfilling prophecy may originate from direct or indirect communication of a mental expectation regarding the probability of a future behavior, thus increasing its likelihood.

Self-instruction Any learning situation in which learners take responsibility for their own learning without relying on an instructor or other leaders of learning.

Self-introduction Introduction made to a group by each member, including their own name and other personal information.

Self-knowledge The HRD competency of knowing one's personal values, needs, interests, style and competencies, and their effects on others.

Self-managed work teams An empowering method of task accomplishment in which the manager supplies the mission and the team takes on all managerial responsibility to complete it.

Seminar An instructor-led learning activity. Often the instructor is an expert or at least highly knowledgeable. Seminars are usually limited to a week or less and focus on a specific topic or problem.

Sensitivity training Methods using intense interpersonal experiences to improve the individual's sensitivity to self and others. Sensitivity training should be conducted under the guidance of a trained person.

Sequential learning An instructional technique that provides for increasingly difficult learning, based on previous knowledge and skills, and on planned desired outcomes.

Seven quality process tools A reference to the most commonly used tools in the quality process. The seven tools are 1) cause and effect diagram, 2) checklist, 3) control chart, 4) graphs (bar, line, and pie), 5) histogram, 6) Pareto diagram, and 7) scatter diagram.

Shaping A technique that reinforces successive approximations, starting with behavior that is already present. Gradually, more difficult material is presented and more sophisticated answers are required. For example, questions the student can answer already are followed by questions that the learner might infer.

Short-range planning The shortest of the planning processes used by organizations. Usually oriented to the following year. Compare with long- and mid-range planning.

Simulation Any representation of an item of equipment, device, situation, system, or subsystem in realistic form. Simulation enables the learner to experience the operation of the target equipment without possibility of destruction of the equipment. The simulation may focus on a small subset of the features of the actual job-world situation.

Situational leadership A model developed by Paul Hersey and Kenneth Blanchard in which the leader provides for the followers what they cannot provide for themselves. The leader identifies the development level of the followers and selects the style which best suits the situation. The followers contract with the leader for the style which best suits their perceived development needs.

Skill Any task-specific ability. A skill is a subset of a task. Skills involve physical or manipulative activities. They often require knowledge for their execution. All skills are actions having special requirements for speed, accuracy, or coordination.

Small group trial Use of an instructional package by a limited number of members of the target population. A trial by a small group, usually under the supervision of an instructional developer, evaluates the effectiveness of the development instructional product to ensure market readiness. Weaknesses are corrected before release for use in the field.

Socialization The process of learning one's role in a setting such as work. Socialization consists of role anticipation, role development, and role stabilization. During the socialization process, individuals progressively internalize the values of their associates.

Society for Human Resource Management (SHRM) An international membership organization for HR professionals. Formerly called the American Society for Personnel Administration.

Soft skill A semi-derisive term to describe abilities not directed toward production of a tangible product. For example, interpersonal skills. This term is used primarily by non-HRD practitioners.

Software Programs that make computers work. Computer programs that deliver content are part of courseware, not software. Compare with hardware and courseware.

Sole source A situation where a consultant or vendor has been identified as the only resource available to provide a needed product or service. Used by organizations to bypass the bidding process when bidding is not appropriate.

Space bubble A concept developed by Edward Hall to describe a zone of personal space that surrounds each person. Intrusion into a person's space bubble will cause discomfort. The concept is useful because people from various cultures have space bubbles of differing sizes. See also cross-cultural instruction and proxemics.

Span of control The number and types of employees and jobs supervised by one person.

Spider-web principle A view of change. The spider-web principle is that a change in any one area is felt throughout other areas, as the vibrations on a strand of a spider web vibrates the entire web.

Springboard A highly visible job within or outside an organization. A springboard job frequently leads to a higher level position in the same or a different organization.

Stakeholder Anyone with a vested interest in the outcome of an activity or project. Stakeholders may support or oppose a particular undertaking. For example, the union may be a stakeholder in a technology upgrade HRD program. Compare with client.

Stand-alone delivery Delivery separate from a large computer system or LAN. Achieved by, and synonymous with, personal computer delivery.

Standard 1) A synonym for criterion. 2) A short, concise statements of expected performance that serves as a gauge for measuring accomplishment. Standards are the subject of a number of U.S. federal agency studies and recommendations for setting industry and skill standards.

Storyboard 1) Documents used for film, video, and computer display planning. A series of sketches resembling a cartoon strip that help visualize the sequence of scenes or views to be presented. Plot, character, and action are all subjects of storyboarding. 2) Sketches of the visuals that are intended to support a presentation. The sketches are used to ensure that the message is supported by the visuals before the visual materials are actually made.

Strategic HRD planning The process of developing a long-range plan for the HRD department. Strategic HRD planning takes into account present strengths and weaknesses and likely future opportunities and threats. Often defined as planning for the period 5-10 years in the future. Also called long-range HRD planning.

Strategic planning A formal process by which an organization determines how it will achieve its purpose over the long term, given expected opportunities and problems presented by the external environment and the strengths and weaknesses of the organization itself. The result is a shared set of beliefs about the organization's future and goals that identifies the functions, priorities, and resources that are necessary to reach those goals.

Stratification In process control, a technique used to identify improvement opportunities. Stratification breaks down single element totals into component categories, classifications, or subgroups based on character.

Structure 1) The characteristic of a group, organization, or system denoted by the hierarchical, physical, or spatial arrangement of the components at any given point in time. 2) The formal means of organization; the grouping of departments, divisions, work groups, jobs, and individuals.

Structured brainstorming A method in which every member of the group must contribute either in turn or pass until asked again in turn.

Succession planning Collective term for programs designed and conducted specifically to ensure that a qualified successor exists for every job in the management hierarchy. Includes HRD as well as non-HRD activities. Succession planning encompasses both replacement and development planning.

Suggestopedia An instructional method, developed by Bulgarian Georgi Lozanov, to provide a short course in language training for adults leaving the country. Suggestopedia is primarily based on relaxation in a conducive learning environment. Suggestopedia features presentation of new material, review, and relaxation. This method is often cited as a basis for a wide range of accelerated teaching techniques, such as accelerated learning, suggestology, and superlearning.

Synergy The concept that the whole is greater than the sum of its parts, developed by Buckminster Fuller. Abraham Maslow applied the concept to his studies of self-actualization people.

System 1) An entity which behaves as a whole because of the interdependence of its component elements. 2) A method or procedure. 3) A network, as for communications.

System approach The comprehensive and rigorous process of developing and conducting a project or activity to accomplish specific outcomes.

Tangible benefit An outcome that can be measured easily, such as reduced training time and increased sales. Tangible benefits usually have economic value.

Target population The group of people for whom a behavior change is intended, usually defined in terms of age, background, and ability. Samples from this population are used in evaluating instructional materials during their development. Sometimes called target audience.

Target population analysis The process of assessing needs of a specific group of individuals. Target population analysis produces a description of the characteristics of that group. One of the parts of a needs assessment. Sometimes called audience analysis.

Task analysis A process of arriving at a step-by-step description of all the performance elements (tasks) that make up a job. Task analysis applies whether the steps of the task are mainly cognitive or psychomotor. Task analysis is done by questionnaires, observations of performance, and interviews with incumbents and supervisors. A term coined by Robert Gagne, it is also referred to as skills analysis. Task and skills analysis are subsets of the complete job.

Teambuilding In organizational development, any of a variety of activities focused on improving work relationships or tasks. Teambuilding is especially used when a new group is formed. It is also common in management and supervisors instruction.

Technical and skills training That area of HRD concerned with learning experiences related to equipment and processes.

Technical competencies Functional knowledge and skills identified in the HRD Roles and Competencies Study. The following competencies are included: adult-learning understanding, career-development-theories-and-techniques understanding, competency-identification skills, computer competence, electronic-systems skill, facilities skill, objectives-preparation skills, performance-observation skill, subject matter understanding, training-and-development-theories-and-techniques understanding, and research skill.

Telecommuting Working at an alternate site instead of commuting to the traditional site. The alternate site may be the worker's home. Typically involving use of a computer for communication with the organization and transmission of work.

Teleconference 1) Two-way electronic communication between two or more groups, or three or more individuals, in separate locations. Includes group communication via audio, audiographs, video, and computer systems. 2) Loosely, a meeting where the participants are at separate locations. A telephone call with three parties would be a very simple teleconference. Some organizations have elaborate facilities for teleconferences. Teleconferencing offers an important alternative to the high cost of travel. 3) At a conference, a teleconference is useful for a general session when an important and significant resource person is invited but cannot be present physically. The resource person may speak to the large group through a telephone hook-up.

Theory X Theory Y A classic theory of management described by Douglas McGregor. Theory X is not "people oriented." It is based on the principle that

people don't like to work. Theory Y is "people oriented." It is based on the principle that people can approach work positively.

T-group A group-based learning exercise to develop the individual's interpersonal skills by studying the effects of behavior and exploring alternative behaviors that might be more effective. T-groups (T for Training) use process observation, games, simulations, structured experiences, and other experiential methods. The T-group is rarely used today, except in a historical context. Also called encounter groups, confrontation groups, awareness groups, Synanon-type groups, discovery groups, sensory awareness groups, sensitivity training, and creativity workshops. See also laboratory training, human relations training, and sensitivity training.

Thinking styles The collective term for various styles that can be associated with the brain dominance profile. These include double dominant cerebral, cerebral right, double dominant right, limbic right, double dominant limbic, limbic left, double dominant left, cerebral left, and creative neutral. See also whole brain learning.

Think tank 1) A synonym for brainstorming. 2) Loosely, a formal or informal group organized for research and development.

Total quality management (TQM) A continuous improvement methodology for every process, supported by management to satisfy the customer. TQM includes every employee using tools, data, and teamwork. Armand Feigenbaum, the originator of the quality costs concept, is sometimes called the "Father of Total Quality Control" because of his assertion that every function in the organization is responsible for quality.

Training manual A document designed for student use during a course and often afterward on the job. A training manual may include preprinted lecture notes, lab/job/worksheets, appropriate drawings and other graphics, and self-check tests.

Training plan A document that includes program information and data concerning the system or equipment program, event, or situation that originated the training requirement, and that describes the training required and the training program(s) needed to satisfy the requirement. Training plans are designed to provide for planning and implementation of training and to ensure all resources and supporting actions.

Transactional analysis (TA) A concept developed by Eric Berne. Considered effective at the applied level, it is also comprehensive at the theoretical level.. It is based on the combinations of the three ego states; parent, child, and adult. The combinations of these states in human interactions is the basis of transactional analysis. The combinations, such as parent-child result in positions such as I'm OK-You're Not OK.

Transparency A specially prepared transparent original containing an image. Used with an overhead projector.

Light from the projector passes through the transparency to form an image on a screen. Also called acetate, foil, and viewgraph. Acetate refers to the plastic sheet used for overhead projection. At one time the transparency sheet was made from acetate.

Turnkey An off-the-shelf product or system that is ready to run as and when delivered-simply turn the key.

Tutorial The most typical form of CAI. The program and the learner interact one-on-one. Ideally, the process advances just as the best tutor might personally conduct the process. One of the modes of CAI. The others are drill and practice, instructional game, modeling, and simulation.

Unlearning Removal of old habits that interfere with the acquisition of new learning. Applicable to the transfer of training process. Also called extinguishing or diminishing.

Unskilled A category of occupations usually involving routine and primarily physical tasks that do not require specialized training.

Unskilled labor Workers in jobs that do not require formal skills, training, or education. For example, housekeeping services for females, military conscription for males, and street vending for both sexes.

Unstructured brainstorming A method in which any member of a group can contribute freely.

Unstructured interview An interview in which the interviewer asks the respondent to expand on answers to the questions. No specific sequence of questions is used.

Upgrading The process of increasing or raising the expected performance, knowledge, and skills of occupations.

Upgrading training Instruction to update individuals. Upgrading training focuses on the knowledge, skills, and attitudes.

User A person who makes use of technology for work rather than for learning.

User-friendly A desirable attribute for any computer system. Implies that the user need not be an expert to use the system and that mistakes are easily overcome or avoided by the system.

Validation Ensuring that a learning activity, instructional product, measurement instrument, or system is capable of achieving its intended aims and functions. For example, validation of instruction includes developmental testing, field testing, and revision of instruction to ensure that the instructional intent is achieved. Validation allows instructional designers to guarantee specified results.

Validity The extent to which a test is a worthwhile measure for its intended purpose. Tests that are valid yield essentially true results. The degree to which a test performs this function satisfactorily is usually called the relative validity. Actions taken to make the test instrument valid are called defending the validity of the instrument. Compare with reliability.

Value-added benefit Any additional benefit to be derived from a system.

Value clarification Helping individuals identify their individual values and how these values may influence their behavior. Value clarification is important in developing self-directed individuals.

Vendor Any organization or individual that sells an HRD product or service to a customer organization. Vendors are always external to (i.e., not part of) the customer organization. Some vendors call themselves "consultants."

Vertical thinking A concept developed by Edward de Bono to describe a thinking method controlled by a preexisting pattern or idea. Vertical thinking displays characteristics associated with left brain hemispheric functions.

Video An instructional medium. Video can be accessed from tape, disc, or semiconductor memory. In some cases, video is meant to include audio and other signals that are part of a complete video signal. Compare with text, audiotape, and CAI.

Video display terminal (VDT) The preferred term for computer display, commonly referred to in its abbreviated form, VDT. VDT is preferred, since it accurately describes a monitor using any display technology such as CRT, LCD, or plasma panel.

Videotape 1) Any video system using cassette or reel-to-reel tape. Currently popular playback systems include 3/4 inch U-matic and 1/2 inch VHS. 2) A medium using a videotape capable of recording a session and then playing it back. Videotape can also be used in conjunction with cable TV or CCTV.

Video teleconference A distance learning method using audio and television images between two or more locations. Video teleconferencing is best for classroom groups located distantly from the instructor. For example, National Technical University courses. NTU transmits by satellite. Compare with audio teleconferencing, and computer conferencing.

Virtual reality (VR) An experience in a computer-generated simulated environment. Virtual reality is particularly used to simulate conditions that do not actually exist, but may also be used to simulate actual potential conditions. Immersive virtual reality uses special peripherals, particularly data gloves and special, close to the user's eyes, computer graphic displays called head-mounted displays (HMD). Immersive VR gives the user the feeling of being present in a scene and able to move around in it. Desktop virtual reality is based on standard desktop computers. Also called artificial reality. See also virtual world.

Virtual world Any environment modeled in a virtual reality system. The virtual world may represent "real" locations and objects or those created for the virtual reality system, including imaginary and yet to be built worlds. Also called synthetic environment.

Vision statement An overall statement of the goal of an organization, usually found at the beginning of that organization's business plan. For example, to become the best HRD department in the hospitality industry.

Visualization Creating dominant mental images of desired future states and envisioning the satisfactions and rewards that would accrue as a result of attaining those states.

Whole brain learning Implementation of brain lateralization and brain dominance technology in the classroom.

Workforce 2000 An influential study by William Johnson and Arnold Packer. It projects U.S. worker demographics, skill levels, and trends at the end of the century, with implications.

Work group A small group of organizationally associated individuals, usually fewer than fifteen. Work groups include everyone who works in the same location and reports to the same supervisor.

Workout A problem-solving meeting. Workouts include 40 to 100 members of an organizational unit and are often held in a retreat setting. The meeting begins with a presentation of the problem by top management. The group uses brainstorming and other techniques to derive recommendations which are presented to top management at the end of the workout. Workouts are often directed at improving the quality and productivity of the organization.

Work rule Defined conduct or behavior that applies in the workplace.

Workshop 1) A limited length learning activity led by an instructor. Workshops focus on improving proficiency in a specific subject. In comparison with a seminar, a workshop is practical and learners expect to have new skills at completion. 2) A practical session designed to illustrate the mechanics of an exercise without necessarily playing it all the way through. 3) A group of professional or vocational persons with a common interest or problem who meet together for an extended period of time. These workshops use study, group exercises, research, and discussion techniques.

Workstation A work location, sometimes confused with learning station. A workstation may feature a computer and any associated input or output devices, based on the particular job need.

WYSIWYG (Pronounced wiz'zy-wig'.) Abbreviation for "What you see is what you get." A computer display that shows the exact appearance of the final printed page. WYSIWYG is important in all applications that are delivered in another media.

Xerox™ Improper synonym, used by some HRD practitioners, for a copy made using the electrostatic process. Xerox is a trademark of the Xerox corporation and should not be used as verb.

Youth Apprenticeship U.S. programs to equip non-college-bound students with the required skills for an exposure to the world of work. Youth Apprenticeship programs include a four-year curriculum that combines academic, technical, and occupational education for students who have completed the 10th grade. Participants are paid wages and complete the program with a high school diploma. Compare with apprenticeship.

Zero-sum game A game in which winning is at the expense of losers. In general, zero sum activities are avoided in HRD.

GLOSSARY OF HUMAN RESOURCE INFORMATION SYSTEM TERMS

Absolute Address A system of programming that uses direct addressing rather than indirect addressing to specify the location of data in the memory.

Access The ability to communicate with a distant computer.

Access Rights The rights a user or computer has to open up a communications pathway with a particular computer, component, or application. Limiting access to specific people, machines, or groups. Access rights are usually controlled through the use of a password and code.

Alpha test The internal test of software under development before external testing or distribution. This term is also applied to development of technology-based courseware.

Analog In technology-based instruction, a technology type that is based on continuous measurement. Analog technology is now being replaced by digital. For example, analog videodisc versus compact disc.

Antivirus Program Software that monitors a computer for viruses by looking for irregularities in a computer system and then comparing its findings to a database of virus information. Viruses not included in the antivirus program's database will go undetected, so it is important to regularly update antivirus programs.

Assembly Language A programming language that allows an application to be written using English syntax. Then an application called an assembler translates the assembly language into machine language so the computer can understand.

Audit A diagnostic examination of the complete computer system to examine system performance, check for viruses and look for any other problems.

Authorization Code A password design for security reasons that verifies the identification of the user.

Backup A copy of a file or files created in case the original is destroyed or damaged.

Backup Server A server used in conjunction with a primary server to make sure there is always a second copy of everything on the network.

Batch processing A method in which all the data are fed to a computer at one time and processed at the same time. Rarely seen in today's interactive computing, batch processing may still be used to process large quantities of inputs, for example in business games.

Batch program A series of commands triggered by a single user command that are carried out one at a time.

Baud The unit of measure of data-transmission speed used for comparison of hardware capabilities for technology-based learning. Baud originated in the era of telegraphy and is now used interchangeably with "bits per second."

Beta test The formal test of under-development courseware and draft documentation by selected users before external testing or distribution. Users test the functionality.

Bit Short for binary digit, which is the smallest unit of computer storage.

Bookmarks User-definable lists that allow a person to display easily a certain location within a document or a page on the World Wide Web. Mouse clicking on a bookmark usually calls up the location it references.

Broadcast To transmit information to more than one person simultaneously.

Browser Software, such as Netscape Navigator or Microsoft's Internet Explorer, that enables a computer user to search for, display, and download the multimedia information that appears on the World Wide Web.

Bulletin Board System (BBS) An on-line computer system you can access through your modem that acts as a central source of information.

Cache A bank of high speed memory set aside for frequently accessed data. Memory cache and disk caching are the two common methods used by PCs.

Cache Card A board inside the computer that provides quick storage.

Cascade An option that organizes the open windows on a computer screen so that they overlap, with the most active window on top.

CD-Erasable (CD-E) A CD format that allows the CD to be erased and reused. CD-Es are said to have a 10-year life span and can be overwritten 10,000 times.

Central Processing Unit (CPU) The computer's control unit or microprocessor. The CPU is a silicon chip that interprets and carries out instructions.

Client/Server Computing systems in which the workload is split between desktop PCs (the client) and one or more larger computers (the server) that are connected via a network.

Debugging In technology-based learning, error identification and correction in any courseware. Identifying and removing errors from computer programs.

Digital Pertains to equipment and processes that use binary numbers to accomplish their purpose. Digital devices are replacing analog devices in technology-based learning.

Digital Video Interactive (DVI) Usually called by its abbreviation, DVI is compact disc format designed for interactive multimedia.

Digitize 1) Converting analog information to digital information. 2) Conversion of a visual image or real object into a format that can be processed by a computer.

Digitizer An input device used to permit rapid input of graphics, normally on a tablet by use of a stylus. Can be used for authoring or student input.

Electronic Mail (E-Mail) Text messages sent through a network to a specified individual or group.

Ethernet A widely used, local area network technology for connecting computers, printers, servers, and other devices in the same building.

Extranet A network built on Internet protocols and operated over the public Internet for private business-to-business communication.

Fax Broadcast Sending a single fax document to many people at once.

Fax/Modem A communications device that allows a PC to fax documents and send data to other modem equipped PCs.

Firewall Software that protects a private network from intrusion via the public Internet.

Generation 1) In technology-based learning hardware, reference to states in product development usually incorporating significant improvements. 2) In all analog media, the number of times a copy is removed from the original. The first generation is made from the original. The second generation copy is made from a first-generation copy. Each generation results in a noticeable degradation of image quality. This applies to audiotape, videodisc, and videotape. The problem does not exist with digital media.

Groupware Programs that permit simultaneous work on a file by more than one networked user. Users can see changes made by any other person as they occur.

High-level language A computer language that permits an action which actually requires several steps inside the computer to be specified by a single command.

Host Computer A network computer to which other computers in the network are connected. A host computer can be set up to do the bulk of the computing on the network and store files and databases.

Hyperlink An icon, graphic, or word in a file that, when clicked with the mouse, automatically opens another file for viewing.

Integrated HR/Payroll System A single computerized database, used by both HR and payroll, eliminating redundant data entry and processing. More powerful than an interfaced system where the HR and payroll databases are actually separate but can share some data.

Interfaced HR/Payroll System Separate computer systems linked to appear to be sharing the same database but actually separate. Transactions put into one system are fed into the other on a scheduled basis.

Interactive System Application programs that respond immediately to input. They work in real time, which means new data is processed as soon as it is entered and the results are available immediately to the user.

Interactive communications In HR, most often used in flexible benefits administration to give employees two-way communication so they can see the results of their choices. Devices used include special PC software programs, telephone voice response systems, and kiosks.

Internet A worldwide collection of interconnected networks that enable users to share information electronically and provides digital access to a wide variety of services.

Intranet A private network, set up within a corporation or organization, which operates over the Internet and may be used to link geographically remote sites.

Information Technology (IT) A general term used to describe any technology that helps to produce, manipulate, store, communicate, or disseminate information.

Integrate Refers to the action of two or more hardware or software components working together as a system.

Job Analysis The process by which HR professionals determine what skills, knowledge and abilities are or will be needed to perform the duties and responsibilities of specific tasks.

Job codes The unique (often numeric) identification for each defined employment task. The term also refers, informally, to the attributes associated with a job title.

Job sharing A relatively new opportunity for workers, in which two or more employees can share a single job, each working part-time or split-shift.

LAN Local Area Network.

Modem Acronym for modulator/demodulator. Lets a computer transmit and receive information over telephone lines. Modems convert analog data into digital data computers can read, and convert digital data into analog data so it can be transmitted over telephone lines.

Mouse In technology-based learning, a hand-held device moved on a desktop or special surface. As a result, the cursor moves in a like manner on the VDT. Pushing a button informs the computer system of the chosen location.

Multitasking The process of having a computer perform multiple tasks simultaneously. During multitasking, some tasks can be performed in the background while working on another program.

Network A set of conjoined computers that can share storage devices, peripherals, and applications. Networks may be connected directly by cable connection, or indirectly by telephone lines or satellites.

Parity Check A PC's process of checking to make sure a data transmission was sent and received correctly.

Peripheral Any device connected to the computer that performs a specific function.

RAM Random Access Memory. A form of computer memory used by applications. Information stored in RAM can be altered by the user and is lost when the computer is shut off.

Relational Database A database that can share information across multiple tables or files. These tables can be linked, or related, by common information.

ROM Read Only Memory. The memory that contains the basic instructions for the computer's microprocessor. Users cannot change this information, and it remains intact when the computer is shut off.

Scanner A peripheral used to produce digitized images of documents and photographs, which can be stored as files and edited on a computer.

Search Engine A server-based application used to search large databases for selected words or phrases. Common search engines use keywords to search for information on the World Wide Web.

Security A system of measures for keeping information on a system safe from corruption or prying eyes. Security can mean anything from a screen saver with password to encrypted data that keeps users from reading information without the proper decoding software.

Sign-on (log-on) 1) The act of entering one's identity into the technology-based system to begin work or study. 2) The name one uses for recognition by a computer.

Terminal A peripheral device that enables a user to interact with a computer and use the power of that computer. Although a microcomputer may be used as a terminal, a terminal falls short of the definition of a computer.

Videoconference A communications system that enables people in separate locations to meet using live video pictures and sound.

Virus A destructive software program that "infects" a computer through a disk or downloaded program.

Wide area network (WAN) A network composed of local area networks (LANs).

INDEX

INDEX

A

Absenteeism:
  excessive, warning about, 494
  figuring costs of, 126
  termination letter for, 495
Accident/Injury Report, 605
Accident Investigation, Supervisor's Report of,
    606-607
Accident reporting, 417-442 (see also Safety)
Active listening, 71
ADA, 84-88, 140, 221-222 (see also Americans
    with Disabilities)
  checklist for employers, 555-557
Addresses and telephone numbers, governmental,
    180-181
Administrative employees under FLSA, 146-147
Ads to recruit workers, 4-10
  advertising agency, using, 10
  "blind" ads, 4
  checklist, 18, 534
  classified ads, learning from, 4-6
  help wanted advertising form, 19
  placing, 6
  sample, 6-9
  television, 4
Adverse impact, 54
Affirmative Action:
  guidelines, 149-150
  planning checklist, 542-543
  plans, 150-153
Affirmative Action Information, 30
Age discrimination charge, letter to EEOC regard-
    ing, 512
Age Discrimination Employment Act (ADEA) of
    1967, 138
Alcohol/drug problems at work, checklist for han-
    dling, 550-551
Alternative dispute resolution (ADR), 450
Americans with Disabilities Act (ADA)of 1990,
    84-88, 140, 221-222
  accommodation letter, sample, 222, 470
  checklist, 221
  "essential functions" in job description, 336
Annual Survey of Occupational Injuries and
    Illnesses, 420-421

Applicant Appraisal Form, 31, 572
Applicant interview checklist, 534-537
  what not to ask, 536-537
Applicant log, computerized, 12
Applicant Rejection Letter, 42, 469
Applicants, letter of reply to, 466-468
  rejection, 469
Application for employment, 21-29, 563-571
  in English, 21-23, 563-565
  in Spanish, 24-29, 566-571
Application forms, 12, 20-29, 66, 67
  Affirmative Action Information, 30
  Applicant Appraisal Form, 31, 572
  Application for Employment, in English, 21-23,
    563-565
  Application for Employment—California
    Addendum, 57, 58
  Application for Employment, in Spanish, 24-29,
    566-571
  Application for Funeral Leave, 594
  Credit Report Processing Authorization Form,
    57, 58
  Fair Credit Reporting Act, 23
Appraisal:
  benefits, 369
  data, evaluation checklist for, 537-540
Appraisal worksheet, 372-373
Approval of Estimated Relocation Expenses and
    Allowances, 576
Arbitration of employment disputes, 456
"At will" employer, 39, 90-91
Audience identification critical to success of
    newsletter, 237
Automated recruiting, 3-4

B

Background checks, 37
Benefit plans, letter to employees regarding annu-
    al report of, 513
Benefits, 325-389 (see also Compensation and benefits)
  new, memo announcing, 516
"Bill of Rights" in testing, 56-57
Binding arbitration, 450
"Blind" ads, 4

C

Civil Rights Act of 1964, Title VII, 137, 138 (*see also* Title VII)
 and job descriptions, 333
Claims processing time explanation letter, 514
Classification method of job evaluation, 342
COBRA memo to employees, sample, 519-522, 524-525
 to terminating employee/dependent, 523
Code of Federal Registry, 138
Communications, employee, 231-259
 through corporate intranets, 235
 handbook for employees, sample, 237-259
  and personnel policy manual, difference between, 237
 newsletter for employees, starting, 236-237
  writing for audience, 237
 personal connection critical to success, 233-235
  channels for implementation, twenty-five, 233-235
Communications programs, checklist for developing, 547-548
Compensation and benefits, 325-389
 benefits, employee, 376-389
  consultants, 376
  costs, 377
  examples, 389
  terms, glossary of, 377-387
  work and family benefits, 389
 changes in compensation programs, 327-328
 deferred compensation, 328
 designing and evaluating program, checklist for, 328-332
  general, 328-329
  job description, 330
  job evaluation, 330
  policies, 331
  salary structure, 330-331
 gain sharing, 328
 job descriptions, 332-341, 347-358
  collecting data, methods of, 333
  do's and don'ts of writing, 334-335
  "essential functions" under ADA, 336
  most important document in compensation program, 332
   and law, 333
  physical/mental demands, sample statements for, 336-338
  preparing, 332
  questionnaire, 333
  sample, 339-341, 347-358
 job evaluations, 342-346
  classification method, 342

Compensation and benefits (*cont.*)
 elements, essential, 343-345
  goals and benefits, 344
  Hay Guide Chart Profile method, 343
  by outside consultants, 342-343
  point method, 342, 345
  ranking method, 342
  undertaking, 345
 job grade system, 345-347
 multiple compensation, 327
 pay-for-performance programs, 327-328, 363-364, 366-376
  appraisal benefits, 369
  appraisal interview, 369-370
  appraisal worksheet, 372-373
  effective, ten keys to, 366-367
  feedback, constructive, 370-371
  goals, 357-368
  KRAs, 366-367
  management by objectives, 368-369
  objectives, setting, 368
  phrases to use, 371-376
  starting, 367
 salary program, model, 359-365
 two-tier contracts, 328
 work and family benefits, 388
Compensation Service, 344, 345
Complaint procedures for employees, letter regarding, 507-508
Complaint/grievance procedures, checklist for, 555
Confidentiality Agreement, 47
 letter, sample, 479
Confidentiality of personnel files, 95, 218-219
Conflict of interest, letter to new employee regarding, 480
Consolidated Omnibus Budget Reconciliation Act (COBRA), of 1986, 139, 162-178
 employees, sample memo, 519-522, 524-525
 to terminating employees/dependent, 523
 notice of amendments, 164-165
Corporate intranets, communication through, 235
Credit Report Processing Authorization Form, 57, 58

D

Death of employee's spouse, sample letter, 526
Deferred compensation, 327-328
Discipline and discharge, handling, 391-416
 action, notification of, sample, 492
 discrimination complaints, preventing, 412-414
  what EEOC and state civil rights agencies look for, 412-414

Discipline and discharge, handling (*cont.*)
    uniformity critical, 414
   forms, 399-408
     Checklist for Termination, 406
     Disciplinary Warning Notice, 402
     Employee Consultation Form, 404
     Employee Warning Notice, 403
     Exit Interview Form, 407-408
     Separation Notice, 405
     Supervisor's Checklist for Effective
       Discipline, 400-401
   harassment, 415-416
    consistency critical, 416
    forms, 415
    options, 416
    policy, 415
    sexual, claims of, 415-416
   just cause, 393
   letters, sample, 409-411
    The Personnel Manager's Complete Model
      Letter Book as reference, 409
    for six-month evaluation, 411
    for suspension without pay, 410
    tips, 409
   notification of action, sample, 492
   performance improvement memorandum, 393-
     396
   policy, determining, 397-399
    sample, 397-399
Discipline, Effective, Supervisor's Checklist and
    Report for, 600-601
Disciplinary Warning Notice, 602
Discrimination complaints, preventing, 412-414
    (*see also* Discipline)
Drug-Free Workplace Act of 1988, 55, 140, 153-157
   deciding on drug/alcohol testing policy, 155-157
Drug problems at work, checklist for handling,
    550-551
Drug testing, pros and cons of, 54-57
   employees, sample memo to, 500

E

EAPs (employee assistance programs), 55, 388
Education Verification Reference, 38, 589
Employee, new, orientation checklist for, 540-542
Employee Absence Report Form, 592
Employee Agreement, 575, 588
Employee Agreement and Handbook
    Acknowledgment Form, 46
Employee Attendance Record, 581
Employee Benefit Program, sample, 582

Employee Benefits Verification Form, 57, 59
Employee Consultation Form, 404
Employee Counseling Activity Sheet, 599
Employee handbook, 13
Employee information and recordkeeping require-
    ments, 97
Employee planning checklist, 532-533
Employee Polygraph Protection Act, 140, 157-158
Employee Retirement Income Security Act
    (ERISA) of 1974, 139
Employee secrecy agreement, memo to manage-
    ment personnel about, 478
Employee Security Acts, state, 143
Employee Transfer Request, 590
Employee verification, letter requesting, 471
Employee Warning Notice, 603
Employee welcome letter, 472
Employment Confirmation Letter, 40
Employment disputes, arbitration of, 456
Employment forms:
   checklist, 14
Employment offer, letter confirming, 465
Employment testing, pros and cons of, 54-57
Employment Verification Letter, 41
Employer's Quarterly Federal Tax Return, Form
    941, 101
Equal Employment Opportunity (EEO) Act of
    1972, 137
   laws, state by state, analysis of, 189-195
Equal Employment Opportunity Commission, 54
   Guidelines, 56
   job-related testing, 56
   offices, 181-182
   policy, 184
   poster, 183
Equal Pay Act of 1963, 101-102, 139
Evaluation of interview/appraisal data, 537-540
Executive employees under FLSA, 145-146
Executive Orders, 138
Exit Interview Form, 407-408, 604

F

Fair Credit Reporting Act, 20, 23
   disclosure, 565
Fair Labor Standards Act (FLSA) of 1938, 101,
    138, 143-149
   administrative employees, 146-147
   executive employees, 145-146
   exempt/nonexempt jobs, 145
    long and short tests, 145
   exemptions, other, 148-149

Fair Labor Standards Act (FLSA) of 1938 (*cont.*)
  professional employees, 147-148
  violations of, 159-160
  who is covered, 144
Family and Medical Leave Act (FMLA) of 1993,
      141, 226-230
  advance notice and medical certification, 223,
      224-225
  enforcement, 223
  job benefits and protection, 223
  paid leave, 223
  reasons for unpaid leave, 223
  return of employee to work, 226-230
  unlawful acts by employers, 223
Federal income tax withholding, 99-100
Federal Insurance Contributions Act (FICA), 98
  and federal income taxes, 100-101
Federal statutes regulating employment, etc., 137-
      142 (*see also* Regulatory)
Federal Unemployment Tax Act (FUTA), 98-99
Feedback, constructive, in performance appraisal,
      370-371
First Aid Report Log, 608
Forms: (*see also* under particular heading)
  discipline/discharge, 399-408
  employment checklist, 14
  recruiting, interviewing, and selection, 14-60
Freedom of Information and Privacy Act of 1974,
      138
Frick Company, 217
Funeral leave, Request for, 594

G

Gain sharing, 328
Government regulations for recruitment and
      employment, 12-13

H

Handbook for employees, sample, 237-259
  and personnel policy manual, difference
      between, 237
Harassment, 415-416 (*see also* Discipline)
Hardship withdrawal letter to employee, 515
Hay Guide Chart Profile method of job evalua-
      tion, 343
Hazards Communications Standards (HCS) of
      OSHA, 419, 422-437
  checklist, 422-423
  guide to accident and injury reporting, 421-437

MSDS (Material Safety Data Sheets), 422
Health Insurance Portability and Accountability
      Act (HIPAA) of 1996, 141-142, 164-165
Health Maintenance Organization Act (HMO) of
      1973, 139
Help Wanted Advertising Form, 19
Hewitt Associates, 457, 458
Human Resources:
  fifty ways to save money in, 529-532
  function, federal regulations for, 185-188
      audit, 132-133
  glossary of terms, 611-642
  manager, question of need for, 446
Human Resources Manager (HRM) merger,
      checklist for, 549-550

I

Illegal employment practices, 89-90
Immigration Form I-9, 44-45, 196-198
Immigration Reform and Control Act, 196-204
  acceptable documents, 199
  Form I-9, 44-45, 196-198
  INS offices, 202-204
  questions and answers, 200-201
Income tax withholding:
  federal, 99-100
  state, 100
Independent contractors, 160-161
  letter, sample, regarding use of, 485
  penalties, 161
  status, 100, 160-161
Individual employee earnings record, 102-103
Injury Report, 605
INS offices, 202-204
Internal job-posting system, 82-84
Internet use by employee, warning about, 499
Interviewing, 1-92 (*see also* Recruiting)
  checklist, 68-70
  evaluation of data, checklist for, 76-78, 537-540
  Interviewing and Selection Handbook, sample,
      61-81
  applicant forms, 66, 67
  applicants, 65
  application, 67
  applications, when not to accept, 81
  "can do" versus "will do" characteristics, 79-
      80
  concepts, basic, 63-64
  decision and implementation, 79-80
  errors, common, 75
  evaluation of data, 76-78

Interviewing (*cont.*)
    inappropriate questions, 74
    interviews, 68-70
    judgment critical, 79
    listening, 78
    questioning techniques, 71
    questions, 72-74 (*see also* Questions)
    resumes, 67
    screening, preliminary, 67
    online, 3-4
    process, 12-13
Intoxication on job, sample termination letter for, 498
Intranets, corporate, communication through, 235

J

Job Bid Form, 85
Job description , 332-341, 347-358 (*see also* Compensation)
    Outline, 15-16, 583-584
Job evaluations, 342-346 (*see also* Compensation)
Job grade system, 345-347
Job offer, making, 39, 90-91
Job-related testing, 56
Job-sharing proposal, 482
Jobs:
    where to list, 5
Just cause, 393

L

Labor relations, 443-461
    alternative dispute resolution (ADR), 456
    arbitration of employment disputes, 456
    human resource manager, question of need for, 446
    key issues, 445-446
    letters, sample, 451-455
    National Labor Relations Board, 447, 448
    outsourcing HR functions, 456-461
        advantages and disadvantages, 458
        defining work to be performed, 460
        employer's experience, 457
        guidelines, 458-460
        partial, 456
        payroll, 457
        RFPs (Requests for Proposals), 459, 460-461
        time sharing, 457
        what is being outsourced, 458

Labor relations (*cont.*)
    plant closings and layoffs, 450-461
        Worker Adjustment and Retraining Notification Act, 450
    union organizer's demand for recognition, handling, 447-450
    union-free status, retaining, 446-450
Layoffs, 450-461 (*see also* Labor relations)
    checklist for preparation for, 552-553
    impending, sample letter to employees about, 486
    notification letter, sample, 487
Leave of absence, sample letter to employee about request for, 484
Leave Request/Return from Leave Form, 593
Letters, personnel, 463-526 (*see also* Personnel letters)
Listening critical in interview, 78
Litigation upon employee termination, checklist to avoid, 551

M

Management by objectives, 368-369
Medical information files on personnel, 96
    privacy of, 218
Medicare, 98
Memos, personnel, 463-526 (*see also* Personnel)
Mental Health Parity Act of 1996, 142
Merger of Human Resource Management (HRM), checklist for, 549-550
Mileage Reimbursement Report, 595
Minnesota Multiphase Personality Inventory (MMPI)
Motivation and Commitment, 345
Mountain States Employers council, 450
MSDS (Material Safety Data Sheets), 422
Multiple compensation concept, 327
Myers Briggs Type Indicator, 55

N

National Labor Relations Board, 447, 448
Nationwide Advertising Services, 10
New employee orientation , 91
    Form, 49-51
    relocation, handling, 91, 92
New hire reporting, 96
Newborns' and Mothers' Health Protection Act of 1996, 142
Newsletter for employees, starting, 236-237
    writing for audience, 237

O

Occupational Injuries and Illnesses Survey Questionnaire, 421
Occupational Safety and Health Act (OSHA) of 1970, 140, 420
Office of Federal Contract Compliance, 12, 54
    guidelines on testing, 56
Omnibus Budget Reconciliation Act of 1986, 139
Orientation for new employees:
    checklist for, 540-542
    schedule, 473-477
OSHA regulations, 417-442 (*see also* Safety)
    Hazards Communications Standards, 419, 422-437 (*see also* Hazards Communications)
    violations, leading, 419-420
Outside consultants for job evaluation, advantages of, 342-343
    guidelines for using, 548
Outsourcing HR Functions, 461
Outsourcing human resources functions, 456-461
    (*see also* Labor relations)
Overtime Hours Worked Report, 579-580

P

Paper and pencil honesty test, 54-55
Pay terminology and definitions, 103-105
Payroll procedures and relevant statutes, 98-103
    (*see also* Personnel recordkeeping)
    deductions, 98-102
Payroll register, 102
Payroll trend report, monthly, 120-123
Personal Data Sheet, 48
Personal Liability and Work Opportunity Act (Welfare Reform) of 1996, 142
Personal privacy and employee rights, 217-220
    versus computer and HRIS, 217-218
    computerized personnel records, 219-220
    and home-based employees, 219
    lawsuits, three steps to avoid, 218-219
    medical records, 218
Pay-for-performance programs, 327-328, 363-364, 366-376 (*see also* Compensation)
Payroll, outsourcing, 457
Payroll Time Report, 578
Performance appraisals, 327-328, 363-364, 366-376 (*see also* Compensation)
    Worksheet, 597-598
Personal communication critical to success, 233-235
Personal Responsibility and Work Opportunity Reconciliation Act of 1996, 96
Personality testing, 55-56
Personnel Action Notice, 577

Personnel checklists, 527-557
    ADA list for employers, 555-557
    affirmative action planning, 542-543
    for applicant interview, 534-537
    communications programs, developing, 547-548
    complaint/grievance procedure, 555
    drug/alcohol problems at work, 550-551
    employee planning, 532-533
    evaluating interview/appraisal data, 537-540
    for Human Resource Management (HRM) merger, 549-550
    Human Resources, fifty ways to save money in, 529-532
    layoff, preparation for, 552-553
    litigation upon employee termination, avoiding, 551
    orientation for new employee, 540-542
    outside consultant, guidelines for using, 548
    safe workplace, maintaining, 554-555
    security activities, 553
    sexual harassment complaints, 543-544
    temporary help, eight uses for, 533
    termination of employee, avoiding litigation, 551
    training and development, 545, 546
    workplace safety, maintaining, 554-555
    in writing recruiting ads, 534
    for yearly salary program, 544-545
Personnel forms, sample, 559-610
    Accident/Injury Report, 605
    Accident Report, Supervisor's Report of, 606-607
    Applicant Appraisal Form, 572
    Application for Funeral Leave, 594
    Approval of Estimated Relocation Expenses and Allowances, 576
    Disciplinary Warning Notice, 602
    Discipline, Effective, Supervisor's Checklist and Report for, 600-601
    Education Verification Reference, 589
    Employee Absence Report Form, 592
    Employee Agreement, 574, 588
    Employee Attendance Record, 581
    Employee Benefit Program, sample, 582
    Employee Counseling Activity Sheet, 599
    Employee Transfer Request, 590
    Employee Warning Notice, 603
    Employment, Application for, 563-571
        in English, 563-565
        in Spanish, 566-571
    Exit Interview, 604
    Expense Reimbursement Request, 596
    Fair Credit Reporting Act, disclosure, 565
    First Aid Report Log, 608
    Injury Report, 605
    Job Description Outline, 583-584
    Leave Request/Return from Leave Form, 593

Personnel forms, sample (*cont.*)
  Mileage Reimbursement Report, 595
  New Employee Orientation, 585-587
  Overtime Hours Worked Report, 579-580
  Payroll Time Report, 578
  Performance Appraisal Worksheet, 597-598
  Personnel Action Notice, 577
  Personnel Requisition, 562
  Quarterly Safety Performance Record, 609
  Supervisor's Checklist and Report for Effective
    Discipline, 600-601
  Supervisor's Report of Accident Investigation,
    606-607
  Telephone Reference Check, 573
  Travel and Expense Reimbursement Request,
    596
  Vacation Request Form, 591
  Workers' Compensation Employee Verification
    Form, 575
Personnel letters and memos, 463-526
  absenteeism, excessive, warning about, 494
    termination letter for, 495
  ADA accommodation letter, 470
  age discrimination charge, letter to EEOC
    regarding, 512
  benefit, new, memo announcing, 516
  benefit plans, letter to employees regarding
    annual report of, 513
  claims processing time explanation, 514
  COBRA memo to employees, sample, 519-522,
    524-525
    to terminating employee/dependent, 523
  company support of employee bowling league,
    517
  confidentiality agreement, 479
  confirming employment offer, 465
  conflict of interest, new employee and, 480
  complaint procedure for employees, 507-508
  death of employee's spouse, 526
  disciplinary action, notice of, 492
  drug testing memo, 500
  employment verification, request for, 471
  hardship withdrawal letter to employee, 515
  independent contractors, use of, 485
  Internet use, warning about, 499
  intoxication on job, termination for, 498
  job sharing proposal, 482
  layoff, impending, informing employees, 486
    notification of, 487
  leave of absence, response to employee request-
    ing, 484
  memo to management re employee secrecy
    agreement, 478
  orientation schedule for new employee, 473-477
  plant closing, informing employees of notice of,
    488

Personnel letters and memos (*cont.*)
  privacy of employee letter to HR manager, 506
  privacy policy of company, 504-505
  rehire and reinstatement of benefits, 481
  replies to applicants, 466-468
  rejection of applicant, 469
  relocation of company, 489
  salary budget, additional, request for, 502
  salary increases when employee on leave of
    absence, 503
  secrecy agreement, memo to management
    about, 478
  sexual harassment memo to manager, 509, 510
    to employee, 511
  substance abuse by employee, 497
  suspension without pay, notice of, 493
  termination for intoxication on job, 498
  theft of company property, termination for, 496
  30-day performance improvement plan, notice
    to employee of, 490
  transfer decision confirmation, 483
  turnover analysis memo to department man-
    agers, 501
  regarding United Way drive, 518
  welcome to new employee, 472
  work performance, unacceptable, 491
*The Personnel Manager's Complete Model Letter
  Book*, 409
Personnel policies, 261-324
  checklist, 264-265
  communication of, 266-267
  implementation of, keys to successful, 263-264
  instructions, key, 267
  sample, 268-324
Personnel policy manual and employee handbook,
  difference between, 237
Personnel recordkeeping, 93-133
  auditing HR function, 132-133
  clause for files, 95
  confidentiality, 95
  costs of recruiting and selection, 124-126
  human resources calculations and reports, 126-131
  medical information file, 96
  new hire reporting mandatory, 96
  pay terminology and definitions, 103-105
  payroll procedures and relevant statutes, 98-103
    deductions, other, 102
    as employee or independent contractor, 100
    Equal Pay Act of 1963, 101-102
    Fair Labor Standards Act, 101
    federal income tax withholding, 99-100
    Federal Insurance Contributions Act (FICA),
      98 (*see also* Federal Insurance)
    Federal Unemployment Tax Act (FUTA), 98-
      99
    individual employee earnings record, 102-103

Personnel recordkeeping (*cont.*)
    monthly payroll trend report, 120-123
    records, 102
    register, 102
    remittance and reporting requirements, 100
    state income tax withholding, 100
    state unemployment compensation taxes, 99
  record retention requirements, 105-119
  requirements, 96-97
  staffing levels, maintaining control of, 120
  telephone requests for information, 96
  terminations, measuring, 127
  turnover, cost of, 126, 127-129
Personnel Requisition Form, 17
Personnel Status Form, 52
Plant closings, 450-461 (*see also* Labor relations)
  letter to employees of notice of, sample, 488
Point method of job evaluation, 342, 345
Policies, personnel, 261-324 (*see also* Personnel)
Polygraph exams, 54
Polygraph Protection Act of 1988, 54, 140, 157-158
Post-Employment Form, 43
Posters required by federal statute, 179, 183-184,
    185-188
Praendix personality test, 55-56
Pregnancy Discrimination Act of 1978, 139
Privacy of employee, sample letter to HR manag-
    er, 506
Privacy policy letter to employee, sample, 504-505
Professional employees under FLSA, 147-148
Profiles International, 37

Q

Quarterly Safety Performance Record, 609
Questioning techniques in interviewing, 71
Questionnaire for job description data, 333
Questions for interview, 72-74
  inappropriate, 74
  for management positions, 73
  sample, 73
  unstructured, 72

R

Ranking method of job evaluation, 342
Record retention requirements, 105
Recordkeeping for personnel, 93-133 (*see also*
    Personnel)
Recruiting, interviewing, and selection, 1-92
  ads, 4-10 (*see also* Ads to recruit)
    Checklist, 534
  advertising agency, using, 10
  automated, 3-4

Recruiting, interviewing, and selection (*cont.*)
  background checks, 37
  best workers, identifying and recruiting, 10-11
  costs of recruiting and selection, 124-126
  disabled, recruiting, 84-88
  drug /employment testing, pros and cons of, 54-
    57
    Drug-Free Workplace Act, 55
  Equal Employment Opportunity Commission
    Guidelines, 56
    job-related testing, 56
  forms, 14-60
    ad checklist, 18
    Application for Employment—California
      Addendum, 57, 58
    application forms, 20-29 (*see also* Application
      forms)
    Applicant Rejection Letter, 42
    Approval of Estimated Relocation Expenses
      and Allowances, 92
    checklist, 14
    Confidentiality Agreement, 47
    Credit Report Processing Authorization
      Form, 57, 58
    Education Verification Reference, 38
    Employee Agreement and Handbook
      Acknowledgment Form, 46
    Employee Benefits Verification Form, 57, 59
    Employment Confirmation Letter, 40
    Employment Verification Letter, 41
    Help Wanted Advertising Form, 19
    Immigration Form I-9, 44-45
    Job Bid Form, 85
    Job Description Outline, 15-16
    New Employee Orientation, 49-51
    Personal Data Sheet, 48
    Personnel Requisition Form, 17
    Personnel Status Form, 52
    Post-Employment Form, 43
    Worker's Compensation Employee
      Verification Form, 57, 60
  illegal employment practices, 89-90
  implementing ideas, 4-6
  internal job-posting system, 82-84
  Interviewing and Selection Handbook, sample,
    57, 61-81 (*see also* Interviewing)
  job offer, making, 39, 90-91
  methods for, effective, 9
  new employee orientation, 91, 92
    Form, 49-51
    relocation, 91, 92
  paper and pencil honesty test, 54-55
  polygraph exams, 54
  procedure, 12-13
  references, giving, 34-35
    telephone reference check, 36

Recruiting, interviewing, and selection (*cont.*)
  relocation of new employee, 91, 92
  selection, successful, seven steps for, 53-54
  sources, 4
  temporary help, using to save money, 88-89
  testing, pros and cons of, 54-57 (*see also ...*
      drug/employment...)
  web sites, use of, 3-4
  where to list jobs, 5
Recruitment and Retention, 345
Reference checks, 34-36
  telephone, 36
Regulatory compliance, 135-230
  addresses and telephone numbers, government,
      180-181
  affirmative action, 149-153
    guidelines, 149-150
    plans, 150-153
  Americans with Disabilities Act (ADA), 140,
      221-222
    accommodation letter, sample, 222
    checklist, 221
  Consolidated Omnibus Budget Reconciliation
      Act (COBRA) of 1986, 139, 162-178
    notice of amendments, 164-165
    sample letters, 166
  Drug-Free Workplace Act of 1988, 140, 153-157
    drug/alcohol testing policy, deciding on, 155-
        157
  Equal Employment Opportunity (EEO) laws,
      state by state analysis of, 189-195
  Fair Labor Standards Act (FLSA) of 1938, 138,
      143-149
  Family and Medical Leave Act, 141, 226-230
      (*see also* Family and Medical)
    advance notice and medical certification, 223,
        224-225
    enforcement, 223
    reasons for unpaid leave, 223
    return of employee to work, 226-230
    unlawful acts by employers, 223
  federal statutes regulating employment, etc.,
      137-142
    Age Discrimination in Employment Act
        (ADEA) of 1967, 138
    affirmative action guidelines and plans, 149-153
    Americans with Disabilities Act (ADA) of
        1990, 140, 221-222 (*see also* Americans with
        Disabilities)
    Civil Rights Act of 1964, Title VII, 137, 138
    Code of Federal Registry, 138
    Consolidated Omnibus Budget Reconciliation
        Act (COBRA) of 1986, 139, 162-178 (*see
        also* Consolidated Omnibus...)
    Drug-Free Workplace Act of 1988, 140, 153-
        157 (*see also* ...Drug-Free...)

Regulatory compliance (*cont.*)
    Employee Polygraph Protection Act, 140, 157-
        158
    Employee Retirement Income Security Act
        (ERISA) of 1974, 139
    Equal Employment Opportunity Act of 1972,
        137, 181-184
    Equal Pay Act of 1963, 139
    Executive Orders, 138
    Fair Labor Standards Act of 1938, 138, 143-
        149 (*see also* Fair Labor...)
    Family and Medical Leave Act (FMLA) of
        1993, 141, 226-230 (*see also* Family and
        Medical Leave Act)
    Freedom of Information and Privacy Act of
        1974, 138
    Health Insurance Portability and
        Accountability Act (HIPAA) of 1996, 141-
        142, 164-165
    Health Maintenance Organization Act of 1973
        (HMO), 139
    Immigration Reform and Control Act of 1986,
        138, 196-204 (*see also*...Immigration
        Reform...)
    Mental Health Parity Act of 1996, 142
    Newborns' and Mothers' Health Protection
        Act of 1996, 142
    Occupational Safety and Health Act (OSHA)
        of 1970, 140
    Omnibus Budget Reconciliation Act of 1986,
        139
    Personal Liability and Work Opportunity Act
        (Welfare Reform) of 1996, 142
    Polygraph Protection Act, 140, 157-158
    Pregnancy Discrimination Act of 1978, 139
    Rehabilitation Act of 1973, 138, 139
    Resource Conservation and Recovery Act
        (RCRA), 141
    sexual harassment guidelines to Title VII, 138
    Small Business Job Protection Act (SBJPA)
        of 1996, 141, 164-165
    Tax Reform Act of 1986, 140
    Technical and Miscellaneous Revenue Act,
        140
    Trade and Competitiveness Act of 1988, 141
    Vietnam Era Veterans Readjustment
        Assistance Act of 1974, 138
    Worker Adjustment and Retraining
        Notification Act, 140
  Human Resources function, 185-188
  Immigration Reform and Control Act of 1986,
      138, 196-204
    acceptable documents, 199
    Form I-9, 196-198
    INS offices, 202-204
    questions and answers, 200-201

Regulatory compliance (*cont.*)
  independent contractors, 160-161
    penalties, 161
    Revenue Act of 1978, 161
    work status, 160-161
  labor relations laws, 143
  personal privacy and employee rights, 217-220
    computer and HRIS, 217-218
    computerized personnel records, protecting, 219-220
    and home-based employees, 219
    lawsuits, three steps to avoid, 218-219
    medical records, 218
  posters required, 179, 183-184, 185-188
  state laws, 142-143
    Employment Security Acts, 143
    Workers' Compensation Acts, 142-143, 205-217 (*see also* Workers' Compensation)
  termination pay requirements by state, 179-180
  unemployment compensation, 217
  what to do for wage-hour investigator visit, 159-160, 163
  Workers' Compensation, 205-217 (*see also* Workers' Compensation)
    checklist, 212
    costs, 209-210
    covered benefits, 206
    as exclusive remedy program, 206-207
    exemptions, standard, 205
    failure to carry, 207
    financing, 208-209
    illnesses/injuries covered, 205-206
    objectives, 205
    offices directory, 213-217
    reform, 209
    requirements, 207-208
    risk financing, 208-209
    Verification Form, 211
    work-related illness/injury liability, 206-207
    workplace injuries under FMLA and ADA, 212
Rehabilitation Act of 1973, 138, 139
  and job description, 333
Rehire and reinstatement of benefits, sample letter, 481
Rejection of applicant, sample letter, 469
Relocation:
  costs, 329
  expenses and allowances, form for approval of, 576
  letter informing employees of, sample, 489
Request for Proposal (RFP), 459, 460-461
Requisition form, 12
Resource Conservation and Recovery Act (RCRA), 141

Resumes, 67
Revenue Act of 1978, 161
Risk financing, 208
RFP, 459, 460-461

S

Safety, accident reporting, and OSHA regulations, 417-442
  guide to reporting, sample, 421-437
  Hazards Communications Standards (HCS) of OSHA, 419 (*see also* Hazards Communications)
    guide to compliance with, 422-437
  obligations for reporting occupational injuries/illnesses, employer's, 420-421
    annual survey, 420-421
  OSHA's leading violations, 419-420
  procedures, basic, 419
  terminology, glossary, 438-442
Safety in workplace, checklist for maintaining, 554-555
Salary:
  budget, additional, request for, 502
  quoting as monthly figure, 13, 39
Salary increase policy for employees on leave of absence, 503
Salary program:
  model, 358-365
  program, yearly, checklist for, 544-545
Screening applicants, 12
Security activities, checklist for, 553
Selection, 1-92 (*see also* Recruiting)
  successful, seven steps for, 53-54
Separation Notice, 405
Sexual harassment:
  claims, investigating, 415-416
  complaints, checklist for investigating, 543-544
  employee, memo to, 511
  guidelines of Title VII, Civil Rights Act, 138
  memo to manager, sample, 509, 510
Small Business Job Protection Act (SBJPA) of 1996, 141, 164-165
Social Security, 98
Staffing levels, control of, 120
Stanton Corp., 54
State income tax withholding, 100
State laws regulating employment, etc., 142-143 (*see also* Regulatory)
State unemployment compensation taxes, 99
Substance abuse by employee, sample letter, 497
Supervisor's Checklist for Effective Discipline, 400-401, 600-601
  and Report, 600-601

Supervisor's Report of Accident Investigation, 606-607
Suspension Letter, sample, 410
Suspension without pay notification, sample, 493

T

Tax Reform Act of 1986, 140
Technical and Miscellaneous Revenue Act, 140
Telephone Reference Check, 573
Telephone requests for personnel information, 96
Television ads to recruit workers, 4
Temporary help:
   eight uses for, 533
   using to save money, 88-89
Termination of employee:
   checklist for, 406
   litigation upon, checklist to avoid, 551
Testing, employment/drug, pros and cons of, 54-57
   "Bill of Rights," 56-57
   Equal Employment Opportunity Commission
      Guidelines, 56
   job-related, 56
Theft of company property, sample termination
      letter, 496
Thirty-day performance improvement plan, sam-
      ple notice to employee of, 490
Time sharing, 457
Title VII, Civil Rights Act of 1964, 137, 138
   affirmative action planning checklist, 542-543
   and job descriptions, 333
Trade and Competitiveness Act of 1988, 141
Training and development checklist, 545, 546
Transfer decision, sample letter confirming, 483
Travel and Expense Reimbursement, Request, 596
Turnover:
   analysis memo to department managers, sample,
      501
   figuring costs of, 126
Two-tier contracts, 328

U

U.S. Search, 37
Unacceptable work performance, sample letter,
      491

Unemployment compensation, 217
   taxes, state, 99
Union organizer's demand for recognition, han-
      dling, 447-450
Union-free status, retaining, 446-450

V

Vacation Request Form, 591
Vendor relationship, establishing, 458-460 (*see also*
      Labor relations)
Vietnam Era Veterans Readjustment Assistance
      Act of 1974, 138

W

Wage-hour investigator visit, 159-160, 163
Web sites, necessary use of, 3
Welcome to new employee, sample, 472
Work performance unacceptable, sample letter, 491
Worker Adjustment and Retraining Notification
      Act, 140, 450 (*see also* Labor relations)
Workers' Compensation Acts, 142-143, 205-217
   checklist, 212
   costs, 209-210
   covered benefits, 206
   Employee Verification Form, 57, 60, 211, 575
   as exclusive remedy program, 206-207
   exemptions, standard, 205
   failure to carry, 207
   financing, 208-209
      purchasing insurance, 208-209
      self-insurance, 208
      third party contracting, 208
   illness/injuries covered, 205-206
   objectives, 205
   offices directory, 213-217
   reform, 209
   requirements, 207-208
   risk financing, 208-209
   Verification Form, 57, 60, 211
   work-related injury/illness liability, 206-207
   workplace injuries under FMLA and ADA, 212
Workplace, checklist for maintaining safety in,
      554-555
Writing job offer, controversy about, 39, 90-91